The Well-Crafted Argument

The Well-Crafted Argument

A Guide and Reader

Fred D. White   *Santa Clara University*

Simone J. Billings   *Santa Clara University*

Houghton Mifflin Company

Boston   New York

Senior Sponsoring Editor: Suzanne Phelps Weir
Senior Development Editor: Martha Bustin
Senior Project Editor: Carol Newman
Senior Production/Design Coordinator: Jodi O'Rourke
Manufacturing Manager: Florence Cadran
Marketing Manager: Cindy Graff Cohen

Printed in the U.S.A.

Library of Congress Control Number: 2001131561
ISBN: 0-618-04549-X

23456789-QF-06 05 04 03 02

Brief Contents

Contents

6 Methods of Critical Reading   124

7 Researching Your Argument   153

Part II Reading Clusters   213

1 What Is the Impact of Cyberspace Technology on Education?   215

3 Can Censorship or Book Banning Ever Be Justified?   317

5 Are Science and Religion Compatible?   461

7   Should Media Violence Be Controlled?   575

8   Can We Preserve Our Privacy in the Internet Age?   631

9 Famous Arguments   689

Roe v. Wade   731

ORIGINAL TRANSCRIPT OF THE ARGUMENT BEFORE THE UNITED STATES SUPREME
COURT

> In 1973, after being denied an abortion in Texas, "Jane Roe" took her appeal to the Supreme Court. Here are highlights from what has become one of the of one of the most important court cases in recent history, and a milestone for women's rights.

The Character of Hamlet's Mother   735

CAROLYN H. HEILBRUN

> In this essay a distinguished scholar and author of *Reinventing Womanhood* reassesses Shakespeare's Queen Gertrude from a feminist perspective.

Preface

The ability to develop and write a well-crafted argument is a valuable and all too rare skill today. Not only can mastery of argumentative writing bring tremendous advantages in academia, in the workplace, and in life, but it can also provide all the satisfactions of self-expression and effective and responsible communication. For these reasons, we wrote *The Well-Crafted Argument: A Guide and Reader*. It equips students with a complete set of skills necessary for writing argumentative essays in a wide variety of contexts. *The Well-Crafted Argument* is based in a process pedagogy that encourages individual voice and vision. At the same time, it introduces models of good writing that provide grounding to inexperienced writers.

Over the years we have used a number of argumentation textbooks in our courses. Time after time, we found that these books left out too much—or put in too much that was not essential in helping students to master argumentative writing. This textbook is distinctive because it contains

- **A thorough yet concise discussion of critical reading strategies.** Critical reading skills can help students better understand and evaluate arguments as well as to do peer reviews and to write and revise their own arguments.

- **An introduction to three principal strategies of argument.** Separate chapters cover instruction in Classical, Toulmin, and Rogerian methods of framing arguments. (Other argumentative texts present only one strategy.)

- **Extensive use of student essays to represent every facet of argumentative writing.** Both in Part I, The Rhetoric of Argument, and in Part II, Reading Clusters, student argumentative essays illustrate different topics and strategies and form the basis for discussions, exercises, and writing projects. No other argumentative textbook contains so many (thirteen) student-written argumentative essays covering so many different topics and strategies.

- **A focus on the writing process as it applies to argumentative writing.** Chapter 1, Anatomy of an Argument, and other chapters within Part I, The Rhetoric of Argument, consider the writing process—gathering ideas, drafting, and revising—in the context of structuring and writing effective arguments.

- **Comprehensive instruction in conducting research for purposes of argument and documenting sources.** Chapter 7, Researching Your Argument, helps students to locate and use both print and Internet resources, to use effective search strategies, and to avoid plagiarism. This chapter also introduces students to interviewing, conducting surveys, and designing questionnaires as ways of obtaining information. Chapter 8, Documenting Your Sources, presents MLA and APA citation styles, with examples.

Additional Distinctive Features

Divided into two parts, a rhetoric and a reader, *The Well-Crafted Argument* provides teachers and students with a wealth of materials and tools for effective argumentative writing, thinking, and reading.

Part I: The Rhetoric of Argument

- **Practical coverage.** Eight brief, readable skills-building chapters cover (a) planning, drafting, and revising argumentative essays; using (b) Classical, (c) Toulmin, and (d) Rogerian models to structure an argument; (e) reasoning effectively and recognizing pitfalls in reasoning; (f) critical reading strategies and evaluating arguments; (g) researching your argument and locating and integrating outside information using print, electronic, and interpersonal resources; and (h) documenting your sources.

- **Reasoning skills covered in context.** This book combines *methods* of effective reasoning with instruction in *errors* of reasoning. Most argument texts present only an out-of-context discussion of the latter.

- **Thorough and pedagogically sound apparatus.** Exercises appear throughout each chapter to reinforce ideas and help students apply what they have just learned in a particular section. Each chapter concludes with a summary, a checklist of protocols relevant to each chapter, and a set of writing projects.

Part II: The Reading Clusters

- **Fresh topics.** Part II presents 72 readings organized thematically into nine clusters. Popular debate topics such as violence in the media and censorship issues appear along with newer, stimulating topics seldom represented in argument texts. These include standardized testing, space exploration, science and religion, and privacy issues. Each cluster includes a wide range of contrasting (not just "opposing") views on issues that students will find intriguing and challenging, as well as refreshing. Issues of immediate relevance to students, such as multicultural education and the effect of technology on education, round out the selections.

- **Readings drawn from a range of sources.** Each cluster of readings includes both mainstream and academic essays. Each cluster includes a student essay on that topic.

- **Famous essays well represented.** A separate cluster contains some of the world's most compelling masterpieces of argument, including Plato's "Allegory of the Cave," Jonathan Swift's "A Modest Proposal," Frederick Douglass's "I Hear the Mournful Cry of Millions," and Rachel Carson's "The Obligation to Endure."

- **Readings from many disciplines.** Readings come from a wide range of academic disciplines: physics, astronomy, biology, anthropology, political science, psychology, education, literature, computer science, mass-media communication, philosophy, religious studies, art, and music. Students thus are made dramatically aware of the fact that argumentative writing is vital to all fields.

- **Effective and interesting apparatus.** Each cluster begins with a brief *Introduction* to the cluster topic and ends with *Connections Across the Clusters* questions, *Writing Projects*, and *Suggestions for Further Reading*. Each reading has a contextualizing headnote and is followed by *Reflections and Inquiries* questions and *Reading to Write* assignments.

The Well-Crafted Argument Web Site

The Well-Crafted Argument has its own Web site at <college.hmco.com>. For instructors, *The Well-Crafted Argument*'s Web site contains sample syllabi, answer keys to select exercises in the text, discussion launchers for the reading clusters, handouts and transparency masters for peer critiquing guidelines and sample essay evaluation sheet, information on other modes of argument such as satire, review, and motivational (with links), and information about where to look for helping in teaching students for whom English is a second language.

For students, the Web site provides resources to supplement topics covered in the text chapters and related topics. For example, the Web site contains additional detail on the Rhetorical Rhombus and on the Toulmin model; an interview with student writers, such as Daniela Gibson; more sample student essays; more examples of logical fallacies; grammar exercises; and an annotation exercise (containing an article to annotate).

In addition to linking students and instructors to the Houghton Mifflin Research Guide and the eLibrary of Exercises, *The Well-Crafted Argument* Web site also provides links for Aristotle and Aristotelian Argument, Toulmin, Carl Rogers, logic, and the eight thematically organized reading clusters in the text.

Acknowledgments

We wish to thank Richard Osberg, our department Chair at Santa Clara University, for his support of this project. We are also grateful to Terry M. Weyna and William R. Billings for their valuable suggestions and encouragement and to Devorah Harris, who expressed enthusiasm for the book from the very beginning.

Throughout the development of this text, many colleagues have been extremely helpful with their suggestions and generous with their time. We gratefully acknowledge the assistance of the following reviewers.

Edmund August, McKendree College

L. Bensel-Meyers, University of Tennessee

Ellen Bernabei, Grossmont College, Miramar College

Nancy Blattner, Southeast Missouri State University

Arnold J. Bradford, Northern Virginia Community College

Sydney Darby, Chemeketa Community College

Lorien J. Goodman, Pepperdine University

Robert W. Hamblin, Southeast Missouri State University

Susan Hanson, Southwest Texas State University

William A. Harrison, III, Northern Virginia Community College

Karen Holleran, Kaplan College

Alex M. Joncas, Estrella Mountain Community College

Erin Karper, Purdue University

Eleanor Latham, Central Oregon Community College

Linda McHenry, University of Oklahoma

William Peirce, Prince George's Community College

Barbara Richter, Nova University

Libby Roeger, Shawnee College

Peter Burton Ross, University of the District of Columbia

Wayne Stein, University of Central Oklahoma

Daphne Swabey, Univeristy of Michigan

Jim Wallace, University of Akron

Kathleen Walsh, Central Oregon Community College

We also wish to thank our students at Santa Clara University and at other academic institutions. Their help has been essential to the creation of this text, and we have learned a great deal from them. We owe a special debt of gratitude to the talented student writers who gave us permission to include their work: Justine Hearn, Daniel Neal, Sheila Gleason, Daniela Gibson, Jarrett Green, Andrea De Anda, Gina Takasugi, Dewey Adams, William N. Boenig, Mark Rodriguez, Chris Garber, and Tina Lennox.

Finally, we thank the staff of Houghton Mifflin, in particular Suzanne Phelps Weir, Senior Sponsoring Editor; Martha Bustin, Senior Development Editor; Janet Young, Development Editor; Carol Newman, Senior Project Editor; Jodi O'Rourke, Senior Production/Design Coordinator; Florence Cadran, Manufacturing Manager; Reba Frederics, Editorial Assistant; and Cindy Graff Cohen, Marketing Manager. They have believed in this project from the beginning and have overseen its evolution in a truly supportive manner.

We have made a special effort to present this challenging and complex material in an engaging fashion, and we welcome all feedback on how this book could be improved in the future. As supporters of the well-crafted argument in all its forms, we also invite users of this book to send in examples of argumentative writing to us, care of Houghton Mifflin College English at 222 Berkeley Street, Boston, MA 02116, for consideration in subsequent editions.

FRED D. WHITE
SIMONE J. BILLINGS
Santa Clara University

The Well-Crafted Argument

Part I

The Rhetoric of Argument

1 | Anatomy of an Argument

Give me the liberty to know, to utter, and to argue freely according to conscience, above all liberties.

—John Milton

The freedom to think for ourselves and the freedom to present and defend our views rank among the most precious rights that we as individuals possess, as the great poet and essayist John Milton knew. The more we know about argument and the more effectively we construct and recognize good arguments and dismiss faulty ones, the more we benefit from this liberty.

Why Argue?

All of us find occasions to argue every day. Sometimes we argue just to make conversation. We argue casually with friends about which restaurant serves the best food, which movies are the most entertaining, or which automobile performs the best or most reliably for the money. Sometimes we engage in arguments that are ongoing in the media, taking positions on topics that are debated in newspapers and magazines and on television, radio, and the Internet. And sometimes we argue in a more analytical manner on issues we think a lot about, such as which political party is most sympathetic to education reform, whether the Internet is a reliable research tool, or how to solve a particular problem. When more is at stake, as in this last type of argument, the chances are greater that we will fail to be persuaded by what we hear or read or become frustrated by our own failure to persuade. We often fail to persuade because we lack evidence to back up our claims or because the evidence we do have is inadequate.

In other words, while casual arguments often consist of little more than exchanges of opinions or unsupported generalizations, more formal arguments are expected to include evidence in support of generalizations if they are to succeed in making strong points, solving real problems, or changing minds.

What Is an Argument?

An argument must possess three basic ingredients to be successful. First, it must contain as much *relevant information* about the issue as possible. Second, it must present *convincing evidence* that enables the audience to accept the writer's or speaker's claim. The more controversial the claim, the more compelling the evidence must be. Third, it must lay out a *pattern of reasoning.* That is, it must logically progress from thesis to support of thesis to conclusion. Before we examine these three elements, though, let us consider a formal definition of argument.

A Formal Definition of Argument

An argument is *a form of discourse in which the writer or speaker tries to persuade an audience to accept, reject, or think a certain way about a problem that cannot be solved by scientific or mathematical reasoning alone.* The assertion that the circumference of a circle is a product of its diameter times *pi* is not arguable because the assertion cannot be disputed; it is a universally accepted mathematical fact. At the other extreme, asserting an unsubstantiated opinion is not stating an argument; it is only announcing a stance on a particular issue. For example, someone in a casual conversation who asserts that public flogging of robbers would be a more effective deterrent than jailing them is voicing an opinion, not presenting an argument. If you respond by saying "Yeah, probably," or "No way—that would contribute to a culture of violence," you are also stating an opinion. If you respond instead by requesting evidence, such as statistics that show a correlation between public punishment and crime rate, you are helping to shape the conversation into a true argument. It is useful to keep in mind that the word *argument* is derived from the Latin word *arguere,* to clarify or prove.

A good argument is not casual. It takes considerable time and effort to prepare. It not only presents evidence to back up its claim but also acknowledges the existence of other claims about the issue before committing to the claim that corresponds most closely to the arguer's convictions. A good argument also guides the audience through a logical, step-by-step line of reasoning from thesis to conclusion. In short, a good argument uses an argumentative *structure.*

Amplifying the Definition

Let us now amplify our definition of argument: An argument is *a form of discourse in which the writer or speaker presents a pattern of reasoning, reinforced by detailed evidence and refutation of challenging claims, that tries to persuade the audience to accept the claim.* Let us take a close look at each of the elements in this definition.

". . . a pattern of reasoning"   This element requires that a good argument disclose its train of thought in a logical progression that leads the listener or reader from thesis to support of thesis to conclusion. It also implies that any unfamiliar

terms or concepts are carefully defined or explained, and that enough background information is provided to enable readers or listeners to understand the larger *context* (interacting background elements) contributing to the argument. For example, to argue that gas-guzzling sports utility vehicles (SUVs) are selling better than fuel-efficient subcompacts does not qualify as an argument because no context for the claim is given. Readers or listeners would ask, "So what?" But if the assertion is placed in the context of an urgent problem—for example, that the enormous popularity of SUVs is rapidly depleting gasoline reserves, which in turn is leading to higher gasoline prices and increased pollution of our national parks—then a valid argument is established.

". . . reinforced by detailed evidence"   In a formal argument, any assertion must be backed up with specific, compelling evidence that is accurate, timely, relevant, and sufficient. Such evidence can be data derived from surveys, experiments, observations, and first-hand field investigations (statistical evidence), or from expert opinion (authoritative evidence).

". . . that tries to persuade the audience to accept the claim"   This last element of the definition brings to mind the ultimate aim of any argument: to convince the audience that the arguer's point of view is a sensible one, worthy of serious consideration if not outright acceptance. To accomplish this aim, arguers often reinforce their evidence with what are known as *appeals*—appeals to authority and traditional values, to feelings, and to reason. In an ideal world, evidence (the hard facts) alone would be enough to persuade audiences to accept the truth of a claim; but in reality, more persuasive force often is needed and appeals are drawn in.

Using Evidence in Argument

Argumentative writing uses two kinds of evidence: indisputable (or factual) and disputable. The first kind refers to matters of public record that anyone can verify. No one is going to dispute the fact that the earth revolves around the sun every 365.25 days, say, or that the state of California was admitted to the Union on September 9, 1850. How such facts are applied is another matter, but the facts themselves are beyond dispute.

But what about disputable evidence? Imagine that a friend's room is filled with art books and reproductions of paintings. If someone asks about this friend's interests, you would reply, "Art!" without hesitation, and cite as evidence the books and paintings. But that evidence is disputable: The books and paintings could belong to a roommate, could be a mere inheritance, or could represent a former interest only recently abandoned.

Just because evidence is disputable, however, does not mean it is unreliable. Such evidence often represents the closest one can get to the truth. Will banning handguns prevent tragedies like the Columbine school shootings? One re-searcher might discover statistical evidence of a correlation between banning guns and reduced crime; yet another researcher could find evidence of a contrary correlation. Different parts of the country or the world, different years, different times of year, different age groups, all represent constantly changing variables that can affect such a correlation. The more aware you are of the possible ways in which evidence may be disputed, the less likely you are to reach facile or prema-ture conclusions.

Using Appeals in Argument

Aristotle in his *Rhetoric* identifies three kinds of appeals:

1. *Ethical:* the appeal to tradition, authority, ethical and moral behavior, which Aristotle terms *ethos;*

2. *Emotional:* the appeal to feelings and basic human needs such as security, love, belonging, health and well-being, which Aristotle terms *pathos;* and

3. *Rational:* the appeal to reason and logic, which Aristotle terms *logos.*

How do appeals reinforce evidence? Say that a writer wishes to argue that if acid rain fallout continues to increase, agriculture in a certain region will be threatened. To argue this claim convincingly, a writer first needs to bring in in-disputable facts—those derived from scientific experiments. These facts would suggest a correlation between increased acidity and rainfall and decreased crop yield. Note that the correlation may be disputable, but it still constitutes valid evidence.

Use of appeals can enhance the persuasive force of the thesis. The writer above, for example, might use one or more of the following appeals:

- An ethical appeal that introduces the testimony of an expert, such as a farmer whose crops have been affected or an industrial chemist who has a professional understanding of the way in which acidity in rainfall can react with soil nutrients.

- An emotional appeal that discusses the basic human need for uncontami-nated food or justifies the fear of cancer many people would have if the situation were not corrected.

- A rational appeal that emphasizes the logical and inevitable consequences of what happens to soil and crops when acid rainfall goes untreated.

Appeals such as these go a long way toward reinforcing the evidence and strengthening the writer's argument.

■ Exercise 1.1

1. Consulting an unabridged dictionary, prepare a critical summary of the terms *argument, debate, dispute,* and *quarrel.* In what ways do the definitions differ? Where do they overlap, and how do you account for the overlap? Supplement these definitions with examples, drawing from your own experiences.

2. Which of the following assertions could be developed into a formal argument, and which could not? Explain your reasons.

   a. A clear link has been established between smoking and lung cancer.

   b. The Surgeon General has determined that smoking is a health hazard.

   c. Studying a foreign language gives children a greater command of their native language.

   d. The more video games children play, the less likely their abstract reasoning skills are to develop properly.

3. List the topics of recent disputes you have had with friends or family. Under each topic, note the claims asserted by each side, followed by any support that had been attempted for each. Next, go back over these topics and list additional support you would give to one or more of these claims if you had been asked to elaborate on them in a more formal manner.

4. Discuss the kinds of evidence writers would want to use to resolve the following controversial assumptions. What problems with definitions might arise in some of these claims?

   a. Adults are safer drivers than teenagers.

   b. More than three hundred species of birds inhabit the Everglades.

   c. The more violent shows you watch, the more likely you are to commit acts of violence.

   d. Male smokers are three times more likely to become impotent than male nonsmokers.

   e. Obscene books should be banned from public school libraries.

5. What types of appeals would be most appropriate for persuading readers of the following assumptions?

   a. Reading stories to children greatly enhances their mental skills as well as their emotional stability.

   b. All work and no play makes Jill a dull girl.

   c. Severer penalties should be imposed on those who abuse animals.

   d. Safety should be anyone's top priority when purchasing a family car.

Communicating with a Purpose

Before we turn to the writing of effective arguments, consider the elements in an act of communication. Any communication act consists of the *writer* or *speaker,* an *audience,* and the *subject* being communicated. This is known as the *Aristotelian* or *Communication Triangle,* as shown in Figure 1.1.

The Aristotelian Triangle reminds us that the act of writing, virtually by definition, involves writing about something to someone—that writing never occurs in a vacuum.

Any act of communication involves a writer or speaker conveying a particular viewpoint to a particular audience in a particular way. We have all had the experience of describing something one way to one person and quite another way to someone else. For example, we might discuss a romantic relationship one way with a friend, quite another way with a parent, and yet another way with a minister, rabbi, or psychologist. The writer or speaker, subject, and audience all shape the communication.

A fourth major element that shapes communication is *purpose.* There are three basic kinds of communication, each with a different purpose:

1. *Referential* or *expository:* communication that primarily aims to inform and explain;

2. *Expressive:* communication that primarily aims to stimulate the imagination, create mood or "atmosphere," and evoke feelings; and

3. *Argumentative:* communication that primarily aims to help skeptical readers or listeners make up their minds about a debatable issue.

These three modes of communication are not mutually exclusive. For instance, writers of arguments must take time to inform readers about the facts underlying a problem. They also must try to make such explanations interesting—perhaps by dramatically re-creating a moment of discovery or by describing the beauty of an observed phenomenon. But argumentative writing

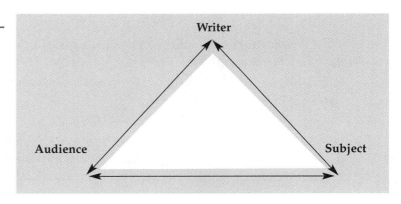

FIGURE 1.1

The Aristotelian or Communication Triangle

does have a unique purpose. Its main aim is to present, support, or challenge a debatable proposition or principle of ethics, taste, propriety, honor, judgment, or spirituality. Such views or principles cannot be proven with experiments or made compelling through descriptive writing alone.

To incorporate this element of purpose, we can transform Aristotle's triangle into a square or, to be a bit more alliterative (to keep the image more firmly in mind), into a *rhetorical rhombus* (see Figure 1.2). Simple as this diagram may seem, it calls to mind a subtle interconnection among the elements; that is, any one element is indispensable to the other three. Thus, the writer's way of seeing the world is made significant by the fact that he or she has a particular purpose for writing here and now; a subject is enriched by the way in which it is made relevant to a particular audience; and so on.

Let us examine each element of the rhetorical rhombus separately, in depth, as it pertains to the writing of effective arguments.

Once you establish that your primary purpose is not expository (to inform) or expressive (to evoke feelings) but argumentative, you will want to consider purpose in that context.

Purpose in an Argumentative Context

The purpose of your argument is the reason *why* you want your audience to agree with your claim and take whatever action is necessary to carry it out. Often, the purpose for wanting to communicate anything is complex. For example, if your claim is that wolf hunting must be stopped (say, by passing laws that prohibit wolf hunting), your purpose might consist of the following:

FIGURE 1.2

Rhetorical
Rhombus

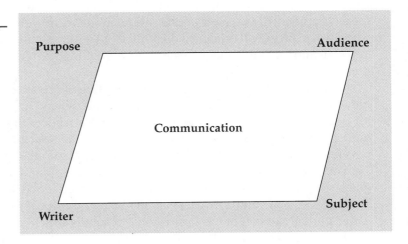

Purpose

Audience

Communication

Writer

Subject

- The facts make it clear to you that wolves are rapidly becoming an endangered species.

- You are convinced that such species endangerment poses a serious threat to the environment.

- You love wolves, and it distresses you to see these beautiful, intelligent animals slaughtered by those who cannot appreciate them.

Purpose, then, is the motivational force that imbues the mere potential for communication with the desire to communicate. In a required writing course, however, purpose becomes even more complicated. Unlike working writers whose purpose for writing a given piece is intrinsically related to the subject, student writers are often motivated by extrinsic matters, such as getting a good grade on the assignment or in the course. While there is nothing wrong with this kind of motivation, it does not quite constitute a bona fide purpose for writing about a given topic.

It is preferable, however, to adopt a professional sense of purpose toward your subject matter. The best way to accomplish this involved, engaged stance is to role-play. *Become* the writer you would like to be. Instead of thinking yourself as a student in a composition course, think of yourself as an expert in the field you are writing about—one who genuinely cares about the topics at hand enough to want your audience to understand them and appreciate them the way you do.

Audience in an Argumentative Context

The people to whom you aim your argument can significantly influence the way you present that argument. For example, two arguments supporting the prohibition of wolf hunting, one aimed at legislators and the other aimed at hunters, would differ greatly from each other. If you were addressing an audience of legislators, you would want to focus on the need for laws that would better protect the environment. If you were addressing an audience of wolf hunters, you would want to explain why it is in the wolf hunters' best interest to stop hunting wolves. You could argue that damage to the habitat would ultimately cause the wolves to die out.

Audience also affects the writing and reading of arguments, in that some arguments may be classified as academic (or scholarly) and others as nonacademic (or popular). Academic arguments are written for fellow scholars affiliated with higher education, although some scholars are "independent"—that is, they are not employed by a college or university and yet pursue similar research projects. The purpose of such writing is knowledge-sharing or idea-sharing; academic arguers say, in effect, "Here is what fellow researchers have determined thus far about the issue at hand; now, here are my views on the matter." A research paper is the student version of the professional scholarly article, in which the scholar carefully and explicitly articulates a claim and provides support for that claim.

TABLE 1.1	Distinction Between Academic and Nonacademic Arguments
Academic Arguments	**Nonacademic Arguments**
Specialized (i.e., discipline-specific), precise language	Nonspecialized, less precise but more accessible language
Formal or semiformal tone	Less formal, more personal tone
All primary and secondary sources explicitly cited and documented, using standard formats (MLA, APA, etc.)	Sources are acknowledged informally, without footnoting
Contributions by other scholars in the field are discussed formally and in detail	Contributions by other writers in the field are discussed briefly
Scholarly audience	General audience

Nonacademic arguments, on the other hand, focus more on reporting the "gist" of new developments or controversies. While academic arguments examine issues in depth and use specialized language to ensure precision, nonacademic arguments tend to gloss over the technicalities and use nonspecialized language, which is less accurate but more accessible to the general public. The chief distinguishing features between academic and nonacademic arguments are outlined in Table 1.1

The more aware you are of your target audience's needs and existing biases, the greater the likelihood that you will address their particular concerns about the topic and, in turn, persuade them to accept your thesis. To heighten your audience awareness, ask yourself these questions:

1. What do my readers most likely already know about the issue? Most likely do not know?

2. How might the issue affect my readers personally?

3. What would happen to my argument if my conclusions or recommendations are accepted? If they are not accepted?

Writer in an Argumentative Context

How, you may wonder, is the writer a variable in the communication, aside from the obvious fact that the writer is the one who presents the argument (the "Communication" that lies at the center of the rhetorical rhombus and is its very reason for being)? Actually, the writer can assume one of many roles, depending on the target audience. Say, for example, that you are trying to convince a friend to lend you $500 to use as a down payment for a summer trip to Europe. Your role here is that of trustworthy friend. If instead you are trying to convince your bank to lend you that same $500, your role becomes that of client or applicant. You are likely to use different language and different support in making your argument to the bank's loan officer than you are to your friend. Similarly writers often are obliged to play different roles, depending on the particular needs of different audiences.

Subject in an Argumentative Context

The subject refers to what the argument (the text) is about. Although the subject remains identifiably constant, a writer might shift the *focus* of a subject to accommodate a particular audience or situation. For example, to convince your friend to lend you $500 for the down payment on that European trip (your argument's subject), you might focus on how the friend could come with you to make for an even more rewarding trip. To convince the bank, you might shift the focus to emphasize future job security and the likelihood of your paying back the loan.

As you study the Classical, Toulmin, and Rogerian models of argument later in this chapter and in the chapters that follow, think about how the rhetorical rhombus applies to each and about how different models place different emphasis on purpose, audience, writer, or subject (PAWS).

Preparing to Compose an Argument

Unlike cooking, which follows a rather fixed sequence of steps, writing arguments (or essays of any kind) is mainly a dynamic, recursive process rather than a linear one. That is, you can start anywhere and return to any stage at any time. You can brainstorm for additional ideas, rework the organizational scheme, wad up and rewrite part of the existing draft, or walk over to the library or log onto the Internet to conduct additional research—and you can do any of these activities whenever you feel the need. Some writers simply do not feel comfortable composing in a linear fashion; some like to compose their endings first, or "flesh out" particular points of an argument as they leap to mind, and then organize them into a coherent sequence later on. Some writers need to map out their ideas in clusters, write outlines, or simply let loose their spontaneous flow of associations via freewriting.

Freewriting to Generate Ideas Rapidly

As you may recall from your earlier composition studies, freewriting is a good way to generate material for an argument. Start writing without any advance planning. Your goal is to let your thoughts run loose on the page; do not concern yourself with organization, sentence structure, word choice, or relevancy to the topic of your argument. You might surprise yourself with how much you already know!

There are two kinds of freewriting: unfocused and focused. In *unfocused freewriting,* let your pen move across the page, recording whatever comes to mind. Try not to pause. In the following example a student, Janis, engages in some unfocused freewriting to stir up ideas about a subject for her argument. She is thinking spontaneously with a pencil, you might say, making no effort to develop a thesis.

> Let's see, I'm supposed to write an argument that would persuade first-year college students what would be the best major in preparation for a particular career. Well, I'm undeclared myself, but want to study law after I graduate, so maybe I could do a comparative analysis of three or four majors that would seem to offer the best preparation for law school (hey, this could help me make up my own mind). Poli sci seems like an obvious possibility, since lawyers need to have a basic knowledge of the way governments work, the nature of public policy, how laws are passed. . . . Also, English, because lawyers need strong communication skills and need to acquire the kind of deep insight into the human heart that great works of literature offer . . . Then I might talk to law students as well as professors in the four different majors—and maybe even practicing attorneys to find out what they majored in as undergraduates, and why. Hey, my aunt is a lawyer! I could talk to her.

Janis knows that she likely will discard most, if not all, of her freewriting; her goal was not to whip out a rough draft or even test out a topic, but to help her mind tease out ideas and associations that otherwise might have remained buried. The goal of freewriting is greater than overcoming not knowing what to say; it includes becoming more receptive to what is possible.

In *focused freewriting*, you write spontaneously as well, but attempt something resembling an actual draft of the essay. Your goal is to generate as much as you know about the topic. It is an excellent way of discovering gaps in knowledge.

Immersing Yourself in the Subject

Imagine spending twenty minutes or so freewriting and getting down on paper everything that comes to mind; you produce several scraggly pages in longhand, or neater ones on a computer. You read them over, highlighting with a marker what seems most relevant and useful. Then you ask yourself these questions: What seems to be the dominant or recurrent trend? What more do I need to know about my topic to write persuasively about it? What kinds of evidence do I need to back up my thesis, however tentative it may be at this stage? In taking these steps, you are preparing to immerse yourself in your subject.

Having relevant information available is important to all writers. Once you know what more you need, you can start looking for information. On the Internet, an enormous quantity of information can be accessed quickly, so it is a good place to begin your research. A strong search engine like DogPile or AltaVista can bring material from any subject onto your screen in seconds. On the other hand, a large percentage of Internet sources will be superficial, dated, or not very relevant to your needs. Balance your Internet research by examining a variety of reliable print sources, such as books, articles, encyclopedias (general as well as subject-specific), handbooks, and specialized dictionaries. For more information about using sources, see Chapter 7, "Researching Your Argument."

Your goal in reading and researching should be to learn all you possibly can about your topic. Familiarize yourself with the differing views experts have about it. Talk to experts. As a college student you are surrounded by them; get in the habit of contacting professors who can give you timely and in-depth information about your topic or suggest material to read. Read and explore as many sources as possible. In other words, immerse yourself in the subject matter of your argument. This involvement will show in your writing and will give the finished paper added depth and vigor.

Using Listing and Clustering

Like freewriting, listing and clustering tap into writers' natural inclination to take a mental inventory of what they already know about a topic as well as to discover what they do not know about it. To list, jot down as quickly as you can ideas (or idea fragments) or names of persons, places, events, or objects. One student prepared the following list as a prelude to writing about the increasing problem of childhood obesity:

> Fast-food chains aggressively target their products to preteen kids.
> TV commercials give wrong impressions.
> Parents too busy to cook.
> Hamburgers often loaded with mayonnaise.
> Burgers, fries, milk shakes, ice cream loaded with fat.
> Parents not paying close enough attention to their kids' diets.

You can use lists to make notes to yourself or to ask questions the moment they occur to you:

> Check how many calories are in a typical fast-food burger.
> How much fat content in a bag of fries?
> What do nutritionists and pediatricians say about the increasing obesity problem?
> Find out how often kids eat fast food, on the average.
> How can kids learn more about this problem in school?

Like listing, clustering helps writers take an inventory of what they know. But clustering also helps writers discover relationships among the ideas they list, a discovery that helps them organize their ideas more efficiently when they begin outlining or drafting their arguments.

FIGURE 1.3 Student Cluster Diagram

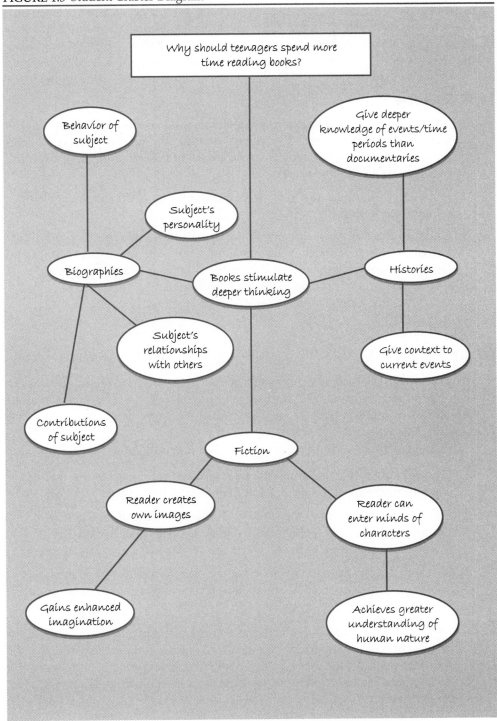

To cluster an idea for an argumentative essay, take a sheet of paper and write down words or phrases; at the same time, keep similar or interconnected words and phrases close together and draw large circles around them to form "clusters." Figure 1.3 shows how one student clustered her thoughts for an argumentative essay on why teenagers should spend more time reading books.

■ **Exercise 1.2**

1. Your science instructor asks you to evaluate the benefits and dangers of vitamin C. Using the Internet, locate information that both supports and challenges claims about the benefits and dangers of this vitamin. Keep a record of the Web sites that you visit.

2. List things you might say in a paper arguing for or against the benefits or dangers of vitamin C.

3. Having gathered potentially useful information about vitamin C and listed things you might want to include in your argument, do a focused freewrite. Do not pause or organize your thoughts or choice of words and phrases. Write rapidly until you have filled at least two handwritten pages.

Organizing the Argument

All writing must be organized or structured. Whether you are relating an experience (*narration*), or explaining an idea or process (*exposition* or *explanation*) or defending a thesis (*argumentation*), you must structure your writing to best communicate with an audience.

Organizing your writing means that you do the following:

1. Introduce the topic (the situation in a narrative; the subject matter to be explained in an exposition or explanation; the problem in an argument)

2. Present the particulars of the situation (the sequencing of incidents in a narrative, elements of a phenomenon in an exposition or explanation; the nature of the problem, followed by the body of evidence, in an argument)

3. Conclude (the outcome in a narrative; the "whole picture" in an explanation; the interpretation, assessment, and recommendations, if appropriate, in an argument)

How you meet these three organizational requirements in an argument depends on the type of model you adopt: the Classical (or Aristotelian/Ciceronian), the Toulmin, or the Rogerian. The chapters that follow examine each model in depth, but for now you merely need to be aware of each one's distinguishing organizational features.

In the *Classical model*, the organizational scheme is predetermined. One begins with an introduction that establishes the problem and states the thesis; next, one analyzes the evidence and refutes opposing views in light of the evidence collected; finally one draws conclusions and provides recommendations.

In the *Toulmin model* (named for the philosopher Steven Toulmin), one shifts emphasis from the argument itself to the arguer. From a Toulmin perspective, truth is not absolute but value-dependent. These values always come into play during the argument, meaning that no one argues for timeless, eternal truths.

In the *Rogerian model* (named for the psychologist Carl Rogers), one shifts emphasis to the social act of negotiating difference through argument. Truth is not only value-based but it must be negotiated cooperatively if argument is to have any constructive social function.

Drafting the Argument

There are several ways to compose a draft. One way of drafting (and, alas, too common) is to put off the task until the day or night before it is due and then to dash off a single draft and proofread it hastily. In general, this is the least productive way of writing. The best writers tend to revise *most* often, not least often.

Another way of drafting is to use an outline as a template. By elaborating on each section of the outline, the drafter takes an important step toward substantive development of the essay. The subsequent rethinking of the argument and the additional research that results becomes more apparent using this method.

A third way is to produce a "discovery draft," which is like freewriting in its spontaneity and in its goal of getting down on paper as much as possible about the topic. However, discovery drafters do have a rudimentary sense of structure and purpose in mind. They believe that, to some extent at least, the things they want to say will fall into place through the very act of writing, and if not, they can rearrange, revise, and edit once they have a rough draft in hand.

Whichever drafting method you choose, allow yourself enough time to reread the draft two or three times and to make marginal notations about possible changes. Mark up a printout of your draft with reminders of what else to include, questions that might help you identify and gather additional evidence, and ideas for changes that will strengthen your argument.

Composing Openings

Openings can be difficult to write because they usually lay out the terrain for the whole argument. Nobody likes to spend a lot of time writing an introduction, only to realize later that it has to be scrapped because the claim or approach has shifted during drafting. But no rule says that you must write your opening first. You can postpone writing the full opening until you have written part of the body of the paper or until you have a firm sense of your paper's shape.

Openings serve two purposes: to introduce the topic and the background information needed to understand or appreciate the topic's seriousness, and to state the thesis.

Consider the following types of openings. Keep in mind that one type can overlap the other (for example, startling openings can be partly anecdotal).

- **Occasional Opening.** An occasional opening refers to a current event or local incident and uses it as the occasion for writing the essay. "In light of the current crisis in Addis Abbaba . . . "

- **Startling Opening.** A startling opening grabs the attention of readers with unexpected information. "While you are reading this sentence, fifty people will die of cigarette-related illnesses in this country."

- **Anecdotal Opening.** An anecdotal opening uses a brief story to engage the reader's attention quickly. An article arguing that some of the most dangerous toxins are found in the home might begin with an anecdote about a toddler lifting an opened bottle of nail polish remover to his lips just as his mother enters the room.

- **Analytical Opening.** An analytical opening launches immediately into a critical discussion of the issue. An argument on the effects of alcohol on the body might open with an explanation of how alcohol damages certain bodily functions.

What makes an opening more appropriate than another? When choosing, consider the four interconnected elements of communication discussed earlier in the rhetorical rhombus. You may find that your subject lends itself more to an analytical opening. Or perhaps the writer's personal experience with the issue leads to an anecdotal opening. Or your purpose to shock readers into accepting the urgency of the matter suggests a startling opening. Maybe the kind of audience you are targeting (impatient to learn the facts? uncertain about the relevance of the topic?) justifies the use of an occasional opening.

Keep in mind that the purpose of your argument, the kinds of readers you are targeting, and the nature of the subject matter are important variables to weigh when you choose a particular type of opening.

■ Exercise 1.3

Discuss the rhetorical techniques used in each of the following openings.

1. The opening to an argument about the significance of the genetic revolution, by a professor of biology:

   Labor Day has come and gone, and I am chagrined to find that I haven't made it through my summer reading. My list comprised only a single book, but a rather unusual one: the text is three billion years old, has six billion

copies in print, runs three billion letters long (about one million pages), and is written entirely in four characters (A, T, C, G) with no spaces or punctuation. The book, of course, is a great classic, *The Sequence of the Human Genome.*
—Eric S. Lander, "In Wake of Genetic Revolution, Questions About Its Meaning," *New York Times,* 12 Sept. 2000: D5.

2. The opening to an argument about the interactive television market, by an editor of *Wired* magazine:

Sports, news, soap operas, Hollywood movies, MTV: Eleven years ago, Rupert Murdoch dynamited the cozy, four-channel world of British television with British Sky Broadcasting, a satellite service that beamed in more choices than the UK had ever seen. Now Sky has exploded another bombshell: interactive television. Using its new Open service, Sky's 1.8 million or so digital couch potatoes can turn on, tune in, and order pizza. Or buy groceries or books or CDs. Or check the weather or scan the movie listings or balance their bank accounts. —Frank Rose, "TV or Not TV," *Wired* March 2000: 246.

3. An essay about a likely future for male-female relations, by a distinguished essayist and novelist:

This could be the century when the sexes go their separate ways. Sure, we've hung in there together for about a thousand millenniums so far—through hunting-gathering, agriculture and heavy industry—but what choice did we have? For most of human existence, if you wanted to make a living, raise children or even have a roaring good time now and then, you had to get the cooperation of the other sex. —Barbara Ehrenreich, "Will Women Still Need Men?" *Time* 21 Feb. 2000: 62.

Composing the Body of the Argument

If you think of your argument's opening as the promise you make to your readers about what you are going to do, then the body of the argument is the fulfillment of that promise. Here you deliver the goods that comprise the subject node of the rhetorical rhombus: the detailed support—facts, examples, illustrations—as well as the emotional, logical, and ethical appeals that collectively demonstrate to your readers that the claim you set forth in your introduction is valid.

How should you proceed in writing out the body of your argument? First, check that the sequence you developed in your outline includes everything you want to say about the issue. Jot down additional notes in the margins if necessary. If you have completed a freewrite or rough draft, now is the time to retrieve those pages and decide what to keep. You may already have more of the draft of your argument completed than you realize!

Many writers find it productive to move back and forth from draft to outline. The outline gives a bird's eye view of the whole scheme; the draft concentrates on the minutiae of point-by-point discussion and exemplification.

Composing Conclusions

A good conclusion enables readers to grasp the full impact of the argument. If the introduction states the claim and the body argues for the validity of the claim by citing evidence for it, then the conclusion encapsulates all those points of evidence, leaving readers with a renewed sense of the argument's validity.

To write an effective conclusion, then, aim to capture in just one or two paragraphs the gist of your argument. Conclusions of short papers need not be long but could be just three to four sentences.

What might you do in a conclusion? Here are two possibilities:

1. Reflect back on the paper.
   - Return to the image or analogy or anecdote you discussed in the introduction and provide a frame for the piece.
   - Restate the thesis to underscore the argument of your essay.
   - Summarize your main points if the argument is complex or the paper is longer than six pages.

2. Broaden the scope beyond your paper.
   - Forecast the future if your main points should prove to be true.
   - Point out the implications of the ideas presented.
   - Exhort your readers to action.

Revising the Argument: A Form of Reevaluation

You have written a draft of your argument, using one of the above methods. Now it is time to revise. "I love the flowers of afterthought," the novelist Bernard Malamud once said. The wonderful thing about writing is that you do not need "to get it right the first time." In fact, you can try as many times as you wish, which is not the case with speaking. Malamud, you will notice, is commenting on the opportunity that revision provides writers with: the opportunity to say it better—more clearly, effectively, or convincingly. And for most writers the very best "flowers" of thought occur only *after* they have written something down.

In revising argumentative essays, attend closely to the ways you have presented the problem, stated your claims, reported the evidence and testimony, represented the challenging views, drawn inferences, and reached reasonable conclusions. What follows is a closer look at each of these steps.

- **Presenting the problem.** Unless you capture the exact nature and full complexity of the problem you are examining, your entire argument is built on a shaky foundation. To determine whether the problem is represented well, question whether the introduction suits the audience and subject (recall the PAWS rhombus) and whether you establish sufficient ethos and pathos for readers to care to read on and to trust you, the writer.

- **Stating the claim.** Just as the problem must be stated clearly, so must the assertions that presumably solve the problem. Ask yourself whether your claim is realistic, practical, and sensible in light of the nature of the problem and the circumstances underlying it.

- **Reporting the evidence.** Facts and statistics—the raw data that comprise evidence—do not carry much meaning outside of a context of discussion. In presenting evidence in support of a thesis, the writer aims to communicate the significance of those facts and figures, not simply to drop them on the page. When revising your discussion of the evidence, ask yourself whether you interpret the data accurately, relate one cluster of data to another clearly enough, and establish your ethos as a careful researcher and thinker on the issue.

- **Refuting challenging views.** When revising refutations, make sure that your writing represents the claims and evidence of the other side as fairly as possible. If you argue from a Rogerian perspective, think of establishing common ground with the audience in terms of shared values (warrants) or of cooperating to reach shared goals. Resist the temptation to omit parts of a challenging perspective because you are not sure about how to refute it. Also, double-check the reliability of your refutation: Does it reveal the limitations or falsity of the challenging view?

- **Drawing inferences and conclusions.** How do you interpret your findings? How clearly do your underlying warrants emerge? Should you give more attention to them? How willing will your readers be to cooperate with you, based on your interpretation of the findings? What else can you say to ensure their cooperation—assuming that you would find such cooperation desirable?

The Pulitzer Prize winning journalist and teacher of writing Donald Murray, in *The Craft of Revision* 2nd ed. (1995), identifies three cardinal virtues of revision:

1. Revision allows one to identify problems to be solved.
2. Revision enables writers to explore the topic more deeply to arrive at new insights into the topic.
3. Revision enhances the brain's capacity for recall and patterning.

Reading to Revise

Reading well, especially in the context of writing, provides you with a wider perspective of your subject and of the many divergent views that give it depth and richness. As a well-read writer, you are in the position of integrating the ideas of different authors into your own views on the subject. Reading and reflecting critically on what you have read also help you to revise more successfully because it forces you to get into the habit of reading your own writing as if it were someone else's. The advantage to beginning your project well in advance of the due date is that you will have the time to do such a critical reading of your drafts.

Using Your Reading Skills in Peer-Critiquing Workshops

You may be given the opportunity to respond critically to other students' drafts. Always read the draft as carefully as you would any published argument. Consider the following criteria as you read the first draft of a peer.

- **Purpose-related issues.** Is the purpose of the draft apparent? Stated clearly enough? Is the thesis (claim) well-stated? Directly related to the purpose?

- **Content-related issues.** Is the scope of the topic sufficiently limited? Does the writer provide enough background information? Provide enough evidence in support of the claim? Provide enough examples and illustrations to support the evidence? Represent challenging views fully and fairly before pointing out their flaws? Are the writer's interpretive and concluding remarks thorough? Does the writer offer clear recommendations, if appropriate?

- **Issues relating to style and format.** Is the writing concise? Easy to read? Are the sentences coherent, well-constructed, varied? Is the level of usage consistent and appropriate for the intended audience? Is the word choice accurate? Are unfamiliar terms defined? Does the writer use subheadings and visual aids where appropriate? Follow proper documentation format?

Types of Revision Tasks

Revising an argument involves a lot more than just "fixing things up"; it also involves re-*seeing* the entire draft from a fresh perspective, checking to make sure that each assertion is fully discussed and that the discussion follows a logical sequence. Here are some different types of revision strategies:

Holistic Revision   F. Scott Fitzgerald liked to speak of "revising from spirit"—that is, revising from scratch after realizing that the first draft is on the wrong track or just does not seem to "click" in your mind. This kind of holistic revision—of revision as re-seeing—makes it more likely that new energy and insights will be infused into the argument. For this kind of revision to work best, you often need to set aside (though not necessarily "scrap") the original draft and start afresh.

Content Revision   When revising for content, you examine your ideas in greater depth than you did during the earlier draft. Typically, you gather more information or return to the original information to process it more efficiently. You may discover that you have underdeveloped an idea, so you would need to provide specific detail to support your claim. Usually, such revisions can be "pasted into" the original draft.

Organizational Revision   Writers often revise to strengthen the structure of their argument. When you revise for organization, pay close attention to the logical progression of your ideas. An argument can be more effective, for example, by saving the most compelling point for last. As for moving coherently and smoothly from one point to the next, make sure you include transitional markers such as "on the other hand," "nevertheless," "in spite of," "according to," "however," and so on.

Strive for the best possible order of ideas, not just the order in which the ideas occurred to you. When an argument unfolds logically, you create what is casually referred to as *flow*. The smoother the flow, the more likely your readers are to follow along and comprehend your argument.

Stylistic Revision   When revising to improve your style, pay attention to the way you sound on paper—to the manner in which you convey your ideas. Stylistic problems include inconsistency in tone of voice (too informal here, excessively formal there), lack of sentence and paragraph variety and emphasis, and use of jargon.

One of the pleasures of writing is projecting something of your individual personality and your own manner of emphasizing ideas, of relating one point to another, and of making colorful or dramatic comparisons. As Sidney Cox writes, "What you mean is never what anyone else means, exactly. And the only thing that makes you more than a drop in the common bucket, a particle in the universal hourglass, is the interplay of your specialness with your commonness" (*Indirections*, 1981:19).

One way to become more adept at constructing sentences and paragraphs is to play around with them. Take any paragraph, your own or someone else's from a magazine article, and rewrite it in different ways, discovering what is possible. You can sense a personality behind Cox's tone of voice, can you not? Look at his syntax, his peculiar word choice. But the point is, if *you* were the one asserting Cox's point, you would have done so in your own manner. For example, you might have expressed the point like this:

People communicate ideas differently because each person sees the world differently. Each person uses language differently. At the same time, all of us who belong to the same culture share a common language. It is a writer's special blending of his or her individual voice with a commonplace voice that makes for a memorable writing style.

In this "revised" passage, the voice has become less conversational and more impersonal. The syntax and word choice seem more formal, which create the impression that the author is speaking to a large audience rather than to a single person.

Proofreading   One of our students once referred to proofreading as *prof-reading*—making sure the essay is ready for the prof's critical eye. Some students mistakenly equate proofreading with copyediting or even with revision in general; but proofreading refers to a very careful line-by-line scrutiny of the semifinal draft to make sure that no errors of any kind are present. The term *proofreading* comes from the profession of printing; a proof is an initial printing of a document that is used for correcting any mistakes. Most desk dictionaries list common standardized proofreaders' marks: symbols and abbreviations that professional compositors use to indicate changes. You already know some of them: the caret (^) to indicate insertion of a word or letter; the abbreviation *lc*, which means change to lowercase (a diagonal line through a capital letter means the same thing). Proofreading is not reading in the usual sense. If you try to proofread by reading normally, you will miss things. An ideal way to proofread is slowly and orally.

Chapter Summary

An argument is a form of discourse in which a writer or speaker tries to persuade an audience to accept, reject, or think a certain way about a problem that cannot be solved by scientific or mathematical reasoning alone. To argue well, a writer uses the three appeals of ethos, pathos, and logos—personal values and ethics, feelings, and logical reasoning—to supplement the facts themselves. The rhetorical rhombus reminds us that every communication act involves targeting a particular audience, whose particular needs and expectations regarding the subject must be met by the writer, and that every act of communication must have a clear, often urgent purpose for establishing communication in the first place.

Good argumentative writing is carefully structured. The three models of argumentative structure—Classical, Toulmin, and Rogerian—represent three different views about the nature and purpose of argument.

Composing arguments is a dynamic process that involves generating ideas, organizing the argument, drafting, revising, editing, and proofreading. These phases of composing overlap and are recursive. Understanding the composing process also means being aware of using different strategies for different parts of the argument, such as openings and conclusions. One final vitally important phase in the composing process is acquiring feedback from peers. Feedback on first drafts is usually immensely valuable in helping writers think more deeply about the purpose, audience, and subject of their arguments.

Checklist

1. Do I clearly understand the four elements of the rhetorical rhombus that comprise the communication act? How each element interacts with the others?

2. Do I understand how the three appeals of ethos, pathos, and logos function in argumentative writing?

3. Do I understand the nature of evidence? Of refutation?

4. Am I familiar with the strategies that comprise the composing process?

5. Have I prepared an outline to prompt me in my drafting?

6. Am I familiar with the different kinds of revision?

7. Have I learned to proofread my drafts carefully?

Writing Projects

1. Conduct an informal survey of students' study habits by talking to your fellow students. How many of them "cram" for exams or write their papers immediately before the assignment is due? What specific strategies do students use when they study? (For example, do they make marginal glosses in their books? Write notes on index cards? Make flash cards? Get together with other students in regular study groups?) Can you correlate methods or habits of study to levels of academic success? Write an essay in which you argue for or against such a correlation, using the responses you have gathered.

2. Write an essay on the role that argumentative writing can play in helping people who disagree about a given issue to arrive at better understanding— or at least at a greater willingness to cooperate. What likely obstacles must initially be overcome?

3. Keep a "writing process log" the next time you write an argument. Describe in detail everything you do when prewriting, composing each draft, revising, and proofreading. Next, evaluate the log. Which facets of the composing process were most useful? Which were least useful?

4. Compose four possible openings, each a different type (occasional, anecdotal, startling, analytical) for your next argument writing assignment. Which opening seems most appropriate for your essay, and why?

5. Prepare an outline (Classical, Toulmin, or Rogerian) for an essay taking a position on one of the following topics:

   a. All bicyclists should (should not) be required by law to wear helmets.

   b. This college should (should not) sponsor formal skateboarding competitions.

   c. More courses or programs in multicultural awareness need (do not need) to be offered at this college.

2 | Using the Classical Model in Your Arguments

> We need the capacity effectively to urge contradictory
> positions . . . not so that we may adopt either of the two (it is
> quite wrong to persuade men to evil), but that we should be
> aware how the case stands and be able, if our adversary
> deploys his arguments unjustly, to refute them.
>
> —Aristotle

Rhetoric, or the art of using language persuasively, has a long history. The work of ancient rhetoricians such as Plato, Aristotle, Quintilian, and Cicero has influenced Western education and literature for nearly two thousand years, shaping public discourse and public life. Though rooted in the past, rhetoric plays an integral role in today's judicial, political, religious, and educational institutions.

Argument in the Ancient World

In the ancient world, rhetoric was taught as oratory (public speaking) and was basic preparation for students entering law, politics, and teaching. Students learned how to communicate a point of view clearly and convincingly. Early rhetoricians, itinerant teachers known as *Sophists,* emphasized the pragmatic skills to be developed in winning an argument. Later, the Platonic school gained ascendancy, valuing philosophical reasoning over mere "training." Plato's student, Aristotle, achieved a sort of middle ground between the idealistic truth-seeking of his mentor and the mercenary pragmatism of the Sophists by viewing rhetoric as the art of finding the best available means of persuasion in a given case—that is, by applying the rigors of philosophical reasoning to actual problems.

In addition to the ancients' everyday uses of argument in law, politics, religion, athletics, and the military, oratorical competitions were held. Individuals or teams would argue an issue, and an impartial judge would determine the winner based on each argument's strengths (much like what happens in debate tournaments today). Debating, we might say, is the "sport" side of argument—a show of argumentative skill for its own sake and valuable for the development of such skill.

Aristotle (384–322 B.C.E.) wrote **Rhetoric.** *It was the first systematic study of argument and reasoning for practical purposes— political, judicial, and ceremonial.*

The Classical Model of Argument

The Classical model for structuring an argument is both simple and versatile. First, here is a look at it in outline form:

    I. Introduction

        A. Lead-in

        B. Overview of the situation

        C. Background

    II. Position statement (thesis)

    III. Appeals (ethos, pathos, logos) and evidence

        A. Appeals: to ethics, character, authority (ethos); to emotions (pathos); to reason (logos)

B. Evidence: citing of statistics, results, findings, examples, laws, relevant passages from authoritative texts

IV. Refutation (often presented simultaneously with the evidence)

V. Conclusion (peroration)

A. Highlights of key points presented (if appropriate)

B. Recommendations (if appropriate)

C. Illuminating restatement of thesis

Organizing Your Argument Using the Classical Model

The Classical argument introduces the problem and states the thesis; it next presents background information in the form of a narrative. It then presents the evidence in support of the thesis, including refutation of opposing views. Finally it reaches a conclusion.

Consider the case of student Justine Hearn, who is writing a paper on the folly of developing a tourist resort in Trinidad and Tobago, an environmentally sensitive twin-island nation in the West Indies. Justine has a good idea of what points she wants to make in her argument but is not sure what sequence to use in laying it out. She understands the Classical structure but is not quite sure how specifically she can make her essay adhere to it. Using the Classical model serves as a heuristic device—a set of hints that may be recast as questions:

1. What is my reason for writing the paper?

2. What is the best way to introduce the problem, given my evidence and audience?

3. What definitions of concepts or explanations will my readers require?

4. What exactly is my position on the matter?

5. How will my readers most likely react? Indifferently? Skeptically? Enthusiastically? How can I deal with it in advance? (For example, if the audience is likely to be skeptical, can I say things that would remove some of their skepticism?)

■ Exercise 2.1

Read Justine's first draft of her argument on how land development damages the ecology of Trinidad and Tobago. Then answer the questions that follow.

Justine Hearn

ECOLOGY VS. LAND DEVELOPMENT IN TRINIDAD AND TOBAGO

The island republic of Trinidad and Tobago in the West
Indies is facing unprecedented land development. It does have
some land preserved, but even this protected land is in danger of
being lost to farming and illegal practices. Thousands of acres
of pristine rain forest are without governmental protection and
are thus left to be destroyed without oversight or penalty.

Although the smaller island of Tobago is home to the world's
oldest legally protected forest, the Crown Point Reserve (1776),
this legacy is not being continued. Instead, it appears that the
government has made its decisions in favor of unchecked development benefiting the tourism and petrochemical industries. There
exists a number of narrowly-based laws, some of which overlap,
that offer environmental protection. However, these laws are not
broad enough or modern enough to carry much weight. Activists
have been petitioning the government to establish a more comprehensive set of laws, but this has yet to be taken seriously
by politicians.

High employment rates—24% of the general public and twice
that for young adults—have created a rift in interests that is
cleaved along social status lines (Julian Kenny and Christine
Toppin-Allahan, Videotaped lecture, Aug. 4, 1995). Environmental
concerns are expressed mostly by those in the upper classes,
while the lower classes are often perceived to be the cause for
certain environmental problems. To best illustrate how the government of Trinidad and Tobago attempts to manage environmental
issues and the societal conflicts that arise from them, an example
of a specific environmental crisis in the Nariva Swamp will
be used.

Squatters—farmers who illegally occupy governmental land—
account for one-fifth of Trinidad and Tobago's population (Kenny
and Toppin-Allahan). The Nariva Swamp and its inhabitants demonstrate the historical struggle between the people's attempt to
establish an adequate livelihood and the government's effort to
uphold established legislation. This state-owned swamp, the only

existing freshwater marsh of its kind in the Caribbean, has become a squatting site of rice farmers. In the 1960s, people began to move into the area to burn and clear Nariva's forest and marshland in order to plant rice. Although this was and still is an illegal practice, farmers continued to move in to take advantage of the open land, encouraged especially by the government's subsidies on locally grown rice. With no budget and little training, Forestry and Wildlife officers had little success in removing the squatters from the land. In fact, the government considered allowing the squatters to purchase the lands they were using, a practice that often takes place on other state-owned lands throughout the islands. In the late 1980s, commercial farmers moved in with heavy equipment to begin large-scale farming, digging canals to regulate water levels, using chemicals, and bulldozing the swamp's forests.

The human health and general pollution laws are the weakest of the environmental legislation. The Public Health Acts, which were established in the 1920s, discuss mosquito control and human waste disposal and regulate pollution in the form of "noxious substances" and "black smoke"—qualities of waste materials that were relevant at the time of the bill's creation but have since lost their bearing. Chemical spills and toxic fumes are not a part of this legislation and are thus not under state jurisdiction.

How might Trinidad and Tobago best solve these serious threats to their environment? It seems that international influences might be one of the best vectors of change, just as the World Bank and Greenpeace influenced the government of Trinidad and Tobago during the early years of the Environmental Management Authority (EMA). However, it is important to the success of the new legislation and ongoing preservation efforts that a sense of imperialism does not develop as a result of the intervention of outside forces. Furthermore, public support is necessary for government legitimacy, but a society will invest in an issue only if its people have at least an elementary sense of security. For many citizens, this would require an improvement in their quality of life, which necessitates the creation of jobs. Yet this leads to the question of sustainability, because a rise in industry

usually results in some form of environmental degradation. If
Trinidad and Tobago's economy were based in the country's biodi-
versity, a sustainable framework for jobs could be created that
would also encourage conservation interests. Ecotourism, bio-
prospecting, and controlled sustainable agriculture would be possible answers in this scenario.

1. What is Justine's thesis? How convincingly does she support it?

2. How relevant to her argument are the statistics that she cites? Are they sufficiently recent? Are they reliable? Are her sources credible? Why or why
   not?

3. Does the solution Justine proposes appear to solve the problem? What alternative solutions does she discuss?

4. Offer suggestions for ways in which Justine could further develop or otherwise strengthen her essay.

Elements of a Classical Argument in Action

Now let us examine each element in detail and see how they operate in a particular argument. Keep in mind that outlines serve to remind writers of the basic
strategy for developing a sound argument; they should not be followed slavishly
as if they were some unalterable blueprint for constructing a house.

Introduction   A good introduction accomplishes three things:

1. It presents the topic of inquiry or the problem requiring attention and perhaps briefly states the thesis.

2. It establishes a clear context for the problem.

3. It engages the reader's attention and desire to get "the whole picture."

Consider the following introduction to an argument against the use of school
vouchers, a system whereby the state promises to pay parents a percentage of tuition for attending a quality school of the parents' choice:

Most Americans believe that improving our system of education should be a
top priority for government at the local, state, and federal levels. Legislators,
school boards, education professionals, parent groups and community organizations are attempting to implement innovative ideas to rescue children
from failing school systems, particularly in inner-city neighborhoods. Many
such groups champion voucher programs. The standard program proposed
in dozens of states across the country would distribute monetary vouchers

(typically valued between $2,500–$5000) to parents of school-age children, usually in troubled inner-city school districts. Parents could then use the vouchers towards the cost of tuition at private schools—including those dedicated to religious indoctrination.

\ Superficially, school vouchers might seem a relatively benign way to increase the options poor parents have for educating their children. In fact, vouchers pose a serious threat to values that are vital to the health of American democracy. These programs subvert the constitutional principle of separation of church and state and threaten to undermine our system of public education.

How well do these two paragraphs meet the criteria for a strong introduction to an argument? First, the author (an anonymous writer for the Anti-Defamation League) introduces the problem: the need to improve our educational system and the fact that vouchers are considered to be a promising solution of that problem. The second paragraph presents the thesis: Vouchers are a bad idea. Finally, the author engages the reader's attention by using strong, dramatic language to convey a sense of urgency to the matter: Vouchers "pose a serious threat to values that are vital to the health of American democracy" and "subvert the constitutional principle of separation of church and state." Such language not only piques interest but it heightens anticipation: How is this writer going to convince me that such an assertion makes sense?

Appeals and Evidence   At the heart of any Classical argument is the evidence, reinforced by the persuasive appeals (see pages 4–6) that will ideally demonstrate, beyond doubt, the validity and reasonableness of the thesis. To be persuasive—that is, to change the minds of readers who otherwise would reject your thesis—facts and appeals must be conveyed in a way that allows readers to see the path by which they lead directly to the thesis.

Let us consider the way in which the three appeals are applied to the argument on school vouchers.

- **Ethos** (the appeal to ethics, character, valid authority). When the school vouchers author argues that a voucher program would undermine the ideals on which this country was founded, he or she is evoking the appeal of ethos: it would be unethical, or a sign of bad character, to undermine what are considered the fundamental ideals of American democracy and liberty. It should be taken for granted, the author implies, that the authority of the U.S. Constitution must always be upheld.

- **Pathos** (the appeal to emotion, compassion, sympathy). By alluding to "a serious threat" that vouchers pose to American values, the author is evoking the appeal of pathos—specifically, the fear of what might happen if states violated the U.S. Constitution.

- **Logos** (the appeal to logic, to sound, reason-based decision making). Note how the author sets up a logical connection between separation of church and state and the American system of public education: If the former is violated, the integrity of the latter is threatened. This is an example of the appeal to logic and reason: There is a logical connection to be made between A and B.

Appeals go a long way toward persuading readers, but strong evidence is also needed. Two kinds of evidence are appropriate to Classical argumentative writing—direct and indirect. *Direct evidence* consists of data from surveys, scientific experiments, and cases-in-point—phenomena that clearly point to a causal agency ("where there's smoke, there's fire"). Facts represent evidence that anyone can check firsthand at any time. *Indirect evidence* consists of formal analytical and mathematical reasoning. Here, the author takes the reader through a step-by-step analysis of, say, causes that lead to inevitable effects.

No matter what type of evidence is used, it must be tested for its relevance, accuracy, thoroughness, and timeliness.

- **Relevance.** The evidence must relate directly to the claims being made. If an argument claims that high school teachers tend subtly to discourage young women from pursuing careers in science or engineering, but then cites instances of that problem only from colleges or private schools, critics would argue that the evidence is not relevant to the claim.

- **Accuracy.** Inaccurate evidence is worse than useless: It can deceive—and even harm. Facts and figures must always be double-checked. Experts or passages from texts must be quoted or paraphrased accurately. Accuracy also requires a degree of precision relevant to what is being argued. It may be acceptable to say "water was brought to a boil" in reference to a recipe, but when describing a chemical experiment involving a water temperature to a precise fraction of a degree, such a statement would be problematic.

- **Thoroughness.** The evidence must cover every facet or implication of the claim. If a writer claims that teenagers in the United States have fewer traffic accidents today than they did ten years ago but then cites accident statistics from only three states, readers rightly would argue that the evidence could be made more thorough by including statistics from all fifty states.

- **Timeliness.** The evidence must be appropriately recent. If a writer argues that teenagers are safer drivers "today" but presents statistics from 1995, then one rightly could argue that the evidence needs to be updated.

Refutation   Closely associated with evidence is refutation, the reference to opposing views and rebutting them. Refuting viewpoints that challenge our own is seldom easy; quite often it is the most difficult stage in writing an effective argument. To refute effectively, we must assume that the challengers are equally convinced of their views. We may be tempted to trivialize or misrepresent an adversarial point by leaving out certain information or giving a faulty interpretation. Disagreements tend to be rooted in deeply personal values and beliefs, so we instinctively try to protect these beliefs. They have worked for us, have stabilized our sense of the world, have helped us cope. Any challenges are avoided. Yet, unless we have the courage to permit these beliefs to be challenged, perhaps modified, maybe even abandoned, learning and personal growth cannot take place.

Knowledge consists not of disembodied facts but of negotiated ideas. What we know we have assimilated from innumerable points of view. The health of our own ideas depends on a steady influx of fresh viewpoints, just as a body of water must be continuously replenished to avoid becoming stagnant. Such receptivity to new ideas requires courage, of course. It is never easy to say of those who argue against us, "Maybe there is some validity to these challenging views; maybe I should adopt some of them."

If after a careful and critical analysis of opponents' arguments we still hold to our overall stance and, in fact, have found flaws in theirs, we are ready to refute them. The aim of refutation is to demonstrate the limitations or errors of challenging views. It is not necessary to establish a distinct boundary between evidence and refutation since evidence may be brought in as part of the refutation process. Notice that in the body of the article on school vouchers (reprinted on pages 36–39), the author refutes the pro-voucher argument by first stating the opposition's rationale and then showing why that rationale is in error:

> Proponents of vouchers argue that these programs would allow poor students to attend good schools previously only available to the middle class. The facts tell a different story. A $2,500 voucher supplement may make the difference for some families. . . . But voucher programs offer nothing of value to families who cannot come up with the rest of the money to cover tuition costs.

The refutation is clearly articulated, but is it convincing? Skeptics probably would demand that the anti-vouchers author supply more in the way of evidence to substantiate the claim that vouchers undermine the integrity of American public schools.

How thorough is the evidence in support of the Anti-Defamation League's thesis that vouchers are harmful? The author brings in important facts that appear to demonstrate the unconstitutionality of vouchers, such as the Supreme Court's quoting of the Establishment Clause or its striking down "education programs that allow parents of parochial school students to recover a portion of their educational expenses from the state." However, much of the argument relies on speculation. There is no way of knowing for sure that the Supreme Court would judge vouchers to be unconstitutional, nor is there any way of knowing for sure that voucher programs "would force citizens—Christians, Jews, Muslims and atheists—to pay for the religious indoctrination of schoolchildren."

Effective argument depends not only on the kinds of evidence used but the degree to which that evidence resolves the stated problem.

Conclusion   The minimal task of a conclusion is to provide a final wisdom about the thesis just argued. Some conclusions summarize the key points of the argument, a strategy that can be much appreciated in a long and complicated argument but may be unnecessary otherwise. Quite often, such summary statements are followed by recommendations for what actions to take. Other conclusions are more speculative: Instead of recommending what should be done, they focus on what *might* be done. And still other conclusions are more open-ended, offering not summative statements but questions for the readers to consider.

The Anti-Defamation League writer on school vouchers does not present as full-fledged a conclusion as he or she does an introduction. Is the conclusion sufficient?

> School voucher programs undermine two great American traditions: universal public education and the separation of church and state. Instead of embracing vouchers, communities across the country should dedicate themselves to finding solutions that will be available to every American schoolchild and that take into account the important legacy of the First Amendment.

The author succinctly restates the problem and leaves the reader with the provocative suggestion found in the concluding sentence. But what sort of solution will solve that complex problem? The author brings the readers no closer to a real solution.

■ Exercise 2.2

Read the complete text of "School Vouchers: The Wrong Choice for Public Education." Then answer the questions that follow.

School Vouchers:

The Wrong Choice for Public Education | Anti-Defamation League

Most Americans believe that improving our system of education should be a top priority for government at the local, state and Federal levels. Legislators, school boards, education professionals, parent groups and community organizations are attempting to implement innovative ideas to rescue children from failing school systems, particularly in inner-city neighborhoods. Many such groups champion voucher programs. The standard program proposed in dozens of states across the country would distribute monetary

---

Source: "School Vouchers: The Wrong Choice for Public Education." Editorial. Anti-Defamation League. 1999. 2 August 2000. <http://www.adl.org/vouchers/vouchers_main.html>. Reprinted by permission of the Anti-Defamation League.

vouchers (typically valued between $2,500–$5,000) to parents of school-age children, usually in troubled inner-city school districts. Parents could then use the vouchers towards the cost of tuition at private schools—including those dedicated to religious indoctrination.

Superficially, school vouchers might seem a relatively benign way to increase the options poor parents have for educating their children. In fact, vouchers pose a serious threat to values that are vital to the health of American democracy. These programs subvert the constitutional principle of separation of church and state and threaten to undermine our system of public education.

Vouchers Are . . . Constitutionally Suspect

Proponents of vouchers are asking Americans to do something contrary to the very ideals upon which this country was founded. Thomas Jefferson, one of the architects of religious freedom in America, said, "To compel a man to furnish contributions of money for the propagation of opinions which he disbelieves . . . is sinful and tyrannical." Yet voucher programs would do just that; they would force citizens—Christians, Jews, Muslims and atheists—to pay for the religious indoctrination of schoolchildren at schools with narrow parochial agendas. In many areas, 80 percent of vouchers would be used in schools whose central mission is religious training. In most such schools, religion permeates the classroom, the lunchroom, even the football practice field. Channeling public money to these institutions flies in the face of the constitutional mandate of separation of church and state.

Supreme Court precedent supports this view. Over 50 years ago, the High Court said that the Establishment Clause requires that "[n]o tax in any amount large or small . . . be levied to support any religious activities or institutions." In 1997, the Court refused to abandon this principle, reaffirming the proposition that the government may not fund the "inculcation of religious beliefs." The Supreme Court has also held unconstitutional government programs that have the effect of advancing religion or of excessively entangling government with religion.

While the High Court has not yet heard a case on vouchers, it has struck down education programs that allow parents of parochial school students to recover a portion of their educational expenses from the state. And the Court has found unconstitutional any parochial schools in a way that might assist those schools in their sectarian missions. For example, it has held unconstitutional programs in which the state paid for certain secular instruction taking place in pervasively sectarian schools when such instruction was provided by the regular employees of those schools. Federal appeals courts have even prohibited the government from lending instructional materials to parochial schools. By subsidizing the tuition paid to schools dedicated to religious indoctrination, voucher programs violate the separation of church and state.

Still, the Constitution leaves substantial room for government programs that result in indirect benefits to religious institutions. For example, the Court has upheld programs that allow parents of children who attend sectarian schools to deduct the cost of tuition from their total income for tax purposes. Further, the Court has not struck down programs like the G.I. Bill, which pays the educational expenses of veterans of the armed forces even if they attend pervasively sectarian universities or divinity schools. These programs, though, are a far cry from the voucher initiatives that would direct public schoolchildren—and tax revenue earmarked for public education—to over-whelmingly religious institutions.

Vouchers . . . Undermine Public Schools

Implementation of voucher programs sends a clear message that we are giving up on public education. Undoubtedly, vouchers would help some students. But the glory of the American system of public education is that it is for *all* chil-dren, regardless of their religion, their academic talents or their ability to pay a fee. This policy of inclusiveness has made public schools the backbone of American democracy.

Private schools are allowed to discriminate on a variety of grounds. These institutions regularly reject applicants because of low achievement, discipline problems, and sometimes for no reason at all. Further, some private schools promote agendas antithetical to the American ideal. Under a system of vouch-ers, it may be difficult to prevent schools run by extremist groups like the Na-tion of Islam or the Ku Klux Klan from receiving public funds to subsidize their racist and anti-Semitic agendas. Indeed, the proud legacy of *Brown v. Board of Education* may be tossed away as tax dollars are siphoned off to delib-erately segregated schools.

Proponents of vouchers argue that these programs would allow poor students to attend good schools previously only available to the middle class. The facts tell a different story. A $2,500 voucher supplement may make the difference for some families, giving them just enough to cover the tuition at a private school (with some schools charging over $10,000 per year, they would still have to pay several thousand dollars). But voucher programs offer noth-ing of value to families who cannot come up with the rest of the money to cover tuition costs.

10

In many cases, voucher programs will offer students the choice between attending their current public school or attending a school run by the local church. Not all students benefit from a religious school atmosphere—even when the religion being taught is their own. For these students, voucher pro-grams offer only one option: to remain in a public school that is likely to dete-riorate even further.

As our country becomes increasingly diverse, the public school system stands out as an institution that unifies Americans. Under voucher programs, our educational system—and our country—would become even more Balkan-ized than it already is. With the help of taxpayers' dollars, private schools would be filled with well-to-do and middle-class students and a handful of the best, most motivated students from inner cities. Some public schools would be left with fewer dollars to teach the poorest of the poor and other students who, for one reason or another, were not private school material. Such a scenario can hardly benefit public education.

Finally, as an empirical matter, reports on the effectiveness of voucher programs have been mixed. Initial reports on Cleveland's voucher program, published by the American Federation of Teachers, suggest that it has been less effective than proponents argue. Milwaukee's program has resulted in a huge budget shortfall, leaving the public schools scrambling for funds. While some studies suggest that vouchers are good for public schools, there is, as yet, little evidence that they ultimately improve the quality of public education for those who need it most.

Vouchers Are . . . Not Universally Popular
When offered the opportunity to vote on voucher-like programs, the public has consistently rejected them; voters in 19 states have rejected such proposals in referendum ballots. In the November 1998 election, for example, Colorado voters rejected a proposed constitutional amendment that would have allowed parochial schools to receive public funds through a complicated tuition tax-credit scheme. Indeed, voters have rejected all but one of the tuition voucher proposals put to the ballot since the first such vote over 30 years ago.

Voucher proposals have also made little progress in legislatures across the country. While 20 states have introduced voucher bills, only two have been put into law. Congress has considered several voucher plans for the District of Columbia, but none has been enacted.

15

A recent poll conducted by the Joint Center for Political and Economic Studies demonstrates that support for vouchers has declined over the last year. Published in October 1998, the Poll revealed that support for school vouchers declined from 57.3 percent to 48.1 percent among Blacks, and from 47 to 41.3 percent among whites. Overall, 50.2 percent of Americans now oppose voucher programs; only 42 percent support them.

Conclusion
School voucher programs undermine two great American traditions: universal public education and the separation of church and state. Instead of embracing vouchers, communities across the country should dedicate themselves to finding solutions that will be available to every American schoolchild and that take into account the important legacy of the First Amendment. ◪

1. Suggest one or more alternative ways in which the Anti-Defamation League author might have structured the essay, keeping within the general framework of Classical organizational strategy. What may gain or lose emphasis as a result of the reordering?

2. Evaluate the author's use of facts and appeals. What additional facts and appeals might have been appropriate?

3. How convincing is the author's evidence that school vouchers would violate the U.S. Constitution?

■ Exercise 2.3

Read "Why School Vouchers Can Help Inner-City Children," an argument by Kurt L. Schmoke, Mayor of Baltimore, in support of school vouchers. Then answer the questions that follow.

| # Why School Vouchers Can Help Inner-City Children | The Honorable Kurt L. Schmoke |

I have been a strong supporter of public education during my tenure as mayor. In 1987 I said that it was my goal as mayor to one day have Baltimore be known as "The City That Reads." In doing that I underscored my commitment to improving all levels of education and getting people in our city focused on lifelong learning.

The state of Baltimore's economy was one of a variety of reasons for this commitment. Thirty years before I came into office, the largest private employer in Baltimore was the Bethlehem Steel Corporation's Sparrow's Point Plant. When I entered into office, however, the largest private employer in Baltimore was the Johns Hopkins University and Medical Center.

This transition meant that though there were jobs available, they would require a level of education that was higher than that which our children's parents and grandparents had to attain. It was clear to me that a commitment to improving literacy and understanding that education is a lifelong process was vitally important to our city.

With this knowledge in mind, I worked to improve our library system and our community college. Additionally, we created a Literacy Corporation to combat illiteracy in our city. In fact, President Bush presented Baltimore with the National Literacy Award in 1992.

In addition to my public responsibility for the Baltimore educational sys-   5
tem, I also have a strong private interest in our city's schools. I have two children who are graduates of city public high schools. In fact, both of my children have at some point while growing up attended both public and private schools, so I have been able to observe my own children in different educational environments.

Source: Schmoke, Kurt L. "Why School Vouchers Can Help Inner-City Children." *Civic Bulletin* 20 August 1999. Lecture. Manhattan Institute. 2 August 2000. Reprinted by permission of The Manhatten Institute. Editing does not distort the speaker's meaning or intentions.

What I've found as a result of my experiences in pursuing a better-educated Baltimore, and a better-educated family, is a major void in current school reform efforts. I believe that the issues of competition and accountability are all too often ignored in efforts to improve public education.

My years of experience in education have led me to be in favor of school choice: quite simply, I believe in giving parents more choice about where to educate their children. My support of school choice is founded in the common sense premise that no parent should be forced to send a child to a poorly performing school.

Unfortunately, however, countless parents, especially in the inner cities, are now forced to do just that. Parents in middle- and upper-class communities have long practiced school choice. They made sure that their children attended schools where they would get the best possible education. There is no reason why this option should be closed to low-income parents.

The consequences of this unfairness are not at all difficult to grasp. As one perceptive observer of urban education has written "Education used to be the poor child's ticket out of the slums. Now it's part of the system that traps people in the underclass."

This was part of the thinking behind what people in Baltimore call my conversion to school choice. It did not happen overnight. It evolved slowly. My belief in school choice grew out of my experiences and, yes, my *frustrations* in trying to improve Baltimore's public schools over the last twelve years.   10

Under my watch as mayor we have tried all sorts of programs to reform the schools. Looking back, some of these programs showed promise, and some of our schools did demonstrate that they were doing a good job of educating our children.

Our successes, however, were still the exceptions, not the norm. I feared that, unless we took drastic action, this pattern would only continue. I considered school choice to be an innovation strong enough to change the course of what was widely recognized as an ailing system.

Why school choice? Two reasons: excellence and accountability. Parents want academic *excellence* for their children. They also want to know that there is someone in their child's school who is *accountable* for achieving those high academic standards.

In most cities in this nation, however, if your child is zoned into a school that is not performing well academically, and where teachers and administrators don't see themselves as being responsible for academic performance, parents have no recourse. Parents can only send their child to that school and hope for the best.

Under a school choice plan, a parent would have options. There would be consequences for a school's poor performance. Parents could pull their children out of poorly performing schools and enroll them someplace else. If exercising this option leads to a mass exodus from certain underachieving   15 schools, schools will learn this painful lesson: schools will either improve, or close due to declining enrollments.

Any corporation that tolerated mediocre performance among its employees, unresponsiveness to the complaints of its customers, and the promotion of a large number of failed products, would not survive in the marketplace very long. What is true of corporations should also be true of poorly performing and poorly run schools.

These are some of the ideas that I expressed when I first came out in support of school choice in a speech at Johns Hopkins University in March of 1996, not as a panacea, but as another way to improve public education. Though I thought my remarks were relatively benign, the speech sparked a great deal of controversy.

One of my own aides even joked that he wanted to see my voter registration card to see if I was still a Democrat. Well, I am still a Democrat and I have no plans to change my political affiliation. I, nonetheless, believe that the Democratic Party should reevaluate its position on school choice issues.

In actuality, choice should not be included in partisan rhetoric. School choice should be about giving our nation's children the best possible educational foundation.

The same week as my speech at Johns Hopkins, I appointed a task force to   20
explore the idea of school choice. I asked the task force to consider the pros and cons of school choice programs in all their variations, including programs such as the system implemented in Los Angeles where parents and students have the freedom to choose any school in the public system. I also asked that they investigate private school voucher plans such as the program in Milwaukee, as well as charter and magnet schools.

The task force released a report in that year which recommended that the Baltimore school system expand magnet schools and initiate a system-wide open enrollment program as a way to provide more educational options for parents and their children.

In my view, the task force unfortunately stopped short of endorsing publicly funded vouchers as a way to achieve the goal of school choice. The group, however, did leave open the door for reconsideration of the voucher issue later on. Meanwhile, the Baltimore city public school system has now implemented a variation of the school choice idea through what is called the New Schools Initiative.

These "New Schools" are very similar to charter schools. They are publicly funded schools that are planned and operated by parents or institutions or other non-traditional sponsors.

I recently spoke at Coppin State University for commencement. Coppin State is an historically black college in Baltimore that started out as a teacher training school. Today, under one of the New School Initiatives, Coppin is managing an elementary school in its home neighborhood drawing on its teaching and research to improve that school.

Now, three years after that Hopkins speech, I continue to believe that   25
choice holds the greatest hope for instilling excellence and accountability in
the nation's public schools.

At that time, as a Democrat and an African-American mayor, I was considered a maverick, or worse, for expressing that idea. No longer. A ground-
swell of support for choice is rising all over the nation, including from some
unlikely quarters. Certainly, there's no greater proof of this than the tremendous response to the Children's Scholarship Fund funded by Wal-Mart heir
John Walton and financier Ted Forstmann.

Under this program, the parents of some 1.25 million low-income children
across the country applied for partial scholarships to help their children attend
private and parochial schools. Civil rights pioneer and former mayor of Atlanta Andrew Young wrote these words in a nationally syndicated newspaper
column shortly after the results of the scholarship drive were announced:
"1.25 million cries for help, voiced by poor, largely minority families, seeking
something most Americans take for granted. A decent education for their
children."

In that column, Young described the collective cry for help as "a moment
of moral awakening" that promises to be just as pivotal in America's civil
rights struggle as Rosa Park's refusal to give up her bus seat in Montgomery,
Alabama more than 40 years ago.

Such moments of moral awakening, Young observed, force us to reevaluate our beliefs and finally to take action. In Baltimore, that particular scholarship program attracted twenty thousand applicants. This represents an
astonishing 44 percent of city children who were eligible.

The conclusions that can be drawn from these figures are unmistakable.   30
The *Baltimore Sun* education editor wrote, "We know now that there's a pent-
up demand for school choice in the city. And we know that poor parents do
care about the education of their children."

In fact, some low-income African-American parents in our city have
shown they care so much that they will even go so far as to look *halfway around
the world* in order to find a good school for their children. The school which I
refer to is called Baraka, which means blessings in Swahili. It's located in rural
Kenya, 10,000 miles and eight time zones from inner-city Baltimore. And it's
funded by a Baltimore-based foundation, The Abell Foundation. The Foundation recruits and selects at-risk seventh- and eighth-grade boys from the Baltimore city public schools to participate in this bold education experiment.

The kids chosen for this program are generally headed for serious trouble.
It is safe to assume that many of the boys in the Baraka program would have
ended up incarcerated, or worse, had they not been selected.

Baraka School is going to begin its fourth year of operation in the fall. With
30 graduates to date, the school is having remarkable success in boosting the
academic achievement of these at-risk youngsters and truly turning around
their lives.

Because of the persistent resistance to school choice by some Maryland politicians, however, the State Education Department has refused to fund the Baraka School project. I do not speak of any extra funding here. I am only talking about taking the state's cost of educating each Baraka student, which would normally have gone to the school that they had been assigned to had they remained in the public system, and allowing it to be used to educate the students in this alternative environment.

The state has absolutely refused. Were it not for the support of the Foundation, the Baraka School, which has done such an excellent job for these young men, would have closed.   35

So, despite greater acceptance of school choice it's certainly premature to declare victory in the public opinion contest. Indeed, criticisms of school choice are as strident as ever and I am sure you have heard the more familiar ones.

Some say that school choice, especially vouchers, will weaken public education. My response is that choice can only strengthen public education by introducing competition and accountability into the mix. Others claim that school choice is undemocratic. My response to them is that choice is in keeping with the aspirations for freedom that formed the core of American democracy. As former Delaware Governor Pete Du Pont once wrote, "It's about the liberty to choose what's best for your children." All of us should have that choice.

Some say that school choice is elitist, or even racist. The truth is that black low-income children are among the prime victims of the nation's failing public schools. African-American parents know this all too well. This is why they have been so open to the idea of school choice.

A recent nation poll released by the Joint Center for Political and Economic Studies found a trend toward growing support of tuition vouchers among African-American parents.

Another common criticism of school choice, and especially vouchers, is that it violates the principle of separation of church and state.   40

A properly structured voucher program is no more a violation of the principle of separation of church and state than is the GI Bill. This program allowed military veterans to use government dollars to attend any university of their choice, public or private, religious or secular.

I am convinced that with time, and through open dialogue, critics of school choice will come to see this movement for what it is: part of an emerging new civil rights battle for the millennium, the battle for education equity. We need to give poor children the same right that children from more affluent households have long enjoyed. The right to an education that will prepare them to make a meaningful contribution to society. It is that simple.

In speaking of battles, and in closing, I remind you of those few words of wisdom from Victor Hugo: "Greater than the tread of Mighty Armies, is an Idea whose Time has Come . . ." As we look to the future, evidence is increasingly compelling, that school choice is such an idea. ◢

1. Critique the essay in terms of (a) the effectiveness of its introduction; (b) the strength of its evidence and appeals; (c) the strength of its refutations; (d) its conclusion.

2. Prepare an outline of your own essay on school vouchers. What will be your thesis? What kind of evidence will you present? How will you refute challenging views?

■ Exercise 2.4

Read the three magazine ads and consider the images they use. Then answer the questions that follow.

1. What are the basic arguments of the magazine ads?

2. What appeals can you identify in them?

3. Is there more than one appeal in a given ad?

GOD, I'M STARVING!

GOD, SO AM I.

☐ Yes, I would like to make a donation to Catholic Charities of Chicago. My donation is $ _____

The ✦ CATHOLIC
CHARITIES
OF THE ARCHDIOCESE OF CHICAGO

☐ Please send me more information on wills and estate planning.

Name: _____

Address: _____

City: _____ State: _____

Zip Code: _____

Send to: Rev. Edwin M. Conway, Administrator, Catholic Charities, 126 N. Desplaines St., Chicago, Illinois 60606

"Starving." So easy to say when you sit down to satisfy your appetite. But it's an empty, hopeless reality for many. Please. Send a check now; leave a bequest in your will later... your willpower can work miracles.

At Catholic Charities, 98.8¢ of each dollar goes to help the needy through 189 services at 96 locations. We helped over a half a million people last year. People of all faiths. The homeless, addicted, abused... and hungry. Victims of unfortunate circumstances who need our help.

Next time you feel "starved," consider those who really are, and help.

Write Rev. Edwin M. Conway, Administrator, 126 N. Desplaines, Chicago, IL 60606, or call 236-5172.

PHOTO: BILL EMRICH

AT A TIME LIKE THIS, WHOSE CELLULAR PHONE WOULD YOU RATHER OWN?

When the name on the phone is AT&T, you're getting something no other cellular phone can give you. AT&T quality and customer service. We back our cellular phones with a 7-day, toll-free Cellular Hotline—for product information, technical help, even next-business-day replacement anywhere in the Continental U.S. Call 1 800 232-5179 for all the details.

DEPENDABILITY BEYOND THE ORDINARY

Available at AT&T Phone Centers and other fine retailers.

OYSTER PERPETUAL
LADY DATEJUST

The Oyster.®

The pearl.

Safe inside the Oyster case of a Rolex Lady Datejust resides a more than 200-component movement of breathtaking complexity and precision. It includes a Perpetual Rotor which transforms the slightest movement into a reserve of power. This rotor, which keeps the mainspring at a constant optimum tension, is so efficient that, even after the timepiece is taken off, it will run for more than a full day. It's just one reason why the more closely one studies this Lady Datejust, the more beautiful it becomes.

Rolex Oyster Perpetual Lady Datejust in 18kt gold with matching Oyster bracelet. For the name and location of an Official Rolex Jeweler near you, please call 1-800-36ROLEX. Rolex, ♛, Oyster Perpetual, Lady Datejust and Oyster are trademarks.

ROLEX

Chapter Summary

The Classical model of argument dates back to ancient Greece and Rome, and it is still used. In effect, the Classical model presents a template, a preestablished structure for framing an argument. It includes these elements:

- An introduction, which presents the claim to be argued and gives necessary background information
- A body of collected data or evidence and appeals, which together attempt to persuade the audience that the claim is convincing, and acknowledgment and refutation of challenging views
- A conclusion, which may summarize key points, reflect on implications and consequences, or make recommendations (if appropriate)

Checklist

1. Does my paper include the elements of Classical argument structure in proper sequence?
2. Does my introduction clearly present my thesis and necessary background information?
3. Have I acknowledged and accurately presented challenging views? Have I refuted them thoroughly?
4. Does my conclusion summarize the key points of my argument, present insightful interpretations, or make appropriate predictions or recommendations?

Writing Projects

1. Using the Classical model of argument structure, write a three-page position paper on one of the following topics:

   a. Students should (should not) be required to take fewer core courses and allowed to take more electives.

   b. First-year composition courses should (should not) be an elective instead of a requirement.

   c. The college bookstore's buyback policy should (should not) be reformed.

2. Using the Classical model of argument, write an essay defending or challenging the value or usefulness of an existing law, policy, or program, such as the electoral college, the National Endowment for the Arts, the banning of prayer from public schools, or the minimum drinking age in your state.

3 | Using the Toulmin Model in Your Arguments

> Rationality has to be understood in terms of formal argumentation.
>
> —Stephen Toulmin

Stephen Toulmin (b. 1922), an English philosopher of science and the history of ideas, developed a system of argument that has proven useful and influential. Toulmin's model of argument is closely associated with the rigor of formal logic and logical reasoning, but it is more flexible and better able to work productively with tentative and value-based judgments, such as the ones encountered in legal and ethical contexts. The Toulmin model calls for making a claim that is debatable; presenting good data and reasons (grounds and evidence) to support this claim; explaining the warrant, or underlying assumptions that connect the claim and the data; qualifying the claim as necessary by acknowledging and responding to counterarguments; and drawing a conclusion.

The Toulmin Model of Argument

The terms we encounter in the Toulmin model immediately call attention to the complexity of social interaction:

- An argument begins with a *claim*, the viewpoint or thesis that you want your readers or listeners to accept.

- To accomplish this goal, you must produce compelling *data*, the grounds or evidence. In formal scientific argument, the data will consist of results obtained from experiments, close observations, or mathematical analyses. In other contexts, the data likely will consist of rules, laws, policies, or highly valued social customs largely shared by the community.

- Next, you need to ask of any argument whether the data or grounds used to support the claim truly are valid. In other words, you must look for a proper *warrant*, a guarantee that the data are based on some sensible or ethical foundation. Anyone can conjure up all sorts of data to support a claim. As Shakespeare in *The Merchant of Venice* reminds us, through the

Stephen Toulmin (b. 1922) is a philosopher of science. His context-based theory of argument provides an influential alternative to rigid, logic-driven theories.

mouth of the merchant Antonio, "The Devil can cite Scripture for his purpose."

- Finally, you must be prepared to bring in a *qualifier* to your claim—that is, be prepared to make an exception to it under certain circumstances. Consider: "The right of free speech must be protected in all situations *except* when it can endanger life or safety, such as yelling 'Fire!' in a crowded theater." The qualification—the exception to the rule—prevents the claim from losing touch with complex social situations.

Now let us examine each Toulmin element in more detail.

The Claim

You know this feature as the thesis, premise, or central assumption. Toulmin chooses to call it the *claim* because that term suggests a thesis or assertion that is particularly *open to challenge.* The term comes from the Latin word *clamare,* to cry out, reminding us of the spontaneity with which claims are often made and hence how easily they can reach human ears and eyes without sufficient evidence to support them. The Latin root also reminds us to pay attention to how open to public scrutiny the claim is likely to be once it is presented as a speech or as a printed document in a periodical or book, on the Internet, in a court of law, or in a college paper.

For an argument to succeed, the writer first must ensure that the claim offered is worthy of deliberation. Some claims are not arguable. For example, it would be foolish to argue seriously that red is a superior color to blue. The claim is too dependent on subjective taste to be arguable. As the Latin maxim goes, *De gustibus non est disputandum*—of taste there is no disputing. But let's say you are an interior decorator and you have studied the effects of color on mood. You might argue that particular colors work best in particular types of rooms within a house. Here the claim is based not on personal taste but on statistical fact: Researchers have shown that pale blue helps relax people; therefore pale blue would be an appropriate color for bedroom walls.

There are two basic types of claims, objective and subjective. *Objective claims* assert that something *actually* exists and present evidence that is demonstrably factual—not only in the sense of scientifically factual but legally factual, as in the case of laws, regulations, and policies. Here are some examples of objective claims:

- Video games heighten a child's hand-eye coordination and visual perception, but they impede the development of language processing skills.

- It is a myth that science is based only on logical reasoning and that art is based only on imagination. Logical reasoning and imagination are equally important to science and to art.

- Those who wish to speak out against the U.S. Constitution have just as much constitutional right to communicate their views in public as those who support the Constitution.

The above claims present themselves as objective truths. But they are not *self-evident* truths; they must be supported with the appropriate evidence before readers can accept them as factual. Thus, before the first claim can be accepted as factual, the arguer must show, for example, that psychologists have compared the learning behaviors of children who play video games with those children who do not and have found enough evidence to establish a causal link between video-game playing and abstract reasoning.

Before the second claim can be accepted as factual, the arguer must provide convincing examples of the way imagination works in science and the way logical reasoning works in art. For example, the arguer might refer to autobiographical statements of scientists such as Albert Einstein or mathematicians such as Jules Henri Poincaré, who at various times obtained scientific understanding through dreams or imaginary "thought experiments."

Before the third claim can be accepted as factual, the arguer must demonstrate how the Constitution, paradoxical as it may seem, actually protects the rights of those who wish to speak out against it. This proof would entail careful analysis and interpretation of selected passages from the Constitution.

Subjective claims, on the other hand, assert that something *should* exist and present evidence derived from ethical, moral, or aesthetic convictions. Someone who argues, for example, that all college students should be required to take at least one course in literature to graduate or that animals should be treated with dignity is making a subjective claim. Although each claim is based on personal values, one cannot dismiss them as a kind of anything-goes relativism. The arguer, for example, might demonstrate that the benefits derived from studying literature improve one's ability to understand human nature, a valuable asset when one interacts with people.

The Data

The Toulmin model demands that writers take pains to ensure that the supporting evidence fully validates the claim. The word *data* suggests "hard facts"—results from experiments, statistics from surveys, as well as historical, legal, and biographical facts. For more indirect kinds of evidence, such as testimonials or interpretations, the term *grounds* or *backing* is more appropriate.

Like claims, data or grounds must be presented as accurately and as unambiguously as possible. Someone who argues, for example, that essay exams test student comprehension of literature better than multiple-choice exams do, and who in so arguing relies on the testimonials of students, would want to make sure that those testimonials contain clear *demonstrations* of better comprehension for students taking essay exams. Or course, the criteria for "better comprehension" would need to be clarified before they could be used as valid grounds for a claim. The criteria might include richly detailed (as opposed to generalized) recollection of the content of literary works; they might also include insightful critical assessment or comparison of the thematic material of the works (as opposed to, say, superficial explanation of its strengths and weaknesses).

The Warrant

A warrant is the assurance that the evidence brought in to support the claim is completely reliable and that it rests on sound principles or values. Thus, just as the data legitimate the claim, a warrant, often implicit in the argument, legitimates the data. As Stephen Toulmin writes, warrants "indicate the bearing of [the] conclusion of the data already produced" (*The Uses of Argument,* 1958: 98). By "bearing" Toulmin is referring to the need for readers to recognize and accept an appropriate direction in which the argument takes shape from claim to data to warrant. Warrants remind us of the humanizing dimension of argument: An argument, no matter how "heated," must always be principled rather than stem from vague or questionable motives.

Let us see how warrants operate in a given argument. Consider an essay in which a student, Melissa, argues for the abolition of letter grades in formal education. Melissa's claim is as follows:

Letter grades should be abolished because they result in unhealthy competition, distract students from truly learning the subject matter, and constitute an inadequate gauge of student performance.

Melissa chooses to support her claim with data that compares the performance of students in a letter-graded class with the performance of students in a Pass/No Pass class. Melissa's warrant might go something like this: "Learning for its own sake is more satisfying to students than learning to achieve predetermined standards of proficiency." Melissa does not need to state this sentence explicitly, but the evidence she uses to support her claim should make the warrant apparent.

We might diagram the relationship between Melissa's claim, data, and warrant as in Figure 3.1.

Compelling warrants are just as vital to the force of an argument as are compelling data because they reinforce the trustworthiness of the data. Unsuccessful warrants often seem disconnected from, or even contradictory to, the evidence. Consider the following claim:

Students should not be required to attend class.

If the evidence presented is the college's pledge to inculcate self-reliance in students, then the warrant—that self-reliance is compromised when professors

FIGURE 3.1 Relationship Between the Claim, Data, and Warrant

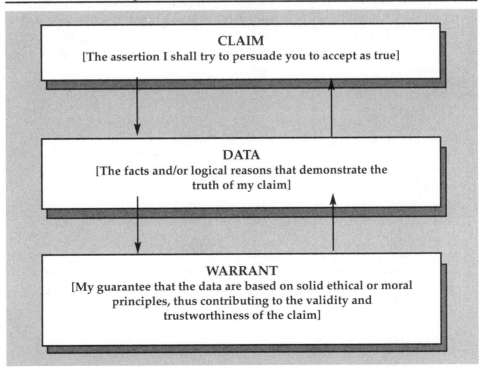

CLAIM
[The assertion I shall try to persuade you to accept as true]

DATA
[The facts and/or logical reasons that demonstrate the truth of my claim]

WARRANT
[My guarantee that the data are based on solid ethical or moral principles, thus contributing to the validity and trustworthiness of the claim]

require students to attend class—would seem contradictory to many readers because it is often assumed that such requirements are designed to *promote* self-reliance.

There are three kinds of warrants, which roughly correspond to the three kinds of appeals in Classical argument: logical or scientific warrants, ethical or forensic-based warrants, and emotional or artistic-based warrants.

1. **Logical or scientific warrants.** These warrants reinforce the trustworthiness of logical progression of scientific reasoning. If a meteorologist predicts a smog alert on the basis of 90-degree temperatures, little or no winds, and heavy traffic, her warrant would be that such a formula for smog predication is reliable.

2. **Ethical or forensic-based warrants.** A warrant is ethical when it relates to values or codes of conduct such as honor, integrity, altruism, honesty, and compassion. If one argues that underrepresented minorities should be allowed the opportunity to attend college even if their admissions test scores are not quite as high as those of the majority of admissions candidates, and uses as evidence the success rate of those given such opportunity, then the warrant is that society is ethically obligated to compensate minorities for past injustices by giving them such opportunities. Where affirmative action measures have become law we could say that the warrant justifies enactment of that law.

3. **Emotional or artistic-based warrants.** If someone argues that profanity in films weakens instead of strengthens his enjoyment of those films and uses personal testimony as evidence, then the arguer's warrant is that such negative reactions to profanity in movies is a reliable criterion for evaluating the strength or weakness of a film.

The Qualifier

Claims are rarely absolute; that is, a claim may be valid in many circumstances, but not necessarily in all. If that is the case, an arguer would want to *qualify* the claim so that her readers would understand how she is limiting its range. For example, someone who claims that dress codes should be eliminated in the workplace might qualify that claim by excluding workplaces where uniforms are required for reasons of security (as is the case with police or military uniforms) or where certain articles of clothing are prohibited for reasons of personal safety (for example, someone cannot wear a necktie when operating heavy machinery). Someone writing about the negative influence of television on learning might qualify the claim by noting that watching television for the specific purpose of studying its negative effects could have a positive benefit on learning.

■ Exercise 3.1

Should the tobacco industry be held responsible for individuals who smoke and become ill because of it? Or should individuals be responsible for their own decisions? Student Daniel Neal decides to take the latter position and shapes his argument according to the Toulmin model. Read Daniel's paper; then respond to the questions that follow.

Daniel Neal

TOBACCO: IGNORANCE IS NO LONGER AN EXCUSE

Any individual who chooses to use tobacco today is making an informed decision. The negative effects of tobacco are known, admitted, and even advertised by tobacco companies. Simply put, ignorance is no longer an excuse for smoking. And since the government has settled with the tobacco companies, ignorance is no longer an excuse for legal action. Because of the tobacco settlement, individuals must now be responsible for the consequences of choosing to use tobacco.

Part of this settlement requires the tobacco companies begin "spending hundreds of millions of dollars on efforts to discourage and deglamorize tobacco use" (Klein 463). Because it will highlight the dangers of tobacco, some argue that this will in fact encourage youth tobacco use. Richard Klein holds that "emphasizing that tobacco is dangerous and disapproved will enhance the glamour, prestige, and attractiveness of cigarettes, particularly among the young" (463). Klein's point is valid: Teenagers are attracted to what is dangerous and disapproved. No one debates that youth tobacco use is undesirable and should be prevented. It is wrong, however, to blame tobacco companies for youth tobacco use for the simple reason that they are not the ones directly selling it to minors. The tobacco companies cannot be held accountable for the actions of independent retailers who choose to sell tobacco to children. Instead of arguing that the settlement will increase youth tobacco use, those who are concerned should attack the way teens get tobacco: dishonest retailers willing to sell tobacco products illegally to minors. The

tobacco settlement has not changed the illegality of underage tobacco use—that minors may choose to smoke illegally is
irrelevant. It is unquestionably positive, however, that the tobacco settlement will fund education efforts so that these
minors, when adults, can make informed and responsible decisions
about tobacco use.

Other critics of the settlement feel that the tobacco industry will receive unfair protection from further lawsuits. In her
essay ". . . Or a Payoff to Purveyors of Poison?" Elizabeth M. Whelan writes:

> Whatever the parties' motivation, the deal that resulted
> gave the tobacco industry a major boost by providing limited
> immunity against future litigation. While technically al-
> lowing smokers (or their survivors) to continue to sue cig-
> arette companies for damages caused by smoking, the
> settlement would put a yearly cap of $5 billion on damages,
> an amount that is a trivial cost of doing business for the
> industry. This cap will serve as a disincentive to future
> plaintiff's attorneys, who will incur enormous costs in any
> challenges they choose to mount against the wealthy tobacco
> companies (467).

If the dangers of tobacco were still concealed by the tobacco
companies, Whelan's argument would be quite valid. However, that
tobacco use is harmful to one's health is plain knowledge today.
Since anyone considering tobacco use today has been fully
informed of the dangers by many sources (including the tobacco
industry) how can anyone but that individual be responsible for
damages resulting from smoking? While Whelan holds that limited
immunity for tobacco companies is a negative thing, it is in fact
quite positive: By setting limits on the liability of tobacco
companies, the government is forcing individuals to take responsibility for their actions. Later in her essay, Whelan continues:
"This is analogous to a scenario in which a corporation admits to
polluting the water supply, pays some damages, then returns immediately to dumping toxins down the well—and gets away with it"
(467). In this analogy Whelan neglects to include a key participant: the individual choosing to use tobacco. Borrowing her

terms, while the well may be toxic, not only is it clearly labeled so, but none is forced to drink from it. The tobacco settlement is quite fair because it places the responsibility for tobacco use into the hands of the informed consumers who use it.

Instead of continuing to demonize the tobacco industry, we should demand that the individuals who choose to use tobacco take personal responsibility for the damages caused by it. Consider alcohol, a substance harmful both when used as intended (killing brain cells) and when abused (driving while intoxicated, alcohol poisoning, alcoholism, etc.). We have, as a society, accepted the idea of individual responsibility for the consequences of alcohol use. It is time we do the same for tobacco. An individual choosing to smoke today must realize that he or she has been amply warned. By providing the tobacco industry protection against future litigation, the tobacco settlement has justly moved the onus of responsibility from the corporation to the informed consumer.

Works Cited

Klein, Richard. "Prohibition II . . ." <u>Wall Street Journal</u> 26 June 1997.

Whelan, Elizabeth M. ". . . Or a Payoff to Purveyors of Poison?" <u>Wall Street Journal</u> 26 June 1997.

1. How effectively does Daniel use the Toulmin method? What might he do differently?

2. Critique Daniel's method of organizing the argument. Which parts of the essay, if any, could he organize more effectively? Why?

Organizing Your Argument Using the Toulmin Model

Preparing to write an argument using the Toulmin model puts you into an intense questioning mode about the nature of your claim, the reliability of your data, and the ethical strength of your warrant.

To begin, write down your claim, data, and warrant. Then jot down questions about each of them. One student, organizing an argument on the hazards of secondhand cigarette smoke, prepares the following list:

My Claim:

Secondhand cigarette smoke is hazardous enough to justify prohibiting smoking in all public places.

Questions About my Claim

1. Is it valid? What makes it valid?

2. Is it practical? Can it actually be acted on?

3. Are there qualifications I must make to my claim?

4. What will be some of the possible challenges to my claim?

5. Who could benefit most from accepting my claim? Benefit least or be harmed?

My Data

1. Statistical information from the American Cancer Society, the American Lung Association, and the American Medical Association

2. The most recent Surgeon General's report on secondhand smoke

3. Personal testimonials of those who became seriously ill as a result of long-term exposure to secondhand smoke

Questions About my Data

1. Do I have sufficient data to support my claim?

2. Are there other important sources of information that I have overlooked?

3. Are my data reliable (not biased or manipulated)? Timely? Accurate?

4. How can I test the data for reliability, timeliness, and accuracy?

5. Which data are the most compelling? Least compelling?

My Warrant

It is more important for people to have the freedom to breathe clean air than for smokers to have the freedom to befoul the air.

Questions About my Warrant

1. Do I really believe that "freedom" in the context of smoking has to be qualified to include freedom from encroaching on one's right to breathe smoke-free air?

2. What other warrants might underlie the one I have identified? Am I too intolerant of smokers? Am I exaggerating the seriousness of the problem?

3. Am I prepared to stand behind my warrant, regardless of how others might challenge it?

The student then prepares the following tentative outline based on this list:

Thesis

Because secondhand smoke is so hazardous, smoking should be banned from all public facilities.

I. Introduction: The problem of secondhand smoke

   A. First example: Woman breathes in secondhand smoke in a restaurant and has an asthma attack

   B. Second example: Child in a shopping mall, allergic to secondhand smoke, becomes seriously ill when a group of smoking teens pass by him

   C. Claim, with allusions to underlying warrants, that secondhand smoke is hazardous enough to justify banning smoking from all public places

II. Data in support of the claim

   A. Scientific data from ACS, ALA, and AMA + discussion of data

   B. Testimonial data from physicians + discussion

III. Deeper considerations (warrants) behind the claim [*Note:* This discussion would approximate refutation in the Classical model but would give more emphasis to a shared value system with the audience.]

IV. Concluding remarks

■ Exercise 3.2

1. For each of the following claims, suggest at least one qualifier, two kinds of evidence, and one warrant. Also suggest a counterclaim with counterdata and a counterwarrant for each.

   a. Our mayor should be removed from office because we just learned that he was once arrested for possession of marijuana.

   b. Any novel that includes the use of racial slurs should be banned from public school classrooms.

   c. Beef in restaurants should be prepared well done regardless of customer preference because of the danger of E. coli infection.

2. Work up two versions of an outline for an essay on improving conditions where you live. Use the Classical model to structure the first outline and the Toulmin model for the second. Which of the two outlines would you use as the basis for the paper, and why?

3. Rewrite each of the following claims by using more specific terms or references. *Example:* UFO sightings are a bunch of nonsense. *Rewrite:* UFO sightings are difficult to document because trick photography is easy to accomplish.

a. Books are an environmental problem.

b. Cats make better pets than dogs.

c. Students should be admitted to college on the basis of merit only.

4. Suggest one or two possible warrants for each of the following claims:

a. All college students should be required to take at least one course in economics.

b. More college courses should be conducted over the Internet.

c. High school sex education courses are inadequate.

■ Exercise 3.3

Read the following essay by Virginia Woolf and identify its claim, data, and warrant.

Professions for Women | Virginia Woolf

When your secretary invited me to come here, she told me that your Society is concerned with the employment of women and she suggested that I might tell you something about my own professional experiences. It is true I am a woman; it is true I am employed; but what professional experiences have I had? It is difficult to say. My profession is literature; and in that profession there are fewer experiences for women than in any other, with the exception of the stage—fewer, I mean, that are peculiar to women. For the road was cut many years ago—by Fanny Burney, by Aphra Behn, by Harriet Martineau, by Jane Austen, by George Eliot—many famous women, and many more unknown and forgotten, have been before me, making the path smooth, and regulating my steps. Thus, when I came to write, there were very few material obstacles in my way. Writing was a reputable and harmless occupation. The family peace was not broken by the scratching of a pen. No demand was made upon the family purse. For ten and sixpence one can buy paper enough to write all the plays of Shakespeare—if one has a mind that way. Pianos and models, Paris, Vienna, and Berlin, masters and mistresses, are not needed by a writer. The cheapness of writing paper is, of course, the reason why women have succeeded as writers before they have succeeded in the other professions.

But to tell you my story—it is a simple one. You have only got to figure to yourselves a girl in a bedroom with a pen in her hand. She had only to move

Source: Woolf, Virginia. "Professions for Women." *The Death of the Moth and Other Essays.* New York: Harcourt, Brace: 1942. 235–242. Copyright 1942 by Harcourt, Inc. and renewed 1970 by Marjorie T. Parsons, executrix, reprinted by permission of the publisher.

that pen from left to right—from ten o'clock to one. Then it occurred to her to do what is simple and cheap enough after all—to slip a few of those pages into an envelope, fix a penny stamp in the corner, and drop the envelope into the red box at the corner. It was thus that I became a journalist; and my effort was rewarded on the first day of the following month—a very glorious day it was for me—by a letter from an editor containing a cheque for one pound ten shillings and sixpence. But to show you how little I deserve to be called a professional woman, how little I know of the struggles and difficulties of such lives, I have to admit that instead of spending that sum upon bread and butter, rent, shoes and stockings, or butcher's bills, I went out and bought a cat—a beautiful cat, a Persian cat, which very soon involved me in bitter disputes with my neighbors.

What could be easier than to write articles and to buy Persian cats with the profits? But wait a moment. Articles have to be about something. Mine, I seem to remember, was about a novel by a famous man. And while I was writing this review, I discovered that if I were going to review books I should need to do battle with a certain phantom. And the phantom was a woman, and when I came to know her better I called her after the heroine of a famous poem. The Angel in the House. It was she who used to come between me and my paper when I was writing reviews. It was she who bothered me and wasted my time and so tormented me that at last I killed her. You who come of a younger and happier generation may not have heard of her—you may not know what I mean by The Angel in the House. I will describe her as shortly as I can. She was intensely sympathetic. She was immensely charming. She was utterly unselfish. She excelled in the difficult arts of family life. She sacrificed herself daily. If there was chicken, she took the leg; if there was a draught she sat in it—in short she was so constituted that she never had a mind or a wish of her own, but preferred to sympathize always with the minds and wishes of others. Above all—I need not say it—she was pure. Her purity was supposed to be her chief beauty—her blushes, her great grace. In those days—the last of Queen Victoria—every house had its Angel. And when I came to write I encountered her with the very first words. The shadow of her wings fell on my page; I heard the rustling of her skirts in the room. Directly, that is to say, I took my pen in my hand to review that novel by a famous man, she slipped behind me and whispered: "My dear, you are a young woman. You are writing about a book that has been written by a man. Be sympathetic; be tender; flatter; deceive; use all the arts and wiles of our sex. Never let anybody guess that you have a mind of your own. Above all, be pure." And she made as if to guide my pen. I now record the one act for which I take some credit to myself, though the credit rightly belongs to some excellent ancestors of mine who left me a certain sum of money—shall we say five hundred pounds a year?—so that it was not necessary for me to depend solely on charm for my living. I turned upon her and caught her by the throat. I did my best to kill her. My excuse if I were to be had up at a court of law, would be that I acted in self-defence. Had

I not killed her she would have killed me. She would have plucked the heart out of my writing. For as I found directly I put pen to paper, you cannot review even a novel without having a mind of your own, without expressing what you think to be the truth about human relations, morality, sex. And all these questions, according to the Angel of the House cannot be dealt with freely and openly by women; they must charm, they must conciliate, they must—to put it bluntly—tell lies if they are to succeed. Thus, whenever I felt the shadow of her wing or the radiance of her halo upon my page, I took up the inkpot and flung it at her. She died hard. Her fictitious nature was of great assistance to her. It is far harder to kill a phantom than a reality. She was always creeping back when I thought I had dispatched her. Though I flatter myself that I killed her in the end, the struggle was severe; it took much time that had better have been spent upon learning Greek grammar; or in roaming the world in search of adventures. But it was a real experience; it was an experience that was bound to befall all women writers at that time. Killing the Angel in the House was part of the occupation of a woman writer.

But to continue my story. The Angel was dead; what then remained? You may say that what remained was a simple and common object—a young woman in a bedroom with an inkpot. In other words, now that she had rid herself of falsehood, that young woman had only to be herself. Ah, but what is "herself?" I mean, what is a woman? I assure you, I do not know. I do not believe that you know. I do not believe that anybody can know until she has expressed herself in all the arts and professions open to human skill. That indeed is one of the reasons why I have come here—out of respect for you, who are in process of showing us by your experiments what a woman is, who are in process of providing us, by your failures and successes, with that extremely important piece of information.

But to continue the story of my professional experiences. I made one pound ten and six by my first review; and I bought a Persian cat with the proceeds. Then I grew ambitious. A Persian cat is all very well, I said; but a Persian cat is not enough. I must have a motor-car. And it was thus that I became a novelist—for it is a very strange thing that people will give you a motor-car if you will tell them a story. It is a still stranger thing that there is nothing so delightful in the world as telling stories. It is far pleasanter than writing reviews of famous novels. And yet, if I am to obey your secretary and tell you my professional experiences as a novelist, I must tell you about a very strange experience that befell me as a novelist. And to understand it you must try first to imagine a novelist's state of mind. I hope I am not giving away professional secrets if I say that a novelist's chief desire is to be as unconscious as possible. He has to induce in himself a state of perpetual lethargy. He wants life to proceed with the utmost quiet and regularity. He wants to see the same faces, to read the same books, to do the same things day after day, month after month, while he is writing, so that nothing may break the illusion in which he is living—so that nothing may disturb or disquiet the mysterious nosings about, feelings round, darts, dashes, and sudden discoveries of that very shy and il-

5

lusive spirit, the imagination. I suspect that this state is the same both for men and women. Be that as it may, I want you to imagine me writing a novel in a state of trance. I want you to figure to yourselves a girl sitting with a pen in her hand, which for minutes, and indeed for hours, she never dips into the inkpot. The image that comes to my mind when I think of this girl is the image of a fisherman lying sunk in dreams on the verge of a deep lake with a rod held out over the water. She was letting her imagination sweep unchecked round every rock and cranny of the world that lies submerged in the depths of our unconscious being. Now came the experience that I believe to be far commoner with women writers than with men. The line raced through the girl's fingers. Her imagination had rushed away. It had sought the pools, the depths, the dark places where the largest fish slumber. And then there was a smash. There was an explosion. There was foam and confusion. The imagination had dashed itself against something hard. The girl was roused from her dream. She was indeed in a state of the most acute and difficult distress. To speak without figure, she had thought of something, something about the body, about the passion, which it was unfitting for her as a woman to say. Men, her reason told her, would be shocked. The consciousness of what men will say of a woman who speaks the truth about her passions had roused her from her artist's state of unconsciousness. She could write no more. The trance was over. Her imagination could work no longer. This I believe to be a very common experience with women writers—they are impeded by the extreme conventionality of the other sex. For though men sensibly allow themselves great freedom in these respects, I doubt that they realize or can control the extreme severity with which they condemn such freedom in women.

These then were two very genuine experiences of my own. These were two of the adventures of my professional life. The first—killing the Angel in the House—I think I solved. She died. But the second, telling the truth about my own experiences as a body, I do not think I solved. I doubt that any woman has solved it yet. The obstacles against her are still immensely powerful—and yet they are very difficult to define. Outwardly, what is simpler than to write books? Outwardly, what obstacles are there for a woman rather than for a man? Inwardly, I think, the case is very different; she has still many ghosts to fight, many prejudices to overcome. Indeed it will be a long time still, I think, before a woman can sit down to write a book without finding a phantom to be slain, a rock to be dashed against. And if this is so in literature, the freest of all professions for women, how is it in the new professions which you are now for the first time entering?

Those are the questions that I should like, had I time, to ask you. And indeed, if I have laid stress upon these professional experiences of mine, it is because I believe that they are, though in different forms, yours also. Even when the path is nominally open—when there is nothing to prevent a woman from being a doctor, a lawyer, a civil servant—there are many phantoms and obstacles, as I believe, looming in her way. To discuss and define them is I think of great value and importance; for thus only can the labour be shared, the difficulties be solved. But besides this, it is necessary also to discuss the ends and the aims for which we are fighting, for which we are doing battle with these formidable obstacles. Those aims cannot be taken for granted; they must be perpetually questioned and examined. The whole position, as I see it—here in this hall surrounded by women practising for the first time in history I know not how many different professions—is one of extraordinary interest and importance. You have won rooms of your own in the house hitherto exclusively owned by men. You are able, though not without great labour and effort, to pay the rent. You are earning your five hundred pounds a year. But this freedom is only a beginning; the room is your own, but it is still bare. It has to be furnished; it has to be decorated; it has to be shared. How are you going to furnish it, how are you going to decorate it? With whom are you going to share it, and upon what terms? These, I think are questions of the utmost importance and interest. For the first time in history you are able to ask them; for the first time you are able to decide for yourselves what the answers should be. Willingly would I stay and discuss those questions and answers—but not tonight. My time is up; and I must cease. ◪

◼ Exercise 3.4

Read Thomas Jefferson's Declaration of Independence and identify its claim, data, and warrant.

Declaration of Independence | Thomas Jefferson

When in the Course of human events, it becomes necessary for one people to dissolve the political bands which have connected them with another, and to assume among the Powers of the earth, the separate and equal station to which the Laws of Nature and of Nature's God entitle them, a decent respect to the opinions of mankind requires that they should declare the causes which impel them to the separation.—We hold these truths to be self-evident, that all men are created equal, that they are endowed by their Creator with certain unalienable Rights, that among these are Life, Liberty and the pursuit of Happiness.—That to secure these rights, Governments are instituted among Men, deriving their just powers from the consent of the governed.—That whenever any Form of Government becomes destructive of these ends, it is the Right of the People to alter or to abolish it, and to institute new Government, laying its foundation on such principles and organizing its powers in such form, as to them shall seem most likely to effect their Safety and Happiness. Prudence, indeed, will dictate that Governments long established should not be changed for light and transient causes; and accordingly all experience hath shewn, that mankind are more disposed to suffer, while evils are sufferable, than to right themselves by abolishing the forms to which they are accustomed. But when a long train of abuses and usurpations, pursing invariably the same Object evinces a design to reduce them under absolute Despotism, it is their right, it is their duty, to throw off such Government, and to provide new Guards for their future security.—Such has been the patient sufferance of these Colonies; and such is now the necessity which constrains them to alter their former Systems of Government. The history of the present King of Great Britain is a history of repeated injuries and usurpations, all having in direct object the establishment of an absolute Tyranny over these States. The prove this, let Facts be submitted to a candid world.—He has refused his Assent to Laws, the most wholesome and necessary for the public good.—He has forbidden his Governors to pass Laws of immediate and pressing importance, unless suspended in their operation till his Assent should be obtained; and when so suspended, he has utterly neglected to attend to them.—He has refused to pass other Laws for the accommodation of large districts of people, unless those people would relinquish the right of Representation in the Legislature, a right inestimable to them and formidable to tyrants only.—He has called together legislative bodies at places unusual, uncomfortable, and distant from the depository of their public Records, for the sole purpose of fatiguing them into compliance with his measures.—He has dissolved Representative Houses repeatedly, for opposing with manly firmness his invasions of the rights of the people.—He has refused for a long time, after such dissolutions, to cause others to be elected; whereby the Legislative powers, incapable of Annihilation, have returned to the People at large for their exercise; the State remaining in the mean time exposed to all the dangers of invasion from without, and convulsions within.—He has endeavoured to prevent the population of these States; for that purpose obstructing the Laws of Naturalization of Foreigners; refusing to pass others to encourage their migrations hither, and raising the conditions of new Appropriations of Lands.—He has obstructed the Administration of Justice, by refusing his Assent to Laws for establishing Judiciary powers.—He has made Judges dependent on his Will alone, for the tenure of their offices, and the amount and payment of their salaries.—He has erected a multitude of New Offices, and sent hither swarms of Officers to harrass our people, and eat out their substance.—He has kept among us, in times of peace, Standing Armies without the Consent of our legislatures.—He has affected to render the Military independent of and superior to the Civil power.—He has combined with others to subject us to a jurisdiction foreign to our constitution, and unacknowledged by our laws; giving his Assent to their Acts of pretended Legislation:—For quartering large bodies of armed troops among us:—For protecting them, by a mock Trial, from punishment for any Murders which they should commit on the Inhabitants of these States:—For cutting off our Trade with all parts of the world:—For imposing Taxes on us without our Consent:—For depriving us in many cases, of the benefits of Trial by Jury:—For transporting us beyond Seas to be tried for pretended offences:—For abolishing the free System of English Laws in a neighbouring Province, establishing therein an Arbitrary government, and enlarging its Boundaries so as to render it at once an example and fit instrument for introducing the same absolute rule into these Colonies:—For taking away our Charters, abolishing our most valuable Laws, and altering fundamentally the Forms of our Governments:—For suspending our own Legislatures, and declaring themselves invested with power to legislate for us in all cases whatsoever.—He has abdicated Government here, by declaring us out of his Protection and waging War against us.—He has plundered our seas, ravaged our Coasts, burnt our towns, and destroyed the Lives of our people.—He is at this time transporting large Armies of foreign Mercenaries to complete the works of death, desolation and tyranny, already begun with circumstances of Cruelty and perfidy scarcely paralleled in the most barbarous ages, and totally unworthy the Head of a civilized nation.—He has constrained our fellow Citizens taken Captive on the high Seas to bear Arms against their Country, to become the executioners of their friends and Brethren, or to fall themselves by their Hands.—He has excited domestic insurrections amongst us, and has endeavoured to bring on the inhabitants of our frontiers, the merciless Indian Savages, whose known rule of warfare, is an undistinguished destruction of all ages, sexes, and conditions. In every stage of these Oppressions We have Petitioned for Redress in the most humble terms: Our repeated Petitions have been answered only by repeated injury. A Prince, whose character is thus marked by every act which may define a Tyrant, is unfit to be the ruler of a free people. Nor have We been wanting in attentions to our British brethren. We have warned them from time to time of attempts by their legislature to extend an unwarrantable jurisdiction over us. We have reminded them of the circumstances of our emigration and settlement here. We have appealed to their native justice and magnanimity, and we have conjured them by the ties of our common kindred to disavow these usurpations, which, would inevitably interrupt our connections and correspondence. They too have been deaf to the voice of justice and of consanguinity. We must, therefore, acquiesce in the necessity, which denounces our Separation, and hold them, as we hold the rest of mankind, Enemies in War, in Peace Friends.—

We, therefore, the Representatives of the *United States of America,* in General Congress, Assembled, appealing to the Supreme Judge of the world for the rectitude of our intentions, do, in the Name, and by Authority of the good People of these Colonies, solemnly publish and declare, That these United Colonies are, and of Right ought to be *Free and Independent States;* that they are Absolved from all Allegiance to the British Crown, and that all political connection between them and the State of Great Britain, is and ought to be totally dissolved; and that as Free and Independent States, they have full Power to levy War, conclude Peace, contract Alliances, establish Commerce, and to do all other Acts and Things which Independent States may of right do.—And for the support of this Declaration, with a firm reliance on the protection of divine Providence, we mutually pledge to each other our Lives, our Fortunes and our sacred Honor. ◪

Chapter Summary

The Toulmin model of argument is valuable because it emphasizes careful reasoning without the constraints of formal logic, the subject matter being too filled with probabilities to be resolved by logic alone. Toulmin argument is tied to the realities of social interaction, particularly of legal courts. This mode of argument recognizes that a claim, whether objective (based on scientific or logical issues) or subjective (based on aesthetic, ethical, or moral issues), must be supported by data (hard facts plus reasoned analysis), which in turn must rest on a warrant (a trustworthy foundation that gives validity to the data).

Checklist

1. Do I state my claim clearly enough for public scrutiny, making sure that it is arguable?

2. Do I qualify my claim, if necessary?

3. Do I have enough data to support my claim convincingly?

4. Are my data reliable, timely, accurate, and sufficient for demonstrating the validity and truthfulness of my claim?

5. Do my data rest on a trustworthy warrant?

Writing Projects

1. Prepare an argumentative essay on a topic of your own or your instructor's choosing that follows the Toulmin model. Include a preliminary synopsis of your argument, divided into four sections: (1) your claim; (2) a qualifier to your claim; (3) your data, subdivided into hard facts and reason-based evidence, both objective and subjective; (4) your warrant, which renders your data trustworthy.

2. Write a Toulmin-based argument in which you defend or challenge the view that anyone elected to public office (mayor, governor, secretary of state, president of the United States, and so on) is obliged to live a morally exemplary life. Be sure to define "morally exemplary."

4 Using the Rogerian Model in Your Arguments

The relationship which I have found helpful is characterized by . . . an acceptance of [the] other person as a separate person with value in his own right, and by a deep empathic understanding which enables me to see his private world through his eyes.

—Carl Rogers

Carl Rogers (1902–1987) was a psychologist of the "humanist" school, seeing co-operative interpersonal relationships as the key to a healthy society. As a therapist, Rogers urged self-realization and believed that to function fully as a person in society, one must be open to new experiences. Rigidity of thought and defensiveness breed intolerance. One way such openness is cultivated is through co-operative methods of communication.

The Rogerian Model of Argument

From Rogers's view, the Classical model of argument and even the more flexible Toulmin model tend to divide people into two camps: proponents and opponents, "good guys" versus "bad guys." The traditional language of argument, for example, is filled with militaristic metaphors: We *win* or *lose* arguments rather than resolve them. We *attack* someone's thesis rather than question points of disagreement. We *marshal* evidence as if gathering troops. Even the seemingly neutral term *debate* is of military origin (from *battre*, to do battle). For Rogers, this combative approach to argument does more harm than good; it generates ill will and antagonism between discussants rather than cooperation.

Finding Common Ground

But, you ask, how can people cooperate or interact harmoniously if they hold diametrically opposed views about an issue? Rogers's answer is that you find a common ground and start from there. Returning to the rhetorical rhombus (see Figure 1.2), we see the emphasis here on *audience*. A paper in the Rogerian mode

Carl Rogers (1902–1987) was known for his "humanist" client-centered approach to therapy. He advocated nonthreatening methods of interpersonal communication.

assumes that readers firmly hold differing views and therefore will resist hearing others' positions. Yet no matter how debatable or controversial a view is, one can locate views on the issue that both can agree on. It might take a while to find them, but they are there. Consider the controversy for and against capital punishment, for example:

- Both sides consider human life to be sacred and precious.
- Both sides feel that capital crimes must be deterred as effectively as possible.
- Both sides agree that someone convicted of a capital crime is a threat to society.

The virtue of finding common ground is that one can isolate and resolve the points of opposition more effectively after identifying the points of agreement because one can reduce any hostility the audience has by demonstrating a true understanding of the audience's perspective.

The Rogerian model modifies the Classical model by emphasizing common ground (points of agreement) *before* calling attention to points of disagreement. The writer's goal is not to win or to prove wrong; it is to work together cooperatively to arrive at an agreed-on truth. From its opening sentence, a Rogerian argument communicates a desire for harmonious interaction rather than combative opposition.

I. Introduction: What is our shared problem? Let's see if we can work together to resolve it.

II. What we agree on.

III. Where we differ: misunderstandings, such as drawbacks or limited application to others' solutions, and the possible reasons behind these drawbacks or limitations.

IV. Possible drawbacks or limitations to writers' solutions, followed by greater benefits of writers' solutions.

V. How we can resolve our differences.

Developing Multiple Perspectives

Rogerian persuasion requires writers to work hard at developing multiple perspectives toward issues. You must be tolerant and respectful enough of differing viewpoints to take the time to fathom the value systems that underlie them. The first step toward achieving this goal, according to Rogers, is deceptively simple: It is *to listen with understanding.*

Listening with understanding is a skill that takes time to develop. You may think you are listening with understanding when you permit challengers to speak their minds, but you may be only allowing them their say rather than genuinely paying close attention to what they are telling you.

Here are some suggestions for listening with understanding, in Rogers's sense of the phrase, that also can be applied to reading with understanding:

* Be as attentive as possible. Assume that the speaker's remarks have value.

* Suspend your own judgments while listening, keeping an open mind so as not to run the risk of prematurely judging the speaker's views before you have the chance to consider them carefully.

* If anything is unclear to you or you find yourself disagreeing with anything, ask questions—but only after the person has finished speaking.

* Try to see the speaker's claims in terms of his or her warrants (underlying values or ideology on which the claims are based). One better understands and appreciates a speaker's position if one is aware of these warrants.

- Think of ways in which the speaker's point of view and your own can somehow work together, despite seeming contradictory. Even if you oppose capital punishment and the speaker supports it, both of you could approach a common ground by thinking of extreme situations on either side that would discourage an inflexible stance.

Using Rogerian argument in conversation is one thing; using it in writing is another. When writing, you do not have your audience in front of you to give you immediate feedback. Instead you have to anticipate questions and counter-responses that challengers would have for you (in other words, automatically consider the needs of your audience). By stressing the audience's needs, you will be more inclined to take a cooperative stance rather than a defensive or combative one.

Arguing cooperatively also means including in your Rogerian essay specific instances in which the differing views are logically sound. That way, you show yourself to have listened well to those perspectives. This in turn prepares your audience for listening more carefully and sympathetically to *your* side of things. You and your audience both become receptive for "give and take."

Organizing Your Argument Using the Rogerian Model

To write an argument based on the Rogerian ideals of cooperation, find common ground with your audience regardless of their views about your claim. You need to become especially sensitive to attitudes and values other than your own. You should desire to reach consensus with your audience on a conclusion rather than to "win" the argument over your "opposition."

As with the Classical and Toulmin models, begin your essay with questions about your audience, the similarities between your views and your audience's (insofar as you are aware of them), and the points at which you differ most, along with possible strategies for resolving those differences.

Consider these questions:

1. Can I be objective enough to represent views and evaluate evidence fairly?

2. How much sense do the points of difference have? Do they make more sense than some of my views? If so, do I have the courage to adopt them, or at least modify them to accommodate my views?

3. Am I genuinely interested in establishing a common ground with my audience? What else can I include that could better facilitate this goal?

When constructing an outline for a Rogerian argument, think in terms of thesis, support of thesis, and concluding judgments based on that support—just as you do when using the Classical and Toulmin models. But with the Rogerian model, you are more concerned with establishing common ground with readers who otherwise would reject the thesis. Here is how an argument using the Rogerian approach might take shape:

I. Introduction to the problem

    A. First scenario: A vignette that illustrates the problem, for example.

    B. Second scenario: Another vignette that illustrates the problem, but one with greater complexity that some solutions wouldn't handle well

    C. Thesis

II. Alternative views worth sharing with the target audience, and why these views are worth considering

III. Points of difference, along with reflection on how to resolve them

IV. Conclusion: The implications of finding a solution in light of the evidence presented, that would benefit everyone, plus discussion of the great benefits derived from the solution that all audience members would most likely find to their liking.

■ Exercise 4.1

Read "Public Funding for the Arts: Time to Correct the Abuses," a Rogerian argument by student Sheila Gleason. Then answer the questions that follow.

Sheila Gleason

PUBLIC FUNDING FOR THE ARTS: TIME TO CORRECT THE ABUSES

A painter receives a $10,000 grant from the National Endowment for the Arts and uses it to create a series of paintings that ridicules sports (one painting shows a gorilla kicking a field goal while gargoyle-faced fans cheer or jeer him on). A sculptor receives an even larger grant to create a twenty-foot high phallus composed of scrap iron. Yet another NEA grantee uses his funding to fill an entire floor of a local gallery with giant photographs of mutilated corpses, titling the exhibit, "Our National Heritage." A composer uses her grant to write a "symphony" consisting entirely of ambulance sirens, jack-hammering, and trashcan banging. These are just four among countless examples of art works that most Americans find offensive and degrading, yet must pay for out of their own pockets through taxes that help support the NEA.

Now, I am a strong believer in government support of the arts. Art, be it music, painting, sculpture, dance, or theater,

expresses the soul of a nation. Art—<u>good</u> art—adds beauty and
meaning to our lives. It is no secret that many talented artists
are unable to support themselves from their artwork alone; that,
without federal grant money, they could not afford to take time
away from their "day jobs" to work on their art. But lately, some
artists have been abusing the system by creating garbage and
calling it "avant garde." They accuse the public of having no
artistic taste, of possessing only cliché ridden ideas of what a
work of art should be like.

Yes, I agree: there are plenty of examples in which the public was dead wrong about innovative art. When Igor Stravinsky's
haunting *Rite of Spring* was first performed, outraged audiences
threw tomatoes at the orchestra. Painters like Picasso and Jackson Pollock were ridiculed in public, and so on. But I refuse to
believe that we cannot draw the line between innovative art and
artless trash. A Picasso painting of a woman whose face is broken
into a grotesque assemblage of triangles may not meet everyone's
definition of art, but it still shows elements of composition and
design and technique. Art, after all, is about seeing things differently, anew, from unusual perspectives.

But show me Robert Mapplethorpe's photograph of a gay man
urinating on his lover and I will tell you that such a photograph
violates the very foundation of art, the expression of beauty,
deep purpose, and deep meaning. Yes, a work of art can be highly
disturbing and still be great. When Oedipus pokes out his eyes
with spikes, the depth of Oedipus's anguish artistically
overrides the violent act itself. No critic would ever call such
violence gratuitous or sensationalistic. But when a so-called
artist produces a painting or sculpture that makes viewers feel
as if they'd just been publicly degraded or humiliated, that
makes them rush out of the gallery in embarrassment, then that
artist has overstepped his or her unwritten covenant with
the public.

Artistic freedom is precious, and no one should attempt to
censor works that appear to violate anyone's definition of art.
But when it comes to public funding for the arts, the consensus
of the people must prevail, and the basic principles of good
art—as the public defines them—must prevail.

1. In what ways is Sheila's essay most Rogerian? Least Rogerian? Why?

2. Where in the essay do you see Sheila attempting to find common ground with those who would likely disagree with her thesis? How well does she succeed?

3. How well does Sheila distinguish between good art and bad? What else, if anything, should she include in her definition of good art?

■ Exercise 4.2

In April 1963, Martin Luther King Jr. was sentenced to a week in jail because of his antisegregationist campaign in Birmingham, Alabama. While in jail, Dr. King wrote the following letter defending his activities to eight members of the Birmingham clergy. As you read this masterpiece of persuasive writing, notice how King makes a concerted effort to seek common ground with his audience and to avoid the "good guys" versus "bad guys" combative stance. Look for specific points of emphasis and specific explanations that make his stance Rogerian. After reading, answer the questions that follow.

Letter from Birmingham Jail | Martin Luther King, Jr.

April 16, 1963

My Dear Fellow Clergymen:
   While confined here in the Birmingham city jail, I came across your recent statement calling my present activities "unwise and untimely."[1] Seldom do I pause to answer criticism of my work and ideas. If I sought to answer all the criticisms that cross my desk, my secretaries would have little time for anything other than such correspondence in the course of the day, and I would have no time for constructive work. But since I feel that you are men of genuine good will and that your criticisms are sincerely set forth, I want to try to answer your statement in what I hope will be patient and reasonable terms.

   I think I should indicate why I am here in Birmingham, since you have been influenced by the view which argues against "outsiders coming in." I have the honor of serving as president of the Southern Christian Leadership Conference, an organization operating in every southern state, with head-

Source: King, Martin Luther, Jr. "Letter from Birmingham Jail." 16 April 1963. Reprinted by arrangement with the estate of Martin Luther King, Jr., c/o Writers House as agent for the proprieter. Copyright 1963 Martin Luther King, Jr., copyright renewed 1991 Coretta Scott King.

quarters in Atlanta, Georgia. We have some eighty-five affiliated organizations across the South, and one of them is the Alabama Christian Movement for Human Rights. Frequently we share staff, educational, and financial resources with our affiliates. Several months ago the affiliate here in Birmingham asked us to be on call to engage in a nonviolent direct-action program if such were deemed necessary. We readily consented, and when the hour came we lived up to our promise. So I, along with several members of my staff, am here because I was invited here. I am here because I have organizational ties here.

But more basically, I am in Birmingham because injustice is here. Just as the prophets of the eighth century B.C. left their villages and carried their "thus saith the Lord" far beyond the boundaries of their home towns, and just as the Apostle Paul left his village of Tarsus and carried the gospel of Jesus Christ to the far corners of the Greco-Roman world, so am I compelled to carry the gospel of freedom beyond my own home town. Like Paul, I must constantly respond to the Macedonian call for aid.

Moreover, I am cognizant of the interrelatedness of all communities and states. I cannot sit idly by in Atlanta and not be concerned about what happens in Birmingham. Injustice anywhere is a threat to justice everywhere. We are caught in an inescapable network of mutuality; tied in a single garment of destiny. Whatever affects one directly, affects all indirectly. Never again can we afford to live with the narrow, provincial "outside agitator" idea. Anyone who lives inside the United States can never be considered an outsider anywhere within its bounds.

You deplore the demonstrations taking place in Birmingham. But your statement, I am sorry to say, fails to express a similar concern for the conditions that brought about the demonstrations. I am sure that none of you would want to rest content with the superficial kind of social analysis that deals merely with effects and does not grapple with underlying causes. It is unfortunate that demonstrations are taking place in Birmingham, but it is even more unfortunate that the city's white power structure left the Negro community with no alternative.

In any nonviolent campaign there are four basic steps: collection of the facts to determine whether injustices exist; negotiation; self-purification; and direct action. We have gone through all these steps in Birmingham. There can be no gainsaying the fact that racial injustice engulfs this community. Birmingham is probably the most thoroughly segregated city in the United States. Its ugly record of brutality is widely known. Negroes have experienced grossly unjust treatment in the courts. There have been more unsolved bombings of Negro homes and churches in Birmingham than in any other city in the nation. These are the hard, brutal facts of the case. On the basis of these conditions, Negro leaders sought to negotiate with the city fathers. But the latter consistently refused to engage in good-faith negotiation.

Then, last September, came the opportunity to talk with leaders of Birmingham's economic community. In the course of the negotiations, certain promises were made by the merchants—for example, to remove the stores' humiliating racial signs. On the basis of these promises, the Reverend Fred Shuttleworth and the leaders of the Alabama Christian Movement for Human Rights agreed to a moratorium on all demonstrations. As the weeks and months went by, we realized that we were the victims of a broken promise. A few signs, briefly removed, returned; the others remained.

As in so many past experiences, our hopes had been blasted, and the shadow of deep disappointment settled upon us. We had no alternative except to prepare for direct action, whereby we would present our very bodies as a means of laying our case before the conscience of the local and the national community. Mindful of the difficulties involved, we decided to undertake a process of self-purification. We began a series of workshops on nonviolence, and we repeatedly asked ourselves: "Are you able to accept blows without retaliating?" "Are you able to endure the ordeal of jail?" We decided to schedule our direct-action program for the Easter season, realizing that except for Christmas, this is the main shopping period of the year. Knowing that a strong economic-withdrawal program would be the by-product of direct action, we felt that this would be the best time to bring pressure to bear on the merchants for the needed change.

Then it occurred to us that Birmingham's mayoralty election was coming up in March, and we speedily decided to postpone action until after election day. When we discovered that the Commissioner of Public Safety, Eugene "Bull" Conner, had piled up enough votes to be in the run-off, we decided again to postpone action until the day after the run-off so that the demonstrations could not be used to cloud the issues. Like many others, we waited to see Mr. Conner defeated, and to this end we endured postponement after postponement. Having aided in this community need, we felt that our direct-action program could be delayed no longer.

You may well ask: "Why direct action? Why sit-ins, marches, and so forth? Isn't negotiation a better path?" You are quite right in calling for negotiation. Indeed, this is the very purpose of direct action. Nonviolent direct action seeks to create such a crisis and foster such a tension that a community which has constantly refused to negotiate is forced to confront the issue. It seeks so to dramatize the issue that it can no longer be ignored. My citing the creation of tension as part of the work of the nonviolent-resister may sound rather shocking. But I must confess that I am not afraid of the word "tension." I have earnestly opposed violent tension, but there is a type of constructive, nonviolent tension which is necessary for growth. Just as Socrates felt that it was necessary to create a tension in the mind so that individuals could rise from the bondage of myths and half-truths to the unfettered realm of creative analysis and objective appraisal, so must we see the need for nonviolent gadflies to create the kind of tension in society that will help men rise from the dark depths of prejudice and racism to the majestic heights of understanding and brotherhood.

10

The purpose of our direct-action program is to create a situation so crisis-packed that it will inevitably open the door to negotiation. I therefore concur with you in your call for negotiation. Too long has our beloved Southland been bogged down in a tragic effort to live in monologue rather than dialogue.

One of the basic points in your statement is that the action that I and my associates have taken in Birmingham is untimely. Some have asked: "Why didn't you give the new city administration time to act?" The only answer that I can give to this query is that the new Birmingham administration must be prodded about as much as the outgoing one, before it will act. We are sadly mistaken if we feel that the election of Albert Boutwell as mayor will bring the millennium to Birmingham. While Mr. Boutwell is a much more gentle person than Mr. Connor, they are both segregationists, dedicated to maintenance of the status quo. I have hope that Mr. Boutwell will be reasonable enough to see the futility of massive resistance to desegregation. But he will not see this without pressure from devotees of civil rights. My friends, I must say to you that we have not made a single gain in civil rights without determined legal and nonviolent pressure. Lamentably, it is an historical fact that privileged groups seldom give up their privileges voluntarily. Individuals may see the moral light and voluntarily give up their unjust posture; but as Reinhold Niebuhr[2] has reminded us, groups tend to be more immoral than individuals.

We know through painful experience that freedom is never voluntarily given by the oppressor; it must be demanded by the oppressed. Frankly, I have yet to engage in a direct-action campaign that was "well timed" in the view of those who have not suffered unduly from the disease of segregation. For years now I have heard the word "Wait!" It rings in the ear of every Negro with piercing familiarity. This "Wait" has almost always meant "Never." We must come to see, with one of our distinguished jurists, that "justice too long delayed is justice denied."[3]

We have waited for more than 340 years for our constitutional and God-given rights. The nations of Asia and Africa are moving with jetlike speed toward gaining political independence, but we still creep at horse-and-buggy pace toward gaining a cup of coffee at a lunch counter. Perhaps it is easy for those who have never felt the stinging darts of segregation to say, "Wait." But when you have seen vicious mobs lynch your mothers and fathers at will and drown your sisters and brothers at whim; when you have seen hate-filled policemen curse, kick, and even kill your black brothers and sisters; when you see the vast majority of your twenty million Negro brothers smothering in an airtight cage of poverty in the midst of an affluent society; when you suddenly find your tongue twisted and your speech stammering as you seek to explain to your six-year-old daughter why she can't go to the public amusement park that has just been advertised on television, and see tears welling up in her eyes when she is told that Funtown is closed to colored children, and see ominous clouds of inferiority beginning to form in her little mental sky, and see her beginning to distort her personality by developing an unconscious bitterness toward white people; when you have to concoct an answer for a five-year-old son who is asking: "Daddy, why do white people treat colored people so mean?"; when you take a cross-country drive and find it necessary to sleep night after night in the uncomfortable corners of your automobile because no motel will accept you; when you are humiliated day in and day out by nagging signs reading "white" and "colored"; when your first name becomes "nigger," your middle name becomes "boy" (however old you are) and your last name becomes "John," and your wife and mother are never given the respected title "Mrs."; when you are harried by day and haunted by night by the fact that you are a Negro, living constantly at tiptoe stance, never quite knowing what to expect next, and are plagued with inner fears and outer resentments; when you are forever fighting a degenerating sense of "nobodiness"—then you will understand why we find it difficult to wait. There comes a time when the cup of endurance runs over, and men are no longer willing to be plunged into the abyss of despair. I hope, sirs, you can understand our legitimate and unavoidable impatience.

You express a great deal of anxiety over our willingness to break laws.   15 This is certainly a legitimate concern. Since we so diligently urge people to obey the Supreme Court's decision of 1954 outlawing segregation in the public schools, at first glance it may seem rather paradoxical for us consciously to break laws. One may well ask: "How can you advocate breaking some laws and obeying others?" The answer lies in the fact that there are two types of laws: just and unjust. I would be the first to advocate to obey just laws. One has not only a legal but a moral responsibility to obey just laws. Conversely, one has a moral responsibility to disobey unjust laws. I would agree with St. Augustine that "an unjust law is no law at all."

Now, what is the difference between the two? How does one determine whether a law is just or unjust? A just law is a man-made code that squares with the moral law or the law of God. An unjust law is a code that is out of harmony with the moral law. To put it in the terms of St. Thomas Aquinas: An unjust law is a human law that is not rooted in eternal law and natural law. Any law that uplifts human personality is just. Any law that degrades human personality is unjust. All segregation statutes are unjust because segregation distorts the soul and damages the personality. It give the segregator a false sense of superiority and the segregated a false sense of inferiority. Segregation, to use the terminology of the Jewish philosopher Martin Buber, substitutes an "I-it" relationship for an "I-thou" relationship and ends up relegating persons to the status of things. Hence segregation is not only politically, economically, and sociologically unsound, it is morally wrong and sinful. Paul Tillich[4] has said that sin is separation. Is not segregation an existential expression of man's tragic separation, his awful estrangement, his terrible sinfulness? Thus it is that I can urge men to obey the 1954 decision of the Supreme Court, for it is morally right; and I can urge them to disobey segregation ordinances, for they are morally wrong.

Let us consider a more concrete example of just and unjust laws. An unjust law is a code that a numerical or power majority group compels a minority group to obey but does not make binding on itself. This is *difference* made legal. By the same token, a just law is a code that a majority compels a minority to follow and that it is willing to follow itself. This is *sameness* made legal.

Let me give another explanation. A law is unjust if it is inflicted on a minority that, as a result of being denied the right to vote, had no part in enacting or devising the law. Who can say that the legislature of Alabama which set up that state's segregation laws was democratically elected? Throughout Alabama all sorts of devious methods are used to prevent Negroes from becoming registered voters, and there are some counties in which, even though Negroes constitute a majority of the population, not a single Negro is registered. Can any law enacted under such circumstances be considered democratically structured?

Sometimes a law is just on its face and unjust in its application. For instance, I have been arrested on a charge of parading without a permit. Now, there is nothing wrong in having an ordinance which requires a permit for a parade. But such an ordinance becomes unjust when it is used to maintain segregation and to deny citizens the First Amendment privilege of peaceful assembly and protest.

I hope you are able to see the distinction I am trying to point out. In no sense do I advocate evading or defying the law, as would the rabid segregationist. That would lead to anarchy. One who breaks an unjust law must do so openly, lovingly, and with a willingness to accept the penalty. I submit that an individual who breaks a law that conscience tells him is unjust, and who willingly accepts the penalty of imprisonment in order to arouse the conscience of the community over its injustice, is in reality expressing the highest respect for law.

Of course, there is nothing new about this kind of civil disobedience. It was evidenced sublimely in the refusal of Shadrach, Meshach, and Abednego to obey the laws of Nebuchadnezzar, on the ground that a higher moral law was at stake. It was practiced superbly by the early Christians, who were willing to face hungry lions and the excruciating pain of chopping blocks rather than submit to certain unjust laws of the Roman Empire. To a degree, academic freedom is a reality today because Socrates practiced civil disobedience. In our own nation, the Boston Tea Party represented a massive act of civil disobedience.

We should never forget that everything Adolf Hitler did in Germany was "legal" and everything the Hungarian freedom fighters did in Hungary was "illegal." It was "illegal" to aid and comfort a Jew in Hitler's Germany. Even so, I am sure that, had I lived in Germany at the time, I would have aided and comforted my Jewish brothers. If today I lived in a Communist country where certain principles dear to the Christian faith are suppressed, I would openly advocate disobeying that country's anti-religious laws.

20

I must make two honest confessions to you, my Christian and Jewish brothers. First, I must confess that over the past few years I have been gravely disappointed with the white moderate. I have almost reached the regrettable conclusion that the Negro's great stumbling block in his stride toward freedom is not the White Citizen's Counciler or the Ku Klux Klanner, but the white moderate, who is more devoted to "order" than to justice; who prefers a negative peace which is the absence of tension to a positive peace which is the presence of justice; who constantly says: "I agree with you in the goal you seek, but I cannot agree with your methods or direct action"; who paternalistically believes he can set the timetable for another man's freedom; who lives by a mythical concept of time and who constantly advises the Negro to wait for a "more convenient season." Shallow understanding from people of good will is more frustrating than absolute misunderstanding from people of ill will. Lukewarm acceptance is much more bewildering than outright rejection.

I had hoped that the white moderate would understand that law and order exist for the purpose of establishing justice and that when they fail in this purpose they become the dangerously structured dams that block the flow of social progress. I had hoped that the white moderate would understand that the present tension in the South is a necessary phase of the transition from an obnoxious negative peace, in which the Negro passively accepted his unjust plight, to a substantive and positive peace, in which all men will respect the dignity and worth of human personality. Actually, we who engage in nonviolent direct action are not the creators of tension. We merely bring to the surface the hidden tension that is already alive. We bring it out in the open, where it can be seen and dealt with. Like a boil that can never be cured so long as it is covered up but must be opened with all its ugliness to the natural medicines of air and light, injustice must be exposed, with all the tension its exposure creates, to the light of human conscience and the air of national opinion before it can be cured.

In your statement you assert that our actions, even though peaceful, must   25
be condemned because they precipitate violence. But is this a logical assertion? Isn't this like condemning a robbed man because his possession of money precipitated the evil act of robbery? Isn't this like condemning Socrates because his unswerving commitment to truth and his philosophical inquiries precipitated the act by the misguided populace in which they made him drink hemlock? Isn't this like condemning Jesus because his unique God-consciousness and never-ceasing devotion to God's will precipitated the evil act of crucifixion? We must come to see that, as the federal courts have consistently affirmed, it is wrong to urge an individual to cease his efforts to gain his basic constitutional rights because the quest may precipitate violence. Society must protect the robbed and punish the robber.

I had also hoped that the white moderate would reject the myth concerning time in relation to the struggle for freedom. I have just received a letter from a white brother in Texas. He writes: "All Christians know that the colored people will receive equal rights eventually, but it is possible that you are in too great a religious hurry. It has taken Christianity almost two thousand years to accomplish what it has. The teachings of Christ take time to come to earth." Such an attitude stems from a tragic misconception of time, from the strangely irrational notion that there is something in the very flow of time that will inevitably cure all ills. Actually, time itself is neutral; it can be used either destructively or constructively. More and more I feel that the people of ill will have used time much more effectively than have the people of good will. We will have to repent in this generation not merely for the hateful words and actions of the bad people but for the appalling silence of the good people. Human progress never rolls in on wheels of inevitability; it comes through the tireless efforts of men willing to be co-workers with God, and without this hard work, time itself becomes an ally of the forces of social stagnation. We must use time creatively, in the knowledge that the time is always ripe to do right. Now is the time to make real the promise of democracy and transform our pending national elegy into a creative psalm of brotherhood. Now is the time to lift our national policy from the quicksand of racial injustice to the solid rock of human dignity.

You speak of our activity in Birmingham as extreme. At first I was rather disappointed that fellow clergymen would see my nonviolent efforts as those of an extremist. I began thinking about the fact that I stand in the middle of two opposing forces in the Negro community. One is a force of complacency, made up in part of Negroes who, as a result of long years of oppression, are so drained of self-respect and a sense of "somebodiness" that they have adjusted to segregation; and in part of a few middle-class Negroes who, because of a degree of academic and economic security and because in some ways they profit by segregation, have become insensitive to the problems of the masses. The other force is one of bitterness and hatred, and it comes perilously close to advocating violence. It is expressed in the various black nationalist groups that are springing up across the nation, the largest and best-known being Elijah Muhammad's Muslim movement. Nourished by the Negro's frustration over the continued existence of racial discrimination, this movement is made up of people who have lost faith in America, who have absolutely repudiated Christianity, and who have concluded that the white man is an incorrigible "devil."

I have tried to stand between these two forces, saying that we need emulate neither the "do-nothingism" of the complacent nor the hatred and despair of the black nationalist. For there is the more excellent way of love and nonviolent protest. I am grateful to God that, through the influence of the Negro church, the way of nonviolence became an integral part of our struggle.

If this philosophy had not emerged, by now many streets of the South should, I am convinced, be flowing with blood. And I am further convinced that if our white brothers dismiss as "rabble-rousers" and "outside agitators" those of us who employ nonviolent direct action, and if they refuse to support our nonviolent efforts, millions of Negroes will, out of frustration and despair, seek solace and security in black-nationalist ideologies—a development that would inevitably lead to a frightening racial nightmare.

Oppressed people cannot remain oppressed forever. The yearning for freedom eventually manifests itself, and that is what has happened to the American Negro. Something within has reminded him of his birthright of freedom, and something without has reminded him that it can be gained. Consciously or unconsciously, he has been caught up by the *Zeitgeist*,[5] and with his black brothers of Africa and his brown and yellow brothers of Asia, South America, and the Caribbean, the United States Negro is moving with a sense of great urgency toward the promised land of racial justice. If one recognizes this vital urge that has engulfed the Negro community, one should readily understand why public demonstrations are taking place. The Negro has many pent-up resentments and latent frustrations, and he must release them. So let him march; let him make prayer pilgrimages to the city hall; let him go on freedom rides—and try to understand why he must do so. If his repressed emotions are not released in nonviolent ways, they will seek expression through violence; this is not a threat but a fact of history. So I have not said to my people: "Get rid of your discontent." Rather, I have tried to say that this normal and healthy discontent can be channeled into the creative outlet of nonviolent direct action. And now this approach is being termed extremist.

But though I was initially disappointed at being categorized as an extremist, as I continued to think about the matter I gradually gained a measure of satisfaction from the label. Was not Jesus an extremist for love: "Love your enemies, bless them that curse you, do good to them that hate you, and pray for them which despitefully use you, and persecute you." Was not Amos an extremist for justice: "Let justice roll down like waters and righteousness like an ever-flowing stream." Was not Paul an extremist for the Christian gospel: "I bear in my body the marks of the Lord Jesus." Was not Martin Luther an extremist: "Here I stand; I cannot do otherwise, so help me God." And John Bunyan: "I will stay in jail to the end of my days before I make a butchery of my conscience." And Abraham Lincoln: "This nation cannot survive half slave and half free." And Thomas Jefferson: "We hold these truths to be self-evident, that all men are created equal. . . ." So the question is not whether we will be extremists, but what kind of extremists we will be. Will we be extremists for hate or for love? Will we be extremists for the preservation of injustice or for the extension of justice? In that dramatic scene on Calvary's hill three men were crucified. We must never forget that all three were crucified for the same crime—the crime of extremism. Two were extremists for immorality, and thus fell below their environment. The other, Jesus Christ, was an extremist for love, truth, and goodness, and thereby rose above his environment. Perhaps the South, the nation, and the world are in dire need of creative extremists.

I had hoped that the white moderate would see this need. Perhaps I was too optimistic; perhaps I expected too much. I suppose I should have realized that few members of the oppressor race can understand the deep groans and passionate yearnings of the oppressed race, and still fewer have the vision to see that injustice must be rooted out by strong, persistent, and determined action. I am thankful, however, that some of our white brothers in the South have grasped the meaning of this social revolution and committed themselves to it. They are still all too few in quantity, but they are big in quality. Some—such as Ralph McGill, Lillian Smith, Harry Golden, James McBride Dabbs, Ann Braden, and Sarah Patton Boyle—have written about our struggle in eloquent and prophetic terms. Others have marched with us down nameless streets of the South. They have languished in filthy, roach-infested jails, suffering the abuse and brutality of policemen who view them as "dirty nigger-lovers." Unlike so many of their moderate brothers and sisters, they have recognized the urgency of the moment and sensed the need for powerful "action" antidotes to combat the disease of segregation.

Let me take note of my other major disappointment. I have been so greatly disappointed with the white church and its leadership. Of course, there are some notable exceptions. I am not unmindful of the fact that each of you has taken some significant stands on this issue. I commend you, Reverend Stallings, for your Christian stand on this past Sunday, in welcoming Negroes to your worship service on a nonsegregated basis. I commend the Catholic leaders of this state for integrating Spring Hill College several years ago.

But despite these notable exceptions, I must honestly reiterate that I have been disappointed with the church. I do not say this as one of those negative critics who can always find something wrong with the church. I say this as a minister of the gospel, who loves the church; who was nurtured in its bosom; who has been sustained by its spiritual blessings and who will remain true to it as long as the cord of life shall lengthen.

When I was suddenly catapulted into the leadership of the bus protest in Montgomery, Alabama, a few years ago, I felt we would be supported by the white church. I felt that the white ministers, priests, and rabbis of the South would be among our strongest allies. Instead, some have been outright opponents, refusing to understand the freedom movement and misrepresenting its leaders; all too many others have been more cautious than courageous and have remained silent behind the anesthetizing security of stained-glass windows.

In spite of my shattered dreams, I came to Birmingham with the hope that the white religious leadership of this community would see the justice of our cause and, with deep moral concern, would serve as the channel through which our just grievances could reach the power structure. I had hoped that each of you would understand. But again I have been disappointed.

I have heard numerous southern religious leaders admonish their worshipers to comply with a desegregation decision because it is the law, but I have longed to hear white ministers declare: "Follow this decree because integration is morally right and because the Negro is your brother." In the midst of blatant injustices inflicted upon the Negro, I have watched white churchmen stand on the sideline and mouth pious irrelevancies and sanctimonious

35

trivialities. In the midst of a mighty struggle to rid our nation of racial and economic injustice, I have heard many ministers say: "Those are social issues, with which the gospel has no real concern." And I have watched many churches commit themselves to a completely otherworldly religion which makes a strange, unbiblical distinction between body and soul, between the sacred and the secular.

I have traveled the length and breadth of Alabama, Mississippi, and all the other southern states. On sweltering summer days and crisp autumn mornings I have looked at the South's beautiful churches with their lofty spires pointing heavenward. I have beheld the impressive outlines of her massive religious-education buildings. Over and over I have found myself saying: "What kind of people worship here? Who is their God? Where were their voices when the lips of Governor Barnett dripped with words of interposition and nullification? Where were they when Governor Wallace gave a clarion call for defiance and hatred? Where were their voices of support when bruised and weary Negro men and women decided to rise from the dark dungeons of complacency to the bright hills of creative protest?"

Yes, these questions are still in my mind. In deep disappointment I have wept over the laxity of the church. But be assured that my tears have been tears of love. There can be no deep disappointment where there is not deep love. Yes, I love the church. How could I do otherwise? I am in the rather unique position of being the son, the grandson, and the great-grandson of preachers. Yes, I see the church as the body of Christ. But, Oh! How we have blemished and scarred that body through social neglect and through fear of being nonconformists.

There was a time when the church was very powerful—in the time when   40
the early Christians rejoiced at being deemed worthy to suffer for what they believed. In those days the church was not merely a thermometer that recorded the ideas and principles of popular opinion; it was a thermostat that transformed the mores of society. Whenever the early Christians entered a town, the people in power became disturbed and immediately sought to convict the Christians for being "disturbers of the peace" and "outside agitators." But the Christians pressed on, in the conviction that they were "a colony of heaven," called to obey God rather than man. Small in number, they were big in commitment. They were too God-intoxicated to be "astronomically intimidated." By their effort and example they brought an end to such ancient evils as infanticide and gladiatorial contests.

Things are different now. So often the contemporary church is a weak, ineffectual voice with an uncertain sound. So often it is an archdefender of the status quo. Far from being disturbed by the presence of the church, the power structure of the average community is consoled by the church's silent—and often even vocal—sanction of things as they are.

But the judgment of God is upon the church as never before. If today's church does not recapture the sacrificial spirit of the early church, it will lose its authenticity, forfeit the loyalty of millions, and be dismissed as an irrelevant social club with no meaning for the twentieth century. Every day I meet young people whose disappointment with the church has turned into outright disgust.

Perhaps I have once again been too optimistic. Is organized religion too inextricably bound to the status quo to save our nation and the world? Perhaps I must turn my faith to the inner spiritual church, the church within the church, as the true *ekklesia* and the hope of the world. But again I am thankful to God that some noble souls from the ranks of organized religion have broken loose from the paralyzing chains of conformity and joined us as active partners in the struggle for freedom. They have left their secure congregations and walked the streets of Albany, Georgia, with us. They have gone down the highways of the South on tortuous rides for freedom. Yes, they have gone to jail with us. Some have been dismissed from their churches, have lost the support of their bishops and fellow ministers. But they have acted in the faith that right defeated is stronger than evil triumphant. Their witness has been the spiritual salt that has preserved the true meaning of the gospel in these troubled times. They have carved a tunnel of hope through the dark mountain of disappointment.

I hope the church as a whole will meet the challenge of this decisive hour. But even if the church does not come to the aid of justice, I have no despair about the future. I have no fear about the outcome of our struggle in Birmingham, even if our motives are at present misunderstood. We will reach the goal of freedom in Birmingham and all over the nation, because the goal of America is freedom. Abused and scorned though we may be, our destiny is tied up with America's destiny. Before the pilgrims landed at Plymouth, we were here. Before the pen of Jefferson etched the majestic words of the Declaration of Independence across the pages of history, we were here. For more than two centuries our forebears labored in this country without wages; they made cotton king; they built the homes of their masters while suffering gross injustice and shameful humiliation—and yet out of a bottomless vitality they continue to thrive and develop. If the inexpressible cruelties of slavery could not stop us, the opposition we now face will surely fail. We will win our freedom because the sacred heritage of our nation and the eternal will of God are embodied in our echoing demands.

Before closing I feel impelled to mention one other point in your statement that has troubled me profoundly. You warmly commended the Birmingham police force for keeping "order" and "preventing violence." I doubt that you would have so warmly commended the police force if you had seen its dogs sinking their teeth into unarmed, nonviolent Negroes. I doubt that you would so quickly commend the policemen if you were to observe their ugly and inhumane treatment of Negroes here in the city jail; if you were to watch them push and curse old Negro women and young Negro girls; if you were to see them slap and kick old Negro men and young boys; if you were to observe

45

them, as they did on two occasions, refuse to give us food because we wanted to sing our grace together. I cannot join you in your praise of the Birmingham police department.

It is true that the police have exercised a degree of discipline in handling the demonstrators. In this sense they have conducted themselves rather "nonviolently" in public. But for what purpose? To preserve the evil system of segregation. Over the past few years I have consistently preached that nonviolence demands that the means we use must be as pure as the ends we seek. I have tried to make clear that it is wrong to use immoral means to attain moral ends. But now I must affirm that it is just as wrong, or perhaps even more so, to use moral means to preserve immoral ends. Perhaps Mr. Connor and his policemen have been rather nonviolent in public, as was Chief Pritchett in Albany, Georgia, but they used the moral means of nonviolence to maintain the immoral end of racial injustice. As T. S. Eliot has said: "The last temptation is the greatest treason: To do the right deed for the wrong reason."

I wish you had commended the Negro sit-inners and demonstrators of Birmingham for their sublime courage, their willingness to suffer, and their amazing discipline in the midst of great provocation. One day the South will recognize its real heroes. They will be the James Merediths, with the noble sense of purpose that enables them to face jeering and hostile mobs, and with the agonizing loneliness that characterizes the life of the pioneer. They will be old, oppressed, battered Negro women, symbolized in a seventy-two-year-old woman in Montgomery, Alabama, who rose up with a sense of dignity and with her people decided not to ride segregated buses, and who responded with ungrammatical profundity to one who inquired about her weariness: "My feets is tired, but my soul is at rest." They will be the young high school and college students, the young ministers of the gospel and a host of their elders, courageously and nonviolently sitting in at lunch counters and willingly going to jail for conscience' sake. One day the South will know that when these disinherited children of God sat down at lunch counters, they were in reality standing up for what is best in the American dream and for the most sacred values in our Judaeo-Christian heritage, thereby bringing our nation back to those great wells of democracy which were dug deep by the founding fathers in their formulation of the Constitution and the Declaration of Independence.

Never before have I written so long a letter. I'm afraid it is much too long to take your precious time. I can assure you that it would have been much shorter if I had been writing from a comfortable desk, but what else can one do when he is alone in a narrow jail cell, other than write long letters, think long thoughts, and pray long prayers?

If I have said anything in this letter that overstates the truth and indicates an unreasonable impatience, I beg you to forgive me. If I have said anything that understates the truth and indicates my having a patience that allows me to settle for anything less than brotherhood, I beg God to forgive me.

I hope this letter finds you strong in the faith. I also hope that circum- 50
stances will soon make it possible for me to meet each of you, not as an inte-
grationist or a civil-rights leader but as a fellow clergyman and a Christian
brother. Let us all hope that the dark clouds of racial prejudice will soon
pass away and the deep fog of misunderstanding will be lifted from our
fear-drenched communities, and in some not too distant tomorrow the radiant
stars of love and brotherhood will shine over our great nation with all their
scintillating beauty.

Yours for the cause of Peace and Brotherhood,

Martin Luther King, Jr.

Notes

[1]This response to a published statement by eight fellow clergymen from Alabama (Bishop
    C.C.J. Carpenter, Bishop Joseph A. Durick, Rabbi Milton L. Grafman, Bishop Paul
    Hardin, Bishop Nolan B. Harmon, the Reverend George M. Murray, the Reverend
    Edward V. Ramage, and the Reverend Earl Stallings) was composed under somewhat
    constricting circumstances. Begun on the margins of the newspaper in which the state-
    ment appeared while I was in jail, the letter was continued on scraps of writing paper
    supplied by a friendly Negro trusty, and concluded on a pad my attorneys were even-
    tually permitted to leave me. Although the text remains in substance unaltered, I have
    indulged in the author's prerogative of polishing it for publication. [King's note.]

[2]**Reinhold Niebuhr** Niebuhr (1892–1971) was a minister, political activist, author, and
    professor of applied Christianity at Union Theological Seminary. [All notes are the
    editors' unless otherwise specified.]

[3]**justice . . . denied** A quotation attributed to William E. Gladstone (1809–1898), British
    statesman and prime minister.

[4]**Paul Tillich** Tillich (1886–1965), born in Germany, taught theology at several German
    universities, but in 1933 he was dismissed from his post at the University of Frankfurt
    because of his opposition to the Nazi regime. At the invitation of Reinhold Niebuhr, he
    came to the United States and taught at Union Theological Seminary.

[5]*Zeitgeist* German for "spirit of the age." ◼

1. King chose to present his views in the form of a letter instead of, say, a manifesto. How might King's choice be explained from a Rogerian perspective?

2. Do any moments in King's letter seem un-Rogerian? How so? What positive or negative effect might they have on his intended readers?

3. Does King use any of the three Aristotelian appeals of ethos, pathos, or
   logos? If so, identify them, and suggest reasons for their use.

4. Where does King most clearly reveal a special effort to reach his audience of
   fellow clergy?

Chapter Summary

A successful argument structured along Rogerian principles, like the Classical and Toulmin models, includes thorough, accurate, and relevant evidence in support of its claim; unlike these models, however, the aim of Rogerian persuasion is not to "win" the argument but to find common ground. Instead of being considered "opponents," those with differing views are encouraged to reach consensus and to enter into a cooperative dialogue with the writer. For such a cooperative dialogue to succeed, arguers need to listen with care and open-mindedness to divergent points of view.

Summary and Comparison of the Classical Toulmin, and Rogerian Models

Classical Model

- Based on philosophical ideals of sound thinking, incorporating the Aristotelian appeals of ethos (ethical principles, recognized authority, and shared values), pathos (stirring of emotions), and logos (dialectical reasoning)

- Follows a predetermined arrangement of elements: An *introduction* that states the problem and the thesis, presentation of the *evidence, refutation* of challenging views, and a *conclusion*

Toulmin Model

- Based on the pragmatics of the judicial system rather than the ideals of philosophical thinking

- Approaches an argument in terms of its *claims* (which are presented more as hypotheses being opened to challenge than as truths to be proven), its *data,* and its underlying *warrants* that make the data trustworthy

- Recognizes the "real world" complexities of an argument; gives special emphasis to refutation

Rogerian Model

- Based on humanistic values that take into account the importance of social cooperation in argument (that is, finding common ground is valued over "beating the opposition")

- Emphasizes points of agreement over points of disagreement

- Urges arguers to cultivate multiple perspectives toward issues

Checklist

1. Do I find common ground with those whose views differ from my own?

2. Do I carefully consider the weaknesses or limitations of my point of view, as well as those of others'? Do I share these with my readers?

3. Is my tone cooperative rather than confrontational?

4. Do I encourage multiple perspectives rather than a singular one toward the issue?

5. Do I treat views with which I disagree respectfully? Do I give more emphasis to the points of agreement than the points of disagreement?

Writing Projects

1. Write an argumentative essay, following the Rogerian model, in which you defend or challenge one of the following issues:

   a. Books, especially textbooks, should be published online.
   b. Because the Second Amendment to the U.S. Constitution gives citizens the right to bear arms, students over the age of eighteen cannot be prohibited from bringing a firearm onto campus if they feel the need for self-protection.
   c. Libraries should become media centers, using their budgets more for electronic resources than for print resources.

2. Write an essay in which you use the Rogerian model to argue for one feasible way of improving living conditions with one or more roommates.

3. Write a comparative evaluation of the Classical, Toulmin, and Rogerian models of argument.

4. Read the following essay, "Who Owns Our Children?" by student Daniela Gibson. Then critique it in terms of her use of Rogerian persuasion.

Daniela Gibson

WHO OWNS OUR CHILDREN?

Every morning when I go to the bus stop, I pass by a poster with a smiling mother and toddler. On the poster, it says, "You are your child's first teacher." Unfortunately, today, many parents feel that this caring and loving relationship with their children is threatened by a dark force—child violence. The reality of this threat is manifested in tragic events such as the shooting at Columbine where two high school students killed twelve students and a teacher, leaving several wounded. In the face of such tragedies, it is not surprising that parents are desperately seeking a cause. Recently, many have turned to the media and argued that violence on TV is responsible for violence among children. Many parents now feel that only TV censorship by the government can bring child violence to a halt.

These parents, together with several journalists, sociologists, and psychologists, see a parallel between TV violence and child violence. In support of their claim, they cite people like David Walsh, director of the National Institute of Media and the Family, who notes that "it is estimated the average American kid has seen 200,000 acts of violence on television by the time he or she graduates from high school" (Hunt). They further refer to Professor Brandon Centerwall whose studies suggest that "when English-language TV came to South Africa in 1975, having previously been banned by the Afrikaans-speaking government . . . there was a spectacular increase in violent crime, most especially among the young" (Kristol). Another argument against TV is that its violence desensitizes both adults and children from the violence in the real world "to the point where nothing is revolting. Where nothing makes us blush" (Jacoby). Arguments like these have let people conclude that "the government . . . will have to step in to help the parents" —a call, of course, for censorship (Kristol).

These reactions are understandable and reflect the fears and concerns of the parents. I think that everybody will agree that violence is bad, that TV can promote violence among young children, and that this is especially the case when TV replaces a parent or other caretaker. It clearly is in the interest of our children and our society that children do not have unlimited access to television. The question is, however, who should be in charge of regulating TV for our children. The government or the parents? I strongly believe that the latter should be in charge. I believe that child violence can only be reduced if parents stop holding the TV media responsible for the violence and instead acknowledge and act upon their responsibilities as parents.

To blame the media for child violence and call for censorship of television is a mistake, for the causal link between child violence and TV has not been sufficiently established and censorship is not only impractical but also dangerous. First, if we see television as the main cause for child violence, we mistake a correlation for a cause. As one author explains: "epidemiological research . . . consists of observing groups of people and then showing statistical associations between their life-styles or behavior and what happens to them later. Scientists know, as the public often does not, that such [. . .] research tells us nothing about cause and effect" (Glasser). The same author continues, "many people will falsely conclude after reading such statistical associations" that "'[t]elevision is the cause' [of violence]." To illustrate the problems with this epidemiological research, let us look at the argument that TV brought violence to South Africa. This claim is based on a correlation of the introduction of English-language TV and an increase in "violent crime, most especially among the young." To say, however, that TV is the cause of the crime is to exclude all kinds of other factors. For example, we know that in the particular case in South Africa, English-language TV had previously "been banned by the Africaans-speaking government." This information suggests tension between the native population and a pro-English movement. Now, I am not saying that I can prove this tension or that it is the real cause for the increase in violence. What I am saying is that we cannot conclude a cause if we only have a simple correlation. To say that English-language TV is the cause for growing violence is to sat that "owning more than one television set caused heart disease" just because an "epidemiologic research showed a statistical association between heart disease and the number of television sets a person owned" (in fact, "[c]linical trials demonstrated that cholesterol, but not the number of television sets one owned, was causally related") (Glasser).

Furthermore, not only are the grounds for TV censorship shaky, but such censorship would also be impractical and potentially dangerous. The following quote points at the impracticality of censorship: "claiming we have to reprogram the media watched by 99.99 percent of us to influence the behavior of 0.01 percent is to be rendered helpless by a much smaller problem" (Jenkins). Although I am not sure about the accuracy of these numbers, I do think that the statement demonstrates well the unwillingness of many people to give up their freedom of watching whatever they want on TV in favor of child sensitive censorship. Furthermore, to trust the government with the regulation of TV programs is also dangerous, for it would be unclear by which and whose standards this censorship would be carried out. The difficulty of finding a standard that corresponds to the values of all parents is demonstrated by the claim of an author who argues that most TV shows are in fact portraying the right values. In support of his claim, he refers to the TV show *Friends* and asks, "Is there a more wholesome group of kids than the cute boys and girls on *Friends*. They are all white and hetero" (Hirschorn). Now, I know several parents who would strongly object to "all white and hetero" as the right message. On the other hand, I also know parents who would endorse such a message. Not only does this disagreement show the difficulty of having someone else than the parents, namely the government, define the "right" values for children, but it also points to the danger of children being indoctrinated with values that conflict with those of their parents.

Being aware of the shortcomings of TV censorship, it is important now to look at the benefits of responsible parenting with respect to TV and violence. I believe that parent regulation of TV shows, a dialogue between parent and child about TV shows, and the offering of alternatives to TV can not only reduce child violence but also increase the happiness of child and parent.

First, responsible parents should regulate the TV exposure of their children. This allows parents not only to reduce the violence their children are exposed to while watching TV but also to monitor the time their children spend in front of the TV. For reasons that I will address under point three, I believe that it is important for the mental and physical health of the child that the time spent in front of a TV is limited. The danger with government regulation is that it might give parents a false sense of security. They think because violence has been censored, TV can no longer harm their children. They will feel comfortable about their children watching TV. Suddenly, the TV has become a convenient babysitter.

But responsible parents know not only what and when their children watch TV but also how they respond to what they see. This brings me to my second attribute of responsible parents: Responsible parents also use TV shows as an opportunity for dialogue with their children. In the case where children actually do watch violence, parents could ask, "Can you imagine how much this must hurt?" to give children a sense of the pain that accompanies violence. And of course, parents should also disagree with the violence shown and tell the child, "I really disagree with the way the character treated his friend. I think it would have been much better if he had talked to him instead of beating him." The point is that watching TV together with your child is more than just a means to shield your child from an overdose of TV violence. It can also be a great opportunity to encourage conversations that foster critical thinking skills and verbal skills and allow parents to understand their children better.

And third, responsible parents should also offer their children alternatives to TV. If a child spends most of his or her time in front of a TV, even if the violence is minimal, the child's physical and mental well-being is threatened. The hour-long sitting prohibits the child from getting enough exercise. Furthermore, the lonely hours in front of the TV would cause the child to become alienated from others and to be less and less able to distinguish reality from the world on TV. On the other hand, spending time with the child on other activities can be very rewarding both for the child and the parent. An example is the weekend my husband and I spent with our five-year-old nephew, Mason. He arrived with a video that he was determined to watch. However, when we suggested going to the park, the video was soon forgotten. Moreover, walking all over the park and visiting the planetarium, aquarium, and playground was time well spent: Mason felt proud that he could keep up with us grown ups without being carried on my husband's shoulders; he got plenty of exercise, not only from the walking but also from the playground; he became completely fascinated with the planetarium; he got the sense that he was important and loved; and he just had a real fun time. At the same time, because this day was full of interaction and talking with Mason, my husband and I learned so much more about our nephew than we would have ever done if we had watched TV. (Also all these activities caused Mason to fall asleep after dinner, so that my husband and I had a calm and restful evening—something that TV would have never accomplished.)

Censorship might shield children from TV violence. But responsible parenting can do the same. And while TV censorship is problematic—its causal grounds are shaky, its practicality and standards are doubtful—responsible parenting is so much more rewarding. When parents not only monitor the shows their children watch and the hours their children spend in front of a TV, but also encourage dialogue about the shows and offer alternative activities to TV, the children will learn to think critically, feel loved, have ample opportunities to release extra energies, and be much happier. And having happier children appears to be the best prevention of violence. In the end, I still believe in the truth of the poster, that "you are your child's first teacher."

WORKS CITED

Glasser, Ira. "TV Causes Violence? Try Again." New York Times 15 June 1994: A19.

Hirschorn, Michael. "The Myth of Television Depravity." New York Times 4 Sept. 1995: A21.

Hunt, Albert R. "Teen Violence Spawned by Guns and Cultural Rot." Wall Street Journal 11 June 1998: 12.

Jacoby, Jeff. "A Desensitized Society Drenched in Sleaze." <u>Boston Globe</u> 8 June 1995: 16.

Jenkins, Holman W., Jr. "Violence Never Solved Anything but It's Entertaining." <u>Wall Street Journal</u> 28 Oct. 1998: 14.

Kristol, Irving. "Sex, Violence, and Videotape." <u>Wall Street Journal</u> 31 May 1998: 28. ◪

5 | Reasoning: Methods and Fallacies

Come now, and let us reason together.

—Isaiah 1:18

As we have seen in the last four chapters, argumentative writing involves the use of many skills: making rhetorical choices regarding audience, purpose, expectations, and the nature of the subject matter; outlining and drafting arguments; deciding to use Classical, Toulmin, or Rogerian methods of argument. This chapter looks closely at another skill of fundamental importance to writers of arguments—reasoning. By working at the development of your ability to think critically and logically, you will be less likely to slip into the pitfalls common to unpersuasive argumentative writing.

Argumentative Reasoning

All arguments are imperfect to some degree. Unlike the tight logic of mathematics, in which a problem is solved methodically and objectively and turns out either correct or incorrect, most genuine arguments are based on complex human situations—complex because they have unpredictable elements. It is one thing to prove that force is equal to the product of mass times acceleration ($F = ma$) or that Socrates is mortal (given the fact that all humans are mortal); it is quite another matter to prove that reading to children, say, dramatically increases their chances of college success. To argue that claim convincingly, you would first need to be aware of variables such as the availability of controlled studies on this topic, the characteristics of the students used in the studies, the types of readings the children had been exposed to, the frequency of being read to, and so on. Because of such complex variables, no argument can be 100 percent beyond dispute.

Thus, opportunities to make an argument stronger than it is always exist. Good arguers, however, strive to create not the perfect argument but the most efficient one—the one that will ethically and logically persuade the readers. An argument, then, is most successful when its weaknesses are minimized as much as possible. As a writer of arguments, you must familiarize yourself with the most common argumentative errors, which are known as *fallacies*.

The Nature of Fallacies

Arguers rarely use fallacies deliberately. Inadvertent lapses in judgment, fallacies usually arise from lack of experience with the subject matter, lack of familiarity with other points of view, and undeveloped methods of argumentative reasoning. Let us examine each of these problems.

- **Lack of experience with the subject matter.** The more informed you are, the more "ammunition" you have to defend your views. Most arguments fail to convince because they do not draw sufficiently from experience (personal experience as well as experience acquired from intensive research). You may feel passionately about the need to save the rain forests, but unless you thoroughly understand the nature of rain forests, the reasons they are so precious, and the ways in which they are so threatened, your argument will lack substance. You would have no choice but to rely on broad generalities, such as "Rain forests are filled with important species." Unless you can name and describe such species and describe their importance, readers are unlikely to be convinced that the assertion was valid.

- **Lack of familiarity with other points of view.** In addition to acquiring a knowledge base about the topic, you also need to be familiar with the range of representative views on that topic. Before you can defend your views on an issue, you need to understand challenging arguments and find reasons why those arguments are not as effective as yours.

- **Underdeveloped methods of argumentative reasoning.** You not only need to be knowledgeable about issues and familiar with the spectrum of views on those issues, but you also need to know how arguments progress logically from one point to the next. In addition to the methods of presenting an argument (the Classical, Toulmin, and Rogerian methods discussed in Chapters 2–4), there are particular *reasoning strategies* or patterns of thinking that enable you to frame an assertion logically.

Strategies of Reasoning

The reasoning strategies most relevant to argumentative writing are as follows:

- **Deduction:** Drawing conclusions from assertions that you know to be true (insofar as you can determine); reasoning from the general to the specific

- **Induction:** Arriving at a conclusion that is based on what you judge to be sufficient (not necessarily conclusive) available evidence; reasoning from the specific to the general

- **Categorization:** Placing an idea or issue in a larger context using the strategies of definition, classification, and division

- **Analogy:** Attempting to enhance the validity of a claim by finding a similar situation in a different context

- **Authorization:** Establishing the validity of a claim by invoking authority, either in the form of personal testimonial from an expert or of preestablished policy or law

- **Plea:** Using emotionally charged expressions of feeling to aid in defending an assertion

The sections that follow look more closely at the ways in which each of these reasoning strategies operates.

Deduction

When you reason deductively, you break down an assertion into formal statements that are logically connected. A *syllogism* is one formula used in deductive reasoning, consisting of a *major premise*, a *minor premise*, and a *conclusion*.

Major premise: All cats meow.

Minor premise: Cordelia is a cat.

Conclusion: Therefore, Cordelia meows.

As this simple example reveals, to reason deductively means to accept the major premise without question. To call the major premise into question ("Is it true that all cats meow?") is to move from deduction to induction, whereby one looks at the evidence leading up to the hypothesis to determine its truthfulness.

In commonplace arguments, an assumption often goes unstated because it is taken for granted that the audience already shares it. From the perspective of formal logic, this is considered an incomplete syllogism; but from the perspective of argumentative discourse, it is considered sufficient and is referred to as an *enthymeme.* Thus, the statement "Cordelia meows because she is a cat" is an enthymeme because the writer takes for granted that the audience accepts the unstated assumption that all cats meow.

Deductive reasoning can be especially powerful when one is refuting a claim. (If you need to refresh your memory about the process of refutation, review the discussion of Classical argument in Chapter 2.) For example, if a friend claims that to accept a government-run program is to reject a free-market economy, you could refute the claim by asserting that a government program and a free-market economy are not as mutually exclusive as the friend's claim implies. Such dichotomous ("either-or") thinking is a commonly occurring example of flawed deductive reasoning. By calling attention to the many-sided complexity of a problem, you raise the consciousness of your audience; you in effect *teach* your readers to recognize the "gray areas" that aren't as conspicuous as the "black and white ones" but that usually bring the truth much closer.

To refute a claim, you may need to do a deductive analysis of the author's reasoning strategies. Here is a five-step method for such analysis:

1. Identify contradictions

2. Identify inconsistencies

3. Identify omissions or oversights

4. Reduce an unsound claim to its logical absurdity (*reductio ad absurdum*) so as to expose the flawed reasoning more conspicuously

5. Identify oversimplifications

Identify Contradictions   Someone asserts that making handgun sales illegal would increase crime because more guns would be obtained illegally. You could reveal a contradiction by showing (using statistics from a reputable survey) how that claim contradicts reality: that crime actually has decreased by a certain percentage in one or more places where such a law had been enacted. Similarly, if a writer asserts that playing video games excessively damages one's ability to think effectively and then proceeds to describe her own experiences with video games in an effective manner, you could point out the contradiction between the authors writing effectively and the alleged damage to her thinking skills from years of playing video games.

Identify Inconsistencies   If you claim that people should give up eating meat but then proceed to eat a bowl of chicken soup, reasoning that such a small quantity of chicken is negligible or that even vegetarians need a "meat break" now and then, you are being logically inconsistent. Or consider this somewhat more complex example: Arlene is against abortion because she equates abortion with murder. However, Arlene agrees that in cases of rape, incest, or grave danger to the mother's life, abortion is permissible. Arlene is being logically inconsistent because her exceptions seem irrelevant to her own definition of abortion as fetal murder.

Identify Omissions or Oversights   A friend advises you not to take a course from Professor Krupp because Krupp gives difficult exams, grades rigorously, and assigns a heavy reading load. At first, you think that these are pretty good reasons for not enrolling in Professor Krupp's course. But then you wonder whether any positive things about this professor might balance out the bad, so you ask: "Did you learn a lot in her course?" Your friend replies, "Oh yes—more than in any other course I've taken." You have just identified a deliberate omission or an accidental oversight in your friend's assessment of Professor Krupp.

Reduce an Unsound Claim to Its Logical Absurdity   Someone argues against a company's policy that employees wear shirts and ties or dresses and skirts by claiming that employees can think well even when dressed casually in jeans and T-shirts. You could refute that claim by taking it to the logical extreme. Why wouldn't the first person show up in pajamas or a swimsuit for work then? The point of the dress code is not to affect one's ability to think but to present a certain image of the company.

Identify Oversimplifications   Recall the earlier example of the friend who argues that a government-run program is never compatible with a free-market economy. This kind of dichotomous thinking oversimplifies the reality of a free-market society such as that of the United States, where government programs such as Social Security and NASA are quite compatible with a market economy. Oversimplification results from an insufficiently investigated or thought-out premise on which the argument rests.

■ Exercise 5.1

1. Examine the following four arguments and describe the method or methods of deductive reasoning that each author is using or representing.

   a. Watching the Republican Party try to come to terms with several million gay voters reminds me a little of my uncle. He's the only family member I'm estranged from, because he regards my sexual orientation as a deliberate rebuke to God. When he heard I had contracted HIV, he told me in a letter, in so many words, that I deserved it and that only the Holy Spirit could cure me. He's also, I might add, a good person: kind, loving, and decent, if not the brightest bulb on the Christmas tree.

   The human question is: How do I get along with him? My human answer: I don't. After his letter about my illness, in which he couldn't even bring himself to ask how I was, I cut him off. In most families with gay members there's something of this sort going on. So I completely understand the impulse to ostracize someone who has decided that a religious fiat, which by definition cannot be challenged, requires him to reject and hurt a loved one.

   In a family, we can get away with such anger and hurt. But in politics such emotionally satisfying options come at a price: impasse, conflict, and little progress. That's why the knee-jerk attempt to turn George W. Bush into a homophobe is, in my view, misguided. It's misguided, first of all, because it's clear he isn't one. And it's misguided also because it will create an atmosphere that, while making a few gays feel better, makes many more worse off. We need to change a paradigm in which one side sees only bigots and the other side sees only perverts. This election presents us with a chance.

   How? The first step is to resist at every opportunity the notion that homosexuals are defined by victimhood. If you look at the agenda of, say, the leading gay lobby, the Human Rights Campaign, you'll see what I mean. Its priorities are laws that protect gays from hate crimes and employment discrimination. Both proposals rely for their effectiveness on the notion that gay men and women be seen as the objects of physical violence and routine oppression in the workplace. But the number of hate crimes perpetrated against gay people is relatively puny, and such crimes are already covered under existing criminal law. And it's ludicrous to look at the gay population and see millions of people who have a hard time finding or keeping a job. In those states where anti-discrimination laws for gays are in effect, the number of lawsuits filed is negligible. But the real harm of these campaigns isn't just that they add new, largely pointless laws; it's that they portray homosexuals as downtrodden and weak.

To put it bluntly, we're not. We have survived a health crisis that would have destroyed—and is destroying—other populations, due in no small part to our tenacity, compassion, and organization. We are represented in almost every major cultural, political, and social organization, often leading them. Gay strength can be seen everywhere—from courageous high school kids organizing support groups to a young lesbian serving as an indispensable aide to Dick Cheney's vice presidential campaign. The media is saturated with gay talent, images, and skill. An honest gay agenda should capitalize on this truth, not flee from it. —Andrew Sullivan

b. If the Darwinian [evolutionary] process really took place, remains of plants and animals [that is, the fossil record] should show a gradual and continual change from one type of animal or plant into another. One of the things that worried Darwin in his day, as well as [what worries] modern evolutionists, was that the fossil record did not supply these intermediate life forms. —Donald E. Chittick

c. Until the census is focused on individuals, not households, the situation of women and children may continue to be distorted—just as it might be if there were only one vote per household. There is such a wide range of constituencies with an interest in Census Bureau policies that journalists have coined the phrase "census politics." But social justice movements haven't yet focused on the fact that census categories also determine what is counted as work, and who is defined as a worker. . . . —Gloria Steinem

d. Aristotle felt that the mortal horse of Appearance which ate grass and took people places and gave birth to little horses deserved far more attention than Plato was giving it. He said that the horse is not mere Appearance. The Appearances cling to something which is independent of them and which, like Ideas, is unchanging. The "something" that Appearances cling to he named "substance." And at that moment . . . our modern scientific understanding of reality was born. —Robert Pirsig

2. Bring in a short article such as a newspaper editorial and discuss it in terms of its use of deductive reasoning. Point out any flaws you see in the deductive reasoning.

Induction

You engage in inductive reasoning when you strive to make sense of things you experience. Unlike deductive reasoning, you do not begin with a premise assumed to be true and then determine a logical foundation for supporting it. Instead, you build a hypothesis out of your observations of phenomena. To return to our simple example of whether all cats meow, the inductive writer would examine the evidence—Cat A, Cat B, Cat C, and so on—until observing enough cats to warrant the conclusion, "Yes, all cats meow," or to reject it ("No, not all cats meow; Siberian tigers are cats, and they growl"), or to qualify it ("Yes, all cats meow, provided they're members of the subgenus *Felix domesticus*").

Because in inductive reasoning the strength of the conclusion rests entirely on the sufficiency of the evidence observed, you must use an adequate number of reliable samples.

Number of Samples   How many samples must be observed before it is reasonable to make the "inductive leap"? Technically, of course, no conclusion arrived at inductively is absolutely indisputable. For that to be the case in our cat argument, for example, you would have to observe every domestic cat on earth! At some point, every inductive reasoner must say, "I have observed enough to draw a reliable conclusion." This decision can be tricky and, indeed, is a major point of disputation in science—which relies preeminently on the inductive method (better known as the scientific method) for testing the validity of hypotheses.

Reliability of Samples   If the purpose of your paper is to argue whether a clear correlation exists between alcohol consumption and health problems, you may decide first to conduct a campus survey to see whether health problems are more frequent among drinking students than among nondrinking ones. In addition to interviewing an adequate number of students from each group (a 20 to 25 percent response rate to your survey from the total student population would be considered substantial), you will want the sample to be reliable in other ways. For example, it should be representative of different groups within the student body. Having only women, only men, only athletes, or only Mormons included would make your sample survey on college drinking unreliable.

Categorization

Without systems of classification and division, we would be unable to make much sense out of reality. Perhaps the best illustration of this is the Linnean system of taxonomy. With its binomial schema (genus name + species name, as in *Felix domesticus* or *Homo sapiens*), all life on earth has been classified. Think for a moment about how valuable such a schema is for understanding the relationship of life forms to each other.

People categorize foods into groups such as savory or sweet, or main course or dessert, to determine what they'll serve for dinner—a useful strategy for knowing what to buy for a dinner party. People break the large category of sports into, say, basketball, and baseball, and then divide those subgroups further into professional and amateur leagues. College football teams would fall into amateur leagues, which then play on their NCAA division level—IA, IAA, IIA, whatever. Imagine the injuries without such classification—an NFL football team playing a IIIA college team! Categorization in sports helps ensure a level playing field.

Categorization is just as important outside of science; for example, we can plan our day better by grouping our activities into "chores," "business transactions," "recreation," etc. However, problems often arise. When people try to categorize human beings neatly according to ethnicity or cultural differences, the danger of stereotyping arises. Superficial differences such as skin color or manner of dress or speech are given more significance than they deserve. Racism, homophobia, and gender-based discrimination are often the ugly results. Categorizing works best when it serves as an initial gauge for differentiating A from B or A and B from C, and so forth. For example, if you were examining the study habits of college students, you might group your sample students by gender or age or major, just in case a correlation between the category selected and the kind of study habits would show up.

Another facet of categorization is definition, which is necessary for "fine-tuning" the distinctions between one thing and another within the same category. The very word *define* means "to determine or fix the boundaries or extent of." (*Random House Webster's College Dictionary.*) Formal definitions make use of categorizing techniques in themselves. In the definition of the word *chaplet,* for example—"a wreath or garland for the head" (*Random House Webster's College Dictionary*)—the first half of the definition ("a wreath or garland") establishes the broad category, or genus, and the second half ("for the head") pinpoints its distinguishing (specific) characteristics.

Analogy

To make an analogy is to draw a correspondence between two things that are superficially different but not essentially different. Analogies are used to enhance comprehension. If you are trying to help readers understand the nature of a radio wave, for example, you might use the more familiar analogy of a water wave. A river and an artery are not superficially alike, but they behave in similar enough ways for one to say that water flows in a river the way blood flows in an artery. A more readily perceived phenomenon like a flowing river is easier to understand than the flow of blood through an artery. The author's goal is to enable ease of understanding over precision of explanation.

However, to say that people are like ants because they swarm in large numbers to sporting events, is to generate a distorted (and demeaning) image of fans' behavior. Using analogy in argumentative writing is a give-and-take situation: You give your readers greater comprehension of the idea, but you take away precision. The rule of thumb, then, is to use analogies carefully.

Authorization

Writers sometimes need to support an assertion by including the testimony of an expert in the field in question. If you are arguing about the dangers of ultraviolet radiation and urging people to consider sunbathing a risky activity due to the alleged link between ultraviolet radiation and skin cancer, you are likely to present empirical evidence from, say, several medical studies. You could also add drama to your claim by quoting a startling statement made by a leading skin cancer expert. In such a situation you are resorting to the ethos, the reliable character, of the expert.

Plea

Emotional response is often highly persuasive. In formal argument, therefore, you may try to persuade your audience to accept your views by way of sympathy or compassion as well as by way of logical reasoning. Thus, if your goal is fundraising for the homeless, you might tell stories about the way homeless people suffer when they have to go without eating for two or three days or shiver during cold winter nights on a park bench. If you wish to emphasize the importance of reading aloud to children, you might create a little scenario in which you dramatize the way that listening to stories delights and heightens the intellectual curiosity of young children who are absorbed in what their parents are reading to them.

Errors in Reasoning: A Taxonomy

Now that we have examined the methods of reasoning, it is time to look closely at the pitfalls that can occur. To some degree errors in reasoning are almost unavoidable because reasoning is a complex mental act that requires a concerted effort to perfect. Nonetheless, the more alert you become to the way in which a given line of reasoning violates a principle of logic, of ethics, or of emotional integrity, the less likely it is that your arguments will be criticized for their fallacies.

Let us begin by becoming familiar with the common fallacies; we then examine each of them in more detail and look at the ways they subtly creep into an argument. We also examine these fallacies to identify faulty logic in the sources we may consult for our topics. Seeing faulty logic in supposedly informed sources helps us to decide not to use such sources ourselves and to know what we can rebut in our opposition's argument.

Errors of Deduction

In this group of fallacies, the line of reasoning that stems from statements assumed to be true are flawed or the statements themselves may be flawed. Many errors in deductive reasoning occur because the author fails to connect premises to conclusions logically. Some common types of deductive fallacies follow.

Fourth Term   Careless arguers sometimes substitute one term for another, assuming the terms mean or suggest the same things, when in fact the terms have different meanings. The way to demonstrate the illogic of such a substitution is to think about the terms in a formal syllogism (the pattern of formal deductive reasoning discussed on page 100–102): major, minor, and middle, as follows:

                    Maj   Mid
Major premise: All **dogs** are **mammals.**

                    Min   Maj
Minor premise: **Rascal** is a **dog.**

                                Min   Mid
Conclusion: Therefore, **Rascal** is a **mammal.**

In any valid syllogism, the major term is the subject that must be equated with both a generic classification (middle term) and an individual one (minor term). In the above example, the major term *dog* is equated with the middle term *mammal* (dog = mammal) and the minor term Rascal (dog = Rascal).

Now consider this syllogism:

All prerequisites for the major in chemistry are difficult.

Chem. 50 is highly recommended for the major in chemistry.

Therefore, Chem. 50 is difficult.

Instead of seeing the major term *prerequisites* appear in the minor premise, a substitute fourth term—*highly recommended*—appears, thus rendering the syllogism invalid (even though in actuality it may be true).

Non Sequitur   In a non sequitur ("It does not follow"), an assertion cannot be tied logically to the premise it attempts to demonstrate. Consider the premise, "Nellie is obsessed with basketball." The reason presented is "because she attends a basketball game every week." The fact that one attends a basketball game every week—or every day—does not in itself demonstrate an obsession. Nellie could be an employee at the arena, or her brother could be one of the players, or she could be a sportswriter, or she could be conducting research on the game of basketball, or she could simply love the game in a positive sense. *Obsession* implies that something in one's behavior is beyond control; if that is the case, then your statements should reflect it: "Nellie is obsessed with basketball because, despite being threatened with losing her job if she doesn't go to work rather than the basketball games, she attends them anyway."

Ad Hominem   An ad hominem ("Against the individual person") is a form of non sequitur in which the arguer argues against an individual's qualifications by attacking his or her personal life or trying to create a negative link between life and work. "Sherwood would not make a good mayor because he spends too much of his free time reading murder mysteries." The reverse situation—*pro hominem*—is equally fallacious, even though it would seldom be reported: "Sherwood would make a terrific mayor because he spends a lot of his time reading the Bible."

Errors of Induction

In this group of fallacies, the process of drawing conclusions or arriving at reliable generalizations based on observed particulars is faulty.

Unsupported Generalization   Generalizing is an important tool for critical thinkers, but a good generalization is derived from evidence. When the evidence is lacking, we say that the generalization is unsupported. *Evidence* in this context refers not only to statistics like trends, tallies, or percentages but also to cases in point. For example, if you read somewhere that more physicians are being sued for malpractice in the current year than in the year preceding, you would be making an unsupported generalization if you neglected to provide statistical support for your assertion. It would also be a good idea to refer to individual cases that *demonstrated* incompetence. Why? Perhaps the increase in malpractice suits was based on other factors, such as more aggressive efforts to sue for malpractice; or perhaps the criteria defining *malpractice* had changed from one year to the next. As a critical thinker, you always need to be aware of alternative possibilities and explanations.

Hasty Generalization   A hasty generalization leaps to a premature conclusion—not because no evidence is provided but because the evidence is insufficient to convincingly support the claim being made. Writers of argument can fall prey to hasty generalization when they do not check out enough cases before reading their conclusion. If you claim, for example, that burglary has increased in your neighborhood and use as your only evidence the fact that two houses on your block have been burglarized, you would be guilty of a hasty generalization—*unless* you could also demonstrate that this number is greater for the same time frame of a year ago. Always make sure your evidence is thorough.

Red Herring   In British fox hunting, red herrings (very odorous) are sometimes dragged across a trail to throw the dogs off scent. This practice serves as a metaphor for raising an issue that has little or nothing to do with what is being argued in order to force the argument in a new direction. For example, say that after listening to a voter's concern that the community's high school needs to receive major funds to upgrade its facilities, a candidate responds, "I understand your concern and have asked the school board to review its policies." The candidate has thrown the voter a red herring by changing the subject from inadequate facilities to the school board's educational policies.

Poisoning the Well   Like the red herring, this fallacy aims to interfere with normal argumentative progression. But whereas the red herring aims to derail an argument in progress, poisoning the well aims to corrupt the argument before it even begins—usually by passing judgment on the quality of the argument before listeners have a chance to evaluate it. If you ask your friends to listen to a debate on whether the public library should be funded for building a videotape collection but then say that one of the debaters will be presenting an argument that has already been successfully repudiated, you would be guilty of poisoning the well with your own evaluation before giving your friends the opportunity to judge for themselves.

Post Hoc ergo Propter Hoc   The phrase (sometimes simply post hoc) means "after the fact, therefore because of the fact." An effect (say, tripping and falling) is attributed to a cause (say, the sudden appearance of a black cat) only because of proximity, not because of any logical connection. The post hoc fallacy forms the basis for superstitious thinking and preempts any effort to determine a logical cause (for example, the ground was slippery or the person who fell was not paying any attention to the ground).

Begging the Question   To beg the question is to state a claim that the speaker assumes is beyond dispute, but in fact is disputable—hence, the speaker begs the question. For example, if a friend says of a TV sitcom, "I enjoy watching those hackneyed shows," she is assuming that there could be no disagreement about the sitcoms being hackneyed—hence she is begging the question "*Are* all such sitcoms hackneyed?"

Slippery Slope   This is an example of induction run rampant. Here a person forecasts a series of events (usually disastrous) that will befall one if the first stated step is taken. Thus, the person who asserts the following is committing a slippery slope fallacy:

> If medical researchers continue to increase human longevity, then the population will soar out of control, mass famine will occur, the global economy will collapse, and the very survival of the species will be threatened.

Factors capable of compensating for the consequences of population increase have not been considered.

Errors of Categorization

In this group of fallacies, arguers tend to see things in terms of black and white instead of color gradations, so to speak—or they confuse one group of objects or ideas with another.

False Dichotomy (Either/Or)   This error of reasoning assumes there are only two options to resolving a given situation, when in fact there may be many. Assertions such as, "If you're not part of the solution, you're part of the problem," "America: love it or leave it," or "If you love nature, then you cannot possibly support industrial development" are examples of dichotomous thinking. To address the last example mentioned, for instance, factors that complicate the industry/nature dichotomy include the fact that recycling, land reclaiming, and alternative energy use (wind, solar, geothermal, biomass) are industries.

Apples and Oranges   We often hear people comparing two things that are not comparable (because they are not part of the same category). A statement like "The physics lecture was not as good as the dinner we had at Antoine's last night" does not convey much meaning. Likewise, it is illogical to claim that Placido Domingo is a better singer than Johnny Cash because opera and country-western are two different kinds of music, with fundamentally different criteria for excellence.

Errors of Analogy

Errors in analogies occur when the analogy distorts, misrepresents, or oversimplifies the reality.

False or Invalid Analogy   An analogy is considered false when it distorts what is essentially true about what is being analogized. If a student dislikes an instructor's strict, regimented classroom tactics and says that the classroom is like Hitler's Third Reich, the student is using a false analogy. Yes, it is true that Hitler used strict military tactics; but that fact alone cannot serve to parallel the situation in a classroom—unless the professor hired secret police agents (Gestapo), put dissenters into horrific concentration camps, and instituted mass extermination plans. Parallel activities of students and professionals often breed false analogies: "It isn't fair that I can't write on anything I want, any way I want. Nobody tells Amy Tan or Stephen King how or what to write!"

Faulty Analogy   Sometimes the analogy we use to parallel an idea or object is something of a half-truth instead of a complete falsehood; that is, it might work in one context, but not in others. To compare human courtship rituals to those of peacocks, for example, might amusingly highlight the similarities, but the differences are too major to take the analogy seriously.

Errors of Authorization

In this group of fallacies, authority figures or their testimonials are used vaguely or erroneously.

Vague Authority   In the sentence, "Science tells us that a catastrophic earthquake will strike Southern California within the next ten years," we would do well to question the term *science*. (In a similar vein, recall the commercial that begins, "Four out of five doctors recommend . . .") We have no idea who or even what authority *science* is referring to since *science* refers to a vast body of disciplines, not any particular authority. To remove the vagueness, the author would have to say something to this effect: "Seismologists at Cal Tech [or better yet, Dr. So-and-So, a seismologist at Cal Tech] predicts that a catastrophic earthquake will strike Southern California within the next ten years."

Suspect Authority   Sometimes it is not easy to tell whether an authority is reliable. Using the above example, if the credentials of the scientist predicting the earthquake are not disclosed—or if her field of expertise is a discipline other than seismology—we have a right to suspect that person's authority.

The Suspect Authority fallacy is encountered most frequently in advertisements. When a film star tells us that a certain brand of shampoo gives a "deep bodied" luster to hair, we wonder what the basis for authority possibly could be, even assuming that everyone agrees on how a "deep bodied" luster looks.

Keep in mind, of course, that such a commercial is not an example of false advertising. The commercial never states that the film star has the proper credentials to evaluate a product's quality, only that the product is the star's personal choice. The audience is left to make any further inferences, such as, "Gosh, if Wilma Superstar uses that shampoo, then it *must* be terrific."

Errors in Pleading

These fallacies stem from erroneous or improper use of the Aristotelian appeals discussed in Chapter 1.

Appeal to Fear   Anyone who has heard commercials for security alarm systems or auto-theft prevention devices is quite familiar with this appeal. The advertiser typically presents scenarios of coming home to find the place ransacked. "Better to be safe than sorry," is the common phrase brandished here. Keep in mind that this appeal becomes an error in pleading when it is excessive or when the scenarios presented are so extreme as to distort reality. If the advertiser for security alarms paints a lurid picture of you and your family being tortured or murdered by burglars, for example, such an appeal to fear likely would be excessive and thus erroneous.

Appeal to the Bandwagon   Appeal to the bandwagon is the fallacy behind peer pressure. "Hey, everyone else is going to the beach today; don't be a nerd and stay cooped up in the library on such a gorgeous day!" Being able to say "no," to maintain your own integrity, and to do what is most responsible and best for you in the long term are hard when you are the only one following that path. If you discover that everyone is suddenly buying or selling shares of stock that you own, the temptation is great to do likewise. It sometimes takes courage to say, "I'm going to think this out on my own and not follow the crowd."

Of course, sometimes an appeal to the bandwagon makes sense, as in the case of sound medical or health-care advice: "Millions of people get their teeth cleaned regularly (because they are far less likely to suffer from gum disease if they do so), so you should get your teeth cleaned too."

Appeal to Ignorance   The basis of the appeal here is that we can decide based on what is *not* known. For example, "We have every reason to believe that Martians exist because we have no way of knowing that they *don't* exit." The problem with this kind of reasoning, of course, is that there is no way to prove or disprove the claim.

One often encounters appeals to ignorance in informal scientific speculation. Have you ever gotten into a conversation about the likelihood of intelligent life on other worlds? You might commonly hear a line of reasoning that goes something like this:

> True, we haven't the slightest blip of evidence that intelligent beings exist beyond earth; but the universe is so vast and our understanding of what the universe could contain is so meager that there must be intelligent life out there somewhere!

Although one might argue that the probability of intelligent life increases in proportion to the size of the field, that probability does not necessarily approach inevitability unless compelling evidence is uncovered (indirect evidence of intelligent habitation, such as industrial pollutants in the atmosphere of a distant planet, for example).

■ Exercise 5.2

1. What is the connection between a method of reasoning and an error in reasoning?

2. State the principal difference between inductive and deductive reasoning.

3. For each of the following passages,

   • give the method of reasoning it belongs to;

   • indicate whether it is an appropriate or erroneous use of that method; and

- if the latter, identify the error and suggest a way to resolve it.
  Note: There may be more than one error in a given passage or no errors at all.

  a. Cats are just like people: They're intensely curious, and they get into trouble as a result of their curiosity.

  b. The idiots who gave my car a tune-up forgot to clean the fuel injection system.

  c. God is beyond logical understanding; therefore, one should never question the truth of God's existence.

  d. All wolves are carnivores. My boyfriend is a wolf. Therefore, my boyfriend is a carnivore.

  e. You must finish eating your broccoli; think of all the starving people in the world.

  f. After interviewing more than a dozen students about their reading habits, I am convinced that students these days do not like to read poetry.

  g. All of my friends who want to attend law school have signed up for the Advanced Argumentation course. Since you plan on going to law school, you should take this course too.

  h. It's a good idea to wash fresh fruit before eating it; the last time I forgot to wash the strawberries I ate, I came down with food poisoning.

  i. Music appreciation classes seem like a waste of time. I know what I like to listen to, and no music expert is going to change my mind about it.

  j. Chicken is much tastier than oatmeal.

  k. Libraries are clearly becoming obsolete because the Internet is growing so rapidly.

  l. To answer your question about whether taxes should be raised, let me first call your attention to the fact that the unemployment rate in this state is lower than it has ever been.

  m. Sound waves, just like light waves, can be low frequency or high frequency.

4. For each of the above passages, suggest ways in which the error, if one exists, may be corrected.

■ Exercise 5.3

Read "Love Is a Fallacy" by Max Shulman, a mid-twentieth-century humorist. In it he attempts to demonstrate logical fallacies in action. Then answer the questions that follow.

Love Is a Fallacy | Max Shulman

Cool was I and logical. Keen, calculating, perspicacious, acute and astute—I was all of these. My brain was as powerful as a dynamo, as precise as a chemist's scales, as penetrating as a scalpel. And—think of it!—I was only eighteen.

It is not often that one so young has such a giant intellect. Take, for example, Petey Burch, my roommate at the University of Minnesota. Same age, same background, but dumb as an ox. A nice enough fellow, you understand, but nothing upstairs. Emotional type, unstable. Impressionable. Worst of all, a faddist. Fads, I submit are the very negation of reason. To be swept up in every new craze that comes along, to surrender yourself to idiocy just because everybody else is doing it—this, to me, is the acme of mindlessness. Not, however, to Petey.

One afternoon I found Petey lying on his bed with an expression of such distress on his face that I immediately diagnosed appendicitis. "Don't move," I said. "Don't take a laxative. I'll get a doctor."

"Raccoon," he mumbled thickly.

"Raccoon?" I said, pausing in my flight.   5

"I want a raccoon coat," he wailed.

I perceived that his trouble was not physical, but mental. "Why do you want a raccoon coat?"

"I should have known it," he cried, pounding his temples. "I should have known they'd come back when the Charleston came back. Like a fool I spent all my money for textbooks, and now I can't get a raccoon coat."

"Can you mean," I said incredulously, "that people are actually wearing raccoon coats again?"

"All the Big Men on Campus are wearing them. Where've you been?"   10

"In the library," I said, naming a place not frequented by Big Men on Campus.

He leaped from the bed and paced the room. "I've got to have a raccoon coat," he said passionately. "I've got to!"

"Petey, why? Look at it rationally. Raccoon coats are unsanitary. They shed. They smell bad. They weigh too much. They're unsightly. They —"

"You don't understand," he interrupted impatiently. "It's the thing to do. Don't you want to be in the swim?"

"No," I said truthfully.   15

"Well, I do," he declared. "I'd give anything for a raccoon coat. Anything!"

My brain, that precision instrument, slipped into high gear. "Anything?" I asked, looking at him narrowly.

"Anything," he affirmed in ringing tones.

I stroked my chin thoughtfully. It so happened that I knew where to get my hands on a raccoon coat. My father had had one in his undergraduate days; it lay now in a trunk in the attic back home. It also happened that Petey had something I wanted. He didn't *have* it exactly, but at least he had first rights on it. I refer to his girl, Polly Espy.

I had long coveted Polly Espy. Let me emphasize that my desire for this   20
young woman was not emotional in nature. She was, to be sure, a girl who excited the emotions, but I was not one to let my heart rule my head. I wanted Polly for a shrewdly calculated, entirely cerebral reason.

I was a freshman in law school. In a few years I would be out in practice. I was well aware of the importance of the right kind of wife in furthering a lawyer's career. The successful lawyers I had observed were, almost without exception, married to beautiful, gracious, intelligent women. With one omission, Polly fitted these specifications perfectly.

Beautiful she was. She was not yet of pin-up proportions, but I felt sure that time would supply the lack. She already had the makings.

Gracious she was. By gracious I mean full of graces. She had an erectness of carriage, an ease of bearing, a poise that clearly indicated the best of breeding. At table her manners were exquisite. I had seen her at the Kozy Kampus Korner eating the speciality of the house—a sandwich that contained scraps of pot roast, gravy, chopped nuts, and a dipper of sauerkraut—without even getting her fingers moist.

Intelligent she was not. In fact, she veered in the opposite direction. But I believed that under my guidance she would smarten up. At any rate, it was worth a try. It is, after all, easier to make a beautiful dumb girl smart than to make an ugly smart girl beautiful.

"Petey," I said, "are you in love with Polly Espy?"   25

"I think she's a keen kid," he replied, "but I don't know if you'd call it love. Why?"

"Do you," I asked, "have any kind of formal arrangement with her? I mean are you going steady or anything like that?"

"No. We see each other quite a bit, but we both have other dates. Why?"

"Is there," I asked, "any other man for whom she has a particular fondness?"

"Not that I know of. Why?"   30

I nodded with satisfaction. "In other words, if you were out of the picture, the field would be open. Is that right?"

"I guess so. What are you getting at?"

"Nothing, nothing," I said innocently, and took my suitcase out of the closet.

"Where are you going?" asked Petey.

"Home for the weekend." I threw a few things into the bag.   35

"Listen," he said, clutching my arm eagerly, "while you're home, you couldn't get some money from your old man, could you, and lend it to me so I can buy a raccoon coat?"

"I may do better than that," I said with a mysterious wink and closed my bag and left.

"Look," I said to Petey when I got back Monday morning. I threw open the suitcase and revealed the huge, hairy, gamy object that my father had worn in his Stutz Bearcat in 1925.

"Holy Toledo!" said Petey reverently. He plunged his hands into the raccoon coat and then his face. "Holy Toledo!" he repeated fifteen or twenty times.

"Would you like it?" I asked.   40

"Oh yes!" he cried, clutching the greasy pelt to him. Then a canny look came into his eyes. "What do you want for it?"

"Your girl," I said, mincing no words.

"Polly?" he said in a horrified whisper. "You want Polly?"

"That's right."

He flung the coat from him. "Never," he said stoutly.   45

I shrugged. "Okay. If you don't want to be in the swim. I guess it's your business."

I sat down in a chair and pretended to read a book, but out of the corner of my eye I kept watching Petey. He was a torn man. First he looked at the coat with the expression of a waif at a bakery window. Then he turned away and set his jaw resolutely. Then he looked back at the coat, with even more longing in his face. Then he turned away, but with not so much resolution this time. Back and forth his head swiveled, desire waxing, resolution waning. Finally he didn't turn away at all; he just stood and stared with mad lust at the coat.

"It isn't as though I was in love with Polly," he said thickly. "Or going steady or anything like that."

"That's right," I murmured.

"What's Polly to me, or me to Polly?"   50

"Not a thing," said I.

"It's just been a casual kick—just a few laughs, that's all."

"Try on the coat," said I.

He complied. The coat bunched high over his ears and dropped all the way down to his shoe tops. He looked like a mound of dead raccoons. "Fits fine," he said happily.

I rose from my chair. "Is it a deal?" I asked, extending my hand.   55

He swallowed. "It's a deal," he said and shook my hand.

I had my first date with Polly the following evening. This was in the nature of a survey; I wanted to find out just how much work I had to do to get her mind up to the standard I required. I took her first to dinner. "Gee, that was a delish dinner," she said as we left the restaurant. Then I took her to a movie. "Gee, that was a marvy movie," she said as we left the theater. And then I took her home. "Gee, I had a sensaysh time," she said as she bade me good night.

I went back to my room with a heavy heart. I had gravely underestimated the size of my task. This girl's lack of information was terrifying. Nor would it be enough merely to supply her with information. First she had to be taught to *think*. This loomed as a project of no small dimensions, and at first I was tempted to give her back to Petey. But then I got to thinking about her abundant physical charms and about the way she entered the room and the way she handled a knife and fork, and I decided to make an effort.

I went about it, as in all things, systematically. I gave her a course in logic. It happened that I, as a law student, was taking a course in logic myself, so I had all the facts at my finger tips. "Polly," I said to her when I picked her up on our next date, "tonight we are going over to the Knoll and talk."

"Oo, terrif," she replied. One thing I will say for this girl: you would go far to find another so agreeable.   60

We went to the Knoll, the campus trysting place, and we sat down under an old oak, and she looked at me expectantly. "What are we going to talk about?" she asked.

"Logic."

She thought this over for a minute and decided she liked it. "Magnif," she said.

"Logic," I said, clearing my throat, "is the science of thinking. Before we can think correctly, we must first learn to recognize the common fallacies of logic. These we will take up tonight."

"Wow-dow!" she cried, clapping her hands delightedly.   65

I winced, but went bravely on. "First let us examine the fallacy called Dicto Simpliciter."

"By all means," she urged, batting her lashes eagerly.

"Dicto Simpliciter means an argument based on an unqualified generalization. For example: Exercise is good. Therefore everybody should exercise."

"I agree," said Polly earnestly. "I mean exercise is wonderful. I mean it builds the body and everything."

"Polly," I said gently, "the argument is a fallacy. *Exercise is good* is an unqualified generalization. For instance, if you have heart disease, exercise is bad, not good. Many people are ordered by their doctors *not* to exercise. You must *qualify* the generalization. You must say exercise is *usually* good, or exercise is good *for most people*. Otherwise you have committed a Dicto Simpliciter. Do you see?"   70

"No," she confessed. "But this is marvy. Do more! Do more!"

"It will be better if you stop tugging at my sleeve," I told her, and when she desisted, I continued. "Next we take up a fallacy called Hasty Generalization. Listen carefully: You can't speak French. I can't speak French. Petey Burch can't speak French. I must therefore conclude that nobody at the University of Minnesota can speak French."

"Really?" said Polly, amazed. *"Nobody?"*

I hid my exasperation. "Polly, it's a fallacy. The generalization is reached too hastily. There are too few instances to support such a conclusion."

"Know any more fallacies?" she asked breathlessly. "This is more fun than dancing even."   75

I fought off a wave of despair. I was getting nowhere with this girl, absolutely nowhere. Still, I am nothing if not persistent. I continued. "Next comes Post Hoc. Listen to this: Let's not take Bill on our picnic. Every time we take him out with us, it rains."

"I know somebody just like that," she exclaimed. "A girl back home—Eula Becker, her name is. It never fails. Every single time we take her on a picnic—"

"Polly," I said sharply, "it's a fallacy. Eula Becker doesn't *cause* the rain. She has no connection with the rain. You are guilty of Post Hoc if you blame Eula Becker."

"I'll never do it again," she promised contritely. "Are you mad at me?"

I sighed deeply. "No, Polly, I'm not mad."   80

"Then tell me some more fallacies."

"All right. Let's try Contradictory Premises."

"Yes, let's," she chirped, blinking her eyes happily.

I frowned, but plunged ahead. "Here's an example of Contradictory Premises: If God can do anything, can He make a stone so heavy that He won't be able to lift it?"

"Of course," she replied promptly.   85

"But if He can do anything, He can lift the stone," I pointed out.

"Yeah," she said thoughtfully. "Well, then I guess He can't make the stone."

"But He can do anything," I reminded her.

She scratched her pretty, empty head. "I'm all confused," she admitted.

"Of course you are. Because when the premises of an argument contradict   90 each other, there can be no argument. If there is an irresistible force, there can be no immovable object. If there is an immovable object, there can be no irresistible force. Get it?"

"Tell me some more of this keen stuff," she said eagerly.

I consulted my watch. "I think we'd better call it a night. I'll take you home now, and you go over all the things you've learned. We'll have another session tomorrow night."

I deposited her at the girl's dormitory, where she assured me that she had had a perfectly terrif evening, and I went glumly home to my room. Petey lay snoring in his bed, the raccoon coat huddled like a great hairy beast at his feet. For a moment I considered waking him and telling him that he could have his girl back. It seemed clear that my project was doomed to failure. The girl simply had a logic-proof head.

But then I reconsidered, I had wasted one evening; I might as well waste another. Who knew? Maybe somewhere in the extinct crater of her mind, a few embers still smoldered. Maybe somehow I could fan them into flame. Admittedly it was not a prospect fraught with hope, but I decided to give it one more try.

Seated under the oak the next evening I said, "Our first fallacy tonight is called Ad Misericordiam." 95

She quivered with delight.

"Listen closely," I said. "A man applies for a job. When the boss asks him what his qualifications are, he replies that he has a wife and six children at home, the wife is a helpless cripple, the children have nothing to eat, no clothes to wear, no shoes on their feet, there are no beds in the house, no coal in the cellar, and winter is coming."

A tear rolled down each of Polly's pink cheeks. "Oh, this is awful, awful," she sobbed.

"Yes, it's awful," I agreed, "but it's no argument. The man never answered the boss's question about his qualifications. Instead he appealed to the boss's sympathy. He committed the fallacy of Ad Misericordiam. Do you understand?"

"Have you got a handkerchief?" she blubbered. 100

I handed her a handkerchief and tried to keep from screaming while she wiped her eyes. "Next," I said in a carefully controlled tone, "we will discuss False Analogy. Here is an example: Students should be allowed to look at their textbooks during examinations. After all, surgeons have X-rays to guide them during an operation, lawyers have briefs to guide them during a trial, carpenters have blueprints to guide them when they are building a house. Why, then, shouldn't students be allowed to look at their textbooks during an examination?"

"There now," she said enthusiastically, "is the most marvy idea I've heard in years."

"Polly," I said testily, "the argument is all wrong. Doctors, lawyers, and carpenters aren't taking a test to see how much they have learned, but students are. The situations are altogether different, and you can't make an analogy between them."

"I still think it's a good idea," said Polly.

"Nuts," I muttered. Doggedly I pressed on. "Next we'll try Hypothesis 105 Contrary to Fact."

"Sounds yummy," was Polly's reaction.

"Listen: If Madame Curie had not happened to leave a photographic plate in a drawer with a chunk of pitchblende, the world today would not know about radium."

"True, true," said Polly, nodding her head. "Did you see the movie? Oh, it just knocked me out. That Walter Pidgeon is so dreamy. I mean he fractures me."

"If you can forget Mr. Pidgeon for a moment," I said coldly, "I would like to point out that the statement is a fallacy. Maybe Madame Curie would have discovered radium at some later date. Maybe somebody else would have discovered it. Maybe any number of things would have happened. You can't start with a hypothesis that is not true and then draw any supportable conclusions from it."

"They ought to put Walter Pidgeon in more pictures," said Polly. "I hardly   110
ever see him any more."

One more chance, I decided. But just one more. There is a limit to what flesh and blood can bear. "The next fallacy is called Poisoning the Well."

"How cute!" she gurgled.

"Two men are having a debate. The first one gets up and says, 'My opponent is a notorious liar. You can't believe a word that he is going to say.' Now, Polly, think. Think hard. What's wrong?"

I watched her closely as she knit her creamy brow in concentration. Suddenly a glimmer of intelligence—the first I had seen—came into her eyes. "It's not fair," she said with indignation. "It's not a bit fair. What chance has the second man got if the first man calls him a liar before he even begins talking?"

"Right!" I cried exultantly. "One hundred per cent right. It's not fair. The   115
first man has *poisoned the well* before anybody could drink from it. He has hamstrung his opponent before he could even start. . . . Polly, I'm proud of you."

"Pshaw," she murmured, blushing with pleasure.

"You see, my dear, these things aren't so hard. All you have to do is concentrate. Think—examine—evaluate. Come now, let's review everything we have learned."

"Fire away," she said with an airy wave of her hand.

Heartened by the knowledge that Polly was not altogether a cretin, I began a long, patient review of all I had told her. Over and over and over again I cited instances, pointed out flaws, kept hammering away without let up. It was like digging a tunnel. At first everything was work, sweat, and darkness. I had no idea when I would reach the light, or even *if* I would. But I persisted. I pounded and clawed and scraped, and finally I was rewarded. I saw a chink of light. And then the chink got bigger and the sun came pouring in and all was bright.

Five grueling nights this took, but it was worth it. I had made a logician   120
out of Polly; I had taught her to think. My job was done. She was worthy of me at last. She was a fit wife for me, a proper hostess for my many mansions, a suitable mother for my well-heeled children.

It must not be thought that I was without love for this girl. Quite the contrary. Just as Pygmalion loved the perfect woman he had fashioned, so I loved mine. I determined to acquaint her with my feelings at our very next meeting. The time had come to change our relationship from academic to romantic.

"Polly," I said when next we sat beneath our oak, "tonight we will not discuss fallacies."

"Aw, gee," she said, disappointed.

"My dear," I said, favoring her with a smile, "we have now spent five evenings together. We have gotten along splendidly. It is clear that we are well matched."

"Hasty Generalization," said Polly brightly.

"I beg your pardon," said I.

"Hasty Generalization," she repeated. "How can you say that we are well matched on the basis of only five dates?"

I chuckled with amusement. The dear child had learned her lessons well. "My dear," I said, patting her hand in a tolerant manner, "five dates is plenty. After all, you don't have to eat a whole cake to know that it's good."

"False Analogy," said Polly promptly. "I'm not a cake. I'm a girl."

I chuckled with somewhat less amusement. The dear child had learned her lessons perhaps too well. I decided to change tactics. Obviously the best approach was a simple, strong, direct declaration of love. I paused for a moment while my massive brain chose the proper words. Then I began:

"Polly, I love you. You are the whole world to me, and the moon and the stars and the constellations of outer space. Please, my darling, say that you will go steady with me, for if you will not, life will be meaningless. I will languish. I will refuse my meals. I will wander the face of the earth, a shambling, hollow-eyed hulk."

There, I thought, folding my arms, that ought to do it.

"Ad Misericordiam," said Polly.

I ground my teeth. I was not Pygmalion; I was Frankenstein, and my monster had me by the throat. Frantically I fought back the tide of panic surging through me. At all costs I had to keep cool.

"Well, Polly," I said, forcing a smile, "you certainly have learned your fallacies."

"You're darn right," she said with a vigorous nod.

"And who taught them to you, Polly?"

"You did."

"That's right. So you do owe me something, don't you, my dear? If I hadn't come along you never would have learned about fallacies."

"Hypothesis Contrary to Fact," she said instantly.

I dashed perspiration from my brow. "Polly," I croaked, "you mustn't take all these things so literally. I mean this is just classroom stuff. You know that the things you learn in school don't have anything to do with life."

"Dicto Simpliciter," she said, wagging her finger at me playfully.

That did it. I leaped to my feet, bellowing like a bull. "Will you or will you not go steady with me?"

"I will not," she replied.

"Why not?" I demanded.

"Because this afternoon I promised Petey Burch that I would go steady with him."

I reeled back, overcome with the infamy of it. After he promised, after he made a deal, after he shook my hand! "The rat!" I shrieked, kicking up great chunks of turf. "You can't go with him, Polly. He's a liar. He's a cheat. He's a rat."

"Poisoning the Well," said Polly, "and stop shouting. I think shouting must be a fallacy too."

With an immense effort of will, I modulated my voice. "All right, I said. "You're a logician. Let's look at this thing logically. How could you choose Petey Burch over me? Look at me—a brilliant student, a tremendous intellectual, a man with an assured future. Look at Petey—a knothead, a jitterbug, a guy who'll never know where his next meal is coming from. Can you give me one logical reason why you should go steady with Petey Burch?"

"I certainly can," declared Polly. "He's got a raccoon coat." ◪   150

1. Shulman ironically relies on fallacies of his own (such as gender stereotyping) as a way of generating humor. Suggest ways in which the piece could be revised without having to rely on such fallacies.

2. How reliable is this piece as a gauge of problematic reasoning among college students? Although its humor is somewhat dated, does it possess enough of an underlying seriousness to warrant further analysis of the reasoning skills of today's college students?

Chapter Summary

Argumentative writing requires careful reasoning, the ability to think critically and logically about the issues you are investigating and to be alert for errors in logic. Such errors—known as fallacies (for example, false analogy and ad hominem)—often arise when writers are not sufficiently knowledgeable about their subject or have not thought sufficiently about possible counterarguments to their thesis. The principal strategies that constitute good reasoning in argument are deduction, induction, categorization, analogy, authorization, and plea. Deduction involves identifying contradictions, inconsistencies, omissions, and oversimplifications as well as reducing unsound claims to their logical absurdity. Induction involves determining a sufficient quantity for the sample as well as determining the reliability of that sample. Categorization involves classifying items according to similar characteristics. Analogy is used to help readers understand a concept by comparing it to one that is simpler and more familiar. Authorization refers to the use of testimony by experts as a supplement to empirical evidence to support claims. Plea refers to use of emotional appeals to motivate readers to take action.

Checklist

1. Is the line of reasoning used in my argument logical and coherent?

2. Do I cover all facets of my argument?

3. Do I anticipate counterarguments?

4. Do I commit any errors in reasoning?

   a. Fallacies of deduction such as fourth term, non sequitur, and ad hominem?

   b. Fallacies of induction such as unsupported generalization, red herring, poisoning the well, and begging the question?

   c. Fallacies of categorization such as false dichotomy and mixing apples with oranges?

   d. Fallacies of analogy such as false analogy and faulty analogy?

   e. Fallacies of authorization such as vague authority and suspect authority?

   f. Fallacies of pleading such as appeal to fear, appeal to the bandwagon, and appeal to ignorance?

Writing Projects

1. Read several newspaper or magazine editorial or opinion pieces on a given topic; then write a comparative evaluation of each piece based on the presence and frequency of deductive and inductive errors in reasoning you detect in them.

2. Write an essay on the importance of good reasoning in establishing healthy human relationships, such as romantic or business relationships, friendships, parent-sibling relationships, and so on. Focus on specific kinds of errors in reasoning that occur, using actual or representative examples.

6 Methods of Critical Reading

A reader must learn to read.
—Alberto Manguel

Reading and writing are intimately related modes of thinking—so intertwined that you really cannot do one without doing the other. Just as writers determine how to approach their subjects by considering their purpose and their readers, so too do readers determine *their* purpose for reading the subject, often working along similar lines to those intended by the writer.

Reading as the Construction of Meaning

Some researchers refer to the symbolic relationship between reading and writing as the *construction of meaning*. That is, readers must process meaning from those symbols on the page that, by themselves, possess no intrinsic meaning.

As readers we also construct meaning beyond what we see on the page before us. For example, when we read through a draft of an argument to revise and edit it, we monitor our sense of direction, the development of the ideas, the coherence (that is, the logical progression of ideas), the clarity, and the larger concerns of persuasiveness and originality.

All of these activities are context-dependent. As the example in Table 6.1 reveals, reading strategies that work well say, in drafting an essay that objectively analyzes the strengths and weakness of a high school exit test may not work when drafting a more subjective essay on why the school should retain or abandon such tests. In the first essay, you need to read for such elements as logical progression of ideas, thorough support of assertions, and fair representation of challenging or alternative views. In the second essay, aware that you are presenting an individual preference, you need to keep an eye out for sufficiently clear (if not always logical) reasons behind your preferences.

Thus, whenever we read, we do a great deal more than simply absorb words like a sponge. In reading others' work, we sometimes think to ourselves, "If I had written this essay, I'd have made this introduction much shorter and put in more examples in the third paragraph—I barely understood it, after all!" Such thinking

TABLE 6.1	Sample Perspectives from Which We Read		
Topic	Perspective 1 (neutral outsider)	Perspective 2 (offensive)	Perspective 3 (defensive)
Value of Exit Tests	To weigh pros vs. cons to pass a fair judgment	I've always been held back by these biased tests!	Tests have always enabled me to show how much I know!

is comparable to what we do as we revise our own work, so clearly we are read-ing another's text from the writer's perspective.

We might also "revise" another's writing when someone asks us about a book or article we've read: "What is Frances Mayes's *Under the Tuscan Sun* about?" In summarizing that contemporary work of creative nonfiction, we would use our own words to shorten a three-hundred-page work to one or two paragraphs. In fact, while you are reading such a text, you are summarizing it to yourself—during the actual reading or during breaks between readings. Thus, to understand a text means, in a sense, to rewrite the author's ideas so that we blend them with our own ideas. Such rewriting is built into the very nature of reading. We cannot truly comprehend a text without doing so.

Active Versus Passive Reading

In the sense that to read means processing written language in order to under-stand it, all reading is "active." But some forms of reading represent a greater challenge to the comprehension process than others. A letter from a loved one may be processed relatively swiftly and efficiently, almost as a photograph would, whereas a demanding legal or technical document of the same length may need to be processed in a much more methodical manner.

When we read primarily for pleasure—whether a novel, a work of nonfic-tion, or a friend's e-mail, we are concerned primarily about content: What is go-ing to happen to the characters in the novel? What is the author's premise in the work of nonfiction? When is our friend's plane arriving at the airport?

But when we read for a purpose besides (or in addition to) pleasure, we need to think more consciously of our reading process so that we can make necessary modifications. Such reading is task-oriented: to find out certain information, to summarize the work, to analyze the structure of the work, to assess the merits of the argument, to determine how the information coincides with our position on the issue.

You can adopt certain strategies to become a more active reader. It may seem strange to think of a "strategy" of reading. The only strategy that leaps to mind is moving our eyes across the page from left to right and top to bottom (for readers of most Western languages). But from a psychological and linguistic perspective, we are pulling off complex feats of cognition. At the simplest level we are doing any or all of the following, more or less simultaneously:

- *Linking* one part of a sentence with another, for example, linking a subordinate clause to a main clause or nouns and verbs to their respective adjectival or adverbial modifiers

- *Tracking* the constantly shifting parameters of meaning from word to word, phrase to phrase, sentence to sentence, paragraph to paragraph

- *Relating* any given sentence or paragraph to a premise or theme, whether implied or explicitly stated

Those are just some of the *basic* strategies. As students of writing, you read not just for understanding but for insight into the way in which an author organizes and develops an argument. This type of active reader needs to do the following:

- Determine the *framework* of the author's argument. What is the claim, data, and warrant?

- Evaluate the *data* (evidence) presented. Is it accurate? Sufficient? Appropriate? Relevant?

- Evaluate the author's *organizational strategy.* Why does the author bring in X before Y and after W? Is the sequence beyond dispute, or is there no clear rhetorical purpose behind the sequence? Should the author have arranged things differently?

- Speculate on the *significance* of what is being argued. What are the short- and long-term consequences of the author's views? If the author argues that searching for life on Mars is a waste of taxpayers' dollars and uses compelling evidence to back up this claim, then the significance of the argument is that it could persuade congressional representatives to vote against funding NASA for such a project.

Each of these cognitive acts works together to comprise active reading. Passive reading, by contrast, means reading without reflecting or "talking back" to the text—that is, without forming questions that can and should be asked of an author who is trying to communicate with us.

■ Exercise 6.1

1. Assess your reading process. What kinds of material do you read actively? Passively? What about the material encourages one mode of reading rather than another?

2. Select a short piece such as a magazine feature or editorial and discuss it in terms of the four concerns of an active reader (framework, data, organizational strategy, and significance).

3. Read a short piece for coherence alone. Explain how the author "glues" sentences and paragraphs together to make them interrelate clearly and meaningfully.

Reading as a Writer of Arguments

Chapter 1 describes the role that supporting data and expert opinion play in building your argument. As you read to find sources of support for your argument, use the following strategies: previewing, in-depth reading, and postreading.

Previewing

Imagine Bob, a first-year student, trying to study for a political science quiz the next day. He's having trouble reading the textbook chapter being tested. It seems like more pages than he has time or inclination to absorb. So he finds his classmate Julie in the library and tells her he's having trouble motivating himself to do all that reading. Julie, who's already read the chapter, encourages him by saying, "Oh Bob, the chapter essentially covers only four points about the economic conditions on the Greek islands comprising Santorini." Relieved that the chapter highlights only four main points, Bob returns to his room motivated to read but also with a sense of how to read the chapter productively. Julie has given him a *preview* of what to expect. Previewing is typically a two-stage process: (1) prereading, and (2) skimming.

Anything worth reading typically requires several readings, so you approach this previewing stage knowing that you will read the assignment more thoroughly later on.

To read as critical thinkers and writers, you must read to ensure that you

- understand the content and progression of the story or argument,

- can determine the rhetorical strategy (for example, the validity and significance of the claim, the data, and the warrant), and

- are able to incorporate the author's views into your own.

Prereading You preread the text to determine its central purpose and approach. You may do this at the beginning of the term, when, standing in line to purchase your textbook, you peruse the table of contents and the introductions to each of the chapters. You also preread when you read the topic sentences of the paragraphs in the introduction. (The topic sentence usually appears either in the first, second, or last sentence.)

To preread an article or chapter from a work of nonfiction, you can rely on the structure that writers in the Western tradition have used for centuries and handed down to the modern college composition course:

- Introduction
- Thesis statement
- Topic sentences
- Transitional paragraphs
- Conclusion

Remember that the purpose of prereading is not to understand the whole piece but to identify the key points of the piece so that when you do read it in its entirety, you already have a clear sense of its framework.

After reading the introduction in full, read the topic sentences of the body paragraphs. These tend to be in one of three spots: first, last, or second. Topic sentences most frequently appear as the first sentences of the paragraphs, just where you have been taught to put them. But they also may occur as the last sentence in the paragraph when the writer has organized the content of the paragraph in an inductive rather than deductive order. And the topic sentence sometimes is the second sentence of the paragraph (the third most frequent position) when the first sentence is transitional, linking the paragraph before to the one that follows. In these cases, you will read both the transitional sentences and the topic sentences. You may need to read a bit of the article or essay to gain a sense of the writer's style—for example, where he or she tends to position the topic sentence.

Here is an example of a paragraph in which the topic sentence appears at the very end, a technique that this particular author, Carl Sagan, uses quite commonly in his writing. This selection is from Sagan's *The Demon-Haunted World: Science as a Candle in the Dark* (1995):

> What do we actually see when we look up at the Moon with the naked eye? We make out a configuration of irregular bright and dark markings—not a close representation of any familiar object. But, almost irresistibly, our eyes connect the markings, emphasizing some, ignoring others. We seek a pattern, and we find one. In world myth and folklore, many images are seen: a woman weaving, stands of laurel trees, an elephant jumping off a cliff, a girl with a basket on her back, a rabbit, . . . a woman pounding tapa cloth, a four-eyed jaguar. People of one culture have trouble understanding how such bizarre things could be seen by the people of another.

The pattern Sagan uses in this paragraph is this: He opens with a question, gives a string of examples to illustrate the basis of the question, and then answers the question, that is, posits the topic sentence. Such rhetorical patterning is a form of coherence that enables readers to follow the strands of a complex discussion.

The final step in prereading is paying close attention to concluding paragraph or paragraphs of the argument. Writers often summarize their main points here. They may also point out implications of the ideas or perhaps let readers know what steps they should take. To return to the chapter from *The Demon-*

Haunted World that focuses on the difficulty of observing nature objectively, we arrive at Sagan's conclusion:

> By and large, scientists' minds are open when exploring new worlds. If we [scientists] knew beforehand what we'd find, it would be unnecessary to go [there]. In future missions to Mars or to the other fascinating worlds in our neck of the cosmic woods, surprises—even some of mythic proportions—are possible, maybe even likely. But we humans have a talent for deceiving ourselves. Skepticism must be a component of the explorer's toolkit, or we will lose our way. There are wonders enough out there without our inventing any.

Sagan not only stresses his central idea about the need to maintain objectivity in the search for truth, he also assures us that the search for truth will reward us with discoveries every bit as wondrous as anything we could concoct.

By following a pattern of prereading, you may not yet fully understand the text, but at this stage you are just trying to provide yourself with an overview. You are also giving yourself a sense of how much energy you will need to invest later on.

Skim-Reading   At this stage, read the article in full, including the parts you have preread. But read swiftly, keeping alert for the key words in each sentence. To skim well, take advantage of your peripheral vision: You do not have to look directly at a word to see it; your eyes notice it just by looking in its general vicinity. Also, you already have an idea of the general parts of the article, and you are fleshing out those generalizations via the specifics that the writer provides. This enables you to grasp more readily the writer's logical progression of ideas and use of evidence. By the time you reach the conclusion, you should feel more comfortable with whatever the author is summarizing or exhorting readers to do.

If the piece you are reading is printed in columns, you probably will make your eyes stop once every other line, approximately following a pattern indicated by the *x*'s in the passage that follows:

x
As you read these two columns,
            x
you'll notice that there are *x's* above
      x
the typed lines, one to the left on the
                  x
first line and then one to the right on
      x
the second line. The *x's* continue to
                  x
alternate down the columns. Fixing

                        x
your eyes on those *x's*, you can see
                              x
the words written below them—not
                  x
just the words directly below the *x's*
                              x
but the words before and after those
                  x
as well. If you were looking just for
                        x
a particular date, such as June 20,

x
2000, then you would be looking just

x
for that particular configuration of

x
numbers. Looking somewhat above

x
the lines rather than directly at

x
the words on the lines helps you

x
not to read the words but more

x
to focus on the particular pattern of

x
words or numbers that you are looking

x
for. (The date of June 20, 2000, was

x
chosen because that's the wedding

x
date of two British friends, Dave and

x
Jenny.) You see how you could sys-

x
tematically skim for just the two

x
occasions of a date-like configuration.

x
Essentially, that's skimming.

In-Depth Reading

The previewing strategies detail methods that you can follow if you wish to lo-cate specific, brief information or to quickly scope out the gist of a piece. As a writer of arguments, you read for other reasons as well:

- *Summarizing* to demonstrate an ability and willingness to present another's ideas in a fair, unbiased way (see "Writing a Summary," pages 131–132)

- *Analyzing* the structure of the piece to understand precisely the logic the writer uses, to determine whether the writer omits some important causal or temporal element, or whether the writer fairly and accurately represents all major viewpoints regarding the issue

- *Assessing* the strengths and weaknesses of the argument and determining the extent to which the writer's position influences your own

- *Annotating* in the margins to maintain an ongoing critical-response dialogue with the author as you are reading (see "Reading with a Pencil," page 133)

Postreading

The purpose for a postread is to reinforce the framework of the whole in your mind and to distinguish between details and main points of a piece. In a postread, you cement in your mind the structure and logic of the piece by going back over it and reviewing its contents. More specifically, follow these steps:

1. Ask yourself, What is the most important thing I learned from this piece, and where is it most clearly expressed? Highlight this passage with a marker and make a marginal note briefly summarizing the passage in your own words. Summarizing helps you reinforce what you have read.

2. Now ask, What evidence does the author use that supports the claim most convincingly? Highlight and annotate this passage as well.

3. Ask finally, What concluding insight does the author leave me with? Again, highlight and then annotate this segment of text in your own words.

Once you get into the habit of previewing, in-depth reading, and postreading articles and essays, you will find it an efficient and satisfying process.

■ Exercise 6.2

1. Read your campus newspaper looking just for the names of people you know well.

2. Preview an article in one of your favorite magazines or from the Clusters in Part II. Write down all the information you obtain from this preview reading. Next, read the article as you normally would and write down any information you had not obtained from the prereading. Write a brief assessment of the value of prereading based on this one experience.

Writing a Summary

One of the most effective ways of reinforcing your comprehension of a piece is to write a formal summary of it shortly after you read it. As you already know, a summary is a concise but accurate rephrasing, primarily in your own words, of the premise of a work. Writing summaries of works you read is a valuable exercise for three reasons:

1. To summarize is to demonstrate (to yourself and to others) the degree to which you understand the piece as the author means it to be understood— realizing, of course, that there is no way of knowing whether one's understanding of an argument corresponds *exactly* to what the author has in mind. Unfortunately, readers sometimes praise or criticize a work based on a misreading or a misunderstanding of what the author is trying to convey. Writing a concise summary of the thesis statement and the principal support statements can help you avoid that problem.

2. Writing a summary helps you better integrate into your knowledge base what you have learned from the piece.

3. Summaries of related articles and books serve as an important resource for a research paper. You may be reading many different sources on a given topic. Summarizing each one immediately after reading the work helps you to internalize the material better and keep various sources straight in your mind. Sometimes you will use these summaries when preparing an annotated bibliography. (See Chapter 8 for how to format an annotated bibliography.)

Typically, a summary is about one-fourth the length of the original, but a special type of summary is referred to as an *abstract*. Abstracts of books are generally a single page long, and those of articles, a single paragraph. Volumes of abstracts, such as *Resources in Education* (which summarizes thousands of articles on education collected in a vast database known as ERIC) and *Chemical Abstracts* (which maintains a similar service for articles on chemistry), are located in your school library and often online.

Writing a summary returns you to the skeletal outline of your essay, where you are better able to isolate the key points. The procedure of summarizing is relatively simple in principle, but in practice it can be tricky. Some pieces are more difficult to summarize than others, depending on whether the key ideas are presented explicitly or implicitly. Here are the steps you should take:

1. Determine the thesis of the essay, rephrase it in your own words, and make that the opening sentence of your summary.

2. Locate the supporting statements. Sometimes these are the topic sentences of each paragraph, but some writers are inventive with paragraph structure. Rephrase the supporting statements in your own words.

3. Write a concluding sentence, paraphrasing the author's own conclusion if possible.

■ Exercise 6.3

1. Do an in-depth reading of the article you preread for Exercise 6.2. How does the prereading help you to absorb the discussion as you encountered it in the in-depth reading?

2. Write a summary of Martin Luther King, Jr.'s, essay, "Letter from Birmingham Jail," found on pages 76–89.

3. After everyone in class has written a summary of the King essay, compare the summaries in small groups. How do they differ? How are they alike? How do you know? What accounts for the similarities among the summaries? What accounts for the dissimilarities? Are the differences and similarities significant? In what way?

4. Consider the differences and similarities found in 3 above to see whether they account for greater accuracy of some summaries.

5. Explain the relationship between summary writing and reading comprehension.

Reading with a Pencil

To help you pay special attention to key ideas during a reading, write marginal comments, underline text, or use visual icons like asterisks, checkmarks, or arrows. Such annotations, or marginalia, enhance your involvement with the reading material and reinforce understanding. (*Note:* Of course, if you are reading library books or books belonging to someone else, do not put a mark of any kind in them. Instead, jot your notes down in a journal.) If you are not in the habit of writing in the margins or in journals, it is a valuable habit to cultivate. Here are some types of marginalia to try:

- *Glosses:* One-sentence summaries of what each paragraph is about.

- *Comparisons:* Notes to yourself reinforcing correspondences you notice. Say you want to compare a passage with something you have read earlier in the piece or in a different piece. The abbreviation *cf.* (Latin for "compare") is most often used; it means compare and/or contrast this passage with such-and-such a passage on such-and-such a page.

- *Questions or reactions:* Spur-of-the-moment concerns you have about an assertion, the validity of the data or other kinds of evidence, or something the author overlooks or overstates.

- *Icons:* These are your own personal symbols—asterisks, wavy lines, checkmarks, bullets, smiley-faces, and so on—that instantly convey to you on rereading whether the passage marked is problematic, or especially noteworthy.

Let us take a look at one possible way of annotating a piece. Study the example that follows.

Say No to Trash | Samuel Lipman

Why is the NEA "Congressionally embattled"?

In canceling the Robert Mapplethorpe exhibition last week, Washington's Corcoran Gallery did more than refuse to show a few raunchy photographs of what the press, unable to print them, primly called "explicit homoerotic and violent images." Because the exhibition was supported in part by public funds from the Congressionally embattled National

1

Source: Lipman, Samuel. "Say No to Trash." *New York Times* 23 June 1989. Copyright © 1989 by The New York Times Co. Reprinted by permission.

Endowment for the Arts, the Corcoran doubtless considered financial self-interest in arriving at its decision. One hopes those responsible are aware that in saying no to Mapplethorpe, they were exercising the right to say no to an entire theory of art.

Or—maybe they were saying no to work that offended the most viewers.

This theory assumes, to quote an official of the neighboring Hirshhorn Museum, that art "often deals with extremities of the human condition. It is not to be expected that, when it does that, everyone is going to be pleased or happy with it." The criterion of art thus becomes its ability to outrage, to (in the Hirshhorn official's words) "really touch raw nerves."

Graffiti also outrages many. Should graffiti be considered art too?

Despite its occasional usefulness, this theory ignores the vast corpus of great art that elevates, enlightens, consoles and encourages our lives. The shock appeal of art is questionable when it encompasses only such fripperies as displaying inane texts on electronic signboards in the fashion of Jenny Holzer; it becomes vastly more deleterious when it advances, as Mapplethorpe does, gross images of sexual profligacy, sadomasochism and the bestial treatment of human beings.

In a free society, it is neither possible nor desirable to go very far in prohibiting the private activities that inspire this outré art. People have always had their private pleasures, and as long as these pleasures remain private, confined to consenting adults, and not immediately injurious, the public weal remains undisturbed. But now we are told that what has been private must be made public. We are told that it is the true function of art to accommodate us to feelings and action that we—and societies and nations before us—have found objectionable and even appalling.

I don't know what "immediately injurious" means.

In evaluating art, the viewer's role is thus only to approve. We are told that whatever the content of art, its very status as art entitles it to immunity from restraint. There are certainly those who will claim that the Mapplethorpe photographs are art, and therefore to be criticized, if at all, solely on aesthetic, never on moral, grounds. Are we to believe that the moral neutrality with which we are urged to view this art is shared by its proponents? Can it, rather, be possible that it is the very content so many find objectionable that recommends the art to its highly vocal backers?

5

Further, there are those who would have us believe that because we are not compelled to witness what we as individuals find morally unacceptable, we cannot refuse to make it

Can any work of art ever be morally neutral?

A key concern: exposure of erotic art to children.

available for others. Taking this position not only ignores our responsibility for others; it ignores the dreadful changes made in our own lives, and the lives of our children, by the availability of this decadence everywhere, from high art to popular culture.

It is undeniable that there is a large market for the hitherto forbidden. Upscale magazines trumpet the most shocking manifestations of what passes for new art. A rampant media culture profits hugely from the pleasing, and the lowering, of every taste.

Just as it is neither possible nor desirable to do much about regulating private sexual behavior, little can be done legally about the moral outrages of culture, either high or popular. But we can say no, and not only to our own participation as individuals in this trash. We can decline to make it available to the public through the use of our private facilities and funds; this, the Corcoran, acting as a private institution, has now done.

There is still more to be done. Acting on our behalf as citizens, our Government agencies—in particular the National Endowment for the Arts—can redirect their energies away from being the validators of the latest fancies to hit the art

Much "great art of the past" was shocking in its day.

market. Instead, public art support might more fully concentrate on what it does so well: the championing of the great art of the past, its regeneration in the present and its transmission to the future. This would mean saying yes to civilization. It is a policy change that deserves our prompt attention. One hopes that the Corcoran, by saying no to Robert Mapplethorpe, has begun the process. ◾

◼ Exercise 6.4

1. Your instructor will distribute a short article for everyone in class to annotate. Then, share your manner of annotating. What useful methods of annotation do you learn from other classmates?

2. Clip a relatively short newspaper story, paste or photocopy it on a sheet of paper, leaving very wide margins, and then annotate the article fully.

Becoming a Highly Motivated Reader

People read for many reasons: to be entertained; to be informed of global, local, and job-related events; to enhance their general knowledge of fields such as history, science and technology, commerce, politics, social developments, and the arts; to improve their personal lives and health.

You, however, have an additional reason to read: to become a better writer. To realize this goal, you must become not only an alert, active reader but a highly motivated one as well.

To acquire a sense of the rich possibilities of argumentative writing, begin to read (if you don't already) any or all of the following material:

- Newspaper editorials and op-ed pieces (familiarize yourself not only with the editorial section of your local newspaper but with that of the *New York Times* and the *Washington Post* as well)

- Essays that appear in magazines and journals noted for high-quality commentary on important issues, journals such as *Newsweek*, *Time*, *Harper's Magazine*, the *Atlantic Monthly*, and the *New York Review of Books*.

- Books that take strong stands on current, intensely debated issues, books such as Harold Bloom's defense of the traditional literary canon in *The Western Canon* (1994), Paul and Anne Ehrlich's counterresponse to the critics of environmentalism in *Betrayal of Science and Reason* (1996), or Carl Sagan's discussion of the dangers of pseudoscience and science illiteracy in *The Demon-Haunted World: Science as a Candle in the Dark* (1995).

You likely are already a motivated reader, or else you could not have made it into college. Your goal now is to capitalize on your already strong reading skills by reading even more widely and avidly. Here are a few suggestions to consider:

1. Begin by thinking of each reading experience—each opportunity to scrutinize an argument—as a chance to recruit more brain cells. It is said that we use only 10 percent of our brain capacity, so there's no danger in running out of cells!

2. Think of each reading experience as yet another opportunity to study a talented writer's craft, an important step toward helping you develop your own craft.

3. Select books for reading that you have intended to read but "never got around to." Do not be overly ambitious; you do not want to disappoint yourself. It is not necessary to give yourself page quotas (for example, a hundred pages a night); that has a way of backfiring when you have an already busy schedule. The key is to read *regularly*, every day, so that reading becomes a habit. And be patient with yourself: It sometimes takes a while for a habit to take hold. After about three or four weeks of "forcing" yourself to read, say, one hour of noncourse-required reading every morning, the ritual will become so engrained that it will feel as natural (and as enjoyable) as eating.

4. Finally, take the time to keep a reading journal. This does not have to be elaborate. After each reading session, take about fifteen minutes to jot down

your reflections on or reactions to the reading you have just finished. In addition to reinforcing your comprehension of the material and your insights into it, the journal will serve as a logbook of your reading experiences.

Once again, it is impossible to overemphasize the importance of reading to learning, to the life of the mind, to what it means to be educated in this complex, information-driven, competitive world. Reading is truly your ticket to the treasures of knowledge and understanding.

■ Exercise 6.5

1. Write a reading autobiography in which you describe your childhood and early adolescent reading experiences and tastes. Note how your tastes in and habits of reading have changed over the years.

2. Keep a record of your reading activities over the next four weeks. Record the time you spend reading each day. List everything you read, but only after you finish reading it (individual chapters can count as separate pieces). Divide the material into "required" and "nonrequired" reading. Do an "active reader" critique of each work (refer back to the list on p. 126). At the end of the fourth week, evaluate your reading. Did your motivation to read improve? When? Did your reading become more efficient? Be as honest with yourself as you can.

3. If you consider yourself a slow or inefficient reader, make a special effort to improve. If it takes you longer than an hour to read fifty pages of a book, you are probably subvocalizing (sounding out one word at a time in your head, as if you were reading aloud). Practice reading *clusters* of words and be sure your pacing is swift and smooth, not jerky. Check to see whether your campus offers classes in speed reading or efficient reading.

4. Keep a reading improvement log. Each day for the next four weeks, record the number of pages you read in a given time (say, half an hour). Do not sacrifice your comprehension as you work on improving your efficiency. The more efficient your reading process, the more your comprehension should improve.

Reading Responsibly

To read arguments responsibly is to engage in a three-step procedure:

1. Read to learn the author's position on the issue

2. Reread to understand fully that position

3. Reread to compare and contrast the author's views with the views of others

Every time we read or listen to someone's views about an issue, we may feel prematurely inclined to agree or disagree. Remaining neutral is sometimes difficult, especially if the writer or speaker presents his or her ideas with passion, eloquence, and wit. As a responsible reader, you do not need to maintain neutrality permanently, only to delay judgment. Before judging an issue, regard any argument as but one perspective, and assume that many perspectives must be considered before a fair judgment can be made.

Reading well is like listening well. Good readers give writers the benefit of the doubt, at least momentarily, and respect the author's point of view, believing it worthy of serious attention (unless the author demonstrates negligence, such as distorting another author's views). But disagreement should never be confused with adversity or contentiousness, even if the author comes across as adversarial. You will comprehend and subsequently respond more successfully if you read the argument attentively, if you assume that the writer has considered the argument's assertions with great care, and if you are willing to give the writer the benefit of any doubts, at least for the time being. Once you have read the argument and reflected on it, go over it again, making sure you have understood everything. Then, before you do a third reading, place the writer's point of view in the context of others' views. The third reading is the critical one in which you ask questions of every assertion, questions that reflect the larger conversation produced by other essays.

■ Exercise 6.6

1. Make a list of ten to fifteen books you plan to read during the quarter or semester. After each title, briefly state your reason for wanting to read the book.

2. Keep a reader's log for each book you read. Each entry might include the following information:

   - Author, title, publication data, and number of pages in the book

   - Dates you began and finished the book

   - Your reason for wanting to read the book

   - The most important things you learned from the book

   - Any criticisms or questions you have of the book

3. Use active reading strategies to read the following editorial on the need to combat global warming. *Preread* the editorial to get a sense of its premise and key points. *Skim* it straight through without critical questioning, allowing the author to present his case without interruption, so to speak. Then *read* the essay in depth, paying close attention to the way in which the writer develops the argument. Finally, *postread* it to reinforce full comprehension.

High Noon

Global warming is here. It is moving as fast as scientists had feared. If it is not checked, children born today may live to see massive shifting and destruction of the ecosystems we know now. They may witness the proliferation of violent storms, floods, and droughts that cause terrible losses of human life.

The good news is that we are not helpless. We can still curb the greenhouse trend. Our next, best chance will come November 13–24 in the Netherlands, when the nations of the world negotiate again over the terms of the global warming treaty called the Kyoto Protocol. If we lose this chance, we may lose momentum for the entire protocol, and with it five or more years of precious time. But if we win a strong treaty in the Netherlands, it will start real movement on the long road to change.

Evidence and Damage

Like trackers on the trail of a grizzly, scientists read the presence of global warming in certain large-scale, planet-wide events. Over the last century, the surface of the planet heated up by about one degree Fahrenheit. More rain and snow began falling worldwide, an increase of 1 percent over all the continents. The oceans rose 6–8 inches. If these numbers applied to local weather, they would be trivial. As planetary averages, they are momentous. The past decade was the warmest in at least a thousand years. A graph of average global temperatures since the year 1000 shows a precipitous rise that starts at about the time of the Industrial Revolution and shoots upward to our own time.

The results may be profound and unpredictable. In altering the climate of the planet, we are playing with a vastly complicated system we barely understand. As Columbia University scientist Wallace Broecker has said, climate is an angry beast, and we are poking it with sticks.

We may already be feeling its anger. Of course, weather happens in spurts, with or without global warming. It is impossible to know whether this storm or that drought was an ordinary event, say the effect of a little extra moisture carried over the West Coast by El Nino, or whether it was a flick of the tail of the global warming beast.

What is certain is that the kinds of catastrophes global warming will cause are already happening all over the world. Hundreds of people died in exceptionally high monsoon floods in India and Bangladesh this fall. Three dozen died last month in mud slides in the Alps; the floodwaters rushing out of the mountains were said to have raised one lake to its highest point in 160 years. A heat wave last year across much of this country claimed 271 lives. Penguins in the Antarctic are finding it harder and harder to find food for their

5

Source: "High Noon." Editorial. *The Amicus Journal.* Winter 2001. National Resources Defense Council. 29 May 2001. Copyright 2001 by NRDC staff. First published in *The Amicus Journal* (www.nrdc.org/amicus). Reprinted by permission.

chicks, as the shrimplike krill they eat grow scarcer in warmer waters. Disease-bearing mosquitoes have moved to altitudes and longitudes they usually never reach: malaria has come to the Kenyan highlands; the West Nile virus thrives in New York City.

If global warming continues unchecked, the next hundred years will be a century of dislocations. Ecosystems cannot simply pick up and move north. Many will break apart as temperatures shift too far and too fast for all their plants and animals to follow. Others, such as alpine tundra, will die out in many places because they have nowhere to go.

According to some climate models, by the year 2100 the southern tip of Florida may be under water and much of the Everglades may be drowned. Vermont may be too warm for sugar maples; wide swaths of the forests of the Southeast may become savannah; droughts may be frequent on the Great Plains. Meanwhile, according to the UN's Intergovernmental Panel on Climate Change, heat-related human deaths will double in many large cities around the world and tropical diseases will spread. Deaths from malaria alone may rise by more than a million a year.

Problem and Solution

There is no scientific question about the cause of global warming. Carbon dioxide and other "greenhouse gases" in the atmosphere trap heat. For millennia, the planet's temperature has moved in lockstep with the concentration of carbon dioxide in the atmosphere. Humans have now increased that concentration by 30 percent since the pre-industrial era, principally by burning oil, coal, and other fossil fuels. Today we have the highest atmospheric carbon concentration since the evolution of Homo sapiens.

The United States is the world's biggest greenhouse gas polluter. We have only 5 percent of the world's population, but we produce more than 20 percent of its greenhouse gases. In the face of climate chaos, we continue to increase our pollution. Power plants are the fastest-growing source of U.S. carbon dioxide emissions, primarily because we are increasing the output from old, inefficient coal plants, many of which don't meet current standards. Cars are   10
another major and growing source.

To stop piling up carbon dioxide, we need to shift to cutting-edge technologies for energy efficiency and for renewable energy from the sun, wind, and geothermal sources. Prosperity doesn't require fossil fuels. According to the American Council for an Energy-Efficient Economy, U.S. carbon intensity (carbon emissions per unit of gross domestic product) has been cut almost in half since 1970. Even during 1997–1999— at the height of an economic boom and with the subsidies and policies that reinforce fossil fuel use still deeply entrenched—the United States achieved a steep decline in carbon intensity, partly through the use of advanced efficiency technologies. Just tightening up national fuel economy standards would eliminate 450 million tons of carbon dioxide per year by 2010.

As the biggest polluter, the United States should take the lead in dealing with global warming. Instead, for most of the past decade, we have obstructed progress. One reason is obvious: the enormously powerful and wealthy fossil fuel lobby, whose campaign contributions subvert the relationship between Congress and the public.

As a result, the Kyoto Protocol is far weaker than it should be. Though many other industrialized countries had pushed for deep cuts in greenhouse gas pollution, U.S. intransigence kept the final agreement conservative. The protocol requires the industrialized nations to reduce their greenhouse gas emissions only 5 percent below 1990 levels by 2012. But for the moment, the protocol is our best hope for nationwide and global progress.

What happens in the Netherlands will be critical in making the Kyoto Protocol work, because the rules on exactly how countries can meet their targets have yet to be written. Three issues stand out:

- The protocol allows a country to meet part of its target by buying greenhouse gas "credits" from nations that emit less than their quota. The negotiators at the Netherlands must make sure that any credits traded represent real pollution cuts, not just paper-pushing.

- The protocol needs strong rules on enforcement. Countries that fail to act and countries with slipshod accounting cannot be permitted to undermine the effort.

- Growing trees absorb carbon, and the protocol allows a nation to meet some of its target by planting trees. The negotiators must make sure that the rules do not permit countries either to raze ancient forests and replant (which releases more carbon than it takes up) or to start counting all the plantings they would have undertaken anyway as new, climate-friendly tactics.

15

The United States must push to eliminate all of these carbon loopholes. If we get a good treaty, it could be the impetus we need to start modernizing our power plants, vehicles, factories, and buildings. Study after study has shown that these steps will create thousands of new jobs and reduce consumers' energy bills. And, for the sake of future generations, it is our responsibility to change our ways.

We have an enormous job to do. It's time to roll up our sleeves and get to work.

To support a strong U.S. position in the Netherlands, contact Undersecretary Frank Loy, State Department Building, 2201 C Street, N.W., Washington, D.C. 20520; phone 202-647-6240; fax 202-647-0753. For more information as the negotiations proceed, see the global warming homepage. ◢

1. Write a one-paragraph summary of the article to ensure that you accurately understand the author's premise and line of reasoning. What is the most

important insight you gain from this editorial? What do you most agree with? Least agree with?

2. How does it compare with other essays you have read on the subject of global warming? Do a subject or keyword search using your library's online catalogue or your Internet search engine, or consult one of the periodical indexes in your library's reference room, such as the *Environmental Index* or the *Reader's Guide to Periodical Literature.* Keep in mind the simple but easily overlooked fact that a single argument is but one voice in a multitudinous conversation. As John Stuart Mill wisely states, "He who knows only his own side of a case knows little." Before you can fully understand the complexities of an issue, let alone take a stance on it, you must become thoroughly familiar with the ongoing conversation, not just with one or two isolated voices.

3. If you had the opportunity to address this topic in an essay of your own, what would be your thesis? How would you defend it? Is there anything missing from the editorialist's argument that should be included? Why do you suppose he omitted it? Out of ignorance? His wish to hide a persuasive contrary view? His assumption that it is irrelevant? Do you find anything in the writer's treatment of the topic that seems especially illuminating, or, on the contrary, misleading or confusing?

4. Rewrite the opening paragraph of the editorial. What expectations does your paragraph set up for your readers? How do they differ, if at all, from the expectation the editorialist sets up with his original opening?

5. Consider the author's style, identifying as many stylistic elements as you can. Examples include use of metaphor, manner of incorporating or alluding to outside sources, manner of emphasizing a point, devices used to connect one idea with another, orchestration of sentence patterns, choices of words and phrases, manner of integrating outside sources, overall readability, and concision. What about his style most delights you? Annoys you? What would you do differently and why?

6. Describe the author's concluding paragraphs. Suggest an alternative conclusion for the editorial.

7. Locate up-to-date information about the Kyoto Protocol. How justifiable is the editorialist's faith in this treaty? How would you rewrite the editorial, if at all, in light of your findings?

Active Reading as Shared Reading

Most of the reading you do is in solitude. However, a significant chunk of learning takes place in social contexts such as classrooms or college learning assistance centers, book discussion groups, or student-coordinated study groups. Whenever possible, arrange to have an in-depth discussion of an assigned essay with another classmate or friend, ideally with two or three other classmates or friends. Here is how to make your reading discussion group most productive:

- After the group reads the piece once, have each person go through it again, following the annotating suggestions given in "Reading with a Pencil," pages 133–135.

- Discuss each writer's strategies identified by the group.

- Discuss the strengths and weaknesses of the argument, keeping tabs on any common ground that is mentioned (see the discussion of Rogerian argument in Chapter 4).

- Also keep tabs on any outside sources mentioned by group members. If at all possible, everyone in the group should consult these sources before trying to reach a consensus (see next point below).

- Attempt to reach consensus, despite differences of opinion. What unified position statement can your group produce that fairly represents the view (by now quite likely modified) of each individual member?

■ Exercise 6.7

1. Reflect on your private reading experience in relation to your public one. What does each reading context contribute toward your understanding and enjoyment of the text? Draw from actual reading experiences that included both a private and a public phase.

2. Does reading with others increase or decrease your comprehension of the text? What do you think accounts for this difference?

Using the Modes of Argument as a Schema for Analysis

To analyze the logic and merits of an argument, first determine which of the predominant general patterns of argument introduced in Chapter 1 and discussed in detail in Chapters 2 through 4—Classical, Toulmin, Rogerian—the argument fits into.

- If the piece follows the Classical (Aristotelian) model, you might ask: Is the intended audience uninformed or well informed on the issue?

- If the piece follows the Toulmin model, you might ask: Are the warrants on solid or shaky ground? Do they need to be made more explicit?

- If the piece follows the Rogerian model, you might ask: Is the tone sufficiently conciliatory to reduce the possibility of reader hostility?

The Importance of Open-Mindedness When Reading

One of the most important attributes that an education affords, along with self-discipline and attentiveness, is open-mindedness—the willingness to suspend judgment until one considers as many differing viewpoints as possible.

Learning to be truly open-minded takes effort. Everyone has deeply rooted beliefs, some of which even border on superstition. When these beliefs are challenged for whatever reasons, no matter how logical the reasons offered are, we resist—sometimes against our own better judgment. Beliefs often operate outside the realm of intellectual control and are entwined with our values and emotions. (Recall the discussion of audience in Rogerian approaches to argument in Chapter 4, pages 70–74.) If, for example, someone in your family earns his or her livelihood in the Pacific Northwest logging industry, you may find it difficult to sympathize with environmentalists who advocate putting an end to logging in that region, even though a part of you wishes to preserve any species threatened with extinction due to continued deforestation.

Being predisposed toward a certain viewpoint is to be expected. Rare is the individual who goes through life with a neutral attitude toward all controversial issues. But one can be predisposed toward a certain view or value system and still be open-minded. For example, you might be highly skeptical of the existence of extraterrestrial creatures and yet be willing to suspend that skepticism to give a writer a fair chance at trying to change your mind. Your willingness to be open-minded may increase, of course, if the author is a scientist or if the body of evidence presented has been shared with the entire scientific community for independent evaluations.

Sometimes we feel defensive when a long-held conviction is suddenly challenged. We may wish to guard the sanctity of that conviction so jealously that we may delude ourselves into thinking that we're being open-minded when we're not. When Galileo made his astronomical discoveries of the lunar craters and the moons of Jupiter known in 1610, he was promptly accused of heresy. We may think, from our enlightened perspective at the dawn of the twenty-first century, that the church was narrow-minded and intolerant, neglecting to realize that at the dawn of the seventeenth century modern science had not yet come into being. Most people's conception of "the heavens" was literally that: the night sky was a window to Heaven, and celestial (that is, heavenly) objects like planets, stars, and the moon all occupied divine niches in that Heaven; they were called the crystal spheres. Galileo's modest telescopic observations revolutionized our conception of the universe, but it did not happen overnight, particularly because Galileo recanted his "heresy"—or, rather, was persuaded to recant by the threat of execution. We know that Galileo never wavered in his convictions because even while under house arrest he continued to write about his discoveries.

The moral of Galileo's story, and the stories of many other daring thinkers throughout history, is that open-mindedness is precious, despite its difficulties. Take a few steps to ensure that you will not judge an argument prematurely or unfairly:

1. Identify and perhaps write down in your notebook the specific nature of the resistance you experience toward the author's point of view. Is it that you're a Republican reading a Democrat's evaluation of a Republican presidential administration? A strict vegetarian or vegan and animal-rights activist reading an article about the importance of preserving the cattle industry? An evolutionist reading an article by a Creationist questioning the validity of the hominid fossil record? Consciously identifying your predisposition helps you approach neutrality and open-mindedness.

2. Allow yourself to accept the author's premise at least temporarily. What are the consequences of doing so? Are there any reasonable facets to the argument? Can you establish some kind of common ground with the author? Does the author perhaps expose weaknesses in the viewpoint that you would advocate?

■ Exercise 6.8

Read the excerpt from Galileo's "Letter to the Grand Duchess Christina." Then answer the questions that follow.

Letter to The Grand Duchess Christina | Galileo Galilei

. . . The reason produced for condemning the opinion that the earth moves and the sun stands still is that in many places in the Bible one may read that the sun moves and the earth stands still. Since the Bible cannot err, it follows as a necessary consequence that anyone takes an erroneous and heretical position who maintains that the sun is inherently motionless and the earth movable.

With regard to this argument, I think in the first place that it is very pious to say and prudent to affirm that the holy Bible can never speak untruth—

Source: Excerpt from Galilei, Galileo. "Letter to the Grand Duchess Christina." *Discoveries and Opinions of Galileo.* Ed. and trans. Stillman Drake. New York: Doubleday/Anchor, 1957. 181–187. Copyright © 1957 by Stillman Drake. Used by permission of Doubleday, a division of Random House, Inc.

Galileo (1564–1642) is here shown lecturing on the Copernican or heliocentric (sun-centered) theory of the solar system. He helped to confirm this theory, with detailed telescopic observations of the movements of Venus, the moons of Jupiter, and sunspots.

whenever its true meaning is understood. But I believe nobody will deny that it is often very abstruse, and may say things which are quite different from what its bare words signify. Hence in expounding the Bible if one were always to confine oneself to the unadorned grammatical meaning, one might fall into error. Not only contradictions and propositions far from true might thus be made to appear in the Bible, but even grave heresies and follies. Thus it would be necessary to assign to God feet, hands, and eyes, as well as corporeal and human affections, such as anger, repentance, hatred, and sometimes even the forgetting of things past and ignorance of those to come. These propositions uttered by the Holy Ghost were set down in that manner by the sacred scribes in order to accommodate them to the capacities of the common people, who are rude and unlearned. For the sake of those who deserve to be separated from the herd, it is necessary that wise expositors should produce the true senses of such passages, together with the special reasons for which they were set down in these words. This doctrine is so widespread and so definite with all theologians that it would be superfluous to adduce evidence for it.

Hence I think that I may reasonably conclude that whenever the Bible has occasion to speak of any physical conclusion (especially those which are very abstruse and hard to understand), the rule has been observed of avoiding confusion in the minds of the common people which would render them contumacious toward the higher mysteries. Now the Bible, merely to condescend to popular capacity, has not hesitated to obscure some very important pronouncements, attributing to God himself some qualities extremely remote from (and even contrary to) His essence. Who, then, would positively declare that this principle has been set aside, and the Bible has confined itself rigorously to the bare and restricted sense of its words, when speaking but casually of the earth, of water, of the sun, or of any other created thing? Especially in view of the fact that these things in no way concern the primary purpose of the sacred writings, which is the service of God and the salvation of souls—matters infinitely beyond the comprehension of the common people.

This being granted, I think that in discussions of physical problems we ought to begin not from the authority of scriptural passages, but from sense-experiences and necessary demonstrations; for the holy Bible and the phenomena of nature proceed alike from the divine Word, the former as the dictate of the Holy Ghost and the latter as the observant executrix of God's commands. It is necessary for the Bible, in order to be accommodated to the understanding of every man, to speak many things which appear to differ from the absolute truth so far as the bare meaning of the words is concerned. But Nature, on the other hand, is inexorable and immutable; she never transgresses the laws imposed upon her, or cares a whit whether her abstruse reasons and methods of operation are understandable to men. For that reason it appears that nothing physical which sense-experience sets before our eyes, or which necessary demonstrations prove to us, ought to be called in question (much less condemned) upon the testimony of biblical passages which may have some different meaning beneath their words. For the Bible is not chained in every expression to conditions as strict as those which govern all physical effects; nor is God any less excellently revealed in Nature's actions than in the sacred statements of the Bible. Perhaps this is what Tertullian meant by these words:

"We conclude that God is known first through Nature, and then again, more particularly, by doctrine; by Nature in His works, and by doctrine in His revealed word."[1]

From this I do not mean to infer that we need not have an extraordinary esteem for the passages of holy Scripture. On the contrary, having arrived at any certainties in physics, we ought to utilize these as the most appropriate aids in the true exposition of the Bible and in the investigation of those meanings which are necessarily contained therein, for these must be concordant with demonstrated truths. I should judge that the authority of the Bible was designed to persuade men of those articles and propositions which, surpassing all human reasoning, could not be made credible by science, or by any other means than through the very mouth of the Holy Spirit.

Yet even in those propositions which are not matters of faith, this authority ought to be preferred over that of all human writings which are supported only by bare assertions or probable arguments, and not set forth in a demonstrative way. This I hold to be necessary and proper to the same extent that divine wisdom surpasses all human judgment and conjecture.

But I do not feel obliged to believe that that same God who has endowed us with senses, reason, and intellect has intended to forgo their use and by some other means to give us knowledge which we can attain by them. He would not require us to deny sense and reason in physical matters which are set before our eyes and minds by direct experience or necessary demonstrations. This must be especially true in those sciences of which but the faintest trace (and that consisting of conclusions) is to be found in the Bible. Of astronomy, for instance, so little is found that none of the planets except Venus are so much as mentioned, and this only once or twice under the name of "Lucifer." If the sacred scribes had had any intention of teaching people certain arrangements and motions of the heavenly bodies, or had they wished us to derive such knowledge from the Bible, then in my opinion they would not have spoken of these matters so sparingly in comparison with the infinite number of admirable conclusions which are demonstrated in that science. Far from pretending to teach us the constitution and motions of the heavens and the stars, with their shapes, magnitudes, and distances, the authors of the Bible intentionally forbore to speak of these things, though all were quite well known to them. Such is the opinion of the holiest and most learned Fathers, and in St. Augustine we find the following words:

"It is likewise commonly asked what we may believe about the form and shape of the heavens according to the Scriptures, for many contend much about these matters. But with superior prudence our authors have forborne to speak of this, as in no way furthering the student with respect to a blessed life—and, more important still, as taking up much of that time which should be spent in holy exercises. What is it to me whether heaven, like a sphere, surrounds the earth on all sides as a mass balanced in the center of the universe, or whether like a dish it merely covers and overcasts the earth? Belief in Scripture is urged rather for the reason we have often mentioned; that is, in order that no one, through ignorance of divine passages, finding anything in our Bibles or hearing anything cited from them of such a nature as may seem to oppose manifest conclusions, should be induced to suspect their truth when they teach, relate, and deliver more profitable matters. Hence let it be said briefly, touching the form of heaven, that our authors knew the truth but the Holy Spirit did not desire that men should learn things that are useful to no one for salvation."[2]

The same disregard of these sacred authors toward beliefs about the phenomena of the celestial bodies is repeated to us by St. Augustine in his next

10

chapter. On the question whether we are to believe that the heaven moves or stands still, he writes thus:

"Some of the brethren raise a question concerning the motion of heaven, whether it is fixed or moved. If it is moved, they say, how is it a firmament? If it stands still, how do these stars which are held fixed in it go round from east to west, the more northerly performing shorter circuits near the pole, so that heaven (if there is another pole unknown to us) may seem to revolve upon some axis, or (if there is no other pole) may be thought to move as a discus? To these men I reply that it would require many subtle and profound reasonings to find out which of these things is actually so; but to undertake this and discuss it is consistent neither with my leisure nor with the duty of those whom I desire to instruct in essential matters more directly conducing to their salvation and to the benefit of the holy Church."[3]

From these things it follows as a necessary consequence that, since the Holy Ghost did not intend to teach us whether heaven moves or stands still, whether its shape is spherical or like a discus or extended in a plane, nor whether the earth is located at its center or off to one side, then so much the less was it intended to settle for us any other conclusion of the same kind. And the motion or rest of the earth and the sun is so closely linked with the things just named, that without a determination of the one, neither side can be taken in the other matters. Now if the Holy Spirit has purposely neglected to teach us propositions of this sort as irrelevant to the highest goal (that is, to our salvation), how can anyone affirm that it is obligatory to take sides on them, and that one belief is required by faith, while the other side is erroneous? Can an opinion be heretical and yet have no concern with the salvation of souls? Can the Holy Ghost be asserted not to have intended teaching us something that does concern our salvation? I would say here something that was heard from an ecclesiastic of the most eminent degree: "That the intention of the Holy Ghost is to teach us how one goes to heaven, not how heaven goes."[4]

But let us again consider the degree to which necessary demonstrations and sense experiences ought to be respected in physical conclusions, and the authority they have enjoyed at the hands of holy and learned theologians. From among a hundred attestations I have selected the following:

"We must also take heed, in handling the doctrine of Moses, that we altogether avoid saying positively and confidently anything which contradicts manifest experiences and the reasoning of philosophy or the other sciences. For since every truth is in agreement with all other truth, the truth of Holy Writ cannot be contrary to the solid reasons and experiences of human knowledge."[5]

And in St. Augustine we read: "If anyone shall set the authority of Holy Writ against clear and manifest reason, he who does this knows not what he has undertaken; for he opposes to the truth not the meaning of the Bible, which is beyond his comprehension, but rather his own interpretation; not what is in the Bible, but what he has found in himself and imagines to be there."[6]

This granted, and it being true that two truths cannot contradict one another, it is the function of wise expositors to seek out the true senses of scriptural texts. These will unquestionably accord with the physical conclusions which manifest sense and necessary demonstrations have previously made certain to us. Now the Bible, as has been remarked, admits in many places expositions that are remote from the signification of the words for reasons we have already given. Moreover, we are unable to affirm that all interpreters of the Bible speak by divine inspiration, for if that were so there would exist no differences between them about the sense of a given passage. Hence I should think it would be the part of prudence not to permit anyone to usurp scriptural texts and force them in some way to maintain any physical conclusion to be true, when at some future time the senses and demonstrative or necessary reasons may show the contrary. Who indeed will set bounds to human ingenuity? Who will assert that everything in the universe capable of being perceived is already discovered and known? Let us rather confess quite truly that "Those truths which we know are very few in comparison with those which we do not know." . . .

Notes

1. *Adversus Marcionem*, ii, 18.
2. *De Genesi ad literam* ii, 9. Galileo has noted also: "The same is to be read in Peter the Lombard, master of opinions."
3. *Ibid.*, ii, 10.
4. A marginal note by Galileo assigns this epigram to Cardinal Baronius (1538–1607). Baronius visited Padua with Cardinal Bellarmine in 1598, and Galileo probably met him at that time.
5. Pererius on Genesis, near the beginning.
6. In the seventh letter to Marcellinus. ◩

1. How convincing is Galileo's effort to reconcile Scripture with his findings?

2. Describe Galileo's attitude toward his audience. To what degree does his manner of supporting his assertions reflect this attitude?

3. How does Galileo connect his different points together? What is his central thesis? Do all of his points relate clearly to this thesis?

4. Why do you suppose Galileo chose to present his argument to a noblewoman and in the form of a letter? Does the letter itself provide any clues?

Chapter Summary

Reading and writing are interconnected modes of thinking. We critically read our own writing (for sense of direction, development of ideas, coherence, clarity, persuasive force, and so on) as well as the writing of others. We construct meaning (a kind of internal writing) when we read in depth—that is, we read actively rather than passively whenever we read critically. To read effectively also means to read in stages: previewing (prereading and skim-reading) to grasp the central purpose of the piece; in-depth reading to understand the content, progression, and rhetorical strategies at work in the piece; and postreading to reinforce the framework of the whole argument. To read effectively also means to respond spontaneously with a pencil, writing marginal glosses, comparisons, and questions in the margins. Finally, reading effectively means to read in a highly motivated manner, as if you are interacting with the author on paper.

Checklist

1. Have I read the assigned essays, as well as the drafts of my fellow students, in three stages: first previewing, then reading in depth, and then postreading?

2. When reading in depth, do I determine the framework of the argument? Evaluate the data presented? Evaluate the author's organizational strategy?

Writing Projects

1. Write a critical response to one of the following quotations about reading.
   a. "To write down one's impressions of Hamlet as one reads it year after year would be virtually to record one's own autobiography, for as we know more of life, Shakespeare comments on what we know." (Virginia Woolf)
   b. "We read often with as much talent as we write." (Ralph Waldo Emerson)
   c. "Camerado, this is no book
      Who touches me touches a man."
      (Walt Whitman)
   d. "To read well . . . is a noble exercise. . . . It requires a training such as the athletes underwent, the steady intention almost of the whole life to this object." (Henry David Thoreau)

2. Write an essay in which you propose ways of improving one's reading strategies. You may want to discuss these strategies in relation to particular types of reading materials.

3. Using what you have learned about the Classical, Toulmin, and Rogerian patterns of argument, construct a list of questions specific to each pattern that you could use to analyze an argument.

7 Researching Your Argument

I have always come to life after coming to books.

—Jorge Luis Borges

Much of the writing you do in college—as well as beyond—requires *research,* which refers to three interconnected activities: (1) searching for and retrieving information you need for your writing project, (2) taking notes, and (3) integrating the necessary information into your paper. These activities not only enable you to strengthen the premise of your argument, but also to acquire in-depth knowledge of the subject.

The Three Faces of Research

Research involves finding information and applying it to your own purposes. One major reason for writing an argument is to present to readers new information and insights into a topic. At the same time, however, readers need to be informed or reminded about the old information to see how the new perspective adds to the discussion of the issue and merits consideration. You therefore must learn as much as possible about your topic and know how to incorporate only the best and most relevant researched data. Sometimes students try to incorporate so much data into their papers that the papers begin to read like mere summaries of what others have written about the topic. Readers want to see your original argument *reinforced* by the findings of others.

Searching before You Research: Taking a Mental Inventory

One of the most important steps in gathering information may seem like the least necessary: making clear to yourself how much you already know about the topic. The step is necessary because a lot of what you learn, if it is not used every day, ends up in the equivalent of deep storage in the brain. Some good ways for retrieving it include listing, clustering, and freewriting—predrafting strategies

described in Chapter 1. These information-gathering techniques help you generate questions, ideas, and "paths" to pursue in your research.

Consider this case in point: Before Marian, a first-year composition student,
sets out to research her chosen topic—possible long-term effects of secondhand
cigarette smoke on children—she opens a blank document in her word processing program and begins freewriting (rapidly recording all that she already knows
or associates with the topic). Ignoring word choice, sentence correctness, or paragraph structure for the moment, Marian focuses only on content.

> My parents both smoked and I remembered coughing a lot when I was around
> them, and sometimes my eyes burned. I never connected my coughing and
> burning eyes to their smoking because I assumed that they would never do any-
> thing to undermine my health. Children can't get away from smoke. In the
> family, are stuck, have no choice in the matter. And then I remember that my
> best friend Julia's parents also smoked, even more than my parents did, and
> that she would cough all the time, and come down with the flu a lot. Not long af-
> terwards (when? what year?), the Surgeon General issued a warning that ambi-
> ent smoke can be just as harmful as firsthand smoke. Question: has
> government done studies comparing effects on children vs. adults? I also read
> recently that medical researchers have established a link between secondhand
> smoke and chronic respiratory illnesses, such as asthma. Question: I wonder if
> the recent upturn in asthma rates in children relates to parents' smoking? I also
> know that some researchers or tobacco industry people or maybe just average
> smokers argue that the connection is exaggerated, people's fears get
> overblown—Question—how to determine how real is the danger?

Marian's freewriting inventory on secondhand smoke is not extensive, but she
has written down enough for questions to start occurring to her—questions that
help direct and focus the research process. Also, the freewriting gets her thinking
about possible opposing views as well as helps her establish a link between her
personal experience with the topic and her more objective knowledge of it.

■ Exercise 7.1

1. Freewrite on one of the following argumentative topics:
   a. Ways to improve my school's fitness center
   b. How to improve the parking situation on campus
   c. Studying to prepare for a career versus studying for the pleasure
      of learning

2. Write down all that you already know about a topic you enjoy reading
   about; then generate a list of questions about aspects of the topic you need
   to know more about.

Focusing Your Research for Argumentative Essays

Once you have a sense of what you need to find out about your topic, you can guide your researching activities with sets of questions to keep your information-gathering activities in focus. Once again, recall the purpose-audience-writer-subject interconnections of the rhetorical rhombus introduced in Chapter 1 (see Figure 7.1).

Generate your questions in the context of each point on the rhombus. If you are arguing against the authenticity of UFO reports, for example, you might generate sets of questions similar to those in the following four sections.

Writer-Based Questions

Writer-based questions enable you to concentrate on your existing knowledge in and understanding of the subject matter and on whether you need to gather more information on it. Here are some examples of writer-based questions:

1. Why is it so important to spend time considering this anti-UFO stance?

2. Do I actually feel strongly one way or another on this issue?

3. How much do I already know about UFO reports?

Audience-Based Questions

Audience-based questions enable you to concentrate on your readers' expectations about the subject matter, on the ways they might respond to your assertions, and on how you might counterrespond to their reactions. Here are some examples of audience-based questions:

FIGURE 7.1

Rhetorical
Rhombus

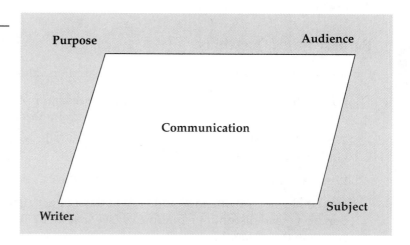

1. Who are the readers I'd like to reach? Those who will support funding of future research on UFOs? Those who are writing the UFO reports to show them their bias?

2. What is my audience's opinion on the authenticity of UFOs? How strongly is that opinion held?

3. What kinds of sources are best suited to my audience? If uninformed, they need background information provided. If hostile, they need to be convinced that I understand their position fully and fairly.

4. What are my audience's main sources of information about UFOs? How reliable are these sources?

5. Exactly how does my audience benefit from reading this essay?

Subject-Based Questions

Subject-based questions focus on the factual content of your topic. Facts are universally verifiable; that is, they can be tested or verified by anyone. They must be distinguished from interpretations, judgments, or conclusions, which are subjective responses *derived* from your analysis of the facts. Here are some examples of subject-based questions:

1. Do existing UFO reports share common elements? Do these elements reinforce authenticity or fraud?

2. What are the *scientific* data for the claims in the most notable UFO reports? How do I know those scientific data are authentic and reliable?

3. What do I need to research to discuss or refute the claims presented by the UFO reports?

4. Do I carefully consider potential challenges to my views and the best way to interpret their validity?

Purpose-Based Questions

Purpose-based questions are interpretive and based on values, for example:

1. What is the thesis (claim) of my essay? Is it sufficiently clear and convincing? (The next section helps you formulate a strong thesis for your papers.)

2. What values (called warrants in the Toulmin model) are implied by the kind of evidence I bring to the claim?

3. What larger implications are conveyed by the thesis?

4. How do I want my intended audience to think or act after reading my paper? To vote to discontinue funding of UFO research? To stop making unsubstantiated claims?

You can see how the answers to questions in these four areas will affect the text, from its content, to its organization, to its tone.

Formulating a Strong Thesis

You already know what a thesis is: It is the main point you wish to argue, the claim you are making and are trying to persuade your audience to accept, using the strongest evidence you can find. However, you may like to gain more skill in coming up with a strong, compelling thesis for your argumentative essays. Here are three steps you can take to ensure that the thesis you come up with is a good one:

1. Write down an assertion (viewpoint, claim) on a particular topic. For example, if your topic is music censorship, you might write down, "Music censorship is wrong."

2. Ask probing questions about the clarity and specificity of your assertion, making sure that you replace vague or ambiguous language with specific, precise language. If the above statement about music censorship appeared as a thesis statement, readers would have some of the following questions:
   - What is meant by *wrong*? Unethical? Illegal? Misguided?
   - What is meant by *music*? The music itself or the lyrics to songs? If songs, then what kinds of songs? Country-Western? Rap? Rock? Jazz? Folk? What about the songs do some people find objectionable? Swear words? Obscenity? Political references? Actions seemingly advocated by the lyrics?
   - What is meant by *censorship*? Bleeping certain words or phrases of certain songs? Restricting sales only to those of a certain age? Banning the music altogether?

3. Turn your assertion into a well-focused, specifically worded thesis statement. For example, "Expurgating or banning rap songs because of their alleged profanity or obscenity is against the law because it violates rights guaranteed by the First Amendment."

By taking the time to examine your trial thesis statement from the point of view of its clarity and specificity, you produce effective thesis statements that in turn help you to produce more effective arguments.

■ Exercise 7.2

1. Generate three questions for each of the four elements of the rhetorical rhombus (purpose, audience, writer, subject) for an essay you have recently finished or one you are currently working on.

2. Imagine that you are writing a paper that argues for the best ways of dealing with sexual harassment in the workplace. Generate questions in each

of these categories: purpose-based, audience-based, writer-based, subject based.

3. Revise each of the following assertions so that they can serve as strong thesis statements:

    a. Water quality needs to be improved.

    b. Males are the dominant sex because they are stronger.

    c. The university should offer more courses for minorities.

Researching Using the Internet

A late twentieth-century invention, the Internet has become, in little more than a decade, the most revolutionary information resource since the invention of printing about 550 years ago. Its dramatic proliferation brings problems, however, as well as benefits. Some sources on the Net are superficial, irrelevant, or unreliable. Usually, you know right away what is junk and what isn't—but sometimes it is not so easy.

You need to acquire an eye for distinguishing between documents that are substantive and relevant and those that are not. Here are a few questions to ask about Internet documents to help you make that distinction:

1. Are the authors experts in their fields? If no biographical information about the authors is included at the site, check the library or search the Web to see whether these credentials are located elsewhere.

2. Do the authors go beyond mere generalized assertions in order to produce useful new knowledge about the subject? For example, if you find an article that argues either for or against the use of exit tests as a condition for high school graduation, does the author back up those assertions with actual data comparing the performance of students who have prepared for such a test with those who have not?

3. Do the authors provide a scholarly context for their arguments? That is, do they relate their points of view to others who have also conducted scholarly inquiry into the subject?

4. Is the subject matter treated seriously and professionally? Be wary of an amateurish tone. For example, in debates over controversial issues such as whether the state should require Creationist doctrine to be given equal standing with evolutionary theory in a high school biology class, one side might easily caricature the other side as "religious fanatics" or "radical atheists." Such pigeon-holing or name calling works against the very purpose of argument, which is to examine both sides of an issue critically, carefully, and responsibly, in order to arrive at a reasonable understanding of what really is or should be. When in doubt, weigh the tone and treatment

of a questionable document with documents you know are authentic and significant.

Useful Types of Internet Resources

The most common types of information resources available on the Internet include listservers, newsgroups, databases and online forums. The sections that follow take a closer look at each of these. *Note:* Regardless which of the below sources you consult, it is always a good idea to double-check information you access, especially when acquiring information from unknown individuals participating in a listserv, newsgroup, or forum.

Listservers

A listserver (more commonly referred to as a listserv) is a discussion group subscription service in which commentary and information about a given topic is exchanged with all members of the group. Listserv members often participate in ongoing conversations or debates over key issues. When a great many experts and enthusiasts from all over the world argue heatedly on a given topic, a wealth of information and viewpoints is generated. For this reason, participation in such discussion groups can be an excellent way of staying informed and developing your argumentative skills at the same time.

Newsgroups

Newsgroups (or usenets) are topic-based electronic bulletin boards. Members with an interest in, say, art history can access useful information that is arranged by subtopic and posted by other members. If you are interested in Italian Renaissance art, for example, you quite likely could find, on a home page menu, a newsgroup devoted to that area.

Databases

Databases are invaluable compilations of sources in a given subject, such as a compilation of books and articles on health care, biochemistry, ancient Egyptian history, economics, or any other subject. Although many databases are accessed online, some of them, like the *Modern Language Association (MLA) International Bibliography of Language and Literature,* the *Readers Guide to Periodical Literature,* and the *Congressional Record Index* continue to be published in hard copy or put on CD-ROM disks. See the reference librarian at your college library when uncertain about locating a particular database for your research project.

The catalogs of most academic and research libraries are available online. The Library of Congress's catalog is also available and contains more than 12 million items. The Library of Congress also has accessible special collections, such as the National Agricultural Library and the National Library of Medicine. Access any of the Library of Congress's catalogs at <http://www.loc.gov>.

Forums

A forum is an ongoing discussion group in real time. Forums exist for just about any subject matter and professional interest imaginable. Such forums can be an excellent way of finding highly knowledgeable people and learning from them, while enjoying interactive conversation with people all across the country or even the world. Be careful, however. The knowledge base of participants varies in these discussions, and some participants may give out misleading information.

Searching on the Web

Searching for information on the Web is easy—almost too easy. All you do is click on a search engine icon at your internet provider's home page or enter a Web address for one of the many existing search engines. Some search engines are more powerful than others, however. Among the most reliable are Google, Web-Crawler, Netscape, Yahoo!, AltaVista and Dogpile. Here are their URL (Uniform Resource Locator) addresses:

<http://www.google.com>

<http://www.webcrawler.com>

<http://www.netscape.com>

<http://www.yahoo.com>

<http://www.altavista.com>

<http://www.dogpile.com>

Every search engine is different. Some, like AltaVista and Dogpile, include brief descriptions of every site called up.

The next step is to type keywords in the narrow blank rectangle provided—and here things can get a little tricky. You need to decide which three or four words come closest to the sort of information you hope to find. Use the most "official" terms you know for your subject. If you are looking for general pro-con arguments on school vouchers, for example, you might enter the keywords *school, voucher,* and *programs*. If you want to find material on vouchers relating to your state, enter the name of your state in the keyword field as well. If you wish to focus on specific concerns within the voucher system, you may need to enter an additional relevant keyword such as *curriculum, class size,* or *teaching excellence.*

Search engines usually retrieve far more sites than you can review in a reasonable time, so you have to be selective. If you're looking for substantive, scholarly commentary, then look for sites from academic institutions. (You can recognize these sites by their URL extension, *.edu*.) Or look for online magazines, or e-zines as they are sometimes called.

Google has a time-saving search option, an "I'm feeling lucky" button that, when clicked on, brings up far fewer hits, but those hits are likely the most relevant to the keywords you have entered.

Another problem to be aware of when searching for relevant sites is timeliness. If you require the latest information, be sure to check the dates of the sites you bring up. Some of them may be several years old.

Useful Web Sites for Writers of Arguments

The list that follows gives some useful Web addresses for your research. Note, however, that Web sites often disappear, are updated, or change their addresses. Consider using a current Internet Yellow Pages (available in most bookstores and libraries) to locate sources.

For Humanities Resources

<http://vos.ucsb.edu/shuttle/general.html>

For Statistics from the U.S. Department of Education

<http://nces.ed.gov/pubsearch/>

For Information on Feminist Issues

<http:www.igc.org/women/feminist.html>

For Health-Related Information from the Center for Disease Control

<http:www.cdc.gov/>

For Information about Population from the U.S. Census Bureau

<http:www.census.gov/>

For Information About Public Policy Issues

<http:www.speakout.com/activism/policy/>

Media Web Sites

<http:www.cnn.com/>   The Web site of the Cable News Network.

<http:www.pbs.org/>   The Web site of the Public Broadcasting Service (educational television programming).

<http:www.npr.org/>   The Web site of National Public Radio.

<http:www.ecola.com/archive/press>   A Web site directory, with links, to newspapers that allow back-issue searches.

<http:www.nytimes.com>   The Web site of the *New York Times.*

<http:forums.nytimes.com>   This Web site takes you to the *New York Times* forums, where you can read numerous postings on dozens of subjects by forum members. By subscribing for free, you can post your own views and responses to the postings of others.

Finally, there are Web sites to help you find information on the Internet, as well as to think critically about available resources:

A Tutorial for Finding Information Online

<http:www.lib.berkeley.edu/TeachingLib/Guides/Internet/FindInfo.html> This site introduces you to the basics of Web searching.

Guidelines for Evaluating Web Sites

<http:www.geocities.com/tucolib/websiteevaluation.htm> A bibliography of online resources for evaluating Web sites.

■ Exercise 7.3

1. Compare the effectiveness of two different search engines, such as AltaVista, Netscape, Dogpile, or Google. Write out a description of their respective strengths and weaknesses.

2. Enter an online forum on a topic that interests you and then write or present a brief report on your experiences. What did you learn about your topic as a result of interacting with other members of the forum?

3. Using the latest Internet Yellow Pages in your college library's reference room, locate three or four Web sites that seem relevant to the topic you are currently writing about. Then go to these sites. Which of them were most useful, and why? Which were least useful, and why?

Researching Using Print Resources

Without doubt, the Internet is a helpful, high-speed information-accessing tool, and its resources are expanding continuously. But hard-copy resources—reference books, trade books, periodicals (specialized and nonspecialized), historical documents, and newspapers—continue to be indispensable. Most academic scholarship continues to be published in traditional print journals, for example, and these articles generally go into much greater depth than their Internet counterparts.

Locating Articles

To locate important article sources, begin with the Expanded Academic Index in your library's electronic catalog. The listing will tell you whether your library carries the periodical that the article is in. If not, you may be able to have your library obtain a fax of it for a nominal fee or obtain a book through inter-library loan.

Other important print periodical indexes include:

General Science Index

Applied Sciences Index

Education Index

Social Sciences Index

Environmental Index

Humanities Index

National Newspaper Index

Using Additional Print Reference Works

In addition to periodical indexes, you may already be familiar with the following hard-copy reference works: encyclopedias (general and specialized), dictionaries, abstracts and digests, handbooks and sourcebooks, and atlases.

Encyclopedias   General or subject-specific encyclopedias are often a good place to begin your formal research because they offer a panoramic view of the topic you are working with and provide references for further reading. An encyclopedia article is essentially a detailed summary of the most important facts about a topic, accompanied by a bibliography. You probably have used general encyclopedias that cover the whole spectrum of knowledge. You may not have used specialized encyclopedias, which are limited to only one subject, such as psychology or religion.

Here is just a small sampling of the kinds of encyclopedias you will find in your library's reference room:

General	Subject-Specific
Encyclopedia Britannica	*Encyclopedia of Environmental Studies*
The Columbia Encyclopedia	*The Wellness Encyclopedia*
Collier's Encyclopedia	*Macmillan Encyclopedia of Computers*
World Book Encyclopedia	*Encyclopedia of Psychoactive Drugs*

Dictionaries   A dictionary provides more than highly concise definitions and explanations; in the case of biographical dictionaries, for example, you will find profiles of notable individuals. Most dictionaries are devoted to words in general, but there are specialized dictionaries as well. Important dictionaries include:

The Oxford English Dictionary

The Merriam-Webster Book of Word Histories

New Dictionary of American Slang

McGraw-Hill Dictionary of Scientific and Technical Terms

A Dictionary of Biology

American Biographical Dictionary

Abstracts and Digests   An abstract is a formal summary of a scholarly or scientific paper. Virtually all disciplines publish compilations of abstracts. Digests are summaries of less formal works such as book reviews. Here is a sampling of abstracts and digests:

Dissertation Abstracts

Ecology Abstracts

Chemical Abstracts

Book Review Digest

Handbooks and Sourcebooks   These types of reference books provide you with guidelines and references for particular disciplines, such as English literature, philosophy, geology, economics, mathematics, and computer science. Some handbooks and sourcebooks are:

Opposing Viewpoints (collections of pro-con position statements on a wide range of topics)

A Handbook to Literature

A Field Guide to Rocks and Minerals (similar Field Guides exist for most subjects in the general sciences)

Atlases   Atlases are collections of maps (of countries, states, cities, the world) and may be historical, topographical (depicting landmasses of different elevations), or geographical (depicting regions in terms of population, natural resources, industries, and the like).

■ Exercise 7.4

1. At your library, consult *Opposing Viewpoints* (see listing under "Handbooks and Sourcebooks") and write a brief summary of each side of a particular

topic that you find interesting. Decide which side is argued most convincingly, and why.

2. Look up a single item in three different encyclopedias or dictionaries. Describe how the coverage differs from source to source.

3. Using *Book Review Digest,* locate three different reviews of a single book and write a comparative evaluation of the three reviews. Which reviewer provides the most useful information about the book's subject matter? About the author?

Gathering Information from E-mail, Telephone Conversations, Interviews, and Surveys

As a college student, you are part of a complex community of educators, researchers, and specialists in numerous disciplines. Name your topic and someone on your college faculty, staff, or student body will be an expert in it. But how do you contact these individuals? Very simply: by e-mail or telephone.

Using E-mail or the Telephone

Obtain a campus phone directory listing faculty and staff and their respective departments or offices; there you will see each person's telephone extension number and e-mail address, along with his or her office location. You can also check your school's Web site to find what specialties are listed for faculty members or to learn where the various offices and departments are on campus so that you can visit them to find out who is an expert in what. Next, e-mail or phone that person, explain who you are and what you are researching, and ask to set up a time convenient for a telephone interview or a personal interview. If the information you require is relatively complex or the person in question is too busy to be interviewed, request an e-mail exchange.

Conducting an Interview

An interview is a focused conversation on a predetermined topic, usually involving the interviewee's personal involvement in the topic being discussed. Interviews can be formal or informal, depending on the nature of the topic and the relationship between interviewer and interviewee.

Information derived from interviews is valuable for two reasons:

1. It is timely (you may be getting "cutting edge" information before it is published), and

2. It provides the opportunity for obtaining personal insights into the subject matter.

Experts can also be extremely helpful in directing you to additional sources and thinking about other aspects of the topic you may not be aware of.

When conducting the interview, keep the following suggestions in mind:

1. Always make an appointment with the person you wish to interview and be clear about what you wish to discuss and why.

2. Prepare questions to ask during the interview, but don't use them rigidly or present them in rote fashion as in an interrogation. Rather, try to work them spontaneously into your discussion. Ask specific, well-focused questions about what you need to know.

3. It is all right to engage in "ice-breaking" small talk, but once the discussion begins, try not to go off on tangents. Remember: You are there to interview the individual, not to have a conversation, so listen more than you talk.

4. Be alert for "spinoff" questions—unanticipated questions that occur to you in light of the way the interviewee answers a previous question. Be sure that spinoff questions are relevant to the topic.

5. Avoid leading questions, whereby your manner of wording the questions reveals a bias on your part. For example, a leading question would be "Wouldn't you agree that the dangers from ozone depletion are highly ex-aggerated?" You want more than a yes or no response anyway.

6. Always ask for clarification of a complex idea or for definition of an unfa-miliar term. Also, ask for the correct spelling of names or terms you are uncertain about.

7. If you wish to record the interview on tape, request permission to do so beforehand. But don't expect to transcribe it all. You will use the tape just to capture precise wording of an elegant or particularly apt phrase, just as when you quote a written source directly.

8. Ask the interviewee for permission to contact him or her for follow-up questions after the interview or perhaps suggest a follow-up interview.

9. Write a thank-you note to the interviewee after the interview: Show that you acknowledge that the individual is a busy person who set aside time for you. Such common courtesy is justified and appropriate. It also makes it more likely that the individual will respond if you need any follow-up help.

Conducting a Survey

To obtain information from a large number of individuals you need to conduct a survey. The first step is to prepare a questionnaire—a set of questions with room on the sheet for answers—to distribute to individuals. These questions should be carefully worded so that (1) the respondents can answer them quickly, and (2) the survey will yield valid and useful information for your purposes.

The second step is to conduct the survey. This may be done via e-mail, using a distribution list so it could be sent, for example, to the entire student body at once or via personal distribution, where you simply question individuals directly or ask them to fill out your questionnaire while you wait.

Designing a Questionnaire

A good questionnaire is a model of relevance, clarity and concision. Word questions carefully, making sure that binary (for example, Yes or No) questions do not stem from a false dichotomy (that is, where answers other than Yes or No are possible). Also, do not word questions that are leading or that conceal a bias. The following is an example of a biased question:

What percentage of old-growth forest should be logged?

_____10% _____50% _____75% _____85% _____100%

This set of options is biased because (1) there is no 0% (the opposite equivalent of 100%), and (2) there is only one option below 50% but two options above 50%. The following is an example of a leading question:

Do you agree that the sexist practices of the Labor Union should be stopped?

_____Yes _____No _____Not Sure

Sexist is judgmental and therefore risks leading the respondent to agree with that judgment. The question should describe actual documented actions that may or may not be judged as sexist, such as "Should the Labor Union continue to deny membership to women?"

It is usually a good idea to avoid questions that readers would not be sure how to answer or that would require long answers. Instead, choose questions that ask respondents to choose among the options you provide:

Which of the following long-term space exploration policies should NASA adopt? (Check all that apply.)

_____Lunar colonization
_____Robot probes of outer planets
_____Human exploration of Mars
_____Lunar-orbiting telescope

Finally, introduce your questionnaire in a brief, courteous paragraph that includes your name, the purpose of your research, and how much time you estimate it will take to answer the questions. Thank them in advance for their time.

Taking Effective Research Notes

The notes you take while reading outside sources for your argument-in-progress will come in handy when you decide which sources you need to integrate into the body of your paper. (See also "Incorporating Outside Sources into Your Argument" on page 172.) The following suggestions will make your note-taking more efficient and productive.

1. Unless you have a laptop computer to take with you into the library, use index cards for taking notes (4" x 6" size is ideal): You can easily shuffle and rearrange them, as well as annotate them. Photocopying articles and passages from books is another option, but photocopying can get expensive and can take as much time as writing out notes. Also, photocopied pages are harder to sort through and review.

2. Write out the complete bibliographic citation for every source you use; that way, you will be able to locate the source again easily if you need to and will be able to prepare your Works Cited page more quickly. Guidelines for citing sources appear in Chapter 8, "Documenting Your Sources: MLA and APA Styles."

3. Read each source straight through to get an idea of all that it includes. Then return to the beginning and copy passages that seem most useful for your needs. Always double-check to make sure you are copying the passage accurately. If you need to omit part of a passage, indicate the omission with ellipsis dots (. . .). If you need to add a word or date to make a quoted passage understandable or coherent, place it in brackets:

   According to the *Cedarville Gazette,* "Last year [2001], the stock market suffered its steepest decline in ten years."

The Role of Serendipity in Research

Writers benefit greatly from methodical research, but not all researching is methodical. Some of it is results from good fortune or a special kind of good fortune call *serendipity.*

Serendipity refers to the capacity for discovering important things in an unexpected manner or in an unexpected place. Serendipity seems most likely to occur when you are immersed in your work. Because your senses are on full alert, you pick up things you might not have otherwise noticed or make connections between two ideas that you would never have made in a less engaged state of mind.

Two students described the following serendipitous discoveries:

Student 1

While I was working on my paper on unfair hiring practices, I happened to notice a news story on the Internet that described how frustrating it is to follow user manuals because their instructions are seldom clear enough. That made a light flash inside my head! Perhaps hiring practices are often unfair because the policies describing them are poorly written!

Student 2

Here I was stumped about how to develop my topic on the way students can study effectively in groups. While I was eating lunch, I overheard two students discussing getting together with their Western Civilization study group to prepare for a midterm. In introduced myself and asked them if they would tell me about how they formed their group, how beneficial they thought it was, and what sorts of pitfalls to avoid.

These examples illustrate the way in which mental alertness and engagement can help you discover new approaches to your topic in unexpected ways.

■ Exercise 7.5

Over the next four or five days, in addition to using methods of methodical researching, do the following:

- Browse for half an hour or so among the library stacks, in subject areas relevant to the topic you are working on.
- Listen closely for connections, however seemingly tangential, while talking with classmates or friends.
- Find some encyclopedia articles related to the topic you are working on and write down any ideas that might be worth incorporating into your essay.
- Review your lecture notes from other classes.

Report on any serendipitous discoveries that you were able to use for your paper. Compare your serendipity experiences with those of your classmates. If you hear of one you have not experienced, then try to experience it for yourself.

Evaluating Your Sources

It is tempting to assume that just because information is published it is reliable. Because that is not the case, unfortunately, you need to ensure that the sources you incorporate into your argument are trustworthy. Evaluate every outside source you incorporate into your paper using these five criteria:

1. *Accuracy* of information presented
2. *Relevance* to your thesis
3. *Reliability* of the author and the periodical that originally published the material
4. *Clarity*
5. *Thoroughness*

The sections that follow consider each criterion in turn.

Accuracy

Factual information needs to be checked for accuracy. Data, such as population trends, the latest nutritional information about a dietary supplement, academic program policies and offerings, and so on, sometimes change so frequently that the print source at your fingertips may not be the most recent information. Carefully check dates of publication, check with the campus specialist, or search the Internet for more current information.

Relevance

Does the information you plan to use in your argument truly contribute to your thesis? If you are writing about the importance of animals in medical research but use information drawn from the use of animals in cosmetic research, there may be a problem with relevance unless you can draw a medical connection to cosmetic use (for example, certain dyes in mascara can cause an allergic reaction).

Reliability

When considering the reliability of information, think about the credentials of the author presenting it. For example, if an author is conveying information about the toxins in local ground water, that person should be a recognized authority in environmental chemistry, not just a local politician.

Clarity

Important data are sometimes presented in such a way that it is difficult to understand. In such cases, you may need to paraphrase the source material instead of quoting it directly, or to quote it directly but add your own explanation afterwards. Technical information, while clear to you, might be confusing to nonspecialized readers. In such cases, you may need to provide a somewhat elaborate interpretation of the data.

Thoroughness

It is important to ensure that your data are not perfunctory bits of quotations or statistics that fail to provide sufficient grounding for your claim. The more debatable your claims, the more you need to provide sufficient data to remove any doubts from readers' minds.

Understanding and Avoiding Plagiarism

From the Latin word for *kidnapper,* plagiarism refers to two connected acts:

1. Using someone else's work, *published or unpublished,* as if it were your own

2. Incorporating someone else's words *or ideas* into your own writing without explicit acknowledgment of authorship or source

You are most likely aware of the seriousness of plagiarism. Quite simply, it is a crime. People's ideas and ways of expressing them are a form of property—intellectual property—and are as worthy of protection from theft as material property. Thus, when a person plagiarizes, he or she is stealing.

Use the following guidelines to determine what kind of material should be acknowledged and what need not be.

1. Paraphrases of someone else's ideas must be acknowledged (that is, cited). Even though you are putting a passage into your own words, you are nonetheless using another's ideas.

2. Any information considered common knowledge does not require acknowledgment. Any facts readily looked up in a least three different sources, such as historical dates, constitute common knowledge. The key word is *readily.* Some factual information is clearly the product of individual research and, as such, not readily available.

3. When you need to quote verbatim (using the author's exact words) be mindful of these pointers:

    a. Quote only what is necessary to convey the author's ideas. Too many or too lengthy quotations can make a paper difficult to read.

    b. Do not rely on quoted material to carry your argument forward. This is a common pitfall of beginning writers. You want your paper to represent *your* way of thinking, not that of the experts you are quoting.

    c. Besides quoting, *comment* on a quotation of one to two sentences or longer. Do not drop a quotation in if your reason for quoting someone else is not patently clear.

    d. Use quotation marks around all material quoted verbatim. If the passage you are quoting runs more than four lines, then place the passage, without quotation marks, in a separate paragraph, indented ten spaces from the main text.

■ Exercise 7.6

1. Label each of the following statements as common knowledge (not requiring acknowledgment) or not common knowledge (requiring acknowledgment).

   a. Some books should be savored slowly, others devoured ravenously.

   b. Like the 1995 flooding of the Rhine, the inundation of the upper Mississippi and Missouri Rivers in 1993 provided a dramatic and costly lesson on the effects of treating the natural flow of rivers as a pathological condition. (Janet Abramovitz, *Imperiled Waters, Impoverished Future:* 16.)

   c. The Battle of Hastings took place in 1066 C.E.

   d. Many educators these days tend to regard the Internet as a cure-all for getting students to read.

2. Choose any one of the arguments from "Part 2: Reading Clusters" and evaluate in writing its evidence in terms of the five criteria: accuracy, relevance, reliability, clarity, and thoroughness.

Incorporating Outside Sources into Your Argument

All writing needs to "flow" for the points to unfold logically and smoothly for the reader. An important element in a smoothly developed argument is a clear link between each general point and the specific reference to outside sources. The writer's text should lead into the quoted material not just with a reference to who made the statement but also with the credentials of the source.

When you are incorporating others' ideas into your argument, you will want to lead into the borrowed material with signals that you are about to use a source to support your claim and that your source is a reliable one for your claim.

To quote or paraphrase? Generally, you should quote another's exact words when one of the following three reasons is true:

1. The precise phrasing is so elegant or apt that you wish to reproduce it intact

2. You are going to focus on the wording itself (or some part of it)

3. You could not rephrase it without significantly changing the meaning or coming close to plagiarizing

If none of those three reasons applies, you probably should paraphrase the source, remembering still to lead into the paraphrased material as you would a direct quotation and to provide appropriate documentation at the end of the paraphrase. Your readers should be able to tell precisely where another's ideas begin and end and where yours begin anew.

Consider the following passage:

> We may be a lot more creative than we realize. "Although we each have nearly limitless potential to live creatively, most people use only a small percentage of their creative gifts." (John Chaffee, *Critical Thinking, Thoughtful Writing,* 1st ed. 64.) Therefore, we should work harder to cultivate these gifts.

Does it seem awkward or clunky to you? Can you tell what causes the awkwardness? Now read the following revision:

> We may be more creative than we realize. As John Chaffee points out in his book, *Critical Thinking, Thoughtful Writing,* "[M]ost people use only a small percentage of their creative gifts" (64). Taking the time to cultivate our creativity thus sounds like a wise investment.

This revised version makes the link between general comment and specific reference smoother and more coherent. Note that the writer trims back some of the original quotation, using only what is essential. The reader is thus able to process the information more efficiently.

Chapter Summary

Argumentative writing often requires research, which is a dynamic multitask process that involves searching for background information and integrating that information effectively into your paper. By acquiring a thorough knowledge of their topics, writers argue their claims more authoritatively. Good research begins with taking a mental inventory and generating questions (writer-based, audience-based, subject-based, and purpose-based) about the topic that need answering. Purpose-based questions lead to formulating a strong thesis. A strong thesis, in turn, helps keep writers on track as they conduct research on the Internet, in the library, and with experts through well-prepared interviews.

Checklist

1. Do I take a thorough mental inventory of my topic?
2. Do I ask myself good writer-, audience-, subject-, and purpose-based questions about my topic?
3. Is my thesis strong and well-focused?

4. Do I screen my Internet and print sources to make sure they meet the criteria for accuracy, relevance, reliability, clarity, and thoroughness?

5. Do I cite sources where necessary? Use proper documentation format?

6. Do I interview experts on campus or elsewhere about my topic?

7. Do I integrate researched information into my argument smoothly and clearly?

Writing Projects

1. Keep a detailed log of all your research-based activities for your upcoming writing assignment. Include idea-generating; initial outlining; initial searches through various print and online reference works (list search engines used); more methodical and focused research, interviews, surveys. Describe your method of preparing the drafts—rough draft, first draft, and subsequent revisions.

2. Write a critical commentary on the usefulness of the Internet as a research tool. Comment on degrees of usefulness of various Web sites and different search engines, as well as the timeliness, reliability, and thoroughness of the information found in selected sites.

3. Write a comparative evaluation of print resources (as housed in your college library) versus Internet resources. Are both resources equally valuable? One more valuable than the other? Defend your assertions as fully as possible using specific examples.

Documenting Your Sources: MLA and APA Styles

> I quote others only the better to express myself.
>
> —Montaigne

Citation of Source Material: A Rationale

You must acknowledge information and ideas taken from sources not your own (commonly referred to as *outside sources*). There are two main reasons for doing so:

1. **Original ideas are a form of property known as *intellectual property*.** Published material is protected from theft by copyright law. Plagiarism, which means to pass off someone else's ideas or writings as your own, is, quite, simply, against the law. Thus, by acknowledging your sources explicitly, you protect yourself from being accused of and prosecuted for copyright violation.

2. **Acknowledging your sources provides an important service to other scholars.** People who read your essays are often interested in consulting the sources you consult to obtain more detailed information.

Which Documentation Style to Use?

The MLA style is commonly used to document sources in writing done within the humanities disciplines (for example, English and the foreign languages). The APA style is commonly used to document sources in writing done within the social sciences (for example, psychology and sociology). Clarify with your instructor whether you should follow the MLA style (see page 176), APA style (see page 193), or some other system. (For example, *Chicago*-style, based on *The Chicago Manual of Style,* 14th edition, is commonly used to document sources in writing done within history and sometimes other humanities disciplines.)

No one expects you to memorize all the details of any particular system of documentation, but you are expected to know how to look up and apply these details each time you write a paper that includes references to other sources. You are expected to know how to follow the instructions and examples given in documentation manuals and to make your citations complete and consistent with the recommendations of an established documentation style. Therefore, get into the habit of checking the proper format either in this chapter or in the other MLA or APA reference manuals listed in this chapter.

A Guide to MLA Documentation Style

The following guide presents the system for documenting sources established by the Modern Language Association (MLA). For more detailed information on how to document a wide variety of both print and electronic sources with the MLA style, see Joseph Gibaldi, *MLA Handbook for Writers of Research Papers*, 5th ed. (New York: MLA, 1999), Joseph Gibaldi, *MLA Style Manual*, 2nd ed. (New York: MLA, 1998), and the MLA Web site at <http://www.mla.org>.

Remember the following about the MLA documentation system:

1. In the body of your paper, you must (a) inform readers of the last name of the author or authors for each source as you use it in your paper, and (b) give the page number where each source appears originally in a larger work. These elements of the MLA system together form what is called the *author/page in-text citation.* Note that no page numbers are needed if your source is an online one or if it is less than a page long.

2. At the end of your paper, beginning on a new numbered page, you must list in alphabetical order by authors' last names, doubled-spaced, all the sources you refer to within your paper. This list is called *Works Cited.*

Before we look at the details of how to cite various types of sources in your text and the way to list them in your Works Cited, let us look at how to present quoted material and how to paraphrase.

Presenting Quoted Material

When quoting or paraphrasing in MLA style, mention the author's surname and indicate the page number of the passage parenthetically. List the page number (or numbers) without the "p." or "pp." abbreviation. If you are citing more than one page number, indicate them in the following way: 15–16; 140–42; 390–401.

Using Quotation Marks and Block-Style Quotation Format

Use double quotation marks around the words quoted if the passage is no more than four lines.

```
According to Charles Lamb, Shakespeare's plays "are grounded
deep in nature, so deep that the depth of them lies out of the
reach of most of us" (7).
```

The title of Lamb's essay, "On the Tragedies of Shakespeare," will appear in the Works Cited, along with more information about the publisher and date of the essay.

Because you are already using double quotation marks to indicate another author's work, substitute single quotation marks for any double quotations that appear in the original author's material.

```
The distinguished teacher of creative writing, Brenda Ueland,
insists that taking long walks is a good way to generate
thoughts: "If I do not walk one day, I seem to have on the
next what Van Gogh calls 'the meagerness'" (42).
```

The end punctuation: close inner quotation, close outer quotation, insert page number of quotation in parentheses, period.

If the passage is four lines or longer, use block-style quotation. Set the passage off as a separate paragraph and indent each line ten spaces from the margin. If you are quoting two or more paragraphs in the block quotation, indent the first line of each an additional three spaces (that is, thirteen spaces from the left margin). Quotation marks are not used with block-style quotations.

```
As Charles Lamb said of Shakespeare's characters,

      they are more the objects of meditation rather than of in-
      terest or curiosity as to their actions, so that . . . while
      we are reading any of his great criminal characters—Macbeth,
      Richard, even Iago—we think not so much of the crimes which
      they commit, as of the ambition, the aspiring spirit, the
      intellectual activity, which prompts them to over-leap those
      moral fences. (12)
```

The period at the end of a block quotation precedes the parenthetical information.

Quoting Verbatim

Do not change punctuation or spelling (for example, changing the British spelling of "colour" to color"). In rare cases in which the author or printer makes a spelling error, follow the error with the Latin word *sic* (meaning "thus") in brackets to indicate that the word appears this way in the original source.

Using an Ellipsis

Indicate omission of any *unnecessary* portion of the passage with an ellipsis—three dots separated from each other by a single space.

Original passage: "The timing, as I mentioned earlier, had to be precise."

Quoted passage, using ellipsis: "The timing . . . had to be precise."

Be certain that the words you omit from a passage do not alter its essential meaning.

Paraphrasing

A paraphrase is a rewording of an author's idea that presents it more concisely or clearly. You must cite the author as if the paraphrase were a direct quotation. Include the author's name and a page number. A paraphrase of the Charles Lamb passage quoted previously might be worded like this:

```
Shakespeare's characters, asserts Charles Lamb, are more ob-
jects of meditation to us than the perpetrators of particular
deeds. Lamb is claiming, in other words, that we regard, say,
the criminal Iago more in terms of his vaulting ambition and
zeal than his crime (12).
```

Make sure your readers will be able to tell which ideas are yours and which are the paraphrased ideas of another author. Do not, for example, merely list a name and page number at the end of a long paragraph. Readers will not be able to tell whether the paraphrase is the last sentence only or the entire paragraph being paraphrased.

Index for Citing Sources: MLA Style

Author/Page In-Text Citations

See the following pages for instruction and examples.

List of Works Cited

See the following pages for instruction and examples.

Citing Print Sources

Using Author/Page In-Text Citations

As you write the body of your paper, you will weave in references to the work of others to support or amplify the points you are making. Make sure that your readers can easily distinguish between your words and ideas, and the words and ideas of others. To create this clear distinction, refer by name to whomever you are quoting or paraphrasing. You can either include the author's name in a lead-in remark:

author's full name mentioned in lead-in remark

```
As Eliot Asinof describes the reaction to the 1919 baseball
scandal, "The American people were at first shocked, then sick-
ened" (197).
```

or you can include the author's name in parentheses with the page number after the quotation or paraphrasing:

```
In reacting to the 1919 baseball scandal, "[t]he American
people were at first shocked, then sickened" (Asinof 197).
```

author's last name mentioned in parentheses   no comma   page number

The preferable style is to use the author's name in your lead-in.

Note the following variations on this pattern, depending on the type of source you are citing and whether you are including the author's name in a lead-in remark.

1. Author Named in Lead-In Remarks.   As long as you mention the author's last name in your lead-in remarks, the only information needed in parentheses is the page number because the full citation will appear in the Works Cited at the end of your paper.

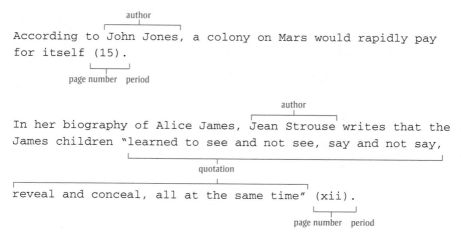

When citing a piece from an anthology or edited volume, cite the name of the author of the piece to which you are referring, not the editor or editors of the anthology.

2. Author Not Named in Lead-In Remarks.   If you do not name the author as you lead into a quotation or paraphrase, place the author's name in parentheses along with the page number of the source.

```
No one person in 1919 knew all of the factors that contributed
to The Black Sox Scandal or could tell the whole story
(Asinof 11).
```
author's last name   no comma   page number

3. Two or More Authors.   If you are citing a work that has two or three authors, mention all their names in your lead-in remarks or in parentheses after the reference.

```
Critical reading involves going beyond simple decoding of the
literal meanings of the written word (Cooley and Powell 3).
```
authors' last names   no comma   page number

If you are citing a work with four or more authors, state the first author's last name and then write "et al." (a Latin phrase meaning "and others").

4. *Multiple Works by the Same Author.* If you are referring to more than one work by the same author, refer to the work's title in your lead-in remarks or include a short form of the title in parentheses, along with the page number.

> In *Teaching a Stone to Talk,* Dillard describes the drama of
> the moon blocking the sun during a total eclipse by saying,
> "It did not look like the moon. It was enormous and
> black. . . . It looked like a lens cover, or the lid of a pot.
> It materialized out of thin air—black, and flat, and sliding,
> outlined in flame" (94).
>   └─┬─┘
>   page number

> One observer described the mystery of the eclipse by saying,
> "If I had not read that it was the moon, I could have seen the
> sight a hundred times and never thought of the moon
> once" (Dillard, *Teaching* 94).
>   └──────────────┬──────────────┘
>   author abbreviated title page number

5. *Works with Anonymous or Corporate Authorship.* Cite works that name no author or editor as follows:

> According to the Consumer Protection Agency, the number of car
> owners who report being cheated by dishonest mechanics has
> dropped by 15 percent in 2000 (7).

6. *Internet Sources.* For most electronic sources, it is not possible to provide a page number in the in-text citation. Instead, check to see if an author's name is given and if there are numbered paragraphs or other text divisions. If so, use these pieces of information in place of page numbers in your in-text citation.

> Some universities have been questioning their use of Aztec
> signs and symbols and the use of mascots like "Monty
> Montezuma" (Weber, par. 6).
>   └───────────┬───────────┘
>   author numbered paragraph

Preparing the MLA List of Works Cited

Definition. The list of Works Cited is an alphabetical listing of all the sources cited or paraphrased or referred to in a paper. The list of Works Cited does not include additional readings, no matter how relevant; however, your instructor may ask you to prepare a separate list of additional readings.

Purpose. The main purpose of the list of Works Cited is to assist readers who wish to obtain more information about the topic by consulting the same sources you have. A secondary purpose is to give readers an opportunity to double-check the accuracy and appropriateness of your quotations and paraphrases. It is possible to quote someone accurately but in a way that misrepresents that author's original intentions—of course, not something you intend to do but may accidentally do.

General Procedure

1. Begin the list of Works Cited on a separate page.

2. Title the page Works Cited and center the heading.

3. List everything alphabetically by author's surname. List the author's surname first. If a work has more than one author, alphabetize the entry according to the surname of the author listed first. If no author is listed, enter the title alphabetically. Titles of books and pamphlets are underscored. Include the city of publication, the abbreviated name of the publisher, and the date of publication.

4. Begin each entry at the left margin. If an entry runs longer than one line, those subsequent lines are indented five spaces.

In the following examples and in the sample student paper beginning on page 186, note the MLA style for citing various types of sources in the list of Works Cited.

Citing Print Sources

1. Single-author Book or Pamphlet

Jones, John. <u>Colonizing Mars</u>. New York: Far Out, 2002.

2. Book with More than One Author

Witt, Linda, Karen M. Paget, and Glenna Matthews. <u>Running as a Woman: Gender and Power in American Politics</u>. New York: Free, 1994.

When more than three authors, use the name of the first author and follow it with "et al."

Johnson, Eric, et al. <u>Smart Shopping</u>. Boston: Lifestyle, 1999.

3. Chapter from a Book:

Blair, John. "The Anglo-Saxon Period." <u>The Oxford History of Britain</u>. Ed. Kenneth O. Morgan. New York: Oxford UP, 1988. 60-119.

4. Government Document

Author Byline Given:

Elkouri, Frank, and Edna Asper. <u>Resolving Drug Issues</u>. Washington: Bureau of National Affairs, 1993.

No Author Byline Given:

United States Department of Health and Human Services. <u>Summary Report of the Graduate Medical Educational National Advisory Committee</u>. Washington: GPO, Apr. 1980.

5. Article from a Periodical

Magazine:

Singer, Mark. "God and Football." <u>New Yorker</u> 25 Sept. 2000: 38-42.

Academic Journal:

Gibson, Ann. "Universality and Difference in Women's Abstract Painting." <u>Yale Journal of Criticism</u> 8 (Spring 1995): 103-32.

Newspaper:

Revkin, Andrew C. "A West African Monkey is Extinct, Scientists Say." <u>New York Times</u> 12 Sept. 2000: A20.

Letter to the Editor:

Kenny, Shirley Strum. "The Useless SAT." Letter. <u>New York Times</u> 19 Mar. 2001: A22.

Unsigned Editorial:

"Flawed Election in Uganda." Editorial. <u>New York Times</u> 16 Mar. 2001: A20.

6. Book Review

Titled Review of a Work

Dowd, Maureen. "The Man in White." Rev. of <u>Hooking Up</u>, by Tom Wolfe. <u>New York Times Book Review</u> 5 Nov. 2000: 6.

Untitled Review of a Work

Warren, Charles. Rev. of <u>The Material Ghost: Films and Their Medium</u>. <u>Georgia Review</u> 54 (Spring 2000): 170-74.

Citing Nonprint Sources

7. Interviews

Personal Interview:

```
Sanders, Dr. Julia. Personal interview. 15 Oct. 2001.
```

Telephone Interview:

```
Ellis, Mark. Telephone interview. 17 Oct. 2001.
```

8. Correspondence

```
Beaumont, Clyde. Letter [or E-mail message] to author.
20 Oct. 2001.
```

If a paper letter is not dated, use the date of the postmark. E-mail messages are dated automatically.

9. Web Pages

Treat sources from the Internet just as you do print sources. Cite the author and the title of the work, publication data such as journal names and volume or issue numbers, and the publication date. In addition, however, you need to give the date the site was last updated (if different from the publication date), the date you accessed the site, and the Web address. The reason for the latter information is that Web sites sometimes disappear or the addresses change.

Periodical Article from Web Page:

```
Sharlet, Jeff. "A Philosopher's Call to End All Paradigms."
Chronicle of Higher Education, Sept. 15, 2000. <http://
chronicle.com-free/v47/i03/03a01801.htm>
Accessed June 24, 2001. Site last updated June 22, 2001.
```

Original Web Page Article:

```
Williams, Anne D. "Jigsaw Puzzles: Not Just for Children Any-
more" (1994) <http://ans.uwaterloo.ca/~museum/puzzles/ jig-
saw/essay.html> Accessed May 28, 2001. Last update
Dec. 7, 2000.
```

Article from a Listserver:

```
"NASA Chief Predicts Scientific Tsunami" <Metanews@meta-list.org>
Oct. 20, 2000.
```

Because listserves are, by definition, accessible only to members of the list, direct citations to them are of extremely limited value. Rather than citing a listserve, the writer should locate any article cited therein at its proper web address, which is accessible to anyone with a computer. Thus, for instance, though the article "NASA Chief Predicts Scientific Tsunami" was originally discovered on the Metanews listserv, it should be cited as follows:

<http://www.space.com/business/technology/business/goldin_
tsunami_001011.htm> Accessed June 23, 2001; updated
June 23, 2001.

10. Television Program:

CNN Evening News. Narr. Bernard Shaw. CNN. 8 Nov. 2000.

11. Recordings

Audiocassette:

Churchill, Winston S. The Great Republic. Audiocassette. Random House Audiobooks, 1998. #RH850.

Videocassette:

Witness. Dir. Peter Weir. Perf. Harrison Ford and Kelly
McGillis. Videocassette. Paramount Pictures, 1985.
Paramount #1736.

Compact Disc:

Von Bingen, Hildegard. Canticles of Ecstasy. Perf. Sequentia.
Deutsche Harmonia Mundi, 1994. #D106292.

When the recording medium is a CD-ROM, that fact is not stated in the entry. It is assumed that the sound recording is made on a CD-ROM unless another medium is indicated.

Sample Student Paper: MLA Documentation Format

1 inch left and right margins

1/2 inch from top of page

Gibson 1

Running head: student name + page number

Name, course, instructor, date; double-spaced

Daniela Gibson

Argumentation

Professor Billings

May 16, 2001

Why We Should Punish

Title, centered

2 spaces between title and first line of text

The caning of a young American in Singapore in 1994 for minor vandalism has added new fuel to a centuries-old debate about proper forms of punishment. Logic demands, however, that prior to the decision of the proper form of punishment, we must decide on the proper aim or purpose of punishment. The views on the proper aim of punishment seem to vary widely. Writers such as Barbara Wootton and H. L. A. Hart believe that the proper aim of punishment is the rehabilitation of the criminal. Others, in contrast, argue for retribution as the proper aim of punishment. Criminal Justice professor Graeme Newman, for example, writes, "Punishment must, above all else, be painful" (40). A third view of the proper purpose of punishment is deterrence, "removing the criminal from activity and serving as a caution to would-be-criminals" (Rottenberg 41). One recently profiled advocate of punishment as deterrence is Joe Arpaio, sheriff of Maricopa County, Arizona (Phoenix area). According to Arpaio, "Jail should be about punishment and the punishment should be so unpleasant that no one who experienced it would even want to go through it again" (Graham 61).

Summary of source

Paraphrased sources; quotation marks not used

Page number reference all that is needed since author mentioned in the discussion

In the following, I would like to posit that the overall function of punishment is to enforce and protect the moral values of a society, a function that appears to be incompatible with the idea of retribution and only partly compatible with the ideas of deterrence and rehabilitation.

Gibson 2

The punishment and the moral values of a society are inseparably linked by the laws of that society. Our laws always reflect and are based on our core values. Most societies recognize the right to life as a core value. In the case of our American society, core values are also the ownership of property and the freedom of speech. Consequently, America has laws that protect private property and the freedom of speech. Theft is against the law and so is violation of the freedom of speech. Furthermore, since these laws are based on values, and values always imply a right and wrong, a trespassing of these laws must have consequences that reflect and uphold these moral judgments. Walter Berns addresses this interdependence between morality and punishment when he writes the following about the death penalty:

> [It] serves to remind us of the majesty of the moral order that is embodied in our law and of the terrible consequences of its breach. . . . The criminal law must be made awful, by which I mean awe-inspiring, or commanding "profound respect or reverential fear." It must remind us of the moral order by which alone we can live as human beings. (12)

Block-style quotation indented ten spaces from margin; double-spaced; no quotation marks used, except for those that appear in the original source, such as in the sixth sentence

Although I do not necessarily agree with the need for the death penalty and "reverential fear," Berns's observation is significant: Punishment, indeed, must always "remind us of the moral order" by which we live, for if the breaking of the law would have no consequences, our moral values would be void (85). If, for example, the violation of the freedom of speech had no consequences, such a violation could take place again and again. But then, it could hardly be called a value since we would not seem to care about it and would not protect it.

Gibson 3

Those in favor of retribution as the aim of punishment agree that a criminal act must have legal consequences for the criminal. Despite this very broad
similarity between retribution and the protection of
moral values, retribution appears impractical and
morally wrong in the context of the American value
system. Advocates of retribution often refer to Kant,
who writes that the principle for legal justice is
"[n]one other than the principle of equality . . . any
undeserved evil that you inflict on someone else among
the people is one that you do to yourself. . . . Only
the law of retribution can determine exactly the kind
and degree of punishment" (qtd. in Berns 18). Such a
view, however, is impracticable, for who would rape a
rapist (and how) for retribution of the crime? In addition to these questions, it seems hardly possible
that the loss of one individual can truly be
retributed by the execution of the murderer.

Yet retribution is precisely the major motive behind capital punishment. The danger with this extreme
form of punishment is irreversible miscarriage of justice, as when an innocent man or woman is sentenced to
death (Berlow) or when racist lawyers eliminate
Blacks, Hispanics, and other racial minorities as potential jurors during jury selection—which was shown
to be the case with Nevada death-row inmate Thomas
Nevius (Amnesty International).

But more importantly, retribution as the goal of
punishment is immoral, at least in the context of our
value system. Mark Costanzo, chair of the Department
of Social Psychology at Claremont McKenna College,
correctly identifies that "[o]ur efforts to mitigate
punishments arise out of the recognition that we must
not sink to the level of the criminal; raping a rapist
would debase us, weaken our moral solidarity, and undermine the moral authority of the state" (23). If we
punish via retribution, the danger is that we would
focus too narrowly on one crime and in doing so would

Reference to a
source quoted
by another
author

References to
Internet
sources

lose sight of the moral code that makes the crime a crime. In other words, the crime would move to the foreground and would overshadow the moral authority that it violates. For example, if someone hits my car, I could exercise the punishment of retribution by hitting that person's car in return. However, doing so fails not only to fix my car but also to ensure me that there is a moral code and its representative law that will protect me from similar instances in the future. Hence, retribution undermines the very same moral law that punishment is supposed to uphold.

In contrast to retribution, which must be rejected as the proper aim of punishment on moral and practical grounds, deterrence appears to be partly compatible with the upholding of moral values. Ernest van den Haag, a retired professor of Jurisprudence, expresses the views of deterrence advocates when he writes that "[h]arsher penalties are more deterrent than milder ones" (114). In his explanation, he draws an analogy to everyday life situations:

> All other things equal, we penalize our
> children, our friends, or our business
> partners the more harshly the more we feel
> we must deter them and others in the
> future from a wrong they have done. Social
> life would not be possible if we did not
> believe that we can attract people to ac-
> tions we desire by giving them incentives,
> and deter them from actions we do not de-
> sire by disincentives. (115)

Van den Haag's analogy works—up to a certain point. Clearly, if we care about our values, we need to protect them, and one way of doing so is to punish offenders as a means of deterrence. And in some situations, deterrence might be the only way of communi-

Gibson 5

cating what is right and wrong. I remember, for example, when I was three years old, I took doll clothing home from preschool. I did so because I liked to play with it more at home, and I did not understand that it was not mine. When my parents found out, they did the right thing: They told me if I ever did that again, I could no longer play with my dolls. In that situation deterrence was necessary since I was too young to understand the concept of private property and its proper relationship to right and wrong; I understood, however, that I wanted to play with my dolls and that I could no longer do so if I would take doll clothing home again.

There is a danger, however, in viewing deterrence as the only proper aim of punishment: it could disconnect that what is feared from what is morally bad, what is desired from what is morally good. The <u>Oxford English Dictionary</u> defines deterrence as "deterring or preventing by fear." If I, when I was old enough to grasp the meaning of right and wrong beyond immediate desires, would have not been taught why it is wrong to take what is not mine, but instead would have been continuously motivated by fear, I could have never developed a deep respect for moral values. Rather, I would have learned to associate fear with my parents' knowledge of my "wrongdoing," but not with the wrongdoing itself. Thus, I would have most likely sought to avoid my parents' knowledge or that of any other authority but not to avoid the deed itself. I believe that this example is generally applicable to deterrence as the main purpose of punishment: Criminals and potential criminals would be taught not that their acts were wrong on moral grounds, but that they should seek to avoid conflicts with authority. But such an attitude would instill in them a distrust for the laws rather than an understanding and respect for the values that they represent.

Another view of punishment is rehabilitation. Rehabilitation in the sense of education seems compatible with and even part of our value system. However, we need to ensure that rehabilitation qua education is not conflicting with other essential values. Costanzo points to the importance that background and circumstances can play in a crime (27). For example, it would seem naïve to expect from a young man proper law-abiding behavior if that man had suffered from "routine beatings from an abusive father" and "grew up in a poverty-ridden, gang-infested neighborhood and received very little in the way of parental guidance or supervision" (31). If that man had committed a crime, rehabilitation that includes a positive alternative to the values or lack thereof of his childhood upbringing seems appropriate. It might not only protect our societal values by preventing further criminal acts by this young man, if the rehabilitation was successful, but it would also reinforce our values, for the effort of rehabilitation shows that we are taking these values seriously and are deeply caring about them.

Yet, as commendable as such rehabilitation efforts are, we cannot allow them to replace other important values such as responsibility and justice. By rationalizing a criminal behavior with the criminal's disadvantageous upbringing, we are in danger of denying individual responsibility, a core value of our society. Further, by granting college loans and "grants," books, "compassion and understanding," to criminals, as one former prisoner demands, we would also commit injustice (Stratton 67). For how could we explain this special treatment to all those who have abided by the law, some even despite their background, but do not enjoy grants, loans, etc.? Because these aims are potentially in conflict with each other and because our highest responsibility is to defend the values of our society, rehabilitation can be an integral part of punishment, but it should never replace punishment.

The discourse about the proper aim of punishment is indeed complex. But exactly because of this complexity, we need to approach the question of punishment step by step. It would be fatal to jump to the question of the proper forms of punishment before the

Gibson 7

question of the proper aim of punishment has been settled. It is absolutely mandatory that the question of
the proper aim of punishment is addressed a priori.
With respect to its answer, if the upholding of the
moral values of a society is any indicator, we should
dismiss retribution, and very cautiously consider deterrence and rehabilitation—but by no means should we
draw any hasty conclusions.

Works Cited

Amnesty International. "Serious Allegations of Racism
      and Injustice in Nevada Death Penalty Case." 6
      April 2001. 30 April 2001 <www.amnesty.org>.
Berlow, Alan. "The Wrong Man." <u>Atlantic</u> Nov. 1999. 6
      Apr. 2001 <www.theatlantic.com/issues/99nov/
      9911wrongman.htm>.
Berns, Walter. <u>For Capital Punishment</u>. New York: Ba-
      sic, 1991.
Costanzo, Mark. <u>Just Revenge</u>. New York: St.
      Martin's, 1997.
"Deterrence." <u>Oxford English Dictionary</u>. OED 2 on CD-
      ROM. Version 1.13 Oxford: OUP, 1994.
Graham, Barry. "Star of Justice: On the Job with Amer-
      ica's Toughest Sheriff." <u>Harper's Magazine</u> Apr.
      2001: 59-68.
Hart, H. L. A. <u>Law, Liberty, and Morality</u>. Stanford:
      Stanford UP, 1963.
Newman, Graeme R. <u>Just and Painful: A Case for Corpo-
      real Punishment of Criminals</u>. London:
      Macmillan, 1983.
Rottenberg, Annette T., ed. <u>Elements of Argument</u>. 6th
      ed. New York: Bedford/St. Martin's, 2000. 569.
Stratton, Richard. "Even Prisoners Must Hope."
      <u>Newsweek</u> 17 Oct. 1994: 67.
van den Haag, Ernest. <u>The Death Penalty Pro and Con: A
      Debate</u>. New York: Plenum, 1983.
Wootton, Barbara. <u>Crime and Penal Policy</u>. London:
      Allen & Unwin, 1978.

Double space
between title
and first entry

Second and
subsequent
lines indented

A Guide to APA Documentation Format

The following guide presents the system for documenting sources established by the American Psychological Association (APA). For more detailed information on how to document a wide variety of sources, both print and electronic, see the *Publication Manual of the American Psychological Association,* 5th ed. (Washington, DC: APA, 2001) and the APA *Publication Manual* at <http://www.apa.org/journals/webref.html>.

Remember the following about the APA documentation system:

1. In the body of your paper, you must (a) inform readers of the last name of the author or authors for each source as you use it in your paper, and (b) give the year of publication. These elements of the APA system together form what is called the *author/year in-text citation.*

2. At the end of your paper, beginning on a new numbered page, you must list in alphabetical order by authors' last names, double-spaced, all the sources you refer to within your paper. This list is called *References.*

Before we look at the details of how to cite the various types of sources in your text and how to list them in your References, let us look at how to present quoted material and how to paraphrase.

Presenting Quoted Material

When quoting or paraphrasing in APA style, indicate the surnames of each author, together with the year the source was published.

```
According to Freud (1900) . . .
```

At the end of the quoted or paraphrased passage, indicate only the page number, preceded by the abbreviation for page ("p.") or pages ("pp.") (the abbreviation "pg." is not standard).

Using Quotation Marks and Block-Style Quotation Format

Use double quotation marks around the words quoted if the passage is forty words long or less.

```
Freud (1900) notes that "in the psychic life there exist re-
pressed wishes" (p. 288).
```

This passage is from *The Interpretation of Dreams,* but it is not necessary to put that information at the end of the quotation because it will appear in the References, along with other relevant publication information.

Because you are already using double quotation marks to indicate another author's work, substitute single quotation marks for double quotations that appear in the original author's material.

```
Henry Petroski (1992) reports that in 1900 "an American patent
was issued to Cornelius Brosnan . . . for a 'paper clip' which
has been regarded in the industry as the 'first successful bent
wire paper clip'" (pp. 62-63).
```

If the passage is more than forty words long, use block-style quotation. Set the passage off as a separate paragraph and indent each line five spaces from the margin. If you are quoting two or more paragraphs in the block quotation, indent the first line of each new paragraph an additional five spaces (that is, ten spaces from the left margin). Quotation marks are not used with block-style quotations.

```
What we recollect of the dream, and what we subject to our
methods of interpretation, is, in the first place, mutilated by
the unfaithfulness of our memory, which seems quite peculiarly
incapable of retaining dreams, and which may have omitted pre-
cisely the most significant parts of their content. (p. 470)
```

This passage is also from *The Interpretation of Dreams.*

Quoting Verbatim

Always double-check to ensure that you have quoted the passage accurately. Do not change punctuation or spelling (for example, changing the British spelling of "colour" to "color"). In rare cases in which the author or printer makes a spelling error, follow the word with the Latin word *sic* (meaning "thus") in brackets to indicate that the word appears this way in the original source.

Using an Ellipsis

Indicate omission of any *unnecessary* portion of the passage with an ellipsis—three dots separated from each other by a single space.

Original passage: According to Clifford Geertz (1973), "We are, in sum, incomplete or unfinished animals who complete or finish ourselves through culture" (p. 49).

Quoted passage, using ellipsis: According to Clifford Geertz (1973), "We are . . . incomplete or unfinished animals who complete or finish ourselves through culture" (p. 49).

Always check to make sure that the ellipsis does not distort the original intention of the author.

Paraphrasing

A paraphrase is a rewording of an author's idea that presents it more concisely or clearly. You must cite the author as if the paraphrase were a direct quotation. Include the author's name and the year of publication. Although APA style does not require that a page number be given with a paraphrase, it suggests that you do so. A paraphrase of the Clifford Geertz passage quoted previously might be worded like this:

```
According to Geertz (1973), humans are incomplete animals who
reach completeness through culture (p. 49).
```

Make sure your readers will be able to tell which ideas are your own and which are the paraphrased ideas of another author. Do not, for example, merely list a name and page number at the end of a long paragraph. Readers will not be able to tell whether the paraphrase is the last sentence only or the entire paragraph.

Index for Citing Sources: APA Style

Author/Year In-Text Citations

See the following pages for instructions and examples.

List of References

See the following pages for instructions and examples.

Citing Print Sources

Using Author/Year In-Text Citations

Introduce outside information smoothly and explicitly so that readers will be able to distinguish between your ideas and the outside source authors' ideas. You provide this clear distinction by referring by name to whomever you are quoting or paraphrasing, as in the following examples.

1. Author Named in Lead-In Remarks

author's full name mentioned in lead-in remark

```
According to Carolyn Heilbrun (1979), womanhood must be rein-
vented (p. 29).
```

So long as you mention the author's last name, the only other necessary information is the page number because the full citation will appear in the References.

2. Author Not Named in Lead-In Remarks

```
One feminist scholar asserts that womanhood must be invented
(Heilbrun, 1979, p. 29).
```

author's last name   date   page number

comma

3. Two or More Authors

authors listed alphabetically separated by commas   date in parens

```
Colombo, Cullen, and Lisle (2001) emphasize that critical
thinking involves cultivating the ability to imagine and the
curiosity to question one's own point of view (p. 2).
```

4. Multiple Works by the Same Author

date followed by letter to indicate the different works

Jones (1998b, p. 130) considers colonization of space a vital
step in human evolution. He even argues that our survivability
as a species depends on it (1998a, pp. 47-51).

date followed by letter to indicate the different works

The letters *a* and *b* following the date indicate the chronological order of publication; thus, Jones's 1998b publication was published later in the year than her 1998a publication. Works by more than one author published in different years are indicated the same way as different authors: (Jones, 1999); (Jones, 2001). When citing two or more different authors sharing the same surname, be sure to include each author's initials: (A. Jones, 1957; C. Jones, 2001).

5. Works with Anonymous or Corporate Authorship

corporate authorship

According to the Consumer Protection Agency (2001), the number
of car owners reported being cheated by dishonest mechanics
dropped 15% in 2000 (p. 7).

6. Internet Sources

Page from a Web site:

According to the Coalition for Affordable and Reliable Energy
(2001), coal fuels more than half the country's electricity
(www.CAREenergy.com).

Web site at end of sentence

Article from an Online Periodical:

author of online article

Farmer (2001) envisions a memory chip that, when implanted,
will give humans the ability to process information one
hundred times faster and more efficiently (www.cyberzine.com/
July 2001).

online periodical

Posting from an Online Forum:

Dr. Charles Taylor (2001), a biologist, claims in an online
forum that human cloning will pose no dangers to cloned

```
person's senses of selfhood because "the mind and personality
can never be cloned" (www.medforum.com).
```

online forum

Note that you do not need to include more than the author's name and the date when citing online sources. Information such as Web addresses will appear in the References.

Preparing the APA List of References

Definition.   The list of References is an alphabetical listing of all the sources cited or paraphrased or referred to in a paper. The list of References does not include additional or recommended readings, no matter how relevant; however, your instructor may ask you to prepare a separate list of supplemental readings.

Purpose.   The main purpose of the list of References is to assist readers who wish to obtain more information about the topic by consulting the same sources you have. A secondary purpose is to give readers an opportunity to double-check the accuracy and appropriateness of your quotations and paraphrases. It is possible to quote someone accurately but in a way that misrepresents that author's original intentions—of course, not something you intend to do but may accidentally do.

General Procedure

1. Begin the list of References on a separate page

2. Title the page References and center the heading.

3. List everything alphabetically by author surname. List the author's surname first, followed by initials. Authors' or editors' full names are not given in APA format. If the work has more than one author, alphabetize according to the surname of the author listed first. If no author is listed, enter the title alphabetically. List the year of publication in parentheses after the authors' names. Titles of books or names of periodicals are italicized; titles of articles use neither italics nor quotation marks. Capitalize only the first word of the title.

4. Begin the first line of each entry flush with the left margin; turnover lines are indented five spaces.

In the following examples and in the sample student paper beginning on page 202, note the APA style for citing various types of sources in the list of References.

Citing Print Sources

1. Single-author Book or Pamphlet

Boorstin, D. J. (1987). *Hidden history.* New York: Harper
     & Row.

2. Book with More than One Author

Witt, L., Paget, K. & Matthews, G. (1994). *Running as a woman:*
     gender and power in american politics. New York: Free
     Press.

In APA format, all authors must be listed in the References. Do not use "et al." to represent authors' names.

3. Chapter from a Book

Blair, J. (1988). The Anglo-Saxon period. In K. O. Morgan
     (Ed.), *The Oxford history of Britain,* (pp. 60-119). New
     York: Oxford University Press.

4. Article from a Periodical

Magazine:

Singer, M. (2000, Sept. 25). God and football. *The New Yorker,*
     76, 38-42.

Academic Journal:

Gibson, A. (1995, Spring). Universality and difference in
     women's abstract painting. *The Yale Journal of Criticism,*
     8, 103-132.

Newspaper:

Revkin, A. C. (2000, Sept. 12). A West African monkey is ex-
     tinct, scientists say. *The New York Times,* p. A20.

Letter to the Editor:

Kenny, S. S. (2001, March 19). The useless SAT. [Letter to the
     editor]. *The New York Times,* p. A22.

Unsigned Editorial:

Flawed election in Uganda. (2001, March 16). Editorial. *The*
     New York Times, p. A20.

5. Book Review

Titled Review of Work:

Dowd, M. (2000, Nov. 5). The man in white. [Review of the book
     Hooking up]. *The New York Times Book Review,* p. 6.

Untitled Review of Work:

> Warren, C. (2000, Spring). [Review of the book *The material*
>   *ghost: films and their medium*]. *The Georgia Review, 54,*
>   170-174.

6. Government Document

Author Byline Given:

> Elkouri, F., and Asper, E. (1993). *Resolving drug issues.*
>   Washington, DC: Bureau of National Affairs.

No Author Byline Given

> United States Department of Health and Human Services. (1980,
>   April). *Summary report of the Graduate Medical*
>   *Educational National Advisory Committee.* Washington, DC:
>   U.S. Government Printing Office.

7. Do not include nonprint sources (interviews, correspondence) in references.

8. Web Pages

Treat sources from the Internet just as you do print sources. Cite the author and the title of the work, publication data such as journal names and volume or issue numbers, and the publication date. In addition, however, you need to give the date the site was last updated (if different from the publication date), the date you accessed the site, and the Web address. The reason for the latter information is that Web sites sometimes disappear or the addresses change.

Periodical Article from Web Page:

> Sharlet, J. (2000 Sept. 15). A philosopher's call to end all
>   paradigms. *The Chronicle of Higher Education.* Retrieved
>   <date>, from: http://chronicle.com/cgi2-bin/printable.cgi

Original Web Page Article:

> Williams, A. D. (1994). Jigsaw puzzles: not just for children
>   anymore. www.ahc.uwaterloo.ca/~museum/puzzles/jigsaw/
>   essay.html

Article from a Listserver:

> NASA chief predicts scientific tsunami (2000). metanews@meta-
>   list.org Oct. 20.

9. Television Program

Turner Broadcasting. (2000, November 8). *CNN evening news.* Atlanta: Cable News Network.

10. Recordings

Audiocassette:

Churchill, Winston S. (Speaker). (1998). *The great republic.* (Audiocassette, Random House Audiobooks #RH 850). New York: Random House.

Videocassette:

Weir, P. (Director). (1985). *Witness.* [Videocassette, Paramount #1736]. Los Angeles: Paramount Pictures.

Compact Disc:

Von Bingen, H. (1994). O choruscans stellarum. [Recorded by Sequentia]. On *Canticles of Ecstasy* [CD]. <city>: Deutsche Harmonia Mundi.

Sample Student Paper: APA Documentation Format

Child Molestation 1   *Running head: short title + page number*

1 inch margins left and right

Jarrett Green

Argumentation

Professor Billings

May 16, 2001

Name, course, instructor, date; double-spaced

Child Molestation: Anything but Your Typical Crime   *Title, centered*

2 spaces between title and first line of text

Give author's name, year, page number if author not mentioned in the sentence

"I've got these urges, and I can't control myself" (Friedman, 1991, p. 2). Although these words come from the mouth of one particular child molester, they easily could have been uttered by thousands of others. Child molesters come in all shapes and sizes, and live in all types of communities—from small farming towns to large metropolitan cities. All child molesters, however, have one very important trait in common: They have an intense sexual fixation with or attraction to children. What makes this trait so dangerous is that it causes immense damage and, at times, destruction to the lives of countless innocent children. Child molestation, unlike any other illegal or stigmatized act, directly attacks our nation's youth—our nation's future. Most states continue to simply imprison child molesters. Some states, on the other hand, have implemented minimal publicity programs that give communities access to information on released child molesters.

The question of how to punish or deal with child molesters is not an easy one. I, however, believe that attaining a proper understanding of the nature of this crime makes its solution crystal clear. Child molesta-

Child Molestation 2

tion is unlike any other crime[1] for two reasons: (1) It has been established to be a physiological and psychological disease, and (2) it requires secrecy and identity concealment. This exceptional combination requires that we treat molesters differently than we treat burglars and car-jackers. More specifically, it requires that we *publicize*[2] child molesters, not to *shame* or *embarrass* them, but to *disable* them.

Child molestation is anything but a typical crime. In fact, it has been established as a physiological and psychological disease. Doctor Kieran Sullivan, Ph.D., an Associate Professor in the Santa Clara University Psychology Department, explains that pedophilia (or the disorder from which child molesters suffer) "is officially recognized as a diagnostic mental disorder by the *DSM IV,* the psychiatrist's bible" (K. Sullivan, personal interview, March 10, 2001). More importantly, Sullivan explains that child molestation is

> the only crime that is actually a psychological disorder. Although we consider serial killers to be "insane," their crime is not a direct manifestation of a physiological/psychological disease. Child molesters, on the other hand, have an overwhelming inner compulsion to engage in sexual interaction with children. It is an ever-present disease that drives them and

Block style quotations (of more than 40 words) are indented 5 spaces from margin and double-spaced

1 If a crime exists that I am presently unaware of that satisfies each of the two stated criteria, it would also be subject to *publicity* as a "punishment."

2 I acknowledge that this use of *publicize* is atypical; however, the need for such a use will become clear later in this paper. Also later in this paper, I will specify the exact manner in which child molesters will be publicized.

Child Molestation 3

controls them. This is what makes child molesters so unique. (K. Sullivan, personal interview, April 10, 2001)

Sharon Rice is a psychiatric nurse who currently
works in the Ohio Veteran's Administration Outpatient
Clinic. She has counseled hundreds of child molesters
throughout her career, both in one-on-one and group
settings. Rice claims that child molesters are

inflicted with a horrible disease. Nearly all of
the child molesters claim that if they are released, they will be unable to not molest
again. Most of them think that pedophilia
should be legalized, as they believe that they
are just giving children love and care. The
others, though, believe their behavior is destructive and harmful toward children—and they
feel incredible guilt and depression for what
they have done. When asked whether or not they
believe they could overcome their feelings if
released, most believed that they could not.
They believed their yearning would eventually
be too powerful for them to control. Child molestation is really a disease that overpowers
the will of the individual. (S. Rice, telephone
interview, April 16, 2001)

Child molestation is obviously a unique crime.
The child molester suffers from a disease that overpowers any and all restrictions (such as society's
ethical standards or the molester's personal

guilt). His[3] external acts are dominated by a physiological and psychological disorder.

Because child molestation is a physiological and
psychological disease, even the harshest prison time
usually fails in deterring the molester from recidi-
vating. The overall rates of recidivism, although very
difficult to determine, are extremely high. One examination, which studied 197 convicted male child molesters, found that 42% of the men were reconvicted
within the next 31 years (Hanson, Steffy, & Gauthier,
1993, p. 646). The study offers the following important clarification:

> Although reconviction rates were used as the
> recidivism criteria in this study, it is likely
> that reconviction rates underestimate the rate
> of reoffending. It is widely recognized that
> only a fraction of the sexual offenses against
> children result in the offender being
> convicted. Consequently, it is possible that
> all of the men in our study could have reof-
> fended but that only about one half got caught.
> (p. 650).

Mary Sue Barone is the Assistant Prosecuting Attorney for the Criminal Division of the Wood County
District in the state of Ohio. During her years as a
prosecuting attorney she has prosecuted nearly every
offense in the book, including numerous child molestation cases. Barone (telephone interview, April 16,
2001) claims that "recidivism rates of child molestation are consistently the highest of any crime,
including drug abuse. It is a disease that plagues a

---

[3]Throughout this paper, I intentionally use the male pronoun in
referring to child molesters since the great majority of child
molesters are male.

Child Molestation 5

child molester for his entire life." When asked whether prison is the proper solution for such a "disease," she replied, "We live in a society of politics. Families and society want to see the child molester locked up. Unfortunately, prison time doesn't seem to do much good the moment the child molester is released." I cannot stress this point enough: Child molestation is a disease—it is a sickness. Locking someone up for six to eight months is not going to suppress the disease. Even if the prison time is harsh, the child molester reenters society with a physiological and psychological urge that remains unimpeded. Thus, the prison's lesson goes in one ear, and the disease throws it out the other. Child molestation is not a typical crime.

The second reason child molestation is an atypical crime is due to the fact that it is inherently dependent on secrecy and identity concealment. Rarely are child molesters strangers who abuse random children at the playground. In nearly all cases, the child molester is the little league coach, the day-care assistant, the family friend, or the next-door neighbor. Everybody assumes that he is a harmless, good person. The child molester conceals his true self. He hides his destructive fantasies and intentions so that he can earn the trust of the child's parents. Having gained the trust of others, he commits the crime. But his crime is dependent on secrecy and concealment of his true identity.

Our current system of throwing child molesters in prison only makes the process by which they conceal their identities easier. We catch child molesters after they have *secretly* damaged or ruined the lives of countless children. Next we *hide* them in prison cells for the length of their terms and then toss them back *without warning* into the world of children. Although mere prison time is undoubtedly a "feel-good" solution, it is really no authentic solution at all.

Child molesters come out of prison and are far too
easily able to reestablish their concealed identities.
They once again hide their molestating selves and,
once again, use this concealment to poison and destroy
the lives of innocent children.

Because child molestation is a truly unique crime
(since it is a *disease* that undermines prison's function as a deterrent *and* it is inherently dependent on
identity concealment), it screams for alternative
state reaction, namely, publicity. Because child molestation is a disease that plagues child molesters,
we cannot release them with the expectation that they
will never molest again. Consequently, we must do all
that we can to decrease the ease by which the disease
controls child molesters' lives and damages children's
lives. Publicity is this road block. It will make it
difficult for child molesters to act on hidden dangerous impulses, since others will be aware of their disease. It will prevent them from succeeding in
manipulatively gaining parents' trust and children's
friendships so as to satisfy their harmful desires.

If we care about the lives of our children, we
must make it as difficult as possible for child molesters to satisfy their harmful impulses through identity concealment. We must prevent them from deceiving
the world into trusting them. We must rob them of the
tools used to molest children: secrecy and identity
concealment. As I explained before, child molesters do
not just molest random kids while in line for the
movies. We can and must obstruct such development of
loyalty and trust by *publicizing* child molesters. Each
child molester, on release from prison, should be publicized by a combination of four "awareness" tactics.
First, newspapers should publish the names and photographs of child molesters as they reenter society.
Second, local television news programs should warn
communities of the release of child molesters. News
programs frequently display the names and snapshots of

Child Molestation 7

so-called "dangerous" citizens (such as people who are currently wanted by the police). Released child molesters are at least as dangerous and arguably more dangerous than on-the-run convicts or prison escapees (depending on the crime, of course). Third, child molesters should be forced under supervision to go door-to-door throughout their entire neighborhood (if not further) and inform people of their danger to children. Fourth, and last, child molesters should be forced to hold up signs (such as "I am a child molester and have recently been released from prison") in popular public locations (such as inside shopping malls or outside movie theatres) in their communities.

The combination of these four "awareness" tactics makes it far more difficult for the child molester reentering society simultaneously to reenter the lives of children. Because the child molester so desperately *needs* his disease covered up if he is successfully to form new relationships with children, *publicizing* his disease will make it far more difficult for him to dupe parents and children into thinking that he is harmless. Thus, publicity does far more than *shame* the child molester (which it may or may not actually succeed in doing); it *disables* him by depriving him of the one tool that he *needs* in order to molest more children: identity concealment.

Disabling child molesters by depriving them of their necessary tool (i.e., identity concealment) is not much different than the ancient punishment of depriving pick-pocketers and thieves of their necessary tool (i.e., their fingers). Pick-pocketers and thieves obviously depended on their fingers in order to commit their crimes. Cutting off their fingers was a simple way of preventing them from repeating their crimes. Similarly, child molesters depend on the concealment of their identities in order to commit their crimes. Depriving them of their concealment via *publicity* is

really the only way we can save countless children
from being sexually molested. Child molestation is
possibly the only crime that fully depends on (which
is to say—is impossible without) the concealment of
identity. For this reason, crimes such as assault and
robbery (which do not depend on the secrecy and deception of identity) should not be countered by publicity. Child molestation is a unique crime. It requires
a unique punishment.

My opponents, at this time, would claim that such
a punishment is unjustifiably excessive. They would argue that although publicity would disable a molester
from molesting, it would also disable him from
successfully seeking and holding a job. Additionally,
because the child molester has *already* served his
time, he now ought to be permitted to reestablish a
normal life, which necessarily involves getting a job
so that he may feed, clothe and house himself. Some,
such as Judith Shepphard (1997), a journalism professor at Auburn University, argue that publicizing child
molesters is indefensible because it constitutes double punishment (37).

I respond by arguing that we must use publicity
against child molesters *in place of* full prison terms.
I am advocating a decrease in (but not elimination of)
prison sentences so that publicity becomes a normal
part of "serving one's time." Thus, my opponents' argument that publicity is unfair because child molesters have *already served* their time is moot. The
publicity with which they will be forced to deal is
not *in addition* to their time; it *is* their time. A
typical "punishment" for child molestation should be
two-pronged: It should begin with a (shortened,
according to today's norms) prison sentence, and conclude with a powerful dosage of public exposure. This
public exposure is obviously not going to help child
molesters get jobs (of course, our current system re-

Child Molestation 9

quires that molesters admit in their job applications that they were convicted of child molestation, which doesn't help this cause much either).

Melvin Watt, the Democratic senator from North Carolina, claims that "our Constitution says to us that a criminal defendant is presumed innocent until he or she is proven guilty. . . . The underlying assumption of this [argument] is that once you have committed one crime of this kind, you are presumed guilty for the rest of your life" (Tougher "Megan's law," 1996). Senator Watt's point demonstrates a blatant misunderstanding of the nature of child molestation. As we established earlier in the paper, child molestation is a physiological and psychological disease from which child molesters suffer. It is not as if they were only *suffering* from the disease the moment they committed the act that led to their convictions. In reality, molesters continuously *suffer* from the disease—it is a mental disorder that they cannot escape. Child molesters are not "presumed guilty" for the rest of their lives; they are, however, presumed dangerous for the rest of their lives. This presumption, due to the nature of molestation, seems fair to make.

The final rebuttal that my opponents make is that publicity violates the convicted child molester's right to privacy. Although at an initial glance this argument appears persuasive, a proper understanding of government-enforced punishment defeats it. If a person assaults another, he is put in prison. Every individual in America has an inalienable right to liberty. We believe, however, that an individual can sacrifice this right by behaving in certain ways (such as by assaulting an innocent other). If we so easily accept that the state can violate an individual's right to liberty, why is it so shocking for me to suggest a punishment in which the state violates the individual's right to privacy? We are simply

When authorship is not given, state title; in this case, no page number is given since the source is from a Web site

Child Molestation 10

accustomed to the violation of liberty (which, by the way, is a truly sacred right). The fact that the right to privacy is not regularly violated by the government (in response to illegal behavior) does not entail that it is unjustifiable. In the case of the child molester, the violation of this right is perfectly justifiable.

Thus, I do not support the publicity of child molesters so that we might slowly eliminate individual rights or eventually revert back to our days of public shaming. I support publicity because it can *disable* and *handicap* people who leave prison prepared, due to their controlling disease, to molest more children. Although it will not put an end to the molestation of children, it will make it far more difficult for child molesters to reenter society and effortlessly start up where they left off.

References

Friedman, S. (1991). Outpatient Treatment of Child Molesters. Sarasota, FL: Professional Resource Exchange.

Hansen, K. R., Steffy, R.A., & Gauthier, R. (1993). Long term recidivism of child molesters. *Journal of consulting and clinical psychology, 61*(4), 646-652.

Shepphard, J. (1997). Double punishment?: Megan's law on child molesters. *American journalism review, 19*(9), 37-41.

Tougher "Megan's law" would require notification. (1996). Retrieved 3 Mar. 2001, from http://www.cgi.cnn.com/ALLPOLITICS. . ./9605/08/sexoffenders/index.shtml.

Title is centered, 2 spaces below page number

Indent second and successive lines of each entry 5 spaces

Entries are listed in alphabetical order by author surname (or by title if no author listed)

Ampersand used before name of last author listed

First word in article title and journal title capitalized; journal title and volume number italicized

Part II

Reading Clusters

1 | What Is the Impact of Cyberspace Technology on Education?

Introduction

In the last decade of the twentieth century, the world came online. Cyberspace became a new realm for human communication and interaction, and this realm continues to develop rapidly—but toward what? Nearly all businesses have Web sites; more and more correspondence is transacted via e-mail; people separated by thousands of miles can sit down together in a cyberspace conference room and conduct their business. It seems as if the very nature of experience itself is being transformed into computerized environments.

What does this bode for education? Ever since the early 1980s, computers have been the conduit for invaluable learning resources, namely information accessing and the virtual classroom.

Information Accessing

The Internet has revolutionized access to information. Thanks to powerful search engines, anyone can call up any kind of information at any time with just a few finger strokes. Not only that, hyperlinks can take researchers to innumerable other related Web sites. But how thorough and reliable is the information obtainable online? It is not easy to generalize about this; it depends greatly on what is being researched. Serious researchers do not limit themselves to online information gathering; instead, they take advantage of traditional research libraries housing millions of books, periodicals, and manuscripts. It sometimes seems as if the Internet is making these more traditional resources obsolete; but that is not likely to happen for a long time, if ever.

The Virtual Classroom

With ever-growing frequency, online instruction at all levels, from elementary school to graduate school, is increasing. In fact, as of June 2001, at least six accredited "virtual universities" offer all of their courses online, including Jones International University (which also calls itself "The University of the Web"), Western Governors University, the Concord University School of Law, and Untext.com.

The readings in this chapter analyze and evaluate the impact of computer technology, actual or potential, on learning. What are the benefits and liabilities? Do the former outweigh the latter, or vice versa? How are educators able to ensure quality of learning? Perhaps the very concept of "educator" will change—but in what way? How compatible are the new computerized learning technologies with the older ones? What legal and ethical concerns arise out of these new learning technologies?

The Battle in Cyberspace | Abby Ellin

As cyberspace (or distance) learning grows in popularity, issues of intellectual property ownership arise. Should the professor who designed the online course or the university who hired the professor—or both—be considered the owner of the course and whatever revenues are generated from it? Who should control online course content? Abby Ellin, a journalist whose column, Preludes, appears in the Money & Business section of the *New York Times*, examines the issue and identifies key points of contention between traditional educators in bricks-and-mortar college classrooms and the new wave of cyber-profs.

In the summer of 1997, Dr. Cyndi Wilson Porter, an assistant chemistry professor at Lakeland College in Sheboygan, Wis., was asked to teach a class online. She hesitated at first—she loved the feel of a classroom, the camaraderie of live communication. She did not want to be an anonymous piece of software somewhere beyond the computer screen.

But she did it, and soon, she said, she fell in love with the interaction. "On the ground, some students respond and others don't; online, everyone does—they have to," she said. "Online, the only way I know you're alive is if you participate, so we set goals of how many times a week students have to respond. It's very exciting."

Three years later, she is the assistant vice president for extended academic programs and the director of Universe Online, a nonprofit virtual arm of the University of the Incarnate Word in San Antonio. Universe Online is starting up this fall and will offer business classes for undergraduates, as well as courses leading to an M.B.A. The online teachers are faculty members and business owners.

Universe Online is one of the many so-called distance-learning programs hovering in cyberspace. According to reports from the United States Department of Education, at least one-third of the 3,500 colleges and universities in the United States offer distance-learning courses; within the next two years, four out of every five are expected to do so.

But neither faculty members nor administrators are sure about some of the issues raised about intellectual property, like who owns and who should control content that appears online. Does the university or the faculty member who created an online course own it? Who retains copyright to the material? The issue did not arise before cybercourses, because the material and the teacher were intertwined. But now many faculty members fear they will lose control over the courses they teach, that their lessons will be modified or prepackaged into a one-size-fits-all lecture by someone at an online institution.

How much freedom does a faculty member have? Professors typically design traditional courses, and decide which readings to assign and what information to deliver. But what happens with an online course, where the methodologies are different?

David F. Noble, a history professor at York University in Toronto, argues that distance learning contributes to the commercialization of academia and that it forces universities to be concerned only with turning a profit.

"Who owns the material you have placed on the Web site or e-mail?" he wrote in an essay called "Digital Diploma Mills: The Coming Battle Over Online Instruction," part of a series that, ironically, he posted on the Internet, at www.communication.ucsd.edu/dl.

"Without a clear and definitive assertion of copyright claims by faculty, the universities will usurp such rights by default."

Dr. Porter disagrees. Educators, she says, "are hired to impart knowledge, to help students learn. Even as a traditional academic, I have never understood the mindset of 'I own this so I should be able to sell it.' As a chemist, I share my knowledge. I didn't invent chemistry or chemical concepts." She added, "Since I am paid by my school to share my knowledge, they in effect are leasing me."

Some universities, on the other hand, are concerned that professors will rake in substantial sums by teaching classes to millions of people across the globe, and that they will not share the tuition with their institutions. They are also worried that some professors will branch out on their own and teach courses for nontraditional institutions like the Global Education Network, a company founded by Herbert A. Allen, a venture capitalist.

That is what happened with Arthur R. Miller, a Harvard Law School professor who provides video courses for the Concord University School of Law, a virtual school founded by Kaplan Inc., the test-preparation company. Professor Miller, who markets many of his Harvard lectures on videocassettes, contended that he was not violating Harvard's policy of not providing course material to another school while still teaching at Harvard, without permission. Harvard said he was. According to Michael Chmura, a Harvard Law School spokesman, the university issued new guidelines last spring, after the conflict

P.C. VEY

How influential will computer-based education become?

with Professor Miller arose, to make clear that it prohibited such online moonlighting. Professor Miller was out of the country and not immediately available for comment, an assistant said.

☑   ☑   ☑

Some universities are signing deals themselves. Unext.com, a virtual university backed by Michael Milken, the former junk bond king, and Lawrence J. Ellison, the chairman of Oracle, has agreements with Columbia University, Carnegie Mellon University, the University of Chicago, the London School of Economics and Stanford University to receive source materials from them for use at an online for-profit virtual university, said Andrew M. Rosenfield, an economist and lawyer who is a lecturer at the University of Chicago Law School and the chief executive of Unext.com. The school also contracts with faculty members at other colleges to provide courses unique to Unext.

Western Governors University, a virtual college, will develop programs that provide academic credit for practical experience, and will utilize course work from institutions throughout the United States.

Still, while colleges and universities have long concerned themselves with   15
patentable items—inventions or medical techniques created in university laboratories—many are unsure about how to proceed with online materials.

"Schools never cared about literary endeavors," said Dan Burk, professor of law at the University of Minnesota in Minneapolis, who is an expert on intellectual property law and cyberlaw. "There was never enough money expected from one." But now that the economics of ownership of academic materials is changing, he says, "the vast majority of universities don't know what they're doing. We have no guidance."

Because the multimedia arena of distance learning is copyrightable subject matter, some academics foresee a lot of money being generated by online courses. For the past three years, for example, Stanford's engineering school has taught 200 courses to students all over the world—at 140 percent of the school's normal tuition. Duke University charges $95,000 for what it calls a Global Executive M.B.A., a 19-month-long program that mixes a month on campus and a month studying abroad with online study. That is considerably more expensive than tuition for the traditional two-year M.B.A. program, which is $28,200 per year.

Administrators at Penn State view their online World Campus as the 25th campus in the university system. Since it opened two years ago, there has been a jump from 70 students to 2,895.

At some schools, faculty members have protested the consideration of courses on the Web. Nine hundred faculty members at the University of Washington signed a petition opposing talk of a virtual university. Professors at Cornell have expressed discomfort with e-Cornell, a for-profit subsidiary to develop and market online courses, said Bill Steele, a university spokesman. Details of the program have not yet been completed.

Beyond the focus on ownership, Dr. Burk cites deeper, more complex issues that are at stake—like career, competition, status and money.   20

If Harvard's Professor Miller took a sabbatical to teach at another bricks-and-mortar institution, "nobody would have cared," he said. But now, "what they're saying is that 'we don't want you to pull a paycheck from Harvard and also teach online.' Harvard's not happy to have its name affiliated with a nonaccredited school."

Mr. Chmura said that the issue was not the linking of names, but assuring that Harvard faculty members give most of their attention to Harvard students. There are also issues of ego and respect. Both came up when faculty members at the University of Chicago were asked by administrators to develop materials for Unext.com. "It makes them sound like they're working for a big corporation, where their bosses can give them an assignment," said Dr. Burk. "They wonder, 'Are we just cogs? Can my dean or department head tell me to create this course as part of my regular duties here? Can I say yes or no?' The real question now is: What's the role of the bricks-and-mortar university, and how is the relationship between the faculty and the university changing?"

Ultimately, the courses those faculty members develop count toward their required teaching load, but they do not earn any extra pay for creating them, said Larry Arbeiter, a University of Chicago spokesman. There is no consensus about many of the questions raised. Some schools have decided to use revenue from online courses as a way of paying faculty. Others are considering the model of the recording and entertainment industries; faculty members would own the rights to online instructional materials and would be allowed to sell materials to online colleges. Some people expect professors to hire agents to broker deals for them.

In May, Duke University's Academic Council approved a policy allowing professors to retain ownership of all courses they create as individuals, but allowing the university to retain ownership of some courses created using university property. The University of Texas has a similar policy, which calls for joint ownership of courses created using the university's funds or personnel.

At the University of Minnesota, faculty members retain ownership of any Web-based courses they create, unless there is a prior agreement to the contrary. Dr. Porter said Universe Online pays a faculty member 5 percent of the tuition it receives for an online course for each of the first five times the course is offered.

25

She said, "There's no difference between online and on-ground teaching other than the actual method of delivery. Instead of standing up and talking, I now type. When I do an online class, I'm still just sharing my knowledge. When I teach a course on-ground, I get paid as part of my salary. When I teach a class online, I also get paid as part of my salary. But everyone wants a piece of the pie." But the issue of dividing the pie is more pressing when, unlike Dr. Porter, the faculty member whose course is offered online does not participate in teaching it, because then he or she will either be paid for assembling the content or not be paid at all.

The American Association of University Professors has drafted model contracts that give faculty members a financial interest in courses that are adapted to online presentations. Dr. Burk of Minnesota predicts that the debate will quiet down soon.

"Part of what's driving this is that these online courses are multimedia intensive, with video, graphics, music, and text," he said. "They're new and hot, and both the institution and faculty seem to think there will be a bunch of money out there. But the reality is that these blockbuster moneymaking gold-rush scenarios probably won't happen. I am hoping people will realize there's not a gold mine and come to their senses." ◨

Reflections and Inquiries

1. Do you agree or disagree with history professor David Noble's assertion that distance learning "contributes to the commercialization of academia"? What does *commercialization* refer to in this context?

2. What was the basis of Harvard University's claim that its law school professor, Arthur Miller, was violating its policy prohibiting its professors from providing course material to another school while still teaching at Harvard? How valid is this claim, in your opinion?

3. Why do you suppose Stanford and other universities charge considerably more tuition for online courses than for traditional ones?

4. Interview a student who has taken an online course or a faculty member who has taught one. What was most satisfying about taking or teaching this course, and why?

5. If you or a friend have ever taken a course online, compare it with a similar classroom-based course. What are the positive and negative aspects of both? Which kind of course seems most valuable to you, and why?

Reading to Write

1. Reread Ellin's article for points you disagree with. For each, explain in one paragraph why you disagree.

2. Write a critique of Ellin's opening segment (paragraphs 1–3). Write an alternative opening to the article.

3. Write a critical evaluation of the online course policies adopted by Duke University and the University of Minnesota, respectively.

The Web Is Not Yet Suitable for Learning | Alfred Bork and David R. Britton, Jr.

Will it soon be possible to acquire a college education partially or even entirely through the Internet? Because of the growing popularity of distance learning, many college administrators seem to be considering such a move. In the following article, however, educators Alfred Bork and David R. Britton Jr. argue that online distance learning is not yet sufficiently developed to replace traditional classroom-based learning. It is crucial, they argue, to distinguish between delivering information and delivering *learning*. Bork is professor emeritus of information and computer science at the University of California, Irvine. Britton was a doctoral candidate at the University of California, Irvine, at the time this piece was written.

Many sites on the Web refer to themselves as *courses*. Doing so is popular at present, with an ever-increasing number of these courses cropping up everywhere. In some universities, administrators pressure the faculty to provide such courses without offering guidelines for how the Internet might best be used for learning.

We've looked at many such courses and come away greatly disappointed. Most of these courses provide little in the way of interaction. Our concern is with situations in which the Web site is intended to be the primary delivery

---

Source: Bork, Alfred, and David Britton, Jr. "The Web Is Not Yet Suitable for Learning." *Computer* June 1998: 115–116. © 1998 IEEE. Reprinted with permission.

method for learning, not when it is a supplement to learning delivered mainly in other ways, such as through lectures.

We are not suggesting that other ways of delivering learning—such as through lectures—are adequate. Distance learning is an important approach for future education, but not as it is currently delivered on the Web.

Information Versus Learning

Those developing courses on the Web often seem to be confused about the difference between delivering *information* and delivering *learning*. This confusion is fed by the longtime use of lectures and textbooks, methods primarily oriented to delivering information, which is simply not enough.

Even before computers—when libraries were the primary information sources—students could access large amounts of information. Merely providing students with information is not sufficient for learning. Good learning material considers, for example, problem solving, intuition, imagination, and creativity as important components of learning.

Problems of Learning

Discussions about learning systems might well begin with typical problems associated with learning, since doing so offers some criteria for evaluating different teaching approaches. In this column, we do not discuss all the major problems that face learning today. But several problems are important in considering new learning possibilities such as the Web.

Learning Is Often Unsuccessful

The first critical problem with learning is that many students do not learn in our *current* educational systems. Evidence for this appears in student grades: Only a small percentage of students make A's. The other students—those not receiving A's—learn only partially or not at all. It is customary to blame this on the students, but doing so is unacceptable.

Benjamin Bloom and his students showed, with experiments conducted in Chicago public schools, that anyone could learn and master any subject. For students to learn well, we must determine what each student does not know and has not learned, and we must offer individualized assistance unique to that student's learning background and style. Bloom did this with individual tutors, but that system (as he knew) was too expensive to be practical.

Many People Need to Learn

The second problem is that we have vast and growing numbers of people who need to learn. We can no longer assume that learning is carried out only in schools and universities; we need to consider learning a lifelong necessity.

Furthermore, at the beginning of this century we had one billion people on earth. Now we have six billion, a number that is still increasing rapidly. With increasingly limited resources, more people than ever need access to learning.

Learning Is Too Costly

A third problem is that learning today is too expensive and is becoming more so. In developing countries, learning often happens only on a very limited scale because these societies cannot afford adequate learning with the methods currently employed.

Even in developed countries, the cost of learning is becoming a problem. Current systems for learning cannot adequately grow to meet society's needs.

Learning on the Web

Given these problems, what can we say about the Web as a delivery method for learning? We see major difficulties with the Web's ability to deliver highly interactive units to students. We also see a problem with the large numbers of students and the networks they'll be using.

Interaction

The major difficulty is the very weak interaction available on the Web today. For students to learn most effectively, they need a high degree of interaction. Effective learning materials continually diagnose student learning problems and provide immediate assistance to address those problems. The Web today provides only low-level interaction. Our languages are our most powerful communication tools. They are certainly not perfect, but they are the best that millions of years of evolution have produced. Finding learning problems in students requires free-form natural-language interaction.

Most current Web material is delivered in HTML. The problem is one of 15 design, however, rather than the particular computer language used. HTML offers only point-and-click interactivity and cannot easily create highly interactive units that actively look for student problems and offer appropriate help. Instead of using HTML's limited capabilities, we need to build systems that can understand natural-language responses from students to analyze the students' difficulties and to take appropriate action.

This type of interaction does not necessarily require artificial intelligence research or techniques. Instead, this type of interaction depends upon careful design by excellent teachers who anticipate typical student responses. We have built such material at the Educational Technology Center.

Because of the Internet's dependence on HTML, the material we see tends to resemble poorly designed books with some hypertext capabilities. These HTML-based books often lack the editing and graphic care that goes into printed books.

Developers often claim that using Java—or other powerful languages—will increase Web interactivity. Indeed, Java goes far beyond mere formatting capabilities. But so far developers have produced little in the way of highly interactive learning, relying instead on Java as a method to overcome some of the formatting limitations of HTML and to add fancy graphics that are often pedagogically useless. To date, Java has not improved learning.

Large Numbers of Students

An advantage of the Web today is that it can reach large numbers of students, but the current Web material cannot identify individual student problems. Other competing technologies can provide this capability and can still reach many learners.

Network Problems

If a larger number of students were to rely on the Web for learning, it must   20
be more responsive, reliable, and available than it is now. At times it can be frustrating to wait for content to download. Sometimes users find it difficult or impossible to access a site, possibly because they are accessing the site at peak times—when a site can't handle the load—or because the site is down. Furthermore, many schools do not have Internet access at all or have only a single line dedicated to the Web.

So far, most Web sites provide little two-way communication, which is essential for highly interactive learning. This type of interaction will be another drain on network resources. No matter how good the learning material is, even a motivated learner may not have the patience to put up with the delays.

These problems may be mitigated by new broadband networks, but broadband's role in education is still uncertain.

Beginning with the Web

Friends tell us that they will first put materials on the Web and then later migrate those materials to CD-ROM. Those developing this type of Web material consider what information to deliver next, but the difference between this approach and effective learning is that good learning material "learns" of student learning problems from an analysis of each student's responses. The result of the analysis allows the learning material to guide the student, in an individualized way, to construct his or her own knowledge.

The difference between providing information and providing learning is great and often leads to entirely different approaches to product development. It seems unlikely, then, that noninteractive material will migrate into highly interactive material.

☑   ☑   ☑

At present, more computers in homes can access CD-ROM than can access   25
the Internet. So it makes sense that other strategies—allowing a much greater degree of interaction—can meet the demands of large numbers of students. We know how to design such learning units, but little funding has been available to do so.

Furthermore, the network delays typical of the Web can be avoided by using CD-ROM. The new DVD-ROM provides far more storage, making it possible to use large amounts of visual material, including video (if it serves pedagogical goals).

When we finally have the technology capable of providing high-quality interaction, we'll be able to retain information about students and track their progress. Some of this information will be subject-specific (such as areas in which the student needs more work), while other information (like user interface preferences) would be uniform—for each student—across all the learning materials used. Use of a network seems the only viable way to ensure that this information survives and is readily accessible.

We have a long way to go before the Web becomes a truly viable option for delivering effective learning. ◪

Reflections and Inquiries

1. How do Bork and Britton distinguish between information and learning? Why is this distinction important?

2. What, according to the authors, are the key problems of learning?

3. What do Bork and Britton consider the major weakness of distance learning? Do you agree or disagree? Why?

4. What must the technology be able to do that it does not already do before distance learning can succeed, according to the authors?

5. What data do the authors present that may need updating? How might this new information affect their thesis?

Reading to Write

1. Which one of Bork's and Britton's assertions do you agree or disagree with the most? Write a one-page rebuttal to it, referring to whatever evidence they use to support that assertion, as well as bringing in evidence to support your own counterassertion.

2. Critique Bork and Britton's conclusion and then rewrite it.

Education on the Web:
A Rejoinder | Patricia Cravener

> The following article by Patricia Cravener, a professor of nursing at Texas Women's University, is a rebuttal to Bork and Britton's piece. The author argues that Bork and Britton rest their argument on obsolete models of distance learning and that existing distance learning programs are already revealing that the technology as well as the pedagogy can work successfully.

Tim Berners-Lee originally conceived of the Web as an efficient way for scholars and scientists to pool knowledge and share information. Many sites on the Web, including course-related academic sites, continue in that tradition. The Web is used to great advantage for information transmission. Its ease of use has extended access to information to huge subpopulations that were formerly unable to use Internet-based file transfer schemes.

Alfred Bork and David R. Britton Jr., after surveying a number of course-related information repositories, came to the conclusion that "the Web is not yet suitable for learning" (*Computer,* June 1998, pp. 115–116). Bork and Britton stated that the technology is not yet capable of supporting high-quality interaction, retaining information about students, or tracking their progress. The error Bork and Britton make is overgeneralizing from the early Web-based distance education to current standards of practice in a field where both technology and instructional design expertise are changing rapidly. In fact, we have had the technology in place for several years.

Integrated Distributed Learning Environments

The state of the art for distance learning projects is based on the use of Web-centric integrated distributed learning environments (IDLEs). Incorporating the application of sound principles of learning/education and appropriate instructional design, IDLEs support extremely high quality, student-centered educational programs for remote learners, making extensive use of the synchronous and asynchronous tools available for Web-based communications. Most of them reside on the server, requiring no proprietary applications on the client side. Distant learners may use any Web browser to engage in collaborative online activities.

Rory McGreal (*Educational Technology Review,* Spring/Summer 1998, pp. 25–31) provides an in-depth assessment of eight IDLE packages and brief descriptions of 15 other commercially available products. Many of the applications are widely used, as is clear from online conversations among distance educators concerning the relative merits of user interfaces, course management capabilities, and the features of different programs. You can subscribe to the Distance Educators Online Symposium by sending e-mail to deos-l@lists.psu.edu.)

Interactive Learning on the Web

Most of what is currently available on the Web is a simple permutation of first-generation distance education: the provision of written information to remote learners engaged in solitary intellectual activities. However, the fact that most faculty use the Web primarily for information transfer no more predicts the potential or carrying capacity of Web-based technology than the first uses of firecrackers precluded the use of combustion devices for space travel.

IDLEs support collaborative online activities that are often improvements over the extent of interactivity available in traditional face-to-face classrooms. However, although the educational technologies that support active learning are easily available and widely used, they continue to be inadequately implemented in academia. Bork and Britton are, therefore, partially correct in their observations along these lines.

A good example of an IDLE is WebCT (http://homebrew1.cs.ubc.ca/webct/), which was developed by the computer science department at the University of British Columbia. It provides good course management tools for faculty and supports a wide range of learning activities and multimedia, including synchronous live chat capacity, student presentation areas, shared group documents, and an asynchronous group conferencing system.

Another example of the high degree of interactivity possible with currently available Web-based instructional tools is Polis, the Project for Online Instructional Support (http://www.u.arizona.edu/ic/polis/). Polis helps students assess their own thinking for clarity, accuracy, precision, relevance, depth, breadth, and logic—intellectual standards wisely accepted as indicators of critical thinking. Faculty members use Polis to provide students with an overview of a controversy. Polis then requires students to make a commitment to and a justification of a perspective on that controversy. Polis then advances a counterargument to the student, who must refute the counter before being presented with either a correct problem solution or a full discussion of the issue from an expert practitioner, as appropriate to the question under consideration.

One of the advantages of Polis is that it engages every student in deliberation, something that rarely happens in conventional classrooms. For assessment and evaluation purposes, Polis provides a record for faculty of individual growth and increasing understanding of complex issues, since the written record of student responses is maintained by server-side software.

Systemic Failure

Failure to use technology appropriately is not the fault of the technology. It is our fault, or more precisely, a fault in our systems. Weak, inadequate use of the Web reflects a pervasive reluctance on the part of many faculty to commit their time, resources, and careers to authentic Web-based teaching and learning.

Reputation

The unfortunate reality is that distance education continues to occupy a very marginal status in academia. Annual evaluation, promotion, and tenure dossiers filled with distance education/distance learning activities are neither highly valued nor well rewarded as indicators of scholarly activity. Distance education is often aligned with extension or community service and is poorly regarded in comparison to traditional classroom-based teaching when it comes time to make decisions about promotion and tenure.

Funding

Other forces also mitigate against faculty learning to use Web-based educational technologies effectively. In most colleges and universities, senior faculty have a substantial stake, and equivalent influence, in budgeting decisions. Funding assigned to new Web-based faculty development projects rarely materializes from new sources of revenue. In most cases, funding that might be dedicated to helping faculty learn new Web-based strategies and software for interactive online teaching would have to be taken from older, more established, more prestigious programs within the college or university. The faculty and administrators who would make that decision are usually the major stakeholders in the traditional system.

Knowledge

Given these facts of academic life, it is more amazing that any department or university *does* have high-quality distance education programs than it is surprising that so few have programs of high quality. After all, the majority of faculty members don't know what educational technology exists to support their instructional designs, don't know how to use it if they have heard of it, don't have time to learn to use it, and wouldn't be likely to be rewarded by their departments or universities for devoting time to the planning, production, and implementation of high-quality Web-based distance learning courses anyway.

Education Versus Information

What we commonly see online, instead of IDLE-based interactive educational programs, are course-related archives of information. These Web resources are often very useful to students, and they save time for the faculty and reproduction expenses for the department. Most even expand students' awareness of related concepts through the inclusion of hypertext links to other Web-based information. Tim Berners-Lee's global information web is solidly in place, but provision of information is not education.

The educational technology exists to link these information sources with dynamic, interactive tools that guide learners to the creation of personal knowledge. The infrastructure to support the technology is in place and is expanding every day.

15

⊿   ⊿   ⊿

While there are plenty of naysayers like Bork and Britton, many others remain hopeful for what the widespread use of IDLEs will do:

- They can provide opportunities for more frequent and timely interactions between students and faculty.

- They can expand options for working together in learning groups far beyond the confines of physical space.

- They can provide a means of access to research libraries, art museums, laboratories, and professional practice sites where students can interact with applications of abstract concepts.

- They can permit each student to receive direct person-to-person feedback by e-mail, to see their instructor's markup responses on drafts of online written work, and to get immediate results from online quizzes.

- They can allow each student to progress at his or her own pace.

The real barriers to excellent Web-based education are not technological, but psycho-social, economic, and political. The Web is already suitable for learning. ⊿

Reflections and Inquiries

1. Summarize Cravener's counterresponse to Bork and Britton's argument. How convincingly does she support her viewpoint?

2. What is an integrated distributed learning environment (IDLE)? How has it been assessed?

3. What five uses is an IDLE capable of?

4. Why does distance learning continue to have low status in the academy, according to Cravener? Suggest ways in which the status can be improved.

5. Cravener asserts that the barriers to quality Web-based learning "are not technological, but psycho-social, economic, and political" (paragraph 17). Do you agree? Why or why not?

Reading to Write

1. Write a critique comparing Cravener's opening to Bork and Britton's. Apart from the views expressed therein, which one do you think is the most effective in terms of engaging the reader's interest and introducing the topic?

2. Write your own opening for an article that refutes Bork and Britton's views.

3. Write a critique of both Cravener's and Bork's and Britton's articles. Pay particular attention to their respective use of evidence, depth of analysis, and clarity of explanation.

Virtual Schooling: Going the Distance— Any Distance—to School | Mary Anne Mather

What advantages can distance learning have for high school students? In the following piece, Mary Anne Mather, a project coordinator for Co-NECT Schools (an assistance organization facilitating school-wide changes in Cambridge, Massachusetts, public schools), examines success stories in four schools around the country. Be sure to note the summary titled "Weighing the Pros and Cons" that Mather includes with this article.

With so many teachers around the world taking advantage of the Internet for telecollaborative projects to enrich their local curricula, it stands to reason that some schools are taking what seems the next logical step—offering complete courses and even diploma programs online. These electronic or virtual schools take a variety of approaches. Some are unscheduled, self-paced, and relatively non-interactive—much like the old correspondence-course model. Others gather a group of students for a defined length of time to interact with one another—either asynchronously (using non-simultaneous approaches such as threaded discussion groups and e-mail) or synchronously (using *Internet relay chat,* video conferencing and other communications involving *real time* exchanges).

The field is so new that many individual schools, consortia, and support organizations are testing methodologies and interfaces with varying degrees of success. All are learning as they are teaching, and are committed to the evolving concept of "school online" as an approach with powerful potential. A close-up look at several virtual schools gives one a better sense of the varied reasons and approaches behind this rapidly growing phenomenon.

Concord Consortium's Virtual High School (vhs.concord.org/)

The Virtual High School Cooperative (VHS), funded by a Technology Challenge Grant from the U.S. Department of Education, is one of the most ambitious K–12 virtual school initiatives. A five-year netcourse development project

---

Source: Mather, Mary Ann. "Virtual Schooling: Going the Distance—Any Distance—to School." *Technology & Learning* April 1998: 30–38. Reprinted with permission from *Technology and Learning,* CMP Media LLC, Manhasset, NY. All Rights reserved, no further duplication or reuse authorized.

started in 1996 by the Hudson, Massachusetts, Public School System and the Concord Consortium (www.concord.org/proj-vhs.html), it is one of the first large-scale projects to create Internet-based courses at the pre-college level. Currently, it serves 43 high schools from 13 states. As of August 1997, there were more than 500 eleventh and twelfth graders registered to take classes.

"In just two weeks, I feel like I know my Virtual High School teacher better than I ever knew any of my face-to-face teachers," a female VHS student enthusiastically proclaims. Another student, who transferred schools due to a family employment change, was able to maintain some educational and social continuity by taking his virtual high school course along.   5

But VSH Director Bruce Droste relates what he feels is an even bigger success story. "A group of students as a whole in 30 different schools, most of them very remote, are able to take courses never before offered in their schools." In Center, Colorado, physics is still offered after the physics teacher left. In Amman, Jordan, and Alaska students take a geometry course previously unavailable to them. And throughout the entire virtual high school, students meet and make friends with people in parts of the world they may never visit.

VHS is an example of an asynchronous interactive course delivery system. "All VHS courses are created with *Lotus Notes* software, housed within *Notes'* LearningSpace educational environment, and delivered to students over the Web," explains Bob Tinker, president of the Concord Consortium. "Within the LearningSpace environment, teachers moderate student discussions and deliver readings, lectures, assignments, and assessments, while students work on and submit personal or collaborative documents, keep journals, use Internet resources, and participate in discussions with their peers." The asynchronous nature of VHS classes allows students from around the world to be in a class together.

Each school in the cooperative contributes a VHS site coordinator and a teacher's time to develop and deliver one VHS netcourse. In turn, the school can enroll up to 20 students in any VHS netcourse. To maintain quality standards, teachers in the instructional pool must successfully complete a graduate-level netcourse on the design and development of network-based courses. The netcourse for teachers gives participating educators exposure to the best educational strategies and current developments in their disciplines. More than that, says Bonnie Elbaum, technical projects consultant for VHS, "Teachers remember what it is like to be a student learning something completely new."

Louine Teague, who designed a geometry netcourse that she teaches from her high school in Lumberton, North Carolina, shared an initial concern. "When I first started preparing VHS lessons I had a sense of panic that I wasn't going to be able to get in everything I wanted." Teague chuckles, "Bruce, the VHS director, wrote me back a message in which he quoted Mark Twain, who had written a really long letter to a friend. At the end of the letter he said, 'I would have written you a shorter letter but I didn't have time.' When you have to be short and concise and to the point . . . your planning is done much more carefully. . . . Sometimes in the classroom we have our children do what we might call busy work. There's no room for busy work in this course."

VHS currently does not deliver core classes that compete with traditional high school offerings. Instead, it is developing specialized courses and interesting electives that expand and enhance, rather than replace, standard curricula. Droste explains, "I don't see this as a substitute for schools as we know them, but rather as a powerful tool for program enrichment." He adds that it offers teachers an opportunity to teach specialized courses that are near and dear to their hearts.

Droste recognizes some additional side advantages to attending virtual   10 school: "All students come away with a clear understanding of technology and how it can relate to their lives as they leap into the 21st century." He goes on to share that it is also a patience builder. "Online learning remains a relatively new frontier, and that so-called 'super highway' is still littered with potholes, if not entire bridges that are out!" Thanks to technology, Bruce Droste, director of VHS, was interviewed overnight from Massachusetts to Brussels!

Future plans for VHS include branching out to include ninth- and tenth-graders and impact far beyond the participating districts. Additional schools interested in joining will be accepted on a partially funded basis, and regional groupings will be mentored with the hope of developing them into independent consortia. Concord Consortium plans to widely disseminate VHS evaluation results as well as information about project-generated curricula, the professional development netcourse, technology, and netcourse designs.

Electronic High School
(www.grand.k12.ut.us/ehs/home.htm)
Grand County School District's Electronic High School in southeastern Utah has ventured into the virtual school business via a very traditional approach to coursework. "We simply took the curriculum used in our alternative high school and placed the assignments on the Internet," says technology director Jolene Morris.

Their reason for going electronic? To help students such as the tenth-graders involved in a daytime networking apprenticeship that will earn them CNE (Certified NetWare Engineer) and MCSE (Microsoft Certified Systems Engineer) certification, and earning power starting at $50,000. Their problem is that the apprenticeship prohibits them from attending daytime classes for the English and social studies courses required for regular graduation. Thanks to Grand County's Electronic High School, they'll take these required courses as independent studies and graduate on time with the class—along with the extra perks the apprenticeship offers.

Electronic High School students complete coursework independently off-line and use the Internet to submit assignments and receive teacher feedback. Currently, print materials and videos are sent to students by mail, but the intention is to rewrite each course to take full advantage of the Internet for content delivery and eliminate the hard-copy materials. Morris explains, "Until a course is rewritten, it is strongly textbook based. You know: Read the chapter, answer the questions at the end, take the test." Interestingly, although course materials and study are offline, all tests are given electronically using *Super Sleuths* testing software (www.grand.k12.ut.us/ehs/ss-adv.htm).

Students in the Electronic High School do not have contact with one an-   15
other, which is one of Morris's concerns, but they can have as much interaction with the teacher as desired by communicating through e-mail and online chat. "We have one student who never contacts us, except to hand in and get more work. Then we have another student who needs help and sends us e-mail two or three times a day."

Morris believes that as electronic schooling continues to mature, and accreditation issues are settled, it will give over to commercial companies rather than public schools that have neither the funding nor personnel to keep such programs operational. Grand County Electronic High School boasts maximum enrollment (25 students) and a waiting list. It has only one teacher supporting as many as 96 courses. Morris muses, "I'm a dreamer, but I hope that the competitiveness nurtured by this development will improve delivery of traditional face-to-face programs, too."

CyberSchool (CyberSchool.4j.lane.edu/)

The students at CyberSchool, a virtual education program administered by Public School District 4J in Eugene, Oregon, are of varied ages and from vastly different parts of the world. Although their circumstances and stories are as different as their geographies, they share a common campus and successful learning experiences at their virtual school.

There's a 47-year-old Japanese executive studying American political systems and a 10-year-old prodigy taking advanced courses. There's the boy who bonded with his grandfather while watching "Tora, Tora, Tora" for his World History Through Film class, and the Russian student studying *War and Peace* who discovered during his first synchronous chat session with American students that the English he was learning from American movies on video was not appropriate for polite conversation. There's the Korean student who enrolled in CyberSummerSchool to accommodate a vacation. The student completed a few lessons in Korea, a few on the U.S. East Coast while visiting relatives, a few lessons on the West Coast, and finished up in Korea upon return home.

CyberSchool is the brainchild of Tom Layton, technology teacher for the district. "While it is true that information retrieval is an important aspect of the Internet, the Internet is also about giving people access to each other," says Layton. "This electronic learning format brings education to the living room where everyone in the family can participate, rather than keeping it in the classroom where only students and their peers take part."

Alice Jagger, a CyberSchool teacher agrees. "We have an enormous reser-   20
voir of primary sources in our grandparents and in people in their 70s and 80s. This is where CyberSchool can provide something unique—it offers a chance

for students to share the place that their family's history has in the history of the world." Layton continues, "To me the big story is that all these kids are taking classes over the Internet and think that it's not all that unusual. It amazes me that they feel this is so natural, and that it fits easily into their vision of normal life as we head to the end of the 20th century."

He hopes that, in the future, distance public education will provide one or two classes each semester for every middle and high school student, adding a dimension of human diversity that the confines of one classroom in a single community just cannot replicate. "Most students in our district are white, middle class, and have known each other since third grade. To have a conversation is almost like talking to yourself. CyberSchool makes it possible to converse with kids who were born in Nagasaki, Berlin, and Moscow—it's an entirely different conversation."

CyberSchool is tuition-based ($300 per semester course) with registration ongoing. As soon as a handful of students "gather" for one course, it begins. Layton is committed to getting public schools onboard as providers as quickly as possible. In the fall of 1997, 45 students accumulated over the course of the semester. The following spring semester, more than that registered right from the beginning. Layton is convinced the novelty of virtual school will soon wear off. "We think it is going to be like the VCR. One week you don't know anybody who owns one, the next week you don't know anybody who doesn't."

And he sees the possibility of a future scenario where large private corporations provide 50 to 100 percent of online classes to families with vouchers in hand, once they discover that the investment to create whole schools online is minimal. Additionally, Layton points out that corporations will not be hindered by a hundred years of agreements, rules, regulations, laws, and public policy that bind public schools.

Layton is enthusiastic about the big picture for electronic schooling. "Distance education finally brings democracy to education. It gives the student in East L.A. or Brentwood or Martha's Vineyard or Harlem or Pakistan an equal opportunity to content curriculum and to people with many perspectives. I believe students who learn with each other will learn from each other. Until now, the single biggest factor influencing the quality of your education was where you live. For the 21st century it is not going to be where you live, but how you are connected."

Monte Vista's On-Line Academy
(monte.k12.co.us/delta/ola/ola1.htm)

The Monte Vista On-Line Academy, based in Colorado, is a program currently   25
in its third and final year of pilot status. Its goal is to "make a difference in the education of Colorado youth who are not currently being served by public education." These students are typically home-schoolers or students who have dropped out of school or been expelled. The On-Line Academy, which is run

out of a parent organization, The Byron Syring DELTA Center, provides an opportunity for approximately 50 Colorado middle and high school students to earn a high school diploma. Up to 40 are funded by the Colorado Finance Act, and the remaining pay tuition.

On-Line Academy is sensitive to equity issues. A participant's ability to provide a computer is not a criterion for program selection. Instead, grants provide computers for needy students, and the cost of Internet dial-up accounts are reimbursed to students who complete the year.

The On-Line Academy incorporates an interesting peer tutoring program that takes advantage of synergies that at-school and at-home students have to offer one another. Peer tutors/student assistants from the regular on-site high school program earn one computer credit for their work. Sixteen to 20 peer tutors interact with online students, and another 11 build Web pages and help construct the online courses. In fact, during the first year of the pilot, the 15 enrolled students actually helped develop the courses they took, building off a strong belief that many educators hold: "If you can teach it, you really know it." Each student contracts with his or her teacher to select classes and set assignment deadlines. The peer tutoring system provides an extra level of support for students who might lack strong parent involvement to keep motivation high.

On-Line Academy maintains a virtual school on the Web called The Schoolhouse, where each subject is represented by a series of Web pages. These pages contain course outlines, assignments, and support information. E-mail and HTML-interfaced instruction are the major forms of communication between students, peers, tutors and instructors. The program has experimented with synchronous Palace Virtual Chat Rooms (www.thepalace.com/), but with less success, and Monte Vista staff believe this type of communication will not become a main focus in any of their courses.

McFadden is committed to the idea of virtual school programs. "We see a huge population of students who are not being served by traditional schools. Our asynchronous program fits their needs. Home-schoolers, expelled students, emancipated students, single parents, and other dissatisfied 'customers' are looking for nontraditional solutions. We expect to see successful alternative programs become even more significant. And we're pleased to be there to participate in this growth and expansion."

Weighing the Pros and Cons

Here, based on interviews with representatives of the virtual schools described in this article, are some of advantages and challenges of schools online.   30

Advantages of Virtual Schools

- Small and rural districts can provide more robust course offerings by supplementing local curriculum with online courses.

- In some cases, public school districts can retain federal per-student funding by servicing a population who might seek alternative education programs to address individual needs, e.g., home-schoolers, the physically disabled, school phobics, and minority language students.

- Home-bound students are able to interact with peers.

- Students can gain a broader perspective by interacting with people in other parts of the country and the world.

- Students can successfully accelerate degree completion or repeat failed courses.

- On their own time, learners can access enrichment content of personal interest.

- A broader range of courses can be offered to a student body without expanding onsite enrollment and requiring facilities expansion.

Challenges of Virtual Schools

- Social interaction can be limited, depending on course structure.

- Authentication of learner input might be questioned.

- Only highly motivated self-starters are entirely successful.

- Real-life responsibilities can take priority over online responsibilities, and students might fall through the cracks more easily.

- System and network breakdowns interrupt instruction time.

- Some schools might look to this type of program for cost cutting, reduction in teacher work force, or as a way to grab students from other districts to keep enrollment up.

- Since online education is still so new, some initiatives are more successful than others, and logistics for ultimate success are still in a testing phase. There is a need to establish netcourse standards to avoid misinterpreting results. ◾

Reflections and Inquiries

1. How, according to CyberSchool creator Tom Layton, can distance learning contribute to student diversity? Do you agree or disagree? Why?

2. What were Grand County School District's reasons for creating a completely online high school curriculum? Do you agree or disagree with these reasons? Why?

3. What important opportunities does distance learning provide that you have not experienced in your own conventional school experience?

4. What is the rationale behind Monte Vista's On-Line Academy's peer tutoring program? Do you think this tutoring would be more or less effective than "real-life" tutoring? Why?

5. Of the reasons disfavoring distance learning that Mather includes in her "Weighing the Pros and Cons" section, which seems most serious, and why?

Reading to Write

1. After investigating at least two distance-learning Web sites mentioned in this article, write a detailed critique of the virtual classroom. Be sure that you represent each author's argument as objectively and as fully as you can.

2. Compare and contrast the curriculum offered by Concord Consortium's Virtual High School with that offered by Monte Vista's On-Line Academy.

The Virtual University | Nicholas Confessore

As educators debate the effectiveness of distance learning, the government continues to fund millions of dollars to schools to develop courses online. Demand is strong because the conveniences are obvious. Why drive dozens of miles to a college campus when you can switch on your computer at home and take the same course? But *is* it the same course? Nicholas Confessore, a staff writer for *The American Prospect* magazine, attempts a balanced view of the distance-learning phenomenon.

Distance learning, education gurus like to say, is as old as the horse and buggy. After all, farmers in the United States and Europe were taking correspondence courses since the time of the industrial revolution. Nevertheless, distance learning's latest incarnation—the "virtual university," replete with the dazzling accoutrements of the information revolution—has recently been the subject of bitter academic debate. When the Colorado-based Jones International University (JIU)—a.k.a. "The University of the Web™"—became, in March, the first fully accredited, entirely online university, the American Association of University Professors promptly dispatched a letter to the accrediting agency to express its "shock and dismay." One Georgetown University professor calls Internet-based distance learning "a new version of a trade school" and, worse, "the joke of the twenty-first century."

Source: Confessore, Nicholas. "The Virtual University." *The New Republic* 4 Oct. 1999: 26–28. Reprinted by permission of *The New Republic*.

But the ten students in Anne Kellerman and Palmer Agnew's virtual classroom are generally content to ignore the furor. After all, each holds down a full-time job, most have more pressing worries such as kids and car payments, and at the moment—week five of "F2058: Internet and Online Teaching Tools"—they are trying to master the vagaries of Web boards, HTML, and RealAudio.

F2058 is one of approximately 150 courses offered by OnlineLearning.net (OLN), a private, Los Angeles-based company loosely affiliated with the University of California at Los Angeles. Though OLN's catalog—which ranges from "D8310T: Accounting for Non-Accountants" to "D7491T: Writing the Situation Comedy"—is heavy on business and information technology, the classes themselves are similar to their low-tech antecedents. F2058 has lectures (which students read online), assigned readings (some in textbooks, some from Web-based sources), projects (group and individual), and discussions (via group e-mail lists). The difference, of course, is that none of the students in F2058 have ever met. Mary Anne Mather lives in Massachusetts; Bill Knapp lives in Jersey City; Mike Pastore hails from Bellevue, Washington; Patrick Lim is in Hong Kong; others are scattered throughout California. For that matter, instructors Kellerman and Agnew live in upstate New York, and the classroom—such as it is—exists on a server in Toronto.

To the students in F2058, at least, the attractions of distance learning are obvious: in education jargon, OLN's classes are almost entirely "asynchronous." Students are expected to read the week's lectures and complete projects on schedule, but exactly when they do so is up to them. Exchanges take place over hours or days—whenever students choose to log on and post a question or response. Students need only a mid-range PC, a modem, and an Internet connection to participate; if you can surf the Web and send e-mail, you can take a class. The classes, in turn, run on relatively simple, self-installing software. You can register online, pay online, and go through orientation online.

Whether Internet-based distance education is as good as traditional education is debatable. That students—particularly working adults—are flocking to such programs is undeniable. In August 1996, OLN had 17 students. This fall, it will have enrolled roughly 6,000 people hailing from every state and 43 countries. By the end of the millennium, predicts OLN's CEO, John Kobara, "we project well over 10,000 in enrollments."

5

☑   ☑   ☑

Internet-based distance learning isn't quite the future of higher education. Though "traditional" four-year and two-year institutions have lately been jumping on the distance-learning bandwagon, the undergraduate degree earned entirely online is still a rarity—even JIU requires that those matriculating in its bachelor of arts program have already earned 60 credits at another, usually non-virtual, university.

The natural market for distance learning lies, instead, within the fastest-growing segment of the otherwise stagnant higher education industry: continuing and professional education for working adults. According to the College Board, almost half of all people enrolled in higher education in the United States are participants in part-time classes or training—one reason why some of the most prestigious universities in the country (including Harvard, Stanford, Duke, Columbia, and the University of Chicago) run continuing education programs, or "extension schools," often at a big profit. Last year, according to the *Chronicle of Higher Education*, New York University's School of Continuing and Professional Studies (SCPS) pulled in revenues of $92 million, while the Harvard Extension School—which serves nearly 60,000 part-time students—earned a hefty $150 million.

Now, many of these schools—and, increasingly, prestigious business schools eager to tap the higher-end "executive education" market—have seized upon distance learning as their brave new world. UCLA's continuing education program, UCLA Extension—which enrolls about 70,000 students per year, earning revenues of roughly $42 million—is the preeminent example. In essence, OLN is a for-profit spin-off of UCLA Extension. Originally founded as Home Education Network to distribute and market videotapes of UCLA Extension's lectures, OLN began offering online classes in 1997, under a licensing and royalty arrangement with the school. Each of the courses OLN offers is also offered by UCLA Extension, and the syllabi are identical. OLN, in turn, has various corporate partners and backers: it is "a Premier Course Provider of the AT&T Learning Network® Virtual Academy," according to its website, and investors include Houghton Mifflin, St. Paul Venture Capital, and the Times-Mirror Company.

Such distance-learning partnerships are becoming increasingly common. Last October, NYU spun off NYU Online, Inc., a private company—to which NYU supplied $1.5 million in start-up capital—that will offer noncredit, online courses to corporate training programs. (NYU's SCPS, in partnership with IBM, also offers 45 online courses through its "Virtual College" program.) Stanford, the University of Chicago, the London School of Economics, Columbia, and Carnegie Mellon have all signed deals with Unext.com, which will "provide state of the art learning engines and knowledge as rapidly as it is created and taught at the world's most respected and distinguished educational institutions." In January, the University of Pennsylvania's Wharton Direct program, a division of the Wharton School of Business, inked a deal with the Los Altos, California, based Pensare, Inc., which will develop and market Wharton-derived online "courseware"—combinations of short lessons, examples, and exercises—to training programs at the likes of Unisys and Hallmark.

☑   ☑   ☑

Here, too, the attractions are obvious. New technologies have greatly accelerated the pace of workplace change, fueling the millennial boom in

10

continuing and professional education. Extension schools can only enroll so many students, but private distance-learning companies can—in theory—fit in anybody who wants to enroll. And why partner with community colleges when you can strike a deal with UCLA? Why develop courseware with Penn State's Smeal business school (ranked number 49 in the country by *U.S. News & World Report*) when you can enlist the prestige and customer-drawing power of Wharton (ranked number two)? Private distance-learning companies get to sell, as one Pensare vice president put it, "well-recognized, branded content," while the universities get a stream of licensing or royalty fees—not to mention a slice of the Silicon Valley gold rush. In 1998, corporations spent about $100 million on Internet-based training; by 2002, according to the International Data Corporation, they will be spending about $6 *billion* per year.

☑   ☑   ☑

Educators are a naturally conservative bunch. So, it's not surprising that many tend to see distance learning as a sort of educational alternate reality where classes become "content," universities become "providers," and corporate representatives speak enthusiastically of "branding." But, for the most part, earlier debates about distance learning are beginning to subside. The prevailing attitude now seems to be one of cautious optimism: distance learning has potential, but, like anything else, it needs to be researched, tested, and reviewed. One measure of the diminishing hostility: In August, the Department of Education announced $10 million in awards to colleges, universities, companies, and nonprofit organizations to "help adults gain access to distance-learning opportunities." "It's not an issue—it's a phenomenon," says Kay Kohl, executive director of the University of Continuing Education Association, "and universities are adapting to it."

But vocal critics remain. Some teachers worry that software and computer companies have managed to fool schools into making massive investments in distance learning and other technologies without any real pedagogical justification. David F. Noble of Toronto's York University, an oft-quoted critic of distance learning, is even more harsh: distance learning is "pedagogically meaningless," he told me. OLN, Noble insists, is "a scam."

Indeed, it is worth wondering what, exactly, is the pedagogical connection between UCLA and OLN—or, for that matter, between UCLA and UCLA Extension. According to UCLA administrators, the extension school curricula are subject to the normal faculty review procedures for any course at UCLA. With syllabi in hand, UCLA Extension then recruits "instructors" (the school prefers to avoid the term "faculty"), 90 percent of whom are adjuncts, to teach the courses, rather than using full-time UCLA faculty. OLN operates similarly: Its courseware is based on UCLA Extension course material, and the teachers are recruited by UCLA and trained by OLN. "The policies that govern our [distance-education] program," notes Robert Lapiner, dean of UCLA Extension, "are identical to the policies that govern our bricks-and-mortar program." But with UCLA Extension-derived courseware sluicing through the Internet, OLN instructors need not be UCLA faculty or even residents of Los Angeles—and, in fact, about 15 percent live elsewhere.

But this is a long way from saying that the teachers are unqualified or the courses are shoddy, as many critics of distance learning seem to imply. Though they lack some of the benefits and job security of tenured faculty, adjuncts and part-timers at UCLA Extension and OLN have either academic or significant professional credentials. Nor does the actual OLN operation quite fit Noble's caricature. "This is the second course I've taken online, and I can assure you it will not be my last," one F2058 student wrote to me in an e-mail. "Look on the map and you'll find that the closest university to me is Chico State—about 75 miles away. . . . The classes are not 'easy'—I have put in every bit as much time and effort into these online courses as I did into my graduate seminars for my master's degree." F2058's teachers, Kellerman and Agnew, are themselves quick to establish that distance learning has its limits. "Nobody thinks that even the best online teaching is as good as [traditional teaching]," they wrote to me in an e-mail. "Our goal is to provide enough interaction . . . to make online education approximately as good as face-to-face education in a typically large class. We strive to overcome the online limitation of using mainly text, with only a few images and a little audio, by eliciting continual, highly active student involvement."

Indeed, during the weeks I followed F2058, Kellerman and Agnew were constantly prodding and responding to their students. Jim Jepsen, the course manager (each OLN class has an "online concierge" to walk students through the software), was never hard to find, and Vi To, the director of course management, answered technical questions in the various class and campus-wide chat rooms so frequently as to appear omnipresent. In addition to offering excellent tech support, OLN, unlike some distance-learning outfits, is fully accredited, which means its students don't have to worry that their credits won't be accepted elsewhere. For that matter, there are no surly registrars at OLN, no dingy classrooms, no lines at the bookstore. There is only a sleek, professional, customer-oriented provider of educational content.

15

☑   ☑   ☑

Still, it's not clear whether a student taking a class at OLN—even a well-designed, fully supported class with dedicated instructors—is even close to getting an experience comparable to that of a student taking a course at UCLA. (For that matter, it's not clear what NYU's non-virtual continuing education students are getting that Manhattan College students are not, or what any student gets out of, say, an accounting class at a brand-name extension school that is much different from what they would get from taking the same class at a good community college.) Moreover, what significance do school names really have, as "branded" educational "content" moves further and further off the campus, away from faculty and into the living room or office cubicle? The real question, then, for consumers of distance learning may not be whether the OLN course is as good as the UCLA course—but, rather, whether it's any better than online courses soon to be offered by North Carolina's Davidson County Community College.

Or maybe not. There is a rapidly growing army of busy professionals who demand reputable continuing education; many of them are more than happy to put up with the potential shortcomings of distance learning in order to enjoy its convenience. And, in a competitive, credential-conscious labor market, a company such as OLN offers an eminently marketable credential: UCLA. "I picked UCLA because their classes looked good and their interface was impressive," one OLN student said in a recent posting to the company's online "student lounge." "[But] the name recognition doesn't hurt," he added. Education is a business—and businesses, after all, have customers, not students. ◢

Reflections and Inquiries

1. According to Confessore, the online courses offered by OLN are "similar to their low-tech antecedents." In what ways? What differences—obvious and perhaps not so obvious—can you point to?

2. Confessore states that Internet-based distance learning "isn't quite the future of higher education." On what grounds does he make this assertion? Do you agree or disagree?

3. What is a "distance-learning partnership"? What advantages can such partnerships have in the success of the programs?

4. How are distance-learning courses reviewed to maintain quality?

5. Would you enroll in distance-learning courses, based on what you've read in this article? Why or why not?

Reading to Write

1. Consider what you reflected individually or discussed in class in response to question 2 above. Write a paragraph in which you support or refute Confessore's assertion, basing your opinion on the evidence he provides.

2. Write a detailed response to one of the criticisms against distance learning that Confessore includes in this article.

Perseus Unbound | Sven Birkerts

In *The Gutenberg Elegies,* award-winning social and literary critic Sven Birkerts calls attention to the haste with which people embrace high technology alternatives to traditional forms of reading and information-gathering—often to the point of abandoning books and traditional humanistic attitudes. The following selection from his book pays particular attention to the danger of sacrificing deep learning, traditionally embodied by books, for lateral learning, embodied by broadcasting and computer media.

Like it or not, interactive video technologies have muscled their way into the formerly textbound precincts of education. The videodisc has mated with the microcomputer to produce a juggernaut: a flexible and encompassing teaching tool that threatens to overwhelm the linearity of print with an array of option-rich multimedia packages. And although we are only in the early stages of implementation—institutions are by nature conservative—an educational revolution seems inevitable.

Several years ago in *Harvard Magazine,* writer Craig Lambert sampled some of the innovative ways in which these technologies have already been applied at Harvard. Interactive video programs at the Law School allow students to view simulated police busts or actual courtroom procedures. With a tap of a digit they can freeze images, call up case citations, and quickly zero-in on the relevant fine points of precedent. Medical simulations, offering the immediacy of video images and instant access to the mountains of data necessary for diagnostic assessments, can have the student all but performing surgery. And language classes now allow the learner to make an end run around tedious drill repetitions and engage in protoconversations with video partners.

The hot news in the classics world, meanwhile, is Perseus 1.0, an interactive database developed and edited by Harvard associate professor Gregory Crane. Published on CD-ROM and videodisc, the program holds, according to its publicists, "the equivalent of 25 volumes of ancient Greek literature by ten authors (1 million Greek words), roughly 4,000 glosses in the on-line classical encyclopedia, and a 35,000-word on-line Greek lexicon." Also included are an enormous photographic database (six thousand images), a short video with narration, and "hundreds of descriptions and drawings of art and archeological objects." The package is affordable, too: Perseus software can be purchased for about $350. Plugged in, the student can call up a text, read it side by side with its translation, and analyze any word using the Liddell-Scott lexicon; he can read a thumbnail sketch on any mythic figure cited in the text, or call up

---

Source: Birkerts, Sven. "Perseus Unbound." *The Gutenberg Elegies: The Fate of Reading in an Electronic Age.* New York: Faber, 1994: 134–140. Copyright © 1994 by Sven Bikerts. Reprinted by permission of Faber and Faber, Inc., an affiliate of Farrar, Strauss and Giroux, LLC.

images from an atlas, or zoom in on color Landsat photos; he can even study a particular vase through innumerable angles of vantage. The dusty library stacks have never looked dustier.

Although skepticism abounds, most of it is institutional, bound up with established procedures and the proprietorship of scholarly bailiwicks. But there are grounds for other, more philosophic sorts of debate, and we can expect to see flare-ups of controversy for some time to come. For more than any other development in recent memory, these interactive technologies throw into relief the fundamental questions about knowledge and learning. Not only what are its ends, but what are its means? And how might the means be changing the ends?

From the threshold, I think, we need to distinguish between kinds of   5 knowledge and kinds of study. Pertinent here is German philosopher Wilhelm Dilthey's distinction between the natural sciences (*Naturwissenschaften*), which seek to explain physical events by subsuming them under causal laws, and the so-called sciences of culture (*Geisteswissenschaften*), which can only understand events in terms of the intentions and meanings that individuals attach to them.

To the former, it would seem, belong the areas of study more hospitable to the new video and computer procedures. Expanded databases and interactive programs can be viewed as tools, pure and simple. They give access to more information, foster cross-referentiality, and by reducing time and labor allow for greater focus on the essentials of a problem. Indeed, any discipline where knowledge is sought for its application rather than for itself could only profit from the implementation of these technologies. To the natural sciences one might add the fields of language study and law.

But there is a danger with these sexy new options—and the rapture with which believers speak warrants the adjective—that we will simply assume that their uses and potentials extend across the educational spectrum into realms where different kinds of knowledge, and hence learning, are at issue. The realms, that is, of *Geisteswissenschaften*, which have at their center the humanities.

In the humanities, knowledge is a means, yes, but it is a means less to instrumental application than to something more nebulous: understanding. We study history or literature or classics in order to compose and refine a narrative, or a set of narratives about what the human world used to be like, about how the world came to be as it is, and about what we have been—and are—like as psychological or spiritual creatures. The data—the facts, connections, the texts themselves—matter insofar as they help us to deepen and extend that narrative. In these disciplines the *process* of study may be as vital to the understanding as are the materials studied.

Given the great excitement generated by Perseus, it is easy to imagine that in the near future a whole range of innovative electronic-based learning packages will be available and, in many places, in use. These will surely include the manifold variations on the electronic book. Special new software texts are already being developed to bring us into the world of, say, Shakespeare, not only glossing the literature, but bathing the user in multimedia supplements. The would-be historian will step into an environment rich in choices, be they visual detailing, explanatory graphs, or suggested connections and sideroads. And so on. Moreover, once the price is right, who will be the curmudgeons who would deny their students access to the state-of-the-art?

Being a curmudgeon is a dirty job, but somebody has to do it. Someone   10
has to hoist the warning flags and raise some issues that the fast-track prose-lytizers might overlook. Here are a few reservations worth pondering.

1. Knowledge, certainly in the humanities, is not a straightforward matter of access, of conquest via the ingestion of data. Part of any essential understanding of the world is that it is opaque, obdurate. To me, Wittgenstein's famous axiom, "The world is everything that is the case," translates into a recognition of otherness. The past is as much about the disappearance of things through time as it is about the recovery of traces and the reconstruction of vistas. Say what you will about books, they not only mark the backward trail, but they also encode this sense of obstacle, of otherness. The look of the printed page changes as we regress in time; under the orthographic changes are the changes in the language itself. Old-style textual research may feel like an unnecessarily slow burrowing, but it is itself an instruction: It confirms that time is a force as implacable as gravity.

Yet the multimedia packages would master this gravity. For opacity they substitute transparency, promoting the illusion of access. All that has been said, known, and done will yield to the dance of the fingertips on the terminal keys. Space becomes hyperspace, and time, hypertime ("hyper-" being the fashionable new prefix that invokes the nonlinear and nonsequential "space" made possible by computer technologies). One gathers the data of otherness, but through a medium which seems to level the feel—the truth—of that otherness. The field of knowledge is rendered as a lateral and synchronic enterprise susceptible to collage, not as a depth phenomenon. And if our media restructure our perceptions, as McLuhan and others have argued, then we may start producing generations who know a great deal of "information" about the past but who have no purchase on pastness itself.

Described in this way, the effects of interactive programs on users sound a good deal like the symptoms of postmodernism. And indeed, this recent cultural aesthetic, distinguished by its flat, bright, and often affectless assemblages of materials may be a consequence of a larger transformation of sensibility by information-processing technologies. After all, our arts do tend to mirror who we are and anticipate what we might be becoming. Changes of this magnitude are of course systemic, and their direction is not easily dictated. Whether the postmodern "vision" can be endorsed as a pedagogic platform, however, is another question.

2. Humanistic knowledge, as I suggested earlier, differs from the more instrumental kinds of knowledge in that it ultimately seeks to fashion a

comprehensible narrative. It is, in other words, about the creation and expansion of meaningful contexts. Interactive media technologies are, at least in one sense, anticontextual. They open the field to new widths, constantly expanding relevance and reference, and they equip their user with a powerful grazing tool. One moves at great rates across subject terrains, crossing borders that were once closely guarded. The multimedia approach tends ineluctably to multidisciplinarianism. The positive effect, of course, is the creation of new levels of connection and integration; more and more variables are brought into the equation.

But the danger should be obvious. The horizon, the limit that gave definition to the parts of the narrative, will disappear. The equation itself will become nonsensical through the accumulation of variables. The context will widen until it becomes, in effect, everything. On the model of Chaos science, wherein the butterfly flapping its wings in China is seen to affect the weather system over Oklahoma, all data will impinge upon all other data. The technology may be able to handle it, but will the user? Will our narratives—historical, literary, classical—be able to withstand the data explosion? If they cannot, then what will be the new face of understanding? Or will the knowledge of the world become, perforce, a map as large and intricate as the world itself?

3. We might question, too, whether there is not in learning as in physical science a principle of energy conservation. Does a gain in one area depend upon a loss in another? My guess would be that every lateral attainment is purchased with a sacrifice of depth. The student may, through a program on Shakespeare, learn an immense amount about Elizabethan politics, the construction of the Globe theater, the origins of certain plays in the writings of Plutarch, the etymology of key terms, and so on, but will this dazzled student find the concentration, the will, to live with the often burred and prickly language of the plays themselves? The play's the thing—but will it be? Wouldn't the sustained exposure to a souped-up cognitive collage not begin to affect the attention span, the ability if not willingness to sit with one text for extended periods, butting up against its cruxes, trying to excavate meaning from the original rhythms and syntax? The gurus of interaction love to say that the student learns best by doing, but let's not forget that *reading* a work is also a kind of doing.

4. As a final reservation, what about the long-term cognitive effects of these new processes of data absorption? Isn't it possible that more may be less, and that the neural networks have one speed for taking in—a speed that can be increased—and quite another rate for retention? Again, it may be that our technologies will exceed us. They will make it not only possible but irresistible to consume data at what must strike people of the book as very high rates. But what then? What will happen as our neural systems, evolved through millennia to certain capacities, modify themselves to hold ever-expanding loads? Will we simply become smarter, able to hold and process more? Or do we have to reckon with some other gain/loss formula? One possible cognitive response—call it the "S.A.T. cram-course model"—might be an expansion of the short-term memory banks and a correlative atrophying of long-term memory.

15

But here our technology may well assume a new role. Once it dawns on us, as it must, that our software will hold all the information we need at ready access, we may very well let it. That is, we may choose to become the technicians of our auxiliary brains, mastering not the information but the retrieval and referencing functions. At a certain point, then, we could become the evolutionary opposites of our forebears, who, lacking external technology, committed everything to memory. If this were to happen, what would be the status of knowing, of being educated? The leader of the electronic tribe would not be the person who knew most, but the one who could execute the broadest range of technical functions. What, I hesitate to ask, would become of the already antiquated notion of wisdom?

◪   ◪   ◪

I recently watched a public television special on the history of the computer. One of the many experts and enthusiasts interviewed took up the knowledge question. He explained how the formerly two-dimensional process of book-based learning is rapidly becoming three-dimensional. The day will come, he opined, when interactive and virtual technologies will allow us to more or less dispense with our reliance on the sequence-based print paradigm. Whatever the object of our study, our equipment will be able to get us there directly: inside the volcano or the violin-maker's studio, right up on the stage. I was enthralled, but I shuddered, too, for it struck me that when our technologies are all in place—when all databases have been refined and integrated—that will be the day when we stop living in the old hard world and take up residence in some bright new hyperworld, a kind of Disneyland of information. I have to wonder if this is what Perseus and its kindred programs might not be edging us toward. That program got its name, we learn from the brochure, from the Greek mythological hero Perseus, who was the explorer of the limits of the known world. I confess that I can't think of Perseus without also thinking of Icarus, heedless son of Daedalus, who allowed his wings to carry him over the invisible line that was inscribed across the skyway. ◪

Reflections and Inquiries

1. What is Perseus 1.0? Why do you suppose Birkerts singles it out for special mention?

2. Birkerts distinguishes between two different areas of study and knowledge. Describe their essential difference.

3. Which of these areas of knowledge does Birkerts consider to be threatened by the new technologies? Do you agree? Why or why not?

4. Summarize the four reservations Birkerts has against pushing ahead with computer-based learning technologies too quickly.

Reading to Write

1. According to Birkerts, knowledge "is rendered as a lateral and synchronic enterprise susceptible to collage, not as a depth phenomenon." In a short essay, discuss what you think he means by this statement and why he considers it a serious problem.

2. Reflect on Birkerts's attitude toward the traditional printed page and toward textual research. In a short essay defend or challenge his attitude.

Neural Implants | Ray Kurzweil

When computer engineer and inventor Ray Kurzweil looks into the future, he sees a world in which computers attain—and then rapidly supersede—human intelligence, thus making way for a new species of intelligent life on this planet. While this may seem too far-fetched for some to take seriously, Kurzweil makes some fascinating and entirely plausible near-future predictions that could make an incredible impact on the way in which humans learn.

I FEEL GOOD WHEN I LEARN SOMETHING, BUT ACQUIRING KNOWLEDGE SURE IS A TE-
DIOUS PROCESS. PARTICULARLY WHEN I'VE BEEN UP ALL NIGHT STUDYING FOR
AN EXAM. AND I'M NOT SURE HOW MUCH OF THIS STUFF I RETAIN.

That's another weakness of the human form of intelligence. Computers can share their knowledge with each other readily and quickly. We humans don't have a means for sharing knowledge directly, other than the slow process of human communication, of human teaching and learning.

DIDN'T YOU SAY THAT COMPUTER NEURAL NETS LEARN THE SAME WAY PEOPLE DO?

You mean, slowly?

EXACTLY, BY BEING EXPOSED TO PATTERNS THOUSANDS OF TIMES, JUST LIKE US.   5

Yes, that's the point of neural nets; they're intended as analogues of human neural nets, at least simplified versions of what we understand them to be. However, we can build our electronic nets in such a way that once the net has painstakingly learned its lessons, the pattern of its synaptic connection strengths can be captured and then quickly downloaded to another machine, or to millions of other machines. Machines can readily share all of their accumulated knowledge, so only one machine has to do the learning. We humans can't do that. That's one reason I said that when computers reach the level of human intelligence, they will necessarily roar past it.

So is technology going to enable us humans to download knowledge in the future? I mean, I enjoy learning, depending on the professor, of course, but it can be a drag.

The technology to communicate between the electronic world and the human neural world is already taking shape. So we will be able to directly feed streams of data to our neural pathways. Unfortunately, that doesn't mean we can directly download knowledge, at least not to the human neural circuits we now use. As we've talked about, human learning is distributed throughout a region of our brain. Knowledge involves millions of connections, so our knowledge structures are not localized. Nature didn't provide a direct pathway to adjust all those connections, other than the slow conventional way. While we will be able to create certain specific pathways to our neural connections, and indeed we're already doing that, I don't see how it would be practical to directly communicate to the many millions of interneuronal connections necessary to quickly download knowledge.

I guess I'll just have to keep hitting the books. Some of my professors are kind of cool, though, the way they seem to know everything.

As I said, humans are good at faking it when we go outside of our area of expertise. However, there is a way that downloading knowledge will be feasible by the middle of the twenty-first century.   10

I'm listening.

Downloading knowledge will be one of the benefits of the neural-implant technology. We'll have implants that extend our capacity for retaining knowledge, for enhancing memory. Unlike nature, we won't leave out a quick knowledge downloading port in the electronic version of our synapses. So it will be feasible to quickly download knowledge to these electronic extensions of our brains. Of course, when we fully port our minds to a new computational medium, downloading knowledge will become even easier.

So I'll be able to buy memory implants preloaded with a knowledge of, say, my French Lit course.

Sure, or you can mentally click on a French literature web site and download the knowledge directly from the site.

Kind of defeats the purpose of literature, doesn't it? I mean some of this stuff is neat to read.   15

I would prefer to think that intensifying knowledge will enhance the appreciation of literature, or any art form. After all, we need knowledge to appreciate an artistic expression. Otherwise, we don't understand the vocabulary and the allusions.

Anyway, you'll still be able to read, just a lot faster. In the second half of the twenty-first century, you'll be able to read a book in a few seconds.

I don't think I could turn the pages that fast.

Oh come on, the pages will be—

Virtual pages, of course. ◢   20

Reflections and Inquiries

1. What does Kurzweil say are the biggest drawbacks or dangers of neural implant technology? Could they be avoided? How?

2. According to Kurzweil, "The technology to communicate between the electronic world and the human neural world is already taking shape" (paragraph 8). What cases in point can you think of that demonstrate Kurzweil's claim?

3. What subjects or courses would you name as most appropriate for neural implant technology? As least appropriate? Why?

4. Assuming that neural-implant technology will be available in your lifetime, how beneficial a learning tool would it be? What makes you think so?

5. Speculate on the possible ways in which neural implant technology would help or hinder the reading of books and magazines.

Reading to Write

1. In this excerpt, Kurzweil uses dialogue format, in which two voices respond to each other. Write a similar dialogue of one to two pages in which you continue the conversation about the benefits or drawbacks of downloading knowledge into a neural net (human or computer or both).

2. Reflect on the part of the conversation that debates the benefits and drawbacks of downloading literature knowledge. Write a dialogue exchange of your own in which you attempt to resolve the issue.

STUDENT ESSAY

You Log On, but You Can't Log Off | Andrea De Anda

Andrea De Anda, who wrote the following essay in her first-year composition course, takes a close look at Internet addiction: what its characteristics are, why it has become a serious problem, and what its long-term consequences might be. As you read this essay, consider how the problem of Internet addiction might be applied to the Internet as an educational tool.

There have been many reported cases of Internet addiction provoking users to lose physical contact with society. One individual, Andrew Stephan, discovered his Internet addiction had caused him to lose contact with the real world:

> I was listening to everything on the speakers of the computer. I no longer used the phone, radio, or television. I read my paper on the *Times* web site. That is how my addiction started. I would wake up and think of what I wanted to do in the Internet. When I went to bed, all I thought about was getting up to log on. . . . People are not realizing that addiction to the Internet can wreak as much havoc in people's lives as alcohol, drugs, and gambling. (26)

There are millions like Stephan who suffer from this problem. Computer addicts can be people who are depressed, lonely, and afraid to go out, in family conflicts, and, generally, people in trouble because they can't leave their computers. Some people think this addiction is one great joke; in reality, this addiction is no joke. It can do as much harm as any other addiction. "News about how Internet Addiction Disorder can ruin lives—broken marriages, lost jobs and so forth . . . many are becoming lonely islands" (Stephan 26). Computer obsessives are depressed, lonely, and generally in trouble. Stephan is "grateful that he can easily click the 'Disconnect' and get some sleep" (26).

Internet Addiction has become a serious problem for users. *Newsweek's* Kendall Hamilton and Claudia Kalb reported, "this is an all-absorbing black hole. Some experts estimate that 2 to 3 percent of the online community—about 200,000 of the estimated 8.6 million consumer users—have serious 'Internet Addictions'" (60). This "all absorbing black hole" is keeping people from making contact and keeping people from creating human relationships.

The net has caused people to become socially isolated. It has influenced users to cut off from genuine human relationships. People begin to depend on the computer for everything so that it soon becomes harmful to their health. According to Kraut, psychologists have documented "a broad decline in civic engagement and social participation in the United States over the past 35 years" due to the Internet (1017). For example, "Citizens vote less, go to church less, discuss government with their neighbors less, are members of fewer voluntary organizations, have fewer dinner parties, and generally get together less for civic and social purposes" (1017). People were reported to become more depressed and lonely when spending most of their time indoors exploring the Internet. The users become so amazed at all the resources available to them that they continue searching for new things on the Internet. Instead of meeting with friends or relatives for coffee or dinner, they send e-mails.

This will become an even greater problem in the future.

5

> Most profoundly—there are the disturbing social implications of a future in which human communication increasingly takes place through

electronic media. Since the nineteenth century, more and more discourse has taken place through the impersonal electronic intermediaries rather than through natural face-to-face communication. Despite these changes, however, personal communication still remained paramount. Whether at work or on daily errands, people still needed to interact. (Mowlana 46)

Family communication changed with computer users. "Different families varied in their use of the Internet, but the amount of communication that an individual family member had with other members of the family did predict subsequent Internet use" (Kraut 1025). According to a research study, "Important findings included that the greater use of the Internet was associated with subsequent declines in family communication" (Kraut 1025).

People need to interact with other people to live a healthy life. When surrounded by loved ones and friends, people become happy and live healthier lives. However, this interaction is decreasing with Internet use. People like this unreal life, but get so caught up in it that they fail to realize that it is hurting them. According to Kraut, "people who used the Internet more subsequently reported larger increases in loneliness" (1025–26). Frequent users also "reported experiencing more stress than usual" (1027). Because stress often triggers depression, and social support is often a buffer protection against depression, people with greater Internet use "were associated with increased depression" (1027).

Human culture has changed along with the innovations of communication. Future research shows that human interaction will decrease considerably, according to Edwin Diamond:

> Researchers are working on electronic substitutes for the daily interactions we take for granted. Work will be done at home and transmitted by modem; shopping will be done over the World Wide Web and paid for by debits to our electronic bank accounts. Even entertainment will take place through the computer screen (42).

The future problems are not the only things to worry about. Chat rooms can be one of the greatest dangers of the Internet. In a chat room, people can become anyone. They could be of different ages and sexes and can have a completely different personality from their own. It could be dangerous to those chatting with these people or to the people creating the personalities themselves. Some eleven-year-old boy can be talking to a fifty-year-old man thinking it is a ten-year-old girl or vice versa. People enjoy having the power to become anyone and refuse to live in the real society and choose to live inside the computer. Human interaction thus reduces here also.

In my own experience, I was trapped in this "black hole." I felt that I had lost the will to leave my computer and log off. I spent an entire night talking to a chatter who called him or herself Bear. I created my own image and I am sure so did he. I could say anything and was held liable for nothing. I got so caught up in this virtual image, that I chatted with a stranger from 11:00 pm

10

until 8:00 am the next morning. I then realized that I had forgotten about the life I actually lived and refused to use a chat room again. It's addictive, just like a dangerous drug.

In today's society, communication is not defined only with verbal person-to-person communication, or through the radio, television, or the telephone, but also by computer networks, fax machines, image recorders, and desktop publishing. The Internet has created the fastest and easiest form of communication; however, even though it makes communication at great distances easier, cheaper, and faster, people suffer emotionally from it. When a person goes out into the world, he or she will be confused as to how to act in front of other people.

The use of the Internet has reduced human contact, which has resulted in psychological problems. When users stop interacting with others in person, they become lonely, depressed, and stressed. They cut any form of contact out when they spend hours on the Internet chatting with people they do not know. Internet users become addicted to the virtual world in which they type and read. Once someone logs on, it becomes very difficult to log off.

Works Cited

Diamond, Edwin and Stephen Bates. "The Ancient History of the Internet." *American Heritage* Oct. 1995: 30–45.

Hamilton, Kendall, and Claudia Kalb. "They Log On, But They Can't Log Off." *Newsweek* 18 Dec. 1995: 60–61.

Kraut, Robert et al. "Internet Paradox: A Social Technology That Reduces Social Involvement and Psychological Well Being?" *American Psychologist* 53 (1998): 1017-31.

Mowlana, Hamid, "The Communication Paradox," *Bulletin of Atomic Scientists* July-Aug. 1995: 40-48.

Stephan, Andrew. "An Internet Addict Confesses." *New York Statesman* 19 June 1998: 26-27. ◢

Reflections and Inquiries

1. What are some of the symptoms of Internet addiction that De Anda refers to? Which of these symptoms seem to be the most serious?

2. Have you ever experienced any of the symptoms of Internet addiction described in this essay? How, if at all, did you deal with the problem?

3. In what way might Internet addiction become an even greater problem in the future?

4. Why, according to De Anda, do chat rooms pose a particularly dangerous problem for participants?

Reading to Write

According to one of the researchers that De Anda cites, frequent Internet users experience increased stress. In a short essay, speculate on why this increase would occur.

Connections Across the Clusters

1. Reflect on the possible impact that distance learning would have on methods of standardized testing (see Cluster 2) or on freedom of speech or censorship of course materials (see Cluster 3).

2. Could distance learning improve or hinder multicultural education objectives (see Cluster 6)?

3. What privacy issues (see Cluster 8) might arise in distance-learning education?

Writing Projects

1. Write an essay in which you defend or challenge the efforts of some educators to preserve traditional classroom education.

2. Propose a set of distance-learning college-level courses for your major. Attach to this proposal a rationale for presenting it online rather than in traditional classrooms.

3. If one is available to you, write a detailed evaluation of an existing online course. Compare it with its traditional classroom counterpart.

Suggestions for Further Reading

Harasim, L., et al. *Learning Networks.* Cambridge: MIT, 1996.

Kiernan, V. "Some Scholars Question Research Methods of Expert on Internet Addiction." *Chronicle of Higher Education* 10 Oct. 1997.

Murray, Janet H. *Hamlet on the Holodeck: The Future of Narrative in Cyberspace.* New York: Free, 1994.

Palloff, Rena M., and Keith Pratt. *Building Learning Communities in Cyberspace: Effective Strategies for the Online Classroom.* San Francisco: Jossey-Bass, 1999.

Rheingold, Howard. *The Virtual Community.* Reading: Addison-Wesley, 1993.

Rose, Ellen. "'This Class Meets in Cyberspace': Women's Studies via Distance Education." *Feminist Teacher* 9 (Fall/Winter 1995): 53–61.

Shattuck, Jessica. "Home(page) Schooling." *Wired* Mar. 1999: 60.

2 Is Standardized Testing a Reliable Method of Assessing Student Performance?

Introduction

High priority has been given to improving the quality of education in the United States; both presidential and vice-presidential candidates in the 2000 campaign vigorously emphasized their support for improving the schools and raising standards of teaching and curriculum. Inevitably, the question of accountability surfaces: Assuming the high standards are adopted, how do we know if they yield the desired results? What should such tests include? What format should they use? What, exactly, do we want them to measure? Perhaps most importantly, how should we use their scores? Should educators use them merely to gauge student progress or, instead, to determine whether students should be placed in "accelerated" or "remedial" classrooms? Should test results determine ongoing state funding? Should they decide whether students graduate early, on time, or not at all?

The following articles reflect a wide range of viewpoints on this exceedingly difficult issue.

Buying Time | Michael Scott Moore

"Any standardized test can be abused," asserts one educator in response to a report that increasing numbers of high school students from high-income families are claiming "learning disabilities" in order to receive extra time to complete the Scholastic Aptitude Test (SAT). In the following article, Michael Scott Moore, a writer for *Salon* and *SF Weekly*, reports on this abuse, which points to an even more serious concern: If students are buying extra time to take the test, what does that tell us about the purpose of such tests?

Source: Moore, Michael. "Buying Time." *Salon.com/books* 9 Feb. 2000. 12 Feb. 2000 <http.//www.salon.com/books/it/2000/02/09/test>. Reprinted by permission of Salon.com/books Feb. 9, 2000. Reprinted by permission of Salon.com.

Should the Scholastic Aptitude Test be scrapped? Richard Atkinson, president of the University of California Board of Regents, thinks so: "I would like to replace the SAT with the high school exit exam," he said in response to a Jan. 9 2000 *Los Angeles Times* report on a growing trend of white, male high school students from affluent families being given "extra time to complete the SAT because of a claimed learning disability."

The article, headlined "New Test-Taking Skill: Working the System," told of how savvy parents find a psychologist willing to make a diagnosis based on small or nonexistent quirks in their child's testing habits.

The University of California is reviewing how it handles scores from learning-disabled students. The College Board, which administers the SAT, says its test isn't the problem, since any standardized test can be abused.

"I didn't really believe this before I started consulting for the College Board," says San Francisco educational psychologist Jane McClure, who has reviewed some of the phony diagnoses. "But there really are some psychologists who will take differences that are within the normal range and call them a learning disability."

The *Times* found a high concentration of "learning disabled" accommodations in wealthy neighborhoods, especially among prep-school students, and a much lower concentration in poor neighborhoods. An accommodation usually means 90 extra minutes for the test (four and a half instead of the usual three hours). The total number of accommodations has risen by 50 percent since 1994. Most accommodations are for valid disabilities, such as dyslexia or attention deficit disorder, but McClure says that recognizing a dishonest diagnosis can be tricky.

"When those reports go to school people who don't have expertise in this area," McClure says, "it's hard for them to tell whether it's legitimate." Any "disabled" diagnosis from a medical doctor carries weight with high schools, testing organizations and colleges, she adds, because no one wants to get sued for assuming a student isn't disabled. A visit to an educational psychologist, legitimate or not, can cost more than $2,000.

On Jan. 19, the University of California president's office announced that its admissions people would review how they read learning-disabled scores (which are flagged with an "N" for nonstandard administration) and reconsider the College Board's criteria for "disability." Throughout the country, only 1.9 percent of students gain extended time, and only a fraction of the diagnoses are found to be dishonest, so the problem is small. But since the end of statewide affirmative action in 1997, the University of California has been pressured by minorities to prove that its admissions process is fair.

"We need to find out now if our admissions officers even [notice] nonstandard test scores," says Carla Ferri, director of admissions for the UC system. "I didn't think that they even looked at the piece of information," meaning the "N" beside the number. Extended-time scores, in other words, may have slid by without a second glance.

Admissions counselors at Harvard and Stanford also say an "N" next to an SAT score would probably go unobserved in the applications-process blizzard. According to Margot Carroll, Harvard's senior admissions officer, "We probably wouldn't notice, just because tests are only one of the things that we look at. And the other parts of the application, such as teacher recommendations and grades, are so important!"

Jean Lippman, Stanford University's senior associate director of admissions, adds, "I think admissions folks always fear that kind of trendy behavior popping up"—like unexplained "N's" next to a test score—"but we're not seeing it." 10

The *Times* counted 47,000 nonstandard tests, out of 2.5 million total, and estimated that only a small fraction—"hundreds or perhaps thousands"— were administered to disingenuously disabled kids. The clue lies in the percentages: While the nationwide fraction of nonstandard tests is only 1.9 percent, the number jumps to nearly 10 percent in some New England prep schools and wealthy districts in California.

"This really pisses me off," says Paul Kanarek, who owns a Princeton Review test-preparation franchise in Southern California. "My fear is that the pressure will build, and kids who are legitimately disadvantaged won't be given the time of day by universities."

Kanarek, a sworn enemy of the Educational Testing Service, says he runs prep classes to undermine the idea that the SAT measures "natural" aptitude. Wealthy families in Orange County pay him to teach their kids tricks to improve their scores, but he also offers free courses for the underprivileged. Kanarek has a single refrain about the test: "Please just acknowledge the fact that the SAT responds well when you throw resources at it. And if one group has them and another one doesn't it's not fair."

The SAT is one of the only national measuring tools around, according to Ferri, the UC admissions director. Her office is mulling a few alternatives such as the American College Test, as well as the exit exam mentioned by Atkinson. The exit exam is a fashionable idea among governors who want to improve accountability in their high schools, and it lies at the heart of Gov. Gray Davis' education reform plan in California.

But officials at the College Board argue that any standardized test will be abused. "I think there's probably more manipulation by schools on state tests than there is on our SAT test," says Beth Robinson, who handles student-disability issues for the College Board. Robinson says that a California exit exam won't compare with applicants from other states and says that the furor over wealthy families exploiting the learning disability label makes "a mountain out of a molehill." According to Robinson, such incidents have declined in the past three years, taking account of the fact that the overall number of tests has risen. "And it doesn't matter what test you're taking," she adds. "If people can find a way to give their kid an advantage, that family will do it, whether it's the SAT or something else." 15

In his new book, "Standardized Minds," journalist Peter Sacks argues that standardized testing is an invalid measuring stick. Sacks describes how former school Superintendent Rudy Crew fooled most of Tacoma, Wash., into thinking he'd conjured up an educational miracle when the city's dismal test scores spiked to improbably high levels. Tacoma is a working-class town with high unemployment, but Crew declared that social conditions were no excuse for low numbers. "I refuse to accept that students are not capable of doing the work," Crew said. He then engineered a set of high scores by ordering that grade-school kids be taught intensively toward Washington's comprehensive test of basic skills.

The experiment succeeded, for a season. Test scores soared, the town rejoiced and Crew, who had delivered on the bottom line, got a renewed contract and a $10,000 raise. Later that year, the New York City school system offered Crew a $195,000 salary and an expensive home to be its chancellor. After Crew moved east, Tacoma test scores plummeted and never recovered. Since Crew wasn't open about his tactics, residents felt tricked.

"I call it buying achievement," Sacks said in a phone interview. "And it seems to me that [test-score] achievement that's bought in this way is so ephemeral, it's kind of a fraud on taxpayers."

In any case, Crew was sly enough to realize that parents, universities, school boards and newspapers respond to test scores the way shareholders scrutinize profit margins. Late last year, New York Mayor Rudy Giuliani forced Crew out of office after a long feud.

Sacks thinks this "corporate model" of measuring minds is false. "It's kind   20
of a losing argument to say that we just need to get rid of all standardized tests," Sacks says. "But in the book, I do argue that we need to create a new paradigm of merit, based on evidence of actual accomplishment." He says evidence from SAT-optional schools like Bates College in Maine shows that a more well-rounded (and expensive) admissions strategy—using grades, essays, portfolios and interviews—brings in freshman classes that are more diverse in race and class and stronger at maintaining high grade-point averages. The same trend exists not just at private colleges with small application pools but at large public institutions that have de-emphasized standardized tests.

"At least in the college admissions context," says Sacks, "schools and counselors can finally stop using the excuse that test scores are the best measurement. This is the richest nation on Earth: Maybe we can hire a few more admissions counselors" to give applicants more personalized attention.

State schools such as the University of Texas and Boalt Hall, UC-Berkeley's law school, have expanded their admissions process in the past few years. The death of affirmative action in those states led to embarrassingly homogeneous freshman classes, and the schools had no choice but to stop using standardized testing as a rigid bureaucratic filter. And the recent mini-scandal over pseudo learning-disabled students may lead to more attention paid to applicants' achievements during high school, at least in the UC system. To

Sacks, however, it's a tiny development "Scrutinizing whether somebody is truly disabled gets into such minutiae," he says. "You have to ask the larger question: What are the tests really telling us in the first place?" ◪

Reflections and Inquiries

1. Moore opens with the question, "Should the Scholastic Aptitude Test be scrapped?" Does his report on the abuse of the test help you answer that question? Explain.

2. Why do the students from affluent families want extra time to take the SAT?

3. Why does Peter Sacks feel that standardized testing is an "invalid measuring stick"? Do you agree or disagree?

4. Why, according to Moore, is it difficult to identify those who falsely claim to be learning-disabled from those who genuinely are?

5. What is Paul Kanarek's reason for running SAT preparation classes?

Reading to Write

Read the online article by Kenneth R. Weiss, "New Test-Taking Skill: Working the System," found by searching for the title at <http://www latimes.com/cgi-bin/>. This article, published in January 2000, covers the same topic as Moore's article. Discuss the similarities and differences between the two articles.

Standardized Testing:
Meritocracy's Crooked Yardstick | Peter Sacks

Is testing a valid way of measuring aptitude and achievement? A growing amount of evidence suggests not, according to Peter Sacks, an education journalist who was nominated for the Pulitzer Prize. In the following article, Sacks describes the antitesting movements of the past forty years and looks at evidence suggesting that standardized tests correlate weakly with actual success in school and encourage educators to emphasize the more superficial aspects of learning.

Source: From Sacks, Peter. "Standard Testing: Meritocracy's Crooked Yardstick." *Change* March/April 1997: 25–31. Peter Sacks is the author of *Standardized Minds: The High Price of America's Testing Culture and What We Can Do to Change It* (Perseus, 2000).

Most Americans have taken standardized mental tests from the day they entered kindergarten. Test scores have told the gatekeepers of America's meritocracy—educators, academic institutions, and employers—that one student is bright, the other is not bright, that one is worthy academically, the other less so. Some, with luck, are able to overcome the stigma of poor performance on mental tests. But others will not.

Indeed, not only is it a stigma, but one that is largely unrecognized in our culture. Meritocracy's gatekeepers brand those who score poorly on standardized tests as somehow deficient, incapable. Psychometricians and educators use quasi-clinical terms for such people: remember the teacher or counselor who patronized an ambitious, competent child as an "overachiever" because her academic performance exceeded what tests predicted? Or recall the handwringing over the "underachiever," the student whose brilliant test scores predicted greater things than what he actually accomplished?

These terms have largely disappeared from public discussion, one result of a revolt against standardized testing over the past 10 or 15 years in the United States. Influential scholars like Harvard's Howard Gardner and Yale's Robert Sternberg have argued forcefully against the narrow views of ability measured by traditional tests. Many educators now sing the praises of new, "authentic" alternatives to standardized testing, such as "performance assessment." Advocates of performance assessment say schools ought to focus on what people can do and less on how well kindergartners, high school students, and prospective teachers can take tests.

But while the anti-testing bandwagon has gathered many adherents since the peak of the revolt around 1980, the wagon itself has crashed head-on into an entrenched system, one obsessed with the testing of American minds. With roots in intelligence testing that go back generations, the mental measurement establishment continues to define merit largely in terms of test-taking and potential rather than actual performance. The case against standardized mental testing may be as intellectually and ethically rigorous as any argument made about social policy in the past 20 years, but such testing continues to dominate the education system, carving further inroads into the employment arena as well, having been bolstered in recent years by a conservative backlash advocating advancement by "merit."

How has the standardized-testing paradigm managed to remain entrenched, despite the many criticisms leveled against it? Like a drug addict who knows he should quit, America is hooked. We are a nation of standardized–testing junkies.   5

The Anti-Testing Movement

Granted, there has been a withering, sustained attack against standardized testing in American education that came on the heels of an explosive growth in such testing during the 1960s. Baby boomers were funneled through the school system and tested to death. After adjusting for inflation, sales of standardized tests to public schools more than doubled between 1960 and 1989, to $100 million a year—even while enrollments were up just 15 percent—according to the U.S. Office of Technology Assessment (OTA). Some estimates of the amount Americans spend on testing—a figure difficult to come by given the fragmented and often private nature of the testing industry—are as high as $500 million annually. Estimates of testing volume are mind-boggling: as many as 127 million tests a year at the K–12 level alone.

The revolt against testing became most aggressive in the late 1970s and early 1980s, culminating in a string of successes for the movement, particularly against aptitude testing for university admissions. There were influential books and reports, such as Stephen Jay Gould's *The Mismeasure of Man*, David Owen's *None of the Above*, James Crouse and Dale Trusheim's *The Case Against the SAT*, and the 1980 Ralph Nader report, *The Reign of ETS*. New York's 1979 "Truth in Testing" law gave takers of standardized mental tests a new floor of protection. Activists and educators launched the National Center for Fair & Open Testing (FairTest), the nation's first organization devoted to protecting the interests of millions of consumers of standardized tests.

These attacks on standardized testing were backed up by a mounting body of evidence that such tests played a key role in a rigged game, one that favored society's well-positioned elites under the guise of "merit." The Nader report focused its attack on the Educational Testing Service (ETS), the tax-exempt organization that makes the Scholastic Aptitude Test (SAT) and other mental tests. "An independent analysis of the dominant testing culture is now coming on the scene," the Nader report enthusiastically observed. "There will be no turning back this time. The shallowness of the ideology and depth of ETS's political power to preserve its way of testing are apparent to increasing numbers of students, parents, educators, administrators, and most refreshingly, to those deprived people who never made it through the first multiple-choice gate."

Since 1980, the anti-testing movement has continued to gain momentum and credibility. One might think the Nader report hit a bull's-eye in anticipating the demise of standardized testing as we know it. But to do so would be to underestimate once again the near magical power that quantification, standardization, and the measuring of minds continue to have over Americans.

The Evidence

A long line of independent academic research bolsters the claims of the anti-testing movement. Much of the research confirms suspicions that such tests thwart rather than help educational reform and that they continue to produce inaccurate—if not biased—assessments of the abilities of many Americans. From this recent work, we know that:

   • *Standardized tests generally have questionable ability to predict one's academic success, especially for certain sub-groups.* Take the Graduate Record Exam (GRE), for instance, the multiple-choice test required for admission or

10

financial aid by most of the nation's graduate programs. Graduate departments use the tests in hopes of predicting a candidate's chances of succeeding in their programs. In an April 1995 "meta-analysis" published in the journal *Educational and Psychological Measurement*, Todd Morrison and Melanie Morrison examined two dozen GRE validity studies encompassing more than 5,000 test-takers over the past 30 years. The authors found that GRE scores accounted for just 6 percent of the variation in grades in graduate school. The GRE appears to be "virtually useless from a prediction standpoint," wrote the authors.

Other studies have focused on the GRE's predictive validity for specific types of programs and for particular institutions, with generally the same findings, whether the program be geology, psychology, or nursing. In their 1992 analysis of the GRE's validity for graduate study in psychology, Edith Goldberg and George Alliger concluded, "Overall, the results . . . do not paint a particularly favorable picture for the validity of the Graduate Record Examination."

In 1994, educational researcher Christine Onasch hypothesized that higher GRE scores would lead to faster completion of a master's degree in geology at Bowling Green State University. But Onasch's data told an opposite story—high scorers actually took longer to complete the degree. As other studies have found, Onasch discovered that a student's undergraduate grades were a far better predictor of graduate school success. The GRE, the author wrote, "is but a one-time measure of the student, which does not realistically indicate (his or her) future success in graduate school." Despite this finding, Bowling Green's geology program has continued to require the GRE.

What about the validity of the SAT, which is required for admission to a great range of undergraduate colleges and universities? Its maker, the Educational Testing Service (ETS), now claims the SAT is not an "aptitude" test but rather an assessment of "developed abilities." Whatever it is, a raft of studies say the test explains (on average) about 16 percent of the variation in actual freshman grades. We know that a student's high school record alone is the best predictor of performance in the first year of college. We also know that the SAT, when combined with high school grades, adds only modestly to the predictive power of high school grades alone.

In statisticians' parlance, Dana Keller, James Crouse, and Dale Trusheim [15] wrote in *Research in Higher Education* in 1994 on the utility of SAT scores: "When the SAT is added to [high school grades] in a way that maximizes the SAT's predictive power, our results strongly suggest that the SAT has considerable statistical redundancy with [grades] in determining who is admitted and who is rejected." This finding appears to hold even at highly selective universities, according to a 1992 study in *Educational and Psychological Measurement* by Jonathan Baron and M. Frank Norman of the University of Pennsylvania.

What is more, standardized tests tend especially to penalize women and many minority students. To an even greater extent than other groups, these subgroups, on average, earn better grades in college than their test scores would predict. Researchers consistently find that adding test scores to the admissions equation results in fewer women and minorities being accepted than if their academic records alone are considered.

Researchers have reached similar conclusions about the validity of standardized testing in the public schools. In a 1993 study, Teresa A. Dais of the University of Illinois commented: "Minorities and students with disabilities, in particular, are suffering as a result of traditional assessment practices, which have proven to be inaccurate and inconsistent, yet continue to be used in prediction, decision-making, and inferences about student performance and lifelong success."

But a fundamental point about the relationship of test scores to academic success is often lost in many psychometric validity studies. It's worth remembering that the SAT, for instance, isn't designed to predict one's ability to succeed at four years of college study—or at life beyond college—but merely to predict freshman grades. When researchers have asked the larger question of how test scores correlate to a student's performance beyond the freshman year, or to broader measures of college success, the case for the SAT becomes tenuous indeed.

In a 1985 study, *Success in College,* published by the SAT sponsor, the College Board, Warren W. Willingham writes: "Can a college effectively recruit and enroll students whom it is likely to regard as most successful four years later by evaluating applicants only on the basis of school rank and test scores? If the institution defines success broadly . . . the answer is no."

When researchers have asked the even more basic question of how well   20
standardized test scores predict one's eventual success in the workplace, the correlations all but disappear. High test scores are pretty good indicators of *participation* in professions such as law, medicine, or university teaching, simply because only high scorers are admitted to a required academic program. But test scores predict little about a person's subsequent real-world capabilities in medicine, law, or teaching. In short, scoring high on standardized tests is a good predictor of one's ability to score high on standardized tests.

• *Standardized test scores tend to be highly correlated with socioeconomic class.* While standardized tests correlate weakly with success in school and work, they correlate all too well with the income and education of one's parents. Call it the "Volvo Effect." The data are so strong in this regard that one can make a good guess about a child's standardized test scores simply by looking at how many degrees her parents have and at what kind of car they drive. Evidence suggests that this relationship holds even across racial lines.

Consider, again, the Graduate Record Exam. The GRE's maker, the ETS, has itself recorded the effects of economic class on test performance. In a January 1994 report for the Exxon Foundation, ETS found that parental income and education have especially strong correlations with test scores. For example, of the nearly 7,000 test-takers who scored between 750 and 800 on the analytical part of the GRE, fewer than 4 percent had fathers who hadn't completed high school. But fully half of these high scorers had fathers with a bachelor's degree or more; of these, some 90 percent had fathers with graduate or professional degrees.

Moreover, when the ETS study held income constant, the often stark differences in test scores between races often diminished dramatically. For example, 25 percent of whites with a family income of $15,000 to $25,000 scored 550 to 599 on the GRE verbal section—identical to the percentage of blacks with those scores in that income bracket.

In a March 1993 report to the Graduate Record Examinations Board, the ETS's Lawrence Stricker and Donald Rock concluded that "it is striking that parental education generally had the most consistent and strongest associations" among several variables, including sex, ethnicity, geographic location, and age.

Similar results on parental education and socioeconomic class hold for the   25
SAT. In a study of California high school students, parental education alone explained more than 50 percent of the variation in SAT scores, according to a 1991 study by Mark Fetler of the California Community Colleges' chancellor's office. College Board data show that someone taking the SAT can expect to score about 30 test points higher for every $10,000 in his parents' yearly income. And, in 1995, the U.S. Department of Education examined the backgrounds of students who made the SAT cut (a minimum score of 1,100) for highly selective colleges. One-third of these high scorers came from upper income brackets, while just 8 percent were from the lower economic rungs.

• *Standardized tests can reward superficial learning, drive instruction in undesirable directions, and thwart meaningful educational reform.* Teachers, researchers, and other educators have expressed widespread disenchantment with the results of several decades of standardized testing in the United States. Evidence strongly suggests that standardized testing flies in the face of recent advances in our understanding of how people learn to think and reason. In the research over the past few years, especially at the K–12 level, one repeatedly finds evidence that traditional tests reinforce passive, rote learning of facts and formulas, all quite contrary to the active, critical thinking skills many educators and employers now believe schools should be encouraging. Many suspect that the tests are themselves powerful incentives for compartmentalized and superficial learning.

Consider, for example, a recent study of college students' testing habits, which suggests that better test-takers tend to think in more superficial ways than those who don't score as well. The study, presented at the National Association of School Psychologists in Seattle in 1994, analyzed SAT scores for some 500 students with respect to their thinking and learning styles: whether they used a "surface approach" (retrieving only required information through rote learning); a "deep approach" (learning for its own sake); or an "achieving approach" (mostly concerned with high grades).

Students who scored highest on the SAT used the surface and achieving approaches more often than the lower scorers; the lowest-scoring students used the deep approach more often than the higher-scoring students. A similar study looked at nearly 700 grade schoolers taking a standardized reading exam in 1992. Eric Anderman of the University of Michigan discovered that students "who valued literacy activities and were learning-focused" tended to do worse on the standardized exams than peers who used more superficial learning strategies. Not incidentally, girls in the study were less superficial in their strategies than boys, more often taking "deeper" cognitive approaches.

At the K–12 level especially, teachers testify that standardized tests don't accurately measure their students' abilities and that widespread practices of "teaching to the test" render test scores virtually meaningless. In 1994, *Educational Policy* published a study on teachers' views of standardized tests. Just 3 percent of teachers in one sample agreed that such tests are generally good, "whereas 77 percent felt that tests are bad and not worth the time and money spent on them." According to the study, about eight in 10 teachers believe their colleagues teach to the tests.

Preoccupied with winning the standardized-testing game for the sake of kudos from parents, the press, and state legislators, schools have often neglected reforms that would promote deeper, more active ways of thinking and learning than are typically captured by multiple-choice tests. The OTA concluded in 1992: "It now appears that the use of these tests misled policymakers and the public about the progress of students, and in many places hindered the implementation of genuine school reforms."

Consider the Lighthouse Project, an effort in a handful of school districts in Ohio to implement new national standards for teaching math that emphasize problem-solving and thinking skills. In a 1994 evaluation of the project, JoAnn Uslick of Kent State University and Carole Walker, coordinator of the Lighthouse Project, reported their disillusionment with traditional standardized tests to measure the efficacy of reforms. "Teachers were in a quandary," the researchers wrote, "because they wanted to fully implement the goals of the program, but they also wanted their students to do well on the standardized tests that their district used."

This widespread tendency of teachers to "teach to the test" might be harmless if the tests were adequate indicators of students' skills, ability, and performance, says educational researcher Bruce C. Bowers. He writes:

30

> However, the main purpose of standardized testing is to sort large numbers of students in as efficient a manner as possible. This limited goal, quite naturally, gives rise to short-answer, multiple-choice questions. When tests are constructed in this manner, active skills, such as writing, speaking, acting, drawing, constructing, repairing, or any of a number of other skills that can and should be taught in schools are automatically relegated to second-class status.

The Shifting Policy Landscape Since 1980

This rich vein of research into the validity, fairness, and efficacy of standardized testing has unquestionably wrought some changes in the assessment landscape. But anti-testing trends have been counterbalanced by a conservative backlash that promises to reinforce standardized testing's continued domination of the educational system.

On the anti-testing side of the policy balance sheet, some of the more significant events of the last few years include the recent elimination of a standardized-testing requirement from the federal Elementary and Secondary Education Act. The law had mandated such tests for allocating federal money for remedial education, the so-called "Chapter 1" program. The stage was set by a 1993 U.S. Department of Education advisory report on the law's reauthorization, observing, as many others have, that "a revolution is taking place in the testing and measurement field." The 1994 revision in the law permits alternatives to standardized tests for Chapter 1. But there are no guarantees that states will implement any alternative assessments.

The rising popularity of performance-based assessment in schools and colleges has contributed to the anti-testing side of the policy ledger, too. As educators became disenchanted with standardized testing, they've managed to implement different ways to evaluate students and educational progress. These alternatives frequently fall under the rubric of "authentic" assessment, the notion that students ought to be judged on the basis of what they can actually do, not how well they take tests. Performance assessment can mean anything from evaluating portfolios of student work or writing samples to art and science projects.   35

The OTA reported earlier this decade that almost half the states (21) had launched performance assessment programs. But it would be an overstatement to conclude that states are embracing the new and abandoning traditional tests. Indeed, most states continue to use traditional standardized tests, supplemented by forays into performance assessment. Only a tiny handful of states, such as Kentucky, Massachusetts, and Vermont, have taken steps to eliminate traditional multiple-choice tests.

On the anti-testing side of the ledger, too, a small but growing number of undergraduate colleges have made standardized admissions tests optional. In April 1995, FairTest counted some 236 such institutions, an increase of 40 in just a year. Most of these colleges are small, private, and not particularly choosy, but there are a handful of selective ones, such as Dickinson and Lafayette in Pennsylvania and Connecticut College. Probably the largest is the California State University system.

But like other universities on FairTest's list, such as Kentucky State, Golden Gate University, and the University of Kansas, Cal State campuses still require the SAT if a student's grades fall below a certain cutoff point. Among graduate or professional schools, FairTest says the usual admissions tests have been dropped at the University of Massachusetts School of Law, the Harvard Divinity School's master's program, and the Harvard Business School.

Traditional tests are still required by the vast majority of graduate and professional programs.

Entrenched or on the Wane?

What, then, are we to conclude from recent developments? Is standardized testing on the wane? Some observers say so. But it would be naive to underestimate the hold that mental measurement has on the American mind. Recent events running opposite to the anti-testing movement suggest that standardized testing remains entrenched and is ready to dig itself in deeper in coming years.

It's worth noting that the mental measurement culture has withstood similar attacks in the past: Walter Lippman wrote a series of articles in *The New Republic* in the early 1920s, warning that the prevalent use of IQ tests in time "could . . . lead to an intellectual caste system in which the task of education had given way to the doctrine of predestination and infant damnation." 40

Some 70 years after Lippman's warning, we got *The Bell Curve.* And tests such as the SAT, the roots of which go back to the very same intelligence tests Lippman condemned, continue to flourish; indeed, they remain the centerpiece, the given, in our "meritocratic" views of who has "merit" and who does not.

This is especially true given the recent assaults on affirmative action in higher education. These include legal challenges and policy changes at the University of California, the University of Texas, the University of Maryland, and at state colleges in Mississippi. Critics of affirmative action argue that people ought to be judged on "merit," not gender or race; to them, the indisputable, "unbiased" criteria for admission are grades and (especially) standardized tests. Abolishing affirmative action means that test scores, regardless of their limits or what educators may think of them, become far more decisive a factor in admissions decisions. This has already happened at the University of California.

And it is happening in Mississippi. In that state, racial preferences in admissions have been abolished; now, any high school graduate with a 3.2 grade point average is automatically admitted. If students' grades are lower, their standardized test scores must be progressively higher to gain admittance. For instance, a grade point average of 2.5 means that a high schooler would have to score at least 16 on the American College Test. (Just a third of blacks meet that cutoff, compared to eight out of 10 whites, *The New York Times* has reported.)

Similarly, under the banner of higher academic standards, recent moves by the NCAA have given new prominence to the already huge role standardized test scores play in determining which athletes get scholarships to attend college. Despite strong opposition from FairTest and other groups, the NCAA recently *raised* the standardized test scores required for athletic eligibility. The NCAA changed its policy contrary to compelling evidence that the real effect of the new rules would be to exclude many minorities from scholarships who nevertheless would have succeeded in college.

"We're seeing a lot of this," says Bob Schaeffer, FairTest's public education director. "People keep believing that to show you're tough or to raise standards means you increase test score requirements, when in fact you're doing 45 neither. You're increasing the potency of severely flawed assessments. In the wake of *The Bell Curve,* there is a revival of the notion that merit equals test scores. To open doors, you need to have certain test scores." According to FairTest, more than 400 colleges and universities continue to use SAT "cut" scores, below which applicants for admission are automatically rejected.

Indeed, in the name of "higher academic standards," a conservative backlash in recent years has resulted in several states shelving efforts at alternative forms of assessment in public schools. In California, Governor Pete Wilson vetoed the reauthorization of the California Learning Assessment System, a decision that FairTest called "a tremendous setback to educational progress." Arizona put its alternative learning assessment program on a one-year hold amid controversy over its effectiveness. The Indiana Legislature defeated proposals to replace multiple-choice tests with essays and short-answer questions.

Or consider what happened when college leaders convened for a closed-door meeting at Harvard last May to mull over their affirmative action strategy in the wake of *Hopwood* v. *Texas.* The *Hopwood* court, aligning itself with the "test scores equals merit" faithful, had assumed that different minimum test scores for different races was proof of wrongdoing. The decision, ominous for affirmative action admissions policies, prompted the president of one elite institution at the Harvard meeting to suggest that the SAT be eliminated from the admission process. But other presidents at the meeting dismissed the suggestion, arguing that dropping the SAT was impossible at this time, that alumni, the press, and the public—long accustomed to the sanctity of tests as a measure of merit—would think colleges were merely relaxing their standards.

When you add up these shifting, often contradictory trends in policy, the net result doesn't look like a standardized-testing establishment that is withering under the heat of popular revolt. Indeed, in many respects, the standardized testing industry has even greater dominance over American lives than it did at the time of the Nader report in 1980. Indeed, just 26 states in 1980 had mandated testing programs for public schools; in 1990, 46 states did so, according to OTA. . . .

What Are the True Costs of Standardized Testing?
Why, then has standardized mental testing managed to continue to explode . . . Why does it remain so entrenched in American life, despite what we know about its validity?

For their part, the educational institutions that continue to buy the tests—   50
the costs of which are born by test-takers or taxpayers—would argue that standardized tests are a cost-effective way to evaluate people. It's obvious; standardized testing is cheap.

But how cheap is it, really? Research findings about the utility of test scores raise profound questions about the social and economic costs of a de facto national policy that has institutionalized the use of standardized tests for college admissions and as the gauge of local and national educational progress. While the tests might be cheap to individual institutions, in many cases these institutions bear neither the direct costs of the tests nor the indirect social costs of testing.

It seems reasonable to question whether the marginal benefits of standardized tests in terms of their predictive validity are worth the hundreds of millions of dollars test-takers and taxpayers spend annually on the exams. Also, a true economic analysis of the nation's de facto testing policy would have to factor the "opportunity cost" of testing: what is forgone when teachers spend inordinate amounts of time teaching to tests that might have minimal connection to what students really need to learn? In one typical urban school district, the OTA valued such lost opportunities at as high as $15 million per test, or $110 per pupil. Compare these estimates to the apparently cheap $6 per student in direct outlays the district normally reports as the "cost" of the test.

Moreover, a cost-benefit analysis would need to account for the social and economic costs of erroneous decisions about people. What are the true economic costs to a nation of wrong decisions about its people's talents?

These are the sort of questions that public policymakers must address before we can conclude that, indeed, standardized testing is "cheap." But even if one were to conclude that standardized testing is the best policy to maximize social benefits versus costs—an empirical question that hasn't been fully answered—there are deeper causes for the continued entrenchment of standardized mental testing in the United States.

"American Tests"

First, Americans are fascinated with mental measurement to a degree that is   55
rare in other countries. In contrast to what Europeans call "American tests," the examinations for college or university admission in other industrial countries are typically essay tests, in which students demonstrate knowledge of various subjects they've learned in the classroom. These tests are not unlike what American educators are now calling "performance assessment." Compared to other countries, Americans appear to be far more obsessed with IQ, the notion that intelligence—most often defined narrowly as logical-analytical ability—is both inborn and representable as a single numerical score.

Indeed, a stroll through any Barnes & Noble superstore speaks volumes about how our culture views intelligence and testing. For $3.95, one can buy *Self-Scoring IQ Tests* or *Self-Scoring IQ Tests for Children,* both written by an official from Mensa, the so-called "genius" club. Or there is *Puzzles for Pleasure: Test Your Intelligence with 102 Mind-Stretching Exercises in Logic, Mathematics, and Precise Reasoning.* Then, take a look at Barnes & Noble's Study Guides section, with its dozens of titles on preparing for an incredible array of standardized school and employment exams. My personal favorite, *Can You Pass These Tests?* includes practice mental tests for getting jobs as Bible scholars, baseball umpires, and even wine tasters.

Similarly, our culture places an exceedingly high value on the notion of potential to achieve, rather than achievement itself. For most Americans, a "gifted" student is one who scores off the charts on aptitude tests, not one who demonstrates advanced practical knowledge on worthwhile endeavors. "We are one of the few societies that place so much emphasis on intelligence tests," Yale psychologist Robert Sternberg told *Skeptic* magazine. "In most societies there is more emphasis on what people accomplish."

Consider, for instance, the mainly poor and black students at Northampton East High School in rural North Carolina. They took their physics and chemistry lessons and built an electric car that in national competitions bested entries from many of the country's elite high schools, whose students typically score far higher on standardized mental tests. Although Northampton East made the best car, any of their competitors who scored a perfect 1600 on their SATs are deemed by cultural norms to have won the meritocratic contest that really counts.

Indeed, the notion that merit and achievement equal high test scores, or that higher "standards" means requiring higher test scores, is repeated constantly in the popular culture. This reinforces the widely accepted legitimacy of standardized tests to rate students, teachers, schools, and colleges.

When New York City schools went shopping for a new chancellor, they hired Rudolph Crew, largely because he was seen as having engineered a big increase in standardized test scores in Tacoma, Washington. Each year, the College Board trots out its list of average SAT scores by state, and the press dutifully reports the rankings as the end all and be all of educational quality. Rarely mentioned are the huge gaps in economic advantage the scores really represent. When a local school district reports on educational progress in its quarterly newsletter, SAT or ACT scores top the charts. Test scores have become so politically charged that a few teachers, besides spending huge amounts of time teaching to tests, have resorted to cheating to make their numbers look good.

In addition, standardized tests serve the economic interests of colleges and universities, particularly their need for prestige, which is often the main asset they have to market to potential "customers." Pick up any of the numerous commercially published guides to colleges, universities, and graduate schools: high among the factors the guides use to rate institutions are average standardized test scores of those admitted. In a sense, Harvard would not be Harvard if those math or verbal SAT scores averaging 750 or so didn't leap from the page at readers of *U.S. News & World Report*. Test scores have become so important to institutions that some have resorted to "fudging" to jack up their averages, feeding the public mythology that high scores are a true measure of institutional quality.

But perhaps most responsible for the grip that mental testing has on America is that it is a highly effective means of social control, predominantly serving the interests of the nation's elites. Most people would agree that, in a democracy, merit is a good basis for deciding who gets ahead. The rub is how you define merit. We've settled on a system that defines merit in large part as the potential to achieve according to test results. It turns out that the lion's

60

share of the "potential" in our society goes to those with well-to-do, highly educated parents. Aristocracies used to perpetuate themselves on the basis of birth and parentage. But America's elites now perpetuate themselves with gatekeeping rules of their own making, rules legitimated by scientific objectivity.

The "beauty part," as Ross Perot might say, is that Americans largely buy into the rules of this rigged game. With the small exception of FairTest, there is little organized opposition to the mental measurement establishment. Besides a few studies over the years, the federal government, which is the only entity with sufficient power to regulate the testing business, has been quiet on the subject, preferring to let private enterprise have its way.

At the peak of the anti-testing revolt in 1978, Sidney P. Marland, a former College Board president and ETS trustee, captured well the notion of the mental test as social control device when he said, "I think that we will continue to have something like the Scholastic Aptitude Test to help millions of young people know something about where they stand in the universe of their peers in terms of intellectual aptitudes and readiness for continued learning." Judging by events in the years since his prognosis, Marland was right. I can only hope that more talented people, like the students at Northampton East High and all of America's "overachievers," will have the chance to prove him wrong. ◪

Reflections and Inquiries

1. According to Sacks, "a stroll through any Barnes & Noble superstore speaks volumes about how our culture views intelligence and testing." What is he referring to?

2. In what ways do standardized tests serve the economic interests of colleges, according to Sacks?

3. What is the Lighthouse Project? What was the reason for launching it?

4. What do standardized test scores reveal about students' thinking and learning styles, according to the National Association of School Psychologists?

5. What is the "Volvo effect"?

Reading to Write

1. Write an essay in which you discuss the implications of the "teaching to the test" phenomenon that Sacks calls attention to in this article.

2. Sacks asserts, "We are a nation of standardized-testing junkies." Write an essay in which you articulate the implications behind this assertion, as Sacks presents them, and whether you agree with them.

Continuing Tensions in Standardized Testing

Thomas Haladyna, Nancy Haas, and Jeanette Allison

The following article summarizes the history of standardized testing in the United States, examines the conclusions about our collective attitude toward testing that emerge from this history, considers the valid versus invalid use of test scores, and examines the effects of testing on students and teachers. The authors are professors of education at Arizona State University West, Phoenix.

Those test scores usually appear on the first page of the newspaper, building a sense of their importance. Students talk about taking the test. Legislators talk about the test scores. School board members either break out the champagne to celebrate high scores or blame the superintendent, who in turn blames the teachers, for low scores. Poor scores prompt editorial writers to lament the sorry state of schools, often criticizing the quality of teaching, as if nothing else contributed. Teachers question the usefulness of the test scores. What are the conditions behind these tests that summon such varied responses?

In this article, the authors examine the tensions resulting from the use of these test scores. Three interwoven themes provide a background for these tensions. The first theme is that mass education was a great social experiment, first tried in the United States in the mid 1800s. The nation sought not only to provide education opportunities to all of its citizens, but also to maintain efficiency in doing so. The second theme is that achievement tests always have been used by the public to evaluate educational progress. Policymakers, including state and national legislators and school boards, make policy decisions and allocate resources based on test scores. It stands to reason that large-scale standardized testing at the national, state and school district levels is likely to continue. The third theme is that U.S. schools have used tests to weed out students and eliminate them from further education opportunities, rather than using tests to identify problems in learning that need intervention. Amid this tension, many students are not being well served—in particular, those who live in poverty and/or lack the language skills necessary to succeed in school and in society. This article examines the roles that educators might play in the future of standardized testing.

A standardized achievement test is designed to provide norm-referenced interpretations of student achievement in specific content areas at certain points in their education careers. Norm-referenced interpretations are relative, showing how students compare with others in the nation.

Source: Haladyna, Thomas, Nancy Haas, and Jeanette Allison. "Continuing Tensions in Standardized Testing." *Childhood Education* Annual Theme (1998): 262–273. Reprinted by permission of Thomas Haladyna, Nancy Haas, and Jeanette Allison and the Association for Childhood Education International, 17904 Georgia Avenue, Suite 215, Olney, M.D. Copyright © 1998 by the Association.

Part One:
A Brief History of Standardized Testing in the U.S.
The impetus for standardized tests emerged in the 1800s and has continued. Problems with standardized testing today are really not very different from old ones.

The Inception of Standardized Testing
The first documented achievement tests were administered in the period 1840 to 1875, when American educators changed their focus from educating the elite to educating the masses. Cremin (1964) pointed out that the earliest tests were intended for individual evaluation, but test results were inappropriately used to compare schools and children without regard for non-school influences. As millions of immigrants came to the United States in the 19th century, the standardized test became a way to ensure that all children were receiving the same standard of education. In fact, however, test results were often used to emphasize the need for school reform (Office of Technology Assessment, 1992).

Ability (Intelligence) Testing
At the turn of the century, the focus shifted from achievement testing to ability testing for the purpose of sorting and classifying students. Schools wanted to identify and weed out students who were not going to succeed academically. Consequently, many ethnic groups new to the United States faced discrimination on the basis of new "intelligence" tests, such as the Binet Intelligence Scale.

In 1922, Walter Lippman wrote a series of articles in the *New Republic* protesting the misuse of standardized ability tests, which echo the protests of current critics. Lippman characterized intelligence tests as

> [a] gross perversion by muddleheaded and prejudiced men. . . . Intelligence is not an abstraction like length and weight; it is an exceedingly complicated notion which nobody has yet succeeded in defining. If the impression takes root that these tests really measure intelligence, that they contribute a sort of last judgment on the child's capacity, that they reveal "scientifically" his predetermined ability, then it would be a thousand times better if all the intelligence testers and their questionnaires were sunk without warning in the Sargasso Sea. (cited in Perrone, 1976, pp. 14–15)

Despite criticism, standardized ability testing quickly took hold in the United States. According to Deffenbaugh (1925), both ability and achievement tests were being used to sort and classify students, reflecting education's lingering elitism, as well as educators' failure to address the problems of low achievers.

The Beginning of Multiple-Choice, Standardized Achievement Tests

As noted earlier, two prevailing goals in American education have been 1) providing equal access to public education and 2) efficient delivery. The drive for greater efficiency turned American schools away from essay tests and toward multiple-choice tests. Critics and test specialists argued vehemently about the strengths and weaknesses of the two types of tests (e.g., O'Dell, 1928), an argument that continues today (Haladyna, 1994; Shepard, 1994).

Technological advances meant that multiple-choice tests could offer test data about many students at a very small cost. This method facilitated comparisons among teachers, schools, school districts and even states. The Stanford Achievement Test is recognized as the first of the large-scale publishers' tests (Haladyna, in press). First published in 1923, it continues to be an acknowledged leader in its field. Other popular standardized tests that can trace their origins to that era include the Iowa Test for Basic Skills (ITBS), the American College Testing Program, Scholastic Aptitude Test, the California Achievement Test and the Metropolitan Achievement Test. The ACT Assessment and the Scholastic Aptitude Test (SAT) became the nation's leading college admissions tests.

Haertel and Calfee (1983) stated that these tests at first only vaguely and generally reflected school learning, without any mention of a curriculum or instructional objectives. Prescriptive and didactic textbooks, however, began to have an influence on the tests. Diagnosis and prescription became central themes in standardized testing. Critics noticed that these tests measured concrete, lower-level school outcomes very well, but neglected more complex types of learning. By the 1950s, the Bloom taxonomy (Bloom, Engelhart, Furst, Hill, & Krathwohl, 1956) emerged, which justified teaching by objectives and raising the quality of testing to measuring more than simple memory-type learning. The biggest disappointment with the standardized achievement test was its remote connection to classroom teaching and the school district curriculum. This mismatch led to a different approach to testing.

10

Criterion-Referenced Testing

Originating from Ralph Tyler's work in the 1930s, teaching and testing by instructional objectives came into vogue in the 1970s. The criterion-referenced test was supposed to be linked to objectives or learning domains that were easily tested. This kind of testing fostered systematic instruction. Proponents of criterion-referenced testing, such as James Popham (1995), called for tests that inform teachers about their successes and failures. Publishers' standardized achievement tests, however, are non-specific and unfocused with respect to the variety of objectives that teachers address in their classrooms. Interest in the criterion-referenced test has waned, because many of its outcomes seemed easy to teach and easy to test. Furthermore, the criterion-referenced test lacked the normative data that nationally normed standardized achievement tests could provide.

Testing in the Latter Part of the 20th Century

Three factors affected standardized testing in the latter part of the 20th century: 1) changing demographics caused by immigration, 2) technological challenges introduced during the Cold War and exacerbated by the computer age and 3) racial inequality. Arthur Jensen (1980) wrote essays and published studies that fueled concern over intelligence and racial differences. Studies show that low degrees of scholastic aptitude (i.e., intelligence) predict low levels of education, and that for most people low levels of education lead to unproductive lives (Herrnstein & Murray, 1994). Reversing this trend, while difficult, continues to be a goal in American education. The question remains: Can we educate *all* students enough so they can function in society in more positive ways?

Problems We Face Today

How do we measure achievement of today's students? For what purposes should standardized achievement tests be used? Do standardized achievement tests adequately measure school achievement, or are performance tests and portfolios more appropriate? Tensions continue to mount as both educators and non-educators seek answers to these questions.

Year after year, polls show that the public wants the information from publishers' standardized achievement tests; 68 percent of respondents to a USA/Gallup poll favor President Clinton's national testing program, and other polls continue to show support for standardized testing (Rose, Elam & Gallup, 1997). Parents are increasingly willing to pay for independent evaluations of their children's achievement in basic skills, as evidenced by the rise of private testing and tutoring centers.

Until a time when they are specifically designed to reflect curriculum and instruction, publishers' standardized achievement tests do not seem to be appropriate measures of instruction or curriculum. They do not reflect how instruction has affected learning and how demographics produces differences in performance. When the achievement tests are given, however, newspapers clamor to publish the scores, and then try to interpret what they mean. Reporters seem to have an innate need to line up the scores from top to bottom and then attempt to make judgments related to the effectiveness of schools. Even college admissions tests are used in this invalid way. The ACT and SAT were never intended to evaluate states or school districts, and the sampling of students is never adequate for this purpose. Nonetheless, members of the press continue to chant the mantra about how schools and, specifically, teachers are failing.

The Message from Testing's History
Four major conclusions emerge from our history of standardized testing:

- Testing has been and will always remain a basis for knowing about how schools affect students, despite the potential for misinterpretation and misuse of test scores

- Two governing principles continue to influence school testing: 1) all students must be given equal opportunities regarding their education and 2) schooling must be offered in an efficient manner

- The increase in the amount of testing, as well as the misuse of test scores, increases tensions in education, to the detriment of children and teachers

- Schooling plays an important role in each citizen's life; those with more education lead more productive lives, and the "quality" of that education is unfairly driven by test scores. (Office of Technology Assessment, 1992)

Standardized testing is entrenched in American education. The public continues to support testing because it perceives that test scores are valid indicators of children's learning. While it seems unlikely that educators will be able to change the public's taste for large-scale standardized tests, it is possible to ensure that the test results are responsibly interpreted and used.

Part Two:
The Role of Professional Organizations
Many national and international organizations have issued position papers or statements on standardized testing, including the: Association for Childhood Education International (1991), Association for Supervision and Curriculum Development (1987), Council for Exceptional Children (1993), National Association for the Education of Young Children (1988), National Association of Early Childhood Teacher Educators (1989), National Association of Elementary School Principals (1989), National Association of State Boards of Education (1988), National Council of Teachers of English (1989), National Council of Teachers of Mathematics (1989), National Commission on Testing and Public Policy (1990), American Psychological Association [APA], National Council on Measurement in Testing, and American Educational Research Association (1985), and the National Education Association (1972). These organizations recognize the mounting evidence that standardized testing often has detrimental and counterproductive effects on children and teachers.

Kamii (1990) summarized the growing concerns of professional organizations, teachers and parents about standardized testing: "[We] are not against accountability. We are all for it. Our reasons for opposing the use of achievement tests are that they are not valid measures of accountability and that they are producing classroom practices harmful to young children's development" (p. ix). Below is the gist of what organizations conclude about standardized testing:

- Testing increases pressure and stress on children, which sets them up for failure, lowered self-esteem and potential health risks

- Testing compels teachers to spend valuable time preparing children to take tests and teaching to the test, undermining what otherwise could be sound, responsive teaching and learning

- Testing limits children's education possibilities, which results in a mediocre curriculum and learning

- Testing discourages social and intellectual development, such as cooperation, creativity, and problem-solving skills, as time is spent instead on learning exactly what appears on the test

- Testing leads to harmful tracking and labeling of children, especially those of minority and low socioeconomic backgrounds.

The professional organizations have stated, in no uncertain terms, that testing does not provide useful information about individual children; yet, test scores often become the basis for making decisions about retention, promotion, kindergarten entrance, ability grouping and special education placements (Council for Exceptional Children, 1993; National Association for the Education of Young Children/Council for Exceptional Children, 1996).

Professional organizations have redoubled their efforts to protect children and teachers. They propose the cessation of all standardized testing below the 4th grade. Realizing, however, that schools are under public pressure to test children, they have made detailed recommendations about testing practices. For instance, the National Association for the Education of Young Children (NAEYC, 1988) issued strong recommendations about the selection, administration, interpretation and use of tests and scores, charging that:

> The most important consideration in evaluating and using standardized tests is the utility criterion: The purposes of testing must be to improve services for children and ensure that children benefit from their educational experiences. The ritual use even of "good tests" (those judged to be valid and reliable measures) is to be discouraged without documented research showing that children benefit from their use. (p. 53)

The above excerpt alludes to something very ironic about testing practices: There is no evidence that supports its pervasive use. What are its direct benefits to children? What great advantage does testing provide teachers?

Professional advocate organizations agree that testing needs to be more humane, meaningful and varied (see, especially, Association for Childhood Education International/Perrone, 1991; Bredekamp & Copple, 1997; Council for Exceptional Children, 1993; National Association for the Education of Young Children, 1988; National Association for the Education of Young Children/Council for Exceptional Children, 1996; Perrone, 1976, 1977, 1981, 1991).

Many educators agree that continuing standardized testing is basically ir-responsible (e.g., Meisels, 1987; Shepard & Smith, 1986; Weber, 1977).

- All standardized testing of children—preschool through later elemen-tary—should cease or at least be severely reduced

- Teachers and parents should oppose all standardized testing especially group-administered tests

- If tests are given, teachers and parents should oppose using test results alone to make any important judgments about a child

- Testing must recognize and be sensitive to individual diversity (age, ability, gender, culture, language and race)

- Tests should be used solely for their intended purpose

- Administrators and teachers must critically evaluate and select tests for validity

- Administrators and policymakers have the responsibility to ensure that schooling is both psychologically and morally prudent for children

- Administrators and teachers must be knowledgeable about interpreting test results, and cautious and conservative when sharing test results publicly.

Increasingly, professional organizations argue that standardized testing is an extremely high-stakes practice in which children's worth is "measured" by a score that is not likely to be validly interpreted. Furthermore, teachers' effec-tiveness is often unfairly judged on the basis of a classroom average. Annual, standardized tests make no allowance for the fact that students' development and cognitive abilities in the early years are uneven. While children's devel-opmental growth is not uniform, standardized test norms are based on aver-age growth without regard to unique developmental patterns. Individual character is lost and children who do not fare favorably on standardized tests (i.e., those with special needs and language barriers) remain "guilty until proven innocent" (Bredekamp & Copple, 1997; Meisels, 1987, 1993; Shepard, 1994; Smith, 1991).

Despite strong support, no convincing evidence exists that standardized testing is beneficial. It can, however, increase chaos and reduce teachers' sense of efficacy (Hartman, 1991; Rosenholtz, 1989). The scope of the curriculum is also reduced. As a result, teachers spend precious time focusing on the me-chanics of test-taking, and . . . on test content (Haladyna, Nolen & Haas, 1991; Nolen, Haladyna & Haas, 1992).

In fact, Perrone (1991) stated that many school districts do not use any standardized testing programs, and they can produce alternative "evidence" of students' productivity and teachers' effectiveness (see also Bredekamp &

25

Copple, 1997; Bredekamp & Rosegrant, 1992, 1995; Meisels, 1993). The use of student portfolios, for example, is gaining many supporters, including parents. The portfolio appears to directly reflect what students are learning in ways that standardized tests never can. One advantage of the portfolio over any test is the perspective of time. A good portfolio shows a student's growth in some important ability, such as writing, over the entire school year. This growth can be assessed by lay persons and parents, without the need for technical data.

Another advantage of the portfolio is that the students' personal written reflections it contains also show how motivation and attitude can affect students' growth. Thus, the portfolio yields a much richer assessment, especially when its contents are directed from a school district curriculum.

Professional organizations need to promote such alternative assessments. More important, organizations must be more active in assessment design, thereby providing school districts and instructional programs with valid and more humane methods to assess students.

Part Three:
Valid and Invalid Interpretations
and Uses of Test Results

The misinterpretation and blatant misuse of test scores is pervasive. Some questions to consider are:

What time span does a test score represent? Test scores can reflect the sum of a child's learning over several years. Most policymakers, however, as well as the lay public, want to know how much learning occurred in a particular school year. A standardized test given once a year is not a good measure of this kind of learning. These standardized tests are not precise enough, nor is instruction geared to reflect exactly what the test measures. At best, we get a rough year-to-year measure of student learning that does not accurately measure the sum of school learning because the school curriculum is seldom specifically correlated to what the test measures. If the curriculum and instruction *did* match the test, we would have another kind of problem, "teaching to the test," which will be discussed in another section.

The causes of a test score or set of scores are complex and difficult to assess. There are, in fact, many causes, some of which reside in school and some of which originate in the home or community. It would be incorrect to attribute test results solely to the teacher's expertise. So many other factors affect test results. In Arizona, for example, 28 percent of the students live in poverty. It is no stretch of the imagination to reason that these students lack the same opportunities the other 72 percent enjoys.

Standardized tests' very name conveys to laypersons a precision that no publisher would support. Each test is a *sample* of a large body of knowledge that teachers often feel compelled to teach. When teachers decide to "teach to the

30

test," a practice that most of them deplore, the interpretation of the test score is corrupted. The standardized test score should never be a precise measure of student learning; it was meant to be merely a general survey instrument.

It has been widely reported that the pressure for unfair accountability causes a number of teachers to tamper with their teaching methods in order to get high scores (Haladyna et al., 1991; Mehrens & Kaminski, 1989; Weber, 1977). While no one is proud of these practices, they are extensive and can be traced to the reductionist thinking that a test score precisely measures a teacher's or school's merit. The invalid interpretation of test scores, coupled with constant public scrutiny and the need for higher performance from chronically low-scoring students, drives some teachers into this unethical trap.

Valid Uses of Test Scores

National rank. One of the major selling points for any standardized survey achievement test is that it can rank students through percentiles. In a competitive world, such information helps shape expectations. We cannot overlook such national ranking, since test scores drive decisions about college admission. Yet, it would be unwise to create false expectations from test performance using national rank, unless mitigating circumstances could explain why certain students scored higher or lower than expected.

Future achievement. The best predictors of future test scores are past test scores. The best predictors of student grades are prior grades. These simple truisms show that a constancy in standardized test scores exists that teaching cannot influence. If these tests truly sample general achievement, then one test score can generally predict future test scores and, thus, future achievement. Intervention or changes may affect future achievement, but test scores are fairly dependable predictors of future test performance.

Curriculum evaluation. At the individual level, a set of test scores is hardly dependable enough to provide good information, but at a school or school district level subscores provide enough information, such as mathematics computation and mathematics problem solving, to furnish central administration and teachers with ideas about student performance relevant to curricula. If the scores for mathematics problem solving are low compared with other areas, the curriculum could be revised, which will, in turn, ultimately change instruction and future test results. This is a positive use of standardized test information. The negative side of this evaluation issue, and a common problem, is that if your curriculum is focused on content and processes that are not well represented on the publishers' tests, then test results can be very misleading about your instructional program's effectiveness.

Policy decisions. The primary education policymakers are school boards and federal and state legislators. They need information to make policies and allocate resources. Standardized test scores provide information that can be useful, but also misleading. A key requirement for making interpretations

35

about the adequacy of student learning and program effectiveness is the linkage of any standardized test to the current curriculum.

In an experiment tried in a small Western school district, the first author met with members of a school district who were trying to justify their programs to an increasingly critical public. An examination of standardized achievement test results showed the district to be slightly above average, reflecting the community's social class and economic wealth. Teachers were asked to examine each test item. The test items were divided into two parts: instructionally relevant and instructionally irrelevant. On relevant items, the district's performance was well above the national average. On irrelevant items, its average was slightly below the national average. The lesson to be learned: if we test what we teach, we are more likely to get positive results than if we test what we do not teach.

Grouping students for instruction. In the early years of the 20th century, schools customarily used test scores to group students for instruction. Students who needed more time and patience were grouped for remedial instruction, while advanced students were permitted to work ahead. Multiage grouping strategies seem to have many positive benefits, according to Ong, Allison and Haladyna (submitted for publication). Since tests scores have good predictive value regarding performance and future performance, it is desirable to have good test information when determining groupings for instruction.

Diagnosis of weak areas in the curriculum. Traditional, standardized test scores provide convincing breakdowns of student performance by specific topics. These breakdowns can help school districts and schools plan for shifts in instructional emphasis to shore up lagging performance in critical areas. If a school's mathematics computation scores are low, a re-emphasis in all the grades might result in a more positive result the following year.

Invalid Uses of Test Scores

Invalid uses of test scores contribute mightily to the increasing tensions associated with standardized testing.

Cash for high test scores. Currently, Arizona is considering legislation that will reward teachers if their students' test scores are high. They would receive a $1,200 bonus in pay. Connecting pay bonuses to students' test performance has a great many flaws, not the least of which is that some teachers and school leaders will do almost anything, even cheat, to achieve a high score (Mehrens & Kaminski, 1989; Nolen, Haladyna, & Haas, 1992). Some educators might then produce fraudulent results by dismissing students who are likely to score low, reading the answers to students, or simply correcting students' answer sheets after the test. Such practices have been well documented, when teachers and other educators feel no recourse other than to tamper with the testing process.

40

Graduation or certification testing. Many states are experimenting with graduation or certification testing. Oregon, for example, has developed the Certificate of Initial Mastery, which requires additional qualifications to receive a high school diploma. Graduation or certification testing is certainly legitimate, because it reflects the public's current interest in having high standards in public schools. It remains to be proven, however, that making pass/fail decisions on the basis of test scores is always valid. The City of Chicago, for example, recently failed 8th-grade students on the basis of test scores from the Iowa Test of Basic Skills.

The schools' failure to provide students opportunities to learn the Iowa Test material, however, may provide a legal basis for striking down such action. How the passing score is set represents another important issue. Downing and Haladyna (1996) identified the types of validity evidence needed in such high-stakes testing and the legal implications of such testing. While states like Oregon go about high school certification using validity evidence as a guidance tool, do all sponsors of such tests stick to the *Standards for Educational and Psychological Testing* (APA et al., 1985)?

Evaluating teaching. Many researchers and experts in teacher evaluation strongly reject the idea of using test scores to evaluate teaching (Berk, 1988; Haertel, 1986). The most common argument against this practice is that students' learning capabilities can be affected by many powerful factors outside of school. Some of these factors are mental ability and social capital (Coleman, 1987), a broad, encompassing concept that includes family and home factors as well as neighborhood factors. Coleman argued that in the most extreme circumstances, no amount of teaching will overcome profoundly low social capital. Teachers from low-income areas already know this. Any progress they make with these vulnerable children will never earn them plaudits as teachers, despite the fact that they heroically work under adverse conditions.

Evaluating schools and school districts. This practice hardly seems defensible, because factors well beyond the teacher's control influence student learning. How, then, can school districts and schools be held accountable for test scores, particularly when the standardized achievement does not sample the domain of instruction found at the school? A good case in point arises in Arizona, where every elementary and secondary school student took a version of the Iowa test. A study by Noggle (1987) showed only a 26 percent correlation between an Iowa test and the state's content standards.

Curriculum alignment. Some schools ask teachers to abandon the regular   45
curriculum in order to prepare students for the standardized achievement test; in other schools, the curriculum is aligned directly with the test (Nolen et al., 1992). Abandoning the curriculum seems to disrupt students and disturb the learning process. Curriculum continuity and coherence are critical in the formative years, especially as children learn how to read and write. Allowing the test to dictate the curriculum results in a watered down curriculum.

Teaching to the test. Nolen et al. (1992) showed that some schools abandon part of the academic year in favor of test preparation, and develop instructional packets to coach students for the test. Suspending normal instruction clearly has a negative effect on student development.

Part Four:
Effects on Students and Teachers

The effects of testing on students and teachers has been studied by Smith (1991), Paris, Lawton, Turner and Roth (1991), and the authors of this article (Haas, Haladyna & Nolen, 1990; Hartman, 1991; Nolen et al., 1992).

Student Effects

Students are adversely affected by standardized tests in three ways: 1) it heightens student anxiety about the testing experience, 2) it decreases student motivation and learning and 3) students, by the time they are in high school, do not believe the tests hold much value (Paris et al., 1991).

Test anxiety. Test anxiety is a chronic problem for as many as 25 percent of all students (Haladyna et al., 1991). Pressure to perform well on tests may exacerbate students' natural anxiety, or create other, related problems. Hartman (1991) and Haas et al. (1990) collected many anecdotal comments from teachers who described their students' test anxiety. The tests left many of the students feeling angry, frustrated, tired and upset. One teacher complained:

> The CAT [California Achievement Test] is a nightmare of testing these children. And I mean a nightmare: Kids crying and throwing up, breaking their pencils, going to the bathroom, saying, "I don't want to come to school" after going 15 minutes of a two-week ordeal. (Hartman, 1991, p. 53)

Another teacher said:

> The children are tense. They don't eat or sleep well the night before the test. Many parents put tremendous pressure on the children to score high. (Haas et al., 1990, p. 50)

Nolen et al. (1992) reported a variety of student problems, including truancy, upset stomach, irritability, crying, wetting or soiling, excessive bathroom breaks, concern over the time limit, "freezing" up on timed parts of the test, headaches, hiding, refusing to take the test, and increased aggression. The prevalence of these incidents, as reported by teachers, ranged from 6.7 percent for wetting and soiling to 44 percent for excessive concern over time limits. The extensiveness of this anxiety is considerable, and would seem to correlate with damage to students' self-concept, and their attitudes toward school and the subject matter.

Loss of valuable learning time. Another dimension of this problem is that the students spend an enormous amount of time studying for, and taking, this test. Nolen et al. (1992) reported that only 12.5 percent of the teachers surveyed at the elementary level spent no time preparing for the test, while others reported spending up to two months in preparation. While this time may be viewed as learning time, students are robbed of time to spend on curriculum-appropriate learning. A junior high school teacher summarized this problem in the following way:

> Because of the standardized test, I found that my creativity and flexibility as a teacher have been greatly reduced. I spend a great deal of time zeroing in on skills that I know are on the test. This leaves only a bare minimum of opportunity to explore writing and enrichment reading. In reviewing the test I find that what I am going over is the same thing that the teachers in one grade lower and one grade higher are covering as well. This makes for a very redundant curriculum. Also, the skills we emphasize before the tests do not help them to perform better on a day-to-day basis. (Haas et al., 1990, p. 63)

The cognitive losses brought on by excessive overstudying of test-specific material may be difficult to assess. The point is, spending class time learning test-specific material detracts from learning other material that needs to be covered.

Inadequate effort or inattention to perform. A number of reports focus on student motivation to perform. A 7th-grade teacher reported:

> This testing is unacceptable. In my homeroom this year out of 28 students, 19 showed up for part of the testing. Many of those students "bubbled" randomly. The situation exists in many classrooms in this district. The students are highly transient and from poor homes. They expect to do poorly and don't try. (Haas et al., 1990, p. 62)

Another teacher said:

> Any little thing could distract them. So it might be a pencil that dropped. It might be something, say we're sitting here and there's a bird out there on the wire and they might look over and see that bird. For ten questions they're looking at the blue jay on the wire and mark anything! . . . Here [the administration] has a test score that they are using to evaluate me on the entire school year and it's all based on the blue jay that was sitting on the rail out there! (Hartman, 1991, p. 66)

Paris et al. (1991) reported lack of student effort to be a problem that increases with age. Students in the early grades think that the test is relevant to measuring what they have learned, but by high school most students know that the test does not reflect their intelligence or learning and has no bearing on their future. They believe tests that really count toward their future are the college admissions tests—the ACT or SAT. Reports indicate that students pay less attention to the test because they are unmotivated or find the tasks too hard.

Effects on Teachers

This section addresses problems that afflict teachers under the conditions introduced by testing. Mary Lee Smith (1991) put it succinctly:

> To understand the perceived effects of external testing on teachers, one needs only to ask. Their statements on questionnaires, in interviews, and during conversations in meetings and lounges reveal the anxiety, shame, loss of esteem, and alienation they experience from publication and use of test scores. (p. 8)

Teachers suffer when standardized tests are used as the sole indicator of student learning. Haas et al. (1990) interviewed nearly 400 teachers, whose comments echoed much of those from Smith's (1991) observations.

Invalidity of test interpretation and use. As stated earlier, test results often are interpreted and used in an invalid manner. If a school's scores are lower than what parents expect, the teachers may be shamed into thinking that they have not done a good enough job. Even teachers who are lucky enough to teach in affluent areas, where test scores are generally very high, may realize they had very little to do with that achievement. Using test scores without a context brings shame and embarrassment to many teachers. They know that it is invalid to use these test scores to hold teachers accountable, but they are powerless in the face of the media commentary and political attacks.

Another factor contributing to the invalidity problem is the presence of children from different cultures who may have English language deficiencies that inhibit learning and affect the measurement of their learning. A 2nd-grade teacher put it this way:

> My students are mostly Native American and Hispanic [of] low SES [socioeconomic status], and as a result are exposed to many hardships. It hardly seems fair to compare their scores to students of the same age who have grown up with a well developed foundation in the English language. I think a national standardized norm-referenced test is a good idea for some things but the results should be taken into consideration with cultural and SES factors. (Haas et al., 1990, p. 102)

A 6th-grade teacher said: "How can the test be appropriate for my Navajo and Hispanic students when the only time they speak English is when they are in school?" (Haas et al., 1991, p. 36).

Teachers seem to be divided roughly into two camps. Both camps admit that the tests reflect poorly on what they teach and how well they teach. Unfortunately, the first camp may resort to some type of strategy to improve student performance on invalid tests, even to the point of cheating. Members of the second camp merely ignore the test and teach according to their beliefs. The second group, while having to endure criticism for low test scores, may still be more satisfied.

Curriculum mismatch. Most teachers recognize that mandated publishers' tests do not match well with state-dictated standards, district curriculum, textbook series or what they themselves deem to be appropriate content. One 1st-grade teacher said:

> I feel that by mandating the standardized test in the primary grades, we are allowing test makers to design curriculum, at least in my district. A much better measure of what children are learning is through the district's curriculum referenced tests. Much valuable time is being lost to test preparation. (Haas et al., 1990, p. 37)

Because the state mandates a test that does not match what teachers are   60 expected to teach, they have to either ignore the state's test and do what they think is professionally and responsibly correct, or cave in and teach to the test. This sets up teachers' sense of apathy that Smith (1991) summarizes as, "Why should we worry about these scores when we all know they are worthless?" (p. 9).

Teacher distress. As reported in the previous section, students suffer from the testing experience. Teachers see firsthand the effects of testing on students, especially young students. These teachers also see the effects of testing on themselves, their colleagues and even the administrators. In the words of a 6th-grade teacher:

> The test adds stress to everyone. In this district administrators are made to think that the test reflects on how well they do their job, which makes them more concerned for themselves than for the children. The children in this school are scared to death because they have been warned by their parents to do well and make them proud. The parents take the results of the test personally, as if they were being evaluated. (Haas et al., 1990, p. 49)

This feeling of remorse about what is happening to students and colleagues seems to gnaw at these teachers. A feeling of hopelessness seems to pervade this atmosphere. It is hard for teachers to be satisfied with their chosen profession when the consequences of published tests can be used against them in so many ways.

Part Five: Where Do We Go from Here?

As we have learned, publishers' standardized achievement tests are not going away. In fact, standardized testing is gaining in popularity, despite its obvious harmful effects. Educators must continue to inform the public about these tests' negative effects, without compromising their integrity or commitment to sound curriculum, good instruction and appropriate assessment. Audiences for this message include: 1) state legislators and school board members, 2) the media, 3) parents, 4) the general public and 5) the few fellow educators who do not understand this message. It is important that educators be united about standardized testing.

What Message Do We Send to These Audiences?

To reiterate, accountability is a good idea. It is important to know where each student stands relative to standards, and to know what to do to help them improve. Simplistic uses of test scores that are only remotely connected to classroom teaching will not achieve this accountability. Test scores alone are not the complete picture, because they ignore environmental factors. What the authors advocate is a broad assessment that includes worthwhile outcomes of student learning, as well as information about factors that exist within and outside of school that affect learning. Additionally, test batteries should be aligned with the curriculum of the school district and instruction.

To advance this continuous dialogue with the public regarding students' education, we support four propositions that guide us toward responsible standardized testing:

Test score interpretations must be valid. Learning is a lifetime endeavor. 65 These standardized survey tests only *sample* the large domain of knowledge. When we see scores, we need to ask what the test measures and what factors probably contribute to this level of performance. In other words, a test score represents only one level of learning out of a very large domain. We must squarely face the fact that these tests are not adequate reflections of a school district curriculum or instructional emphasis at the classroom level. As a measure of lifelong learning, we might want to speculate about which factors contributed to high or low performances. Some of these factors are: the quality and quantity of instruction, motivation, cognitive ability, amount and quality of family support, attitude, adequacy of instructional materials, and quality of educational leadership, both within the school and at the district level. Do not make judgments simply from a test score. Be careful about assigning a single cause to test scores, such as the teacher being solely responsible for the student outcomes. Such irresponsible interpretation unfairly judges teachers and children.

Test score uses must be valid. Insist that test scores be used only for valid purposes. Ask for evidence about the validity of any test use. Evaluating teachers on the basis of test scores is invalid, because no evidence can show that the test is well-matched to instruction; nor can it be shown whether other, non-school factors were taken into account. Test scores are simply inadequate to the task of evaluating teaching and teachers. Tests that are supposed to keep students accountable for their education are defensible if students are given adequate preparation for the test, as well as remedial instruction, when necessary.

Keep standardized tests standardized. Once the standardized test is accurately interpreted and used fairly and defensibly, the administration of the test ought to be standardized, as well. Too many reports from all parts of the

United States concern educators who capitulated to the pressures of being accountable by doing something unethical. To reiterate:

- Do not teach to the test. Do not alter the curriculum to conform to the test's content.

- Do not change the test administration times or conditions.

- Determining who should be tested should be spelled out as part of policy. Excluding certain students from testing is one way to inflate test scores, which may lead to invalid interpretations.

- Excluding students from testing is sometimes appropriate, however, as when the test result does not validly reflect students' knowledge. Language barriers, emotional difficulties, health and illness factors, and physical and mental handicaps are prominent factors that may hinder students' ability to perform well. The exclusion should be standardized from class to class, school to school, and district to district.

Examine and evaluate the consequences of standardized testing. Students should not take tests unless the interpretations and uses of test results are fair and useful. If it is shown that the consequences of testing have harmful effects on students, then such testing cannot be justified. As pointed out in Part Three, many educators have argued that standardized testing below grade 3 seldom provides true measures of student ability or development.

In addition, the reporting of test scores by racial or ethnic categories seldom serves useful purposes. These reports often perpetuate negative stereotypes of minority groups, masking relevant factors, such as poverty, that may account for a poor performance. If test interpretation and use lead to unequal treatment of students instead of providing equal opportunities, then we must take steps to resolve the problem. More and more states, for example, are adopting stiff high school graduation requirements. If students are not instructed adequately, then large numbers of students will not complete high school. Test scores already tell us that the most likely group of students destined to fail these graduation tests will be those living in poverty and those with the added task of trying to learn to read, write, speak and understand English. As we examine and evaluate the consequences of standardized testing, we will probably continue to offer the public what they demand, but we should insist that the testing is done in a manner that does not harm those whom the tests are intended to serve.

70

References

American Psychological Association, American Educational Research Association, National Council on Measurement in Education. (1985). *Standards for educational and psychological testing.* Washington, DC: American Psychological Association.

Association for Children Education International/Perrone, V. (1991). On standardized testing. A position paper. *Childhood Education, 67,* 131–142.

Association for Supervision and Curriculum Development. (1987). Testing concerns. In *Forty years of leadership: A synthesis of ASCD resolutions through 1987* (pp. 17–19). Alexandria, VA: Author.

Berk, R. A. (1988). Fifty reasons why student achievement gain does not mean teacher effectiveness. *Journal of Personnel Evaluation in Education, 1*(4), 345–364.

Bloom, B. S., Engelhart, M. D., Furst, E. J., Hill, W. H., & Krathwohl, D. R. (1956). *Taxonomy of educational objectives.* New York: D. McKay.

Bredekamp, S., & Copple, C. (Eds.) (1997). *Developmentally appropriate practice in early child-hood programs* (Rev. ed.). Washington, DC: National Association for the Education of Young Children.

Bredekamp, S., & Rosegrant, T. (Eds.). (1992). *Reaching potentials: Appropriate curriculum and assessment for young children: Volume 1.* Washington, DC: National Association for the Education of Young Children.

Bredekamp, S., & Rosegrant, T. (Eds.). (1995). *Reaching potentials: Transforming early child-hood curriculum and assessment: Volume 2.* Washington, DC: National Association for the Education of Young Children.

Coleman, J. S. (1987). Families and schools. *Educational Researcher, 16,* 32–38.

Council for Exceptional Children. (1993). *Division for Early Childhood recommended practices: Indicators of quality in programs for infants and young children with special needs and their families.* Washington, DC: Author.

Cremin, J. (1964). *The transformations of the school: Progressivism in American education, 1876–1957.* New York: Vintage Books.

Deffenbaugh, W. S. (1925). *Uses of intelligence tests in 215 cities. City School Leaflet No. 20.* Washington, DC: Bureau of Education, U.S. Department of the Interior.

Downing, S. M., & Haladyna, T. M. (1996). Model for evaluating high-stakes testing pro-grams: Why the fox should not guard the chicken coop. *Educational Measurement: Issues and Practice, 15,* 5–12.

Haas, N. S., Haladyna, T. M., & Nolen, S. B. (1990, April). *War stories from the trenches: What teachers and administrators say about the test.* Paper presented at a symposium at the annual meeting of the National Council on Measurement in Education, Boston.

Haertel, E. (1986). The valid use of student performance measures for teacher evaluation. *Educational Evaluation and Policy Analysis, 8,* 45–60.

Haertel, E., & Calfee, R. (1983). School achievement: Thinking about what to test. *Journal of Educational Measurement, 20,* 119–130.

Haladyna, T. M. (1994). *Developing and validating multiple-choice test items.* Hillsdale, NJ: Lawrence Erlbaum Associates.

Haladyna, T. M. (in press). *Review of the Stanford Achievement Test* (8th ed.). Mental Mea-surement Yearbook.

Haladyna, T. M., Nolen, S. B., & Haas, N. S. (1991). Raising standardized achievement test scores and the origins of test score pollution. *Educational Researcher, 20*(5), 2–7.

Hartman, J. A. (1991). *How mandated student assessment programs affect kindergarten teachers: Two steps forward, three steps backward.* Unpublished doctoral dissertation. Urbana, IL: The University of Illinois.

Herrnstein, J., & Murray, C. (1994). *The bell curve: Intelligence and class structure in American life.* New York: Free Press.

Jensen, A. R. (1980). *Bias in mental testing.* New York: The Free Press.

Kamii, C. (Ed.). (1990). *Achievement testing in the early grades: The games grown-ups play.* Washington, DC: National Association for the Education of Young Children.

Mehrens, W. A., & Kaminski, J. (1989). Methods for improving standardized test scores: Fruitful, fruitless, or fraudulent? *Educational Measurement: Issues and Practices, 8,* 14–22.

Meisels, S. J. (1987). Uses and abuses of developmental screening and school readiness testing. *Young Children, 42,* 4–6, 68–73.

Meisels, S. J. (1993). Remaking classroom assessment with The Work Sampling System. *Young Children, 48*(5), 34–40.

National Association for the Education of Young Children. (1988). Position statement on standardized testing of young children 3 through 8 years of age. *Young Children, 43*(3), 42–47.

National Association for the Education of Young Children/Council for Exceptional Children. (1996). *Guidelines for preparation for early childhood professionals.* Washington, DC: Authors.

National Association of Early Childhood Teacher Educators. (1989). Resolution: Testing in the early years. *The Journal of Early Childhood Teacher Education, 10*(1), 16–17.

National Association of Elementary School Principals. (1989). Standardized tests. In *Platform 1988–1989* (p. 7). Alexandria, VA: Author.

National Association of State Boards of Education. (1988). *Right from the start.* Alexandria, VA: Author.

National Commission on Testing and Public Policy. (1990). *From gatekeepers to gateways: Transforming testing in America.* Chestnut Hill, MA: Boston College.

National Council of Teachers of English. (1989). Testing and evaluation. In *NCTE forum: Position statements on issues in education from the National Council of Teachers of English* (pp. VI:1–VI:4). Urbana, IL: Author.

National Council of Teachers of Mathematics. (1989). *Curriculum and evaluation standards for school mathematics.* Reston, VA: Author.

National Education Association. (1972). Moratorium on standardized testing. *Today's Education, 61,* 41.

Noggle, N. L. (October 1987). *Report on the match of the standardized tests to the Arizona Essential Skills.* Tempe, AZ: College of Education.

Nolen, S. B., Haladyna, T. M., & Haas, N. S. (1992). Uses and abuses of achievement test scores. *Educational Measurement: Issues and Practices, 11,* 9–15.

O'Dell, C. W. (1928). *Traditional examinations and new type tests.* New York: Century.

Office of Educational Research and Improvement. (1996). *Youth indicators 1996.* Washington, DC: U.S. Department of Education.

Office of Technology Assessment. (1992). *Testing in American schools: Asking the right questions.* Washington, DC: Author.

Ong, W. S., Allison, J. M., Haladyna, T. M. (submitted for publication). *A comparison of reading, writing and mathematics achievement in comparable single-age and multi-age classrooms.*

Paris, S., Lawton, T. A., Turner, J. C., & Roth, J. L. (1991). A developmental perspective on standardized achievement testing. *Educational Researcher, 20,* 12–20, 40.

Perrone, V. (1976). *On standardized testing and evaluation.* Olney, MD: Association for Childhood Education International.

Perrone, V. (1977). *The abuses of standardized testing* (Fastback 92). Bloomington, IN: Phi Delta Kappa Educational Foundation.

Perrone, V. (1981). Testing, testing, and more testing. *Childhood Education, 58,* 76–80.

Perrone, V. (1991). *Standardized testing. ERIC Digest.* Urbana, IL: ERIC Clearinghouse on Elementary and Early Childhood Education.

Popham, W. J. (1995). *Classroom assessment: What teachers need to know.* Boston: Allyn & Bacon.

Rose, L. C., Elam, S. M., & Gallup, A. C. (1997). The 29th annual Phi Delta Kappa/Gallup poll of the public's attitudes toward the public schools. *Phi Delta Kappan, 79*(1), 41–58.

Rosenholtz, S. J. (1989). *Teacher's workplace: The social organization of schooling.* New York: Longman.

Shepard, L. A. (1994). The challenges of assessing young children appropriately. *Phi Delta Kappan, 76*(3), 206–212.

Shepard, L. A., & Smith, M. L. (1986). Synthesis of research on school readiness and kindergarten retention. *Educational Leadership, 44*, 78–86.

Smith, M. L. (1991). Put to the test: The effects of external testing on teachers. *Educational Researcher, 20*, 8–11.

Weber, G. (1977). *Uses and abuses of standardized testing in the schools.* Washington, DC: Council for Basic Education. ◪

Reflections and Inquiries

1. Why did schools in the United States shift focus from achievement testing to ability testing at the beginning of the twentieth century? What effects has this had?

2. What factors led schools to prefer multiple-choice tests over essay tests?

3. What is "criterion-referenced" testing? Why has interest in it diminished?

4. Why have some professional organizations called for an end to standardized testing below the fourth grade?

5. Why do some schools ask teachers to abandon a standard curriculum to prepare for the standardized achievement test? Do you support this practice? Why or why not?

Reading to Write

1. After reviewing the authors' summaries of what they believe are valid versus invalid uses of test scores, write an essay that argues whether the valid uses outweigh the invalid uses or vice versa.

2. Write an essay on test anxiety after reading the articles on that topic cited by the authors: Haas et al. (1990) and Hartman (1991). How serious a problem is it? Draw from your own experiences with test anxiety if you wish.

Standardized Exams Get an "A" | Gene Koretz

Because educators have been questioning for decades the validity and usefulness of standardized testing, they have looked for ways to correlate test results with actual student achievement. In the following news story, Gene Koretz, a *Business Week* writer on economic trends, reports on recent progress in this area.

Source: Koretz, Gene. "Standardized Exams Get an 'A': They Seem to Enhance Learning." *Business Week* 30 June 1997: 32. Reprinted from June 30, 1997 issue of *Business Week* by special permission, copyright © 1997 by The McGraw-Hill Companies, Inc.

Should U.S. elementary and high schools develop national curriculum standards and state or nationwide tests to assess student achievement in core subjects? President Clinton and a number of governors are supporting the idea, but the key issue is whether such exams really promote student learning, as proponents claim.

To find out, economist John Bishop of Cornell University recently looked at how students from various countries performed on international tests on science and mathematics. Analyzing the results of the Third International Mathematics & Science Study, which tested 7th and 8th graders from 39 nations in 1994 and 1995, he found that students from countries that had standardized mandatory exams did significantly better than those from countries that lack such tests—performing, on average, at a grade level higher in both subjects.

An analysis of the International Assessment of Educational Progress administered to 8th grade students from 15 nations in 1991 yielded similar results. Moreover, students from Canadian provinces mandating standard curriculum-based exams significantly outperformed students from provinces that lacked such tests. And surveys of Canadian school administrators and students revealed more intensive emphasis on science and math instruction in the provinces requiring tests. Students there also spent more time reading for pleasure and watching science programs on TV than their peers in the other provinces.

All of which, concludes Bishop, suggests that President Clinton and other advocates of statewide or national curriculum-based tests are on to something.

Reflections and Inquiries

1. Being a news story, this piece cannot be expected to present as much evidence as a full-fledged analytical article would in proving that standardized testing can enhance learning. That said, how useful is the evidence that Koretz does refer to? What additional information do you need?

2. How do you interpret the word *significantly* in the context in which John Bishop uses this word? (See paragraphs 2 and 3.)

3. What do you suppose is the "something" that advocates are on to?

Reading to Write

Write a short essay assessing the nature of the influence that testing has on the quality of classroom instruction, as revealed by the Canadian surveys referenced by Koretz.

Eliminating Standardized Tests in College Admissions

The New Affirmative Action?   Rebecca Zwick

How reliable are standardized test scores for predicting student performance? What does a psychometric investigation—an investigation that focuses on the psychological and sociological dynamics of test-taking and the way these dynamics are reflected in the test scores—reveal about the accuracy of standardized tests in predicting academic achievement regardless of ethnicity? What would happen if colleges decided to eliminate Scholastic Aptitude Test (SAT) scores from consideration and placed more emphasis on grade point averages (GPAs) or other indicators of academic performance? Rebecca Zwick, a professor of education at the University of California, Santa Barbara, reports the results of her formal investigation of these key concerns in the standardized testing controversy.

College enrollment figures aren't ordinarily big news, but the 1998 freshman enrollment numbers for the University of California's most prestigious campuses were startling enough to warrant headlines. At the University of California, Berkeley, African American enrollment dropped by more than 60% from 1997 levels, and Latino enrollment dropped by nearly 50%. UCLA experienced dramatic decreases as well.[1]

Since the passage in 1996 of California's Proposition 209, which banned consideration of race or ethnicity in admissions decisions at public colleges and universities, University of California educators have feared just such a plunge in minority representation and have been considering ways to counteract it. In 1997 the university settled on an apparently simple solution: eliminate the SAT as a criterion for admissions. "We . . . have evidence that the SAT loses us 2,000 Latino students this year alone," said Eugene Garcia, dean of the School of Education at Berkeley in a 1997 interview.[2]

Although the university's enthusiasm for eliminating the SAT may have faded, admissions testing remains a source of controversy. A new document from the U.S. Department of Education, "Nondiscrimination in High-Stakes Testing" (still in draft form), advises that colleges may be in legal jeopardy if they rely too heavily on standardized test scores in making admissions or financial aid decisions. The president of the University of California, Richard Atkinson, said in a March 1999 interview that he "would be prepared to forget that SAT" if the newly approved California high school exit examination proves to be a good test.[3] And a bill that would deemphasize the role of standardized testing in admissions decisions (S.B. 145), introduced for the second

Source: Zwick, Rebecca. "Eliminating Standardized Tests in College Admissions: The New Affirmative Action?" *Phi Delta Kappan* Dec. 1999: 320–324. © 1999, Rebecca Zwick. This article first appeared in the December 1999 issue of *Phi Delta Kappan.* Reprinted by permission of the author.

time in January 1999, awaits action in the California senate. (An earlier version of the bill, introduced in 1998, passed both houses of the legislature but was vetoed by the outgoing governor, Pete Wilson.)

Meanwhile, Texas has been grappling with the effects of the *Hopwood* decision, which banned the use of race in admissions programs, and the state of Washington has been faced with the consequences of Initiative 200, a Prop 209 clone that was passed in 1998. These political developments have provoked a reconsideration of the role of tests in college admissions and have focused serious attention on two questions: Are standardized admissions tests biased against minorities, as is often argued? Would eradicating these tests produce a more ethnically diverse freshman class?

The Question of Bias

Differences between racial and ethnic groups in their performance on standardized tests—including the SAT (from the Educational Testing Service) and its competition, the ACT (from ACT, Inc.)—have been analyzed extensively, both in academic journals and in the popular press. Researchers, social theorists, and politicians have offered an array of reasons for these score differences, ranging from socioeconomic, cultural, linguistic, and genetic factors to test bias. A recent inflammatory contribution to this literature was *The Bell Curve*, by Richard Herrnstein and Charles Murray, which was published in 1994 and encouraged consideration of genetic explanations for group differences in test scores.[4] But the controversy has not been limited to the *reasons* for the differences in performance. Even the matter of determining which groups are advantaged by standardized tests is less straightforward than it first appears.

In the popular press, the existence of bias in admissions tests is typically assumed to be demonstrated by the persistent pattern of differences between racial groups in average test scores. The idea that score differences are sufficient evidence to establish bias is reflected in the original language of the California standardized testing legislation that is currently under consideration. According to the initial version of the bill, "a test discriminates . . . if there is a statistically significant difference in the outcome on test performance when test subjects are compared on the basis of gender, ethnicity, race, or economic status."[5] Another example of the view that score differences are sufficient evidence for test bias can be found at a website maintained by *Time* and the Princeton Review, a test preparation company: "Studies show persistent . . . race bias in both the SAT and the ACT. . . . The SAT favors white males, who tend to score better than all other groups except Asian-American males."[6]

When academic researchers investigate the fairness of the SAT, however, they don't ordinarily focus on the average scores achieved by each ethnic group. Instead, they consider another aspect of the test results: How well does the SAT predict college grades for each group? Researchers have typically found that using the SAT to predict first-year college grade-point averages (GPAs) results in a *more positive* prediction for black and Latino test-takers than is warranted; that is, the predicted grades tend to exceed the actual grades for these groups.

5

For example, a 1994 College Board study found that "there were, on average, underpredictions [of college GPAs] for Asian American students (and to a lesser extent, white students) and overpredictions for American Indian, black and Hispanic students."[7] In other words, SAT scores tended to predict higher college grades than were actually attained by African American, Latino, and American Indian students and lower grades than were actually attained by Asian American and white students. In discussing the recurrent finding of inflated predictions for African Americans, Robert Linn, an eminent educational researcher, noted in 1983 that this result is "contrary to a commonly held expectation that tests are unfair to certain minority groups in the sense that they give a misleadingly low indication of the likely performance . . . in school. The overprediction finding suggests that, if anything, just the opposite is true."[8] In their widely acclaimed 1998 book, *The Shape of the River,* William Bowen and Derek Bok also include an extensive discussion of this phenomenon.[9]

What's the real story about differences in ethnic group performance on the SAT? Do black and Latino test-takers tend to score lower, or are predictions of their college grades based on their SAT performance inflated? Paradoxical as it may seem, *both* these patterns have characterized SAT results for many years.

The 1994 College Board study provides a useful context for illustrating these seemingly contradictory results. This research, based on 1985 data from 45 colleges, represents the most detailed and painstaking analysis of the utility of the SAT as a predictor of college grades. A portion of the results—those for African Americans, Asian Americans, Latinos, and whites—are given here. The much smaller American Indian group is not included. (See Table 1.)

The average SAT scores, high school GPAs, and college GPAs show substantial differences across groups. Average SAT scores are higher for Asian American and white students than for African American and Latino students. The difference is more dramatic for the math score than for the verbal score.

10

TABLE 1   Average SAT Scores, High School GPAs, and College GPAs, by Ethnic Group

	African American	Asian American	Latino	White	Overall
SAT (verbal)	436	484	462	513	505
SAT (math)	466	595	516	564	559
High school GPA	3.18	3.58	3.43	3.40	3.41
College GPA	2.14	2.80	2.37	2.66	2.63
Number of test-takers	2,475	3,848	1,599	36,743	44,849

Source: Adapted from Leonard Ramist, Charles Lewis, and Laura McCamley-Jenkins, *Student Group Differences in Predicting College Grades: Sex, Language, and Ethnic Groups* (New York: College Entrance Examination Board, College Board Report No. 93-1; ETS Research Report No. 94-27, 1994), p. 9.

The average SAT math score for Asian Americans is about 130 points higher than the average SAT math score for African Americans.[10] (The 1998 SAT results reveal similar patterns.) If a difference in average performance were considered sufficient to demonstrate test bias, then these findings would appear to show bias against African American and Latino test-takers. (If this were the sole criterion, we would have to conclude that high school and college grades were biased as well.)

However, in the world of psychometrics, the assessment of test bias is conceptualized differently. Group performance differences can arise for many reasons that are not a function of the test itself—unequal educational opportunity being the most obvious—so the absence of such differences is not considered a criterion for test fairness. Instead, traditional psychometric analysis focuses on another question: Is the test an effective and accurate predictor of college GPAs for all groups? (Here we consider only ethnic groups, but other demographic groups—males, females, native and non-native speakers of English— are ordinarily examined as well.)

The first step in the psychometric investigation is to assess the validity of the test for students as a whole. Does the SAT lead to better prediction of college grades than could be obtained using high school grades alone? Typically, the effectiveness with which SAT verbal scores, SAT math scores, and high school grades can jointly predict college grades is evaluated through linear regression analysis, a standard statistical procedure that is used in a variety of prediction applications. The regression analysis yields an equation for predicting college grades from high school grades, SAT math scores, and SAT verbal scores (each multiplied by a weighting factor and then added up). Predictive effectiveness is measured by the degree of correspondence between the predicted college grades and the actual college grades. The analysis can then be repeated using high school grades alone as a predictor. Comparing the results of the two analyses yields an estimate of the "value added" by using SAT scores.

After these analyses are completed for the entire group of students, the next step is to perform a separate prediction analysis within each ethnic group and to compare the resulting equations across groups. The College Board study evaluated various combinations of the three key predictors of college grades. Consistent with earlier research, the results showed that high school grades and SAT scores are important predictors in all ethnic groups and that including the SAT did lead to better prediction than using high school grades alone.[11] Research conducted at the University of California in 1997 produced the same conclusion.[12] In the College Board study, prediction was somewhat more effective for white and Asian American test-takers than for African American and Latino test-takers, regardless of which combination of predictors was used. In the African American group, unlike the other groups, SAT scores alone provided slightly more effective prediction than high school grades alone.

Although test validity research involves the computation of separate pre-   15
diction equations for each ethnic group, admissions decisions within a college
are ordinarily made by means of a common prediction equation for all ethnic
groups. Will the use of a single equation result in systematic over- or underprediction of college grades for certain groups? This can be determined by
comparing the actual first-year college grades to the predicted grades (obtained using the equation based on all students). Table 2 shows the average
differences between actual college GPA and predicted college GPA for each
group. A minus sign indicates overprediction (actual grades lower than predicted grades); a plus sign, underprediction (actual grades higher than predicted grades).

By definition, the equation will, on average, predict perfectly for the overall group. The white results will necessarily be similar since whites constitute
about 82% of the total group in the study. But how do the results stack up for
the remaining ethnic groups? Whether SAT score, high school GPA, or a combination is included in the equation, the results for Asian American test-takers
are slightly underpredicted, while the results for African American and Latino
test-takers are overpredicted. It is worth noting that overprediction is mitigated by the use of the SAT—it's even worse when only high school GPA is
used. For example, college GPAs for African Americans are overpredicted
by an average of .35 when only high school GPAs are used as predictors.
When SAT scores are included in the prediction equation, the average overprediction is reduced to .16.[13]

What explains the overprediction? A variety of reasons have been advanced, including differences across groups in high school courses taken or in
the stringency of high school grading practices, differences across groups in
the choice of college curriculum, and a greater incidence in ethnic minority
groups of life difficulties that interfere with academic performance in college.

The results of the College Board study mirror the general findings of SAT
validity research from the last several decades. First, for all ethnic groups, tests

TABLE 2   **Average College GPA Minus Average Predicted College GPA**

Predictors in Equation	African American	Asian American	Latino	White	Overall
High school GPA	−.35	+.02	−.24	+.03	0
SAT (verbal and math)	−.23	+.08	−.13	+.01	0
High school GPA plus SAT (verbal and math)	−.16	+.04	−.13	+.01	0

Source: Adapted from Leonard Ramist, Charles Lewis, and Laura McCamley-Jenkins, *Student Group
Differences in Predicting College Grades: Sex, Language, and Ethnic Groups* (New York: College Entrance
Examination Board, College Board Report No. 93-1; ETS Research Report No. 94-27, 1994), p. 15.
*The scale of the GPAs is 0–4.

do contribute to the prediction of college performance as measured by college GPA. Second, there's some evidence of ethnic group differences in the effectiveness and accuracy of prediction. Third, it's possible for a group to have lower average test scores than other groups and still receive inflated predictions of later performance. The overriding conclusion is neither new nor earthshaking: in crafting a college admissions policy, tests serve as useful, but far from perfect, tools.

Would Eliminating the SAT Improve Ethnic Diversity?

If colleges removed the SAT from admissions criteria, what would be the likely result? This is the very question addressed in a December 1997 report issued by the Office of the President, University of California.[14] It was based on supplementary analyses of data from a study conducted by the California Postsecondary Education Commission (CPEC).[15] Transcripts, test scores, and demographic information from a 6% random sample of 1996 graduates of California public high schools were analyzed to determine the effect of applying various admissions criteria. The study issued by the Office of the President considered how eliminating standardized admissions tests would affect the rates of "UC eligibility," which is based on the completion of certain college-preparatory courses, the GPA for those courses, and (if the GPA is below 3.3) scores on the SAT or ACT.

The study's conclusion was surprising to some: eliminating the admissions test requirement, when combined with other mandated features of admissions policy at the University of California, would produce very small changes in the eligibility rates for Latinos (from 3.8% to 4.0%), African Americans (from 2.8% to 2.3%), and Asian Americans (from 30% to 29%). The largest change would be an *increase* in the eligibility rate for whites (from 12.7% to 14.8%).[16]

The analysis that produced these projections of eligibility rates incorporated the provisions of the Master Plan for Higher Education in California, which mandates that 12.5% of the state's high school graduates be declared "UC eligible." If the admissions test requirement were dropped, the minimum GPA for the required college-preparatory courses would need to be raised, a change that leads to the predicted effects on eligibility rates. Dropping the SAT, while simultaneously ignoring the "12.5%" requirement, increased eligibility to 18.7% overall, while leaving the pattern of ethnic-group eligibility virtually unchanged. (This analysis, as well as many of the conjectures in this article, is based on the implicit assumption that eliminating the SAT would not have a substantial impact on high school grading practices. Some educators have raised the concern that rampant grade inflation would occur if the SAT requirement were lifted, rendering high school grades useless as an admissions criterion.)

The minimal changes in the predicted eligibility rates for African American and Latino students are less remarkable in light of the finding that "low test scores rarely are the only reason for a student's ineligibility."[17] In fact, the

CPEC report on eligibility shows that only 2.5% of California public high school graduates were ineligible solely on the basis of inadequate test scores. Most students—62.6% of graduates overall—were ineligible because they had "major course omissions" or grade deficiencies or because they attended "schools that did not have a college-preparatory curriculum approved by the University." The percentage of students ineligible for these reasons was higher for African Americans (77%) and Latinos (73.6%) and lower for whites (58.7%) and Asian Americans (39%). Another 13.7% of graduates overall were ineligible because they were missing "only a few" (no more than three) of the required college-preparatory courses.[18]

Because the pattern of ethnic group differences in average high school GPA is usually similar to the pattern of average admissions test scores, an admissions policy that excludes tests but continues to include high school grades is unlikely to produce dramatic change. A case in point is the so-called 4% plan, which will go into effect at the University of California in 2001. The plan offers admission to the top 4% of graduates of every California high school who have completed the required college-preparatory courses, regardless of their test scores. Analyses have predicted that the plan will have "little impact on racial proportions at UC, since any increases in numbers of black, urban students [will] be matched by increases in white, rural students."[19] Keith Widaman, chair of the universitywide committee that developed the plan, told the *San Francisco Chronicle* that implementing the plan will probably have only a minor effect on the percentage of black and Latino applicants admitted.[20]

The indisputable fact is that both high school grades and scores on admissions tests are reflections of the same education system, with all its flaws and inequities. In a recent colloquium on the future of affirmative action, Christopher Edley, a professor of law at Harvard University and a consultant to President Clinton on issues of race, noted, "The SAT simply recapitulates . . . all of the class advantages, all of the access advantages . . . in the K–12 experiences of the student."[21] The same can also be said of high school grades. By using grades rather than SAT scores as an admissions criterion, said sociologist Christopher Jencks in a 1989 essay, "You are simply substituting tests designed by high school teachers for tests designed by the Educational Testing Service."[22] A college admissions system that relies heavily on either tests or high school grades, then, cannot be the path to the eventual elimination of disparities in educational opportunity.

While there is little basis for concluding that standardized admissions tests are biased against ethnic minorities in the psychometric sense—in fact, they tend to overpredict performance for African American and Latino students—it is clear that an overreliance on tests and other traditional measures of achievement in admissions can perpetuate the underrepresentation of certain groups by, as author Ellis Cose has put it, rewarding "those who have already been well schooled."[23] The *Hopwood* decision, Proposition 209, and similar initiatives exacerbate the problem by removing one method of increasing access to higher education for people of color.

A point on which individuals of every political stripe can agree is that, ultimately, we must fix "the pipeline"—that is, improve K–12 education so that
college applicants will be better prepared. But this viewpoint has drawn an
impatient response from some educators. "Obviously," says Edley, "we all
would prefer the great day in which the pipeline is repaired and students of all
kinds show up at our doorsteps prepared, ready, eager to take the best of what
we have to offer. But that day is not with us. What do we do in the meantime?"[24]

One avenue for change in the admissions process is the consideration of
alternative definitions of college success. Although it has long been argued
that the first-year college GPA is not the only outcome of interest, no other criterion has gained wide use. Remaining within the realm of grades, GPA in a
student's area of specialization and GPA at graduation have been proposed as
alternative criteria. The 1994 College Board study found that the grades
earned in individual college courses may be more promising outcome measures than GPA. Other possible criteria are successful completion of the first
year of college or successful completion of the bachelor's degree. What distinguishes students who attain these milestones from those who do not? Among
the student attributes that warrant further investigation are motivation, perseverance, ability to overcome an adverse environment, and "spike talents" in
particular areas. We need research to determine how best to measure these
characteristics and how to assess their predictive value.

Of course, none of these approaches is guaranteed to improve the ethnic
balance on U.S. campuses. As a society we must determine whether we believe that diversity is beneficial per se—a view that is distinct from the argument that diversity be promoted as a way of righting past or present wrongs.
If we support President Clinton's contention that "there are independent educational virtues to a diverse student body,"[25] then we should adopt the goal of
diversity explicitly by considering an applicant's membership in an underrepresented group to be a "plus" in the admissions process.

Mounting legal barriers to such explicit consideration of ethnicity have
given rise to the idea that eliminating the SAT can serve as a form of covert affirmative action. Although it is certainly possible to design a workable admissions policy that does not include standardized tests, as some 15% of four-year
colleges have done, it is not sound policy to eliminate admissions tests in the
hope of indirectly furthering a social policy goal. In California, the perennial
hotbed of the affirmative action debate, we now know that failure to complete
required college-preparatory courses—rather than low test scores—is the
main barrier to admission to the University of California for members of all
ethnic groups. In any case, both test scores and high school grades are reflections of the very same disparities in educational opportunity. Eliminating
standardized tests and relying more heavily on high school achievement in
admissions decisions simply cannot result in a dramatic change in the ethnic
diversity of the student body. In short, dismantling admissions test requirements as a backdoor affirmative action policy cannot work.

Notes

1. Kenneth R. Weiss, "Fewer Black and Latinos Enroll at UC," *Los Angeles Times*, 21 May 1998, pp. A-3, A-24.
2. Richard Lee Colvin, "Q & A: Should UC Do Away with the SAT?," *Los Angeles Times*, 1 October 1997, p. B-2.
3. Kenneth R. Weiss, "Use of Sat Tests May Not Pass with UC Regents," *Los Angeles Times*, 24 March 1999, Sect. B.
4. Richard J. Herrnstein and Charles Murray, *The Bell Curve* (New York: Free Press, 1994).
5. "Legislative Counsel's Digest, S.B. 1807: Standardized Testing," available from the website of the California State Senate, www.sen.ca.gov, 18 February 1998.
6. "The Best College for You," available from the *Time*/Princeton Review website, www.review.com, April 1997.
7. Leonard Ramist, Charles Lewis, and Laura McCamley-Jenkins, *Student Group Differences in Predicting College Grades: Sex, Language, and Ethnic Groups* (New York: College Entrance Examination Board, College Board Report No. 93-1; ETS Research Report No. 94-27, 1994), p. 32.
8. Robert L. Linn, "Predictive Bias as an Artifact of Selection Procedures," in Howard Wainer and Samuel Messick, eds., *Principles of Modern Psychological Measurement: A Festschrift for Frederic M. Lord* (Hillsdale, N.J.: Erlbaum, 1983), p. 33.
9. William G. Bowen and Derek Bok, *The Shape of the River: Long-Term Consequences of Considering Race in College and University Admissions* (Princeton: Princeton University Press, 1998).
10. Ramist, Lewis, and McCamley-Jenkins, p. 9.
11. Ibid., p. 31.
12. Judy A. Kowarsky, *University of California Follow-up Analyses of the 1996 CPEC Eligibility Study* (Oakland: Office of the President, Student Academic Services, University of California, December 1997), p. 25.
13. Ramist, Lewis, and McCamley-Jenkins, p. 15.
14. Kowarsky, op. cit.
15. *Eligibility of California's 1996 High School Graduates for Admission to the State's Public Universities: A Report of the California Postsecondary Education Commission* (Sacramento: California Postsecondary Education Commission, 1997).
16. Kowarsky, p. 2.
17. Ibid.
18. *Eligibility of California's 1996 High School Graduates*, pp. 50–61.
19. "Senate Looks into Making Top 4% of Students in Each High School UC-Eligible," *Notice: A Publication of the Academic Senate, University of California*, March 1998, pp. 1–3.
20. Pamela Burdman, "UC Regents Dubious About New Admissions Proposal," *San Francisco Chronicle*, 15 May 1998, p. A-21.
21. Christopher Edley, quoted in Daren Bakst, ed., *Hopwood, Bakke, and Beyond: Diversity on Our Nation's Campuses* (Washington, D.C.: American Association of Collegiate Registrars and Admissions Officers, 1998), p. 81.
22. Christopher Jencks, "If Not Tests, Then What?," in Bernard R. Gifford, ed., *Test Policy and Test Performance* (Boston: Kluwer Academic Publishers, 1989), p. 117.
23. Ellis Cose, *Color-Blind: Seeing Beyond Race in a Race-Obsessed World* (New York: HarperCollins, 1997), p. 117.
24. Edley, quoted in Bakst, p. 80.
25. "A Dialogue on Race with President Clinton," *Newshour with Jim Lehrer*, 9 July 1998, available from the website of the Public Broadcasting Service, www.pbs.org.

Reflections and Inquiries

1. What, besides average scores achieved by different ethnic groups, do researchers investigate when trying to determine the fairness of the SAT? Why?

2. What does a psychometric investigation of test bias disclose about the differences in average test scores among ethnic groups?

3. What is the "4% plan" that the University of California launched in 2001? Why is it unlikely, according to one researcher, that this plan will be able to change racial proportions at UC?

4. How does Zwick account for the tendency of test scores to over- or under-predict actual achievement?

Reading to Write

1. Using the data reported by the CPEC, defend or challenge a move to eliminate SAT testing as a way of predicting academic achievement for African-American, Latino, and Asian-American students.

2. Defend or challenge Zwick's conclusion that getting rid of admissions test requirements would fail as a "backdoor affirmative action policy."

Should the SAT Account for Race? | Nathan Glazer *Yes*
Abigail Thernstrom *No*

Few would disagree that a college education should be within the grasp of all young people, regardless of their race, ethnicity, gender, or socioeconomic class. Yet, due to a wide range of inheritable disadvantages, such as growing up in an inner-city environment, attending poor schools, and growing up with little or no parental guidance, some students' chances of getting into college are slim.

What, if anything, can educators and legislators do to help? Affirmative action is one possibility: require that a certain percentage of underrepresented minorities be admitted without regard to test scores such as the Scholastic Aptitude Test (SAT), which is unfavorable to certain ethnic groups. But critics of affirmative action consider any kind of racial targeting wrong, even when the purpose is to compensate for past injustices.

Source: Glazer, Nathan, and Abigail Thernstrom. "The End of Meritocracy: Should the SAT Account for Race? ["Yes" (Glazer); "No" (Thernstrom)]" *The New Republic* 27 Sept. 1999: 26–29. Reprinted by permission of the author.

The following debate considers another possibility: equalize the testing playing field with a scoring handicap called a "Strivers" score. Students of underrepresented ethnic groups who come from inner-city areas, for example, would have extra points added to their actual test results. In effect, affirmative action ideals would kick into effect at the testing stage.

Nathan Glazer, who supports the use of a Strivers score, is a contributing editor of *The New Republic*; Abigail Thernstrom, who argues against it, has coauthored the book, *America in Black and White: One Nation, Indivisible* (1997).

YES

This month [Sept. 1999], the Educational Testing Service (ETS), creator and marketer of the SAT—the most widely used test of academic ability and the key measure that colleges and universities take into account when making admissions decisions—announced that it is developing a "Strivers" score, an adjustment of the SAT score to take into account a student's socioeconomic background and race, increasing the scores of those whose socioeconomic background or race is considered to put them at a disadvantage. Colleges and universities will be able to use the new Strivers score, if they wish, in making their admissions decisions. The ETS will offer institutions both a "race-blind" model, which includes only social, economic, and educational factors, and a model that also takes into account race—that is, whether the applicant is black, Hispanic, or Native American. ETS's chief competitor, the American College Testing Program, which produces a test used by many institutions instead of the SAT, will be developing a similar model.

Clearly, these developments are a response to the crumbling of the legal support that colleges and universities have relied upon to justify the almost universal practice among selective institutions of giving some kind of preference to black and Hispanic students. And, just as surely, critics of racial preference in college admissions will not be mollified by the new Strivers score • and other, similar new strategies. If the formula using race is factored into admissions decisions, the new procedure will be just as legally vulnerable as the existing formal or informal preferences for race that have been struck down by a federal appeals court ruling in a University of Texas case and are now being challenged in an important University of Michigan case. Nor, one would think, would the new approach survive in the courts of the states—California and Washington—where popular referenda have forbidden the states and their agencies, including colleges and universities, to take race into account when making admissions decisions.

And, if the Strivers score without the race factor is used, present statistical patterns show that it will be less effective in identifying black students who may qualify for admission than the score that includes race as part of the formula. For race is indeed a factor in reducing test scores, independent of family wealth, education, and the other socioeconomic factors. It has a particularly strong independent effect in reducing scores for blacks, and, for most institutions, increasing the number of black students is a higher priority than increasing the number of Hispanic students.

What is most striking about the development of the Strivers score is the evidence it gives us of the strength of the commitment to maintaining a higher number of black and Hispanic students in selective institutions than would qualify on the basis of academic promise alone. It is not only the testing agencies that show this commitment. They are, after all, responding to their customers, the educational institutions, whose presidents and administrations universally support racial preference in admissions. They may call it "diversity," a softer and more benign term, but what diversity in practice means is more blacks than they would admit under admissions procedures that didn't take race into account. Writing in *National Review*, Stephan Thernstrom, a strong critic of racial preferences, informs us with disapproval that "[William] Bowen and [Derek] Bok argue [in their study of racial preference *The Shape of the River*] that administrators barred from using racial double-standards in admissions will elect to lower standards for all applicants so as to secure enough non-Asian minorities in the student body."

While this is not quite their position—it is, rather, that administrators will   5
do what they can to maintain the number of black students even when legal bans on taking race into account exist—the fact is that it is not administrators alone who will do this in the effort to evade the clear effect of the elimination of race preference. The Texas legislature voted that the state university should

Standardized testing is a major education industry. How necessary is it?

consider the top ten percent of the graduating class of every Texas high school eligible for the state university, a far more radical lowering of the standards for eligibility than any university administrator would have proposed.

Even more remarkably, the Regents of the University of California, who had earlier voted that race could not be taken into account in admissions decisions, have voted that the top four percent of the graduates of every California high school should be eligible for admission to the state university system! The Texas and California actions both radically expand the number of black and Hispanic students eligible for the state universities, for in both states there are many high schools almost exclusively Hispanic and black in composition that would not be capable of producing students eligible for the top branches of the state university without the new policies.

The faculties of colleges and universities have not played much of a role in all this. Faculty members critical of racial preferences berate their colleagues for not speaking up—indeed, faculty members rarely speak up when a controversial issue does not affect them directly. But recent surveys show that the critics of racial preference will not get much support from university faculties. Although a recent survey of 34,000 faculty members conducted by the Higher Education Research Institute of the University of California at Los Angeles does not ask the racial preference question directly, it does ask whether "promoting diversity leads to the admission of too many underprepared students." Only 28 percent of respondents agreed. And 90.5 percent of respondents agreed with the following statement, admittedly not much more controversial than arguing the virtues of motherhood: "A racially/ethnically diverse student body enhances the educational experience of all students."

Thus college and university faculty and administrators, state legislatures, and the ruling political bodies in charge of public universities all seem to have a commitment to maintaining the number of black and Hispanic students receiving higher education, and, bluntly, are willing to take evasive action to do it. They will use substitutes for race—and, if one substitute does not work, they will look for others. If focusing on applicants who live in a poor neighborhood doesn't help—perhaps there are too many Asians in one poor California neighborhood or another—they will try focusing on applicants who live in housing projects. One way or another, the commitment to enrolling more blacks than would qualify based on academic criteria alone will be pursued.

I believe this commitment, however cloaked in subterfuge it may be, is a valid one. True, it has been clear from the beginning of affirmative action that the majority of the American population—and even a very substantial part of the black population—does not like the idea of making an individual's fate dependent on his or her race or ethnic background. We are all, in principle, in favor of a race-blind society, and clearly that is an important principle, one that we all hope to realize in time. But it has turned out that the use of strict race-blind admissions procedures will radically reduce the number of black students, and in lesser measure the number of Hispanic students, in the selective institutions of higher education—key institutions of our society. This can only

serve to further divide non-Asian minorities and whites and to further postpone the day when we can achieve a truly race-blind, fully integrated society.
And this is simply too high a price to pay for adhering to the principle of race-
blind admissions today.

☑   ☑   ☑

If, then, one accepts that admitting more non-Asian minorities than would   10
make the cut through academic criteria alone is a legitimate goal, the Strivers
score is not such a terrible way to achieve it. The new score, which is simply an
adjustment of the actual SAT score, is based on the common observation that
students from wealthier and more educated families, from well-to-do suburbs,
from high schools with better students, and the like, will on average do better
on the SAT than students from poorer and less-educated families and from
worse high schools—the circumstances of a disproportionate number of minorities. It stands to reason that a student from a materially and educationally
impoverished environment who does fairly well on the SAT and better than
other students who come from a similar environment is probably stronger
than the unadjusted score indicates. In the past, those colleges and universities
whose admissions staffs and procedures permitted individual evaluation of
applications took such factors into account informally. With the new Strivers
score, they will have a statistical tool that includes no fewer than 14 characteristics that are expected to affect SAT scores. It will, of course, be up to individual institutions to decide whether they want to make use of the Strivers
adjustment, just as individual institutions now determine how much weight
the SAT score should have in the admissions decision. Still, the Strivers score
may make what was essentially an intuitive system more rational.

Of course, there's a strong possibility that it may not survive the inevitable
legal challenges. It also remains to be seen just how effective the new approach
will be at maintaining or increasing the number of black and Hispanic students in our colleges and universities. For instance, it's possible that the main
effect may be instead to increase the number of Asians, in which case the effectiveness of the Strivers adjustment would undoubtedly be reviewed.

But even if the Strivers score approach does not succeed, its introduction
has highlighted the need for institutions under legal attack to improve the informal and messy procedures that they have been using to raise their enrollment of minority students. Perhaps we can bury the overt emphasis on race
while trying to reach the same objective; perhaps race can become the dirty little secret we are trying to take account of without directly saying so.
Hypocrisy in the matter may be no minor gain. But it is clear that, for some
time, if we are to maintain the appearance of being one nation when by many
measures we are, in fact, two, a pure race-blind policy will be so strongly resisted that racial preference will by some means prevail.

NO

The Educational Testing Service (ETS) calls them "strivers." They could just as well be called the "but for" kids: kids who would have done better on their SATs *but for* . . . their racial or ethnic identities, their families' income, the quality of their schools, and so forth. Or so ETS believes. These and other circumstances call for college admissions officers to treat these students' scores differently than they otherwise would, the company suggests. Never mind that selective colleges already take such factors into account when weighing student applications. That inevitably subjective process is inadequate, ETS apparently believes. Schools with high admissions standards need further instruction and a tool to help read scores properly. "A combined score of 1000 on the SATs is not always a 1000," Anthony Carnevale, an ETS vice president who heads the Strivers project, has said. "When you look at a striver who gets a 1000, you're looking at someone who really performs at a 1200."

The students ETS has in mind are those who have done better than their demographic profile would predict. Carnevale suggests the low score is, in effect, a false negative, but ETS has evidently decided to leave the actual process of readjusting scores up to the schools themselves. It will provide the unadjusted score and a statistical formula that colleges can use to convert it to the Strivers number, should they so choose.

Or so it seems. In the wake of negative press, the company released an obfuscating memo denying any current "program or service based upon the Strivers research." But it did not rule out offering a "program or service" once its final report is completed—in about two months. "Researchers" have been "studying the effect of considering additional background information" in order to "provide a richer context for candidates' scores," the memo explained. "ETS is committed to continuing a dialogue about fairness and equity in higher education."

That ongoing "dialogue" has largely been prompted, of course, by the end of the use of racial preferences in admissions decisions in public higher education in Texas, California, and Washington states. Although University of Michigan President Lee Bollinger recently declared diversity to be "as vital as teaching Shakespeare or mathematics," the University of Michigan's own race-based admissions processes will soon be on trial in a federal district court. Suits against other elite colleges (all of which sort students on the basis of race and ethnicity) are sure to follow. But ETS may be riding to the schools' partial rescue with a formula that gives a pseudo-scientific imprimatur to setting lower SAT standards for "disadvantaged" students.

ETS broadens the definition of disadvantage beyond race and ethnicity and is said to be working on two formulas. One will factor in race. The other will reportedly focus on only such variables as the employment status of the student's mother and the kinds of electrical appliances and number of books in the student's home, as reported—accurately or inaccurately—by the student. Thus, the University of California and the handful of other schools that are no longer allowed to make race-based admissions decisions will be able to use it. A formal acknowledgment that disadvantage comes in all colors and many forms would certainly be a step forward. But not a very big one. Expanding the universe of preferential admits does not solve the basic problem. ETS is simply adding more variables to a victimology index and reinforcing the already-too-widespread belief that demography is destiny. And once you start factoring in variables that lead to disadvantage, where do you stop? Should you take into account an applicant's birth order? Her relationship with her parents? The psychologists haven't even gotten into the act yet.

☑   ☑   ☑

Of course, literally no one believes that SAT scores alone should determine who gets into which schools. And, in fact, no college entirely ignores the "context" that ETS wants to stress. But does ETS really want high schools telling a black kid in the Bronx that no one expects him to do as well as the Vietnamese immigrant in his class? Should a teacher say to a white student from a low-income family, "I'll count your C in math as an A? You come to the test with a disadvantage; I understand."

Across the nation, states are getting serious about promoting high academic standards in their elementary and secondary schools. But, in Massachusetts and elsewhere, anti-testing voices have argued that it is simply unfair to expect suburban skills in urban schools with high concentrations of non-Asian minority kids. Teachers, critics say, are being asked to achieve the impossible. Moreover, the Office of Civil Rights in the U.S. Department of Education has recently weighed in with an attack on all high-stakes testing as potentially discriminatory.

Without doubt, school is easier for children who grow up in affluent and educated households. And yet, without tough tests and uniformly high expectations, the academic performance of black and Hispanic children—which, on average, is woefully behind that of whites and Asians—is unlikely to improve. ETS is proposing to send the worst possible message to these kids: If you start out in life with less, we expect less of you—today, tomorrow, maybe forever. The die has been cast. The fix is in.

The students who meet high academic expectations in the kindergarten-through-twelfth-grade years are likely to do well on the SATs, and for most students those tests are excellent predictors of how they will fare in college. As a consequence (as Carnevale surely knows), a score of 1000 is simply not the same as 1200; the lower-scoring student is less academically prepared. Even a score of 1200 means a rough academic ride for students at universities such as Princeton and Stanford, where the median SAT score exceeds 1400.

If elite schools want to become nonselective, or if they want to choose their matriculants randomly from the pool of applicants with scores over, say, 1000, who could object on grounds of principle? Needless to say, their fancy professors and devoted alumni might not like the idea. The physics professor who is a Nobel laureate generally wants to teach high-powered students, and the alumni like the prestige that accompanies highly selective admissions. A more random system would let in plenty of strivers, but the schools themselves would change. Students who were less prepared would require less rigorous courses—unless the colleges suddenly became willing to flunk them out.

ETS is obviously trying to suggest otherwise. Strivers (by definition) have tried harder and thus can do as well as the kid with the much higher SAT, the testing service implies. The disadvantaged student with a score of 1000 will do just as well as the privileged one who got 1200.

Well, maybe, in some cases. But the notion rests on a questionable assumption—namely that a score of 1000, when it beats a racial or other group norm, represents extraordinary effort. That may not be the case. Perhaps the student from an impoverished family who seems to have beaten the SAT odds is simply good at taking standardized tests. Or perhaps her parents have intangible qualities that the ETS formula has failed to capture. It is even possible that she didn't try hard enough—that she is underperforming relative to her intellectual gifts. Her score may reflect academic talent, not hard work. In fact, if ETS is serious about finding the kids who really "strive," it might make much more sense to look at grade point averages, adjusted for the difficulty of the courses taken. Arguably, it is the student with a low SAT score but a high GPA who has demonstrated dedication and perseverance—true grit.

In addition, there is no evidence that students who outscore peers with the same demographic characteristics will experience exceptional intellectual growth in college. In general, for unknown reasons, black students, for instance, earn substantially lower grades in college than their SATs would lead us to predict. (This is one of the buried but depressing facts contained in William Bowen and Derek Bok's pro-affirmative-action book, *The Shape of the River.*) Another recent study, which focused on University of San Diego undergraduates, looked not only at blacks and Hispanics but also at the records of students who attended impoverished high schools, came from low-income families, or lived in neighborhoods with few college graduates. These disadvantaged youths also underperformed, by the measure of their SAT scores.

Most important, why should the measure of achievement be a group norm? Asians do better than whites on math SATs; should whites who outperform the white group norm be given special preference? Should a high-scoring Asian be rejected from MIT if she beats the non-Asian competition but scores lower than Asians in general? In fact, both Asians and Jews will suffer under any leveling scheme that penalizes applicants who come from more prosperous and better-educated homes. These two groups are strikingly overrepresented on elite campuses today, precisely because they score so high on the SATs. Asians constitute only four percent of the population, but they represent almost a quarter of all students scoring above 750 on the math SATs, with the result that they make up nearly one-fifth of the student body at Harvard and a quarter or more at MIT and Cal Tech. It appears that the end of racial preferences in California has primarily benefited Asians.

25

ETS is perfectly right, of course, to say that race, ethnicity, and socioeconomic status correlate with SAT scores. And SAT scores, the company should add, correlate with college performance. Instead of trafficking in group stereotypes, endlessly tinkering with scores, giving extra points for this or that sort of disadvantage, and pretending lower-scoring students are competitive when they are not, why not just educate the kids? Does ETS believe good schools are an impossible dream? Shame on it, if it does. ◪

Reflections and Inquiries

1. According to Glazer, those who criticize racial preference in college admissions are not expected to support the Strivers score option. Why not?

2. What reasons does Glazer give that make the Strivers score option a valid one?

3. Glazer feels that measure of achievement should not be a group norm. Why not? Do you agree or disagree?

4. Thernstrom considers the Strivers score option subjective and inadequate. Why?

5. In Thernstrom's view, ETS is merely reinforcing the belief that demography is destiny. What does she mean by that? Do you agree or disagree?

6. How would the Strivers score option affect "elite" universities like Princeton, according to Thernstrom? Would you consider this change a good one? Why or why not?

Reading to Write

1. Write a one- to two-page critique of each debater's use of evidence to support his or her respective claims.

2. Drawing from the information both authors provide and supplementing it with additional background reading, write a position paper in which you recommend that colleges use or not use Strivers scores as a criterion for admission.

Standardized Testing of Young Children 3 Through 8 Years of Age

National Association for the Education of Young Children

The following document, prepared for elementary education teachers, is a position statement—more accurately, a summary of a position statement—on the appropriate use of standardized tests with young children. Being a summary of a position, it does not include analysis or evidence in support of the assertions set forth as guidelines. As you study this document, imagine yourself as a member of the target audience. How useful would this document be?

The purpose of this position statement is to guide the decisions of educators regarding the use of standardized tests with young children 3 through 8 years of age. These administrative decisions include whether to use standardized testing, how to critically evaluate existing tests, how to carefully select appropriate and accurate tests to be used with a population and purpose for which the test was designed, and how to use and interpret the results yielded from standardized tests to parents, school personnel, and the media.

NAEYC believes that the most important consideration in evaluating and using standardized tests is the *utility criterion:* The purpose of testing must be to improve services for children and ensure that children benefit from their educational experiences. Decisions about testing and assessment instruments must be based on the usefulness of the assessment procedure for improving services to children and improving outcomes for children. The ritual use even of "good tests" (those that are judged to be valid and reliable measures) is to be discouraged in the absence of documented research showing that children benefit from their use.

The following guidelines are intended to enhance the utility of standardized tests and guide early childhood professionals in making decisions about the appropriate use of testing.

- All standardized tests used in early childhood programs must be reliable and valid according to the technical standards of test development (AERA, APA, & NCME, 1985).

- Decisions that have a major impact on children, such as enrollment, retention, or assignment to remedial or special classes, should be based on multiple sources of information and should never be based on a single test score.

Source: "Standardized Testing of Young Children 3 Through 8 Years of Age." National Association for the Education of Young Children. 16 March 1998. 18 Feb. 00 <http://www.naeyc.org/resources/position_statements/pstestin.htm>. Position statement; adopted November 1987. Reprinted with permission from the National Association for the Education of Young Children.

- It is the professional responsibility of administrators and teachers to critically evaluate, carefully select, and use standardized tests only for the purpose for which they are intended and for which data exists demonstrating the test's validity (the degree to which the test accurately measures what it purports to measure).

- It is the professional responsibility of administrators and teachers to be knowledgeable about testing and to interpret test results accurately and cautiously to parents, school personnel, and the media.

- Selection of standardized tests to assess achievement and/or evaluate how well a program is meeting its goals should be based on how well a given test matches the locally determined theory, philosophy, and objectives of the specific program.

- Testing of young children must be conducted by individuals who are knowledgeable about and sensitive to the developmental needs of young children and who are qualified to administer tests.

- Testing of young children must recognize and be sensitive to individual diversity. ◪

Reflections and Inquiries

1. What does the NAEYC consider the most important concerns that teachers should keep in mind when using standardized tests with young children?

2. The guidelines given are intended "to enhance the utility of standardized tests." What does this mean?

3. NAEYC urges teachers to use tests in a way that will enable children to benefit from their educational experiences. In what ways might the children benefit, as some of the guidelines imply?

4. How useful are NAEYC's seven guidelines? What, if anything, needs further explanation?

Reading to Write

Write a critique of NAEYC's guidelines. Suggest revisions or additions to the guidelines if you feel they are warranted. Explain the reasons for your recommendations.

Why Are the "Standards" So Low in Education? | Gina Takasugi

We hear a great deal about the pros and cons of standardized testing from educators, but what about from students? Gina Takasugi, a student at Santa Clara University, provides us with a college student's perspective on the usefulness of tests in the public schools by comparing such tests with the learning experience they are supposed to reflect.

Schools have been putting too much emphasis on standardized tests. Having a single test to analyze students' knowledge defeats the point of education. During pre-school and first grade, learning was interesting because activities were hands-on and we were doing things that intrigued us. As we grew up, textbook reading and memorization became the standard.

Education is about expanding one's knowledge in many areas, not making fourteen-year-olds memorize useless facts about some war that broke out. Students need to learn about the ideas *behind* the war, how the war may have arisen because of social, economic, and cultural conditions at the time. Knowing who bombed Pearl Harbor, which is the kind of question that gets asked on a standardized test, is not what is essential. Do those students know the reasons behind the bombing, or what society can to do prevent such a thing from happening in the future?

My best friend, Anna, and I attended different high schools in Seattle. During our junior year we both took U.S. History Honors. My teacher was passionate about teaching *concepts* of history, not facts. The respect he earned from his students was unparalleled. He made us want to learn about the history of our country and wonder what else there was to learn. One day, he began class with the question, "What do *you* want to learn today?" After a few minutes of astonishment and contemplation, hands rose eagerly. Halfway through the class, he explained this approach to learning as one of Rousseau's. Like Rousseau, he involved us with philosophical thinking. By involving us that way, we were excited to learn.

My friend Anna had a teacher who gave tests every Friday on the readings she'd been assigned. Although both of our schools used the same textbook, I read a total of two chapters throughout the year while Anna had to read fourteen chapters. Today Anna recalls, "It was a bunch of busy-work. We didn't have time to know anything. Fridays consisted of turning in the 'Chapter Review' and then taking the chapter test." When the time came to take standardized tests, Anna knew more factual events about history, but I had a better understanding of it. Anna, in theory, should score higher because she covered so much more factual textbook information than I. My class concentrated more on material that cannot be measured with a standardized test. Anna hated her junior-year history and I loved mine.

People think that standardized testing raises academic standards and pro-   5
motes accountability in the public schools ("Trouble"). If students were required to pass a standard test for grade advancement or graduation, teachers would emphasize memorization of dates and teach out of the text in order to give all students a fair chance. It would also mean that a portion of school time would have to be wasted teaching "tricks" for test taking. If education were reduced to test coaching, important learning would be overlooked. "But who can blame a teacher or school for orienting the lesson toward helping students pass those tests with high marks? The temptation to teach students to do well on standardized tests is almost unavoidable when performance on such tests is how entire school systems are evaluated" (Trouble"). If students are tested regularly by standard tests, then grades and scores are over-emphasized.

Even if standard tests were a good analysis of one's knowledge, there are many factors that can lead to a bad test-taking day. Putting someone under the stress of "you must pass this test before you can graduate from high school" can lead him or her to do poorly on that specific day. Taking a test is highly stressful and requires a lot of energy and concentration. If, for any reason, you are not in your best condition, your test results will very likely suffer. One test given on a random day does not evaluate a student's knowledge of a given subject. Therefore, it should not hold such importance for that student's future. Imagine sitting in a room taking a test that determines if you are allowed to graduate. One person near you is tapping a pencil while another seems to have a terribly runny nose. Every distraction causes you to lose your train of thought and have to re-read the terrible analogy: "Mast is to Sailboat as Shakespeare is to A, B, C, or D." You don't even know what option C means and your neighbor's sniffling is almost on a beat. You are losing concentration rapidly. And that can result in being ineligible to graduate.

One of three things happen on a multiple choice question: (A) One knows the answer; (B) one makes an "educated guess" because the past few weeks in school have been spent learning tricks; or (C) one makes a blind guess. Congratulations if one knows the answer. If that student makes a successful educated guess, then he or she wasted too much time in school learning such tricks. If the student randomly guesses the correct answer, then that student's learning is not being accurately judged.

I am a freshman in college, where learning is greatly appreciated. But in high school teachers need to support and motivate an appreciation for learning. Chapter-by-chapter memorization and weekly tests do not accomplish this. When students learn in depth they learn about culture and reality, not dates and isolated facts. Today, while many people work on school reform, they need to rethink the idea of standardized tests.

"By having skilled teachers assess student academic performance over time   10
through portfolios, projects and exhibitions, not one-shot tests, we can achieve
genuine accountability and improve student learning. That is the sort of reform
all of our children deserve" (Neill). Deep involvement with subject matter
would be beneficial to everyone. Students would learn more successfully and
institutions would be moving students forward in a truly meaningful way.

Works Cited

Neill, Monty. "High-Stakes Testing Flunks." 7 Sept. 1999.
    <http://www.fairtest.org/k12/High-stakes%20oped.html>.
Trouble with Standardized Tests. Ask Jeeves website.
    http://www.askjeeves.com/main/askjeeves.asp?ask-standardized+
    testing&x=188y=14.>(January 2001). ☑

Reflections and Inquiries

1. Compare your experiences with standardized testing with Takasugi's. Are
   they similar or different? Do your experiences lead you to support or challenge Takasugi's thesis?

2. Do you agree with Takasugi that memorizing facts is a waste of time? Why
   or why not?

3. What tricks of test-taking do you suppose Takasugi has in mind? Do you
   agree or disagree that they are mere tricks or that they defeat the purpose
   of learning?

Reading to Write

Obtain a recent SAT test from the Educational Testing Service, Princeton,
New Jersey, and study it carefully. Then write a detailed critique of its effectiveness as a gauge of learning. Be sure you anticipate and refute challenging views when supporting your claims.

Connections Across the Clusters

1. Speculate on the relationship between ethnicity and classroom performance
   in an effort to explain the causes of low SAT scores among certain ethnic
   groups. Consider obstacles in multicultural education contexts, such as
   inadequate learning environment and lack of opportunity for nonnative
   speakers of English to acquire fluency in English. See Cluster 6.

2. Might certain aspects of admissions and IQ testing be considered an invasion of privacy? See Cluster 8.

Writing Projects

1. Conduct an in-depth study of a standardized admissions test such as the SAT, ACT, MCAT, or LSAT. Examine it for racial or ethnic bias or for its ability to predict academic performance.

2. Write an essay on the usefulness or uselessness of IQ testing of young children. Allude specifically to the latest version of an actual test, such as the WISC test.

Suggestions for Further Reading

Gifford, Bernard R., ed. *Test Policy and Test Performance.* Boston: Kluwer Academic, 1989.

Gronlund, Norman. *Measurement and Education in Teaching.* New York: Macmillan, 1965.

Herrnstein, Richard J., and Charles Murray. *The Bell Curve.* New York: Free, 1994.

Kohn, Alfie. *The Case Against Standardized Testing: Raising the Scores, Ruining the Schools.* Portsmouth: Heinemann, 2000.

Lehmann-Haupt, Rachel. "Scans: Real Tests for Kids." *Wired* 1999. Oct. <http://www.wired.com/news/news/culture/story/7571.html>.

McLaughlin, Kenneth F. *Interpretation of Test Results.* Washington: U.S. Dept. of Health, Education, and Welfare, 1964.

Owen, David. *None of the Above: The Truth Behind the SATs.* Lanham: Rowman & Littlefield, 1999.

Perrone, Vic. *The Abuses of Standardized Testing.* Bloomington: Phi Delta Kappa Educational Foundation, 1977.

Weiss, Kenneth R. "New Test-Taking Skill: Working the System." <http://www.latimes.com/cgi-bin/>.

Yardley, Jim. "A Test Is Born." *New York Times/Education Life* 9 Apr. 2000: 32–36.

3 | Can Censorship or Book Banning Ever Be Justified?

Introduction

Issues of censorship are interwoven with issues of individual freedom, freedom of the press, freedom of speech, and fundamental human rights in a democratic society. Philosophers, church leaders, political leaders, confronting the potential impact of unrestrained individual voices on the harmony and stability of the state, often turn to censorship as a regulatory device and protection against anarchy. The counterresponse, of course, is that when ideas or books (the permanent repository of ideas) are repressed, no matter how potentially "dangerous" they might be, democracy is threatened.

The problem is further complicated when censorship issues are placed in specific social contexts, such as schools or colleges (public or private), the press, or corporate security. Should inflammatory ("hate") speech or works like *Mein Kampf* or *The Turner Diaries*, both of which advocate white supremacy at all costs, including genocidal war, be banned? After all, the latter book was in the possession of Timothy McVeigh, the convicted Oklahoma City terrorist bomber, although it was never determined that its ideas significantly influenced his decision to blow up the Murrah Federal Building, killing 168 men, women, and children. Where does one draw the line between "speaking one's mind" about, say, a public official's allegedly poor performance and defaming that person (a legitimate basis for a lawsuit)? Should students or faculty be permitted to communicate ideas and opinions that most people would consider offensive? The following selections present a rich assortment of opinions on this multifaceted and deeply debated issue.

Campus Speech Issues | Martin P. Golding

Perhaps the trickiest part of settling freedom-of-speech issues is deciding what exactly constitutes "speech." Should the freedom to yell "Fire!" in a crowded theater be protected by the First Amendment when there is no fire? Is it unconstitutional for airport security to prohibit joking about firearms when passing through the metal detectors? Well, then, some would argue, why should Ku Klux Klan members or sympathizers retain their right to speak? Isn't it true that racist speech is tantamount to a physical assault on some people?

Some argue that college communities should adopt speech codes that would ensure a comfortable learning environment for all students. Others counter that students be able to speak their minds and learn to deal with audience reactions, for that is how learning takes place. In the opening chapter of his book, *Free Speech on Campus,* Martin P. Golding, a professor of philosophy and of law at Duke University, examines the rationale behind college speech codes.

From time to time, the Congress of the United States has considered an amendment to the Constitution that would allow Congress and the states to prohibit the physical desecration of the American flag. Were the amendment to be approved (it would need the vote of two-thirds of each House and three-fourths of the states), it would have the effect of reversing the decision of the Supreme Court in the case of *Texas v. Johnson* (491 U.S. 397 (1989)), which held that a statute designed to protect the flag violated the free speech provision of the First Amendment: "Congress shall make no law . . . abridging the freedom of speech or of the press. . . ." Gregory Johnson had burned a flag in protest at the 1984 Republican National Convention. Yet as Justice William J. Brennan wrote:

> If there is a bedrock principle underlying the First Amendment, it is that the Government may not prohibit the expression of an idea simply because society finds the idea itself offensive or disagreeable.

The Court's decision was met with a great deal of outrage, for as the Court itself recognized, the flag is the "unique" symbol of national unity. Hence the move by Congress to reverse the decision.

This so far unsuccessful move has been met by opposition, much of it coming from people who revere the flag and deplore its desecration. They see the proposal as contrary to the "bedrock principle," perhaps just the thin edge of the wedge toward eroding an essential American freedom. It is somewhat

---

Source: Golding, Martin P. "Campus Speech Issues." *Free Speech on Campus.* Lanham, MD: Rowman & Littlefield, 2000. 1–13. Reprinted by permission.

ironic, though, that a number of these same people have no hesitation in supporting campus speech codes. While there may be a difference between a government's restriction of the expression of an idea and a college's or university's imposition of a speech code (a difference that evaporates in the case of a public institution), there clearly is some dissonance here. A double standard seems to be at work. But there are complications. Many people may be more resentful of the government's attempts to restrict free speech than a university's.

A university is more of a special-purpose institution, and restrictions on expression, it is sometimes argued, fit in with its aims: restrictions on speech are necessary to promote a "comfortable learning environment." The airing of certain ideas is therefore acceptable, while airing others that are offensive to one or another group is not. Some proponents of speech codes insist that it is not the ideas in the abstract that are of concern so much as "verbal behavior" that may cause hurt. The simplistic old adage, "Sticks and stones may break my bones, but names will never harm me," is rejected. The proscription of certain offensive and disagreeable ideas, or the mode of their expression, is therefore appropriate. Or so it is maintained.

While speech codes have varied in details, these interrelated arguments or sentiments seem to be basic considerations. Another related claim is that punishing "hate speech" teaches people that racism or other prejudice is unacceptable and can bring about tolerance and sensitivity.[1] A school's failure to institute a speech code, it is sometimes said, is tantamount to an endorsement of bigotry and racism. It has also been claimed that the Fourteenth Amendment ("nor shall any State . . . deny to any person within its jurisdiction the equal protection of the laws") mandates that students be protected from demeaning and denigrating speech if they are to be—and feel—equal on campus.[2] At perhaps a lesser level, it has been argued that some Supreme Court opinions legitimize prohibition of certain forms of offensive speech.[3] Whether arguments for speech codes can be sustained is something we examine later.

In line with the above considerations and claims, three basic models of codes have been noted: the fighting words approach, the emotional distress theory, and the nondiscrimination/harassment option.[4] (1) "Fighting words" were forbidden as student misconduct by a University of California code. These are defined as personally abusive epithets inherently likely to provoke a violent reaction whether or not they actually do so, and they constitute harassment when they create a hostile and intimidating educational environment. (2) A University of Texas at Austin code made it a university offense to engage in racial harassment, defined as "extreme or outrageous acts or communications that are intended to harass, intimidate or humiliate a student or students on account of race, color or national origin and that reasonably cause them to suffer severe emotional stress." (3) A third type of code emphasizes "discriminatory harassment." Thus, a proposed code at the University of Massachusetts would have made it a violation for any member of the university community to engage in verbal or physical conduct that the targeted individual or group "would find discriminatorily alters the conditions" for participation in the activities of the university, on the basis of race, color, and national or ethnic origin. The third approach seems the most commonly used, but they all overlap in extent.

Of course, a public college or university, as an agency of government, is required to conform to the provisions of the First Amendment. It is to such an institution that Justice Brennan's bedrock principle applies. In a number of important instances campus speech codes have been struck down by the courts.[5] Private institutions are in a different situation, however. They have more leeway in enacting speech codes.[6] Furthermore, one can easily imagine a church-connected college imposing a speech and conduct code that prohibits on-campus expressions that do not conform to its official beliefs and practices (e.g., opposition to abortion). The courts probably could not disallow such a code, for that may interfere with another First Amendment right, the school's right of "free exercise" of religion.

The similarities and differences that obtain among public, private, and church-connected colleges and universities suggest a broad topic for analysis: the aims of institutions of higher learning. For it is in the context of these aims that arguments for and against campus speech codes take place. Obviously, the topic is too large for full treatment here, but it cannot be avoided entirely. For we are concerned, as it were, with the "constitution" of institutions of higher learning and the extent to which it does contain, or ought to contain, something like Justice Brennan's bedrock principle. . . .

Also, although the bedrock principle of the First Amendment applies head-on only to public institutions, there is much to be gleaned from some of the debate over how far it reaches. The fact is that not all kinds of speech are constitutionally protected, for instance, obscene speech and terrorist threats. Analogies to free speech jurisprudence are frequently found in the speech code literature, even in the case of nonpublic colleges and universities, many of which proclaim their commitment to principles of freedom of expression and inquiry. That they are found is hardly surprising. While George Washington did not receive the Ten Amendments on Mount Vernon, they nevertheless are as close to being our civil religion as anything. So although the First Amendment applies only to governments and their agencies, we often encounter the complaint of people who have been suspended from a private institution, because of an opinion they have expressed, that their right of free speech has been violated.

The issue of free speech on campus is broader than that of speech codes alone. Speech codes are typically directed at students. Academic freedom, on the other hand, is a concept that applies, first of all, to the corporate, institutional autonomy of a university or college, its freedom to determine who shall teach, who shall be admitted, and what shall be taught. Most importantly, however, it refers to the freedom of the individual faculty member to express his or her views (however unpopular with the trustees or college administration) on extramural matters, e.g., on questions of general or local politics, and freedom from reprisal for positions taken.[7] In this respect, the term refers to free speech "off campus," as it were, though such expression might occur on the campus. The status of tenure is regarded as vital to protect this aspect of academic freedom. In fact, many faculty members do not have tenure, and their protection derives from the respect for academic freedom maintained by the intellectual culture of the university.[8]

In another sense of the term, "academic freedom" is associated with the   10
university as a marketplace of ideas and the free speech provision of the university's constitution. . . . In this sense the term refers to political positions and ideological assertions "on campus," positions and assertions expressed in the course of teaching and class discussion or debate. An instructor in economics might be a proponent of the free market or of Marxism and teach from one or the other perspective, and a student might take a contrary position. With regard to an instructor, the term also covers the freedom (jus docens, the right to teach) of a qualified faculty member to control the contents of his or her courses and research, subject to the limits of professional ethics. Academic freedom in this sense may come into conflict with the institutional autonomy of the university, its freedom to determine what shall be taught. Although trustees and administration should not interfere with academic freedom, that doesn't mean "anything goes." Trustees and administration have the responsibility of seeing that standards of scholarship are not eroded; "academic freedom" shouldn't become a mindless device for avoiding this responsibility.[9]

All these aspects of academic freedom border on the battle being fought over the curriculum and "multicultural education." Although some of the arguments voiced in this encounter are germane to the issue of free speech on campus, they will only be glanced at here.[10] In trying to understand the scope of the university as a marketplace of ideas, we shall, however, consider whether there are grounds for *excluding* a subject or field from the university.

Because of the campus disturbances that were common in the 1960s and '70s, "academic freedom" was extended to include the right of students to attend classes and invited lectures free from disruption by students who disapprove of the ideas being expressed therein. Instances of such disruption have occurred in recent years, as well as in the 1980s. On many campuses, conduct codes forbid disruption of classes and lectures, but these provisions seem to be selectively enforced.

The freedom of qualified faculty members to control the content of their courses can raise a free speech issue in another way, as is illustrated by an item in the *New York Times* (May 11, 1994). Under the headline "A Sexual Harassment Case to Test Academic Freedom," there is a report on events that allegedly took place in a class at the Chicago Theological Seminary. The professor, Gordon Snyder, told a story, from the Babylonian Talmud, regarding a man who falls off a roof and accidentally "penetrates" a woman. The point of the story, presumably, was that in the opinion of the Talmud the man is free from sin because his act was unintentional. (Examination of the source will show that the story has nothing at all to do with sin but rather with whether the man is civilly liable for degradation.) A female student believed that the story justified brutality toward women, and she charged the professor with "creating an intimidating, hostile or offensive environment"—he had engaged "in verbal conduct of a sexual nature." The upshot of the incident was that the professor was severely censured by the seminary and had his course placed under strict supervision.

While it is impossible to comment on this incident without having more information, it is easy to see that the outcome could have a "chilling effect" on the conduct of this course and other courses taught at the school. The ethics of teaching does place limits on professors, and the control that they may have over their courses should not be the same thing as professorial whim. Still, it is plain that sexual harassment regulations can raise campus free speech concerns. And they can raise them for students, too. In fact, there appears to be a trend to use anti-harassment regulations as a way of restricting speech, analogous with prohibitions in Employment Law.[11]

By the beginning of 1995 more than 350 American colleges adopted or   15
tried to adopt a speech code. Although, as noted, the speech-restrictive provisions of codes at several public institutions have been invalidated by the courts, many of them remain on the books unchanged, perhaps for public relations or "feel good" reasons. While some codes appear to be merely aspirational, others designate punishments for violations, anything from censure to expulsion. Offenders (faculty or student) may sometimes also be required to undergo a process of sensitivity training. Sensitivity and diversity training is one of the growth industries on American campuses, bringing with it a corps of (often high-priced) so-called sensitivity and diversity consultants and facilitators. On many campuses such training is a mandatory part of freshman orientation. Some of the practices that have been reported strike me as bizarre; for instance, requiring students to sit quietly while all sorts of slurs are thrown at them. Certain techniques strike me as ethically questionable, to say the least, such as embarrassing or shaming students to the point of tears. If speech codes forbid anything, it should be these sorts of practices.

As objectionable as sensitivity training may be, it raises an important general question: Is moral education part of the university's function, and if so, what shape should it take? More specifically for our purposes, do speech codes have a role to play in the process? The former question raises the large issue of curriculum, which is beyond the scope of this book. The latter question is dealt with indirectly in other chapters. We should keep in mind, of course, that the issue of speech codes is only part of the subject of free speech on campus.

At this point it will be useful to list a number of examples of incidents that are used to raise campus free speech issues. Except for one, all are given here more or less as they are reported in the literature. Almost all of them have occurred in the past ten years. It is sometimes said that the campus speech debate has largely consisted of a rehashing of the same few alleged horror stories whose existence is attested to by anecdotal evidence at best. While a lot of rehashing has occurred, it is my distinct sense that the "alleged horror stories," i.e., incidents of successful or attempted suppression or regulation of speech, are many and not few. But, in an important respect, whether they are many or few really doesn't matter. The incidents raise questions of principle and underlying rationale, which merit discussion in their own right. These questions are the subject matter of this book. Although I shall be looking at real-world incidents, it is not intended as a work of reportage.

(1) A group of students hangs a banner reading "Homophobia Sucks" across the entrance to a building.

(2) A male student wears a sweatshirt with the words "Fuck Women."

(3) One student calls a student who is of Asian descent a "Gook" and says that there are too many of his kind at the university.

(4) In a class on race relations in the United States the lecturer refers to a group as Indians rather than Native Americans. As a result the class is disrupted.

(5) In order to prevent its circulation, a black student takes copies of an independent campus newspaper; a previous issue contained an article about blacks that he found offensive and "full of lies."

(6) A university adopts a rule that prescribes punishment for "derogatory names, inappropriately directed laughter, inconsiderate jokes, and conspicuous exclusion from conversation."

(7) In the campus newspaper, an advertisement is published that denies the occurrence of the Holocaust.

(8) A black student association withdraws its invitation to a speaker who reportedly gave an anti-Semitic speech on another college campus.

(9) A new course proposed by a professor is turned down by the college curriculum committee on the grounds that it is ethnocentric and its syllabus is not sufficiently multicultural. When the instructor objected to such "thought control," her dean declared the objection a threat to academic freedom.

(10) In a legal studies class on the Thirteenth Amendment the instructor refers to the black students as ex-slaves. He is required to make a public apology and attend a "sensitivity and racial awareness" session.

(11) A mathematics professor writes a letter to the student newspaper about date rape; he states that female students who accept invitations to male students' dormitory rooms must bear some responsibility for such alleged rapes. The professor is temporarily suspended.

(12) A professor of biology writes a letter to the student newspaper condoning premarital intercourse between consenting students. The professor is dismissed from his position.

(13) A student newspaper runs a cartoon making fun of affirmative action, for which one of the editors is suspended. A student editor at another school writes an article that criticizes the suspension; he, too, is suspended.

(14) In a project for a course on contemporary issues in feminist art, some women students distribute posters around the university with the names of fifty men chosen at random from the directory, under the heading "Notice: These Men Are Potential Rapists."

(15) A fraternity stages an "Ugly Woman" contest in which one member dresses as a black woman: he wears stringy black hair in curlers, uses pillows to pad his chest and buttocks, and speaks in slang that parodies blacks. As a result, various sanctions are imposed by the university on the fraternity.

Except for one case, the second, these incidents, or incidents like them, are reported to have occurred on North American college or university campuses in the past few years.[12] I used the second case as an example in an undergraduate course. We were discussing John Stuart Mill's defense of free speech in his famous essay *On Liberty,* and I brought up the 1971 Supreme Court case of *Cohen v. California* (403 U.S. 15). Cohen had been convicted in a California court of violating a disturbing-the-peace statute by "offensive conduct." He had worn a jacket bearing the words "Fuck the Draft" in a Los Angeles courthouse corridor. He testified that he did so as a means of informing the public of the depth of his feeling against the Vietnam War and the draft. A majority of the U.S. Supreme Court decided that Cohen's right to freedom of expression had been violated and reversed his conviction.[13]

My class (thirty or so students, mostly seniors, about ten of them women) readily agreed with the result in *Cohen.* Well, I asked, suppose a student wore a sweatshirt emblazoned "Fuck NAFTA" around the Duke campus (the North American Free Trade Agreement was being debated in Congress at the time). Again, my students had no difficulty in saying it should be allowed—a clear case of "political" speech, they said. Well, then, what about a sweatshirt with "Fuck Women"? A brief moment of disquiet could be sensed. Well, what about it? Somewhat to my surprise, given the line being broadcast in many quarters of the campus regarding male-female relations, there was general agreement that this sort of speech or conduct should not be punishable. Even the ten women who were present agreed with that view; at least none of them openly dissented. Unfortunately, I did not pursue the issue. I could at least have inquired whether they thought their view was widely shared by Duke undergraduates. (I think that the general reaction would be quite vocal and negative.) But I was too diffident to press the example. I rarely use the mentioned four-letter word in my own speech, even less in a class, and in more than thirty years of teaching I don't think that I ever uttered it as many times as that day. I did suggest that a generation used to cable television and R-rated movies may have become inured to such language, but that universities and colleges, students and faculty both, perhaps should be held to higher standards of speech and conduct than the rest of society. Because of my diffidence, however, I moved on to other, less discomforting examples. (The concern with single words may seem rather old-fashioned, the sort of thing for which kids would get their mouth washed out with soap. In fact, many speech codes focus on single words, so-called derogatory names.)

Because of my diffidence I also failed to take up a related topic, the possible "chilling" effect on freedom of expression—was my diffidence due in part to that chilling effect? was I committing a verbal sexual assault? will I use this example again in a class? I would not venture to predict whether the students' reaction would be the same, next time.

In order to elicit some of the issues inherent to our subject, it will be useful to look at a few of our opening examples. It will not be necessary to expound each of them with the same degree of detail. Some of them overlap, anyway.

Example (1) is reported as an actual incident at a college in the northeast. A father visiting his son there asked the president of the college whether it would be all right if a group of students hung a banner with the slogan "Homosexuality Sucks" on a college building. "That could never be tolerated," he answered.[14] (As stated, it is not important whether any of this occurred exactly as reported.) Why it couldn't be tolerated isn't clear to me. Perhaps the president merely wanted to avoid dealing with the ruckus that would be aroused. But *shouldn't* it be tolerated? If one banner is the expression of an idea, isn't the other (its opposite) also the expression of an idea? And if it is permissible to express one idea, shouldn't it be permissible to express the other? Various observers of campus goings-on have said that a "double standard" often operates in cases of this kind.[15] Suppose, in example (7) for instance, there is a move to forbid, punish, or (as has been done) severely censure the publication of Holocaust-denying advertisements. Should it matter that they contain blatant falsehoods, as long as they are an expression of ideas? How should such cases be handled?

More fundamentally, though, we need to consider whether there is a principled basis for distinguishing acceptable from unacceptable speech. This is no easy matter, and in the end we may not be able to formulate such a principle, which could be a point of great consequence. Is "Sucks" acceptable on a campus banner, no matter what it is that is supposed to "suck"? The fact is that there may well be levels of unacceptable speech, ranging, as it were, from

20

felonies to misdemeanors. A form of speech may be unacceptable yet not something that should be punishable, as some members of my class seemed to believe in example (2). Is "inappropriately directed laughter," example (6), the sort of thing that should be punished? On one campus a student was suspended after laughing when someone called another student a "faggot" in his presence.

Moreover, much may depend on the context. In the late 1960s and early '70s, expletives and vulgarities were uttered in classrooms in order to cause a disruption; they now are frequently used in student newspapers, and even by some faculty in classes, as a matter of course. But what about "derogatory names"? In example (3), it will be noticed, a derogatory name was directed against a specific person, while in example (10), as described above, the name was used in reference to a group. Should that make a difference to whether a name is acceptable? Of course, regarding these two examples, it could be argued that there isn't much if any difference between them, for in (10), calling the black students "ex-slaves," the name was used in reference to a *present* group. But suppose someone announces more generally that there are too many "Gooks" at the university? Should that be regarded as the expression of an "idea" and hence tolerable, however unacceptable the mode of expression? Suppose the student had merely said that there were too many Asians at the university? The poster with the fifty names, example (14), seems to be the expression of an idea, but does that make it tolerable? If it had said "Notice: All men are potential rapists," would that make it more tolerable?

What makes a name a "derogatory name" anyway? Various kinds of   25
speech (e.g., false accusations) plainly have the capacity to cause harm in a given context. But if, as the old adage has it, "names will never harm me," perhaps what makes a name derogatory and unacceptable is that the recipient of the name finds it *offensive*—it hurts in a way, even if it doesn't harm. Sometimes, however, the recipient may find a name to be offensive while the deliverer does not. Apparently this was the case in example (10); the instructor did not think it offensive to call the black students "ex-slaves," and he did not *intend* to give offense. (In the actual incident, he initially spoke the word to a particular black student who couldn't recite the Thirteenth Amendment to the U.S. Constitution; as an ex-slave, the instructor said, he and all the other blacks should know the amendment's contents. As a Jew, the instructor later explained, he didn't mind being called an ex-slave, for as the annual Passover service states: "We were slaves in Egypt. . . .") If certain words or forms of expression are to be deemed unacceptable and possibly punishable—but only if uttered with an intention to offend—it has seemed crucial to many commentators that there be some standard of offensiveness that is not dependent exclusively on the feelings of those people to whom the remark is directed. For example, some students at a major state university, which had a speech code, complained that they were offended when they were called "rednecks." Some administrators decided that the word itself is not offensive, but were they the right judges?

Examples (10) and (4) should be compared. A number of students in the classroom were upset because the lecturer used the word "Indian" instead of "Native American," and they made it difficult for him to finish out the course. Assuming that there were no Native Americans in the audience who might have taken offense (in fact, I've met Native Americans who prefer to be called Indians), and assuming that no offense was intended, there would seem to have been no wrong committed.

On the other hand, certain words in our language are recognized as intrinsically derogatory names or deprecatory words, e.g., "stupid." Should we say, instead, "cognitively challenged"? These words have negative connotations and express "con" rather than "pro" or neutral attitudes. It is easy to compile a list of them. But the status of many words is far from clear. Perhaps "Indian" falls into the unclear or neutral category, though there are some people who strongly prefer to be called Native Americans, just as there are some people who prefer to be called African Americans rather than blacks. Whether a name has an intrinsically derogatory status will often be controversial, and it might be argued that the recipient, in such a case, just has to tolerate any offense he or she feels. Some words are generally recognized as derogatory and yet do not always cause offense. It is imaginable that someone might not be offended by being called a "nerd." "Zero tolerance" of *any*thing that *any*body finds offensive, which is a principle found in a few campus speech-regulation policies, clearly creates havoc with free speech.

Aside from the problems raised by offensive words and derogatory names, there are perhaps more important free speech issues raised by "ideas" that offend or are unacceptable at least in some sense. For the notion that certain ideas are unacceptable has as its complement the notion that only certain ideas are acceptable. In effect, this duality was noted regarding the banner in example (1), assuming that the expression of an idea was involved. But it is also present in other examples: taking copies of a newspaper (5), the Holocaust-denying advertisement (7), withdrawing an invitation to speak (8), the letters about date rape and premarital sex (11), (12), and the cartoon (13). Though each of these cases probably raises a particular free speech issue, there is in each one an implicit reference to a complementary pair of acceptable and unacceptable ideas.

Consider, for instance, example (13). A student editor was suspended after writing an article criticizing the suspension of a student editor at another school who ran a cartoon making fun of affirmative action. Of course, one can easily imagine that the cartoon was in bad taste, a not infrequent characteristic of the "humor" that pervades college publications. But how significant should that be? It is hard to believe that the second student editor would have been suspended had he written an article *supporting* the suspension. Apparently, advocacy of affirmative action is acceptable but expressing one's opposition to it is not.[16]

This example and the others just cited raise an important and difficult issue about universities. To what extent should they remain neutral as between

30

conflicting ideas and values? Can they in fact be neutral? Isn't the promotion of certain ideas and values implicit in the very concept of a university? Does it matter if a certain idea is regarded as a blatant falsehood? and by whom? Example (7), the Holocaust-denying advertisement, is a case in point. What, in any event, is the distinction between the expression of an idea and the expression of an attitude (the use of derogatory names), and of what relevance is it? Whether there is a workable distinction is, I believe, a crucial question in the campus speech debate. Attitudes generally reflect the beliefs and opinions one holds, which is one reason why outlawing even deliberate attempts at humiliation could be problematic.

Example (15), which occurred at a public university, raises the interesting issue of the speech–conduct distinction. It generally is agreed that conduct (behavior) is more subject to government regulation and restriction than speech is. But it turns out that conduct will sometimes be regarded as a kind of speech and therefore qualify for First Amendment protection—namely, so-called "expressive conduct," conduct that expresses an idea or attitude. Johnson's burning of the flag and Cohen's wearing of the "Fuck the Draft" slogan were held by the Supreme Court to fall into this category. And so did the incident of example (15), according to the federal court that heard the case: "[The] Fraternity's skit, even as low-level entertainment, was inherently expressive and thus entitled to First Amendment protection."[17] Some proponents of speech codes, however, argue in the other direction. They maintain that speech itself can at times be regarded as a form of conduct and therefore become subject to regulation in the way that other conduct is. Should we accept this argument?[18]

We have not discussed all of the examples given in the detail they deserve. The number listed easily could have been multiplied, especially if we include instances of hoax "hate crimes." But enough has been said to indicate the problems, some of which will turn up in our examination of arguments for speech codes in chapters 4 and 5.[19]

What we need to do now is to consider some fundamentals of the "constitution" of institutions of higher learning (colleges and universities, though "university" is the term we shall generally use) and, particularly, why a free speech provision—something like Justice Brennan's bedrock principle—is a vital element of it. Having such a provision, however, does not by itself resolve all the speech issues that might come up, any more than the words of the First Amendment of the U.S. Constitution do. In order to resolve campus speech issues, recourse must be had to the provision's underlying rationale or justification, and even then problems could remain. (It should be kept in mind that speech codes are only one aspect of the topic, free speech on campus.) That rationale is rendered by the notion of the university as a marketplace of ideas.

Notes

1. See Richard Delgado, "Words That Wound: A Tort Action for Racial Insults, Epithets, and Name-Calling," 17 *Harvard Civil Rights-Civil Liberties Law Rev.* (1982), 148–49.

With slight editorial changes and the elimination of some footnotes, this article is reprinted in M. J. Matsuda, C. R. Lawrence III, R. Delgado, and K. W. Crenshaw, *Words That Wound. Critical Race Theory, Assaultive Speech and the First Amendment* (Boulder, Colo.: Westview Press, 1993), 89–110. Three articles from this book are discussed below, in chapters 4 and 5. There is no agreed-on definition of "hate speech," and it is sometimes used interchangeably with "offensive speech." Judging from the literature, though, we can take it to mean: any form of expression (or communication), verbal or nonverbal (e.g., posters, parades, insignia, picket lines) regarded as offensive to racial, ethnic, or religious groups or other discrete minorities (e.g., homosexuals), or to women.

2. See Mari J. Matsuda, "Public Response to Racist Speech: Considering the Victim's Story," 87 *Michigan Law Rev.* (1989), 2320–81. With slight editorial changes and the elimination of some footnotes, this article is reprinted in *Words That Wound*, 17–52.

3. *Chaplinsky v. New Hampshire*, 315 U.S. 568 (1942) ("fighting words," words that "by their very nature inflict injury" and words that "tend to incite an immediate breach of the peace," are not protected by the First Amendment); *Beauharnais v. Illinois*, 343 U.S. 250 (1952) (upholding the constitutionality of a 1917 Illinois group libel law). For a discussion of the erosion of these decisions, see Samuel Walker, *Hate Speech: The History of an American Controversy* (Lincoln: University of Nebraska Press, 1994).

4. See Robert M. O'Neil, *Free Speech in the College Community* (Bloomington: Indiana University Press, 1997), 7–11, for a discussion of the differences. O'Neil's clearly written book covers more topics than we do here, and focuses on public colleges and universities and issues of constitutional law.

5. For an excellent study of the cases, see Timothy C. Shiell, *Campus Hate Speech on Trial* (Lawrence: University of Kansas Press, 1998). The opinion of the court in *Doe v. Univ. of Michigan,* 721 F. Supp. 852 (E.D. Mich. 1989) (speech code effectively declared unconstitutional) is given in appendix A.

6. In February 1995, a judge of the Santa Clara County (California) Superior Court struck down the Stanford University speech code on the basis of California's 1992 Leonard Law: Private educational institutions may not discipline a student "solely on the basis of . . . speech or other communication that when engaged in outside the campus is protected from government restriction by the First Amendment." The Stanford code, enacted in 1990, prohibited "personal vilification of students on the basis of their sex, race, color, handicap, religion, sexual orientation or national and ethnic origin." There is no Leonard Law in other states, but some individual state constitutions contain speech protections that may apply to private colleges and universities.

7. As put in the 1940 American Association of University Professors *Statement of Principles on Academic Freedom and Tenure:* "When they [teachers] speak or write as citizens, they should be free from institutional censorship or discipline. . . ."

8. Academic freedom is a large subject, on which much has been written. See Richard Hofstadter and Walter P. Metzger, *The Development of Academic Freedom in the United States* (New York: Columbia University Press, 1955). A bibliography from 1940 and articles of historical, legal, and philosophical interest may be found in 53 *Law and Contemporary Problems* (Summer 1990), Freedom and Tenure in the Academy: The Fiftieth Anniversary of the 1940 [American Association of University Professors] Statement of Principles.

9. Academic fields and faculties are generally self-governing and they have the initial responsibility of showing that the "emperor has no clothes." But faculties are notoriously weak (and weak-kneed). The slogan of "academic freedom" too easily becomes a way of avoiding judgments of academic merit. But the issue can have complex dimensions; more about it in a later chapter.

10. I have never met a faculty member who is opposed to the teaching of non-Western cultures, languages, and literatures. What is opposed by many faculty is the ideology and policy of multiculturalism, an expression of which is contained in Stanford University's *Affirmative Action Plan* (October 16, 1991): "The Office for Multicultural Development is predicated upon the knowledge that our society is composed of independent, multi-racial/multi-ethnic peoples and that our future requires new thinking and new structures which incorporate diversity as a means to harmony, unity, and equity. Moreover, diversity is fundamental to the pursuit of excellence and knowledge. In understanding and accepting this reality, Stanford University begins a transformation to ensure that multiculturalism is infused into (not appended to) all aspects of teaching, research, planning, policies, practices, achievement, and institutional life. It is the mission of the Office for Multicultural Development to develop the multicultural model of the future and guide Stanford University through the transformation."

   Cited in David O. Sacks and Peter A. Thiel, *The Diversity Myth* (Oakland, Calif.: The Independent Institute, 1995), 24. The authors demonstrate the dependence of Stanford's multiculturalism on an animus against Western culture and ideals. ("Hey hey, ho ho, Western Culture's got to go!") Statements similar to the one cited are found at other universities.

11. See Shiell, n. 5. This topic is treated in chapter 5.

12. Example (12) goes back to 1960. It is very doubtful that such a letter would result in dismissal today, whether from a public university or from most private institutions. More than likely, it would not be written, and if written, not attract attention. In the 1950s a number of faculty members were dismissed or not renewed because of political positions they had taken, because of failure to sign loyalty oaths, because of political affiliations, or because of refusal to testify before government committees (e.g., the House Un-American Activities Committee) about their political affiliations. I have chosen to focus on more recent examples. Example (12) is mentioned because it reminds us of how much historical context counts, when compared with example (13).

13. At some point in First Amendment jurisprudence, the term "freedom of expression" began to be often substituted for the term "free speech." (Even striptease in bars has been claimed to be constitutionally protected expression.) And once we move to "self-expression," political or nonpolitical, it seems that Mr. Cohen has a pretty good case. As Justice John M. Harlan II said in *Cohen:* "We cannot sanction the view that the Constitution, while solicitous of the cognitive content of individual speech, has little or no regard for that emotive function, which, practically speaking, may often be the more important element of the overall message sought to be communicated."

14. College and university administrations do have a large degree of control over the placement of banners, announcements, posters, etc., on campus property, though that control may be subject to First Amendment free speech guarantees in public institutions. Compare the removal of a Malcolm X mural, with anti-Semitic symbols, from a wall at San Francisco State University. In this instance, the university had paid for the mural, and therefore had the right to remove it. *Herald-Sun,* Durham, N.C., May 29, 1994, G8.

15. Employment of a double standard is a kind of hypocrisy, which occurs when a purportedly general standard is applied in one way to one individual or group and differently (or not at all) to another. Such hypocrisy is not infrequent on college campuses, e.g., when administrations condemn newspaper thefts by some groups but not by others, or when they condemn expression of one controversial idea ("Homosexuality Sucks") but not the expression of another ("Homophobia Sucks").

16. Since a public university is subject to the First Amendment, any allowable restriction (e.g., reasonable time, place, and manner restrictions) on speech must be "viewpoint neutral."

17. *Iota Xi Chapter of Sigma Chi Fraternity v. George Mason University,* 993 F.2d 386 (4th Cir. 1993). At a nearby university some male students sponsored a context to find the "Biggest JAP on Campus." "JAP" is a derogatory term referring to a stereotypical Jewish American Princess. I do not know whether the school disciplined these students. JAP baiting incidents have been reported on a number of campuses. Slogans such as ZAP-A-JAP and SLAP-A-JAP have been worn on students' T-shirts, for instance. Compare example (2).

18. See appendix B, Speech and Speech Acts.

19. Example (8) wasn't discussed at all. When the invitation was withdrawn, some people said that the speaker's First Amendment rights had been violated. This claim rests on a misunderstanding. Just as a private association has no duty to provide a speaker with a forum, so may it withdraw an invitation, if there are good grounds for doing so. Regarding example (9), the reader should make his or her own judgment after reading the next two chapters. ◨

Reflections and Inquiries

1. How does Golding distinguish between "free speech" and "speech codes"?

2. Is it useful to draw a distinction between "expression of ideas" and "verbal behavior"? Why?

3. In light of the fact that obscene language is not protected by the First Amendment, defend or challenge Golding's examples of students' use of obscene slogans on articles of clothing as a form of protest. What about Golding's own use of such examples in his classroom?

4. Examine the fifteen examples of freedom-of-speech incidents that Golding lists. Which of these examples, if any, deserve First Amendment protection? Which do not? Explain your reasons.

Reading to Write

1. Write an essay in which you support or argue against the adoption of a campus speech code. Allude to examples from Golding's article, as well as from your own experience, to make your case.

2. After rereading Golding's commentary on derogatory names, write a position paper in which you defend or challenge the motion that "derogatory" in this context is too subjective to prohibit in a speech code.

Precarious Prose | Donna A. Demac

To what extent do threats of libel suits affect freedom of the press? Will journalists exercise excessive self-censorship to avoid them and, in so doing, compromise their constitutional right to speak their minds freely? In the following
selection, Donna A. Demac examines the impact of litigation on this freedom.
Demac is an attorney and a professor at New York University, where she
teaches courses in copyright law and in international communications. She
has published books and articles on public access to information and is a
member of the National Coalition against Censorship.

In 1980 Richard Hargraves wrote an editorial for the Belleville, Illinois, *News
Democrat* criticizing the chairman of the local county board for breaking his
campaign promise not to raise taxes. The piece, printed in the paper's "Viewpoint" section, argued that the official "did absolutely nothing to protect your
interests" and was "nothing more than another patronage-oriented political
hack." The angered official sued for libel; Hargraves and the newspaper were
found guilty, and damages of more than $1 million (later reduced to $200,000)
were awarded.[1]

This case is one of hundreds brought over the past decade in which journalists, broadcasters, publishers, movie producers, and others have been sued
for exercising what they believed was their constitutionally guaranteed right
of free expression. No genre of expression has been exempt. Television newscasts, editorials, history books, biographies, and even novels and cartoons
have been subjected to libel suits brought by public officials, celebrities, and
others who find themselves depicted in ways that displease them. Suits
against student publications are also on the rise.[2]

In many instances, enormous sums are at stake. Since 1980 juries have
awarded libel plaintiffs damages of $1 million or more in at least thirty cases.
A 1984 study by the Libel Defense Resource Center found that the average jury
award for libel damages was triple that allowed in product liability and medical malpractice cases.

Libel is defined as communication—words or pictures—that tends to expose someone to public ridicule, shame, or contempt, or otherwise damages a
person's reputation. Traditionally, severe penalties have been imposed for libel, in recognition of the embarrassment and possible loss of income associated with defamatory statements.

Some libel cases have a degree of legitimacy, such as the suit of actress   5
Carol Burnett against the *National Enquirer* for a story falsely reporting that she
had been drunk and disorderly in public. However, libel suits are frequently

Source: Demac, Donna A. "Precarious Prose: The Threat of Libel Suits." *Liberty Denied:
The Current Rise of Censorship in America.* New Brunswick: Rutgers UP, 1988. 23–36.
Reprinted by permission.

brought for reasons that are, at best, tangential to the protection of someone's reputation. Some plaintiffs have political aims or are interested in discouraging or punishing unfavorable coverage; others may simply be fishing for damage awards.

Even in those cases in which the allegations of libel are found to be without merit, libel suits are costly to defend. In this climate it is not surprising that many publishers and broadcasters have become particularly cautious about the content of what they produce. Libel lawyers are consulted more frequently, and media executives are demonstrating a tendency to avoid potential problems by toning down controversial material—especially investigative reporting—or "spiking" it altogether.[3]

While this trend toward self-censorship is difficult to measure, there is no doubt that it has deprived the public of valuable news and information. Simply the threat of a libel suit has intimidated many members of the Fourth Estate and the resulting atmosphere has shifted discussion of controversial issues from public forums to the courts. This "chilly" climate in effect creates a type of immunity for powerful public figures.[4] The overall result is a crippling of free and open discourse.

From Sedition to Sullivan

> We'd better tone this down or George III will sue us for libel.
>
> —Caption of cartoon by Auth of the *Philadelphia Inquirer*, April 20, 1985, showing Revolutionary War leaders looking at the Declaration of Independence

Although libel is regarded today as an issue that involves celebrities and individual public figures, the origins of the concept are bound up with the right to criticize the government. In pre-Revolutionary America, colonial authorities frequently used laws prohibiting "seditious libel" to squelch dissent.

These statutes, based on British jurisprudence, mandated harsh penalties for any statement that was deemed to be defamatory, even if it was true. The rule went unchallenged until 1735, when the lawyer defending printer John Peter Zenger, who had published a statement criticizing the unpopular governor of New York, successfully persuaded a jury that Zenger should not be convicted if the published statement was found to be accurate. In acquitting Zenger—and rejecting the existing law—the jury helped establish the principle of a free press in America.

While the Zenger verdict bolstered the country's spirit of independence, it 10 did not rapidly transform the law of libel. In fact, even well into the twentieth century libel remained an offense of "strict liability" in most states, meaning that the truth defense had to overcome a heavy presumption of injury.

The doctrine of seditious libel resurfaced in the new nation with the Sedition Act of 1798. A deliberate attempt by the Federalist Party to suppress opposition to its programs, the act made it a crime to publish "false, scandalous, and malicious writing or writings against the United States, or either house of the Congress . . . or the President."

Once the law was passed, leaders of the Adams administration moved to enforce it against written and oral statements of the Republicans. Threats were issued, and editors were jailed.

The Sedition Act expired after two years, but opposition to government policies remained punishable under a succession of congressional statutes, presidential orders, and court decisions.

The U.S. system remained ambiguous about the extent to which it was permissible for citizens to criticize the government. James Madison advocated uninhibited public debate, regarding it as the best means of arriving at an accurate assessment of the state of the nation. Thomas Jefferson, who spoke against the crime of seditious libel when he was out of office, voiced no objection when it was used against those who criticized him during his presidency. Justice Oliver Wendell Holmes, who wrote stirring and profound opinions on First Amendment freedoms, rationalized the use of the Sedition Act of 1918 to imprison the socialist Eugene Debs for his speeches advocating resistance to military conscription for World War I.

Thus, for nearly two centuries after the founding of the country, state and federal libel laws remained in place to discourage blunt criticism of elected officials. The Supreme Court sanctioned them, ruling as late as 1942 that libelous statements, along with obscenity and "fighting words," fell outside the protection of the First Amendment.[5]

All this changed in 1964, when the Court ruled on a libel complaint brought against *The New York Times* by a police commissioner in Montgomery, Alabama. L. B. Sullivan had sought $500,000 in damages in connection with an advertisement published in the *Times* on March 29, 1960, by civil rights leaders and activists who were seeking to draw attention to the desegregation battles then raging in the South. The ad noted that student leaders had been expelled from schools and "loads of police armed with shotguns and tear gas ringed the Alabama state college campus."

Though Sullivan was not mentioned by name, he claimed to be identifiable, and thus defamed, in his role as Montgomery police commissioner. But Sullivan's chief complaint was broader than anything that could be called libel. As an ardent segregationist, he was hostile to the media, which were helping to make the civil rights movement a burning national issue. His lawsuit against the *Times*, which won success under the laws of Alabama, was intended to discourage press coverage of the struggle for desegregation.

In a landmark decision, the Supreme Court overturned the *Times's* conviction in the lower courts and rejected the Alabama libel law. The Court ruled that Sullivan could not prevail against the newspaper even if the ad contained inaccuracies (which it did), unless the newspaper itself was shown to have had reckless disregard for the accuracy of the statements it published. A free and robust press, the Court said, needed to operate without fear of being prosecuted and incurring heavy legal fees each time an error was made.[6]

The Sullivan case was clearly of extraordinary importance to the civil rights movement, and it continues to be of unparalleled significance for the

15

free press.[7] Yet the decision failed to answer a diverse array of relevant questions. How, for example, could it be proven that a publication acted in "reckless disregard" of the truth? Did this standard apply to all libel plaintiffs, or only to public officials? What difference would it make if the alleged defamation was contained in a news article, a cartoon, or a novel?

In subsequent years, the Court at first seemed to raise the level of protection for media libel defendants. The "reckless disregard" standard established for Sullivan, a public official, was ruled to apply also to public figures. Then it was established that private citizens who alleged libel carried a lesser burden, and needed only to show that the journalist (or writer, filmmaker, etc.) had been negligent. But how could it be determined whether one was a public or a private figure? The major difference, the Court said, depended on the extent to which the disputed media coverage was voluntary or involuntary, and on the allegedly defamed person's ability to respond through the media, short of going to court.

Other Supreme Court decisions have made the press more vulnerable to libel actions. Especially disheartening was a 1979 ruling that gave libel plaintiffs access to editorial notes, records of reporters' conversations, and other material that might be relevant to a finding of reckless disregard. This single decision made libel suits far more expensive and time-consuming to defend. Many weeks are now necessary before trial in order to review the material furnished by both sides. In this process the meticulous journalist who has kept extensive notes may encounter particular difficulty because he or she must supply such documents to the other side during pretrial discovery proceedings. At the same time, pressure is exerted on the reporter to reveal the identities of confidential sources. The dynamics of the process have made libel suits attractive to those plaintiffs who seek to attack the credibility of particular publications or journalists.

Where Libel Litigation Is Alive and Well

Despite the Sullivan ruling, the use of libel laws by public officials to challenge the media has flourished at the state and local levels. One hot spot has been Philadelphia, where as many as fifteen libel suits at a time have been brought by former mayors, judges, prosecutors, and even a member of Congress. The *Philadelphia Inquirer* is perhaps the most besieged paper in the country. During the 1980s, its reporters and editors have spent innumerable and costly hours on libel litigation and suffered jury awards as high as $4 million.

In 1987 a television station in Mobile, Alabama, was sued for $5 million by the president of the county commission. At issue was a newscast in which the station had presented footage of a public hearing. One of the participants in the hearing had made false assertions, which the station recognized and took care to rebut in follow-up statements. Nonetheless, a state court ruled the broadcast libelous.

National figures sometimes try to use state libel laws to their advantage. In 1984 then Senator Paul Laxalt of Nevada filed a $250 million suit against

McClatchy Newspapers for an article reporting that profits had been skimmed from a casino at a time when Laxalt was its principal owner. McClatchy viewed the action as an attempt to deter the rest of the media from pursuing the story and filed a countersuit. Soon after a federal judge ruled in April 1987 that the writer of the story did not have to reveal his sources, the two parties settled the suit; Laxalt received no damages.

Even when libel complaints are settled out of court or are decided in favor of the defendants, the sheer time and expense required to prepare a defense often has a chilling effect on future coverage.[8] In addition to the phenomenon of self-censorship, a publication that has been sued for libel may also find it more difficult to gain access to newsmakers and sources. A newspaper or other media outlet that has been sued for libel may find that regardless of the outcome it has been made into a pariah.

Even at the federal level, the Sullivan decision has not completely protected the media from attack. Under the rubric of national security the government has frequently attempted to punish the press for reporting embarrassing or sensitive information. . . .

The direct use of libel laws also has been employed by former government officials. For instance, David Atlee Phillips, a former CIA official, sued Donald Freed and Fred Landis, authors of *A Death in Washington,* and their publisher, Lawrence Hill & Company, for $210 million for linking him to the Washington murder of former Chilean ambassador Orlando Letelier.[9] Phillips also used the popular "national security" argument in refusing to answer questions from defense attorneys during the pretrial discovery process.[10] The case was settled out of court after the authors agreed to retract the allegations against Phillips publicly.

The ability of the government and former officials to hide behind rationales like "national security" puts into question the entire legitimacy of libel laws with respect to public figures. In fact, some critics have called for what amounts to a deregulation of political speech through the abolition of the right of public officials to bring libel suits.[11]

Lancing the Press

The attempt by journalists to defend themselves against the growing wave of libel actions has been inhibited by a strong public displeasure with various media practices. Libel plaintiffs often win popular support because they reinforce the notion that the press is an arrogant, monolithic institution guilty of sensationalism for the sake of profit, the glorification of gossip, and the invasion of individual privacy. The status and glamour that the press, particularly investigative reporters, enjoyed in the wake of the Watergate affair have receded greatly during the conservative national political atmosphere of the 1980s.

The extent to which investigative journalism is under siege was demonstrated in a suit against the Alton, Illinois, *Telegraph,* after two of its reporters sent a confidential memo to federal law enforcement officials; the memo contained information about a local builder who was suspected of having links to organized crime. Although this information was never published, the memo made its way to the Federal Home Loan Bank, and as a result the builder's line of credit was cut off. Apprised of the memo, he sued for libel and was initially awarded $9.2 million in damages. The *Telegraph* subsequently went into Chapter 11 bankruptcy as a result of the high legal fees and is now under new management. Both of the reporters involved in the case have left the newspaper, which is now less inclined to do investigative reporting.[12]

As the Illinois Hargraves case indicated, newspapers have been prosecuted for editorial opinion as well as for statements of fact, and this offers perhaps the clearest indication of how libel suits strike at the heart of a free press. The danger was anticipated by James Madison in an attack on the Sedition Act:

> It must be obvious to the plainest minds, that opinions and inferences, and conjectural observations, are not only in many cases inseparable from the facts, but may often be more the objects of prosecution than the facts themselves.[13]

News stories and editorials are not the only categories of journalism to be hit with the libel weapon. The *Chicago Tribune* and its architecture writer were sued by real estate developer Donald Trump for poking fun at his ambition to build the world's tallest building. Cartoonist Paul Szep of *The Boston Globe* has been sued for libel some half-dozen times in his career; a $3.6 million suit against him was filed by former Massachusetts governor Edward King. In a case that went all the way to the Supreme Court, fundamentalist preacher Jerry Falwell sued *Hustler* magazine for a satirical feature. The issue at stake was whether Falwell could claim damages for "emotional distress" even though the jury had found that the satire—a tasteless parody of a liquor ad that depicted Falwell as a drunkard having sex with his mother in an outhouse—was not libelous because it was in no way believable. The high court was not sufficiently swayed by Falwell's embarrassment. In February 1988 the justices voted 8 to 0 in favor of *Hustler* and gave a ringing endorsement of the right to criticize public figures, even if it involves statements that are "outrageous" or offensive.

Rewriting History in the Courts

It was in 1984 that two of the most momentous libel trials of the age got under way, both in New York City. The first case was brought by retired General William Westmoreland against CBS in response to a television documentary that charged that Westmoreland, during his tenure as commander of U.S. troops in Vietnam, allowed falsified intelligence data on the war to be sent to his superiors at the Pentagon. Although evidence indicated that the journalistic standards of the CBS documentary were sometimes questionable, Westmoreland dropped the suit before a verdict was reached.

The other case was a $50 million suit brought by Israeli general Ariel Sharon against *Time* magazine for the way it had depicted his connection to the massacre by Lebanese Phalangist soldiers of hundreds of Palestinian civilians.

In this case, too, there were revelations of sloppy journalistic practices. But both Westmoreland and Sharon had a larger purpose than protecting their reputations and correcting factual errors. Civil libertarians agreed that both cases were deliberately designed to attract major media coverage with the aim of trying to remold public opinion regarding two highly disputed subjects: U.S. involvement in Vietnam and the Israeli invasion of Lebanon. Westmoreland and his financial backers, including several New Right organizations, clearly hoped to revise the public record on the failure of the military to assess the deterioration of its position in Vietnam adequately. Sharon hoped to obscure the fact that an Israeli commission had found him "indirectly responsible" for the massacres at Sabra and El Shatila. In both cases the plaintiffs were seeking to use the libel laws to rewrite history.

Some plaintiffs seek to draw attention away from critical accounts of their actions by bringing libel charges based on an incidental personal issue. Perhaps the most celebrated instance of this sort was the case brought against Peter Matthiessen for his book *In the Spirit of Crazy Horse*, which deals with the confrontation that took place between government officials and Native American activists in South Dakota in the 1970s. Angered at statements about him in the book, South Dakota governor William Janklow sued the author and his publisher, Viking, for libel, asking for $25 million in damages. The complaint focused on Matthiessen's references to old allegations that Janklow had raped a young Indian girl during his time as a legal services attorney on the Rosebud Indian Reservation. The rumors had been in circulation since 1967 and had been considered and dismissed by the FBI, which Matthiessen also noted.

Janklow sued not only Matthiessen and Viking but also *Newsweek* for mentioning the charges in an article it had carried about *In the Spirit of Crazy Horse*. In addition, Janklow personally telephoned booksellers in several states, threatening to sue them as well unless they stopped selling the book; he actually did bring suit against several bookstores in South Dakota. The inclusion of the booksellers greatly expanded the potential impact of this case; no court, however, has been willing to accept the argument that booksellers have a responsibility to vouch for the accuracy of their inventory.

Matthiessen and Viking were also hit with a $25 million libel suit brought by David Price, an FBI agent who claimed that *In the Spirit of Crazy Horse* defamed him. In January 1988 a federal district court dismissed that suit, ruling that authors have a right to publish "an entirely one-sided view of people and events." Judge Diana E. Murphy gave judicial endorsement to writing on controversial subjects by holding that "speech about government and its officers, about how well or badly they carry out their duties, lies at the very heart of the First Amendment." In 1989 Janklow's suit was also dismissed by a judge who found that Matthiessen had not shown reckless disregard of the truth.

Libel as Intimidation

During the last ten years, for every relatively legitimate libel suit, dozens have been intended purely to intimidate. Cult organizations are especially fond of this tactic. Lyndon LaRouche, Synanon, and the Church of Scientology all have brought aggressive libel suits clearly aimed at discouraging press coverage of their activities.

LaRouche, a onetime leftist who veered to the extreme right, brought a $20 million suit against the publisher of a small New York City weekly called *Our Town* and its reporter Dennis King, who had written a series of investigative articles about LaRouche entitled "Nazis on the Rise." Though the case was dismissed, King says that the very fact that it was brought, along with numerous other libel suits by LaRouche, have made it difficult to find publishers who will buy articles about him and his organization.

In 1984, as NBC was about to air a program about LaRouche, he attempted to suppress it by filing a $100 million libel suit in federal court against the network, several staffers, Dennis King, the Anti-Defamation League of B'nai B'rith, and others who had helped in preparing the piece. During months of trial preparation, LaRouche's people engaged in various forms of harassment, including picketing against an NBC reporter and claiming she was a prostitute, and distributing a bogus newspaper to King's neighbors—with his photo on the front page—that maligned his sexual practices. The court found the suit to be an entirely frivolous attempt to intimidate reporters and, after a countersuit filed by NBC, ordered LaRouche to pay several million dollars in damages.

In another incident, Synanon sent some 1,000 letters to wire services, publishers, and broadcasters, threatening to take legal action if corrections were not made regarding virtually every story printed about the organization in 1978 and 1979. During this period, Synanon members were being tried for attempted murder after a rattlesnake had been placed in the mailbox of an attorney involved in a suit against Synanon.

Small and alternative publishers are especially vulnerable to this sort of threat. The Jackson, Mississippi, *Advocate* was hit with a libel suit by the National Alliance Party, an action the paper believes was a deliberate attempt to put it out of business.

Libel actions meant to intimidate also have been brought by people and organizations who are considered quite reputable. Landlords have sued tenants for statements made about them, and employers have sued their employees. In a case that reached the Supreme Court, the owner of Bill Johnson's Restaurants in Phoenix filed a libel charge in relation to leaflets that had been distributed on a picket line organized by waitresses who were calling attention to what they said were management's mistreatment of employees and "unwarranted sexual advances." The case was dismissed in the lower courts as a thinly veiled effort to prevent workers from engaging in legitimate collective activity, but when it reached the Supreme Court it was reinstated on the grounds that employers were entitled to their day in court.[14]

The Court's decision in this case has given a green light to employers who   45
seek to suppress the free speech of labor. In one instance libel charges were
brought against a group of workers at the American Motors Corporation plant
in Kenosha, Wisconsin, who were issuing a newsletter called *Fighting Times.*
The $4.2 million suit was brought by company foremen who were criticized in
the publication, but it was later revealed to have been paid for by American Motors.

Celebrity Suits and Libelous Fiction

An inevitable result of the boom in reporting and book publishing about
celebrities has been an expansion in the number of libel suits. Cases brought
by subjects of "juicy" articles, books, and broadcasts who did not like the way
they were portrayed have become a staple of entertainment news. It is tempting to believe that many of these suits are brought solely to elicit even more
publicity for the subject, but they can set dangerous legal precedents. Perhaps
most disturbing was the threat by Frank Sinatra to sue author Kitty Kelley *before* she began writing a biography of him.

Legal conflicts can arise even when the subject is collaborating with the
author. A striking example involves a $15 million action brought by Jeffrey
Macdonald, who was convicted in the late 1970s of the murder of his wife and
two children. While he was appealing the conviction, Macdonald looked for
someone to write his story and signed a contract with the writer Joe McGinniss. Although it was not stated in the contract, Macdonald assumed that
McGinniss would support his claim of innocence in the murders.

McGinniss, however, reached a different conclusion in the book *Fatal Vision,* which became a bestseller and the basis for a television miniseries. Macdonald sued McGinniss, alleging fraud, emotional distress, and other injuries.
In August 1987 the suit ended in a mistrial when jurors failed, after twenty
hours of deliberation, to agree on a verdict. Later that year the case was settled
for $325,000. Macdonald told reporters that he felt vindicated, while the
lawyer for McGinniss insisted that his client's book stood "untarnished."

People also have brought suits charging that they were libeled by works of
fiction. For example, a California psychologist who conducted nude encounter
sessions was awarded $75,000 in damages from a novelist who had partici-
pated in one of these sessions and later wrote a fictionalized account of it.
Courts in different states, however, have differed as to the merit of such actions. A New York court, considering the complaint of a writer's former girl-
friend, found no basis for her claim that she had been libeled in his novel.

The problem with such suits is that they pose a great threat to the creative   50
process. Most works of fiction bear at least some resemblance to the writer's
personal experiences, which, after all, is the raw material of literature. How,
then, can the appropriate degree of attention be paid to individual reputation
without stifling creativity? As Judge Irving Kaufman has written:

Simply according artistic works the same protection as nonartistic works may not be sufficient to protect creativity. After all, the very essence of artistic expression is invention and artists necessarily draw on their own experience. But if the rules of liability are unclear, artists will not be able to know how much disguise is sufficient to protect their claims from the claims of those who may see themselves in the portrayals.[15]

It's sometimes difficult to understand why plaintiffs go to the trouble of bringing libel suits. The initial indignation at reading what is considered a scurrilous article or book or broadcast is understandable. But given the mixed record of libel litigation, potential plaintiffs have little reason to believe they will be totally vindicated. In the quest for what is likely to be at best a partial court victory, plaintiffs spend huge amounts of time and money, which, in light of the fact that most large jury awards are later reduced on appeal by more than seventy-five percent, are unlikely to be recovered even if a plaintiff wins.

Whether or not libel litigation provides satisfaction to plaintiffs, the fact that the phenomenon is so widespread has created a troubling challenge to free speech. The Supreme Court ruling in the Falwell case was encouraging. Cartoonist Garry Trudeau was so pleased that he drew in a Supreme Court seal of approval on a Doonesbury strip that ridiculed the recently disclosed sexual indiscretions of Jimmy Swaggart.

Yet the ruling does not remove the threat posed by the use of libel suits to intimidate. As long as we have libel laws that allow public figures to drag their critics into court, free speech will remain inhibited. As Martin Garbus, Floyd Abrams, and other legal experts in the field have argued, significant changes in libel litigation procedures are needed to remove the curbs on public discourse imposed by rampant libel suits.

Notes

1. Hargraves served several days in jail for his refusal to disclose the names of confidential sources.
2. See "Liability and the Student Press," *Student Press Law Center Report*, Fall 1985, p. 29.
3. Robert Picard, "Self-Censorship Threatens U.S. Press Freedom," *Index on Censorship*, March 1982.
4. See Michael Massing's analysis of libel trends in "The Libel Chill: How Cold Is It Out There?" *Columbia Journalism Review*, May/June 1985.
5. Chaplinsky v. New Hampshire, 315 U.S. 568 (1942).
6. *The New York Times v. Sullivan*, 376 U.S. 254 (1964).
7. A fuller treatment of the Sullivan case and its importance can be found in Anthony Lewis, "Annals of Law: The Sullivan Case," *The New Yorker*, 5 November 1984.
8. Floyd Abrams, "Why We Should Change Libel Law," *The New York Times Magazine*, 29 September 1985, p. 34.
9. This action was paid for by an organization formed in 1981 to finance suits by former intelligence agents. See Eve Pell, "Taking C.I.A. Critics to Court," *The Nation*, 17 October 1981.

10. Jack Anderson, "When Spies Go to Court," *The Washington Post*, 12 June 1983.
11. Gilbert Cranberg, "Burying the Libel Hatchet," *Washington Journalism Review*, January/February 1988; Martin Garbus, "Abolish Libel—The Only Answer," *The Nation*, 8 October 1983.
12. Cindy Skaugen, "A Profitable, yet Cautious *Telegraph*," *The State Journal-Register* (Springfield, IL), 12 May 1985.
13. *Elliot's Debates on the Federal Constitution*, vol. 4, p. 575.
14. Nat Hentoff, "Libel and Labor, Bill Johnson's Restaurant Serves Up a Chill," *The Progressive*, November 1983.
15. Irving R. Kaufman, "The Creative Process and Libel," *The New York Times Magazine*, 5 April 1987. ☑

Reflections and Inquiries

1. In what ways does excessive litigation against allegedly damaging articles and books present a "troubling" challenge to free speech?

2. How serious a problem is self-censorship? In what ways, if any, does it interfere with the Fourth Estate (for example, the practice of professional journalism)?

3. What justifies the charge of libel? Which of Demac's examples seem to you to be most justifiable for being the basis of a lawsuit? Which seem least justifiable or unjustifiable?

4. Why are most lawsuits for libel not worth pursuing?

Reading to Write

The federal court dismissed the lawsuit against Peter Matthiessen and his publisher, Viking, for alleged damages to the reputation of a South Dakota governor. Write a paper in which you defend or challenge the rationale behind this decision.

Banned Books: Two Case Histories | Nicholas J. Karolides

The following selection consists of two case histories of famous banned books: Richard Wright's *Black Boy*, and Kurt Vonnegut's *Slaughterhouse-Five*—two out of more than one hundred represented in the volume from which these cases were selected, and these just on political grounds. Other volumes in the series include *Banned Books: Literature Suppressed on Religious Grounds*, on Sexual

---

Source: From Karolides, Nicholas J. "Banned Books: Three Case Histories." *Banned Books: Literature Suppressed on Political Grounds*. New York: Facts on File, 1998. 43–50, 414–422.

Grounds, and on Social Grounds. Each of the cases is divided into two sections: a summary of the book and a summary of its censorship history. Nicholas J. Karolides teaches at the University of Wisconsin, River Falls.

Black Boy

Summary

"My days and nights were one long, quiet, continuously contained dream of terror, tension and anxiety. I wondered how long I could bear it." So concludes chapter 13 (there are 14) of Richard Wright's autobiography, expressing the crescendo of his feelings before finally in the last chapter achieving his secret dream of escaping the South to the North.

Subtitled "Record of Childhood and Youth," the memoir begins when he is four years old and takes him into his nineteenth year. His accounts of his experiences and relationships reveal how he has been shaped and conditioned, the person he has become.

Wright's childhood was one of trauma and indignity, narrowness and poverty. The family moved frequently, first from the plantation of his birth,

Richard Wright (1908–1960) is an African American novelist and social critic whose books dramatize racial injustice.

where his father was a sharecropper, to Memphis. Other moves resulted from his father's abandoning his wife and two sons for another woman. These moves took the family to lower-rent accommodations, to new locations in search of jobs, or to relatives where they lived on their sometimes grudging charity. Such dependence became virtually permanent after his mother at quite a young age suffered a stroke that caused paralysis of her legs.

Dominant childhood memories are of hunger, deficiency and fear. With the father's departure, there was no income until his mother was able to find work. Hunger, constant and gnawing, haunted the family; when food was available, it was insufficient in both quantity and nutrition. Often there was not enough money to heat their shack. Sometimes young Richard's mother brought the two boys to work with her; they stood in the corner of the kitchen where she was a cook, smelling the food but unable to eat. There was not enough money for clothes; ashamed of Richard's destitute appearance, his mother would not send him to school.

Beatings appear to have been "automatic" responses of adults toward children for misbehavior or stubborn resistance. Young Richard, an intractable, willful child, is often birched or strapped by his mother (before her illness) and relatives. Uncles and aunts attempt also to browbeat him into submitting to their wills. A parallel violence is evident in contacts with neighborhood gangs and in schoolyards. Richard, the new kid, the outsider, has to prove himself before he can gain entrance.

The sense of abandonment, exacerbated by being placed in an orphanage when his mother could not afford to take care of the two boys, and the feelings of loss—though perhaps not understood—were affective in forming Richard's personality. These dovetailed with his frequent outsider status; opportunities for deep and lasting relationships were thwarted by both the frequent moves and the suppressive attitudes of the significant adults. Warmth, tenderness and encouragement were lacking, except sporadically from his mother.

Religion was another source of agony and emotional browbeating, particularly during the period when he lived in his grandmother's house. Despite his young age, he resisted his grandmother's efforts to commit him to her fear-evoking religion, refusing to be bullied into submission. When his equally rigid and devout aunt, who is also his teacher, struck him across the knuckles with a ruler because she assumes he, rather than a devout classmate, is guilty of littering the floor, he vowed not to allow it a second time. When she came at him at home with a switch, he fought her off with a kitchen knife, fighting, in effect, for his sense of justice and independence.

A contrasting strand is woven through the autobiography: young Richard's curiosity, his eagerness to learn to read and the rapidity with which he learned. He began to pick out and recognize words in his playmates' schoolbooks at age six; in about an hour's time, the coalman taught him to count to 100. He questioned about everything. His school attendance started late and was erratic; he was past 12 before he had a full year of formal schooling. But once fully enrolled, he excelled, graduating as the valedictorian of his class. Books became his salvation, both an escape from his tormenting environment and an avenue to a dreamed of future: "going north and writing books, novels." Books opened up the world of serious writing, opened up for him the life of the mind and encouraged his conviction to live beyond the constraints of the South.

Richard Wright acknowledges his limited contacts with whites during his early years. By age nine, a dread of whites had grown in him, fueled by frightening tales of repression, of the Ku Klux Klan and his family's experiences. His first jobs with whites when he is a young teenager corroborate his impressions of their meanness and mistreatment, projecting their view that blacks are children or idiots and less than human. A significant realization is his understanding that "the entire educational system of the South had been rigged to stifle" the aspirations of the black citizens.

As he gains experiences in the white world, Wright learns to keep secret   10
his dream of going north and becoming a writer. It takes him considerably longer than his school and work acquaintances to learn appropriate obsequious mannerisms, language and tone. His ignorance causes him to lose employment and to suffer harm. Part of his "problem," as a friend notes in his sixteenth year: "'You act around white people as if you didn't know that they were white.'" Wright silently acknowledges this truth:

> . . . it was simply impossible for me to calculate, to scheme, to act, to plot all the time. I would remember to dissemble for short periods, then I would forget and act straight and human again, not with the desire to harm anybody, but merely forgetting the artificial status of race and class.

His friend continues: "You know, Dick, you may think I'm an Uncle Tom, but I'm not. I hate these white people, hate 'em with all my heart. But I can't show it; if I did, they'd kill me."

Richard Wright did learn to control his public face and voice to a greater extent, but not without a sense of shame, tension and mental strain. While the latter dissipated somewhat in the more urbane atmosphere of Memphis, he was frequently reminded of the need to be guarded. These experiences and responses reveal Wright's growth and cultural assimilation. They also reveal the survival training induced in blacks by the white threat: deception, dishonesty, lying and irresponsibility.

When contemplating his present life and his future, Wright sees four choices: rebellion, organizing with other blacks to fight the southern whites; submitting and living the life of a genial slave, thus denying that his "life had shaped [him] to live by [his] own feelings and thoughts"; draining his restlessness by fighting other blacks, thus transferring his hatred of himself to others with a black skin; and forgetting what he's learned through books, forgetting whites and finding release in sex and alcohol. In this context, he continues:

I had no hope whatever of being a professional man. Not only had I been so conditioned that I did not desire it, but the fulfillment of such an ambition was beyond my capabilities. Well-to-do Negroes lived in a world that was almost as alien to me as the world inhabited by whites.

Finally, however, "sheer wish and hope prevailed over common sense and facts." Planning with his mother, brother and aunt, he takes the step; he boards the train bound for Chicago.

Censorship History*

Richard Wright was not unfamiliar with the threat of censorship. A member of the Communist Party in 1940 when *Native Son* was published, he was threatened with expulsion because at least one party leader sensed a fundamental disagreement between the party's views and those expressed in the book. Wright had been saved by its popularity and acclaim, making Wright too important a member to lose. Wright had recognized other attempts by the party to constrain his thinking. In 1940 he renounced his affiliation with the party.

The Special Committee on Un-American Activities, the Dies Committee, had investigated him and called him subversive. Wright had also been the target of a top-priority investigation of the FBI regarding his affiliation with and activities for the communist party. Wright knew that his neighbors had been questioned. These events had preceded the publication of *Black Boy*. In the 1950s Richard Wright was identified unfavorably before the House Un-American Activities Committee and cited by the committee as belonging to one or more "fronts." According to existing directives, his work should have been withdrawn from U.S. libraries overseas.

Black Boy as originally submitted, titled *American Hunger*, included Wright's Chicago experience. Initially accepted by Harper & Row, his editor later informed Wright that the book would be divided: the first two-thirds, the experiences in the South, would be published separately from the experiences in the North, Chicago and New York. Initially, Wright accepted this suggestion without question; Constance Webb, Wright's biographer, notes, however, that subsequently, he felt "in his whole being that his book was being censored in some way." He considered the possibility that Harper & Row did not want to offend the Communists, since the United States and the USSR were then allies, or that the Communist Party itself was exerting some influence over the publisher. He determined to find a way to publish the omitted final segment of his manuscript.

At the time of publication, despite its being a Book-of-the-Month Club selection and achieving both broad readership and significant acclaim in reviews, Mississippi banned it; Senator Bilbo of Mississippi condemned the book and its author in Congress:

15

---

*This censorship history was augmented by the research and writing of Dawn Sova.

Black Boy should be taken off the shelves of stores; sales should be stopped; it was a damnable lie, from beginning to end; it built fabulous lies about the South. The purpose of the book was to plant seeds of hate and devilment in the minds of every American. It was the dirtiest, filthiest, most obscene, filthy and dirty, and came from a Negro from whom one could not expect better.

The autobiography has created controversy in school districts in all regions of the United States. Most of the challenges have been of mainly local interest, while one case received national attention and created precedent. In 1972, parents in Michigan objected to the book's sexual overtones and claimed that it was unsuitable for impressionable sophomores, which resulted in the removal of the book from classroom use. In 1975, the book was removed from Tennessee schools for being obscene, instigating hatred between the races and encouraging immorality.

Complaints against five books, including *Black Boy*, were filed in November 1975 in East Baton Rouge, Louisiana, by Babs Minhinnette, chairperson of Concerned Citizens and Taxpayers for Decent School Books. This complaint emerged out of a controversy over the removal of two books, one by the school board and the other by the principal. This controversy had led to the adoption in May 1975 of a policy to handle objections. Subsequently, however, in September 1975, the school board had ordered a search for books and materials containing obscenity, filth or pornography. Teachers and librarians criticized the search order, claiming it was a reversal of the policy adopted in May. The challenge to the five books by the Concerned Citizens chairperson was perceived as an attempt to test the new review procedure. The committee voted 6–1 to reject the request to remove the books after a review conducted in late November.

A comparable situation developed in Nashua, New Hampshire, in 1978. As a result of a complaint against the use of *Black Boy* in the ninth grade of the high school in Nashua, a review committee recommended that the book be removed from this grade level and that it be used only in elective courses in grades 11 and 12. The controversy over *Black Boy* and *Ms* magazine gave rise to questions about the appropriateness of certain textbooks in schools across the state and gave impetus to the formation of a new organization, Concerned Citizens and Taxpayers for Better Education. This group's intention was to monitor books used in classes of several communities, from which its members were drawn, in order to safeguard "traditional Judeo-Christian values" in the schools.

In September 1987, Nebraska Governor Kay Orr's "kitchen cabinet" met with leaders of a citizens' group, Taxpayers for Quality Education. The group made recommendations to the governor regarding curriculum, strategies for teaching reading and school administration. It also indicated it would monitor books in school libraries and recommend reading lists. George Darlington, president of Taxpayers for Quality Education, identified *Black Boy* as one of the books that should be removed, asserting it had a "corruptive obscene nature" and citing the use of profanity throughout and the incidents of violence. He noted that such books "inflict a cancer on the body of education we want our children to develop." The book was removed from library shelves, then returned after the controversy abated.

The Anaheim (California) Secondary Teachers Association in September 1978 charged the Anaheim Union High School Board of Trustees with having "banned thousands of books from English classrooms of the Anaheim secondary schools." The trustees, acting on a recommendation of the district's administration, had removed more than half of the reading material available to English teachers. *Black Boy* was among the books banned from the classroom and from school libraries. The board's president, James P. Bonnell, claimed that the 270 books remaining on the grade 7 to 12 list were "adequate." Teachers were instructed to simply store the book, along with others, and cautioned that they were not permitted to provide the books for supplemental reading or to discuss the books with students. The local school board warned teachers that they risked dismissal if they taught any of the banned books. The result of the confrontation was the mounting of a recall campaign: petitions were circulated to enforce a re-election ballot for Bonnell and another trustee and "Notice of Intent to Recall" papers were served on these individuals. The recall election was successful in unseating these trustees.

In a landmark case, the autobiography was one of 9 books that the school board of the Island Trees (New York) Union Free District removed from the junior and senior high school libraries in 1976; two books were removed from classrooms. The other books were *The Best Short Stories by Negro Writers, The Fixer, Go Ask Alice, Slaughterhouse-Five, Down These Mean Streets, A Hero Ain't Nothin' But a Sandwich, Laughing Boy, The Naked Ape, Soul on Ice* and *A Reader for Writers.* Condemned with broad generalizations, the books were charged with being "anti-American, anti-Christian, anti-Semitic, or just plain filthy." As entered in the court record, the specific objections to *Black Boy* concerned the use of obscenity and the anti-Semitic remarks and other ethnic slurs, in such passages as the following: "We black children—seven or eight or nine years of age—used to run to the Jew's store and shout: . . . Bloody Christ Killers/Never trust a Jew/Bloody Christ Killers/What won't a Jew do/Red, white and blue/Your pa was a Jew/Your ma a dirty dago/What the hell is you?"

The controversy began in March 1976 when the chair of the Long Island school board, Richard J. Ahrens, using a list of "objectionable" books and a collection of excerpts compiled by Parents of New York United (PONY-U), ordered 60 books removed from the Island Trees School District High School Library. Teachers indicated that two of the books, *The Fixer* and *The Best Short Stories of Negro Writers,* had been removed from classrooms, where they were being used in a literature course. The local teachers union did file a formal grievance against the board, alleging a violation of the provisions of academic freedom in the union contract. A group of residents also objected to the censorship, stating they would protest to the state commissioner of education.

In defense against the protests of parents and students, the school board appointed a committee made up of parents and teachers to review the books and to determine which, if any, had merit. The committee recommended that seven of the books be returned to the library shelves, that two be placed on restricted shelves and that two be removed from the library, but the school board in July ignored these recommendations and voted to keep all but two of the books off the shelves. It authorized "restricted" circulation for *Black Boy* and circulation without restriction for *Laughing Boy.* The others would be "removed from . . . libraries and from use in the curriculum," that is, not to be assigned as required, optional or even suggested reading, although the books might still be discussed in class. The vote was unanimous on most titles. Ahrens said, "It is not only our right but our duty to make the decision, and we would do it again in the face of the abuse heaped upon us by the media."

Five students—one junior high school and four senior high school—filed suit on January 4, 1977, against the school district, seeking an injunction to have the books returned to the library shelves. The students challenged the censorship, claiming that the school board had violated their constitutional rights under the guise of protecting their social and moral tastes.

A federal district court decision handed down in August 1979 (*Pico v. Board of Education*) favored the school board. U.S. District Court Judge George C. Pratt rejected what he termed "tenure" for a book; in effect, he ruled that school boards have the right to examine the contents of library materials in order to determine their "suitability." At the center of the controversy was the constitutional role of the school board in public education, particularly in selection of content in relation to the perceived values of the community.

> In the absence of a sharp, focused issue of academic freedom, the court concludes that respect for the traditional values of the community and deference to the school board's substantial control over educational content preclude any finding of a First Amendment violation arising out of removal of any of the books from use in the curriculum.

After a U.S. Circuit Court of Appeals decision to remand the case for trial—in a 2–1 vote—the school board requested a review by the U.S. Supreme Court, which was granted. The appellate court had concluded that the First Amendment rights of the students had been violated and the criteria for the removal of the books were too general and overbroad.

The Supreme Court justices, sharply divided in a 5–4 decision (*Board of Education, Island Trees Union Free School District v. Pico*) upheld the appeals court. The Supreme Court mandated further trial proceedings to determine the underlying motivations of the school board. The majority relied on the concept that the "right to receive ideas" is a "necessary predicate" to the meaningful exercise of freedom of speech, press and political freedom. Justice Brennan, writing for the majority (which included Justices Marshall, Stevens and Blackmun; and Justice White with qualifications), stated: "Local school boards have broad discretion in the management of school affairs but this discretion must be exercised in a manner that comports with the transcendent imperatives of the First Amendment."

> Our Constitution does not permit the official suppression of *ideas*. . . . If [the school board] *intended* by their removal decision to deny [the students] access to ideas with which [the school board] disagreed, and if this intent was a decisive factor in [the school board's] decision, then [the school board] *intended* by their removal decision to deny [the students] access to ideas with which [the school board] disagreed, and if this intent was a decisive factor in [the school board's] decision, then [the school board] have exercised their discretion in violation of the Constitution. . . . [emphasis in original].

> [W]e hold that local school boards may not remove books from school library shelves simply because they dislike the ideas contained in those books and seek by their removal to "prescribe what shall be orthodox in politics, nationalism, religion, or other matters of opinion". . . . Such purposes stand inescapably condemned by our precedents.

In their dissenting opinion, Chief Justice Burger and Justices O'Connor, Powell and Rehnquist issued a warning as to the role of the Supreme Court in making local censorship decisions: "If the plurality's view were to become the law, the court would come perilously close to becoming a 'super censor' of school board library decisions and the Constitution does not dictate that judges, rather than parents, teachers, and local school boards, must determine how the standards of morality and vulgarity are to be treated in the classroom." Thus, in their reluctance to place the Supreme Court in the position of local censor, the conservative justices recommended that the task of setting local community standards remain in local hands.

The controversy ended on August 12, 1982, when the Island Trees school board voted 6–1 to return the nine books to the school library shelves without restriction as to their circulation, but with a stipulation that the librarian must send a written notice to parents of students who borrow books containing material that the parents might find objectionable. The board also delayed action on whether *The Fixer* by Bernard Malamud would be returned to the curriculum.

Slaughterhouse-Five; or the Children's Crusade: A Duty Dance with Death

Summary

Many years after World War II, Kurt Vonnegut visited Bernard V. O'Hare, a friend from the war, to discuss the destruction of Dresden. The Allied forces annihilated Dresden with so much firepower that it resembled the ruins one might imagine seeing after an atomic bomb had been dropped. Vonnegut and other American prisoners of war (POWs) survived the ordeal in "Schlachthof-funf," Slaughterhouse-Five, a cement fortress originally used as a stockyard killing shed. The two men later returned to Dresden, which, along with personal experience, provided Vonnegut with material to write his "famous book about Dresden."

Billy Pilgrim, the protagonist, was born in Ilium, New York, in 1922. He served in the army as a chaplain's assistant. After his father is accidentally killed in a hunting accident, Billy returns from furlough and is assigned as an aide to a regimental chaplain whose assistant has been killed. However, the chaplain is killed in the Battle of the Bulge, leaving Billy and three other Americans lost wanderers deep in German territory. One of the other Americans, Roland Weary, is an antitank gunner who has been plagued throughout his life by being the unpopular person everyone likes to ditch. More than once Weary pushes Billy out of the line of enemy gunfire, but Billy is so exhausted and in such poor condition that he does not realize his life has been spared. This attitude infuriates Weary, who "had been saving Billy's life for days, cursing him, kicking him, slapping him, making him move." Weary and the other two in the quartet, both scouts, have become "The Three Musketeers" in Weary's mind. However, as Weary's obsession to keep the hallucinating Billy alive grows, the scouts' contempt of Billy and Weary also grows, and they ditch

Kurt Vonnegut (b. 1922) is well-known for his novels, which satirize war, avarice, and all-around human stupidity.

Billy and Weary. Weary is set on destroying Billy, but just as he is about to send his heel crashing through Billy's exposed spine, the two are discovered by a band of German soldiers and taken as prisoners of war.

Billy and Weary are searched, deprived of their weapons and valuables and paraded away to a cottage that has been transformed into a holding place for POWs. The men are placed with about 20 other Americans. For a propagandist technique, Billy is singled out and photographed as an example of how the American army prepares its men for the war. The Germans and the POWs travel on and meet with more POWs until they form a human river. They arrive at a railyard and are separated by rank, privates with privates, colonels with colonels, and so on. Billy and Weary are separated, but Weary's continuous testimony of how Billy was responsible for the breakup of "The Three Musketeers" eventually spreads to the car where Billy is being held, causing a general feeling of hatred from the occupants of the car toward Billy. On the ninth day of their journey, Weary dies of gangrene. On the tenth day the train finally stops and the occupants are released into a prison camp. Billy is the next to last to leave his car. A corpse stays behind.

The men are stripped, they shower and their clothes are sanitized. Among them is Edgar Derby, a middle-aged man whose son is fighting in the Pacific theater, and Paul Lazzaro, a tiny shriveled-up man who is covered with boils. Both men were with Weary when he died; Derby cradled his head, and Lazzaro promised to enact revenge upon Billy. The men are given their clothes and dogtags, which they must wear at all times. They are led to a shed that houses a number of middle-aged Englishmen who had been POWs since near the beginning of the war. Unlike their American counterparts, however, the Englishmen have made the most of their imprisonment by keeping themselves in shape and properly groomed. They have also cleverly hoarded enough rations that they can afford to trade with the Germans for supplies like lumber and other building materials that they use to maintain their shed.

In poor condition and in a hallucinatory state, Billy is billeted in the hospital portion of the British compound, which is in reality six beds in another room of the shed. Here he is injected with morphine and watched by Derby, who reads *The Red Badge of Courage* to pass the time. Billy awakens from his morphine-induced sleep, not knowing where he is or what year it is. Derby and Lazzaro are sleeping in adjacent beds. Apparently Lazzaro's arm has been broken for stealing cigarettes from an Englishman, and he is now lecturing Billy and Derby on how he will someday enact revenge for that and for Weary's death, for which he holds Billy responsible.

The Americans are informed by the head Englishman that they will be "leaving this afternoon for Dresden—a beautiful city. . . . [they] needn't worry about bombs. . . . Dresden is an open city. It is undefended, and contains no war industries or troop concentrations of any importance." The Americans arrive to find that what they have been told is true. They are led to a cement fortress that had been a slaughterhouse of livestock and is now their dwelling place—"Schlachthof-funf." The Americans are assigned to work in a factory

35

that produces malt syrup enriched with vitamins and minerals, to be used by pregnant German women.

Four days later, Dresden is destroyed. Billy, some Americans and four German guards are safe in the underground slaughterhouse while the entire city is fire-bombed. As they emerge the next afternoon, "the sky was black with smoke. The sun was an angry little pinhead. Dresden was like the moon now, nothing but minerals. The stones were hot. Everybody else in the neighborhood was dead." The soldiers order the Americans to line up in fours, and they all march away until they come to a country inn that is far enough removed from Dresden to not have been affected.

Two days after the war ends, Billy and five other Americans ride back to Dresden, looting through abandoned homes and taking as many souvenirs as they please. The Russians come along soon afterward and arrest the Americans, who are sent home on the *Lucretia A. Mott* two days later.

Throughout his war experience, Billy Pilgrim is a time traveler. His trips stem from a few incidents, namely, when he is near death or when he is on drugs. As he is being pushed along by Weary, he travels in time forward and backward. For example, he goes back to when he was a boy, when he and his father were at the YMCA. His father wanted to teach Billy how to swim by using the "sink-or-swim" technique. Pushing him into the deep end, Billy ended up "on the bottom of the pool, and there was beautiful music everywhere. He lost consciousness, but the music went on. He dimly sensed that somebody was rescuing him. [He] resented that." From the pool he goes forward in time to 1965 to visit his mother in Pine Knoll, a rest home; then he returns to 1958 to his son's little league banquet; from there he goes ahead to a New Year's Eve party in 1961, where he is caught cheating with another woman; finally he is back in the German outland being shaken against a tree by Weary.

While under the morphine-induced sleep in the British-run prison camp, Billy travels through time to 1948, to the veterans' hospital near Lake Placid. He is being introduced by Eliot Rosewater, a former infantry captain, to the works of Kilgore Trout, a little-known science fiction writer who will become Billy's favorite author and whom Billy will meet some years later. Billy also goes ahead to a time when he is 44 years old and a captive in the zoo on Tralfamadore. The Tralfamadorians, telepathic beings who live in four dimensions and have a firm understanding of the concept of death, have captured Billy and put him into a "human exhibit," where he is naked in a setting consisting of furniture and appliances from the Sears & Roebuck warehouse in Iowa City, Iowa. Not long after Billy is captured, the Tralfamadorians capture a female earthling, Montana Wildhack, a 20-year-old motion picture star whom they hope will mate with Billy. In time she gains Billy's trust and they mate, much to the awe and delight of the Tralfamadorians.

Not long after their sexual experience, however, Billy wakes up. It is 1968, and he is sweating profusely because his electric blanket is on the highest setting. His daughter had laid him in bed upon his return from the hospital, where he had been placed after being the lone survivor in a plane crash in

Vermont, en route to an optometrists' convention in Canada. His wife, the former Valencia Merble, is the daughter of a well-to-do optometrist, who had placed Billy in charge of his business in Ilium, thus making Billy a wealthy man. She died while rushing to visit Billy in the hospital after the plane crash, apparently from carbon monoxide poisoning.

Billy Pilgrim drives to New York City the next day, hoping to be on a television show so he can tell the world about the Tralfamadorians. Instead, he ends up on a radio talk show where the topic is "Is the novel dead or not?" Billy speaks of his travels, Montana, the Tralfamadorians, multiple dimensions and so on, until "He was gently expelled from the studio during a commercial. He went back to his hotel room, put a quarter into the Magic Fingers machine connected to his bed, and he went to sleep. He traveled back in time to Tralfamadore." Billy Pilgrim dies on February 13, 1976.

Censorship History

As one of the most censored books of the past 25 years according to Lee Burress, *Slaughterhouse-Five* can boast dozens of cases when students, parents, teachers, administrators, librarians and members of the clergy have called for the removal or destruction of the Vonnegut novel for one or many of the following reasons: obscenity, vulgar language, violence, inappropriateness, bathroom language, "R-rated" language, un-Godliness, immoral subject matter, cruelty, language that is "too modern" and an "unpatriotic" portrayal of war.

June Edwards focuses on the charge of parents and the religious right: [45] "The book is an indictment of war, criticizes government actions, is anti-American, and is unpatriotic." This charge defies the reason why Vonnegut wrote the novel, which was to show that "there is nothing intelligent to say about a massacre." Edwards supports this position by also countering the final two arguments: "Young people may refuse to serve in future combats after reading about the horrors of war in novels like *Slaugherhouse-Five* . . . , but this does not make them un-American. They do not want their country to engage in violence, to exterminate whole populations, but to find other ways to resolve conflicts."

Nat Hentoff reports that Bruce Severy, the only English teacher in North Dakota's Drake High School in 1973, used *Slaughterhouse-Five* in his classroom as an example of a "lively contemporary book." Severy submitted the text to the superintendent for review and, after receiving no response, went ahead and taught it. A student's objection citing "unnecessary language" led to a school board meeting where the text was denounced and labeled "a tool of the devil" by a local minister. The school board decided that the novel would be burned, even though no board member had read the entire book. Severy, after discovering his contract would not be renewed, stated, "A few four-letter words in a book is no big deal. Those students have all heard these words before; none learned any new words. I've always thought the purpose of school was to prepare these people for living in the 'big, bad world,' but it evidently isn't so." Severy, with help from the American Civil Liberties Union, sued the school district; the following verdict was reached in an out-of-court settlement: 1) *Slaughterhouse-Five* could be used by teachers in Drake High School in connection with the teaching of English in grades 11 and 12; 2) Severy's performance could not be in written or oral terms deemed unsatisfactory; and 3) Severy was awarded $5,000.

The Librarians Guide to Handling Censorship Conflicts gives a detailed account of the suits and countersuit of *Pico v. Board of Education,* Island Trees Union Free School District cases of 1979, 1980 and 1982. It is noted for being the first case of school library censorship to have reached the Supreme Court. The case stemmed from the actions of school board members attending a meeting in 1975 of Parents of New York United (PONY-U), where one of the issues concerned "the control of textbooks and library books in the schools." Using a list that contained books considered objectionable in other high school libraries, Richard Ahrens, then president of the school board, along with board member Frank Martin, descended upon the school library one evening to see which listed books were shelved there. They discovered nine, including *Slaughterhouse-Five.* At a subsequent meeting in February 1976 with two high school principals, the board decided to remove the nine books, along with two others from the junior high school. That decision prompted a memo from Superintendent Richard Morrow, which stated, "I don't believe we should accept and act on someone else's list. . . . we already have a policy . . . designed expressly to handle such problems." At the March 30 meeting, President Aherns disregarded the memo and ordered the books removed from the district's libraries. After the media got word of the brewing controversy, the board wrote a rebuttal which stated:

> This Board of Education wants to make it clear that we in no way are BOOK BANNERS or BOOK BURNERS. While most of us agree that these books have a place on the shelves of the public library, we all agree that these books simply DO NOT belong in school libraries where they are so easily accessible to children whose minds are still in the formulative [sic] stage, and where their presence actually entices children to read and savor them. . . .

Superintendent Morrow responded that it was "wrong for the Board—or any other single group—to act to remove books without prolonged prior consideration of the views of both the parents whose children read these books, and the teachers who use these books to instruct . . . and to by-pass the established procedure for reviewing the challenged books." On April 6 the board and Morrow voted to appoint a review committee of four parents and four teachers to review the books and make recommendations concerning their future status. In the meantime, Morrow requested that the books be returned to the shelves until the review process was completed. They were not. In subsequent meetings, the review committee determined that six of the 11 books, including *Slaughterhouse-Five*, should be returned to the school shelves. Three were not recommended, and two others couldn't be decided upon. However, on July 28, the board in an open meeting voted to return only one book, *Laughing Boy*, to the shelves without restrictions and one, *Black Boy*, with restrictions despite the committee's stance. Aherns stated that the other nine books could not be assigned as required, optional or suggested reading, but could be discussed in class.

A lawsuit was filed on January 4, 1977, by Stephen Pico and other junior and senior high school students, who were represented by the New York Civil Liberties Union. Pico claimed that First Amendment rights had been violated via the board's removal of the books.

As entered in the court record, the school board condemned the books as   50
"anti-American, anti-Christian, anti-Semitic, and just plain filthy"; it cited passages referring to male genitalia, to sexuality, to lewd and profane language and to sacrilegious interpretations of the Gospels and of Jesus Christ. According to Leon Hurwitz, "A federal district court gave summary judgment for the board, but an appellate court remanded the case for a trial on the students' allegations." The Supreme Court to which the school board appealed this decision, in a 5–4 decision, upheld the appellate court, rejecting the idea that "there are no potential constitutional constraints on school board actions in this area." The case came full circle on August 12, 1982, when the school board voted 6–1 to return the books to the school library shelves, with the stipulation that the librarian send a notice to the parents of any student who might check out a book containing objectionable material. (For further discussion of this case, refer to the censorship history of *Black Boy*.)

Many other incidents have occurred throughout the seventies, eighties and nineties concerning *Slaughterhouse-Five*. According to *Banned Books: 387 B.C. to 1987 A.D.*, an unidentified Iowa town's school board in 1973, the same year as the Drake burning, ordered 32 copies burned because of objectionable language. The teacher who assigned the text had his job threatened. In McBee, South Carolina, a teacher using the text was arrested and charged with using obscene materials.

Newsletter on Intellectual Freedom reports that a review committee in Lakeland, Florida, in 1982 voted 3–2 to ban *Slaughterhouse-Five* from the Lake Gibson High School library, citing explicit sexual scenes, violence and obscene language. The complaint originated from a board member and was backed by then Polk County Deputy School Superintendent Cliff Mains, who stated that the book review policy maintained the decision's legal validity.

On May 27, 1984, in Racine, Wisconsin, William Grindeland, the district administrative assistant for instructional services, barred the purchase of *Slaughterhouse-Five*, stating, "I don't believe it belongs in a school library." Unified school board member Eugene Dunk countered, "Denial of quality reading materials for our youngsters is criminal." This stirred up a heated controversy, which was compounded by the board's banning of five textbooks, three in social studies and two in home economics, on June 12. Board member Barbara

Scott proposed that a "reserved list" be developed that contained books for which written parental permission would be required for students to check them out. Meanwhile, the Racine Education Association threatened to take legal action and file a lawsuit in federal court against the Unified school board if the book was banned. REA Executive Director Jim Ennis said the suit's goal would be to "prevent the school board from excluding 'contemporary and relevant literature' from Unified libraries and courses." On June 14, a committee of administrators did recommend that the school district purchase a new copy of *Slaughterhouse-Five,* and also recommended a new library book selection policy, which called for the formation of a committee consisting of parents, librarians and directors of instruction, who together would be responsible for the selection of new library materials. This news prompted the REA to hold off on any legal action against the school district.

On May 15, 1986, Jane Robbins-Carter, president of the Wisconsin Library Association, wrote to inform the Racine Unified School District that a resolution of censure had been developed "due to the conflict between the policies and practices of the District as they relate to library materials selection and purchase and the principles of intellectual freedom as supported by the Library Bill of Rights of the American Library Association." The charges stemmed from the actions undertaken by William Grindeland, which allowed him "the authority to delete orders for library materials 'not in keeping with the standards of the selection policy,'" to use "vague and subjective criteria" in choosing what materials could be used and to refer "requests for materials of a highly controversial nature . . . to the public library, local bookstores or newsstands." Robbins-Carter added that "the censure will remain in effect until such time as the Board of Education adopts a revised Library Materials Selection and Purchase Policy." The Racine Unified School District adopted a policy in June 1985; on December 9, the Racine Unified School District's Library Materials Review Committee voted 6–2 to place *Slaughterhouse-Five* under limited access to students with parental permission. Grindeland, a member of the committee that reviewed the book, said, "I objected to the book being in a school library, and I still do. But restricting it is a good compromise."

In October 1985, in Owensboro, Kentucky, parent Carol Roberts filed a complaint stating that *Slaughterhouse-Five* was "just plain despicable," referring to the passages about bestiality, Magic Fingers and the sentence, "The gun made a ripping sound like the opening of the zipper on the fly of God Almighty." She had also prepared a petition with the signatures of over 100 parents. In November, a meeting consisting of administrators, teachers and parents voted unanimously that the text remain on the school library shelves. Judith Edwards, director of the city schools' department of instruction, commented that the committee "felt the book was meritorious." In April 1987, in LaRue, Kentucky, the LaRue County Board of Education refused to remove *Slaughterhouse-Five* from the school library shelves despite numerous complaints citing foul language and deviant sexual behavior. Principal Phil Eason defended the book, stating that it "show[s] the obscenity of war," and "We don't make them [the people opposing the text] read them [books in the library]."

In August 1987, in Fitzgerald, Georgia, school officials decided that a policy used to ban *Slaughterhouse-Five* from all city schools would also offer the same protection against other "objectional" materials. The book was permanently banned by a 6–5 vote after Farise and Maxine Taylor, whose daughter had brought the book home, filed a formal complaint in June, citing that "[I]f we don't do anything about it, they're putting that garbage in the classroom and we're putting our stamp of approval on it."

In February 1988, in Baton Rouge, Louisiana, school board member Gordon Hutchinson stated that he wanted to ban *Slaughterhouse-Five*, and all books like it, which he described as being "a book of dirty language." The complaint was brought to his attention by parent Brenda Forrest, whose daughter had selected the book from a suggested reading list at Central High School. Baton Rouge District PTA President Beverly Trahan commented, "You can get into some very serious problems with book bans." Dick Eiche, executive director of the East Baton Rouge Association of Educators, echoed Trahan's view supporting the book. School Board President Robert Crawford, a Vietnam veteran, agreed with Eiche and Trahan's views when he stated, "I think it's dangerous to start banning books. We could clean out the libraries if we wanted to." In March, Superintendent of Schools Bernard Weiss said a committee would be formed to evaluate the book. The 12-member committee voted 11–0 with one abstention to retain the book. Community member Bill Huey stated, "I can hardly believe this community . . . is even discussing removing a book from library shelves. I don't want to live in a community that sanctions bingo and bans books."

Banned in the U.S.A.: A Reference Guide to Book Censorship in Schools and Public Libraries cites an attack against *Slaughterhouse-Five* that occurred in 1991 in Plummer, Idaho. Parents objected to the book's use in an 11th-grade English class, citing profanity. Because the school had no policy in effect to deal with the challenge, an official ordered that the book be removed from the school and that the teacher using the book throw away all copies. ◪

Reflections and Inquiries

1. After reading the censorship histories of the two books, decide which complaints against each book seem (a) most legitimate, (b) most illogical, and (c) most difficult to evaluate. Be prepared to give sound reasons for your assertions.

2. *Slaughterhouse-Five* is among the century's most censored book for political reasons. Why is this the case, in your opinion?

3. To what degree does the author's reputation affect the decision to ban a book, in your opinion? You may wish to consult additional cases in Karolides's book to get a better sense of this.

Reading to Write

How legitimate are parents' rights to have questionable books removed from the public schools their children attend? Take a pro or con stance in a short essay.

Panama City, Florida: Darkness in the Sunshine State | Herbert N. Foerstel

Book censorship has succeeded in the United States because of widespread opinion that publishers should maintain certain standards of decency, such as avoidance of graphic depictions of human situations especially of a sexual nature and of profane language. From the late nineteenth century onward, as Herbert N. Foerstel points out, "private virtue became public virtue." In the twentieth century, special-interest groups put pressure on state governments to ban certain books from schools. Despite obvious violations of the First Amendment, these groups often have succeeded. In 1990, the Thomas Jefferson Center for the Protection of Free Expression noted that a double standard existed in American society: A great many Americans were not willing to extend the right of free speech to printed matter. This led the Center to declare that the First Amendment is "in perilous condition across the nation" (Foerstel xiv). In the following selection, Foerstel examines a particularly disturbing book censorship case that seemed to threaten the very fundamentals of public school education. Foerstel is head of the Engineering and Physical Sciences Library at the University of Maryland.

One of the nation's more recent and disturbing bookbanning incidents occurred in Panama City, Florida, a beach town within what is called the "Redneck Riviera." Greater Panama City has a population of about 120,000, served by over 125 churches that advertise their healing powers in the Yellow Pages. This Bible Belt town has only grudgingly accepted the cosmopolitan influences of the local air force base, a navy research laboratory, several colleges, and a branch of the University of Florida. Panama City was to witness the familiar battle between religious fundamentalists, who wanted to teach children *what* to think, and teachers, who wanted to teach children *how* to think.

Gloria Pipkin was an eighth-grade English teacher in Panama City. When she first arrived at Mowat Junior High School, the English Department had the students spending most of their time identifying nouns and verbs in grammar

---

Source: Foerstel, Herbet N. "Panama City, Florida: Darkness in the Sunshine State." *Banned in the U.S.A.: A Reference Guide to Book Censorship in Schools and Public Libraries.* Westport: Greenwood, 1994. 42–53. Copyright © 1994 by Herbert N. Foerstel. Reproduced with permission of Greenwood Publishing Group, Inc. Westport, CT.

workbooks, and the few textbooks that were used ignored all twentieth-century literature. Pipkin says the kids hated this arrangement, and so did the teachers. But then a new chairman of her English Department, Ed Deluzain, arrived from Florida State University (FSU), bringing with him new ideas for teaching English to kids, ideas that encouraged children to read and write, not just to learn grammar by rote. Gloria Pipkin and her friend ReLeah Hawks had heard of these teaching techniques, which utilized books that children actually enjoyed reading, including "young adult novels" written for and about adolescents. Soon all eleven teachers in the Mowat English Department were enthusiastically reading and discussing the novels.

In 1982, Gloria Pipkin became the chairman of the Mowat English Department, and under her leadership, the teachers introduced books by Mark Twain, George Orwell, Anne Frank, and Robert Cormier, while organizing paperback book swaps and book fairs at the school. The teachers created minilibraries within each classroom, purchased with their own money or income they earned from selling soft drinks at football games. Books from the classroom libraries were passed out to kids, allowing them to sample books at random and replace them as they wished. The students became excited over their reading, and they also began to write prolifically. The students in Pipkin's eighth-grade class even wrote and bound their own novels. In a countrywide writing contest. Mowat students won all five first-place prizes, and eleven of fifteen prizes overall. Mowat ninth-graders soon achieved twelfth-grade reading comprehension, vocabulary, and grammar, well ahead of students at any other junior high school in the county. In 1985, the National Council of Teachers of English designated the Mowat English Department a "Center of Excellence," 1 of only 150 secondary schools in the United States and Canada to be so designated, and the only one in Florida.

Then the censors descended. In 1985, Marian Collins, grandmother of a Mowat Junior High School student, wrote to Bay County School Superintendent Leonard Hall, complaining that the novel *I Am the Cheese*, by Robert Cormier, contained vulgar language and advocated humanism and behaviorism. *I Am the Cheese* tells the story of a teenage boy whose family is put in a witness protection program after his father testifies against members of the Mafia. The book had been named as one of the best young adult books of 1977 by *Newsweek, The New York Times,* and *School Library Journal.* Hall immediately ordered Mowat principal Joel Creel to ban the book. Two months after Collins's original letter to Hall, she wrote again, complaining that *I Am the Cheese* was still being used at Mowat. She also wrote Principal Creel, asking why he had not complied with the superintendent's order to remove the book. Collins's daughter, Claudia Shumaker, then joined her mother's censorship campaign, and now mother, daughter, and granddaughter were in the fray. The Shumakers objected to the book's occasional profanity and the "subversive" suggestion that government agents could be involved in a murder plot.

Soon a few other parents began complaining about vulgarity in some of   5
the books their children had acquired from the book fairs or borrowed from

the classroom libraries. During the summer of 1985, the Mowat teachers did their best to accommodate them without altering the curriculum or their classroom libraries. They met regularly with concerned parents to explain their programs. They encouraged students whose parents objected to a book used in class to choose an alternative book. Also, written parental permission was required before any student could attend a book fair or read challenged books. But none of this could placate Claudia and Robert Shumaker, whose daughter was in ReLeah Hawks's English class. When they saw the classroom, with books lining the walls, they were dismayed. "It's like walking into a B Dalton with desks," complained Claudia Shumaker, who described some of the books as "immoral" and "blasphemous." She said she didn't allow her children to see any movie they wished, so why should she have them exposed to books they shouldn't see?

The previous April, when ReLeah Hawks had assigned *I Am the Cheese* to her class, she sent a letter to parents, warning that the book was "difficult" and asking permission for their children to read it. If they disapproved of the book, an appropriate alternative would be assigned. When all parental responses were received, eighty-eight parents gave permission, and four, counting the Shumakers, rejected the book. Teacher Hawks saw the vote as an endorsement of Cormier's novel, and she anticipated no difficulty in assigning alternative reading for the other four students. Later she reflected, "How could I know that this was the first step in a long and terrible process that would lead to full-scale censorship and the virtual dismantling of our program?"

The Shumakers were not willing to accept alternative books. They claimed that if their daughter read an alternative book, she would be ostracized. Therefore, on the advice of Superintendent Hall, Claudia Shumaker filed an official complaint against *I Am the Cheese* and another novel used at Mowat, Susan Pfeffer's *About David*. Creel immediately withdrew both books from use in all schools in the county, pending judgment by a review committee.

The teachers felt personally offended. "There was a lot of hurt and a lot of rage too," recalls teacher Sue Harrell. ReLeah Hawks had to tell four classes that they couldn't read the book she had been touting all year. Gloria Pipkin warned, "If they take our books away and start giving us the books they want, then the kids won't read. We want to make them literate, life-long readers. We're co-learners. We're participating with the kids in the process of reading and writing." But Pipkin was not discouraged. "I was really pleased," she says. "At last it was in the open, and there was a forum where it could be heard and we could respond."

In her formal challenge to *I Am the Cheese,* Claudia Shumaker stated that "the theme of the book is morbid and depressing. The language of the book is crude and vulgar. The sexual descriptions and suggestions are extremely inappropriate. Our children's minds are being warped and filled with unwholesome attitudes by reading worthless materials." She attached photocopies of offending passages containing words like *hell, shit, fart,* and *goddamn.* Her challenge to *About David,* a book about teenage suicide, said the subject should be handled through prayer at home, rather than in school. She added, "If the teaching of Christian morals and code of decency is illegal in the school system, then the teaching of the Humanist religion's code of immorality is also illegal."

By the time the District Review Committee, composed of administrators, teachers, and parents, got around to judging *I Am the Cheese,* several Mowat English teachers had drafted a six-page rebuttal to Shumaker's challenge, signed by ten of the eleven members of the department. The rebuttal acknowledged that it was the right of parents to decide what their child may or may not read and that students were therefore free to choose an alternative to *I Am the Cheese.* 10

On May 20, 1986, the review committee issued its report, describing *I Am the Cheese* as a high-interest young adult novel that encourages reading, critical thinking, and class discussion. The committee recommended that the use of *I Am the Cheese* be continued with young adults. But the final judgment was left in the hands of Bay County School Superintendent Leonard Hall, who was in no hurry to make a difficult decision. He allowed the school year to pass without action on the challenge, thus effectively keeping *I Am the Cheese* out of the classrooms.

Even so, Charles Collins, Claudia Shumaker's father, was enraged over the recommendations of the review committee. Collins, a wealthy beach-front developer and former school board member, called the novels used in the Mowat schools "trashy" and "obscene," recommending instead the Nancy Drew mysteries and the Bobbsey Twins books. He regarded Mowat's book fairs and classroom libraries as part of the humanist conspiracy to take over American education. After the review committee recommended retention of *I Am the Cheese,* Collins stepped up his attacks on Mowat's schools, taking out a large ad in the local newspaper that began: "Your child's textbooks—Have you read them?" The ad printed a few excerpts from *I Am the Cheese* and another Cormier novel, *The Chocolate War,* and concluded by saying, "If you believe these books should be banned, mail the attached coupon." School officials were quickly inundated with letters and phone calls.

In a newspaper interview, Collins complained: "There's no respect in this county any more. You cannot go down the halls of the high schools and junior highs without hearing the dirtiest language you ever heard in your life. I believe these filthy little books are the cause."

The Mowat teachers responded by calling a meeting on May 27, 1986, inviting all students, teachers, and parents. On the morning of the meeting, Superintendent Hall stormed into the Mowat English Department, accusing teachers of inflaming the students. Hall told the teachers not to discuss the First Amendment with their students and not to answer any student questions on the book controversy. He then ordered the teachers to tell the students not to attend the meeting. "The issue is a parental issue," said Hall. "It is not a student issue. I think the parent should speak for his or her child. . . . We feel like they're at an impressionable age. They're not mature enough to recognize that the books are an invasion of their rights to have literature that is not full of obscenities in the classroom." The meeting was attended by nearly 300 parents and an unexpected TV crew. There were some protesters present, but two thirds of the speakers expressed support of the school's English program. Many parents thanked the teachers for inspiring their children to read. One father told the crowd, "A strange thing has happened to my son since he's been going to Mowat. I've caught him reading. Sometimes on weekends. I also caught him writing a letter to his grandmother without my telling him to do it." After the meeting, the teachers were optimistic, but they had no way of knowing what was in store for them.

On June 5, 1986, as summer vacation began, Hall announced that despite the review committee's recommendation to accept *I Am the Cheese* the book could not be used in Bay County schools, nor could any other material not specifically approved by the board be used in the future. Hall's announcement began with the statement that the school district would not use instructional materials that contain vulgar, obscene, or sexually explicit material. His proposal specifically required that all materials not formally adopted by the state be approved by the school superintendent and the principal before use in the schools. Even after approval, a challenged book would automatically be withdrawn from use until a series of review boards had decided its fate.

The edict not only banned the Cormier novel but eliminated virtually every book that had been used during the past year, as well as all classroom libraries. Even literary classics that had been taught for years were excluded under the new policy. All that remained for classroom use were a few old English textbooks. Many teachers were left with no books that could legally be used. ReLeah Hawks recalls: "Eleven dumbfounded, award-winning English teachers sat listening to our Superintendent tell us our program no longer existed. There was an overpowering feeling of helplessness as we realized that everything not on the state-adopted textbook list was being banned."

In opposition to Hall's proposal, Gloria Pipkin organized a group of teachers, librarians, and book lovers calling themselves CHOICE (Citizens Having Options in Our Children's Education). To Pipkin, the forces recruited by Collins were fighting the concept of critical thinking. "They want kids to read well enough to follow directions and write well enough to take dictation," she said. On the other side, Charles Collins began working full-time with church women circulating petitions against "obscene books."

On a hot August evening in 1986, the school board met to consider Hall's proposal and make the ultimate decision on the challenged books. Several hundred people packed the room, made all the hotter by the TV lights. After the board's attorney read the proposal, Hall himself presented the board with a stack of antiobscenity petitions that he claimed contained 9,000 signatures. Pipkin told the board of the successes of the English program. Another teacher pointed out that Bay County's program for children with learning disabilities used thousands of "unapproved" materials, each of which would now require a laborious review. The president of the teachers union noted that under the

15

proposed guidelines, teachers would spend most of their time writing justifications for their books. An FSU professor read a long list of authors—from
Shakespeare to Tennessee Williams—whose works would be banned under
Hall's proposal. Several Mowat students spoke in defense of their teachers
and the controversial books. But a woman opposing the challenged books rose
to declare that she and her followers had prayed two hurricanes away during
the previous year, and there would be grave consequences if the schools continued to profane the name of God.

After almost five hours of haggling, the board voted to approve Hall's policy, with a minor modification. Any books used during the previous year
could be used in the coming year, after which they would all be subject to title-
by-title official approval. Even that concession would not apply to two
books—*I Am the Cheese* and *About David*. Those books remained banned.

Gloria Pipkin decided to submit a request to reinstate *I Am the Cheese* in   20
ReLeah Hawks's class. She wrote a rationale and submitted it to Principal
Creel. Creel rejected her request, saying the book was not appropriate for the
age-group, that it contained vulgar or obscene language and might tend to encourage seventh- or eighth-graders to rebel against parental authority. Pipkin
then wrote to Hall, asking him to override Creel, and when Hall refused, she
wrote to the school board requesting a hearing.

But in the meantime, the bookbanning process proceeded apace. When
the school year began in September 1986, Hall appeared in the library of the
Lynn Haven Elementary School and browsed through the periodicals, looking
for a magazine called *Young Miss.* Hall had heard that one issue of the magazine contained a story on abortion. After Hall left, the librarian received a
phone call from the assistant principal, saying that Hall wanted the magazine
removed from the shelf. The librarian picked three issues of *Young Miss* off the
shelves and threw them in the trash. Librarians at other elementary schools
did the same. When the teachers' union protested the removal of library materials without following official procedures, the local TV station, an NBC affiliate, assigned reporter Cindy Hill to cover the story. When her report was
aired on TV, Hill received several irate phone calls demanding that she
drop the story. She was told to stop bothering Leonard Hall, a good, God-
fearing man.

But Hill smelled a good story. She went to the school board to check on the
9,000 signatures Charles Collins had claimed during his petition drive. She reported that there were only 3,549 signatures, many of which were not registered Bay County voters. She also discovered that many people had signed the
petition three or more times. In some cases, heads of family had signed the
names of all family members, including children.

Immediately after Hill's report aired on the evening news, calls came in attacking her as a "Communist," "atheist," and the "daughter of Satan." One
caller recited: "Roses are red, violets are black. You'd look good with a knife in
your back." The calls continued for several days, and on the morning of October 25, when Hill stepped out of her apartment, she came across a gasoline-

soaked carpet with a burned match atop it. The following morning, at about 3:00 A.M., Hill was awakened by her smoke alarm to find her living room filled with smoke. She fled her apartment and called the police, who concluded that a flammable liquid had been poured under her door and then lighted.

A nervous Cindy Hill called Gloria Pipkin, who invited the young reporter to move in with her family for a few days. Soon thereafter, Pipkin's husband noticed the hood of Hill's car open in the driveway and discovered evidence of tampering. A few nights later, Hill's car suddenly stalled on a dark stretch of highway. When a policeman examined the engine, he noticed that three of the four sparkplug wires had been pulled loose.

After Hill received a phone call telling her, "Satan will get revenge," Pipkin staked out Hill's apartment to catch any intruders. She did surprise someone tampering with Hill's car, but the intruder fled to his car in the adjoining parking lot and disappeared. A note had been left on Hill's car warning, "Beware of the bomb." When the police arrived, they found a tape-covered device sitting on the engine, ticking. The police evacuated several apartments, sealed off the area, and summoned the bomb squad. The "bomb" turned out to be a fake, but that did not calm Pipkin's nerves. Charles Collins ridiculed the incident, first saying, "It may have been a practical joke." He then announced: "I don't believe anything. The thing in her car was just a joke. The fire didn't burn anything. It just smoked. That's a good way to get your apartment painted by the landlord. I'm thoroughly disgusted with these trite little people in this county." Referring to the Mowat teachers, Collins said, "They ought to be fired, run out of the county and gotten rid of for insubordination."

On a November afternoon, after a long day teaching and coaching the school's "Knowledge Bowl" team, Gloria Pipkin checked her school mailbox. There, amid the departmental notices and memos, Pipkin noticed an envelope addressed with letters crudely cut from magazines. She opened the envelope and unfolded a note, again written in letters cut from magazines. The note read:

> Woe to those who call evil good and good evil, who put darkness for light and light for darkness, who put bitter for sweet, for they have revoked the law of the Lord. For this you all shall DIE. One by one. Hill, Hawks, Farrell, Pipkin.

Pipkin took the letter to the Panama City police. She later showed it to the other women threatened in the note. They were terrified. Hill talked of moving, and Farrell, a divorced mother of a teenager daughter, was worried that there was no one to protect them. Hawks, who was pregnant, wondered if she should send her five-year-old son to his grandparents. Pipkin said: "Three-quarters of me, the rational side, realizes that it's probably a trick to scare us, but part of me is afraid." She wondered if it was time for her to quit. After reflection, she concluded, "I'm in this to the bitter end."

On November 12, 1986, when the school board met to consider her request to reinstate *I Am the Cheese*, Gloria Pipkin was not optimistic. Collins and the

25

Shumakers were in the front row. There was some doubt about whether Pipkin would even be allowed to speak. The board chairman asked her if she was going to be speaking as a citizen or as a teacher, and Pipkin said it would be difficult for her to separate those roles. The chairman reminded her that as an employee of Mowat Junior High School she was obliged to follow the edicts of the principal and superintendent. Only after Pipkin said she had followed those edicts did the acting school board attorney state, "I think that since she's on the agenda, she has a right to speak." Pipkin then told the board, "Despite the fact that the board attorney . . . recently informed me that no right of formal appeal exists under the new policy, I am here today requesting that you restore this powerful tool to our curriculum. Make no mistake about it, *I Am the Cheese* has been banned in the Bay County School System because the ideas in it are offensive to a few." Charles Collins then attacked the book and suggested that Pipkin's actions might be cause for dismissal. "If teachers are unhappy then they should resign," said Collins. "We would ask this board to reprimand the teachers." Collins warned that if the teachers continued to oppose the bookban, "the board should dismiss the teachers and let them find another job."

When all speakers had finished, the board chairman denied Gloria Pipkin's request to reconsider *I Am the Cheese.* In addition, the board approved a policy requiring all nontextbook materials to be formally approved by the principal, the superintendent, and the school board.

The next morning, Pipkin returned to her eighth-grade classroom. One of   30 her students asked her if they could talk about censorship. Pipkin said they could if they wanted to. A number of students asked if Pipkin was going to be fired, and she assured them that a teacher couldn't be fired for simply talking to the school board. One student said, "I think they ought to keep you, not in spite of what you're doing but *because* you're doing it." Some students criticized Principal Creel, but Pipkin defended him, saying he was under enormous pressure.

"We lost *I Am the Cheese* and we're mad," said one girl.

"What would happen if we just started reading the book next Monday?" asked another student.

"I'd be fired," said Pipkin.

"I think you should take us to another state and teach us the book," suggested a girl.

"The sad thing about it," said Pipkin, "is that similar things are happening all over the country."

"About *I Am the Cheese?*"

"About a lot of different books," Pipkin said.

Indeed, Superintendent Hall was not finished with his plan to cleanse the Bay County schools of "bad language and ideas." Early in 1987, Hall cited a single vulgarity in Farley Mowat's *Never Cry Wolf* as sufficient reason for banning it. "If you say a single vulgar word, you've said it," proclaimed Hall. "If you steal a penny, you're still a thief, or is it only when you steal $500,000?"

In May 1987, Hall extended this purist notion of vulgarity by announcing a new three-tier book classification system by which all schoolbooks would be judged. Hall's new system divided all the world's literature into three categories: books with no vulgarity; books with a "sprinkling" of vulgarity; and books with "oodles" of vulgarity. Hall declined to define *sprinkling* or *oodles*, but he quickly issued a list of sixty-one books in Category III, claiming they either contained vulgarity or the word *goddamn* and must henceforth not be taught or discussed in Bay County classrooms. Banned titles included classics by Sophocles, William Shakespeare, Charles Dickens, Charlotte and Emily Brontë, Ernest Hemingway, Geoffrey Chaucer, George Orwell, John Steinbeck, Tennessee Williams, and a host of other prominent writers.

There was widespread concern that Hall's continuing crusade would finally destroy Bay County's acclaimed English program. Some students wore black arm bands to school as a protest, and the Panama City Commission unanimously urged that the bookban be lifted. The Bay County Public Library decided to assemble a "Banned Books" display, prominently featuring the books that Hall had banned from classroom use. The public librarian said Hall had moved his censorship to a new level that required some response from the community. "[H]e's gone beyond imaginative fiction for young people to the classics of our culture. The censorship craze has definitely moved from amusement to concern, grave concern."

On May 12, forty-four Bay County teachers, parents, and students chose to file a class action suit in federal court against Superintendent Hall, Principal Creel, and the school board, arguing that the bookban was a violation of their First Amendment rights. A student, Jennifer Farrell, was first among the plaintiffs, and the case went forward as *Farrell v. Hall* (1988). The day after the suit was filed, the PAW, which provided legal representation for the plaintiffs, met with the school board in an attempt to negotiate changes in the school's book review policy. A subsequent board meeting produced a revised policy, allowing teachers to assign any books that had been used in 1986–1987, as long as they were recommended by the principal.

Farrell v. Hall asked the court specifically to restore *I Am the Cheese* and the other books still excluded and to declare the ban on classroom libraries to be unconstitutional. The board claimed that their compromises on the book review policy now rendered *Farrell* moot, but the plaintiffs pointed out that *I Am the Cheese* and other books were still banned at Mowat because of Hall's earlier prohibitions. The plaintiffs noted that the new policy provided no time limits for board response to requests to use particular materials, thus allowing officials to effectively veto requests by delaying a decision. For example, while *Farrell* was in progress, Gloria Pipkin resubmitted a rationale for teaching *I Am the Cheese*. This time, Creel and the county curriculum officials approved the book, but Hall again rejected it, and the board upheld his action. The plaintiffs therefore asserted that it was disingenuous for Defendant Hall to claim the controversy over *I Am the Cheese* was moot or that the defendants' minds were open on these matters.

In particular, the plaintiffs argued that Hall had excluded books solely because they conflicted with his religious beliefs, and the new policy would not prevent such actions in the future. Hall's *motivation* in banning books thus became essential to the case, and the plaintiffs brought witnesses before the court to testify on Hall's religious agenda in the schools. Hall's public statements were cited to demonstrate his intention to bring Christian values to the schools of Bay County and remove library books and curricular materials that involve subjects such as feminism, consumerism, environmentalism, and racism. Hall had earlier stated that he had removed *I Am the Cheese* because it gave a negative picture of a department of the U.S. government, prompting a local journalist to ask, "What will they protect Bay County children against next? The depressing knowledge of the size of the federal debt?" Even when Hall claimed to be banning books solely because of "vulgar" language, he failed to define what he meant by that characterization, allowing him to use language as a pretext to ban books on religious grounds. The plaintiffs concluded that the school board had acted improperly in allowing the superintendent to exercise such broad authority over the selection and rejection of books.

On July 18, 1988, Judge Roger Vinson of the U.S. District Court issued an order that supported some of the plaintiff's claims while rejecting others. Judge Vinson said Hall had admitted that his actions were motivated by his personal conservative beliefs, such as an obligation to restore Christian values to the county's schools. Vinson noted:

> Hall thinks that one vulgarity in a work of literature is sufficient reason to keep the book from the Bay County school curriculum. Hall's opposition to *I Am the Cheese* arises solely from his personal opposition to the ideas expressed in the book. He believes it is improper to question the truthfulness of the government. Thus, students should not be presented with such ideas.

Vinson refused to dismiss the case, ruling that the school board's use of the revised policy continued most of the activities to which the plaintiffs objected. On the other hand, Vinson continued the courts' long tradition of support for broad school board authority, finding that the removal of books on the basis of a single vulgarity was within the board's authority. Vinson said the review policy itself was acceptable to the court because school boards have the right to regulate the content of school libraries, including classroom libraries, in any way they wish. Their decisions can be challenged if they are made for illegal or arbitrary reasons, but the policy itself is legal. On the other hand, Vinson did *not* dismiss the complaint that *I Am the Cheese* and other books had been removed in an effort to suppress the ideas in them.

As both sides began preparing their arguments for trial, Leonard Hall announced that he would not run for reelection as superintendent, and on December 31, 1988, his term expired. Judge Vinson ruled that Hall's successor, Jack Simonson, automatically replaced Hall as a defendant, and a suspension was granted to attempt a resolution of the dispute out of court. By this time, the community was beginning to turn against Hall's draconian censorship. The Panama City mayor complained, "New business will not want to come to a place like this." The influential *St. Petersburg Times* warned:

> Local control of schools is an important part of public education, but it has limits of reasonableness. Depriving students of knowledge by the widespread banning of books is not a reasonable element of local authority. Unless the book banners are stopped in Bay County, there's no telling how far they'll go.

After three years of settlement negotiations between the school board and PAW, a further revision of the policy for approving instructional materials was approved by all. Time limits were set for each stage of the review process, and teachers were allowed to appeal denials of their requests for new materials. The new policy detailed a procedure for handling challenges to materials already in the classroom and ensured that parents would be notified of any complaints against materials in time for them to respond. The settlement negotiated under Vinson's order had the appearance of compromise, but the board's review policy was changed in a direction favorable to the *Farrell* plaintiff's *only* because the board agreed to it. In reality, Vinson's order had followed the decisions of other courts involved in textbook controversies, affirming the board's almost unlimited power over the curriculum.

40

Soon after Superintendent Hall left office, the terms of two of the five school board members expired, and their successors gave the board a potential 3–to–2 majority for a more liberal textbook policy. Fortunately, the reconstituted board countermanded Hall's exclusion of sixty-four literary classics in time to allow their use when classes began in September. But the educators who had endured this protracted censorship struggle were not around to savor the victory. Principal Creel had left Mowat Junior High School to head a brand-new junior high school in Bay County, and all eleven English teachers who had earned their department national awards had resigned. Today, the Mowat English Department is no longer listed as a "Center of Excellence" by the National Council of Teachers of English. ◪

Reflections and Inquiries

1. What did Gloria Pipkin and her fellow teachers do to get their students excited about their reading?

2. What did parents find objectionable about the novel *I Am the Cheese?*

3. What rationale did Pipkin give in defense of *I Am the Cheese?* Can you think of other rationales she also might have used?

4. One of the parents claimed that students were talking filthy because they were reading similar language in the books. Support or challenge this claim.

Reading to Write

People often want to ban books because they are vulgar, immoral, or blasphemous. Study the definitions of these words in an unabridged dictionary such as the *Oxford English Dictionary*, and then write an essay in which you examine how these terms should apply or not apply to novels that parents often attempt to have banned.

A Letter to the Chairman of the Drake School Board | Kurt Vonnegut, Jr.

One of America's best-loved novelists, Kurt Vonnegut, is famous for novels that satirize the human condition from unusual perspectives. His most famous novel, *Slaughterhouse-Five*, which focuses on the brutality of World War II, has been banned from numerous schools and libraries primarily because of its use of offensive language. In 1973, after the school board in Drake, North Dakota, literally burned the book, Vonnegut wrote the following letter to the chairman of the Drake school board.

My novel *Slaughterhouse-Five* was actually burned in a furnace by a school janitor in Drake, North Dakota, on instructions from the school committee there, and the school board made public statements about the unwholesomeness of the book. Even by the standards of Queen Victoria, the only offensive line in the entire novel is this: "Get out of the road, you dumb motherfucker." This is spoken by an American antitank gunner to an unarmed American chaplain's assistant during the Battle of the Bulge in Europe in December 1944, the largest single defeat of American arms (the Confederacy excluded) in history. The chaplain's assistant had attracted enemy fire.

So on November 16, 1973, I wrote as follows to Charles McCarthy of Drake, North Dakota:

Dear Mr. McCarthy:

I am writing to you in your capacity as chairman of the Drake School Board. I am among those American writers whose books have been destroyed in the now famous furnace of your school.

Certain members of your community have suggested that my work is evil. This is extraordinarily insulting to me. The news from Drake indicates to me

---

Source: Vonnegut, Kurt. "Letter to Charles McCarthy, Drake School Board." *Palm Sunday.* New York: Delacorte, 1981. 4–7. Copyright © 1981 by Kurt Vonnegut. Used by permission of Dell Publishing, a division of Random House, Inc.

that books and writers are very unreal to you people. I am writing this letter to let you know how real I am.

I want you to know, too, that my publisher and I have done absolutely nothing to exploit the disgusting news from Drake. We are not clapping each other on the back, crowing about all the books we will sell because of the news. We have declined to go on television, have written no fiery letters to editorial pages, have granted no lengthy interviews. We are angered and sickened and saddened. And no copies of this letter have been sent to anybody else. You now hold the only copy in your hands. It is a strictly private letter from me to the people of Drake, who have done so much to damage my reputation in the eyes of their children and then in the eyes of the world. Do you have the courage and ordinary decency to show this letter to the people, or will it, too, be consigned to the fires of your furnace?

I gather from what I read in the papers and hear on television that you imagine me, and some other writers, too, as being sort of ratlike people who enjoy making money from poisoning the minds of young people. I am in fact a large, strong person, fifty-one years old, who did a lot of farm work as a boy, who is good with tools. I have raised six children, three my own and three adopted. They have all turned out well. Two of them are farmers. I am a combat infantry veteran from World War II, and hold a Purple Heart. I have earned whatever I own by hard work. I have never been arrested or sued for anything. I am so much trusted with young people and by young people that I have served on the faculties of the University of Iowa, Harvard, and the City College of New York. Every year I receive at least a dozen invitations to be commencement speaker at colleges and high schools. My books are probably more widely used in schools than those of any other living American fiction writer.

If you were to bother to read my books, to behave as educated persons would, you would learn that they are not sexy, and do not argue in favor of wildness of any kind. They beg that people be kinder and more responsible than they often are. It is true that some of the characters speak coarsely. That is because people speak coarsely in real life. Especially soldiers and hardworking men speak coarsely, and even our most sheltered children know that. And we all know, too, that those words really don't damage children much. They didn't damage us when we were young. It was evil deeds and lying that hurt us.

After I have said all this, I am sure you are still ready to respond, in effect, "Yes, yes—but it still remains our right and our responsibility to decide what books our children are going to be made to read in our community." This is surely so. But it is also true that if you exercise that right and fulfill that responsibility in an ignorant, harsh, un-American manner, then people are entitled to call you bad citizens and fools. Even your own children are entitled to call you that.

I read in the newspaper that your community is mystified by the outcry from all over the country about what you have done. Well, you have discovered that Drake is a part of American civilization, and your fellow Americans can't stand it that you have behaved in such an uncivilized way. Perhaps you will learn from this that books are sacred to free men for very good reasons, and that wars have been fought against nations which hate books and burn them. If you are an American, you must allow all ideas to circulate freely in your community, not merely your own.

If you and your board are now determined to show that you in fact have wisdom and maturity when you exercise your powers over the education of your young, then you should acknowledge that it was a rotten lesson you taught young people in a free society when you denounced and then burned books—books you hadn't even read. You should also resolve to expose your children to all sorts of opinions and information, in order that they will be better equipped to make decisions and to survive.   10

Again: you have insulted me, and I am a good citizen, and I am very real. ◪

Reflections and Inquiries

1. How would you describe the tone of Vonnegut's letter to Charles McCarthy? Is it angry? Upset? Respectable? Sarcastic? A little of each? Something else? What is noteworthy about the tone of the letter?

2. What do you consider to be the most important point that Vonnegut makes in his letter? How convincingly does it come across?

3. Imagine that you are a member of a junior high school book-selection committee. Would you vote to ban Vonnegut's book on the basis of the sentence that he quotes from it? Why or why not?

4. To what extent does Vonnegut consider the views of the Drake school board? Should he have been more sympathetic to them? Explain. You may wish to review Rogerian argumentative strategies in Chapter 4.

5. What seem to be the major factors underlying a public school board's decision to ban books? Which of these factors, if any, seem valid to you?

Reading to Write

Write a letter to Vonnegut in which you support or take issue with his response to the Drake school board.

Against Pornography | George P. Elliott

One of the most difficult issues in the censorship controversy is how to define terms like *obscenity* and *pornography*. Only after a concept is defined accurately can one determine how to deal with it as a social matter. Thus, if a work is judged to be pornographic, and *pornography* is defined as injurious to people in ways that can be clearly explained, it would follow that any work so defined ought to be banned, if not rendered illegal altogether. In the following essay, George P. Elliott, the distinguished British novelist and essayist, makes an effort to come to terms with the concept of pornography and how to determine its effect on society.

Pornography is like a squalid, unnecessary little country which owes its independence to a vagary of history. But, though pornography is seldom of much importance, it may be of considerable interest, for to talk about it is unavoidably to talk about the Great Powers adjacent to it. Pornography speaks the language of Art; in recent centuries it has come within the sphere of influence of the Law; Psychology and Morals have vested interests in it. Moreover, occasionally pornography becomes genuinely important—when it is used as a seat of operations by the erotic nihilists who would like to destroy every sort of social and moral law and who devote their effective energies to subverting society as such. One who undertakes to discuss pornography finds himself, willy-nilly, falling back upon some of his ultimate positions in matters aesthetic, social, psychological, ethical. If a reader agrees with these opinions, he is likely to view them as principles; if he disagrees, prejudices. Here are some of mine.

Before plunging ahead, I had better indicate two mutually antagonistic dispositions, one liberal, the other conservative, in my opinions on pornography. On the one hand, I favor the liberal view that the less power the state and the police have over us private citizens the better, that the less the state concerns itself with the individual's thoughts, entertainments, and sexual actions the better, and that we should do what we can to keep from drifting toward totalitarianism. In other words, let us have no censorship because it strengthens the state, which is already too strong. Also let us have none because most of the things that in fact get censored are less harmful than some of the things that do not—for example, large-circulation newspapers and magazines. Society is harmed far less by the free circulation of a book like *Fanny Hill* than it is by routine and accepted practices of the daily sensationalist press: let a man inherit ten million dollars, pour acid on his wife, or win a Nobel Prize, and reporter and photographer are made to intrude upon him and his family and then to exhibit to public view in as gross a manner as possible his follies,

Source: From Elliott, George P. "Against Pornography." *Harper's* March 1965: 51–58. Copyright © 1965 by George P. Elliott. Originally appeared in *Harper's*. Reprinted by permission of Georges Borchardt, Inc.

shames, or just plain private affairs. Such invasions of privacy are not only allowed, they are allowed for the purpose of letting the public enjoy these same invasions vicariously, all in the name of freedom of the press. I believe that this accepted practice has done more damage to society as a whole and to its citizens individually than massive doses of the most depraved pornography could ever do. So much for my liberal views.

On the other hand, I favor the conservative view that pornography exists among us and is a social evil, though a small one. That is, in a good society of any sort I can imagine—not some daydream utopia where man is impossibly restored to sexual innocence but a society populated with recognizable, imperfectible men—in a good society there would be active opposition to pornography, which is to say, considerable firmness in the drawing of lines beyond which actions, words, and images are regarded as indecent. Furthermore, the opinion that pornography should not be restrained I regard as being commonly a symptom of doctrinaire liberalism and occasionally an evidence of destructive nihilism.

A liberal suspicion of censorship and a conservative dislike of pornography are not very compatible. Some sort of compromise is necessary if they are to live together. Their marriage will never be without tensions, but maybe the quarrel between them can be patched up well enough for practical purposes.

Originally the word pornography meant a sort of low erotic art, the writing of and about whores with the intention of arousing a man's lust so that he would go to a whore, but some centuries ago, the word, like the practice itself, came to include considerably more than aesthetic pandering. It has come to overlap with obscenity, which originally meant nothing more than the filthy. Obscenity still means that primarily, but notions about what is filthy have changed. Defecating and urinating, instead of being just low and uninteresting, came to be viewed as filthy, obscene, taboo. Apparently, down in the underworld of taboo, things and functions easily become tinged with sexuality, especially functions as near the genitals as urinating and defecating. In any case, since in common practice no clear distinction is made between pornography and obscenity, I am offering, for the sake of convenience, a definition in which the single word pornography is stretched to include most of obscenity. The definition is mine, but not just mine; it also reflects the usages and attitudes of my society.

Pornography is the representation of directly or indirectly erotic acts with an intrusive vividness which offends decency without aesthetic justification.

Obviously this definition does not just describe but also judges; quite as obviously it contains terms that need pinning down—decency, for example. But pornography is not at all a matter for scientific treatment. Like various other areas of sexual behavior in which society takes an unsteady, wary interest—homosexuality, for example, or fornication or nudity—pornography is relative, an ambiguous matter of personal taste and the consensus of opinion. The grounds for this definition are psychological, aesthetic, and political.

The Criterion of Distance

Psychologically, pornography is not offensive because it excites sexual desire; desire as such is a fine thing, and there are happy times and places when desire should be excited and gratified freely and fully; moreover, even in inappropriate times and places there is plenty of free-floating desire abroad in the world; it doesn't take pornography to excite excesses of desire among young men and women. Nor is pornography offensive because, in its perverted and scatological versions, it excites disgust; in the proper context disgust serves the useful function of turning us from the harmful. Psychologically, the trouble with pornography is that, in our culture at least, it offends the sense of separateness, of individuality, of privacy; it intrudes upon the rights of others. We have a certain sense of specialness about those voluntary bodily functions each must perform for himself—bathing, eating, defecating, urinating, copulating, performing the sexual perversions from heavy petting to necrophilia. Take eating, for example. There are few strong taboos around the act of eating; yet most people feel uneasy about being the only one at table who is, or who is not, eating, and there is an absolute difference between eating a rare steak washed down by plenty of red wine and watching a close-up movie of someone doing so. One wishes to draw back when one is actually or imaginatively too close to the mouth of a man enjoying his dinner; in exactly the same way one wishes to remove oneself from the presence of a man and woman enjoying sexual intercourse. Not to withdraw is to peep, to pervert looking so that it becomes a sexual end in itself. As for a close-up of a private act which is also revolting, a man's vomiting, say, the avoidance-principle is the same as for a close-up of steak-eating, except that the additional unpleasantness makes one wish to keep an even greater distance.

Pornography also raises aesthetic questions, since it exists only in art—in painting, literature, sculpture, photography, theater—and my definition implies that it is offensive aesthetically. The central aesthetic issue is not whether certain subjects and words should be taboo but what distance should be maintained between spectator and subject. Because of our desire to withdraw from a man performing private acts and our doubly strong desire to withdraw from a man performing acts which are not only private but also disagreeable or perverted, we wish aesthetically to remain at a certain distance from such acts when they are represented in art. Nothing whatever in human experience should, as such, be excluded from consideration in a work of art: not Judas betraying Christ nor naked starved Jews crowded by Nazi soldiers into a gas chamber nor a child locked by his parents in a dark closet for months till he goes mad nor a man paying a whore to lash him with barbed wire for his sexual relief nor even husband and wife making love.

Nothing human is alien to art. The question is only, how close? But the criterion of distance is an extremely tricky one. Aesthetically, one good way to keep a spectator at a distance from the experience represented by an image is to make the image artificial, stylized, not like us. If it is sufficiently stylized, it may be   10 vivid and detailed and still keep a proper distance from the viewer. One would normally feel uneasy at being with a lot of men, women, and children engaged in every imaginable form of pleasurable erotic activity. Yet the vivid throngs of erotic statues on certain Indian temples create in the viewer no uneasiness but are simply delightful to look at. The viewer is kept at a considerable remove by the impossible poses and expressions of the statues; he cannot identify with the persons performing the acts. For the statues do not represent lustful, passionate, guilty, self-conscious, confused people like you and me, but pure beings to whom all things are pure, paradisal folk who are expressing their joy in generation and the body by erotic acts: these are stylized artifices of blessedness. Another way of keeping the spectator at a proper distance from a private experience is to give very little of it—make the image small, sketch it in with few details. One does not want to be close to a man while he is defecating nor to have a close-up picture of him in that natural, innocent act—not at all because defecating is reprehensible, only because it is displeasing to intrude upon. One would much rather have a detailed picture of a thief stealing the last loaf of bread from a starving widow with three children than one of Albert Schweitzer at stool. However, Brueghel's painting "The Netherlandish Proverbs" represents two bare rear ends sticking out of a window, presumably of people defecating into the river below, and one quite enjoys the sight—because it is a small part of a large and pleasant picture of the world and because the two figures are tiny, sketched in, far away.

To be sure, a satiric work of art may purposely arouse disgust in its audience. Even the breast of a healthy woman is revolting when inspected too closely, as Swift knew when he had tiny Gulliver revolted by every blemish on the breast of the Brobdingnagian wet nurse suckling the baby. Our revulsion at the description of her breast sticking out a good six feet, with a nipple half the size of a man's head, is necessary to Swift's satiric purposes, and it is kept within bounds by his reminding us that if proportions had been normal—if Gulliver and she had been about the same size—both he and we would have been pleased by the sight of her breast. When the artist's purpose goes to the limit of satire and he intends, as Swift does in the fourth book of *Gulliver's Travels,* to disgust us with man as such, then he will force us right into the unpleasantly private, as Swift gets us to contemplate the Yahoos copulating promiscuously and lovelessly, besmeared with their own excrement. The aesthetic danger of such powerful evocations of disgust is that the audience may and often does turn not only against the object of the artist's hatred but also against the artist and work of art for having aroused such unpleasant emotions. Swift, just because he succeeds so powerfully, is often reviled for his misanthropy in the voyage to the Houyhnhnms; the fourth book of *Gulliver's Travels* is even called a product and proof of madness—which is convenient and safe, for of course the fantasies of a madman may be pathetic and scary but they don't apply to us, *we* are sane.

The Erotic Used—and Misused

There is a special problem raised by realism, because it aims to present people as they actually are. How can a realistic artist be true to his subject if he is forbidden direct access to an area of human behavior which is of considerable importance? The aesthetic problem is for the realistic artist to represent these actions in such a way as to lead to understanding of the characters without arousing disgust against them or a prurient interest in their activities. When he can accomplish this very difficult feat, then he is justified in including in a realistic work of art representations that would otherwise be pornographic. Here are two instances of intimate erotic acts realistically represented, one of a kiss which is pornographic, the other of a copulation which is aesthetically justified and hence is not pornographic.

In the movie *Baby Doll*, made by Elia Kazan, a healthy young man and woman who desire one another embrace. By this point in the movie the spectator is convinced that their lust is powerful but banal, and a brief and somewhat distant shot of their embracing would adequately suggest to him how intensely they wanted to consummate their desire. Instead, he is subject to a prolonged series of images, especially auditory images, the effect of which is to arouse his own lust and/or disgust, to no aesthetic end. The kiss becomes so severed from characters and plot that the spectator does not care how the couple are related, but cares only that they are given over to desire, and he is encouraged by the very depersonalization of that desire to give himself over to a lust of his own. He may be excited to want some sort of sexual activity with the next available person, but, more probably, observing and sharing in that movie embrace becomes a kind of substitute sexual activity on the part of the spectator. For, just because the scene in *Baby Doll* arouses its spectator vicariously and in a theater, the chief appetite it whets is not for casual fornication but for more voyeurism—which is good at least for the movie business. Even if *Baby Doll* were a good work of art, as it surely is not, this episode in itself would remain aesthetically unjustified and therefore pornographic, and would merit censoring.

The other example of an intimately presented erotic act is from the novel *Pretty Leslie* by R. V. Cassill. The reader is given an emotionally intense account of a young man and woman copulating in an abnormal way; the man hurts the woman, and the reader understands how he does it and why she lets him do it. This would seem to be essentially pornographic, yet it is not. The art of this novel redeems its ugliness. The reader is not encouraged to use this episode as an incitement to casual fornication or voyeurism. Instead, what is aroused in him is a profound understanding of the characters themselves, of a kind he could have got in no other way. To understand what these people were like, how they were connected, and why they did what they did to each other, the reader must be close to them as they make love, and because he knows this is necessary for his understanding, he will not use either the episode or the whole novel for pornographic ends, unless he himself is already perverted. In *Baby Doll* a natural private act, by being brought close for no legitimate reason, excites an uneasy desire whose satisfaction can only be indiscriminate or perverse. In *Pretty Leslie* the account of an unnatural private act is not so close as to create disgust but is close enough to lead toward moral understanding and aesthetic satisfaction: there is no other possible way for the novelist to accomplish this legitimate end, and the emphasis he gives the episode is in proportion to its contribution to the whole novel.

The aesthetic problem has been stated succinctly by Jean Genet. As a professed immoralist and enemy of society, he has no compunction about using pornography and in fact he once made a pornographic movie. But as a writer, he has this to say about his art (in an interview in *Playboy* magazine for April 1964): "I now think that if my books arouse readers sexually, they're badly written, because the poetic emotion should be so strong that no reader is moved sexually. In so far as my books are pornographic, I don't reject them. I simply say that I lacked grace."   15

Nothing said thus far would justify legal suppression, official censorship. The effect of pornography in a work of art is aesthetically bad, but it is no business of the state to suppress bad art. The effect of pornography on an individual psyche is that of an assault, ranging in severity from the equivalent of a mere pinch to that of an open cut; but in the normal course of things one can avoid such assaults without much trouble, and besides the wounds they make are seldom very severe one by one, though they may be cumulatively. To be sure, there are people who want and need pornography just as there are those who want and need heroin, but such a secret indulgence is not in itself socially dangerous. Here again, the state has no business intruding: a man's soul is his own to pollute if he wishes, and it is not for the state to say, "Be thou clean, be thou healthy, close the bathroom door behind you." It is only when pornography becomes public that, like dope, it takes on a sufficiently political cast for censorship even to be considered. It is unlike dope in that it sometimes acquires political overtones by being used ideologically, when put in the service of nihilism. But in one important respect it is like dope: it usually becomes public by being offered for sale, especially to the young.

Sell It Under the Counter

The classic example of pornography is a filthy picture: it is ugly; it is sold and displayed surreptitiously; it allows the viewer to intrude vicariously upon the privacy of others; it shows two or more men and women posing for money in front of a camera, in attitudes which sexual desire alone would lead them to assume in private if at all. An adult looking at such a picture roused to an excitement which may lead either to revulsion or to satisfaction, but whatever his reaction, he should be left alone to decide for himself whether he wants to repeat the experience. The state has no legitimate political concern with his private vices. But the effect on young people of such a picture, and especially of a steady diet of such pictures, is another matter. A common argument against allowing young people to have unrestricted access to pornography runs somewhat as follows.

About sex the young are curious and uncertain and have very powerful feelings. A filthy picture associates sexual acts with ugly, vicarious, and surreptitious pleasure, and helps to cut sex off from love and free joy. At the most, one experience of pornography may have a salutary effect on the curious, uncertain mind of an adolescent. To be shown what has been forbidden might provide him a considerable relief, and if he has feared that he is warped because of his fantasies, he can see how really warped are those who act on such fantasies. Moreover, by his own experience he can learn why pornography is forbidden: experience of it is at once fascinating, displeasing, and an end in itself, that is to say, perverse. However, too many experiences with pornography may encourage the young to turn their fantasies into actions ("in dreams begin responsibilities") or to substitute fantasies for actions, and so may confirm them in bad habits.

Whatever the validity of this argument, it or something like it is the rationale by which our society justifies its strong taboo against exposing children to pornography. For my own part, I would accept the argument as mostly valid. The state has no business legislating virtue: indeed, one of the symptoms of totalitarianism is the persistent attempt of the state not just to punish its citizens for wrongdoing, but to change their nature, to make them what its rulers conceive to be good. But patently the state has the obligation to protect the young against the public acts of the vicious.

This means that, in the matter of the sale and display of pornography, the state, the apparatus of the law, should have two effective policies. It should strictly forbid making pornography accessible to the young: "No One Under 18 Admitted." But as for pornography for adults, the law should rest content with a decent hypocrisy: "Keep it out of the marketplace, sell it under the counter, and the law won't bother you."   20

An assumption underlying such policies is that a certain amount of official hypocrisy is one of the operative principles of a good society. It is hard to imagine a civilized society which would not disapprove of adultery, for the maintenance of the family as an institution is one of the prime concerns of society, and adultery threatens the family. Yet, on the other hand, imagine living in a country in which the laws against adultery were strictly enforced—the informing, spying, breaking in upon, denouncing, the regiment of self-righteous teetotalers. What is obviously needed here is what we have: unenforced laws. Only an all-or-none zealot fails to distinguish between the deplorable hypocrisy of a man deceiving his neighbors for his own gain and the salutary hypocrisy of a government recognizing the limits beyond which it should not encroach upon its individual citizens. Another assumption underlying these recommendations is that the censorship of simple pornography for adults will never be very effective. There is a steady demand for it, and it is not important enough to prosecute at much expense. The main function of laws against adult pornography is to express disapproval of it.

Clearly the logic of this argument leads to prohibiting certain books and works of art that are now legally available in some parts of the country. For example, in some localities the courts have refused to prohibit the sale of *Fanny Hill*. This refusal seems to me quite irresponsible on any grounds other than a general refusal to censor pornography, for by any meaningful definition *Fanny Hill* is pornographic. Such story as there is in the novel exists for no other purpose than to provide occasions for detailed accounts of sexual encounters, and these accounts are the only passages in the book with power to stir the reader's emotions. The characters are very simple types without intrinsic interest, and Fanny herself is little more than a man's fantasy of female complaisance and sexual competence. The one literary quality which has made the book celebrated is a certain elegance of style; compared to most simple pornography it reads like a masterpiece, but to anyone familiar with eighteenth-century English prose it reads like several other third-rate novels. Surely the world is not in such need of third-rate eighteenth-century English fictional prose as to allow this consideration alone to justify the public sale of a work of sheer pornography. What else would justify its sale is hard to imagine. To deny that the book is pornographic or to say that its literary value redeems its pornography, is to blur distinctions, and for an august court of law to do so is for the state to abrogate one of its functions. An essential and conservative function of the state is to say, "Thou shalt not," to formulate society's taboos. Unless I am seriously mistaken, in this instance the court, speaking for the state, has refused to draw a clear line which corresponds to society's actual customs. In our culture the place for nudists is in a nudist colony, not on the city streets, and the way to sell books like *Fanny Hill* is under the counter, not over it. In the name of enlightenment and sexual permissiveness, the state is violating an actual taboo, and the reaction to many such violations may very well be a resurgence of that savage fanaticism which burns books and closes theaters.

What to Censor, and Why

I am going to defer a consideration of the nihilistic use of pornography, which would logically come next, and instead look at certain borderline questions of enforcing censorship. The censoring of unquestionable pornography is of little interest; it pretty directly reflects what decent society considers indecent at a given time; it is custom in action. But the censorship of borderline pornography demands discrimination and philosophy, without which censorship can degenerate into puritanical repressiveness of the kind there has been quite enough of during the past two or three centuries.

Thus far, my argument on what to censor and why has led to a legal position which is at least within hailing distance of common practice in the United States now. To purveyors of raw pornography our practice says in effect:

bother your neighbors, especially children, and you will be punished; leave others untroubled by your vice and you will be viewed with disapproval by the law but left alone. This attitude is fine till one gets down to cases, but once it is a matter of wording and enforcing a law, the question must be answered: how is one to distinguish between pornographic and decent art? Still, such lines must be drawn if there are to be laws at all, and they must, in the nature of things, be arbitrary. As I see it, a more manageable form of the question is this: who should do the censoring? Whatever the answer to this question may be, whatever the best method of censoring, one thing is clear—our present method is unsatisfactory.

As things stand, an object is banned as pornographic on the judgment of some official in customs or the postal service or else by some police officer prodded by a local zealot. In most cases this judgment presents little difficulty: even civil-liberty extremists who are opposed to all censorship on principle blanch when they are confronted with genuine hard-core pornography, the unarguably warped stuff, the bulk of the trade. But sometimes there is the question of assessing the value of a work of art, and for this task the bureaucrats and policemen who are presently empowered to decide are unqualified.

Should *Fanny Hill* be offered to the public freely? When society has said *no* for generations and when judges and literary critics cannot agree on the question, it is wrong to allow a police sergeant to decide the matter. If a duly constituted public authority says, "*Fanny Hill* shall not be sold in this state," then the policeman's duty is clear: arrest the man who displays it for sale. But to leave to bureaucrats and policemen the task of making all the delicate discriminations necessary in deciding whether the novel should be censored in the first place, is genuinely irresponsible of society at large and of legislators in particular. To be sure, cases are brought to court. But the laws offer such vague guidance that far too much depends on the quirks of the judge or jury at hand. *No censorship might be preferable to what we have now.*

In fact, a strong case can be made for removing all censorship of pornography. Here are six arguments for abolishing censorship. The first three seem to me valid. (1) No law can be framed so as to provide a clear and sure guide to bureaucrat, policeman, judge, and jury. (2) It is very hard to demonstrate that pornography does in fact injure many people severely, even adolescents, for if the desire to break taboos is satisfied imaginatively, it is less likely to issue in antisocial acts. (3) The less power the state and the police have the better.

There are three further arguments against censorship which are commonly used but which I find less persuasive. (1) Decent citizens can by their very disapproval segregate pornography without assistance from the state. But, in an age as troubled as ours and with so much private indiscipline and theoretical permissiveness in sexual matters, there is little reason to suppose that the moral disapproval of decent citizens would actually stop the public distribution of pornography. (2) It is arguable that some people are rendered

25

socially less dangerous by having their sexual tensions more or less satisfied by pornography, tensions which unrelieved might well lead to much more antisocial acts. True, but pornography, if it is to help those who need and use it, must be outside the law, clearly labeled *shameful;* if society has any respect for them, it will sternly assure them that what they are doing is nasty by passing a law against it, and then will pretty much leave them alone. (3) In the past, censorship has not succeeded in keeping books of literary value from being read but has only attached an unfortunate prurience to the reading of them. But the prurience attached to reading pornography derives less from breaking a law than from violating the taboo which caused the law to come into existence.

Goodman's Lovely Daydreams

There is another argument, more important and erroneous than any of these six, which is commonly advanced in favor of abolishing censorship. It hinges on a mistaken liberal doctrine about the nature of sexual taboos. According to this doctrine, sexual taboos, like fashions in dress, are determined by local custom and have as little to do with morality as the kinds of clothes we wear. However—the argument goes—people frequently mistake these sexual taboos for ethical rules, and pass and enforce laws punishing those who violate the taboos. The result is a reduction of pleasure in sex and an increase of guilt, with an attendant host of psychological and social ills. The obvious solution is to abolish the taboos and so liberate the human spirit from its chief source of oppression and guilt. At the moment in America, this ultimately Rousseauistic doctrine finds extensive elaboration in the writings of Paul Goodman, and is present to some degree in the writings of many other intellectuals.

It presents a considerable difficulty: by supposing that the potent and obscure emotions surrounding sexual matters derive from unenlightened customs, it holds out the hope that enlightened views can liberate us from those customs so that sex in every form can become healthy and fun for all. This is a cheery, optimistic view, not unlike the sweet hopefulness of the old-fashioned anarchists who thought that all we have to do, in order to attain happiness, is to get rid of governments so we may all express our essentially good nature unrestrained. Such ideas would show to advantage in a museum of charming notions, along with phlogiston and the quarrel about how many angels can dance on the head of a pin, but turned loose in the world they sometimes cause a bit of trouble. Sexual anarchism, like political anarchism before it, is a lovely daydream. But it has come to be a part of fundamental liberalism, and so a part of the body of doctrines accepted by more and more of the rulers of the nation. Conceivably the First Amendment will be taken literally ("Congress shall make no law . . . abridging the freedom of speech or of the press") and many or all legal restraints against pornography may in fact be removed. But I believe that so far from eliminating sexual taboos, such an official under-

30

mining of them would only arouse the puritans to strengthen the bulwarks; the taboos would be made more repressive than ever; and many of the goods of liberalism would be wiped out along with and partly because of this utopian folly. Decent people had better learn now to censor moderately, or the licentiousness released by liberal zealots may arouse their brothers the puritan zealots to censorship by fire.

A civilized method of censoring is feasible. One does not have to imagine a utopian system of extirpating pornography through some sexual revolution—an Eden of erotic innocence in which prohibitions will be unnecessary because social relations will be as they should be. In our actual, historical United States, in which perversions and pornography flourish, one can imagine a better method of restraining pornography, which is yet within the framework of our customs and procedures. It would operate somewhat as follows.

All decisions about what is legally pornographic in any of the arts are in the custody of boards of censors. A board is elected or appointed from each of three general categories of citizens: for example, a judge or lawyer of good repute; a professor of art, literature, or one of the humanities; and a social worker, psychologist, or clergyman. These are not exciting categories; but in them, if anywhere, are likely to be found citizens whose own opinions will reflect decent social opinion and who are also capable of making the various discriminations the task calls for. Obviously it is necessary to keep sexual anarchists off the board; just as a person is disqualified from serving as a juror in a murder case if he is against capital punishment, so one would be disqualified from serving on a board of censors if he were against censoring pornography.

A board of censors must never look to a set of rules of thumb for guidance—not, as now, to the quantity of an actress's body that must be covered. Is a burlesque dancer's breast indecent from the nipple down or is it only the nipple itself that offends? That way foolishness lies. Rather, the censors must look only to their own personal experience with a given work of art for only in such experience can art be judged. For this reason, the censors should be people for whom society's taboos are part of themselves, not something in a code external to them. No photograph, drawing, book, stage show, or moving picture is banned by the police except at the instruction of this board. Its decisions, like those of every quasi-official public agency, are subject to appeal to the courts, but the Supreme Court would do all it could to dodge such cases. *The banning is deliberately hypocritical: out of sight out of mind, so long as children are not molested.*

The aesthetic and moral principles guiding the board are roughly these: distance and effect. At the distance of a movie close-up, a kiss between husband and wife can be pornographic. If a child and adult are sitting side by side watching a stage performance of a witty Restoration comedy of adultery, they are at altogether different distances from the play, the adult closer than the child; but at a marionette performance of a fairytale melodrama they reverse distances, the child closer this time and the adult farther away. As for effect on the spectator, this consideration is only slightly less tricky than distance. The question to be asked is whether a story intrudes on the privacy of its characters in order to give the reader vicarious and perverse sexual excitement or in order to provide him with a sympathetic understanding which he could have got in no other way. These criteria of distance and effect—these rubber yardsticks—apply to the parts as well as to the whole, so that a novel or a movie of some aesthetic merit may be judged as censorable in part. In a movie the part is excisable with more or less aesthetic harm to the movie as a whole; with a book, if the board decides the gravity of the offense outweighs such literary excellence as the whole book may possess, the book is banned—not burned, just no longer offered for public sale.

This system is scarcely watertight; it presents plenty of opportunity for   35
contradictions and revisions; it has tensions built into it. But it would not be likely to become troublesome politically; for, without strengthening the state, it provides a better way than the present one for our society to enforce certain inevitable taboos. Civilization behaves as though men were decent, in full knowledge that they are not. ◢

Reflections and Inquiries

1. Elliott confesses to harboring "two mutually antagonistic dispositions, one liberal, the other conservative," regarding pornography. What is the crux of each view? Does he manage to find a way to link them together logically? If so, how feasible is the synthesis?

2. Can there be a clear-cut way of distinguishing between pornographic and decent art? Why or why not? Just how valid are "pornographic" and "decent" as criteria for evaluating art?

3. Elliott presents three valid reasons for removing all censorship of pornography. Do you agree or disagree with these reasons? Why?

4. How sensible, in your opinion, is Elliott's plan for establishing a board of censors to evaluate works of art? What difficulties might such a board run into?

Reading to Write

In a short essay, evaluate the usefulness of Elliott's definition of pornography. How would you modify his definition? Be sure to justify your changes.

Comic Book Censorship and the Comic Book Legal Defense Fund | Dewey Adams

Adult comic books, like popular novels, have an enormous readership; unlike popular fiction, though, comic books have become targets of censors. As Dewey Adams, a junior at the University of South Carolina, points out in his investigation of comic book censorship, the only person ever to be convicted of obscenity in the United States was a comic book artist.

Americas's most cherished law is the First Amendment to the United States Constitution. America is a land where artists are free to express themselves in any form and espousing any beliefs with little or no censorship. The idea of an American artist being convicted and serving a sentence for the obscenity of his art is unthinkable to most Americans. However, on June 27, 1997, this is exactly what happened to Mike Diana (Romenesko). It was on this date that the United States Supreme Court denied Diana's request for an appeal to his case. What did Mike Diana create that was so horrible? Some comic books. What can be so bad about comic books? Well, Diana's comics featured very little story content and an excess of mangled, disfigured bodies, and graphic sexual content, but he was not distributing his comics to minors. In fact, he was hardly distributing them to anyone. His largest print run was only 200 copies, but Diana's comic *Boiled Angel* became comic book's most recent martyr in the fight against censorship, a fight that has been raging for fifty years (Romenesko).

From Lil' Abner to Spiderman to Spawn, comics have been on the fringe of mainstream society and viewed as mere entertainment for youths, and because of this have been used as a scapegoat for youth delinquency and forced to meet stringent censorship criteria. Perhaps the most appalling consequence of this misconception is the lack of artistic respect given to comic book creators. Comic creators and retailers who offended the gods of the legal bureaucracy had no champion until 1990, when the Comic Book Legal Defense Fund was officially formed (Comic Book Legal Defense Fund). The following pages discuss the history of comic book censorship, the CBLDF's contributions to the censorship battle, and the story of Mike Diana as a case in point.

Many historians attribute the beginning of American comics to the appearance of Lil' Abner in the 1890's. This famous comic strip was the first nationally popular one of its kind and was later collected and reprinted in book format. However, comic book historians look to early 1922 and Embee Distributing Company's *Comic Monthly* (Goulart). This publication was also just reprints of newspaper comic strips, but it was an ongoing series and set the standard for comic book proportions and length. The 1930's saw the birth of such comic legends as Superman, Batman, and Captain America (Feiffer). These comics were truly created exclusively for children, and adults paid little attention to the magazines. Truly, the adults of America had more important things to worry about—the Great Depression and World War II, for example. However, at the end of World War II American adults turned their attention to comics and persecuted the medium much like television has been persecuted in the past twenty years.

In August of 1950 a survey among "interested groups" proved that 70% of the people surveyed did not believe that there was a correlation between crime in comics and crime among youth. So, the Senate released the findings and was done with it. Despite the lack of public support, Congress continued to investigate the industry, using the United States Postal Service as their watchdogs. In the spring of 1954 the Senate Subcommittee on Juvenile Delinquency began investigating the comics industry for its influence on the growing delinquency among America's youth (Nyberg). Two of the main comics on trial were crime comics, like *Crime Must Pay the Penalty, Crime Suspense Stories,* and *Shock Suspense Stories*—especially a story called "The Whipping," about racism. All stories used in the trial involved good triumphing over evil or another positive social message, like the anti-racism message of "The Whipping," but the prosecution misrepresented the comics by taking scenes and dialogue out of context and presenting only part of the story to the jury. Despite all of the attempts of the Subcommittee's leader, Estes Kefauver, the finding were inconclusive and the official report read: "Surveying the work that has been done on the subject, it appears to be the consensus of the experts that comic-book reading is not the cause of emotional maladjustment in children" (U.S. Congress).

Despite the Senate's negative findings, the comic book industry was   5
scared and decided to begin self-regulation. In 1954 the Comics Magazine Association of America was formed and, subsequently, the CMAA Comics Code (Lent). This code was very stringent and placed many restrictions on comic books. A few of the rules include: Crime and criminals shall never be glamorized or portrayed in a sympathetic manner; drugs shall not be involved in the story in any way, shape, or form; racial, religious, gender, physical abnormalities, or any other form of slurs shall not be used. These restrictions were unchallenged until 1971. In 1971 Marvel Comics was asked by The Society for a Drug-Free America to create a story in *The Amazing Spiderman* that depicted the evils of drug use. But the comics code did not allow for drug content in *any* form in comic book stories, not even if the content was necessary to show the evils of drug use. Marvel faced a dilemma: publish its first comic book not ap-

proved by the code, or do a story that gave a much needed social message. Marvel was one of the big two comic book publishers and it knew that offending the CMAA could hurt its sales and lead to further scrutiny of their other publications, but they published the story anyway (Daniels). This issue and its overwhelming success led the CMAA to revise its comic book code.

With the trials of the 1950's behind the comic book industry and the victory of 1971, the 1970's and early 1980's were a prosperous time in the comic book industry. The government took a hands-off approach to industry regulation, the CMAA revised and loosened its Comic Book Code, and the rest of America paid no attention. Unfortunately, the 1990's would see an end to that attitude that necessitated the formation of the Comic Book Legal Defense Fund.

The Comic Book Legal Defense Fund was formed in 1990 from the leftover funds raised by the comics community to defend Friendly Frank's, a comic store in Lansing, Illinois, whose owner, Frank Mangiaracina, was arrested for selling "obscene comics." The Comic Book Legal Defense Fund's guiding principle is "comics should be accorded the same constitutional rights as literature, film, or any other form of expression." Denis Kitchen, publisher of Kitchen Sink Press and self-proclaimed "self-publisher gone bad," is founder and president of this organization that has comic book legends Peter David, definitive Incredible Hulk writer of almost twelve years, and Frank Miller, the creator of Batman: The Dark Knight Returns, on its board of directors. Comics creators like Neil Gaiman and Kurt Busiek have also aided the CBLDF.

In its nine years of official existence the CBLDF has aided many cases. One of the most important was *Mavrides v. California Board of Equalization*. Paul Mavrides is a Californian, creator of *The Fabulous Furry Freak Brothers*. In 1991 the California Board of Equalization, the organization in charge of ensuring creator royalty receipt and taxation of said receipts, erroneously awarded Paul Mavrides with $80,000 in royalties (Mavrides). Mavrides notified them of their mistake, but the California BOE used this incident to investigate the nature of and classification of Mavrides's profession. The BOE decided that Mavrides and other California-based comic book creators were not artists, but independent contractors who had to pay tax on the sale of their product. Mavrides and the CBLDF contested that comic creators were artists and creations were original pieces of art, which are sales-tax exempt. A legal battle ensued. The court case cost approximately $75,000, and the amount in question was only $1,400, but Mavrides said: "The money consistently has been the least important matter to me. I was more in fear of the domino effect it would have had both on comic publishers and my colleagues in the comics field" (Comic Book Legal Defense Fund).

One of the CBLDF's blemishes is the obscenity trafficking conviction of the owners of Planet Comics in Oklahoma City, Oklahoma. This conviction is considered a blemish not because the store owners were convicted. The CBLDF has lost cases before and they were disappointing, but nothing like this. On September 5, 1997, just days before the trial, the two owners, Michael Kennedy and John Hunter, signed a plea bargain in the state of Oklahoma. It is the CBLDF's policy to only take cases when the defendants will plead innocent. If convicted, Kennedy and Hunter could have faced up to five years in prison, but the plea bargain allowed them to serve a suspended three-year sentence, but cost the CBLDF a lot of credibility (Comic Book Legal Defense Fund, 1999).

The CBLDF's most publicized case to date is *Diana v. Florida.* The beginnings of the case are disputed; some say the Gainesville police first learned of Diana's work when a secretary at a public school got one of Diana's original pages jammed in a copier. Diana was working at the school as a janitor and was illegally copying his underground comic book, *Boiled Angel,* when one of the pages got stuck (Romenesko). Others think that Diana came under scrutiny when a man in California had his car searched, and a copy of *Boiled Angel* was found that included drawings of dead bodies that were positioned much like the victims of unsolved serial killings at the University of Florida (Rogers). Either way, Diana's drawings got him in a lot of trouble. He was accused of child molestation and even arrested for the serial killings his drawings supposedly resembled. In March of 1993 Diana was served a summons for obscenity based on the materials found during the Gainsville murder investigation. On March 25, 1994 he was found guilty of obscenity after a mere ninety minutes of jury deliberation (Rogers, 1997). Diana appealed his case all the way to the Supreme Court, but to no avail. So, he stands as the only American artist ever convicted of obscenity. His punishment has been severe to say the least. He is not allowed within 500 yards of any minor, has had to pay over $3,000 in fines, attend a journalism ethics class, have a psychiatric evaluation, do 1,248 hours of community service, and is on probation for three years. Anytime during this probation Diana's home or Diana himself may be subjected to searches without a warrant or notification, and if he possesses any "obscene" material, he could face a prison sentence. This means that Mike Diana is not allowed to draw anything that may be offensive even if what he does with it is place it in the garbage can (Romenesko). If you would like to see some of Mike Diana's work that has not been censored, then go to <http://www.testicle.com/mikediana.htm.>

Comic books stand poised to break their way out of the basements of socially maladjusted pubescent boys, and into the living rooms of mainstream America. Even the academic community is beginning to recognize the value of comic books. Universities and colleges around the country are beginning to offer courses based solely on comic book literature or at least using comic books as part of the class curriculum (Busbee). Hopefully, these two developments will change America's opinion of comic books; from the medium designed primarily for children, to a valid form of expression for adults to communicate their beliefs and ideas. Then, censorship in the medium should diminish from the current strict regime to become a loose commonwealth of ideas, beliefs, and most of all, truly free speech.

Works Cited

Busbee, James. "Wizard U." *Wizard Comics.* Vol. 1, no. 80. 1988.

Comic Book Legal Defense Fund. 1999. <http://www.cbldf.org>.

Daniels, Les. *Marvel: Five Fabulous Decades of the World's Greatest Comics.* New York: Abrams, 1991.

Feiffer, Jules. *The Great Comic Book Heroes.* New York: Dial, 1965.

Goulart, Ron. *The Great Comic Book Artists.* New York: St. Martin's, 1986.

Lent, John. *Pulp Demons: International Dimensions of the Postwar Anti-Comics Campaign.* New Brunswick: Farleigh-Dickinson UP, 1999.

Mavrides, Paul. Why Me? (Part 2). 1996. <http://www.darkcarnival.com/DCOLarchive/cbldf.paul.fly.htm>.

Nyberg, Amy Kiste. *Seal of Approval: The History of the Comics Code.* Jackson: UP of Mississippi, 1998.

Rogers, Adam. "Arrested Development." *Wizard Comics.* Vol. 1, no. 74. 1987.

Romenesko, James. "The Mike Diana Saga." 1994. <http://php.indiana.edu/~mfragass/diana_obscure.html>.

United States Senate. Subcommittee to Investigate Juvenile Delinquency. *Interim Report: Comic Book Juvenile Delinquency.* 84th Cong., 1st sess. Washington: GPO, 1955. ◢

Reflections and Inquiries

1. What is Adams's thesis? Where does it appear most explicitly? How successfully does he defend it, in your opinion?

2. Why have comic book artists come under so much censorship, in your view?

3. Adams devotes a considerable amount of time to discussing the history of comic book censorship. How necessary is this discussion to Adams's argument?

4. Why do you suppose the comic book industry opted for self-censorship despite the Senate's conclusion in 1955 that comic book reading did not cause emotional maladjustment in children?

5. Should comic books be subjected to certain restrictions? If you agree they should be, what should those restrictions include? If not, why not?

Reading to Write

1. Adams notes that some colleges and universities offer literature courses that include comic books either partly or exclusively. Try locating, online, course descriptions, syllabi, and perhaps instructor profiles for such courses. Write an essay that (a) describes the range of such course offerings and (b) evaluates their content based on the descriptions, syllabi, and profiles.

2. If you are a reader of adult comics, write a critical evaluation of one of your favorite series. Use some or all of the following criteria: writing and story-

telling quality, artwork, originality. Comment also on anything that you or other readers might find offensive about the series. Is the offensive material merely sensationalistic or a necessary part of the story? Could it have a negative effect on some of its readers? Why or why not? You might find the following studies of comic book artistry—presented in comic format—useful: *Understanding Comics* (1993) and *Reinventing Comics* (2000), both by Scott McCloud.

Connections Across the Clusters

1. In what ways can censorship and book banning become a multicultural issue? See Cluster 6. A privacy issue? See Cluster 8.

2. Should certain kinds of media violence (see Cluster 7) be subject to censorship? What kinds, and why?

3. Discuss censorship of ideas in terms of the effort of some teachers and legislators to ban the teaching of evolution alone, or the teaching of special Creation alone, from the science classroom. See Cluster 5.

Writing Project

Hundreds of books have been banned from U.S. schools in the past decade, for various reasons: Defiance of authority, use of offensive language, and sexual situations are the usual reasons. Visit "The One Hundred Most Frequently Challenged Books of 1990–1999" at <www.ala.org/alaorg/oif/top100bannedbooks. html>. Choose one of these banned books, read it if you haven't already, and write an essay in which you support or argue against the rationale for its being banned.

Suggestions for Further Reading

Casey-Webb, Allen. "Racism and Huckleberry Finn: Censorship, Dialogue, and Change." *English Journal* Nov. 1993: 22–34.

Goodman, Paul. "Pornography, Art, and Censorship." *Commentary* Mar. 1961: 203–12.

Haight, Anne Lyon, and Chandler B. Grannis. *Banned Books: 387 B.C. to 1978 A.D.* 4th ed. New York: R. R. Bowker, 1978.

Jalongo, Mary Renck. "Censorship in Children's Literature: What Every Educator Needs to Know." *Childhood Education* 67 (Spring 1991): 143–49.

Lawrence, D. H. *Sex, Literature, and Censorship.* New York: Viking, 1959.

Pease, Edward C. "A Purple Yearbook and Free Speech on Campus." *Chronicle of Higher Education* 19 Nov. 1999: A80.

Widmer, Eleanor, ed. *Freedom and Culture: Literary Censorship in the 70s.* Belmont: Wadsworth, 1970.

4 | Is Space Exploration Worth the Expense?

Introduction

For many people, the answer to the question posed by this cluster is an unqualified "no." Why spend billions of dollars exploring other worlds, launching expensive telescopes into orbit, building space stations, or searching for signs of life beyond the earth when those funds could be used for improving things on this world, such as helping to alleviate hunger, poverty, homelessness, and drug abuse for starters?

This is an entirely legitimate response. Few would disagree that more could be done to combat human suffering—if not globally, then at least in our own country. And yet, must one endeavor exclude another? Why can't we eliminate human suffering *and* explore space (and pursue any or all of other worthy government-funded endeavors as well)?

One of the problems many people have with space exploration is that they do not understand how it can be beneficial, other than satisfying curiosity. Even though the space age is nearly half a century old (it began October 4, 1957, when the Soviet Union launched Sputnik I, the first artificial satellite), many still associate space exploration with science fiction-like fancifulness—nice for escapist entertainment but hardly relevant to solving the practical problems of the world.

The following selections present a variety of perspectives on the practicality of space exploration. Some express undiluted enthusiasm for what space has in store for humankind; others consider the matter more cautiously. All the authors, however, acknowledge the complexity of the issue.

Flowers for Mars | Christopher P. McKay

Mars. The very name fires the imagination of space enthusiasts who believe that it is our destiny to explore and colonize other worlds. And Mars is the most promising planet to explore because it holds much promise for colonization and for conducting exciting scientific research. Ever since a Martian meteorite harboring a possible fossil microscopic organism was discovered on Earth in 1997, scientists have directed their attention to Mars as the likeliest place beyond Earth where life may currently exist. Photographs of the Martian surface from orbit reveal long riverbed-like formations, most likely caused by running water in Mars's distant past. Where liquid water ran, life may have evolved.

In the following article, Christopher P. McKay, a NASA scientist whose specialty is astrobiology, explains why sending flower seeds to Mars and allowing them to grow there is a good idea.

Life is the reason that Mars is interesting to us: we search for the possibility of life early in that planet's history and try to determine the potential of Mars as a home for life in the future. Ultimately perhaps the Martian surface could support a planetary-scale biosphere.

The near-term robotic exploration of Mars is the first step toward realizing this vision. Robotic probes provide us with background information about Mars: where to search for evidence of past and present life and how to assess the future biological potential of the planet.

One important way to assess the biological potential of Mars is to send life there. Thus, a goal for the near-term robotic program ought to be to send a seed to Mars and to grow it into a plant—ideally a flowering plant—using to the extent possible the sunlight, soil, and nutrients available in the Martian environment.

Why do such an experiment if the laws of physics and chemistry are the same on another planet? Isn't testing on Earth adequate? Certainly testing on Earth is important, but we gain technical as well as psychological reassurance by demonstrating viability on Mars.

NASA has a long tradition of flying technology demonstration missions. *Mars Pathfinder* was such a mission. On a future lander mission, NASA plans to fly a unit to test oxygen production from atmospheric carbon dioxide on Mars. A module capable of growing a single plant from seed would also be a demonstration mission.

The best design for a plant growth module for Mars would make use of the Martian soil, with nutrients added as necessary. Carbon dioxide and water would be obtained from the Martian atmosphere, and the natural sunlight on Mars would provide for photosynthesis. Because of the lower pressure on Mars, the plant would need to be in a small pressure vessel—its own little

5

Source: McKay, Christopher P. "Flowers for Mars." *The Planetary Report* Sept./Oct. 2000: 4–5. Reprinted by permission.

spacesuit. The design of this miniature greenhouse would allow light to enter and, true to its name, provide greenhouse warmth during the day. At night the growth module may need to draw on heat generated by the main spacecraft to keep the plant warm. The plant's growth and flowering would be monitored using the lander camera. Initial designs by groups at the University of Colorado and the Jet Propulsion Laboratory have shown that such a unit can be constructed. We could therefore send life to Mars on the next lander.

There are many reasons for sending a flower to Mars. First, it would be highly symbolic. This plant would be the first organism from Earth to play out its existence on another world. It would be a true biological pioneer, an important step for life on Earth expanding to other planets. More practically, a plant growth module would directly test the toxicity of the Martian soil. It would also demonstrate the effectiveness of Martian carbon dioxide and water for a Martian greenhouse. These are essential steps toward a full-scale greenhouse to support a human base. Moreover, the growth of a plant in the Martian environment would help alleviate concerns about the danger of contaminating the Earth by the return of Martian samples.

In all these respects a plant growth model would serve as a biological precursor to human exploration. Indeed, when humans go to Mars, it would make sense for them to arrive at a site that has already established a biologically based life support system, tested and fully operating—robotically. As on Earth, we humans function best when surrounded by other life-forms.

A simple plant growth module would not be in violation of the planetary

Scientists continue to design or conceptualize ingenious robot probes such as this "Rose Lander," intended to test the ability of flowers to grow in the harsh Martian environment.

protection policy. NASA abides by the policy established in 1967 to prevent the inadvertent contamination of Mars by terrestrial microorganisms. For the *Viking* missions this involved the complete sterilization of the spacecraft. However, these missions showed that environmental conditions on the surface of Mars were hostile to life. No organism known could grow or reproduce under Martian conditions. As a result the requirement for sterilization was replaced with a limitation on the number of microorganisms on spacecraft surfaces to less than 300 per square meter.

The original purpose of the planetary protection policy was to preserve   10
extraterrestrial environments as objects of scientific study. We appreciate that the accidental contamination of an alien ecosystem has ethical implications that extend beyond scientific exploration. Sending life beyond the Earth is an important step and not one we would want to take without consideration of consequences.

The planetary protection guidelines do not explicitly prevent the controlled transport of biological materials to Mars or the use of biological materials in controlled experiments aboard spacecraft. A plant growth unit could be constructed in accordance with the bioload limits of the present planetary protection policy. In fact, to be sure it functions as intended, the system might well exceed these limits and even be treated to eliminate nearly all bacteria.

By developing ways to send life to Mars consistent with the goals of the planetary protection policy, a near-term plant experiment would pave the way for future research and study on the planet. Most important, the growth of a single flower on Mars would be a powerful symbol of the long-term goal of expanding life beyond the Earth, first to Mars and then elsewhere. It would rival the image of the Earth from space—the pale blue dot—as a symbol of our place and future in the universe. ◪

Reflections and Inquiries

1. What reasons does McKay give for sending flower seeds to Mars? Do you agree that this is a worthy experiment to undertake? Why or why not?

2. What is the purpose of NASA's planetary protection policy? Why would sending seeds to Mars not violate this policy?

3. Earlier explorations of Mars disclosed surface conditions that are hostile to life. If this is true, why try to grow plants there?

Reading to Write

This article probably raises several concerns people have about exploring Mars. Write an essay in which you "take to task" some of the assumptions McKay makes—for example, of committing to a long-term goal of "expanding life beyond the Earth."

Why Send Humans to Mars? | Carl Sagan

One of the century's greatest popularizers of science, particularly astronomy, Carl Sagan is the author of *The Dragons of Eden* (1977), which received the Pulitzer Prize, *Cosmos* (1980), which became a highly successful twelve-part PBS television series, and *The Demon-Haunted World: Science as a Candle in the Dark* (1995). A long-time advocate of Mars exploration, Sagan presented his case at a Scientists' Hearing on Space Policy in the U.S. Senate, October 1990. The following article is Sagan's adaptation of that Senate presentation.

On July 20, 1989, the twentieth anniversary of the Apollo 11 landing on the moon, President Bush announced a long-term direction for the U.S. Space Program. Called the Space Exploration Initiative (SEI), it proposes a sequence of goals that includes a space station, a return of humans to the Moon, and then the first landing of human beings on Mars. In a more recent statement, Mr. Bush has set 2019 as the target date for the first footfall on that planet.

SEI has been criticized first with regard to continuity of commitment. It extends five or so presidential terms of office into the future, assuming the average presidency is one and a half terms. That makes it easy for a president to attempt to commit his successors, but leaves in question how reliable such a commitment might be.

Second, there is concern about whether NASA, which has recently experienced great difficulty lifting a few astronauts 200 miles above the Earth—as well as other well-publicized problems—can safely send astronauts on an arcing year-long trajectory to a destination 100 million miles or more away.

And finally, there is the question of where, in terms of practical politics, the money is supposed to come from. The costs for SEI have been variously estimated, ranging as high as $500 billion.

I would like to stress that it is impossible to estimate costs before you have   5
a mission design. And the mission design depends on such matters as the size of the crew; the extent to which you take mitigating steps against possible solar and cosmic radiation hazards, or zero gravity; and what risks you consider acceptable with the lives on board. Other relevant uncertainties are the amount of redundancy in equipment; the extent to which you want to use closed ecological systems or just depend on the food, water, and waste disposal facilities you've brought with you; the design of roving vehicles for the Martian landscape: and what technology you carry to test the ability to live off the land for later voyages.

Source: Sagan, Carl. "Why Send Humans to Mars?" *Issues in Science and Technology 7* (Spring 1991): 80–85. Copyright 1991 by the National Academy of Sciences. Reprinted with permission from *Issues in Science and Technology.*

Clearly, these issues powerfully affect cost, and until they are decided it is absurd to accept any figure for the cost of the program. On the other hand, it is equally clear that the program will be extremely expensive.

The Call of Mars

For me, Mars has been calling since childhood. Voyages to other worlds seem to me the natural continuation of the long history of human exploration. The Earth itself, except for the sea bottoms, is now all explored. At this same moment, our technology permits us to go to other worlds. So of course that's where we'll go, sooner or later.

In the long term, self-sustaining human communities on other worlds would be a step more significant than the colonization of the land by our amphibian ancestors some 500 million years ago, and the descent from the trees by our primate ancestors some 5 to 10 million years ago. It would be a transforming event in human history, in the history of life on Earth. But that doesn't mean it has to happen today. It will also be a transforming event if it happens 100 years from now.

I have been advocating human missions to Mars with some vigor since 1984. With the Planetary Society's "Mars Declaration" it became clear that a stunningly ecumenical group of American leaders also supported such a program, and after a short time we found that the Soviets were embracing it as well. Human exploration of Mars is prominent in the 10 stated long-term technological goals of the USSR, and President Gorbachev on a number of occasions has announced that he would like to pursue it jointly with the United States.

What I had in mind, in the height of the Reagan "evil empire" days, was   10
to establish a common constructive goal for the nuclear superpowers as a means of binding the two nations together, and sharing a purpose of truly historic proportions. The trouble is that the world has not remained static. New developments have emerged. The first is that the U.S. and Soviet economies are in much worse shape than was generally recognized in the Reagan years, and either nation's ability to spend enormous amounts of money on such a goal is now a relevant question.

Also, a joint human mission to Mars was promoted as a way of creating a shared and worthy goal for the two Cold War adversaries; but the Cold War is now over. In fact, U.S./Soviet relations have recently been at their warmest point since the end of World War II. The two nations still have some 55,000 nuclear weapons between them, though, 25,000 of which are in hair-trigger strategic readiness; and it is therefore possible that benign shared objectives extending decades into the future are still very important for the well-being of the global civilization.

I don't believe that the increased budgetary problems and the thawing of the Cold War are significant enough changes to actually scuttle the case for going to Mars. But they do work, at least incrementally, to weaken the argument.

My own chief misgiving is that there are now other matters—clear, crying national needs—that cannot be addressed without major expenditures; while, at the same time, there is an extremely limited discretionary federal budget. Such matters include the disposal of chemical and radioactive wastes, energy efficiency, alternatives to fossil fuels, declining rates of technological innovation, the collapsing urban infrastructure, the AIDS epidemic, homelessness, malnutrition, infant mortality, education—there is a painfully long list, and money is needed to address all of these matters, which endanger the well-being of the nation.

Nearly every one of these matters could cost hundreds of billions of dollars, or more, to address. Indeed, alternatives to the fossil-fuel economy clearly represent a multitrillion-dollar investment, if we can do it. And every now and then there are unexpected little fiscal perturbations provided by private and public corruption, such as the savings and loan scandal.

Saving Money

If there were 20 percent more discretionary funds in the federal budget, I prob-   15
ably would not feel so worried about advocating such enormous expenditures in space. If there were 20 percent less, I don't think the most diehard space enthusiast would be advocating anything like SEI. If, to take a more extreme example, half the people in the Sudan are in immediate danger of starvation, a conscientious board of directors of the Khartoum Art Museum will not be advocating increased government spending to purchase art—no matter how convinced they are of the social benefits of art. You can have life without art, but not vice versa. Surely there is some point at which the national economy is in such dire straits that sending people to Mars is unconscionable. The only difference there might be between me and other enthusiasts for human missions to other worlds is where we draw the line. But surely such a line exists, and every participant in such a debate should stipulate where that line should be drawn, what fraction of the GNP for space is too much.

If we're talking about a relatively minor increment to the NASA budget in order to accomplish SEI, then perhaps it's inappropriate to make zero-sum arguments. But if we advocate, say, $300 billion spent for SEI, that's $300 billion unavailable for other pressing national needs. That amount is essentially the present NASA budget devoted exclusively to SEI for the next 20 years. If the cost of SEI is to be added on, then we're talking about doubling the NASA budget.

So if we are convinced that sending humans to Mars is important for the human future, the key to getting there is to save money. For example, some propose that with alternative technologies and more lenient bureaucratic restrictions, quick, dirty, and incredibly cheap missions of humans to the Moon and Mars are possible. In the review panels I'm familiar with—including the White House/National Space Council "Blue Ribbon" Committee on the President's Human Exploration Initiative, as it was then (November 1989) called—such proposals have been thought stimulating but somewhere between unconvincing and specious. Nevertheless, there might be new technologies, missed by a hidebound NASA, that could produce enormous savings. If such technologies are mature and accessible, they may be critical in sending humans to Mars in the next few decades.

Failing this, the only way for the United States to go is to do it cooperatively. NASA would then commit to something like SEI, but scale back substantially on such technologies as space stations and heavy-lift vehicles, where substantial capability is in hand in other countries—especially, the Soviet Union. If the cost of going to Mars were shared equally among, say, the Soviet Union, the European Space Agency, Japan, and the United States, the cost for each nation might become low enough for the project to be feasible. Without such cooperation, the program may remain wholly *in*feasible.

I must confess to being perplexed by those who assert that such cooperation can never be accomplished, or if it can, we will not save any money because of interface and communications problems. If this is the only way we can get to Mars, we should be devoting substantial technical, bureaucratic, and social resources to finding ways to resolve such difficulties. If the Cold War could be made to wind down, if some semblance of true democracy could be introduced in Eastern Europe, we can solve interface and communications problems.

The Standard Justifications

But beyond discussions of costs, even reduced costs, we must also identify benefits. And since there are major and valid social and environmental demands on the discretionary federal budget, it seems to me that advocates of SEI have to address whether, in the long term, it is likely to mitigate any of them. Let me list the standard set of justifications given for SEI and indicate my own sense of whether they are valid, invalid, or indeterminate: 20

Clearly, such a set of missions will enormously improve our knowledge of the planet Mars, including any results of the search for present or past life. The program is very likely to help clarify our understanding of the environment of our own planet, as robotic missions have already done; the history of our civilization shows that the unfettered pursuit of basic knowledge is the way the most significant practical advances have come about. On the other hand, it is very hard to argue that humans are essential for such a goal. Robotic missions, given high national priority and equipped with improved artificial intelligence, seem to me entirely capable of answering, as well as astronauts can, all the questions we need to ask—and at 10 percent of the cost, or less.

It is alleged that "spinoff" will occur—huge technological benefits that would otherwise not come about—thereby improving our international competitiveness and our domestic economy. But this is an old argument: Spend $75 billion to send Apollo astronauts to the Moon, and we'll throw in a free nonstick frying pan. One can clearly see that if we are after frying pans, we can invest the money directly and save almost all of that $75 billion.

The argument is specious for other reasons as well, one of which is that Teflon technology preceded Apollo. The same is true of cardiac pacemakers and other purported spinoffs of the Apollo program. But the central point here is that if there are some technologies that we urgently need, then spend the money on developing them. Why go to Mars to do it?

Then there is education, an argument that has proved very attractive in the White House. Doctorates in science peaked somewhere around the time of Apollo 11, maybe even with the proper phase lag after the beginning of the Apollo program. The cause-and-effect relationship is perhaps not demonstrated but it's not implausible. But so what? If we are interested in improving education, is going to Mars the best route? Think of what we could do with $100 billion in terms of teachers' training and salaries, school laboratories and libraries, scholarships for disadvantaged students, research facilities, and graduate fellowships. Is it really true that the best way to promote science education is to go to Mars?

Another argument is that SEI will give the military-industrial complex something approaching worthy work, thereby diffusing the temptation to use its considerable political muscle to exaggerate external threats and pump up defense funding. The other side of this coin is that by going to Mars we maintain a standby technological capacity that might be important for future military contingencies. Of course, we might simply ask those guys to do something directly useful for the civilian economy. But as we saw with Grumman buses and Boeing/Vertol commuter trains, the aerospace industry experiences real difficulty in producing competitively for the civilian economy.

There are other justifications offered for SEI. It is argued that the ultimate solution to world energy problems is to strip-mine the Moon down to a depth of a few microns, return the solar-wind-implanted Helium-3 back to Earth, and use it in fusion reactors. What fusion reactors? Even if this were possible, it is a technology 50 to 100 years away. Our energy problems need to be solved at a less leisurely pace.

Even stranger is the argument that we have to send human beings into space in order to solve the population crisis on Earth. But 250,000 more people are born than die every day—which means that we would have to launch 250,000 people per day into space to maintain the present world population. This appears to be somewhat beyond NASA's present capability.

Finally, there is a set of less tangible arguments, many of which, I freely admit, I find attractive and resonant. The idea of an emerging cosmic perspective, of understanding our place in the universe, of a highly visible program affecting our view of ourselves—this might have extremely important benefits for us in clarifying the fragility of our planetary environment and in recognizing the common peril and responsibility of all the nations and peoples of Earth. SEI would provide exciting, exploratory, adventure-rich, and hopeful prospects for young people who are ordinarily provided by the mass media and by the incompetence and corruption of politicians with the most dismal view of what their future might be.

I've mentioned the importance—somewhat diminished with the end of the Cold War, but still very great—of binding the United States and the USSR in a grand, long-term common endeavor.

And then there is the "because-it's-there" argument: Mt. Everest explored by robots would have aroused minimal public enthusiasm, but when humans first conquered it, that was another story. Maybe. But robotic technology is going to make enormous progress in the next few decades. Imagine, for example, comprehensive data from several sites on Mars used to construct a Martian virtual reality—so that many people on Earth could have the visual and tactile sensation of walking on and exploring Mars. With appropriate data processing, it is possible that robotic missions will, by 2019, generate public appeal fully competitive with human missions.

Another argument, used by President Bush, suggests that it is human destiny, manifest destiny, or maybe just American destiny to go to other worlds. Well, it's a very brave person who claims to know what is written in the book of destiny. This is essentially a religious argument, and not everyone is an adherent of this faith.

When I run through such a list and try to add up the pros and cons, bearing in mind the other urgent demands on the federal budget, to me it all comes down to this question: Can the sum of a large number of individually inadequate justifications and some powerful but intangible justifications add up to an adequate justification?

I don't think any of the items on my list of purported justifications is demonstrably worth $500 billion, certainly not in the short term. On the other hand, every one of them is worth something and if I have 10 items or so and each of them is worth $50 billion, maybe it adds up to $500 billion. If we can be clever about reducing costs and making true international partnership work, the justifications become more compelling. I don't know how to do this calculus, but it seems to me that this is the kind of issue we ought to be addressing.

Steps for the Here-and-Now

Until a national debate on this topic has transpired, until we have a better idea of the rationale and the cost/benefit ratio of SEI, what should we do? My suggestion is that we pursue R&D projects that can be justified on their own merits or their relevance to other goals and that can also contribute to human mission to Mars should we decide to go. Such an agenda would include:

- U.S. astronauts on the Soviet space station *Mir* for joint flights of gradually increasing duration, aiming at one to two years.

- Reconfiguration of the proposed U.S. space station *Freedom* to study the long-term effects of the space environment on humans, and make maximum use of knowledge gained from *Mir*.

- Early implementation of a rotating or tethered "artificial gravity" module on *Mir* or *Freedom*.

- Enhanced studies of the Sun, including a distributed set of probes in heliocentric orbit, to monitor solar activity and give the earliest possible warning to astronauts of hazardous solar flares.

- Development of a nonreusable heavy-lift vehicle. Present launchers cannot even duplicate the successes of the 1976 Viking and the 1977 Voyager missions, and the shuttle is inadequate and unsafe as the workhorse for SEI.

- U.S./Soviet and multilateral development of *Energiya* technology for the U.S. and international space programs. Although the United States is unlikely to depend primarily on a Soviet booster rocket, *Energiya* has roughly the lift of the Saturn V that sent the Apollo astronauts to the Moon. The United States let the Saturn V assembly line die, and it cannot readily be resuscitated. The USSR is eager to sell *Energiya* technology for hard currency.

- Vigorous pursuit of joint projects with NASDA (the Japanese space agency) and Tokyo University; the European Space Agency; and GLAV-COSMOS (the Soviet space agency) and the USSR Academy of Sciences; along with Canada and other nations. In many cases these should be equal partnerships, not the United States calling the shots. They could range from joint working groups for choosing landing sites on Mars to joint missions in low-Earth orbit. One of the chief objectives should be to build a tradition of cooperative competence.

- Technological development—using state-of-the-art robotics and artificial intelligence—of rovers, balloons, and aircraft for the exploration of Mars, and implementation of the first international rover/return sample mission.

- Vigorous pursuit of new technologies such as constant-thrust propulsion to get us quickly to Mars; this may be essential if the radiation or microgravity hazards make one- to two-year flight times too risky.

- Intensive study of near-Earth asteroids, which may provide preferable intermediate time-scale goals for human exploration than does the Moon.

- A greater emphasis on science—including the fundamental sciences behind space science, and the thorough reduction and analysis of data already obtained—by NASA and other space agencies.

The above recommendations add up to a tiny fraction of the full cost of SEI, but if implemented, they would help us to make accurate cost estimates and better assessment of SEI's dangers and benefits. They would permit us to maintain a vigorous pace toward human missions to Mars without prematurely commiting to the specific hardware of those missions. Most, perhaps all, of these recommendations have strong justifications, even if we were sure we were unable to send humans to any other planet in the next few decades.

In the meantime, the most important step we can take toward Mars is to make significant progress on Earth. Achieving even modest improvements in the serious social, economic, and political problems that our global civilization now faces could release enormous resources, both material and human, for furthering space exploration and other worthy goals. ▰

Reflections and Inquiries

1. How appropriate is Sagan's plan for cutting the high cost of planetary exploration, in your opinion?

2. Sagan felt that a joint U.S.–Soviet Mars exploration project (this was in 1990, before the Soviet Union fell) would improve cooperation between the two superpowers. Do you think a joint U.S.–Russian Mars exploration project would be beneficial today? If so, in what way? If not, why not?

3. What does Sagan mean by "spinoff" benefits that could result from Martian exploration?

4. Why does Sagan argue against premature commitment to a Mars exploration project? Do you agree or disagree with his reasons?

Reading to Write

Review the benefits of exploring Mars that Sagan mentions. Do you agree that they are benefits? Argue your premise in a short essay.

The Moon Shot and Congressional Critics | James L. Kauffman

The U.S. space program has always been fraught with controversy. Any kind of space venture is hugely expensive, and the odds are always fairly high of a billion-dollar project literally going up in smoke due to a technical failure. There is also the matter of practicality. Benefits from space exploration, if any, take a long time to be realized—and they can be considerable. The following selection takes us back to 1963, the last year of the Kennedy era when congressional debates over funding the hugely expensive Apollo program were taking place. Was the venture a reckless waste of tax dollars, or was the United States facing a genuine crisis (for example, in national defense or global influence?) that only a successful lunar exploration program could resolve? James L. Kauffman teaches Speech Communication at Indiana University.

Source: From Kauffman, James L. "The Moon Shot and Congressional Critics." *Selling Outer Space: Kennedy, the Media, and Funding for Project Apollo, 1961–1963.* Tuscaloosa: Univ. of Alabama P, 1994. 118–127. Reprinted by permission.

In 1963, serious criticism of Project Apollo arose within Congress for the first time. Two groups, one composed of social liberals, the other of military hawks, attacked the space program on a variety of diverse grounds, yet both groups called for a slowdown in the program's pace. Project Apollo met its greatest resistance in the Senate. On 10 May 1963 the staff of the Senate Republican Policy Committee released a report critical of the space program. It challenged the basic justifications for the moon shot and proposed that the government could better use the money to solve human problems on earth. The report's main thrust was that the program had proceeded too quickly. Calling for a slowdown in the attempt to reach the moon, the document proposed that the country would receive more value if "we take it easy and try to accomplish our ultimate purpose step by step."

The loudest and most persistent criticism of the space program in the Senate came in 1963 during the debate over NASA's appropriation bill. The critics, social liberals like J. William Fulbright (D., Ark.), Joseph S. Clark (D., Pa.), Maurine B. Neuberger (D., Ore.), and Ernest Gruening (D., Alaska) wanted to slow the program's pace, thereby saving money that could be used to solve social ills. Fulbright led the charge. He questioned the administration's "excessive emphasis on space in relation to other national programs," most notably in education and employment. Like Fulbright, Senator Ernest Gruening viewed solving the unemployment problem as crucial to the nation. He was "far more concerned" with the 5 million unemployed in the country than with landing "men on the moon at the earliest possible date." Joseph Clark, a critic, tried to dramatize the enormous cost of the lunar program by arguing that for the cost of one of Project Apollo's "Cadillac sized modules," the government could rebuild "a fair sized city from the ground up."

In 1963, Representative Louis C. Wyman (R., N.H.) and William Fulbright offered amendments to cut NASA's appropriations. Wyman proposed a $700 million reduction, cutting $550 million from Project Apollo and an additional $150 million from lunar and planetary exploration. He explained the objective of his amendment in the following way: "It will defer, it will stretch out, it will delay a moonshot program and this we should do." He called the current schedule a "crash program." The bill gained some support in the House but lost 132–47.

Fulbright, the most vocal critic in 1963, took a similar position. In offering an amendment that would cut 10 percent across the board from research and development, construction of facilities, and administrative costs, Fulbright explained that his amendment attempted to "allow time to re-evaluate the goal of trying to reach the moon in this decade and to proceed on a more deliberate and thoughtful basis." He did not object to the moon shot, he insisted. "I merely object," Fulbright announced, "to our trying to go tomorrow." The amendment lost in the Senate in a surprisingly close vote, 46–36.

The first substantive debate over Project Apollo centered around questions of political prestige and national defense. A poll of House members in early 1962 found that many believed the space program "questionable except

5

when viewed from the standpoint of the cold war," suggesting the success of administration arguments on the issue. Yet the administration had a lot of help from the congressional committees on the floor. Representative Albert Brooks (D., La.), for example, chairman of the House Committee on Science and Astronautics until his death in late 1961, opened the NASA authorization debate that year by citing the importance of the moon shot for America's prestige around the world. Brooks called the space program one of America's "strongest weapons" in the "ideological struggle with communism for the mind of man." Similarly, Representative J. Edward Roush (D., Ind.) cited checking communist expansion as justification for supporting a lunar landing. The moon shot, Roush declared, gave America a chance to "go on the offensive in a peaceful way in this great battle in the cold war." Perhaps Representative H. R. Gross (R., Iowa) best summed up the opinion of many members: "In this cold war fight with the Communists, the new battlefield is space." Thus the moon shot came to represent a test of national vitality. Losing it would greatly reduce America's prestige and influence overseas. Representative David S. King (D., Utah) characterized outer space as a "showcase" in which the world would judge the United States, while Senator Clinton Anderson (D., N.M.), who became chairman of the Aeronautical and Space Sciences Committee in 1963, argued that losing the race to the moon with the Soviets would be "disastrous" for American prestige abroad. The administration's most reliable advocate, Representative Olin E. Teague (D., Tex.), pointed to the "uncommitted" nations and what effect losing the space race would have on them. "If we flunk the space test," Teague concluded, "our prestige will dwindle away to nothing."

Critics of the moon shot, however, were not about to concede its symbolic value in the cold war. Perennial advocate of increased social programs, Senator William Fulbright attacked the lunar landing program on the grounds that "not a single nation" had succumbed to Soviet influence "because of communist successes in space." The prestige garnered from landing on the moon would be "fleeting," he insisted, and he characterized the moon mission as a "9-day wonder of history, a gaudy sideshow in the real work of the world." Only a small group of his colleagues seemed to share Fulbright's opinions. Senator Joseph Clark was among the few agreeing that there was an "immature" attitude behind the space race; he compared it to a "high-school cross-country race."

Other critics alleged that partisan politics, not national prestige, best explained President Kennedy's support for a moon shot. Representative Thomas M. Pelly (R., Wash.) suggested that Kennedy was more worried about his own prestige "since he took office." Pelly called the moon shot a "costly political stunt." Representative James D. Weaver (R., Pa.) likewise blasted the narrow political motivations of the president, insisting that the Kennedy administration challenged the Soviets to a lunar race to divert public attention away from "the fiasco of the Bay of Pigs." Kennedy, moreover, left himself and NASA open for attack about the sincerity of their earlier cold war arguments when he proposed a joint U.S.-U.S.S.R. moon mission. A joint venture would eliminate the competitive aspects of the program. Worse yet, it would also eliminate another of the advocates' main justification for a manned moon mission: national defense.

The greatest challenge to Project Apollo came in response to arguments that it would enhance the defense of the country. One can divide the members of Congress into three camps on the defense issue surrounding the program: those who supported the defense value of a moon shot, those who questioned the defense value of a moon shot and wanted to scale back the space program, and those who questioned the value of a moon shot and wanted greater emphasis placed on a military space program.

Space committee members led those defending the contribution of Project Apollo to the country's national security. Olin Teague, chairman of the House Subcommittee on Manned Space Flight, cited national security as the "most important reason for going to the moon." If America's defense did not "depend" upon a moon shot, Teague added, he would not favor the program as much as he did. When critics began challenging the moon shot in 1963, Teague impatiently insisted that more than "90 percent" of the House members "know" Project Apollo enhances national security, and "that is why most of them support it." Space committee members, such as Senator Stuart Symington (D., Mo.) and Representatives George Miller (D., Calif.), James G. Fulton (R., Pa.), Albert Brooks (D., La.), and Emilio Daddario (D., Conn.), joined Teague in justifying Project Apollo in the same terms. They argued that America could not let the Soviets, or any other hostile power, control outer space. Doing so would jeopardize America's security.

A small but vocal group in 1963 began to challenge the military value of going to the moon. Senators William Fulbright and Joseph Clark, joined by the eternal congressional gadfly Senator William Proxmire (D., Wis.), questioned the contribution that Project Apollo made to the country's security. These critics came well prepared. In addition to marshaling their own evidence from respected sources, they also cited criticisms voiced in the Senate space committee hearings but ignored in the committee's 1963 reports. Critics relied heavily on the concerns of scientists like Dr. Harold Urey and Dr. Polykarp Kush, two of the ten experts who appeared before the Senate Committee on Aeronautical and Space Sciences. During debate over NASA's appropriations in 1962 and 1963, Fulbright and Proxmire consistently challenged administration charges that the moon shot would help America's defense. In a 1962 speech, Proxmire pointed out the superiority of land-based missiles over space or moon-based missiles. Firing an object "moving at such fantastic speed in space, or even to fire from the moon," he noted, "would result in all kinds of handicaps, all kinds of limitations" not imposed on delivering the same payload from earth. Proxmire cited numerous experts to support his position: Dr. James R. Killian, president, Massachusetts Institute of Technology and former science adviser to Eisenhower; Dr. Lee A. DuBridge, president, California Institute of Technology; and Dr. Harold Brown, director, Defense

10

Research and Engineering. Not only did these men question the value of space weapons, they also questioned the military need for manned space vehicles. Proxmire went so far as to say that space spending could have an "adverse effect" on American national security.

Senator William Fulbright joined Proxmire in attacking the military rationale for the program. In a speech delivered on 19 November 1963 Fulbright called the military justification for a moon shot "minimal." Fulbright cited General Maxwell Taylor, chairman of the Joint Chiefs of Staff, and Nobel laureate Dr. Harold Urey, who said the moon shot would have no direct bearing on America's military security. Furthermore, he introduced the testimony of General Curtis LeMay, chief of staff of the air force, who viewed ground weapons as the most effective and least costly. Characterizing the manned moon mission as "not essential to the Nation's security," Fulbright, like Proxmire, called for a reduction in space spending. Senator Stuart Symington, a space booster, attempted to counter Fulbright's charges, arguing that the people in the military whom he respected the most understood the "vital importance" of space to national defense. Symington noted that the military had never been known for its "unanimous decisions" and insisted that it was not uncommon for the three military branches to have three entirely different ideas about a military issue. This argument also proved handy in answering the last group of critics the administration faced—those who agreed that Project Apollo made a minimal contribution to national defense but saw great defense potential in a different sort of program.

Since NASA's inception, a small group in Congress began calling for a greater emphasis on a military program to counter the Soviets' growing military space program. Quintessential cold warrior Senator Barry Goldwater (R., Ariz.), joined by Senator Howard W. Cannon (D., Nev.), demanded a greater emphasis on military uses of space, cautioning that the Soviets did not make a distinction between military and civilian programs. George Miller, chairman of the House space committee, defended the administration's position, declaring that "our defense officials are not dolts." Miller echoed Symington's argument that the "real cause" of the "squabble about the military in space" was an "inhouse difference of opinion in the Military Establishment." The movement for a greater military emphasis gained momentum in 1963 as six Republican congressmen attached a minority report to the report of the House Committee on Science and Astronautics calling for greater emphasis on military exploitation of inner space. During floor debates, additional members joined in pushing for a greater emphasis on inner space. James Weaver's comments typify those of the critics. America can only wage the "cold war" with the "Communists," Weaver warned, "if our space program progresses with national security as its prime goal." Frustrated with lack of support for his position, Weaver demanded that NASA administrator James Webb either realign America's space "objective" to national security or resign. Viewing the moon shot as a public relations gambit, Weaver declared that "Congress and the public can no longer tolerate public relations gimmicks and doubletalk concerning the space program and our space gap when our national security is threatened." These critics wanted national security as the first priority of America's space program. Representative Donald Rumsfeld of Illinois stated their desire clearly: "This country should direct itself toward inner space and not place our top priority in the direction of the moon."

One cannot overestimate the significance that members of Congress placed on the cold war and defense arguments in debate on the floor of Congress. The House perhaps best demonstrated its distrust of the Soviets and the depth of its cold war sentiments by passing an amendment prohibiting the administration from entering into a joint space effort without the consent of Congress. The amendment, offered by Thomas Pelly, won a narrow victory, 125–110, but it was one of the few times that the administration's space policy was flatly rejected in Congress.

Space committee members also had to defend the administration's position on the floor of Congress against attacks on the scientific value of the manned lunar program. On the floor, the scientific arguments in favor of the program were much the same as in the committees. Representative Emilio Daddario (D., Conn.) argued that the space program would contribute greatly to America's "knowledge of the basic sciences." Likewise, Senator Margaret Chase Smith (R., Maine), whose letter to Chairman Clinton Anderson prompted the committee hearings of the ten distinguished scientists in June 1963, proposed that the scientific fallout from the moon shot might surprise the country. The "valuable scientific knowledge that we gain on the way to putting a man on the moon," she conjectured, "could very well be far more significant than the end objective." Representative James Fulton even predicted that the program would create "urgent demands for more knowledge from science." Finally, George Miller, a onetime critic of the program, relied heavily on the scientific appeal, especially when the program started coming under attack in 1962. On three different occasions in 1962, Miller felt it necessary to tell fellow congressmen that the space flights were not shows or stunts but "serious scientific experiments."

Armed with testimony from many of the scientists who testified before the space committees, critics raised serious challenges to the scientific value of Project Apollo. Again, one finds Fulbright, Proxmire, Cannon, and Thomas Pelly (R., Wash.) at the forefront of the attack. Pelly, for example, questioned the scientific contribution of a manned lunar landing. "A high percentage of the scientific fraternity," Pelly proclaimed, "find fault with the Apollo program on many specific scores." He went on to cite numerous scientists, among them Dr. Philip Abelson and Nobel laureates Dr. Harold Urey and Dr. Polykarp Kush, who refuted Project Apollo's scientific contribution. Pelly concluded by advocating that the United States send instruments to the moon instead of a man, since they cost less and would gather the same amount of scientific information. Similarly, Fulbright used the testimony of distinguished scientists to challenge the scientific justifications of a moon shot. No scientists,

15

he declared, justify Project Apollo's "pace" or "cost as esential to scientific objectives."

Proxmire, supported by Cannon, went beyond merely questioning the scientific objectives of the program to argue that Project Apollo might actually hurt American science, education, and industry by stealing scientists away from those areas. America, he submitted, already suffered from a shortage of scientific manpower. Project Apollo would only exacerbate the problem. In mid-1962, Proxmire offered an amendment to NASA's appropriations bill establishing a commission to study the impact of NASA's programs on scientific manpower in the United States. Responding on behalf of the space committees, Senator Robert S. Kerr (D., Okla.) insisted that Proxmire had greatly overstated the shortage and that the president already had a commission overseeing the question of scientific manpower. The Senate rejected Proxmire's amendment 83–12.

Space boosters ultimately tried to refute the scientific criticisms of the administration's space policies by raising questions of expertise and credibility. Ken Hechler (D., W.Va.), for example, a member of the House space committee, submitted that the congressmen raising scientific objections were not "scientists" and therefore could not make an informed opinion on many aspects of the program. "Let our experts run this program," Hechler implored. "Let us not substitute our layman's judgment for theirs." Chairman Clinton Anderson attempted to denigrate the testimony of many of the scientists themselves, characterizing it as motivated by self-interest. Anderson called the disagreement among the scientific community "an understandable expression of parochial interest." Many scientists critical of the space program were upset because they wanted their disciplines to receive funding. "Any scientist worth his salt," Anderson explained, "should be an advocate for his own discipline." Thus, in one full swoop, Anderson tried to make all scientific criticism suspect. Interestingly, by Anderson's logic, one would have to assume that scientists who advocated the program also did so out of "parochial interest."

Supporters of the administration's space program encountered similar opposition when they argued that Project Apollo would stimulate the economy. Appealing to the average American by arguing that Project Apollo would create new jobs and stimulate economic growth, Olin Teague characterized the program as "stimulating employment to a degree little recognized by most people." Teague claimed that it created "millions" of jobs if one included those in education and industry along with jobs related directly to NASA. Other advocates emphasized how the moon shot would create new consumer goods and whole new industries. Albert Brooks warned that America's "economic and material well-being" depended "in no small degree" on what the country accomplished in the space program. Olin Teague metaphorically summarized the space committee's view on the economic impact of the program during the 1963 debates over NASA's authorization bill. The space program "started the blood coursing a little more fervently through the arteries of our economy," Teague stated. It started the industry's "pulse" "beating like a drum." Teague concluded by predicting that the space program would trigger a "new industrial revolution."

Critics of the administration's space program questioned the impact of the moon shot on the civilian economy. William Fulbright charged that the space program might actually "become a drain on the civilian economy," jeopardizing America's position in "world trade." He countered the notion that the moon shot would stimulate industry by pointing out that American "aerospace industries," where the country spent its billions of space dollars, did not need "stimulation." Representative Louis Wyman (R., N.H.) attacked the relationship between NASA and big business, arguing that it had become too cozy. Stating that certain businesses had a vested interest in the space program's growth, Wyman insisted that a number of the contracting companies had become "propagandists for NASA and the moonshot." Not surprisingly, the most vocal economic critic was William Proxmire. He agreed with space advocates that the program would stimulate the economy. But, he noted, it would be "bought at a stiff price in higher taxes." In 1962, Proxmire attacked NASA for its lack of competitive bidding. Warning that the lack of bidding harmed small business and led to bigger contracts and greater concentration among the few big businesses who received space contracts, Proxmire offered an amendment to the Senate appropriations bill that would force NASA to adopt more competitive bidding for its contracts. Administration space supporters Robert Kerr and Stuart Symington responded to Proxmire's charges, arguing that the amendment would cause unnecessary red tape and that only big businesses had the money necessary for the research, design, and manufacturing needed for the new space equipment. The amendment gained some support but lost 72–23.

Finally, space boosters argued on the floor of Congress that the manned   20
lunar program would have a positive impact on education in America. James Fulton advanced the education argument in mid-1963, proposing that the space program forced American universities to demand "higher scholastic achievement through greatly improved curriculums" so that its graduates would be useful to NASA, the DoD, government, and to "society as a whole." Super space booster Olin Teague concurred, calling the space program a "gigantic spur to our education system." Fulbright and Proxmire challenged the educational argument, warning that the program would only drain much needed science teachers away from the universities. The educational argument undoubtedly had great popular appeal, testifying once again to the concern in the floor debates with public justification.

Critics of the administration's manned lunar space program clearly offered serious and legitimate arguments on the merit of the program. Always armed with expert testimony, critics argued forcefully against the scientific, military, economic, and educational justifications of a manned lunar landing. Despite these objections, Congress continued to provide overwhelming support for Project Apollo, appropriating billions for the manned lunar effort from 1961 to 1963. How does one account for this? Why did the critics have so little influence? The answer may lie in the ultimate justification for the manned lunar landing during congressional floor debates: the promise of a great frontier adventure. As in the rhetoric of the Kennedy administration and the popular mass media, the frontier adventure story seemed to transcend and overwhelm debate on the merits of the Kennedy administration's plan. ◪

Reflections and Inquiries

1. Why did the Senate Republican Policy Committee criticize the plans for Project Apollo in 1963? Do you agree or disagree with their rationale?

2. Some critics accused President Kennedy of staging a costly political stunt with the Apollo program. In your opinion, to what extent did partisan politics influence Kennedy's decision to fund the Apollo program?

3. How credible is the argument that the Apollo program was important to national defense?

4. Why did many scientists at the time find fault with the Apollo program?

5. What were the arguments for and against the notion that the Apollo program would stimulate the economy?

Reading to Write

Review the negative versus positive effects of the Apollo program. Then write an essay arguing whether the program was necessary or whether the United States could have met Soviet competition in space some other way.

Research and Development for Whose Benefit?

The Relationship Between NASA and the Users of Earth Resources Data | Pamela Mack

How can the short-term or long-term benefits of government-sponsored technological developments be determined? Is it possible to screen proposed research and development projects for their likely effectiveness or ineffectiveness without resorting to blind trial and error costing U.S. taxpayers billions of dollars? In the following article, Pamela Mack, a professor of history at Clemson University and an expert in the history of technology, examines this issue in the context of the Landsat satellite program that was used for acquiring data about the earth's agricultural and geological resources.

Landsat satellites provide new information about our world by collecting data in the form of sophisticated images of the surface of Earth. These can be utilized for geology, agriculture, land-use mapping, and other resources management fields. Yet the U.S. Earth Resources Satellite Program has developed slowly, with much opposition. Five Landsat satellites have been launched since 1972, and the project has been officially declared operational and turned over to private industry. Yet today, more than twenty years after the origins of the program, its future is still uncertain. Many of the key difficulties for Landsat have arisen in the relationship between research and development and the practical use of the satellite data.

Themes

The central question for the study of government development of technology should be: what determines whether new technology will be effectively used? Effective or ineffective use of a technology has often been explained simply by technical faults or organizational problems. Rather than using just one of these factors to explain effectiveness, this study will seek to explain it on the basis of the interaction of the process of technological change with the needs and organizations that form a context for that change. The central focus is thus on how the government context affects the relationship between research and development and the use of technology.

Landsat is a particularly interesting case for such an examination of the transition from research and development to application and diffusion be-

---

Source: Mack, Pamela. "Research and Development for Whose Benefit? The Relationship Between NASA and the Users of Earth Resources Data." *A Spacefaring Nation: Perspectives on American Space History and Policy.* Eds. Martin J. Collins and Sylvia D. Fries. Washington: Smithsonian Institution Press, 1991. 207–24. Reprinted by permission.

cause the development and the use of Earth resources satellites were divided among NASA and a variety of different government agencies and other institutions. Research and development were assigned to NASA, while other agencies and organizations were the ultimate users of the technology. Landsat, like weather and communications satellites, but unlike most other space projects, required NASA to deal with users outside the agency who would put the space technology to practical use. NASA had the responsibility for research and development of space applications, but it was generally assumed that the space agency would turn over operational programs (those ready for routine use) to the agency concerned with the related application (for example, the weather bureau would take over weather satellites). Many of the controversies of the Landsat project grew out of disagreements over what voice the users should have in the development of the project and at what point it should be turned over to the users.

This division between research and development and use raised a variety of challenges. It meant that the transition from development to use could not be handled as informally as in a single institution, making it easier for the historian to examine. It also made interagency politics the major tool for mediating between the interests of the research and development team and the interests of the users. Such interagency politics can be either creative or destructive; in the case of Landsat it became destructive with the addition of pressures resulting from general political opposition to the space program in the late 1960s and 1970s. The government context thus at times meshed with the process of technological change in ways that increased the difficulty of technological innovation. Yet it is by no means clear that Landsat could have been better handled by private industry; NASA had the opportunity to develop the Landsat program to bring the most benefits rather than the most profit.

How can the interaction between technological change and the government context be broken down into more manageable pieces for analysis? Let us first look at these two elements in isolation, and then try to put the matrix together to see the interaction. For the Landsat case, technological change can be divided roughly into four stages: research and development of the satellite and of equipment on the ground to process the data coming from the satellite, testing the resulting system and developing ways of applying the new data, persuading people to use the applications, and creating a truly operational permanent system. My larger study of Landsat is concerned only with the first three stages; this paper examines in detail part of the first stage, analyzing cooperation between developers and users during the development process.[1]

The strength and weakness of a research and development agency like NASA lies in its freedom to innovate boldly. As a government agency, NASA could seek to develop a satellite system that would bring broad benefits from improved resource management, even though it was clearly not going to be quickly profitable. More specifically, because NASA was an independent research and development agency, NASA engineers had the freedom to investigate the potential of various technologies before worrying about the requirements of the users. The space agency had an interest in developing the best possible system, rather than throwing something together to meet user demands that might reflect only current expectations rather than the true potential of the technology. At its best, this approach can bring unexpected benefits from technological breakthroughs. At its worst, an independent research and development organization can end up pursuing technological sophistication for its own sake when a simpler, less expensive, system would better meet the needs of the users.

The process of bringing the technology into use can be divided into two tasks: developing applications and cultivating users. NASA had to help develop methods of applying Landsat data, in cooperation with the research and development branches of the agencies that would ultimately use the operational satellite. Some of these agencies wanted a larger role in Landsat, but NASA tended to want to keep control of the project and the design, and limit the users to the development of applications. Later on, in seeking to encourage use of the data, NASA managers learned the hard way that publicizing a new technology and funding scientific research to show its potential were not sufficient to convince organizations to adopt it for everyday use. NASA had little experience with selling new technology, and it showed. It is often assumed that this is an area where private industry would have an advantage. However, some government agencies have developed impressive skill in encouraging innovation, most notably the extension program of the Department of Agriculture. Therefore, the problem lay not in government agencies per se, but in NASA's role as a research and development agency without a clearly developed relationship with a constituency.

To look at the same story from a different perspective, it is crucial to recognize that the government context is far from monolithic; it can be viewed on a variety of levels, from philosophies of government to management policies within an agency. The word "politics" often includes not only electoral politics but also the relationships between branches and agencies of the government. Using that broad definition, there are many types of politics that affect government projects. None of these can be examined in isolation, but the emphasis of my work is on the relationships between agencies. Other studies have concentrated on other levels: a deeper treatment of the Presidential politics of the space program can be found in John M. Logsdon's *The Decision to Go to the Moon* and W. Henry Lambright's *Presidential Management of Science and Technology: The Johnson Presidency.*[2]

The broadest level of analysis shows competing philosophies of government. One nagging controversy in the Landsat project was whether the whole thing was properly a government enterprise or whether it should be left to private industry. Ideally, the government sponsored technological development for the public good when the benefits were too diffuse or too far in the future for private industry to be willing to sponsor the new technology.[3] Opinions about what fell within this definition depended on attitudes toward the relative roles of government and private industry.

The highest stage of the government hierarchy played a much smaller role in Landsat than in more expensive and popular space projects. Landsat cost only about $32 million through the launch of the first satellite, so it was too small to get much attention from the highest levels of government. What little authority was exerted over Landsat from above NASA came mostly from the President through the Office of Management and Budget, which negotiates with federal agencies their share of the budget the President proposes to Congress. The Office of Management and Budget opposed Landsat both because of a presidential policy of seeking to cut government spending and because of specific opposition at the budget bureau to Earth resources satellites. Landsat received occasional support from the presidential level when NASA appealed to Presidents Nixon and Carter to prevent devastating budget cuts. But each President who gave the project support also expected it to serve his own policy interests, whether they were improving international cooperation or diminishing the size of big government. Congress, particularly the House Subcommittee on Space Science and Applications under the leadership of Congressman Karth, gave the project more consistent support. However, Congress could not oversee the project in as much detail as could the Office of Management and Budget. Congress occasionally reversed a damaging budget cut, but NASA's top policymakers could not appeal directly for such a change because they had to be loyal to the administration that had appointed them.

Because Landsat received little attention from political decisionmakers, decisions had to be thrashed out between the interested agencies, with NASA taking a dominant role as lead agency for the project. Landsat was shaped by two kinds of interagency politics. One of the functions of government bureaucracy is to make decisions on grounds of the good of the nation, rather than just profit or technological feasibility. The process of interagency politics at its best is a process for negotiating decisions among competing priorities that use scarce resources. Because of the many interests involved, the Landsat project required a large amount of this kind of decisionmaking.

But Landsat was also influenced by another kind of interagency politics. Government agencies seek to increase their own importance by increasing their budgets and the number of projects they control (they may have to do this simply to obtain the influence necessary to achieve their broader missions), and a project can be hurt or helped by this competition for power for reasons independent of the merit of the project.[4] In an interagency project, each agency is monitored by its branch of the Office of Management and Budget and its congressional committee to determine how well that agency uses its funds to meet its own objectives. Few mechanisms exist for rewarding agencies that work together effectively toward larger goals. In the Landsat case, NASA had to deal with the different interests of the Departments of Defense, the Interior, and Agriculture, and the Office of Management and Budget. Agencies had interests

10

both in whether stress was put on the experimental or operational nature of the project and in specific technologies. For example, the Department of Defense did not want reconnaissance satellite technology revealed by civilian use; the Department of Agriculture wanted the satellite to carry the sensor most useful for agricultural research and survey. Interagency politics caused special problems for Landsat because NASA managers had little experience in working cooperatively with other agencies on practical projects.

In the Landsat project, NASA had to deal not only with other government agencies but also with a variety of organizations that the space agency hoped would eventually make practical use of Landsat data. NASA had little experience in dealing with constituencies and clients other than politicians, scientists, and the aerospace industry. NASA sponsored a variety of programs to encourage the use of Landsat data, but the agency was disappointed by the results. The interactions of technology and context are particularly clear in the case of NASA's attempt to encourage the use of Landsat data by state and local governments. Such users could give NASA valuable political support, but they were hard to convince to use Landsat data because they were particularly inexperienced with and suspicious of advanced technology. The importance of skillful technology transfer and early involvement of the users is one of the most important lessons to be learned from Landsat.

The interaction of technological change and the government context depends on historical circumstances, so the Landsat case study can only raise questions, not prove a model. It does raise two issues in particular that provide good examples of the interaction of the various stages and levels discussed above. As seen above, one central theme of the Landsat case was what influence the needs of the users had on the design of the technology. NASA was not strongly bound to user requirements by either its institutional framework or its prior experience. The interaction between the government context and technological change can be examined by asking how effectively NASA's relationship with the users provided the coordination needed for beneficial technological change.

The second issue is a related question that came up repeatedly during the   15
Landsat project: the timing of the transition from experimental to operational Earth resources satellite programs. Research groups and users not only had different priorities but also had different concepts of the process of technological change. Because NASA had responsibility for research and development but turned operational programs over to the appropriate user, the space agency had an interest in prolonging the experimental phase of a project as long as possible while the agencies that would take a project over had an interest in defining the project as operational as soon as possible. But this was not the only use to which definitions of experimental and operational phases were put. The Bureau of the Budget used a narrow definition of an experimental project to constrain Landsat by requiring that the system built be ade-

quate only to test the concept, not for routine use. In addition, the definition of the project as experimental for more than ten years scared away potential operational users and reduced the pressure to bring it into effective use. The definition of the phases of technological change thus became a tool of the conflicting interests of the organizations involved.

These issues suggest that one of the most important factors in determining the effectiveness of a new technology is how closely the goals of the developers and the definition of the stages of technological change are integrated with the needs of the users. To prove this whole proposition requires a much broader examination of the history of Landsat than is possible here. This paper will examine only one facet of the story: the relationship between the user agencies and NASA in the definition of Landsat.

User Agencies and the Origins of Landsat

Although NASA involved potential users of Earth resources satellites in the Landsat program only to the extent of supporting research at a few federal agencies, those agencies attempted, with limited success, to play a major role in the program. While the space agency depended on the user agencies for some scientific research, it did not always agree with them about what their role in the overall program should be. NASA-funded experiments generated so much enthusiasm among groups of scientists at the Department of Agriculture and the Department of the Interior about the potential of satellite data for agricultural and geological studies that the user agencies became strong lobbyists for an accelerated satellite program. The Department of the Interior took the lead in an attempt to pressure NASA to speed up the program that reflected interagency power-playing, different ideas than those held by NASA and the Department of Defense about what an Earth resources satellite should do and what technology it should use, and a sensitivity to the needs of at least a small part of the potential user community for Landsat data. Not surprisingly, NASA managers wanted to design the program with as little interference from outside as possible, but the process of interagency politics enabled some compromises to be made among conflicting interests. The question addressed here is not whether interagency politics reflected or subverted national policy, but how interagency negotiations shaped the developing Landsat project and the technology used for Landsat.

In 1963, a NASA geologist working on background work for Apollo, Peter Badgley, received authorization to investigate the use of space for Earth resources research. One of his first steps was to fund research at the agencies that could potentially use Landsat data to help fulfill their assigned missions. He transferred NASA research funds to the Departments of Agriculture and the Interior for agricultural and geological research and provided funds to the Naval Oceanographic Office to investigate using a satellite for oceanography. This last area of research was transferred from the Naval Oceanographic

Office to the National Oceanic and Atmospheric Administration when that agency was created in 1970. It led eventually to Seasat, a satellite designed for oceanographic research, launched in 1978.

Contracting with other agencies for research was standard NASA procedure. The Army Corps of Engineers and the U.S. Geological Survey had already contributed special skills to the Apollo program and had been reimbursed by NASA, so it seemed logical to call on the Departments of Agriculture and the Interior for scientific expertise in the field of Earth resources.[5] That NASA paid the departments for their services rather than bringing them in as partners in the enterprise shows that NASA considered itself solely responsible for space research and development. The departments found this arrangement useful because as operating agencies, they had difficulty funding their own advanced research. NASA's other goal was to enlist the political support of these potential beneficiaries for NASA's new applications program to help persuade the Bureau of the Budget and Congress of the value of the program.

Most of the funding provided by NASA to the Department of the Interior for Earth resources research went to one of its branches, the U.S. Geological Survey. The U.S. Geological Survey used this funding to assign a group of scientists to investigate potential applications of remote sensing from space and to determine specifications for an Earth resources satellite and additional experiments on Apollo Applications missions. In 1966 Badgley asked the Geological Survey to prepare a summary evaluation of the potential value of an Earth resources satellite for geology, cartography, and hydrology. The Geological Survey scientists reported that remote sensing from space would be very valuable in these fields and should be developed quickly.[6]

By mid-1966 the group at the Department of the Interior became impatient with NASA's lack of progress toward defining a satellite system. The leaders of this discontent were a geologist in the Geologic Division of the Geological Survey, William Fischer, and hydrologist Charles J. Robinove. NASA had been discussing Earth resources experiments for the human spaceflight program and small, medium, and large orbiting Earth resources observatories for at least a year without actually approving any project. The scientists at the Geological Survey believed that the experiments under consideration at NASA were too diverse and sophisticated; the Geological Survey group wanted a simple, useful satellite as soon as possible.

NASA managers, in the meantime, had many reasons to proceed slowly with an Earth resources satellite. Earth resources experiments for the Apollo Applications program also had to be developed, taking time and energy away from work toward an automated satellite. More importantly, NASA may have had a secret agreement with the Department of Defense or the National Security Council to go slowly on Earth resources satellites.[7] The details of this policy, if it existed, will not be available until information on reconnaissance satellites is declassified. There is, however, evidence of much discussion in late

1965 and early 1966 of what resolution could be used without classification problems.[8] This suggests that the relationship between reconnaissance satellites and Earth resources satellites was an issue at that time.

Despite this policy problem, Badgley and Leonard Jaffe, head of NASA's applications programs, were sensitive to the demand for the speedy development of an Earth resources satellite. They continued the Earth resources research program and tried to speed things up by arguing to their superiors that NASA needed to reorient itself toward practical missions.[9] By 1966 the program had a good foothold in NASA, although not a great deal of support from the agency's policy makers, and NASA scientists were aware of growing interest outside the agency. In an August 1966 memo pushing for authorization to develop a small orbiting Earth resources observatory, Badgley pointed out that the user agencies wanted an operational satellite in 1970 instead of in 1974–1975 as NASA officials intended. Badgley stressed that NASA should take a leading role in the program, including providing research funds to other agencies, because strong leadership was particularly important for a satellite that would collect data for many agencies. He pointed out that the benefits of studying Earth resources from space could help justify the space program if Earth resources experiments lived up to their promise, and that application "is an area which NASA is holding up to Congress as very promising, and one which needs strong support."[10] The same memo mentioned a fact that was to come as a shock a month later: the Geological Survey was considering asking Congress for money in fiscal year 1968 for construction of a small satellite, for a launch possibly as early as 1969. The Survey, according to Badgley, considered photographic and television sensors and the necessary communications system "to be already operational for space use" for needs in the fields of geology, hydrology, cartography, and geography.[11] Officials in the higher levels of NASA did not absorb Badgley's warning.

An August 1966 meeting of representatives from NASA (including Jaffe), the Geological Survey (including Fischer and Robinove), the Agency for International Development, the Department of Agriculture, and the Naval Oceanographic Office clearly brought out the Survey's concerns. The Geological Survey and the Agency for International Development expressed enthusiasm about using data collected from space for resources studies in Latin America. This discussion had been partially motivated by a State Department paper that suggested studying the feasibility of using a spacecraft to collect Earth resources data over South America.[12] Jaffe, with caution typical both of NASA's position and his own personality, warned "about overenthusiasm on [the] part of underdeveloped nations for new and exotic techniques, with concomitant exclusion of proven methods."[13] Fischer discussed the idea of a Department of the Interior Earth Resources Observation Satellite, based on an RCA proposal using a newly developed very-fine resolution television camera. In a memo on the meeting, Jaffe concluded that "USGS would like to budget for an 'operational' satellite as soon as possible to establish jurisdiction."[14] In other words, he suspected that the Geological Survey was making a move to insure that it would control the eventual operational satellite system. In the meeting, Jaffe suggested that the user agencies should develop data requirements; NASA would consider what sort of satellite would meet those requirements after "certain decisions" were made. Those decisions, presumably classified, were expected in September.[15] Jaffe's remarks implied a lengthy experimental phase under NASA's control, very different from the quick development of an operational satellite that the Department of the Interior wanted.

The Department of the Interior wanted to control an Earth resources satellite program both because it believed that data from such a satellite would help the agency fulfill its mission and because, like most agencies, it sought to increase its own areas of responsibility, and thus its size and power. By mid-1966 Fischer and Robinove at the Geological Survey had a good idea of what an Earth resources satellite could do and who could use it. They were frustrated by NASA's rapidly changing ideas for a variety of Earth resources satellites, without any approved project in progress. Fischer and Robinove wanted to force NASA to commit itself to building the small satellite they believed would be most useful.[16] Their first step was to go to William D. Pecora, director of the Geological Survey, with the idea that the Department of the Interior might develop its own operational Earth resources satellite. In an interview, Robinove described why Pecora liked this idea:

> Now Bill Pecora . . . recognized that this concept technically was one that, if it worked, there would be a very, very large payoff. It would be very worthwhile doing and something that would be good for the country to have this information. . . . And also being a very astute politician he recognized that if we took the leadership, the Geological Survey and the Department of the Interior stood to gain simply by being a good forward-looking agency.[17]

Fischer, Robinove, and Pecora presented the idea to the Secretary of the Interior, Stewart L. Udall, arguing that the satellite would be useful to other branches of the Department of the Interior in addition to the Geological Survey. They quickly convinced Udall of the merits of an Interior satellite program. According to Fischer, Udall may have liked the idea in part because he resented the amount of government money going to military and space programs rather than to the preservation of natural resources and undeveloped areas that he valued so highly.[18]

The enthusiasts at the Department of the Interior prepared a plan in secret, and most observers were shocked when Udall unilaterally announced on September 21, 1966, that the Department of the Interior planned a program of Earth Resources Observation Satellites (EROS). At a news conference, Pecora described EROS as an evolutionary program beginning in 1969 "with television cameras flown in an orbit that will cover the entire surface of the earth repeatedly."[19] While the proposed satellite had many of the features eventually

25

incorporated in Landsat, the announcement appears to have been largely a political move designed to accelerate NASA's program. In fact, as William Fischer remembered one reaction to the announcement: "Pecora had no more resources than the Prince of Liechtenstein with which to launch that satellite."[20]

NASA leaders were upset over Udall's announcement, nonetheless.[21] The threat they saw was typical of interagency conflict; the Department of the Interior appeared to be attempting to take over a function that clearly belonged to NASA, the development of a new satellite system. NASA's only mission was research and development; if other agencies developed their own space systems they would take away NASA's reason for being. Fischer remembered one NASA official telling an Interior official: "If you so much as used a nickel of NASA's money to write that press release I'll see you in jail."[22] The negative reaction was not limited to NASA. Willis H. Shapley, who had moved from the Bureau of the Budget to NASA in September 1965, reported that Udall was nearly fired because the Department of the Interior announcement was in conflict with national policy so secret that Udall had not been informed of it.[23] Pecora said a few years later that he, too, had feared he would lose his job.[24] At least in retrospect, however, the reaction was not entirely hostile. Many people at NASA remembered the EROS announcement as a "good friendly bureaucratic maneuver to get the guys moving and doing something instead of just talking."[25]

NASA responded through official channels. Peter Badgley's office received the Department of the Interior announcement a few days before its release, and immediately sent it up the hierarchy to NASA Administrator James E. Webb, who discussed it with President Lyndon B. Johnson on September 20.[26] An announcement by the Secretary of the Interior required a response from a high level in NASA. Deputy Administrator Robert C. Seamans Jr. wrote to Udall on September 22, presenting what appears to be a decision from above about which agency would control the program:

> At this time, I believe that all affected agencies are fully aware of the potential value of such a program as EROS and of the enthusiasm with which the Department of the Interior has approached the applications of space technology to the hard problems of natural resources measurement. NASA is anxious to work closely and effectively with your Department in developing and testing this exciting application of technology prior to the decision to establish an operational system. Since many agencies are interested in pursuing similar efforts, and since there are a number of critical considerations involved (especially in the area of international relations), NASA is being assigned "lead agency" responsibility in *experimental* space applications for civil functions.[27]

NASA was allowed to define Earth resource satellites as experimental, even though the Department of the Interior claimed that some sensors were ready for operational use. Seamans's letter stressed the experimental nature of the project, cautioning that a "careful research and development effort must precede operational systems decisions if we are to assure that performance lives up to promise."[28] Thus NASA kept control of Earth resources satellites for an experimental phase of unspecified length.

The Department of the Interior continued to press NASA for a commitment to an operational satellite as soon as possible. After a meeting with Webb, Seamans, and Jaffe, Under Secretary of the Interior Charles F. Luce wrote to Seamans:

> Our staff are quite optimistic that the state of the art has advanced to the point that we are ready for an operational system which we have called the EROS program. In staff discussions with Mr. Jaffe and his people we should be able to establish whether our optimism is justified.[29]

On October 21, 1966, Luce transmitted to Seamans performance specifications titled "Operational Requirements for Global Resource Surveys by Earth Orbital Satellites," calling for an operational system by the end of 1969.[30] These specifications were reasonable; in fact, they closely resemble those for the experimental satellite that was eventually developed. When NASA provided no immediate reply, Pecora and Fischer continued to discuss an operational satellite to be launched in 1969. When Pecora led a discussion of Earth resources satellites at a November 1966 meeting with officials from the Organization of American States, Jaffe (the NASA representative at the meeting) worried that Pecora was promising too much. Jaffe's memo on the meeting states:

> We agree on all points except whether anyone had the authority to hold out promise of an operational earth resources survey satellite as early as 1968 or 1969. Pecora took the position that since after the EROS public announcement no one specifically told them to stop, that they had every right to pursue and talk about EROS. We agreed that a policy clarification is required.[31]

The operational satellite that Pecora hoped to have in 1969 indeed turned out to be an elusive goal that has still not fully been realized today.

NASA's response to the Department of the Interior's October data specifications was written in January and officially transmitted to the department in April in the form of a letter from Seamans to Luce. It stressed the need for an experimental program, stating that: "orderly development and flight qualification and testing of subsystems and sensors in an experimental development program permit assurances that the technology base exists on which to build the operational systems."[32] The comments attached to the letter described a system that could meet the requirements, but saw the need for significant development of sensor, data storage, and data transmission technologies before they would be ready for a satellite.[33] Thus NASA defined a long research and development program.

30

The announcement of the EROS program caused NASA to accelerate its Earth resources research and development program. Although NASA officials were slow to respond to the requirements provided by the Department of the Interior in October, Interior's announcement generated wide interest in the press, forcing the space agency to show at least steady progress. For example, an article in *Technology Week* in February 1967, headlined "Earth Resources Satellite Far From Reality," pointed out that since NASA had not yet asked for any development funds, an experimental satellite could not be launched until the early 1970s.[34] Negative articles continued to appear for months. Jaffe explained to NASA Associate Administrator Homer Newell that an October 1967 article in *Aerospace Technology* "is obviously based on partial information resulting from the aftermath of the Department of Interior's EROS press release" and stated that relations with the Department of the Interior "are extremely good at the moment."[35] A draft memo from Pecora to Luce in June also stressed good relations, but explained:

> The ungracious reception by Administrator Webb of the Secretary's announcement hindered full cooperative efforts for several months. The visit to Houston by the Secretary has helped measurably to alter Mr. Webb's views. Until some helpful statement by NASA appears, the technical press will continue to refer to NASA's earlier unfavorable position.[36]

By mid-1967, the Department of the Interior and NASA had officially agreed on policy, but not necessarily on how they construed it. An Interior offer to participate in funding was met with the response that it would be discussed further "if it proves desirable to proceed with an experimental satellite system."[37] In June, Pecora wrote, "We continue to speak in terms of 'experimental system,' leaving the concept of 'operational system' for some distant time schedule."[38] The Department of the Interior described the project as a joint research and development effort. NASA simply assumed lead agency status and went ahead with the development of a satellite proposal.[39]

The group of enthusiasts at the Geological Survey felt that they had lost the battle but won the war. That is, their announcement had resulted in the acceleration of activities at NASA. They had also established the EROS program, which continued to serve as an institutional base for satellite studies at the Department of the Interior even when NASA was given responsibility for all satellite projects. However, they had also crystallized the opposing interests of some of the other agencies potentially involved by pushing for control of an operational Earth resources satellite. The Department of Agriculture had an equally valid interest in the program. This point became significant quickly, particularly when the time came to choose the sensors for the satellite.

Conclusions

The conflicting interests of the participating agencies were a fundamental problem visible from the beginning of the Landsat project. NASA defined its interest as control of the experimental phase of the project and tended to see this phase as a long, incremental process of development. The user agencies wanted an operational satellite as soon as possible, so that they could justify their interest by using the data in the routine execution of the missions they had been given by Congress. Even the Department of Defense was apparently involved, struggling behind the scenes to protect its interests by keeping the reconnaissance satellite program free from controversy. Obviously, an understanding of the relationship between NASA and the user agencies requires a broader examination of the Landsat project than space has allowed here. But this portion of the story can suggest that the Landsat project suffered from lack of creative management of the unavoidable tensions between developers and users of technology.[40] In various forms those tensions have caused many of the problems that have reduced the effective use of Earth resources satellite technology in the United States.

Notes

1. This paper is based on my larger study, *Viewing the Earth: The Social Construction of the Landsat Satellite System* (Cambridge: MIT Press, 1990).

2. John M. Logsdon, *The Decision to Go to the Moon: Project Apollo and the National Interest* (Cambridge: MIT Press, 1970); W. Henry Lambright, *Presidential Management of Science and Technology: The Johnson Presidency* (Austin: University of Texas Press, 1985). For more general information on NASA management, not focused on the highest political level, see Arnold S. Levine, *Managing NASA in the Apollo Era* (Washington, D.C.: NASA SP-4102, 1982).

3. The classic example is weather forecasts, which are subsidized by the government because they provide widespread benefits. Those benefits are diffuse in the sense that they are difficult to measure and it would be impossible to fund the weather bureau by charging fees to the individuals who benefit from better forecasts. More formally, the concept of public good has many different definitions, as illustrated in Glendon Schubert, *The Public Interest: A Critique of the Theory of a Political Concept* (Glencoe: The Free Press, 1960). My working definition, which I think follows the most common usage at NASA, is that the public good is the long-range benefit of the society, balancing the interests of organized and unorganized interest groups, as opposed to the short-range benefit of industry or other individual interest groups. (Professor Schubert would probably characterize this definition as somewhere between social engineering and psychological realism.)

4. A strongly stated and useful discussion of the effect of agency self-interest on Landsat can be found in W. Henry Lambright, "ERTS: Notes on a 'Leisurely' Technology," *Public Science* (August/September 1973): 1–8.

5. Homer E. Newell to Dr. Thomas B. Nolan, Jan. 19, 1975; "SM Reading file" folder, box 52, accession 74-663, record group 255, Washington National Records Center.

6. Interview with Charles J. Robinove, EROS Program Office, Reston, VA, July 31, 1978. "EROS Program—Issue Paper," attachment to David S. Black to James E. Webb, November 21, 1967; "Related Sciences 3, ERTS/EROS, NASA/Interior Collaboration," 77-0677 (33), RG 255, WNRC.

7. Interview with Willis H. Shapley, American Association for the Advancement of Science, Washington, D.C., August 13, 1979.

8. Edward Z. Gray to Director, Manned Space Science, "Pete Badgley's White Paper on Remote Sensing," October 18, 1965; Peter C. Badgley to Deputy Director, Space Applications Programs and Director of Meteorology, "Guidelines for Meeting with DOD Relative to Geography Program," March 30, 1966; "Response to Supplementary Questions Raised by Associate Deputy Administrator in Connection with Schultze (BoB) Letter to Webb Re FY '68 Budget Backup Materials," March 30, 1966; all in "Documentation—Earth Resources" folder, History Office, NASA Headquarters.

9. Leonard Jaffe to the record, "Commentary Delivered by Mr. Leonard Jaffe at the Airlie House Planning Seminar, June 1966," July 8, 1966; biography file on Leonard Jaffe, History Office, NASA Headquarters; Peter C. Badgley to the record, "Relative Funding Support by NASA and the Earth Resources User Agencies Over the Next Several Years," August 10, 1966; "Documentation—Earth Resources" folder, History Office, NASA Headquarters.

10. Badgley, "Relative Funding Support . . ." August 10, 1966.

11. Ibid.

12. "Space Applications Program, May 23, 1967," program review document; Donald P. Rogers's files, NASA Headquarters.

13. Robert G. Reeves to the Record, "Meeting at the U.S. Geological Survey (USGS), 10 am, August 25, 1966," August 31, 1966; "Documentation—Earth Resources" folder, History Office, NASA Headquarters.

14. Leonard Jaffe to the Deputy Administrator, "Meeting at the U.S. Geological Survey, August 25, 1966, Regarding Remote Sensing and South America," September 6, 1966; "Documentation—Earth Resources" folder, History Office, NASA Headquarters.

15. Reeves, "Meeting at the U.S. Geological Survey . . ." August 31, 1966.

16. Robinove interview. Interview with William Fischer, EROS Program Office, Reston, Virginia, August 8, 1978.

17. Robinove interview.

18. Fischer interview.

19. Office of the Secretary, U.S. Department of the Interior, News Release, "Earth's Resources to be Studied from Space," September 21, 1966; "EROS Program—Creation" folder, EROS Program Office files.

20. Fischer interview.

21. Ibid.

22. Ibid.

23. Shapley interview.

24. Charles P. Boyle to John F. Clark, "Highlights of NASA Hearing Before the House Subcommittee on Space Science and Applications, March 19, 1969," March 20, 1969; "ERS, ERTS" folder, Information Processing Division Files, Goddard Space Flight Center.

25. Interview with Marvin Holter, ERIM, Ann Arbor, Michigan, May 15, 1981.

26. Peter C. Badgley to the record, "Interior Department News Release on Earth Resources Observation Satellite (EROS)," September 29, 1966; "Documentation—Earth Resources" folder, History Office, NASA Headquarters.

27. Robert C. Seamans Jr. to Stewart L. Udall, September 22, 1966; "Related Sciences 3, ERTS/EROS, NASA/Interior Collaboration" folder, History Office, NASA Headquarters.

28. Ibid.

29. Charles F. Luce to Robert C. Seamans Jr., October 7, 1966; "Related Sciences 3, ERTS/EROS, NASA/Interior Collaboration" folder, 77-0677 (33), RG 255, WNRC.

30. Charles F. Luce to Robert C. Seamans Jr., October 21, 1966, with attachment "Operational Requirements for Global Resource Surveys by Earth-Orbital Satellites: EROS Program," "Related Sciences 3, ERTS/EROS, NASA/Interior Collaboration" folder, 77-0677 (33), RG 255, WNRC.
31. Leonard Jaffe to the record, "Meeting at Organization of American States (OAS) on Applicability of Remote Sensor Satellite Programs for Latin America, November 3, 1966," November 15, 1966; "Landsat 1 Documentation" folder, History Office, NASA Headquarters.
32. Robert C. Seamans Jr., to Charles F. Luce, April 7, 1967; "Landsat 1 Documentation" folder, History Office, NASA Headquarters.
33. "Specific Comments on October 21 Letter From C. F. Luce to R. C. Seamans," January 14, 1967, attachment to Robert C. Seamans Jr. to Charles F. Luce, April 7, 1967; "Landsat 1 Documentation" folder, History Office, NASA Headquarters.
34. John Rhea, "Earth Resources Satellite Far From Reality," *Technology Week* 20 (February 13, 1967): 34–37.
35. L. Jaffe to Dr. Newell, "Article on the Earth Resources Satellite in *Aerospace Technology*, October 9 Issue," October 13, 1967; "Related Sciences 3, ERTS/EROS, NASA/Interior Collaboration" folder, 77-0677 (33), RG 255, WNRC.
36. W. T. Pecora to the Under Secretary, "Status of EROS Program," June 15, 1967; William Fischer's Significant Documents file, EROS Program Office.
37. Charles F. Luce to Robert C. Seamans Jr., April 24, 1967; "Related Sciences 3, ERTS/EROS, NASA/Interior Collaboration" folder, 277-0677 (33), RG 255, WNRC. Robert C. Seamans to Charles F. Luce, June 1, 1967; William Fischer's Significant Documents file, EROS Program Office.
38. Pecora, "Status of EROS Program," June 15, 1967.
39. Stewart L. Udall to James E. Webb, September 9, 1967; James E. Webb to Stewart L. Udall, December 1, 1967; both in "Landsat 1 Documentation" folder, History Office, NASA Headquarters.
40. For a comparison of Landsat with communications and weather satellites see Pamela E. Mack, "Satellites and Politics: Weather, Communications, and Earth Resources," in *A Spacefaring People: Perspectives on Early Space Flight*, ed. Alex Roland (Washington, D.C.: NASA SP-4405, 1985). ◼

Reflections and Inquiries

1. What was controversial about the Landsat project? What steps were taken to resolve the controversy?

2. What are the four stages of technological change that Mack identifies in the context of the Landsat project? Can these stages be applied in other technological contexts? Give at least one other example.

3. Why does Mack call NASA's freedom to innovate boldly a weakness as well as a strength? Does she convince you? Why or why not?

4. To what extent did the needs of the users influence the design of the Landsat project?

Reading to Write

Write a paper analyzing NASA's use of its funding for space exploration. Aim for a balanced report: ineffective uses as well as effective ones. Use the Internet to locate more up-to-date information than what Mack provides.

Space: You Can't Get There from Here | Neil de Grasse Tyson

People who dream about space as the "last frontier" that promises unending adventure and discovery may not pause to consider expense. In the following article, Neil de Grasse Tyson, an astronomer and director of New York City's Hayden Planetarium, reconsiders the likelihood of space exploration in terms of its prohibitive costs. Tyson is the author of *Just Visiting This Planet* (1998).

From listening to space enthusiasts talk about space travel, or from watching blockbuster science fiction movies, you might think that sending people to the stars is inevitable and will happen soon. Reality check: It's not and it won't—the fantasy far outstrips the facts.

A line of reasoning among those who are unwittingly wishful might be, "We invented flight when most people thought it was impossible. A mere sixty-five years later, we went to the Moon. It's high time we journeyed among the stars. The people who say it isn't possible are ignoring history."

My rebuttal is borrowed from a legal disclaimer often used by the investment industry: "Past performance is not an indicator of future returns." Analysis of the problem leads to a crucial question: What does it take to pry money out of a population to pay for major initiatives? A quick survey of the world's famously funded projects reveals three common motivations: praise of person or deity, economics, and war. Expensive investments in praise include the Great Pyramids, the Taj Mahal, and opulent cathedrals. Expensive projects launched in the hope of economic return include Columbus's voyage to the New World and Magellan's round-the-world voyage. Expensive projects with military or national defense incentives include the Great Wall of China, which helped keep out the Mongols; the Manhattan Project, which designed and built the first atomic bomb; and the Apollo space program.

When it comes to extracting really big money from an electorate, pure science—in this case, exploration for its own sake—doesn't rate. Yet during the 1960s, a prevailing rationale for space travel was that space was the next frontier; we were going to the Moon because humans are innate explorers. In

Source: Tyson, Neil de Grasse. "Space: You Can't Get There from Here." *Natural History* Sept. 1998: 74–78. Reprinted with permission from *Natural History,* September 1988. Copyright the American Museum of Natural History.

President Kennedy's address to a joint session of Congress on May 25, 1961, he waxed eloquent on the need to reach the next frontier. The speech included these oft-quoted lines:

> I believe that this nation should commit itself to achieving the goal, before the decade is out, of landing a man on the moon and returning him safely to the earth. No single space project in this period will be more impressive to mankind, or more important for the long-range exploration of space; and none will be so difficult or expensive to accomplish.

These words inspired the explorer in all of us and reverberated throughout the decade. But nearly all of the astronauts were being drawn from the military—a fact I could not reconcile with the rhetoric.

Only a month before Kennedy's Moon speech, Soviet cosmonaut Yuri   5
Gagarin had become the first human to be launched into Earth orbit. In a rarely replayed portion of the same address, Kennedy adopts a military posture:

> If we are to win the battle that is now going on around the world between freedom and tyranny, the dramatic achievements in space which occurred in recent weeks should have made clear to us all, as did Sputnik in 1957, the impact of this adventure on the minds of men everywhere who are attempting to make a determination of which road they should take.

Had the political landscape been different, Americans (Congress in particular) would have been loath to part with the money (more than $200 billion in 1998 dollars) that accomplished the task. In spite of Kennedy's persuasive phrases, the debates that followed on the floor of Congress demonstrated that funding for Apollo was not a foregone conclusion.

A trip to the Moon through the vacuum of space had been in sight, even if technologically distant, ever since 1926, when Robert Goddard perfected liquid-fuel rockets. This advance in rocketry made flight possible without the lift provided by air moving over a wing. Goddard himself realized that a trip to the Moon was finally possible but that it might be prohibitively expensive. "It might cost a million dollars," he once mused.

Calculations that were possible the day after Isaac Newton introduced his law of universal gravitation show that an efficient trip to the Moon—in a craft escaping Earth's atmosphere at a speed of seven miles per second and coasting the rest of the way—takes about a day and a half. Such a trip has been taken only nine times—all between 1968 and 1972. Otherwise, when NASA sends astronauts into "space," a crew is launched into Earth orbit a few hundred miles above our 8,000-mile-diameter planet. Space travel, this isn't.

What if you had told John Glenn, after his historic three orbits and successful splashdown in 1962, that in thirty-seven years, NASA was going to send him into space once again? You can bet he would never have imagined that the best we could offer was to send him into Earth orbit again.

Space. Why can't we get there from here?

Let's start with money. If we can send somebody to Mars for less than $100   10 billion, then I say, let's go for it. But I have a friendly bet with Louis Friedman, the executive director of the Planetary Society (a membership-funded organization founded by the late Carl Sagan, and others, to promote the peaceful exploration of space), that we are not going to Mars any time soon. More specifically, I bet him that there will be no funded plan by any government before the year 2005 to send a manned mission to Mars. I hope I am wrong. But I will only be wrong if the cost of modern missions is brought down considerably, compared with those of the past. The following note on NASA's legendary spending habits was forwarded to me by a Russian colleague:

> THE ASTRONAUT PEN
> During the heat of the space race in the 1960s, the U.S. National Aeronautics and Space Administration [NASA] decided it needed a ballpoint pen to write in the zero gravity confines of its space capsules. After considerable research and development, the Astronaut Pen was developed at a cost of approximately $1 million U.S. The pen worked and also enjoyed some modest success as a novelty item back here on earth. The Soviet Union, faced with the same problem, used a pencil.

Unless there is a reprise of the geopolitical circumstances that dislodged $200 billion for space travel from taxpayers' wallets in the 1960s, I will remain unconvinced that we will ever send *Homo sapiens* anywhere beyond Earth's orbit. I quote a Princeton University colleague, J. Richard Gott, a panelist who spoke a few years ago at a Hayden Planetarium symposium that touched upon the health of the manned space program: "In 1969, [space flight pioneer] Wernher von Braun had a plan to send astronauts to Mars by 1982. It didn't happen. In 1989, President George Bush promised that we would send astronauts to Mars by the year 2019. This is not a good sign. It looks like Mars is getting farther away!"

To this I add that, as we approach the millennium, the only correct prediction from the 1968 sci-fi classic *2001: A Space Odyssey* is that things can go wrong.

Space is vast and empty beyond all earthly measure. When Hollywood movies show a starship cruising through the galaxy, they typically show points of light (stars) drifting past like fireflies at a rate of one or two per second. But the distances between stars in the galaxy are so great that for these spaceships to move as indicated would require traveling at speeds up to 500 million times faster than the speed of light.

The Moon is far away compared with where you might go in a jet airplane, but it sits at the tip of your nose compared with anything else in the universe. If Earth were the size of a basketball, the Moon would be the size of a softball some ten paces away—the farthest we have ever sent people into space. On this scale, Mars (at its closest) is a mile away. Pluto is 100 miles away. And Proxima Centauri, the star nearest to the Sun, is a half million miles away.

Let's assume money is no object. In this pretend-future, our noble quest to   15
discover new places and uncover scientific truths has become as effective as
war for drumming up funds. If a spaceship sustained the speed needed to escape Earth—seven miles per second—a trip to the nearest star would last a
long and boring 100,000 years. Too long, you say? Energy increases as the
square of your speed, so if you want to double your speed, you must invest
four times as much energy. A tripling of your speed requires nine times as
much energy. No problem. Let's just assemble some clever engineers who will
build us a spaceship that can magically summon as much energy as we want.

How about a spaceship that travels as fast as *Helios B*, the U.S.-German solar probe that was the fastest-ever unmanned space probe? Launched in 1976, it
was clocked at nearly 42 miles per second (150,000 miles per hour) as it accelerated toward the Sun. (Note that this is only one-fiftieth of one percent of the
speed of light.) This craft would cut the travel time to the nearest star down to a
mere 15,000 years—three times the length of recorded human history.

What we really want is a spaceship that can travel near the speed of light.
How about 99 percent the speed of light? All you would need is 700 million
times the energy that thrust the Apollo astronauts on their way to the Moon.
Actually, that's what you would need if the universe were not described by
Einstein's special theory of relativity. But as Einstein correctly predicted, while
your speed increases, so too does your mass, forcing you to spend even more
energy to accelerate your spaceship to near the speed of light. A back-of-the-
envelope calculation shows that you would need at least 10 billion times the
energy used for our Moon voyages.

No problem. These are very clever engineers we've hired. But now we
learn that the closest star known to have planets is not Proxima Centauri but
one that is about fifteen light-years away. Einstein's theory of special relativity
shows that, while traveling at 99 percent of the speed of light, you will age at
only 14 percent the pace of everybody back on Earth, so the round-trip for you
will last not thirty years but about four. On Earth, however, thirty years actually do pass by, and everybody has forgotten about you.

The distance to the Moon is 10 million times greater than the distance
flown by the original *Wright Flyer,* built by the Wright brothers. But the Wright
brothers were two guys with a bicycle repair shop. *Apollo 11*, the first moon
landing, was two guys with $200 billion and ten thousand scientists and engi-
neers and the mandate of a beloved, assassinated president. These are not
comparable achievements. The cost and effort of space travel are a consequence of space's being supremely hostile to life.

You might think that the early explorers had it bad, too. Consider Gonzalo   20
Pizarro's 1540 expedition from Quito across Peru in search of the fabled land
of oriental spices. Oppressive terrain and hostile natives ultimately led to the
death of half Pizarro's expedition party of more than 4,000. In classic account
of this ill-fated adventure, *History of the Conquest of Peru*, William H. Prescott
describes the state of the expedition party a year into the journey:

> At every step of their way, they were obliged to hew open a passage with their axes, while their garments, rotting from the effects of the drenching rains to which they had been exposed, caught in every bush and bramble, and hung about them in shreds. Their provisions spoiled by the weather, had long since failed, and the live stock which they had taken with them had either been consumed or made their escape in the woods and mountain passes. They had set out with nearly a thousand dogs, many of them of the ferocious breed used in hunting down the unfortunate natives. These they now gladly killed, but their miserable carcasses furnished a lean banquet for the famished travelers.

On the brink of abandoning all hope, Pizarro and his men built from scratch a boat large enough to take half the remaining men along the Napo River in search of food and supplies:

> The forests furnished him with timber; the shoes of the horses which had died on the road or had been slaughtered for food, were converted into nails; gum distilled from the trees took the place of pitch; and the tattered garments of the soldiers supplied a substitute for oakum. . . . At the end of two months, a brigantine was completed, rudely put together, but strong and of sufficient burden to carry half the company.

Pizarro transferred command of the makeshift boat to Francisco de Orellana, a cavalier from Trujillo, and stayed behind to wait. After many weeks, Pizarro gave up on Orellana and returned to the town of Quito, taking yet another year to get there. Pizarro later learned that Orellana had successfully navigated his boat down the Napo River to the Amazon and, with no intention of returning, had continued along the Amazon until he emerged in the Atlantic. Orellana and his men then sailed to Cuba, where they subsequently found safe transport back to Spain.

Does this story* have any lessons for would-be star travelers? Suppose one of our spacecraft with a shipload of astronauts crash-lands on a distant, hostile planet—the astronauts survive, but the spacecraft is totaled. The crew adopts the spirit of our sixteenth-century explorers. Problem is, hostile planets tend to be considerably more dangerous than hostile natives. The planet might not have air. And what air it does have may be poisonous. And if the air is not poisonous, the atmospheric pressure may be 100 times higher than on Earth. If the pressure is okay, then the air temperature may be 200° below zero. Or 500° above zero. None of these possibilities bode well for our astronaut explorers, but perhaps they can survive for a while on their reserve life-support system. Meanwhile, all they would need to do is mine the planet for raw materials; build another spacecraft from scratch, along with its controlling computers

---

*I thank Steve Napear, deputy director of the San Diego Supercomputing Center, for calling my attention to the Pizarro story and its relation to the challenges of space travel.

(using whatever spare parts are musterable from the crash site); build a rocket fuel factory; launch themselves back into space; and then fly back home.

I needn't dwell on the absurdity of this scenario.

Perhaps what we really need to do is to engineer life-forms that can survive the stress of space and still conduct scientific experiments. Actually, such "life" forms have already been created. They are called robots. You don't have to feed them. They don't need life support. And most importantly, they won't be upset if you don't bring them back to Earth. People, however, generally want to breathe, eat, and eventually come home.

It's probably true that no city has yet held a ticker-tape parade for a robot. But it's probably also true that no city has ever held a ticker-tape parade for an astronaut who was not the first (or the last) to do something or go somewhere. Can you name the two *Apollo 16* astronauts who walked on the Moon? Probably not. It was the second-to-last moon mission. But I'll bet you have a favorite picture of the cosmos taken by the orbiting robot known as the *Hubble Space Telescope*. I'll bet you remember the images from the Mars robotic lander, *Pathfinder*, and its deployed rover, *Sojourner*, which went "six-wheeling" across the Martian terrain. I'll further bet you remember the *Voyager*'s images of the Jovian planets and their zoo of moons from the early 1980s.

In the absence of a few hundred billion dollars in travel money, and in the   25
presence of hostile cosmic conditions, what we need is not wishful thinking and science fiction rhetoric inspired by a cursory reading of the history of exploration. What we need, but may never have, is a breakthrough in our scientific understanding of the structure of the universe, so that we might exploit shortcuts through the space-time continuum—perhaps through wormholes that connect one part of the cosmos to another. Then, once again, reality will become stranger than fiction. ◢

Reflections and Inquiries

1. What made the public so supportive of the Apollo program despite its formidable expense? In your opinion, would the public today be as supportive for a human mission to Mars or beyond? Why or why not?

2. What might be done to at least partially cut costs in a space program?

3. What has been Hollywood's take on the plausibility of interstellar exploration? What is the actual likelihood of travel to the stars?

4. Why would an actual interstellar voyage be virtually impossible to fund, even if the technology were available?

5. What would be the most feasible way of exploring space, according to Tyson? Do you agree or disagree? Why?

Reading to Write

Argue whether the enormous expense involved in space exploration is worth it. Can such expense be justified as a worthy investment? In what? What suggestions regarding less costly (though more technologically sophisticated) ventures that Tyson makes seem worth pursuing, if any?

What Should We Do with the Moon? | Fred Guterl

Strange as it sounds, manned lunar exploration is both a part of American history—a series of expeditions took place nearly forty years ago—and an activity for the future. Should we colonize the moon? Use it as a platform for missions to Mars and beyond? Use it as a scientific research station? Mine its natural resources? In the following article, Fred Guterl, a science writer and senior editor of *Discover* magazine, examines these endeavors and the steps being taken to achieve them.

Shortly after the National Aeronautics and Space Administration was formed in 1958, its engineers began visiting elementary schools in the leafy suburbs of Washington, D.C., to practice inspirational speeches in front of kids. The space program hadn't yet hardened into a race against the Soviets. It was still pictured as a journey of exploration, one that would eventually lead to colonizing first the moon, then Mars and the rest of the solar system. At least, that's the way Gregory Bennett remembers the message the NASA guys gave to his third-grade class.

From that day on, Bennett was wedded to the space program. The Mercury shots thrilled him. Gemini entranced him. But nothing beat Apollo. It wasn't just Neil Armstrong's "small step for man" or the *Apollo 13* cliff-hanger. The missions opened up spectacular vistas of an alien world, culminating in 1972 with Eugene Cernan and Harrison "Jack" Schmitt's 18-mile, 22-hour jaunt throughout the breathtaking Taurus-Littrow Valley, just southeast of the Sea of Serenity, a 3.7-billion-year-old, 350-mile-wide lava-flooded valley.

But then Cernan and Schmitt parked their *Apollo 17* rover, walked up the steps of their lunar module, sealed the door, and blasted off back to Earth. With the lack of atmosphere, it would have taken only a few minutes for the dust kicked up by their rocket exhaust to settle on the equipment they left behind. But once covered, it lay there undisturbed, a lunar version of Miss Havisham's wedding cake. It lies there still.

Source: Guterl, Fred. "What Should We Do with the Moon?" *Discover* Sept. 1998: 73–84. Fred Guterl/© 1998. Reprinted with permission of *Discover* magazine.

Over the passing decades, Bennett has grown into a man with thinning hair and a full beard and the gentle mien of a giant plush bear. Now he is in his late forties, and on a typical day he can be found in meetings at NASA's Johnson Space Center in Houston. The photo ID hanging from his neck identifies him as an employee of Boeing, NASA's primary contractor for the International Space Station, where he is senior principal engineer for extravehicular activity (EVA) operations. In other words, when it comes to figuring out how astronauts are going to assemble the station, Bennett is the Man. He gives the impression of being one of those fortunate souls who gets paid for having fun. This good nature, however, masks a decades-long grudge.

"Apollo was worse than an anticlimax," he says. "It showed that space is   5
nothing but a political football, which it always was. Building space colonies was never on NASA's shopping list." Bennett tries to propel these lines with vitriol, but he can't muster very much. He is not a bitter man. He loves his day job. And even though it does little to satisfy his longing for the moon, there's always his other identity to fall back on. On evenings and weekends, Bennett is one of the leaders of what you might call a lunar underground, a group called the Artemis Society, which is bent on circumventing the politics and bureaucracy of NASA and striking out on its own for the moon. Bennett probably knows more than anyone how this might be done; he has written hundreds, maybe thousands, of pages of plans, and he is the unlikely chief executive of a commercial company, Lunar Development Corporation, empowered to execute them. "I figure we can put a man on the moon for about $1.5 billion," he says matter-of-factly. After an awkward silence, he adds: "We're going to do it. We are going to the moon."

Bennett and his cohorts are not the only ones packing their bags. After decades of neglect, the moon is once again becoming an object of human enterprise. Suddenly, just about everybody, it seems, is trying to get there, including a motley collection of entrepreneurs and dreamers here in the United States.

Everyone, that is, except NASA. The only people who have ever gotten us to the moon have no interest in going back: they have their hands full with the space station, and their eyes cast in the direction of Mars. With NASA on the sidelines, and with no cold war in sight, those listening to Bennett's pitch could be forgiven for wondering how a new lunar program might be structured and who, in this day of budget cuts and belt-tightening, would be willing to pay for it. And why?

☑   ☑   ☑

Wendell Mendell attended the Twenty-Ninth Lunar and Planetary Science Conference last March at the Johnson Space Center, as he has attended just about every moon conference since the mid-1960s, when he was a planetary scientist for the Apollo missions. Mendell, whose thin white beard makes him look like a wizened garden gnome, still works for JSC's Planetary Science

Branch, and he is one of the leading advocates for putting people on the moon. He also knows firsthand how difficult it is to get the lunar bandwagon rolling.

Back in the early 1980s, Mendell and his colleagues spurred NASA-affiliated engineers and scientists to think about and plan a return mission to the moon. The result was the first Lunar Base Symposium in Washington, D.C., in 1984. Momentum flagged after the *Challenger* explosion in 1986 but picked up again in 1989 when President Bush made a Kennedyesque speech challenging NASA to go to Mars. NASA responded with a 30-year plan that used the space station and the moon as starting points. Unfortunately, the price tag—$500 billion to $600 billion—triggered the gag reflex in Congress.

But Mendell has quietly continued to plug the moon, writing articles such as "Lunar Base—Why Ask Why?" He wants to go not for national pride but for another equally old-fashioned reason: knowledge. The moon has much to teach us, he says, about the origins of the solar system. "Fifty years ago, if you looked at Lake Manicouagan in Quebec on a map and remarked that it was awfully round, scientists would have told you that it is a crypto-volcano—a volcano crater with no apparent volcano. In those days, everything was a volcano. Now we know it's an impact site—we understand that terrestrial processes are altered by the space environment. In this sense, the moon is a geologic time machine. It underwent some of the processes that Earth underwent, but then it just stopped. It is a record of the early days of the solar system, just waiting to be read."

So far scientists don't know much more than the broad outlines of that history. Even the moon's origin is far from being settled. Over the past 15 years, many have come to agree with the so-called Big Whack theory, which holds that about 4.5 billion years ago a rogue planet roughly three times the size of Mars collided with Earth. Most of the asteroid broke apart or vaporized and wound up being incorporated into Earth, while chunks of Earth vaporized, cooled, and coalesced into the moon. This would account for the moon's seemingly being made of the same material as Earth's mantle, why Earth and the moon spin about each other with more angular momentum than any other planet-moon system, and why the moon appears to have no iron-rich core. It also explains the relative dearth of lunar "volatiles"—materials, such as hydrogen, helium, and water, that have low boiling points and that a collision would have vaporized. But the Big Whack theory still has many loose ends that only a trip to the moon could tie up.

At NASA these days, however, Mendell and his colleagues are voices in the wilderness. When it comes to sending people to space, the moon is still pretty low on NASA's list of priorities—far below Mars, for example. But wouldn't the moon be a good place to practice getting to Mars? "On Mars, you'd need a technology that can go for three years without maintenance," says Mendell. "You need to develop a lot of know-how. And if you miss a launch, you have to wait 26 months for another. Sure, you can put people in

10

Antarctica and pretend they're on Mars, but psychologically the moon is much better preparation, and psychology is important in determining how people can live in space."

John Connolly, an engineer in NASA's Exploration Office, doesn't rule out a trip to the moon. "Some people think we'll never get to Mars without first going to the moon," he says. "Others think it would just get in the way, sucking up money that should go toward getting us to our ultimate destination. I tend to be somewhere in the middle. But the scientific rationale for going back is not sufficient. Frankly, moon bases aren't even on our radar screen. We've looked into them, and you could design one, but the question is, why would you even want it? The only reason you'd want to go to the moon is to verify things you'd need to go to Mars."

Even if we could do it on a shoestring—say, for $1.5 billion, about 1 percent of what Apollo cost, adjusted for inflation—Connolly doesn't think it would fly at NASA. "There are very few things we'll spend a billion dollars on just because they're cool," he says.

A casual stroll through the meeting rooms at the Lunar and Planetary   15
Science Conference revealed a similar bias: lively, packed sessions devoted to the *Mars Global Surveyor,* to the meteorites that may or may not harbor signs of Martian life, and to images of Jupiter and its liquid moon Europa. The handful of sessions on the moon, by contrast, were sparsely attended and vaguely melancholy. After all, how excited can you get about new ways to interpret 25-year-old moon rocks? There was one glaring exception, though: the summary of data from the *Lunar Prospector* orbiter.

Back in January, only weeks before the conference convened, the probe had arrived in lunar orbit and started making detailed maps of the surface. The biggest jewel in a treasure trove of scientific data was the first incontrovertible evidence of water on the moon—about a billion tons of it, more even than moonstruck optimists had expected.

To be sure, water on the moon is a great scientific find and gives evidence of impacts by primordial water-bearing comets. A comet striking the moon would have vaporized, cooled, and settled onto the surface as frost. The sun's powerful rays would have evaporated most of it, except for a few deposits in deep craters at the poles, where steep walls would have blocked the almost horizontal sunlight.

But even scientists are more excited by the practical implications of water for future moon colonies. Not only is it essential for survival, but its constituent elements, hydrogen and oxygen, happen to make the most potent of rocket fuels.

Water on the moon has given the lunar underground a fillip. "Primarily, the existence of water opens people's minds to going to the moon," says Alan Binder. "It doesn't seem like such a foreign place. It's like finding gold. California could have been settled without the gold rush, but it sure helped."

Binder is a dapper, white-haired 58-year-old who usually wears a pinstripe   20
suit, and for good reason. He has potential investors to impress. A planetary
scientist turned entrepreneur, Binder was the driving force behind the scrappy,
650-pound *Prospector* orbiter, which, costing less than $63 million to design,
build, launch, and maintain from the ground, definitely abides by NASA's
"faster, better, cheaper" dictum. The orbiter itself is a model of thrift and mod-
esty. It is small—it has only five instruments on it, short of the dozen or so
needed to map the whole surface—but that made it easier to launch cheaply.
"We could have done the job in one payload," says Binder, "but we decided to
get it done in bits and pieces. So we'll need to send up three more payloads."

Binder had been trying to piece together private financing for *Prospector*,
but when investors failed to materialize, he persuaded NASA to foot the bill.
Now, after *Prospector*'s resounding success, he hopes to raise private money for
future moon-mapping missions. Binder is developing a new spacecraft that can
accept an array of scientific instruments built by outside organizations—research firms or university scientists—even more readily than did *Prospector*,
and without having to engage in the kind of engineering give-and-take that
jacks up the cost of doing business with NASA. "The idea is that this thing is
like a VW," he says. "We want to build them cheap and mass-produce them."

☑   ☑   ☑

But what's the point of these missions? It couldn't just be the science, could it?
Binder looks and sounds like a man who's out to make a buck, and he is able
to sustain this impression for perhaps 15 minutes before he reveals more elaborate motivations. He is, to put it plainly, nuts about space. "You can't explore
the moon without mapping it first," he says. "That's the first step. Once we've
done that, we'll start working on sending landers—extremely simple landers,
using only existing hardware." The next step is leaving things on the moon—
equipment, robots, dwellings—and little by little build up lunar bases.

Eventually, Binder wants to start factories on the moon, churning out hydrogen or basalt bricks. He's not talking about a moon base now but a whole
industrial infrastructure in space—the moon as industrial park. At present it
costs about $2,000 a pound to launch a payload into low Earth orbit. If you're
going to need goods in space, why not make them there? "Slowly but surely,
you'd build up the capabilities to survive by yourself on the moon," Binder
says. "And slowly but surely, the way our forefathers did in the New World,
we'd build up an industrial capacity in space. The moon opens up the solar
system. If you have industrial capacity to build from lunar materials, the
moon could be a harbor. You could go there first, on your way to Mercury,
Venus, or Mars."

Meanwhile, Binder has to get his fledgling enterprise off the ground. To do
so, he must overcome a formidable obstacle. He has to convince investors that
he'll be able to extract enough money from scientific institutions to make his

venture work. That won't be easy. Scientists are notorious for having access to very little money. And would the NASA establishment—particularly the Jet Propulsion Laboratory, which runs NASA's scientific missions—happily step aside while private firms muscled in on its territory? "JPL would squash you like a bug if you were a competitor to its feeding stream," says Mendell.

Mendell doubts that scientific arguments alone are ever going to get us back to the moon. In 2003 the Japanese plan to launch the first of a series of four lunar landers and an accompanying orbiter to make detailed maps of the moon's gravity field. But there's no saying when the subsequent missions will go up and what they'll do. And the prospect of sending people is remote. An insider says that manned missions may take another 20 years.

What's needed, Mendell thinks, is something to get people excited about space, something that bypasses reason and appeals directly to passion. What could excite the passion of a large, wealthy, democratic people with a lot of time on their hands?

"There's a lot of talk about putting a five-kilometer-long optical interferometer on the moon," he says. An interferometer is a row of telescopes trained on the same object, so that when the images are combined in a certain way, they are able to resolve details much finer than any single telescope could. Scientists have long wanted to put an interferometer on the moon because the lunar surface, quiet except for vibrations from micrometeorites—tiny meteorites the size of sand grains—would provide a convenient, easy-to-service base. "You'd need to measure the impact of micrometeorites and compensate for them, and for that you'd need to put a seismometer on the moon, because measuring these vibrations is something you can't do now.

"And do you know how you could finance it?" Mendell pauses and leans forward, the better to deliver the punch line. "You could start a lottery based on what the seismic data for the day were going to be. If people will bet on a random number, why wouldn't they bet on the movement of a seismometer needle on the moon?" He's even thought up a name for his lunar lottery: he'd call it Lunar Powerball.

Mendell, of course, did not invent the idea of exploiting the moon for its entertainment value. Rather, it seems to be percolating up from some deep wellspring of common consciousness. Mendell got the idea for Lunar Powerball while talking with an executive from Shimizu, a big Japanese construction company with an interest in building in space. Somebody there was telling him about an idea to finance construction of a moon base by holding lunar bulldozer races, which would raise money from sponsors and television rights. Another executive from the same firm came to Mendell with an idea to put a camera on the moon to film Earth rising on the first day of the millennium. Mendell politely pointed out a small flaw: Earth doesn't rise on the moon. Since the moon doesn't rotate relative to Earth, Earth always stays fixed in the sky. Mendell informed the executive, however, that the moon has a slight wobble, which means that from the east or west limbs, Earth would periodically dip below the horizon and rise back up again. Of course, it takes one lunar day—29 Earth days—for Earth to dip and come up again, so it would all happen very slowly. Think of watching the sun setting 29 times slower.

But the lightbulb really went on when Mendell first heard about Celestis Corporation, the Houston-based company that launched Timothy Leary's ashes into orbit last year. "Funeral homes have these binder notebooks that clients look through, and there's a section near the back that talks about paying extra for, you know, putting your loved one's ashes at the eighteenth hole of his favorite golf course, or in the Andes Mountains, or whatever. Celestis made a package that slips right into the binder. They had to go through all the hoops to break into that business. It wasn't easy, but they did it. And they said they would make a profit after the first launch. They have had two. Now *that's* a business model."

The question is, who is going to do for the moon what Celestis did for ashes in orbit?

Denise Norris, a former computer-industry consultant turned entrepreneur, is chief executive officer of Applied Space Resources, a private firm she formed with the goal of putting together a lunar sample-return mission. The idea is to build a cheap lander, plunk it down in the Sea of Nectar, and bring back about 20 or 30 pounds of moon rocks. She'll sell more than half to scientific organizations for $3,000 to $5,000 per gram, but she'll put aside several pounds to sell as souvenirs. "I think we could get about $200 for a moon rock the size of a dried pea," she says.

Norris insists that the project wouldn't require any new technology; after all, the Soviet Union did a robotic sample return with their *Luna* landers back in the 1970s. The total cost of the project would be $50 million to $60 million, depending on the type of launcher used. And there may be commercial spin-offs. "We could take the landing simulator and make a game out of it. We could even have a contest to see who could do the best job on the simulator. The winner would get to watch the launch." Like a whole host of would-be lunar entertainment czars, she is currently trying to raise capital for the venture.

Then there's LunaCorp, a private firm cofounded by David Gump, the former publisher of a space-industry newsletter who got hooked on the idea of putting together a space mission. He wants William "Red" Whittaker, a roboticist at Carnegie Mellon, to build a moon rover with "telepresence," which would be controlled from Earth via joystick—preferably by an adolescent in an arcade in an amusement park somewhere. Thanks to high-bandwidth electronic communications technology, it would be your eyes and ears on the moon, going wherever you want it to go for as long as you want to pay for the privilege of operating it. "Using telepresence, we're getting more of a democratic approach," he says. "Millions of people could switch into the bodies of the robots." After nine years on the stump, Gump has succeeded in raising "a little bit of money."

Oddly enough, Europe almost boasted the first venture to squeeze enter-   35
tainment out of the moon. It started in utter seriousness when Dutch astronaut
Wubbo Ockels had an epiphany on the space shuttle *Challenger* in 1985. "You
get in this machine and eight minutes later you are above the atmosphere," he
says. "Earth looks so small and fragile. It looks like a park. And then it becomes perfectly obvious that you must do whatever you can to preserve it,
and also to lessen your dependence on it."

Ockels spent seven years putting together an alliance of European commercial firms and the European Space Agency to send a lander to Aitken Basin
on the moon's south pole. At 1,350 miles in diameter and 1.8 miles deep on average, it is one of the biggest craters in the solar system. There is a point where
the west rim of the Shackleton crater, a smaller crater within the basin, inter-
sects with the rims of two other craters, forming a peak about 4,000 feet above
the basin floor. Ockels calls this "the peak of eternal light" because it is thought
that the sun falls on this patch of ground day and night, virtually year-round.
Solar panels placed on the peak could provide continuous power to a nearby
moon base, which could use the power to mine ice deep within nearby craters.

Ockels wanted to start modestly by sending a small lander equipped with
a video camera to celebrate the millennium. But last March, politicians denied
the funding. "I was flabbergasted," he says. "I thought this plan was so fantastic. It really looked like it was snowballing."

☒   ☒   ☒

Nobody thinks bigger than Greg Bennett, though, when it comes to mining the
moon's entertainment resources. He and the other several hundred or so
members of the Artemis Society have put together a plan that is all-American
and very contemporary—and doesn't rely on wringing money from space-
happy investors. "Look at it this way," he says. "Disney is bigger than NASA.
Disney's annual profits are now bigger than the budget for the space-station
program. When I realized that, it made me think we've been approaching
space in the wrong way all along."

Before he even starts building a spaceship, he wants to get a revenue
stream going. He's started Lunar Traders, a retail store that sells memorabilia
about the Artemis Society's mission to the moon. He is also busy developing
story treatments for movies and television. "Like a documentary about doing
the Artemis project itself," he says, "or the lives of the people who'll be going
to the moon." And then there's *Artemis* magazine, which will be about—you
guessed it—the Artemis Society's efforts to reach the moon. The magazine will
be launched soon, Bennett says assuringly. He spoke only the other day to the
publisher, who's putting out the magazine from his apartment in Brooklyn,
but "I wasn't able to pin him down." Once it's up and running, though, he'll
sell it on the stock market, using the bounty to further the mission.

"When we get enough money coming in, then we'll build something," he   40
says. "It's a very Disney-ish approach."

Bennett admits that it will be four or five years before he even begins designing a spaceship, and it'll be years more before it flies. A lot can happen in that time. If that day ever comes, however, it will have been worth waiting for. There'll be no grainy black-and-white television pictures, no mumbo jumbo about history in the making. If you think that Bennett is using tourism merely to jump-start a serious moon program, think again. In his vision, tourism is the sine qua non of the development of the moon, and the entire solar system for that matter.

Let's assume, for argument's sake, that the angels of the free market take a shine to Bennett. The year is 2012. After the inevitable fits and starts, Lunar Traders has made a killing in space memorabilia, *Artemis* magazine has surpassed *Discover* in circulation and has been sold for many tens of millions, and Bennett has opened an office in Hollywood, cutting deals left and right with movie producers desperate for footage to satisfy the public's insatiable appetite for moon flicks. Investors flock to Bennett for a piece of *Artemis: The Movie*. Finally he is free to build his spaceships. The launch date arrives. The cameras are rolling.

To keep his overhead low, Bennett first has his astronauts hitch a ride to the space station, either on the space shuttle or some other launcher, and then switch to a lunar transfer vehicle. This would consist of a Spacehab module—a type of small space lab built privately for NASA—modified to include rocket engines and a lunar lander. The lunar transfer vehicle takes the astronauts on the three-day journey from Earth orbit to lunar orbit and then remains there while they proceed down to the surface. No need for a command module pilot in this day of intelligent robots.

On the lunar surface, much work has already been done. Housing, in the form of three Spacehab modules, is already in place. A robot rover has been methodically burying the modules in regolith—lunar dirt—to protect them from the −240 degree lunar night, from the sun's harsh rays, and from the continuous barrage of micrometeorites. The robot pauses long enough to film the astronauts as they land.

It promises to be quite a sight. The three astronauts make the two-hour trip from lunar orbit down to the surface sprawled out on an open platform, like fish on a platter, with a rocket engine stuck on the bottom. "The flight would pose no greater hazard to the crew than two hours of surface EVA," Bennett writes. (Still, it's better than the version NASA's Connolly thought up back when the moon was still a plausible destination. He had the astronauts standing upright, hanging to straps for dear life.)

The first thing Bennett's astronauts do is check out the landing site, gather a few moon rocks—and turn on their camcorders. A high priority of business is to get stock footage for the inevitable documentaries and other entertainment vehicles that are financing the operation. Since the astronauts have already undergone rigorous training in acting school, they have no trouble enacting scripts for scenes in movies.

45

After that, Bennett's plans get a little dreamy. They start with lunar resorts: "Getting people up there would cost, oh, maybe $100,000 per person,"
Bennett says. "It'd be like a luxury capital tour of Europe. It's about
what you'd spend to go to Mount Everest. If you had a resort on the northeast
corner of Mare Crisium, there's a place called Angus Bay where you could go
spelunking."

The real apple of his eye would be to discover one of the long lava caves
that scientists believe may be commonplace. Of course, none of these lava
tubes has been discovered. (That's probably because nobody's looked very
hard. Only one Apollo mission took a deep core sample, and that went down
only about three feet.) Rather, scientists infer their existence from rills—long,
snaking valleys formed from lava flows, which presumably were frequent in
the moon's early days. These lava rivers would have begun to cool quickly,
starting with a thin crust on top, which then insulated the lava below, keeping
it warm. Since lunar lava is more "watery" than lava on Earth, the warm lava
can eventually flow elsewhere, leaving a vast underground cavern. Most rills,
in fact, are probably collapsed lava tubes.

The idea is to find one of these caves, seal it off, and pump in air. The cave
would provide protection from radiation—a natural lunar habitat. "We'd like
to pressurize a cave," Bennett says. "Some of them may be many miles long.
Here you'd be in this cave, but it'd feel like outdoors, because the roof would
be the height of clouds. You'd have one-sixth the gravity—that's the greatest
part. You could put on some wings and actually fly through it. You could do
anything you'd want to do at a luxury resort, and more."

For people to have any real fun at all on the moon, you would want to let   50
them walk around outside, and for that you'd need some kind of protective
garment. NASA spends $10 million on one pressurized suit, so something
cheaper, and perhaps more idiot-proof, would have to be made. "I'm sure we
could build space suits that a tourist wouldn't be able to kill himself in—with
enough dexterity to bend down and pick up some rocks, but with not quite the
dexterity of astronauts," says Bennett.

Once people had checked into their rooms, they'd naturally want to take a
tour, just to get themselves oriented. Bennett envisions a network of gondola
chairs that would take people around to the most interesting sights. "If you're
touring the moon, you might want to visit all the Apollo sights. It'd be a big
trip—the moon's a big place; it has the land area of Africa—so you'd have
these pressurized gondola chairs to the major sights." The gondolas, similar to
the ones at ski resorts in the Alps, would ride on overhead cables. Of course,
you can't have tourists tramping all over Neil Armstrong's footprints, so
you'd keep people to sightseeing trails laid out within big, pressurized clear
plastic tubes on stilts.

Ice-skating could also see the light of lunar day. "A gal in Artemis is a skater,
and she'd like to see a skating rink on the moon," says Bennett. "It would be in-
describably beautiful. Can you imagine a triple axel in one-sixth gravity? Think

of any sport, for that matter, involving people. You could jump six times higher than you ever could on Earth, and a ball would fall six times slower."

And Bennett hasn't ruled out having fun with science: observatories on the far side of the moon would have many advantages because the moon would act as a natural shield. Radio telescopes would be free of radio, television, and other electromagnetic interference from Earth. You could build optical telescopes much larger than the Hubble Telescope, and they'd be more stable, more accurate, and easier to fix. "Observatories are just entertainment for scientists," he says.

⬛   ⬛   ⬛

Bennett doesn't admit the possibility that the moon will fail to be developed. Of far greater concern is the prospect of people like Jack Schmitt getting his way. Schmitt, of course, was the last person to get to the moon, but he is also a geologist, and he is now aiming to stake his claim in the coming moon rush.

Schmitt's plan relies on the development of a practical technology for generating energy from nuclear fusion—in particular, a form of fusion that uses an isotope of helium called helium 3. Since helium 3 fusion would emit far fewer nasty neutrons than conventional fusion, some scientists favor it as more practicable. But making helium 3 is difficult: you have to knock a neutron out of the nucleus of conventional helium 4, which can't be done artificially in great quantity. And although the sun makes a lot of helium 3 and sends it out by solar wind, it gets lost in the hurly-burly of Earth's atmosphere. The moon, however, has no atmosphere. The same solar wind has been depositing helium 3 in the lunar regolith for billions of years, so that there is more than a million tons of it—enough to generate 20,000 trillion watt-years, roughly ten times the amount of energy you'd get by burning off all the fossil fuels on Earth.

And it's all there for the taking. All you'd need to do is dig up the lunar dirt and heat it to 1100 degrees, at which point the helium 3 would evaporate. While you were at it, you could continue heating the dirt to 1650 degrees, burning off the oxygen that makes up about 40 percent of the regolith by weight. And to power these operations lunar day and night, you could put a solar power plant in the Aitken Basin on the south pole, on top of the "peak of eternal light." All in all, Schmitt believes that a helium 3 mining and fusion operation could be set up for $10 billion to $15 billion over the next 15 years or so. "That's an investment on the order of the Alaskan pipeline or the Eurotunnel," he says.

You might expect one of the few people who have firsthand experience of the moon to be enthusiastic about the idea of sending tourists, but Schmitt is skeptical. "The first thing you'd want to do, if you were going to take tourists, is spend a fair amount of time—say, six months—doing what astronauts would call training. You can get sick if you don't control yourself right in space, at least before adaptation. Anybody who gets into an unusual situation has to know enough not to panic. It's a new environment for the human species. These people who are talking about tourism haven't factored in all the things you'd have to do. Someday it's going to happen," Schmitt says, "but I suspect it will piggyback on a commercial effort."

Bennett and other members of the "tourism first" camp realize the importance of having space industry. The oxygen for tourists to breathe, the hydrogen to fuel their rockets, and the solar power to heat and cool their rooms would have to come from somewhere. Once you have a healthy tourism business going on the moon, it would make sense to have also developed a healthy moon economy. "Perhaps the moon would be the Hong Kong of the solar system," says Bennett. "Ships would land there; interplanetary trading companies would have their headquarters on the moon." All sustained by tourism.

But the difference is one of emphasis. "I almost hope that helium 3 fusion power doesn't get developed too quickly," says Bennett. "The helium 3 on the moon would be worth a fortune, and the moon would be developed like a mining town. I would rather develop the moon's character as a tourist center than as a rough mining town, where everybody hates their job. I'd rather see it developed like Honolulu."

Which way will prevail on the moon? Mining or tourism? Production or consumption? Although nobody is even close to leaving Earth, already it seems clear that the final arbiter of what we should do with the moon will most likely be the free market. If the coming decades are anything like this one, don't count entertainment out. "It's really not such a radical idea," says Bennett. "In the past, explorers would go out and explore, and they'd bring back stories. Then the Hudson Bay Company would come in and do the trading. Never mind that the entire human species is at stake. We're doing this for fun." ◼

60

Reflections and Inquiries

1. What is the Artemis Society? Why is it important for someone like Gregory Bennett?

2. Why does NASA, which first enabled us to reach the moon, show little interest in returning?

3. According to Wendell Mendell, what valuable knowledge does the moon have to teach us? How practical is this knowledge?

4. In what ways could the public become enthusiastic about lunar exploration once again? How sensible are these reasons?

5. What is the significance of lunar lava caves, assuming they exist at all?

Reading to Write

Write an essay on the feasibility of lunar colonization through the efforts of private industry. Draw from your own outside reading in addition to the information Guterl provides.

Some Thoughts on SETI | Christopher Chyba

People have often wondered whether life, especially intelligent life, exists beyond Earth. Ever since 1960 there have been organized efforts to answer that question. Radio telescopes have been used to detect artificial signals from the stars—such as radio transmissions or television broadcasts—that would prove the presence not only of intelligent life but of technologically advanced civilizations. Despite the growing sophistication of signal-detecting radio telescopes, no such signals have been found, except for a very few unexplained—and never redetected—anomalies. But because there are billions of possible channels and billions of places to search, it could take a long time before anything is detected—assuming there is anything out there to detect. In the following essay, Christopher Chyba speculates on reasons for engaging in such a search. Chyba holds the Carl Sagan Chair for the Study of Life in the Universe at the SETI Institute and is a consulting professor in the Department of Geological and Environmental Sciences at Stanford University.

What are the prospects for there being other intelligent technical civilizations in our galaxy? Discoveries in the past few years have certainly increased the likelihood of extraterrestrial *life*. In just the past few years we have learned that planetary systems are not uncommon, if not necessarily similar to our own. We have learned that liquid-water oceans, such as that likely to exist under the icy surface of Europa, may well exist on worlds heated from within—even if those worlds are otherwise too far from their stars for liquid water to be possible. Finally, it's becoming increasingly clear that Earth harbors a subsurface microbial biosphere, some of which may be capable of surviving independently of surface conditions. Earth's deep biosphere makes Mars and Europa seem more plausible as venues for life.

But what are the prospects of extraterrestrial *intelligence?* Here our ignorance remains profound. Before touching on new insights into this question, it is worth recalling some of the old arguments.

Source: Chyba, Christopher. "Some Thoughts on SETI." *The Planetary Report* May/June 1999: 6. Reprinted by permission.

The Fermi Paradox

The Fermi paradox is the suggestion that if extraterrestrial civilizations were widespread, one of them would have visited us by now. A more recent version is that were there many technological civilizations even slightly older than ours, one or another of them should by now have colonized the galaxy using self-replicating intelligent probes. Since that hasn't happened, the argument goes, they—extraterrestrial civilizations—don't exist. However, unless these probes' creators truly wished the entire galaxy—including their own resources—to be consumed, they would have built in some process to limit their machines' otherwise remorseless, exponential replication. In this case, resolving the Fermi paradox degenerates into interminable arguments over alien psychology: what limits would other civilizations place on the danger of exponential replication by robot probes?

Or would other limits inexorably evolve? Our world remains full of green plants, despite the presence of abundant, mobile, self-replicating "machines" (called insects) that feed on them. The insects are held in check by predators. The same could be true for the putative galaxy-eating robots: robot predators may have evolved for them as well. With these sorts of arguments, the entire discussion enters the realm of the ineffable; we simply cannot resolve it on the basis of anything we know.

How Rare Is Intelligence?

A more interesting argument, I believe, has been posed by those biologists who view intelligence on Earth as an extraordinarily unlikely event, an event contingent on a list of very special and peculiar circumstances. If we could rewind the tape of life and start again from the beginning, they suggest, nothing like humans would ever evolve. Earth has seen multiple, independent evaluations of such highly selected capabilities as flight and sight, but intelligence, the argument runs, is not analogous to these. Intelligence has evolved only once among the very, very many species that have ever existed here. 5

Yet I find that this argument has a whiff of the tautological about it. Isn't it likely to be the case that the first intelligent species on the planet would look back over the history of life and ask why it, among all others, was first?

And what of the dolphins? Those dolphins with the largest brains in relation to their bodies are, by this measure, brainier than was *Homo habilis*—one of our tool-using ancestors. Are we really the only intelligence on Earth, or do we share this planet with intelligent, marine mammal species? If so, it is humbling to think that we have made so little progress in communicating with them. In any case, dolphin intelligence is not technical. Dolphins will never build radio transmitters or explore the planets.

But if multicellular life arose more than half a billion years ago, why has it taken this long, and the evolution of so many different species, for *technical* intelligence to arise just once? In this line of questioning, too, I am concerned about human myopia. Let's think about the total length of time over which multicellular life is likely to exist on Earth. The Sun is growing brighter, and in about 2 billion years our oceans will likely boil into a runaway greenhouse and Earth may become uninhabitable. Until that time, however, it seems likely—not certain—that multicellular life is here to stay. (It would be an impressive extinction indeed if every rat, every worm, every clam, every giant squid, and every cockroach were to disappear.) Multicellular life on Earth therefore seems likely to endure *in toto* for more than two-and-a-half billion years. From this perspective, technical intelligence arose on Earth *early* in the history of multicellular life—in the first 20 percent or so of its history. The observation that intelligence is a latecomer to the scene seems based in the human perspective.

Extinction Cycles and SETI

There may be a kind of cosmic selection operating against planets that do not evolve technical intelligence. All that we now understand about planetary formation assures us that habitable worlds like our own will face ongoing collisions with objects similar to our comets and asteroids. On Earth, collisions big enough to cause a mass extinction—like that 65 million years ago at the end of the age of the dinosaurs—are statistically expected to occur every 100 million years or so. Any biosphere that does not evolve an intelligence capable of recognizing and responding to this impact hazard will therefore be catastrophically disrupted, on average, every 100 million years. If a mass extinction ensues, new niches and evolutionary paths open. Only biospheres in which technical intelligence evolves will have the chance to avoid this cycle of destruction and regeneration. Planetary biospheres with technical civilizations may, in this sense, be selected over those without them.

Each of these arguments is intriguing; I find none to be compelling. The seemingly interminable nature of these arguments reflects how little we know about intelligence. Therefore, I believe, the search for extraterrestrial intelligence is fundamentally an empirical problem. The best we can do is search. ◪   10

Reflections and Inquiries

1. What is the Fermi paradox? Why is it a sufficient basis for deciding whether alien civilizations exist beyond Earth, according to Chyba?

2. How likely an event was the origin of multicellular life on earth? How does this relate to the question about the existence of extraterrestrial life?

3. Why does Chyba find none of the theories about the origin or presence of life in the universe compelling enough to guide us in our search for extraterrestrial intelligence?

4. How does Chyba answer the question, "Why has it taken [so] long . . . for *technical* intelligence to arise" on Earth? Do you agree with this answer? If not, how would you answer the question?

Reading to Write

Speculate in a short essay on why you think intelligent life exists or does not exist elsewhere in the universe. Explain in your essay what you mean by *intelligent*: *intelligent* in the sense of human intelligence (embracing art, religion, science, technology) or something very different? Allude to points raised by Chyba and other astronomers and biologists.

In Search of a Space Policy That Goes Somewhere | Pat Dasch

The first decade and a half of the space age, from the 1957 Soviet launching of Sputnik I, the first artificial satellite, to the last Apollo moon landing in 1971, was fueled by political pressures. Because of mutual distrust on both sides of the Iron Curtain, one of the most accelerated technological advancements in American history had taken place. And the cost was horrendous; there was no time to consider economical ways of achieving predominance in space. But times have changed. In the following article, Pat Dasch, Executive Director of the National Space Society, argues that we need a nongovernmental body, free of bureaucratic entanglements, to coordinate the commercial and scientific potentials of space.

The Mars mission failures of 1999, and the subsequent Young Report issued March 14 of this year, have led to a re-evaluation of the Mars program. That has left some lingering questions: What direction should space exploration and development take in the future? And what role should national and state government play in that development?

The space world is changing fast. Gone is the era when space activities were conducted exclusively by government agencies venturing boldly where no one else dared or cared to go. Today, communications giants dominate low Earth orbit, and visionary entrepreneurs are lobbying for land grants on the moon and clarification of resource extraction and utilization legislation on bodies in outer space.

The space race with the Russians dominated the first 20 years of NASA's existence; the space-station program, which has sought to engage our former Russian adversaries in peaceful pursuits, has been the dominant program in the second half of the agency's history. Expanding the frontiers of science and technology should shape the role of NASA for the future. We need a space pro-

---

Source: Dasch, Pat. "In Search of a Space Policy that Goes Somewhere." *IntellectualCapital.com*, 27 April 2000. Reprinted by permission of the author.

gram that goes somewhere and space policy to take us there. We should focus on removing key barriers on the route to space development.

Developing Past the Man on the Moon

Currently no single body is responsible for coordinating policy between the various space sectors. This has led to disconnects and unnecessary reinvention and competition.

A single body with responsibility for policy development, such as a re-vamped and redefined National Space Council, would actually stimulate ac-celerated development. This body should include representatives from the research community, the military establishment and the commercial space business community, as well as the usual agency representatives from NASA, National Science Foundation, National Oceanic and Atmospheric Administra-tion, etc. This panel could facilitate a smooth and speedy transition from a civil-space program immersed in and encumbered by the massive cost of op-erations to one that undertakes only cutting-edge research and development. 5

True creativity in developing space business infrastructure will come from the commercial world of Wall Street and corporate America. A broad-based space business-development council should be formed to advise the govern-ment at the highest level on commercial space development and to foster new commercial space business initiatives.

February's government report on "Future Management and Use of the U.S. Space Launch Bases and Ranges" opens the way for involving commer-cial operators in launch facility upgrades. Upgrading launch ranges, creation of spaceports (with federal and state support) with competitive pad turn-around times and customer-friendly support facilities are essential if the United States is to win back a greater share of international launch business.

Some Priorities

A reduction in the cost of getting to orbit is key to improved and increased space commerce and exploration. We have been launching spacecraft in the same manner—with controlled explosions—since the beginning of the space age 50 years ago. U.S. suppliers are relying increasingly on Russian know-how and hardware for access to space. New forms of propulsion and reusable launch vehicles are long overdue. NASA should coordinate development of new launch technologies and the use of new materials in collaboration with the best researchers in our universities.

Cautioned by the technical challenges and expense of the International Space Station (ISS), the Clinton administration's space policy makes no com-mitment to a humans-in-space program beyond the International Space Sta-tion even though the most valuable contribution of the space station is advertised to be research on long duration space flight—research that is most helpful for future human ventures in space.

What is the problem with talking about the future? Is it a question of po-   10
litical priorities, or is it a more fundamental lack of vision? The Apollo program was a major achievement and a source of great national pride. It was
borne of a unique moment of international tension and not a model for the future. Those with the responsibility to shape the future are not required to make
a Kennedy-style commitment to land humans on Mars, but they have a responsibility to set clear objectives for the disbursement of public tax dollars.

NASA has many notable scientific achievements to its credit, but it is pride
in human achievement that fuels public support of space exploration. Mars
Pathfinder grabbed public attention because it represented a first step in our
return to the Red Planet—a robotic precursor to an ultimate human mission
to the most Earth-like planet we know. With the current opportunity to reexamine the Mars science program we should acknowledge that while searching for signs of ancient life on Mars we are also looking toward introducing
human life to the Red Planet. And we should ensure that the experiments carried on missions over the next decade represent a well-coordinated program
that focuses on life and living on Mars.

At the same time, it is time to stop embracing just one program at a time
in the humans-in-space arena. It is time to recognize that space is a place, and
we are already operating there routinely—just check your pager.

Future human missions likely will have major commercial components—
vehicles owned or managed by private operators and laboratories provided
by multinational concerns. A commercially based return to the moon is already under consideration among space entrepreneurs. A commercially established lunar outpost should be utilized for research, development and testing
for an eventual human mission to Mars. Plans for human reconnaissance of
near-Earth asteroids should be outlined. NASA should be empowered to lay
the roads to these new frontiers. An addition of 1% per annum to the NASA
budget, earmarked for a commitment to our future in space, would enable
steady if limited progress on this vital work.

Space Is a Place

The current protective regulatory environment, especially with respect to export of spacecraft or components, fails to recognize the international aspect of
space business and the multinational nature of many of our most successful
space businesses. The degree of international networking in space business,
from components, to financing, to insurance, requires a new regulatory framework to avoid irreversible damage to U.S. performance in this fastest growing
business sector.

Not only have we been slow to recognize the harmful impact of current   15
export legislation, but Congress also has been slow in acting on legislation
needed to accommodate the new space age. There is need for intensive work
on the international front to revise anachronistic statutes (such as the Moon
Treaty of 1979, written at a time that anticipated only government-run space

enterprises) and to introduce new laws and treaties to provide a framework that enables space commerce. Anything less will inhibit space commerce and the attendant economic growth and technology development that will flow from the new era of space exploration and exploitation.

The New Space Age has arrived and promises to be a powerful force in the economy. NASA's agenda and the legislative and regulatory environment must be coordinated to best leverage and the new space dynamic for technology leadership and economic success. The most powerful driver will be a commitment to a vision for the future. Space is a place; we should plan to lead the way there. ◪

Reflections and Inquiries

1. Dasch asserts that we should "remove key barriers" on the route to space development. What barriers is he referring to? Why are they barriers?

2. How would a revamped and refined National Space Council stimulate accelerated development? What evidence, if any, does Dasch bring in as support for his claim?

3. According to Dasch, "True creativity in developing space business infrastructure will come from the commercial world . . . of corporate America." Do you agree or disagree? What do you suppose Dasch means by "true creativity" in this context?

Reading to Write

1. Write a position paper in which you agree or disagree with Dasch's claim that "space is a place," in the sense that it is as much a realm for human habitation as Earth.

2. What priorities would you set for the space program over the next decade? Defend your project choices as fully as possible, taking into account likely objections.

Is Space Travel Worth the Expense? | William N. Boenig

A perennial problem in determining one's stance on a controversial issue is how to sort out valid information from misinformation, and how to distinguish between truths, half-truths, rumors, and outright falsehoods. William Boenig, a first-year engineering physics student at Santa Clara University, decided that exactly this kind of sorting out was needed before one could properly evaluate U.S. space exploration or justify its expenses. His analysis leads him to believe that the answer is a qualified "yes"—our destiny in space seems inevitable, but we must try harder to privatize costs.

The reality of space travel—finally on our horizon after millennia of people have gazed up at the cosmos in wonderment and awe. Could the coming decades witness the development of a permanent human presence in orbit around our Earth and even on our nearest planetary neighbor, Mars? Or will the prospects of extending our footprints beyond our native soil wither in the face of overwhelming opposition? The answers to these questions will manifest themselves in the scientific and sociopolitical forces that compete for limited resources and power. More specifically, space exploration supporters' success in maneuvering around economic obstacles and setbacks will dictate how quickly and to what extent, if at all, we can call ourselves a space faring people.

Since the beginning of our nation's space program almost half a century ago, opponents to space travel more often than not have succeeded in curbing most development and exploration projects by citing astronomical price tags. Estimates running into the hundreds of billions of dollars and time commitments spanning several decades have made space travel an easy target for policy makers and the public who seek to increase funding for their own causes. Simply put, for many, space exploration has not proved to be worth the expense, but recent indications show the economic tide beginning to turn in favor of space exploration.

The economic reality that progress depends on a new, more cost effective approach to funding space projects has spurred scientists, economists, and policy makers to change their old methods of balancing mission goals with the tight budgets available. The way they see space has dramatically changed, too. Instead of a hostile, barren no-man's-land of unimaginable expanse, space, when viewed from our evolved technological standpoint, abounds with resources that we can turn into economic and social opportunities here on Earth.

For much of our space history, methodologies for accomplishing projects have remained unchanged, and for this reason many people automatically perceive the endeavors aimed at space as too expensive, too inefficient, and too far removed from the important issues affecting people every day. But the new strategies designed to replace the old hold promise for making space travel worth the expense. Therefore, we need to differentiate them from antiquated notions so we can make informed decisions with regard to supporting space exploration. Now more than ever before, space projects stand better chances of seeing realization.

A brief identification of the goals of these projects might help clarify some common misconceptions. First, feasible space exploration refers to those projects that current or emerging technologies can accomplish. Beneath this heading lie human and robotic trips to the moon and Mars. On the periphery of these serious and doable endeavors, on the other hand, are what science writer Neil de Grasse Tyson refers to in his article "Space: You Can't Get There from Here" as the "unwittingly wishful" dreams of others with less than realistic goals (74). The allure of space for some inevitably sparks the imagination, and speculation of traveling throughout the galaxy in starships and interacting with other civilizations sometimes seems like the actual, serious plans of a few. But we should not mistake these whimsical aspirations for the serious work of private industry and government agencies. For the most part, missions to explore our solar system and investigate the workings of our universe have been solidly grounded in tangible, scientific method, and continued exploration most likely will apply its limited funds toward realistic goals.

One reason many reject the justifications for space exploration rests on their comparison of such a project to similar historical events. Wendell W. Mendell, a leading advocate for exploring the usefulness of the moon for future space missions, has observed, "The expectations of the advocates of human exploration are usually couched in the language of the Apollo experience" (107). As a result, many opponents to space exploration remember the negative parts of the Apollo program—high cost, lack of public support, etc.—and automatically apply them to current and future efforts to go to space. For instance, according to James L. Kauffman, author of "The Moon Shot and Congressional Critics," America's space program came under harsh scrutiny in 1963 for its large budget appropriation in relation to such other national concerns as education and unemployment (119). The force with which the space program thrust itself into the national priority inevitably put it at odds with other competing programs. In relation to common social concerns, the high-minded plan to go the moon seemed intangible to most, especially because most individuals obviously lacked a personal stake in the "space race" with the Soviets. Similarly, many people, especially policy makers, found the Kennedy administration's motivations for enacting such a bold plan at least a little bit suspect. One poll of House members in early 1962 revealed most found the space program "questionable except when viewed from the standpoint of the cold war" (Kauffman 120). Despite vociferous opposition to the program, Kauffman suggests the promise of adventure in a new frontier seemed sufficient to maintain support for the Apollo program for the extent it lasted.

Several factors during the decade of the 1960s set the stage for Apollo's eventual demise. Mendell relates the difficulties encountered by the Apollo program to those experienced by other totally new technologies in tentative political environments. For instance, the modernity of the technology for its time required extensive new designs and testing (Mendell 107). The fact that only a few systems were produced and that few components from current technologies found application in the final product (almost everything had to be designed from scratch) further skyrocketed the cost. Such costs eventually brought about the project's cancellation shortly after the main success of the *Apollo 11* landing. Also, the severance of funds to the aerospace industry, despite coming from government policy makers, did not improve the program's popularity. The late 1960s showed how little political momentum—Kennedy's announcement to the world that the nation had set its eyes on the moon— could be relied upon to see such a project through to its completion.

Looking at plans for space exploration in terms of similar endeavors in history can have its downfalls, especially if the historical comparison was fraught with issues that would impede any progress today. For the time in which it was completed and the magnitude of the actual accomplishment itself, the Apollo program overcame great odds. But in today's environment, an approach other than sheer political will would be in order. Despite the preceding emphasis on the economic, political, and social conditions surrounding the Apollo program, its benefits to science remain substantial to this day and should not be overlooked. Likewise, science propels much of the impetus to continue space exploration. As a more stable platform than almost any political environment could provide, science deserves particular attention as a legitimate justification for space exploration's expense, especially since our society and economy are built upon a foundation of scientific and technological advances.

Carl Sagan, one of this century's most notable scientists, wrote, "the history of our civilization shows that the unfettered pursuit of basic knowledge is the way the most significant practical advances have come about" (82). Because so little of space has been explored and studied, even in our immediate vicinity, it holds a wealth of scientific knowledge waiting for discovery. And, as with most scientific findings, the potential for solving practical problems might not seem immediately evident. Yet the benefits for tomorrow from today's efforts often surprise us. One need only reflect on the century's technological advancements. For instance, scientists studying the applications of mathematics to electrical engineering in the 1930s formed the foundation for the technology that drives our computers today (Britannica.com). One can draw a line between space exploration and any other form of traditional scientific inquiry. Thus, the question might arise, how can we put a price tag on the scientific value of space exploration when the fruits of our efforts remain unknown to us now? A couple of examples of how space has contributed to our understanding of Earth provide a glimpse into the potentials awaiting us in space.

Throughout history people have sought to understand the mechanisms shaping the surface of the Earth. The fact that even up to fifty years ago we lacked several basic geological theories shows how much progress remains to be made in what some might see as a well established and mastered field (Guterl 75). For example, Mendell points out how an established geological theory was proved incorrect in light of data obtained through the use of space vehicles. According to him, "'if you looked at Lake Manicouagan in Quebec on a map and remarked that it was awfully round, scientists would have told you that it is a cryto-volcano—a volcano crater with no apparent volcano'" (qtd. in Guterl 75). However, by comparing images obtained from the moon via satellites and via the Apollo missions to pictures of circle-shaped lakes on Earth taken from high altitude, geologists found striking similarities between meteorite impact sites on the moon and these lakes. As we learned, the lake in Quebec, and many others like it around the world, were formed not by ancient volcanoes, but by meteorites. As a result of taking our scientific uncertainties into space, Mendell follows, "'[we now] understand that the terrestrial processes are altered by the space environment. In this sense, the moon is a geologic time machine'" (qtd. in Guterl 75). In other words, our planet and everything living on it are subject to the very same forces affecting our neighbor, the moon. But, unlike the Earth, the moon remains relatively undisturbed from the elements which erase geologic history from our surface. A glimpse at the moon, in essence, is a glimpse of Earth billions of years ago.

But what about Earth now and in the future? In yet another example of how space exploration can help us better understand our own planet, scientists have begun to look toward Mars to learn about the changes in weather patterns we are experiencing here on Earth. Support for the theory that the greenhouse effect is causing global warming has reached the point where even the United Nations has expressed its concerns regarding the repercussions which are expected with this trend—not in a thousand years, or several hundred for that matter, but within the next century. Preliminary analysis of the data obtained from satellite missions to Mars provides details of our nearest planetary neighbor's annual climatic cycle involving the formation and disappearance of large polar ice caps. The implications of this limited information, along with all the rest obtainable in more missions, would be like no other knowledge obtained from our vicinity in space. Scientists point out evidence of ancient rivers and other surface water on Mars, suggesting that perhaps it once behaved how Earth does now. Using data from more missions to Mars to augment our own limited information about the history of our climatic history, we could make more accurate and well informed predictions as to what to expect here in the future. Our preparations in terms of environmental and economic policy and infrastructure could save us huge amounts of money. If

10

we view the opportunities available to us through space exploration in these terms, then the question becomes, at what point in our technological development does *not* exploring space begin adversely to affect us?

Many people see economic rules as setting the pace for our exploration of space, and rightly so. No other factor in the world of policy-making carries as much sway as funding, and when political forces enter the scene, space projects tend to end up with less public funds than they initially set out to obtain. Opponents of the space program, Mendell observes, can use its high cost against it in the political arena (108). Space agencies have recognized the political pressure to keep costs down and, in response, have encouraged their scientists to "think out of the box" (Mendell 107). For instance, Don Goldin, the current NASA administrator, asked scientists if a return mission to the moon could be accomplished for less than 1% of the original cost of about $200 billion (in today's value) (Mendell 107). "The imposition of a very low ceiling reflects political realities," Mendell asserts, but Goldin's effort to find a low-cost alternative to space travel reflects the willingness with which supporters of space exploration will conform to guidelines to reach their objectives (107).

The economic conditions in the world today differ vastly from those during the Apollo program. And, as a favorable result of space exploration, the market elements exist for substantially reduced mission costs. In a preceding argument, several elements of the Apollo program were said to have greatly contributed to its high cost, but those elements either don't exist today or have reversed and have become favorable for space exploration. For instance, unlike the political atmosphere of the early 1960s, today does not see international rivalries spurring huge space projects, with economics taking a back seat to national pride. Rather, economic forces dictate the speed and to what extent a project will see completion. Also, the entire Apollo program was directed by a government agency, NASA, partly because of the enormous quantity of public funds at stake and partly because of the complexity of the project. If the same project were initiated today, perhaps policy makers would entertain the possibility of integrating the project into private industries so as to increase institutional efficiency, minimize delays, and increase the chances of completion. Therefore, a new self-sustaining industry could develop, the revitalized economy could provide jobs, and the space project could escape the possibility of a premature political death.

Furthermore, the current boom in telecommunications and global positioning system satellites demonstrates the viability of private investment in space technologies already (Mendell 109). Up to $10 billion in private shareholder money goes toward any single project, and with solid sums of money of that magnitude at stake, market forces cascade down through every related industry (Mendell 109). For instance, the launch industry expects reduced launch costs with every new project, and launch capacities increase, too, with larger payloads (Mendell 109). In addition, Mendell explains, from a technological point of view it takes the same amount of energy to move a satellite in regular low Earth orbit to an operational position as it takes to move that same satellite to the moon (109). Current launchers possess that capability. Mendell believes, "in another decade the projected commercial launch capability will grow to the point where trips to the Moon can be purchased competitively . . . even if no *publicly funded, government-managed* exploration program is initiated" (109).

The concept of privately funded space projects in the form of telecommunications satellites and strategic systems has proved successful and holds much promise for growth and expansion into other facets of space projects. Meanwhile, federal agencies, most notably NASA, have explored ways to reduce their risks and costs in similar and other different, innovative ways. For instance, the losses of the *Mars Climate Observer* and the *Mars Polar Lander* in recent years have proved grossly costly and embarrassing for the agency. As a result, the idea of privatizing some of its operations has provided an attractive option. In fact, the concept has already been tested with a project credited with making one of the most significant discoveries since the beginning of space exploration: the discovery of water on our moon. The *Lunar Prospector* was a model for NASA's "faster, cheaper, better" mentality toward space travel and exploration. At only $63 million to design, launch, and maintain from the ground, it demonstrated the feasibility of making an extremely low cost yet highly successful satellite (Whittington). The *Prospector*'s success, this time with government funding, might encourage private investment in similar projects in the future, where federal agencies and institutions could contract for the scientific data obtained from private ventures.

The economic potential of space exploration and transportation holds some promise, but, one might ask, where does *human* exploration, such as to Mars, fit into the plan? Couldn't robots do the same job for a tenth of the cost and without the safety risk? Well, for human exploration of Mars, one can argue that the impetus lies in the scientific value of first-hand exploration, in addition to what Sagan refers to as the natural desire to proceed outward into space in exploration as technology allows (81). In his essay "Why Send Humans to Mars?" Sagan admits there exist theoretically more cost efficient alternatives to sending humans to Mars (e.g., robots), yet asks, what if Mt. Everest was explored by robots? It would have "aroused minimal public enthusiasm" and would have remained in the minds of many as nothing more than a glorified project to satisfy the abstract curiosities of a few scientists (83). Again, the burden falls on mission designers to address the primary obstacle to simply starting the project—cost. 15

But the requirement has contributed to a subtle yet widespread shift in how they view Mars. Instead of grappling with how to supply a crew with more than two years worth of supplies and enough fuel for the trip over and back, they are now beginning to look at Mars in terms of its resources and how they can reduce mission complexity and cost and increase safety. For instance, probes sent to Mars before the launch of any crew from Earth could begin making fuel for their return trip home. The crew wouldn't leave Earth until the probes had made enough fuel to ensure their safe return. Similarly, habitation, equipment, and labs sent ahead of time could make everything ready for their survival, thus reducing the size and complexity of the actual crew's spacecraft and further lowering the cost. Also, the opportunity exists for us to test these new technologies in a real space environment that is nearby and cost effective—the moon. With *Prospector*'s discovery of water in the polar regions, the moon could serve as the perfect test site and could even function as the primary location for making rocket fuel. Overall costs turn out lower when we have less to lift off Earth. And, with the previously mentioned prediction by Mendell that small payload transportation to and from the moon is just a decade away, such testing for redundancy and safety would not put a burden on the Mars mission's overall budget (109). This proposal for a Mars mission demonstrates how various proposed solutions to space challenges can complement each other to most efficiently accomplish the objective.

The economic constraints put on space exploration have inevitably led to the question, "Is space exploration worth the expense?" Pragmatically speaking, many would argue the millions, and sometimes billions, of dollars going into publicly funded space programs could better benefit other national priorities. For them, their conception of current and future space projects based on the methodologies of the Apollo program misrepresents the evolution, especially recently, of the space program. Now, not only is low cost a priority, but it is a requirement without which any successful mission can take place. Also, the economic, sociopolitical, and technical environments in which space programs operate are more favorable and stable than ever before, and dynamic and innovative advocates for space exploration steadily find solutions to policy makers' challenges.

For science, the allure of space has awakened a deeper understanding of the workings of the universe, yet we have but scratched the surface. From an economic point of view, market demands have already pushed certain infrastructures into space, where technology provides them with the greatest return for their investment. As trends indicate, and as it becomes economically feasible, be it for scientific, economic, or discovery purposes, space exploration will happen. And, finally, as Sagan puts it:

> The idea of an emerging cosmic perspective, of understanding our place in the universe, of a highly visible program affecting our view of ourselves—this might have extremely important benefits for us in clarifying the fragility of our planetary environment and in recognizing the common peril and responsibility of all the nations and peoples of Earth. (83)

Is space travel worth the expense? I ask, down what path are we destined to travel? You decide.

Works Cited

Britannica.com. 2000. Encyclopedia Britannica. 20 Mar. 2001 <http://www.britannica.com/bcom/eb/article/2/0,5716,117722+2+109626,00.html?query=history%20computers>.

de Grasse Tyson, Neil. "Space: You Can't Get There from Here." *Natural History* Sept. 1998: 74–78.

Guterl, Fred. "What Should We Do with the Moon?" *Discover* Sept. 1998: 73–78.

Kauffman, James L. "The Moon Shot and Congressional Critics." *Selling Outer Space: Kennedy, the Media, and Funding for Project Apollo 1961–1963*. Tuscaloosa: U Alabama P, 1994. 118–27.

Mendell, Wendell W. "Role of Lunar Development in Human Exploration of the Solar System." *Journal of Aerospace Engineering* 11 (Oct. 1998): 106–10.

Sagan, Carl. "Why Send Humans to Mars?" *Issues in Science and Technology* 7 (Spring 1991): 80–86.

Whittington, Mark R. "A New Way to Explore Space." *Space Policy Digest* Mar. 2000. 15 March 2001 <http://www.spacepolicy.org/page_mw0300.html>. ◪

Reflections and Inquiries

1. According to Boenig, what are some of the misconceptions that people have about the space program? How well does the author convince you that they are misconceptions?

2. Why, according to Boenig, have many people not supported human exploration of the moon?

3. Exactly what sorts of benefits can space exploration yield? In what way are they benefits?

4. Boenig claims that "one can draw a line between space exploration and any other form of traditional scientific inquiry." What does he mean by this assertion?

Reading to Write

In your background reading of space exploration, identify current projects such as searching for life on Mars, studying solar flares, planning for lunar colonization, experimenting with new rocket propulsion systems and the like. Decide whether these projects are worth pursuing. Write a pro or con paper defending your views.

Connections Across the Clusters

1. Examine human exploration of space from a multicultural perspective (See Cluster 6.) How well represented have women and persons of color been in U.S. space programs? How well represented are they now?

2. What influence, if any, has space exploration had on religious experience? (See Cluster 5.) What influence could it have? Do you consider the aims of

space exploration to be antithetical or complementary to the aims of religion? Why?

Writing Projects

1. Write a detailed proposal for a lunar or Martian colony. How would it be self-sustaining? What activities should it give priority to? What demographic characteristics should it have?

2. Write a position paper in which you argue for or against the effort to establish a human colony on the Moon or on Mars.

3. Write a position paper supporting or challenging the purposefulness of searching for intelligent life beyond Earth.

Suggestions for Further Reading

Anderson, Charlene M. "Human Exploration of Space: Fact and Fantasy." *The Planetary Report* July/Aug. 2000: 18–19.

Greeley, Robert. *Planetary Landscapes*. 2nd ed. New York: Chapman, 1994.

Huntress, Wesley T., Jr. "Grand Challenges for Space Exploration." *The Planetary Report* Mar./Apr. 1999: 4–6.

Lemonick, Michael D. *Other Worlds: The Search for Life in the Universe*. New York: Simon, 1998.

Macvey, John W. *How We Will Reach the Stars*. New York: Collier, 1969.

Miller, Ron, and William K. Hartmann. *The Grand Tour: A Traveler's Guide to the Solar System*. Rev. ed. New York: Workman, 1993.

Morrison, Philip. "Beginnings of Galactic Exploration." *The Planetary Report* May/June 1999: 4–5.

Murray, Bruce. *Journey into Space*. New York: Norton, 1989.

Sagan, Carl. *Cosmos*. New York: Random, 1980.

———. *Pale Blue Dot: A Vision of the Human Future in Space*. New York: Random, 1994.

5 | Are Science and Religion Compatible?

Introduction

In the seventeenth century, when modern science was born, it was feared that new insights into the eternal mysteries of the universe derived from experimentation and telescopic observation would sound the death knell for religious faith. Before modern science brought new truths, what we now call "outer space" was literally considered Heaven. But if outer space was merely an extension of ordinary space, populated by other worlds made of ordinary matter, then where was Heaven? And where was God?

Ever since 1610 when Galileo turned his telescope to the moon and Jupiter and beheld evidence that other worlds were earthlike, not heavenlike, scientists and theologians have debated the relationship between scientific revelations and theological ones. Galileo himself, a devout Catholic, struggled with the issue, asserting that there must be some way to reconcile divine revelation (for example, as manifested in the Old and New Testaments) with what he had seen through the telescope.

Today, despite our increased understanding of the nature of things—or perhaps because of it—scientists and theologians are finding more common ground. Albert Einstein, one of the greatest scientists of all time, insisted that the sensation of the mystical and the beautiful is fundamental to the pursuit of science. Mystery, one could argue, is built into the very fabric of nature, as quantum mechanics would imply. The following cluster of essays provide an overview of this exciting interdisciplinary inquiry, which in recent years, with regard to creationism versus evolution, has been hotly debated in schools, the political arena, and even in the courtroom.

A Designer Universe? | Steven Weinberg

Does the material universe show signs of having been deliberately designed? That is, can we find evidence in nature not only of God's existence but of God's active involvement in the process of creation? Steven Weinberg responds to this centuries-old theological problem from the perspective not only of contemporary physics and cosmology, but of world history. Weinberg is an eminent physicist—he received the Nobel Prize in 1979 and the National Medal of Science in 1991—and is a professor in the Departments of Astronomy and Physics at the University of Texas, Austin.

I have been asked to comment on whether the universe shows signs of having been designed. I don't see how it's possible to talk about this without having at least some vague idea of what a designer would be like. Any possible universe could be explained as the work of some sort of designer. Even a universe that is completely chaotic, without any laws or regularities at all, could be supposed to have been designed by an idiot.

The question that seems to me to be worth answering, and perhaps not impossible to answer, is whether the universe shows signs of having been designed by a deity more or less like those of traditional monotheistic religions—not necessarily a figure from the ceiling of the Sistine Chapel, but at least some sort of personality, some intelligence, who created the universe and has some special concern with life, in particular with human life. I suppose that this is not the idea of a designer held by many people today. They may tell me that they are thinking of something much more abstract, some cosmic spirit of order and harmony, as Einstein did. They are certainly free to think that way, but then I don't know why they use words like "designer" or "God," except perhaps as a form of protective coloration.

It used to be obvious that the world was designed by some sort of intelligence. What else could account for fire and rain and lightning and earthquakes? Above all, the wonderful abilities of living things seemed to point to a creator who had a special interest in life. Today we understand most of these things in terms of physical forces acting under impersonal laws. We don't yet know the most fundamental laws, and we can't work out all the consequences of the laws we do know. The human mind remains extraordinarily difficult to understand, but so is the weather. We can't predict whether it will rain one month from today, but we do know the rules that govern the rain, even though we can't always calculate their consequences. I see nothing about the human mind any more than about the weather that stands out as beyond the hope of understanding as a consequence of impersonal laws acting over billions of years.

Source: Weinberg, Steven. "A Designer Universe?" *New York Review of Books* 21 Oct. 1999: 46–47. Rpt. in *The Best American Science Writing 2000.* Ed. James Gleick. New York: HarperCollins/Ecco, 2000. 239–248. Reprinted by permission of the author.

There do not seem to be any exceptions to this natural order, any miracles. I have the impression that these days most theologians are embarrassed by talk of miracles, but the great monotheistic faiths are founded on miracle stories—the burning bush, the empty tomb, an angel dictating the Koran to Mohammed—and some of these faiths teach that miracles continue at the present day. The evidence for all these miracles seems to me to be considerably weaker than the evidence for cold fusion, and I don't believe in cold fusion. Above all, today we understand that even human beings are the result of natural selection acting over millions of years of breeding and eating.

☑   ☑   ☑

I'd guess that if we were to see the hand of the designer anywhere, it would be in the fundamental principles, the final laws of nature, the book of rules that govern all natural phenomena. We don't know the final laws yet, but as far as we have been able to see, they are utterly impersonal and quite without any special role for life. There is no life force. As Richard Feynman has said, when you look at the universe and understand its laws, "the theory that it is all arranged as a stage for God to watch man's struggle for good and evil seems inadequate."

True, when quantum mechanics was new, some physicists thought that it put humans back into the picture, because the principles of quantum mechanics tell us how to calculate the probabilities of various results that might be found by a human observer. But, starting with the work of Hugh Everett forty years ago, the tendency of physicists who think deeply about these things has been to reformulate quantum mechanics in an entirely objective way, with observers treated just like everything else. I don't know if this program has been completely successful yet, but I think it will be.

I have to admit that, even when physicists will have gone as far as they can go, when we have a final theory, we will not have a completely satisfying picture of the world, because we will still be left with the question "why?" Why this theory, rather than some other theory? For example, why is the world described by quantum mechanics? Quantum mechanics is the one part of our present physics that is likely to survive intact in any future theory, but there is nothing logically inevitable about quantum mechanics; I can imagine a universe governed by Newtonian mechanics instead. So there seems to be an irreducible mystery that science will not eliminate.

But religious theories of design have the same problem. Either you mean something definite by a God, a designer, or you don't. If you don't, then what are we talking about? If you do mean something definite by "God" or "design," if for instance you believe in a God who is jealous, or loving, or intelligent, or whimsical, then you still must confront the question "why?" A religion may assert that the universe is governed by that sort of God, rather than some other sort of God, and it may offer evidence for this belief, but it cannot explain why this should be so.

In this respect, it seems to me that physics is in a better position to give us a partly satisfying explanation of the world than religion can ever be, because although physicists won't be able to explain why the laws of nature are what they are and not something completely different, at least we may be able to explain why they are not *slightly* different. For instance, no one has been able to think of a logically consistent alternative to quantum mechanics that is only slightly different. Once you start trying to make small changes in quantum mechanics, you get into theories with negative probabilities or other logical absurdities. When you combine quantum mechanics with relativity you increase its logical fragility. You find that unless you arrange the theory in just the right way you get nonsense, like effects preceding causes, or infinite probabilities. Religious theories, on the other hand, seem to be infinitely flexible, with nothing to prevent the invention of deities of any conceivable sort.

Now, it doesn't settle the matter for me to say that we cannot see the hand   10
of a designer in what we know about the fundamental principles of science. It might be that, although these principles do not refer explicitly to life, much less human life, they are nevertheless craftily designed to bring it about.

☑   ☑   ☑

Some physicists have argued that certain constants of nature have values that seem to have been mysteriously fine-tuned to just the values that allow for the possibility of life, in a way that could only be explained by the intervention of a designer with some special concern for life. I am not impressed with these supposed instances of fine-tuning. For instance, one of the most frequently quoted examples of fine-tuning has to do with a property of the nucleus of the carbon atom. The matter left over from the first few minutes of the universe was almost entirely hydrogen and helium, with virtually none of the heavier elements like carbon, nitrogen, and oxygen that seem to be necessary for life. The heavy elements that we find on earth were built up hundreds of millions of years later in a first generation of stars, and then spewed out into the interstellar gas out of which our solar system eventually formed.

The first step in the sequence of nuclear reactions that created the heavy elements in early stars is usually the formation of a carbon nucleus out of three helium nuclei. There is a negligible chance of producing a carbon nucleus in its normal state (the state of lowest energy) in collisions of three helium nuclei, but it would be possible to produce appreciable amounts of carbon in stars if the carbon nucleus could exist in a radioactive state with an energy roughly 7 million electron volts (MeV) above the energy of the normal state, matching the energy of three helium nuclei, but (for reasons I'll come to presently) not more than 7.7 MeV above the normal state.

This radioactive state of a carbon nucleus could be easily formed in stars from three helium nuclei. After that, there would be no problem in producing ordinary carbon; the carbon nucleus in its radioactive state would spontaneously emit light and turn into carbon in its normal nonradioactive state, the state found on earth. The critical point in producing carbon is the existence of a radioactive state that can be produced in collisions of three helium nuclei.

In fact, the carbon nucleus is known experimentally to have just such a radioactive state, with an energy 7.65 MeV above the normal state. At first sight this may seem like a pretty close call; the energy of this radioactive state of carbon misses being too high to allow the formation of carbon (and hence of us) by only 0.05 MeV, which is less than one percent of 7.65 MeV. It may appear that the constants of nature on which the properties of all nuclei depend have been carefully fine-tuned to make life possible.

Looked at more closely, the fine-tuning of the constants of nature here   15 does not seem so fine. We have to consider the reason why the formation of carbon in stars requires the existence of a radioactive state of carbon with an energy not more than 7.7 MeV above the energy of the normal state. The reason is that the carbon nuclei in this state are actually formed in a two-step process: first, two helium nuclei combine to form the unstable nucleus of a beryllium isotope, beryllium 8, which occasionally, before it falls apart, captures another helium nucleus, forming a carbon nucleus in its radioactive state, which then decays into normal carbon. The total energy of the beryllium 8 nucleus and a helium nucleus at rest is 7.4 MeV above the energy of the normal state of the carbon nucleus; so if the energy of the radioactive state of carbon were more than 7.7 MeV it could only be formed in a collision of a helium nucleus and a beryllium 8 nucleus if the energy of motion of these two nuclei were at least 0.3 MeV—an energy which is extremely unlikely at the temperatures found in stars.

Thus the crucial thing that affects the production of carbon in stars is not the 7.65 MeV energy of the radioactive state of carbon above its normal state, but the 0.25 MeV energy of the radioactive state, an unstable composite of a beryllium 8 nucleus and a helium nucleus, above the energy of those nuclei at rest.[1] This energy misses being too high for the production of carbon by a fractional amount of 0.05 MeV/0.25 MeV, or 20 percent, which is not such a close call after all.

▪   ▪   ▪

This conclusion about the lessons to be learned from carbon synthesis is somewhat controversial. In any case there *is* one constant whose value does seem remarkably well adjusted in our favor. It is the energy density of empty space, also known as the cosmological constant. It could have any value, but from first principles one would guess that this constant should be very large, and could be positive or negative. If large and positive, the cosmological constant would act as a repulsive force that increases with distance, a force that would prevent matter from clumping together in the early universe, the process that was the first step in forming galaxies and stars and planets and people. If large and negative the cosmological constant would act as an attractive force increasing with distance, a force that would almost immediately reverse the expansion of the universe and cause it to recollapse, leaving no time for the evolution of life. In fact, astronomical observations show that the cosmological constant is quite small, very much smaller than would have been guessed from first principles.

It is still too early to tell whether there is some fundamental principle that can explain why the cosmological constant must be this small. But even if there is no such principle, recent developments in cosmology offer the possibility of an explanation of why the measured values of the cosmological constant and other physical constants are favorable for the appearance of intelligent life. According to the "chaotic inflation" theories of André Linde and others, the expanding cloud of billions of galaxies that we call the big bang may be just one fragment of a much larger universe in which big bangs go off all the time, each one with different values for the fundamental constants.

In any such picture, in which the universe contains many parts with different values for what we call the constants of nature, there would be no difficulty in understanding why these constants take values favorable to intelligent life. There would be a vast number of big bangs in which the constants of nature take values unfavorable for life, and many fewer where life is possible. You don't have to invoke a benevolent designer to explain why we are in one of the parts of the universe where life is possible: in all the other parts of the universe there is no one to raise the question.[2] If any theory of this general type turns out to be correct, then to conclude that the constants of nature have been fine-tuned by a benevolent designer would be like saying, "Isn't it wonderful that God put us here on earth, where there's water and air and the surface gravity and temperature are so comfortable, rather than some horrid place, like Mercury or Pluto?" Where else in the solar system other than on earth could we have evolved?

Reasoning like this is called "anthropic." Sometimes it just amounts to an assertion that the laws of nature are what they are so that we can exist, without further explanation. This seems to me to be little more than mystical mumbo jumbo. On the other hand, if there really is a large number of worlds in which some constants take different values, then the anthropic explanation of why in our world they take values favorable for life is just common sense, like explaining why we live on the earth rather than Mercury or Pluto. The actual value of the cosmological constant, recently measured by observations of the motion of distant supernovas, is about what you would expect from this sort of argument: It is just about small enough so that it does not interfere much with the formation of galaxies. But we don't yet know enough about physics to tell whether there are different parts of the universe in which what are usually called the constants of physics really do take different values. This is not a hopeless question; we will be able to answer it when we know more about the quantum theory of gravitation than we do now.

20

☑   ☑   ☑

It would be evidence for a benevolent designer if life were better than could be expected on other grounds. To judge this, we should keep in mind that a certain capacity for pleasure would readily have evolved through natural selection, as an incentive to animals who need to eat and breed in order to pass on their genes. It may not be likely that natural selection on any one planet would produce animals who are fortunate enough to have the leisure and the ability to do science and think abstractly, but our sample of what is produced by evolution is very biased, by the fact that it is only in these fortunate cases that there is anyone thinking about cosmic design. Astronomers call this a selection effect.

The universe is very large, and perhaps infinite, so it should be no surprise that, among the enormous number of planets that may support only unintelligent life and the still vaster number that cannot support life at all, there is some tiny fraction on which there are living beings who are capable of thinking about the universe, as we are doing here. A journalist who has been assigned to interview lottery winners may come to feel that some special providence has been at work on their behalf, but he should keep in mind the much larger number of lottery players whom he is not interviewing because they haven't won anything. Thus, to judge whether our lives show evidence for a benevolent designer, we have not only to ask whether life is better than would be expected in any case from what we know about natural selection, but we need also to take into account the bias introduced by the fact that it is we who are thinking about the problem.

This is a question that you all will have to answer for yourselves. Being a physicist is no help with questions like this, so I have to speak from my own experience. My life has been remarkably happy, perhaps in the upper 99.99 percentile of human happiness, but even so, I have seen a mother die painfully of cancer, a father's personality destroyed by Alzheimer's disease, and scores of second and third cousins murdered in the Holocaust. Signs of a benevolent designer are pretty well hidden.

The prevalence of evil and misery has always bothered those who believe in a benevolent and omnipotent God. Sometimes God is excused by pointing to the need for free will. Milton gives God this argument in *Paradise Lost*:

> I formed them free, and free they must remain
> Till they enthral themselves: I else must change
> Their nature, and revoke the high decree
> Unchangeable, eternal, which ordained
> Their freedom; they themselves ordained their fall.

It seems a bit unfair to my relatives to be murdered in order to provide an opportunity for free will for Germans, but even putting that aside, how does free will account for cancer? Is it an opportunity of free will for tumors?

I don't need to argue here that the evil in the world proves that the universe is not designed, but only that there are no signs of benevolence that might have shown the hand of a designer. But in fact the perception that God cannot be benevolent is very old. Plays by Aeschylus and Euripides make a quite explicit statement that the gods are selfish and cruel, though they expect better behavior from humans. God in the Old Testament tells us to bash the heads of infidels and demands of us that we be willing to sacrifice our children's lives at His orders, and the God of traditional Christianity and Islam damns us for eternity if we do not worship him in the right manner. Is this a nice way to behave? I know, I know, we are not supposed to judge God according to human standards, but you see the problem here: If we are not yet convinced of His existence, and are looking for signs of His benevolence, then what other standards *can* we use?

The issues that I have been asked to address here will seem to many to be terribly old-fashioned. The "argument from design" made by the English theologian William Paley is not on most people's minds these days. The prestige of religion seems today to derive from what people take to be its moral influence, rather than from what they may think has been its success in accounting for what we see in nature. Conversely, I have to admit that, although I really don't believe in a cosmic designer, the reason that I am taking the trouble to argue about it is that I think that on balance the moral influence of religion has been awful.

This is much too big a question to be settled here. On one side, I could point out endless examples of the harm done by religious enthusiasm, through a long history of pogroms, crusades, and jihads. In our own century it was a Muslim zealot who killed Sadat, a Jewish zealot who killed Rabin, and a Hindu zealot who killed Gandhi. No one would say that Hitler was a Christian zealot, but it is hard to imagine Nazism taking the form it did without the foundation provided by centuries of Christian anti-Semitism. On the other side, many admirers of religion would set countless examples of the good done by religion. For instance, in his recent book *Imagined Worlds,* the distinguished physicist Freeman Dyson has emphasized the role of religious belief in the suppression of slavery. I'd like to comment briefly on this point, not to try to prove anything with one example but just to illustrate what I think about the moral influence of religion.

It is certainly true that the campaign against slavery and the slave trade was greatly strengthened by devout Christians, including the Evangelical layman William Wilberforce in England and the Unitarian minister William Ellery Channing in America. But Christianity, like other great world religions, lived comfortably with slavery for many centuries, and slavery was endorsed in the New Testament. So what was different for anti-slavery Christians like Wilberforce and Channing? There had been no discovery of new sacred scriptures, and neither Wilberforce nor Channing claimed to have received any supernatural revelations. Rather, the eighteenth century had seen a widespread increase in rationality and humanitarianism that led others—for instance, Adam Smith, Jeremy Bentham, and Richard Brinsley Sheridan—also to oppose slavery, on grounds having nothing to do with religion. Lord Mansfield, the author of the decision in *Somersett's Case*, which ended slavery in England (though not its colonies), was no more than conventionally religious, and his decision did not mention religious arguments. Although Wilberforce was the instigator of the campaign against the slave trade in the 1790s, this movement had essential support from many in Parliament like Fox and Pitt, who were not known for their piety. As far as I can tell, the moral tone of religion benefited more from the spirit of the times than the spirit of the times benefited from religion.

Where religion did make a difference, it was more in support of slavery than in opposition to it. Arguments from scripture were used in Parliament to defend the slave trade. Frederick Douglass told in his *Narrative* how his condition as a slave became worse when his master underwent a religious conversion that allowed him to justify slavery as the punishment of the children of Ham. Mark Twain described his mother as a genuinely good person, whose soft heart pitied even Satan, but who had no doubt about the legitimacy of slavery, because in years of living in antebellum Missouri she had never heard any sermon opposing slavery, but only countless sermons preaching that slavery was God's will. With or without religion, good people can behave well and bad people can do evil; but for good people to do evil—that takes religion.

In an e-mail message from the American Association for the Advancement of Science I learned that the aim of this conference is to have a constructive dialogue between science and religion. I am all in favor of a dialogue between science and religion, but not a constructive dialogue. One of the great achievements of science has been, if not to make it impossible for intelligent people to be religious, then at least to make it possible for them not to be religious. We should not retreat from this accomplishment.

Notes

1. This was pointed out in a 1989 paper by M. Livio, D. Hollowell, A. Weiss, and J. W. Truran ("The anthropic significance of the existence of an excited state of 12C," *Nature,* Vol. 340, No. 6231, July 27, 1989). They did the calculation quoted here of the 7.7 MeV maximum energy of the radioactive state of carbon, above which little carbon is formed in stars.

2. The same conclusion may be reached in a more subtle way when quantum mechanics is applied to the whole universe. Through a reinterpretation of earlier work by Stephen Hawking, Sidney Coleman has shown how quantum mechanical effects can lead to a split of the history of the universe (more precisely, in what is called the wave function of the universe) into a huge number of separate possibilities, each one corresponding to a different set of fundamental constants. See Sidney Coleman, "Black Holes as Red Herrings: Topological fluctuations and the loss of quantum coherence," *Nuclear Physics*, Vol. B307 (1988), p. 867. ◢

Reflections and Inquiries

1. What does the opening paragraph reveal about Weinberg's attitude about the universe being designed?

2. Weinberg "does not see any exceptions" to the natural order of things—that is, he sees all that is, including the human mind, "as a consequence of impersonal laws acting over billions of years." How does Weinberg support this claim?

3. Why does Weinberg feel that physics is in a better position than religion to give us a more satisfying explanation of the world?

4. What events in human history have made Weinberg doubtful that a benevolent Creator could exist?

5. Do you agree or disagree with Weinberg's assertion that "with or without religion, good people can behave well and bad people can do evil; but for good people to do evil—that takes religion"?

Reading to Write

1. Write an analysis of Weinberg's use of logical reasoning to defend his thesis. Does his argument contain any logical fallacies? If so, identify them. (See Chapter 5, Reasoning: Methods and Fallacies.)

2. Weinberg alludes to a number of sophisticated scientific concepts such as carbon synthesis, the cosmological constant, and the anthropic principle. Do additional background reading in these concepts, and then write a paper evaluating Weinberg's use of them to defend his thesis.

The Search | Gerald L. Schroeder

A theologian as well as a physicist, Gerald L. Schroeder attempts to reconcile Scripture with the findings of modern science, as did Galileo nearly four hundred years earlier. "Both; scientific and religious traditions," he writes, "are systems of thought that seek the truth." Of course, "truth" in religion is very different from "truth" in science. In the former, truth is revealed and witnessed; it is also felt deeply and intuitively within. In science, no assumptions (hypotheses) attain the status of truth unless they can be verified by anyone at any time. Yet, according to Schroeder, "The Bible . . . can be as demanding as the research of science." Read the following selection and see whether you agree.

Know what to answer a skeptic.
—Talmud

Source: Schroeder, Gerald R. "The Search." Genesis and the Big Bang. New York: Bantam, 1992. 11–26. Copyright © 1990 by Gerald Schroeder. Used by permission of Bantam Books, a division of Random House, Inc.

For the last few years, I have had a continuing debate with my son Joshua. By the age of eight, Josh had already completed five years of biblical study. He had been taught to relate to the Bible in its most literal sense, and so for him, and for many of his teachers, the age of the universe is exactly the age derived from the generations as they are listed in the Bible. This comes to approximately 57 centuries. For them, the cosmological estimate of the age of the universe, some 15 billion years, is a preposterous fiction. According to a literal reading of the Bible, six days is stated as the time between "the beginning" and the appearance of man—and six days it is. As we shall learn, the forebears of this same biblical tradition were well aware that a theology devoid of knowledge of the physical universe was (and is) a contradiction in terms. The implications of general relativity and Doppler shifts in light are an essential part in understanding the opening chapters of Genesis. Although the insights provided by modern science have yet to be assimilated by many contemporary teachers of Genesis, we shall find that they are a help rather than a hindrance toward the rapprochement of the secular and nonsecular.

The discrepancy between the 5700-year biblical age of the universe and the 15-billion-year scientific estimate might not have caused the family debate that led me to write *Genesis and the Big Bang* had there not been one, almost extraneous, circumstance in our lives. That circumstance was a nearby archaeological dig.

For three years we lived in Zikhron Ya'aqov, a village on the Carmel range overlooking Israel's coastal plain. The plain is bounded on the west by the Mediterranean. A few kilometers inland from the shore, the massive limestone outcrop of the Carmel range rises abruptly to form the plain's eastern boundary. It is a wonderfully productive area. This is especially true of the region between Zikhron Ya'aqov and Haifa. Here rows of avocado and orange trees, heavy with foliage and fruit, border the blue-green waters filling acres of fishponds. These ponds share space with white-specked fields of cotton. The productivity of the area is probably not new. Archaeological evidence indicates that this land has provided its material abundance to man and his predecessors for tens of thousands of years.

A few kilometers north of our village, among scrub growth halfway up the steep face of Mt. Carmel, the yawning black openings of several particularly large caves appear as sentinels overseeing the coast. On two or three occasions, my family and I have scrambled up Mt. Carmel to explore the archaeological digs within the caves. It is these digs that are the source of my continuing debate with Josh.

Here artifacts and fossils of that prehistoric animal, Neanderthal man, 5 have been found. For the theologian steeped in a superficial reading of Genesis, these fossils may be Neanderthal, but they have nothing to do with man!

For the paleontologist, the age of the fossils also presents a problem, but of a different sort. The bones of Neanderthal man are too old to date using carbon-14 methods. So much of the original skeletal carbon-14 has decayed (one-half the original content decays radioactively each 5,600 years) that the small amount of carbon-14 remaining cannot be reliably measured. The bones' location within geologically known strata gives them an estimated age of 60,000 years. For Josh and for many other people, Jew and Christian alike, a 60,000-year archaeological history is at least 54,000 years in error. It is totally at odds with a literal understanding of the opening chapters of the book of Genesis.

But this discord between archaeology and theology is neither necessary nor valid. As I have studied the details of biblical and scientific texts, I have reached what was for me an enlightening and unexpected conclusion: The biblical narrative and the scientific account of our genesis are two mutually compatible descriptions of the same, single, and identical reality. My goal in this book is to explain that compatibility to expert and layperson alike.

Simply stated, I will discuss here the first week of Genesis. To the literalist, these first six days can be a problem. Fossils place the appearance of beings with humanlike features at well over the 60,000-year age of the Neanderthal fossils of the Carmel caves. Although dating the time of Peking man's existence has the same types of problems as those encountered when dating the remains of Neanderthal man, the archaeological estimate is that these humanlike animals lived some 300,000 years ago. Their home, near Cho-k'ou-tien, China, was in a group of limestone caves quite similar to those found in the Carmel range. *Homo erectus,* the genus and species to which Peking man belonged, made its appearance 1.5 to 2 million years ago. Because of this antiquity, only a few nearly complete *Homo erectus* skeletons have been found. One of these, located in what is now an arid region of Kenya, is the Lake Turkana Boy. It is estimated that the lad lived his twelve years of life 1.6 million years ago. Looking at this fossil, it is clear that, except for the shortened forehead, these early hominids had features so similar to modern humans that they could go unnoticed if they walked on a busy city street.

But does mankind's history really stretch back a million years, or even several tens of thousands of years? A strictly literal view of the Bible would say no. To the literalist, there was no prehistoric man. Adam was the first man and he was formed some 5700 years ago from the dust of the Earth (Gen. 2:7).

Part of the contradiction between archaeological evidence and biblical tradition is semantic, originating in the use of the word *man*. Archaeologists use the term to describe prehistoric animals that had some, but not necessarily all, of the features of modern man. Biblically speaking, the term *man* is applicable only to Adam and his progeny. It is, however, no secret that the divergent views of science and tradition are based on differences far more fundamental than the definition of words. In fact, most biblical commentators accept that the meaning of words of the Bible, especially as in the creation story, must be understood in accordance with their context. "The terms for *water, darkness, wind, heavens,* and *earth* as used in the first ten verses of Genesis have meanings that are quite different when used later on in the Bible. It is the calendar

10

of the early universe that raises a discrepancy far more difficult to explain than the variances in terminology.

Entire herds of fossilized rhinoceroses, their calves nestled between their legs in nursing position, have been dated by the potassium-argon content of the volcanic ash that buried them, as having lived 10 million years ago. Dinosaurs have been firmly established, at least according to paleontologists' data, to have roamed the Earth for 100 million years, becoming extinct some 65 million years ago. The simplest forms of life, the early prokaryotic (nucleus-free) bacteria and blue-green algae, make their first fossil appearance in earliest sedimentary rocks. These are dated as being 3 to 4 billion years old. The oldest rocks are only some 600 million years older. These are the original igneous rocks.

The length of this fossil record certainly seems to contradict the relatively brief period of creation and genesis presented by the Bible. And yet the fossil record covers only a fraction of the age that current cosmological observations ascribe to our universe. Where do the preponderance of paleontological and astronomical data, indicating an Earth some 4.5 billion years old and a universe that reaches back 10 to 20 billion years, fit into traditional biblical scholarship? At first it would appear that these findings put paleontology hopelessly at odds with the Bible. For the total cosmic evolution from the creation (the "In the beginning . . ." of Genesis 1:1) to the appearance of Adam gets only a bit more than five biblical days.

As an affirmation of faith, the literalist can explain the paleontological finds as having been placed in rocks at creation by the Creator. They might be there to satisfy man's need to rationalize the nature of the world, or to test man's belief in the biblical narrative. This argument, while impossible to disprove, is the weakest of reeds (Isa. 36:6) in a world full of explosive and convincing discovery.

Some theologians argue that the methods of paleontological dating are flawed. These methods depend on measurements of radioactive decay (see Table 1). They claim that the rates of decay today are not the same as in prehistoric times. If this were true, the ages of fossils or rocks could not be estimated from current measurements of radioactivity.

Again, it is impossible to disprove the idea that patterns of radioactive decay have changed during the past few thousand years. But the very concept of a fickleness in nature is contrary to all modern evidence. Our experience with the laws of nature, including those that govern radioactivity, is that they are unchanging. Imagine the bedlam of our lives if we were forced to test the consistency of gravity each time we put a glass on a table or the rate of passage of time in our Newtonian system each time we had an appointment to keep. The constancy of nature's laws is an integral part of life as we experience it. In fact, we base our entire life pattern on the assumption that the laws of nature are predictable.

TABLE 1	How the Radioactive Decay of Carbon Is Used to Date a Fossil				
	Atoms		Atoms		Atoms
Carbon-14	0000 0000 0000	first 5600 years	00 00 00	second 5600 years	0 0 0
Carbon-12	0000 0000 0000	first 5600 years	0000 0000 0000	second 5600 years	0000 0000 0000

Two of the types of carbon found in all living things are referred to as carbon-12 and carbon-14. Both carbon-12 and carbon-14 act the same way as far as the chemical reactions of life are concerned, but carbon-14 is radioactive and carbon-12 is not. During every 5600 years, half of the carbon-14 atoms decay. Therefore, from the time that a plant or an animal dies, the ratio between the amounts of carbon-14 and carbon-12 is constantly decreasing. During the first 5600 years following death, the ratio decreases by half because half the carbon-14 decays in this period. During the next 5600 years, this ratio again decreases by half so that at the end of this period the carbon-14 to carbon-12 ratio will be one-fourth of the ratio that existed at the time of death. This continual decrease proceeds as long as any carbon-14 remains. By measuring the ratio of carbon-14 to carbon-12 in a fossil, it is possible to estimate the amount of time that has passed since death. Two assumptions are necessary to use radioactivity as a means of dating: The rates of decay must always have been the same as they are now and the ratio of carbon-14 to carbon-12 (or whichever other radioactive elements are being used) at the moment of death must be known. We assume that the initial ratio of carbon-14 to carbon-12 in plants and animals has always been similar to what it is today.

But we need not reconcile biblical tradition and the findings of science with weak reeds. It is possible to maintain faith in the validity of the Bible and also to accept that the cave on Mt. Carmel *does* have 60,000 years of history layered in the deposits on its floor and that this cave was a dwelling place of the prehistoric creature we have labeled Neanderthal man.

Both scientific and religious traditions are systems of thought that seek the truth. Religion bases its search for truth within knowledge believed to have been attained by revelation. Science seeks the same truth by evaluating interactions observed in our physical world. Often, it is not realized that gaining an accurate understanding of the Bible is an endeavor that can be as demanding as the research of science. The biblical text is tersely cogent and yet "it speaks in the language of man." Included in the seemingly simple accounts of mankind's development and encounters with the Creator are concepts that, we see by hindsight, were to guide the Western world for over 3000 years and to speak to civilizations that stretch from a tribe of just-freed slaves trekking through an unsown desert (Jer. 2:2) to modern man circling the Earth in a space capsule.

To the questions that science has posed to tradition there are answers, but they emerge only from a serious probe of the science and an understanding of the tradition that goes well beyond the literal biblical text.

◪   ◪   ◪

The realization that biblical scholarship and the natural sciences are closely related is not new—but it is still important. "Study astronomy and physics if you desire to comprehend the relation between the world and God's management of it." This deep insight into sources of knowledge was written in the year 1190 by Moses Maimonides (*The Guide for the Perplexed*). Thousands of years earlier, the author of the book of Ecclesiastes warned, "If the iron is blunt and he does not sharpen its edge, then he must exert extra effort, but," he continued, "wisdom increases his skill" (Eccles. 10:10). Although it is true that, as the Psalmist wrote, "The heavens tell of the glory of God and the firmament tells the works of His hands" (Ps. 19:2), it is also a reality that understanding the story that these heavens tell is no small task.

To reach our goal of understanding the interplay, the intimate connection, between the Divine and the natural, we will need more than a love for the Bible; we also need a knowledge of the natural sciences. Maimonides compared those who understand the blending of the natural and the Divine to royal subjects being within the throne room of their exalted king, while those seeking an understanding of the Bible but lacking an understanding of the natural sciences were subjects groping *in vain* for the outermost gate of their king's palace. [20]

Without an understanding of nature, the Earth appears to be the center of the universe. Man appears to be able to solve all material problems and learn all details. His works become his gods. Galileo's probing of space with the telescope dispelled the first notion. Heisenberg's uncertainty principle dispelled the second. Unfortunately, we are at times still shackled to the third notion of our works being our gods.

If we are to approach the "throne room" of which Maimonides wrote, we will have to understand at least part of the physics and chemistry of inert and living forms of matter. We must deal with exotic-sounding concepts such as *entropy* and *general relativity*. To be certain that we consider only established principles in the natural sciences, I have imposed limits on the sources of information we use. These are publications of leading scientists in their fields, including works by physicists and cosmologists such as Albert Einstein, Steven Weinberg, Stephen Hawking, Edwin Taylor, John Archibald Wheeler, and Alan Guth; geophysicists such as A. G. W. Cameron, Frank Press, and Raymond Siever; and biologists and molecular chemists such as George Wald and Francis Crick.

When we seek an understanding of the biblical text, we are confronted with the abbreviated manner in which episodes are recorded in the Bible. This succinct form has made interpretive explanations of the text an integral part of biblical study. In Jeremiah (23:29) we read: "Behold, My words are as fire, says the Lord, and as a hammer that shatters the rock." Based on the parallel context of these two phrases, the Talmud teaches that "just as a hammer breaks a rock into many pieces, so can a single biblical passage have many meanings." The result is that there is a plethora of opinions on each biblical passage.

In this book, I deal almost exclusively with information contained in the Five Books of Moses, that is the Pentateuch, or in Hebrew, the Torah. The validity and import of these five books, and really of the entire Old Testament, is shared by Jew and Christian alike. Because of this shared heritage, it has been possible here to rely on commentaries that are in essence nonsectarian in that they embrace beliefs held in common by the Judeo-Christian tradition.

Only a few biblical commentators have withstood time's test. Four are accepted by Jew and Christian alike as guiding lights in the interpretation of the book of Genesis. It is on these four that I rely. They are Onkelos (ca. C.E. 150), Rashi (Solomon ben Isaac, C.E. 1040–1105, France), Maimonides (Moses ben Maimon, C.E. 1135–1204, Spain, Egypt; also known as Rambam), and Nahmanides (Moses ben Nahman, C.E. 1194–1270, Spain, Israel; also known as Ramban). Because their commentaries were written long before the advent of modern physics, we avoid the folly of using interpretations of tradition that may have been biased by modern scientific discoveries. 25

Onkelos translated the Five Books of Moses into Aramaic. Aramaic was the common language of the Middle East during the centuries that preceded and followed the start of the common era. It was the language routinely spoken by Jews of the period in which the debates in the Talmud were recorded. This included the time of Jesus. Aramaic, a semitic language, is sufficiently similar to Hebrew to allow it to serve as a linguistic cross-reference. By translating the Hebrew into Aramaic, Onkelos provided definitions to words, the meanings of which had become obscure. This source is still in such standard use that it is referred to as "the translation."

Rashi's trailblazing commentary on the Bible made available to all students interpretations of biblical words and phrases that hitherto had been accessible only to students learning with leading scholars.

Maimonides, in his *Guide for the Perplexed* (1190), discussed aspects of the Bible that, as the title suggests, perplexed students and laypersons. The sections of the *Guide* relevant to our study deal with aspects of Genesis and include the time shortly after the initial act of creation.

Nahmanides, teaching in the century after Rashi and Maimonides, had the benefit of their scholarship coupled with his personal training in tradition and mysticism. He believed that a full understanding of the origins of the universe was contained in the Bible as received by Moses. The information was written either explicitly or by hints taken in some instances from the very form of the written text.

> Hear counsel and receive instruction in order that you will become wise. (Prov. 19:20)

In recent times an unusual orientation has arisen among many who are eager to evaluate the relevance of the Bible to daily life. There is the misconception that an understanding of the text comes to one as a natural heritage, as if we are bequeathed it genetically along with the instinct to breathe or the 30 ability to reason. The most simplistic meanings are assumed to be adequate and study of commentaries thereon is considered superfluous. Now this presents an interesting inconsistency in how we evaluate information.

The paleontologist shows that the brontosaurus bones he has examined have a scientifically confirmed age of 80 million years and, an adherent to the theory of evolution, interprets these and other fossils to demonstrate a theory of evolution. But there is no *dynamic* pro-Darwinian evidence in the fossil record. Neither the fossils nor the variety of life that surrounds us provides any proof of one species changing into another, or a development of complex life forms from earlier, more simple forms. The incomplete data are analyzed and interpreted, and we now feel secure, based on these interpretations, that life did indeed start with a few simple morphologies and develop over millennia to the seemingly infinite variety of today's living forms.

Similarly, the cosmologist interprets spectra of starlight to prove that the universe is 10 to 20 billion years old and in a state of rapid expansion. But a literal interpretation of the star-filled sky, whether viewed by eye or by telescope, is that the Sun and Moon and planets move and all other celestial bodies occupy fixed, unchanging positions. Perhaps three or four times per thousand years one of these tiny specks of light we call stars gets brighter and then fades to oblivion. But for the most part, the heavens are quiescent. They give the *literal* appearance of a steady-state system, not one in expansion as *interpretations* of cosmological data imply.

On the basis of a literal "reading" of the physical world, we might discard the claims of scientists to a deeper understanding of our universe. But such literal interpretations of the heavens or of biology are never used by scientists. Interpretation is an integral, indeed essential, part of scientific inquiry.

This flow between the apparent and the actual holds for biblical study as well. A literal reading of the Bible reveals only a part of the wealth of information held within the text. Every major theological treatise that has withstood the test of time promulgates the need for an understanding of the biblical text in a way that is compatible with *both* literal and interpretative meanings.

Laws of physics, especially those describing the flow of time and matter, are often difficult to conceptualize. They are, however, amenable to proof. What might be called the laws of divine science, that is, the validity of biblical interpretations, are considerably less open to proof. In fact, they are usually taken (or rejected) on faith.

If we are not to construct arguments of gossamer, we must tackle some of the more rigorous aspects of theology. These theological concepts are even more difficult to integrate into our thought processes than those of physics and cosmology. We all have an emotional stake in religion. Be it pro or con, our psyches will resist changes in our perceptions of the Bible's meaning. The most basic theological concept that we require as a background to our discussions is the realization that the Bible includes a range of knowledge, only part of which is immediately obvious from the actual text. Perception of this information requires an interpretive understanding of the text.

35

An analogy of such interpretation might be a layman reading a text written in scientific notation. For example, the statement 10^3 could be read as a typographical error for 103. To the trained scientist, it is obvious that 10^3 is read as 1000. The information held within the biblical text, but beyond the literal reading of the words, was as obvious to those versed in biblical interpretation as the fact that, to anyone who knows scientific notation, 10^3 means 1000 and not 103.

In his summary of the Torah (Deut. 31), Moses in effect calls out for interpretation of the text by referring to the entire Torah as a poem. Because the text is clearly not written in the form of a poem, this reference appears to relate not to form but to "the essence." The meanings of poems go well beyond the literal text and include subtleties held within the words and even the form. This is what Maimonides taught in regard to Proverbs 25:11, "A word fitly spoken is like apples of gold in a filigree vessel of silver"—the vessel (the literal meaning of the text) is beautiful and valuable, but the golden apples held within the vessel (the inner meanings of the text) are even *more* beautiful and valuable.

Nahmanides taught that the subtleties found in the Torah go even beyond those of a poem, reaching to the very shapes of the letters. In the "Introduction" to his *Commentary on Genesis,* he stated that everything that was transmitted to Moses was written in the Torah explicitly or by implication in words, in the numerical value of the letters, as bent or crooked letters, or their crownlets. This was implied in the verse from the Song of Songs (1:4): "The King has brought me into His chambers." This verse informs us that in the Bible, the king, God, has given mankind the knowledge of God's way in the universe, God's chambers, as it were. We need only know how to interpret the Bible.

Because of the importance accorded not only to the content of the Bible, but also to its form, to this day the addition or removal of a single letter, or even the changing of the shape of a letter, invalidates an entire Torah scroll. For a text containing 304,805 letters, this was and is an extraordinary demand of precision. Torah scrolls are still written only by specially trained *sofreim,* or "writers of the Book." The parchment and even the ink most be specially prepared for use in the scroll. 40

With the establishment of the State of Israel, scrolls of the Five Books of Moses have been brought together from communities separated in time since the exile of Jews from Jerusalem and in space by the thousands of miles between the Arabian peninsula and Western Europe. Perhaps the most extreme of the reunions was the return of the Yemenite community to Israel. The Jewish community of Yemen had a residence in Arabia since the destruction of the Temple in 586 B.C.E.

The texts and forms of the scrolls from the Arabian peninsula differed in only one aspect from those saved from the Holocaust of Europe. The cover of an Arabian scroll is rigid and as such it holds the scroll in a vertical position when opened to be read or studied. The cover of a European scroll is soft cloth and because it offers no support, the scrolls when opened are placed horizontally on a table. But as for the actual content and form, they are one and the same. If indeed the Torah as revealed at Sinai contained concealed information, the faithfulness by which the *sofreim* transmitted the text across the generations has ensured that this information is still potentially available.

Unfortunately we no longer have the skills to lay open all the hints within the Bible. We have, however, the teachings of the sages who tapped this information. The topics of these teachings range from the cleansing of a clay pot to the creation of the universe. As we shall see, combined they present an ancient account of our cosmic roots, which are remarkably similar to those presented by current cosmology and paleontology.

☒   ☒   ☒

In a manner that parallels the unfolding of deeper meanings within the Bible, the advances achieved by scientific research during the last 50 years have brought major changes in our understanding of our universe, its age, origin, and development. Well into the twentieth century, both astronomers and physicists believed the age of the Earth to be measured in millions, not billions, of years. Oceanographers gave the origin of the ocean waters as condensation from a primeval cloud that surrounded a once molten Earth. Biologists gave the source of life as the result of random associations of molecules such as ammonia and methane, that eventually through trial and error grew to be amino acids, the structures of life, and then life itself. Spacial dimensions and the passage of time were considered absolute, fixed, and mathematically true. As the core sciences of physics, chemistry, and mathematics made their way into what were once primarily descriptive fields of astronomy. geology, and biology, the age of the Sun was found to be measured in billions and not millions of years; the amount of water able to be contained in a cloud surrounding a molten Earth was found to be a small fraction of the water now present in the world's oceans; the time for random associations even of optimal, chemically advanced molecules (such as amino acids) to form the simplest bacterium was found to be possible only in times that equaled or exceeded the entire age of the universe—not merely the time the Earth, or even the solar system, has existed. But most extraordinary of all, the rate of time's passage and the spacial dimensions of objects were found to be not at all fixed but instead to vary in a grand manner that depends on the relation of the observer and the observed.

These new scientific insights might have been uncomfortable for traditionalists of science. They represented radical departures from the ideas prevalent at the time. In sharp contrast to this, for scholars who understand biblical tradition, each advance has increased the compatibility of science and theology.

For over 3000 years following the revelation at Mt. Sinai, the Western world had based its traditional concept of the origin of the world on the opening chapters of Genesis. This posed no intellectual problem because there was

45

no challenge from a credible outside source that staked an equal claim to fundamental truths. It was a time when the family tree showing a few generations could satisfy a desire to understand one's position within the world. Remaining questions were answered by a religion that came neatly packaged in prayer books and a pastor's sermon. Then came the scientific enlightenment, and physics and cosmology claimed to provide the fundamental truths concerning our existence. Cosmologists measured the age of the universe to be 10 to 20 billion years and not the approximately 5700 years calculated from the dates given in the Bible. Paleontologists discovered evidence of a gradual evolution in the forms of life. This evolution extended over billions of years, not a few days. Man became merely the latest addition to the tree of life. Finally, the crushing blow: All life was found to have a single and extraordinarily complex genetic code—clear indication of man's evolution from bacteria.

Since the rise of scientific thinking and discovery, particularly in the late nineteenth and early twentieth centuries with the giant intellectual leaps taken by Einstein, Bohr, Planck, and others, the issues surrounding the very early universe have become crucial to our understanding of mankind's place on Earth, the nature of the cosmos, and the meaning of Genesis.

For the average layperson, Jew or Christian, there must necessarily be a conflict between science and biblical tradition. Is the biblical story of Creation the ultimate metaphor? Is it to be taken as literal truth? How can we reconcile the observable facts of paleontology and the laboratory proofs of the equations of Einstein with the very essence of Judeo-Christian faith—the biblical story of the first six days?

Have these seemingly unequivocal scientific revelations sounded the death knell for religious tradition as we have known it? Are the worlds of science and religion mutually exclusive?

The truth is just the opposite. The newly won knowledge of the universe 50 is in fact the fertile ground for tradition's flowering.

It is essential to bear in mind that science has *not* provided explanations for the two principal starting points in our lives: the start of our universe and the start of life itself. When we try to describe the conditions at that crucial interface between total nothingness and the start of our universe, we are confronted with a point of space having infinitely high density and infinitely small dimensions. In the language of physics, such a point is called a singularity. Singularities cannot be handled mathematically in the dimensions we experience: the length, width, and height of things and the passage of time. Changing to imaginary dimensions of time allows the math to be handled but does nothing to remove the fact that an untenable singularity existed in real time at the Big Bang.

We might bypass this problem of a beginning by hypothesizing that there was no beginning, that the universe has been here forever. But even that does not work. This would require an infinite number of cycles in which the universe expanded, then contracted and reexploded to start a new Big Bang cycle. But, as we shall learn, this is thermodynamically not possible. There could not have been an infinite number of cycles if any of the material world were to remain. Because we are very much here in our tangible forms, along with all the other material stuff of the world, there must have been a beginning sometime in the finite past. But we cannot understand how, scientifically.

The answers provided by science for life's origins are no more satisfying than those provided for the universe's origins. Since the monumental "Conference on Macro-Evolution" was held in Chicago in 1980, there has been a total reevaluation of life's origins and development. In regard to the Darwinian theory of evolution, the world-famous paleontologist of the American Museum of Natural History, Dr. Niles Eldridge, unequivocally declared, "The pattern that we were told to find for the last one hundred and twenty years *does not exist.*" There is now overwhelmingly strong evidence, both statistical and paleontological, that life could *not* have been started on Earth by a series of random chemical reactions. Today's best mathematical estimates state that there simply was not enough time for random reactions to get life going as fast as the fossil record shows that it did. The reactions were either directed by some, as of yet unknown, physical force or a metaphysical guide, or life arrived here from elsewhere. But the "elsewhere" answer merely pushes the start of life into an even more unlikely time constraint.

For decades, many scientists have presented the misconception that there are rational explanations for the origins of the universe, life, and mankind. The shortcomings of the popular theories were merely swept under the rug to avoid confusing the issues. The knowledge that scientists do *not* have these explanations has now been coupled by the awareness of the fossil record's failure to confirm Darwin's (or any other) theory of the gradual evolution of life. The demonstration of these misconceptions has brought many scientists and laypersons to an uncomfortable realization: The problems of our origins, problems that most of us would have preferred to consider solved by experts who should know the answers, in fact have *not been solved* and are not about to be solved, at least not by the purely scientific methods used to date.

During my three decades as a scientist active in applied nuclear physics and oceanography, and a 25-year immersion in the study of biblical tradition, I have found that there *are* answers to the questions posed by my son Joshua. What was for me the most exciting discovery in this search is that the duration and events of the billions of years that, according to cosmologists, have followed the Big Bang and those events of the first six days of Genesis are in fact one and the same. *They are identical realities that have been described in vastly different terms.*

The scientific and theological sources that led me to this realization are not the intellectual reserve of an elite in either discipline. Rather they are a heritage readily available to all who seek them. Using these sources, we can complete what might otherwise be a perplexing search for our cosmic roots. The result can be, for skeptic or believer, Jew or Christian, a fresh understanding of the key events in the life of our universe and in one's personal genesis as well. ◪

Reflections and Inquiries

1. In what way can modern scientific theories, such as those of relativity and paleontology, help rather than hinder efforts to achieve harmony between science and religion?

2. According to Schroeder, part of the reason for the contradiction between archaeological evidence and Scripture is *semantic*. What does he mean by this? What examples does Schroeder cite? What examples of your own can you add?

3. Discuss the role of Scriptural interpretation as a way of establishing harmony between religion and science. Is there a Scriptural sanction for interpretation over literalism? If so, what?

4. Schroeder claims that people have "an emotional stake in religion." What does he mean by this? Is it possible for people to have an emotional stake in science as well?

Reading to Write

In a short paper, reflect on the prospects of science and religion achieving greater harmony. Allude specifically to points raised by Schroeder.

The Anaesthetic of Familiarity | Richard Dawkins

Science has often been accused of ruthlessly removing mystery and beauty from the world. The title of Richard Dawkins's book, *Unweaving the Rainbow*, from which the following selection is taken, echoes a lament of John Keats from his poem "Lamia" that could serve as the outcry of all who accede to the notion that science is coldly, inhumanly rational:

Philosophy [i.e., science] will clip an Angel's wings
Conquer all mysteries by rule and line,
Empty the haunted air, and gnomed mine—
Unweave a rainbow . . .

Dawkins, an eminent evolutionary biologist and currently the Charles Simonyi Professor of the Public Understanding of Science at Oxford University, argues against this thesis by claiming that science is itself filled with the miraculous, the beautiful, the wonderful.

To live at all is miracle enough.
—Mervyn Peake, *The Glassblower* (1950)

We are going to die, and that makes us the lucky ones. Most people are never going to die because they are never going to be born. The potential people who could have been here in my place but who will in fact never see the light of day outnumber the sand grains of Arabia. Certainly those unborn ghosts include greater poets than Keats, scientists greater than Newton. We know this because the set of possible people allowed by our DNA so massively exceeds the set of actual people. In the teeth of these stupefying odds it is you and I, in our ordinariness, that are here.

Moralists and theologians place great weight upon the moment of conception, seeing it as the instant at which the soul comes into existence. If, like me, you are unmoved by such talk, you still must regard a particular instant, nine months before your birth, as the most decisive event in your personal fortunes. It is the moment at which your consciousness suddenly became trillions of times more foreseeable than it was a split second before. To be sure, the embryonic you that came into existence still had plenty of hurdles to leap. Most conceptuses end in early abortion before their mother even knew they were there, and we are all lucky not to have done so. Also, there is more to personal identity than genes, as identical twins (who separate after the moment of fertilization) show us. Nevertheless, the instant at which a particular spermatozoon penetrated a particular egg was, in your private hindsight, a moment of dizzying singularity. It was then that the odds against your becoming a person dropped from astronomical to single figures.

The lottery starts before we are conceived. Your parents had to meet, and the conception of each was as improbable as your own. And so on back, through your four grandparents and eight great grandparents, back to where it doesn't bear thinking about. Desmond Morris opens his autobiography, *Animal Days* (1979), in characteristically arresting vein:

> Napoleon started it all. If it weren't for him, I might not be sitting here now writing these words . . . for it was one of his cannonballs, fired in the Peninsular War, that shot off the arm of my great-great-grandfather, James Morris, and altered the whole course of my family history.

Morris tells how his ancestor's enforced change of career had various knock-on effects culminating in his own interest in natural history. But he really needn't have bothered. There's no 'might' about it. *Of course* he owes his very existence to Napoleon. So do I and so do you. Napoleon didn't have to shoot off James Morris's arm in order to seal young Desmond's fate, and yours and mine, too. Not just Napoleon but the humblest medieval peasant had only to sneeze in order to affect something which changed something else which, after a long chain reaction, led to the consequence that one of your would-be ancestors failed to be your ancestor and became somebody else's instead. I'm not talking about 'chaos theory', or the equally trendy 'complexity theory', but just about the ordinary statistics of causation. The thread of historical events by which our existence hangs is wincingly tenuous.

> When compared with the stretch of time unknown to us, O king, the present life of men on earth is like the flight of a single sparrow through the hall where, in winter, you sit with your captains and ministers. Entering at one door and leaving by another, while it is inside it is untouched by the wintry storm; but this brief interval of calm is over in a moment, and it returns to the winter whence it came, vanishing from your sight. Man's life is similar; and of what follows it, or what went before, we are utterly ignorant.
>
> The Venerable Bede,
> *A History of the English Church and People* (731)

This is another respect in which we are lucky. The universe is older than a hundred million centuries. Within a comparable time the sun will swell to a red giant and engulf the earth. Every century of hundreds of millions has been in its time, or will be when its time comes, 'the present century'. Interestingly, some physicists don't like the idea of a 'moving present', regarding it as a subjective phenomenon for which they find no house room in their equations. But it is a subjective argument I am making. How it feels to me, and I guess to you as well, is that the present moves from the past to the future, like a tiny spotlight, inching its way along a gigantic ruler of time. Everything behind the spotlight is in darkness, the darkness of the dead past. Everything ahead of the spotlight is in the darkness of the unknown future. The odds of your century being the one in the spotlight are the same as the odds that a penny, tossed down at random, will land on a particular ant crawling somewhere along the road from New York to San Francisco. In other words, it is overwhelmingly probable that you are dead.

In spite of these odds, you will notice that you are, as a matter of fact, alive. People whom the spotlight has already passed over, and people whom the spotlight has not reached, are in no position to read a book. I am equally lucky to be in a position to write one, although I may not be when you read these words. Indeed, I rather hope that I shall be dead when you do. Don't misunderstand me. I love life and hope to go on for a long time yet, but any author wants his works to reach the largest possible readership. Since the total future population is likely to outnumber my contemporaries by a large margin, I cannot but aspire to be dead when you see these words. Facetiously seen, it turns out to be no more than a hope that my book will not soon go out of print. But what I see as I write is that I am lucky to be alive and so are you.

We live on a planet that is all but perfect for our kind of life: not too warm and not too cold, basking in kindly sunshine, softly watered; a gently spinning, green and gold harvest festival of a planet. Yes, and alas, there are deserts and slums; there is starvation and racking misery to be found. But take

5

a look at the competition. Compared with most planets this is paradise, and parts of earth are still paradise by any standards. What are the odds that a planet picked at random would have these complaisant properties? Even the most optimistic calculation would put it at less than one in a million.

Imagine a spaceship full of sleeping explorers, deep-frozen would-be colonists of some distant world. Perhaps the ship is on a forlorn mission to save the species before an unstoppable comet, like the one that killed the dinosaurs, hits the home planet. The voyagers go into the deep-freeze soberly reckoning the odds against their spaceship's ever chancing upon a planet friendly to life. If one in a million planets is suitable at best, and it takes centuries to travel from each star to the next, the spaceship is pathetically unlikely to find a tolerable, let alone safe, haven for its sleeping cargo.

But imagine that the ship's robot pilot turns out to be unthinkably lucky. After millions of years the ship does find a planet capable of sustaining life: a planet of equable temperature, bathed in warm starshine, refreshed by oxygen and water. The passengers, Rip van Winkles, wake stumbling into the light. After a million years of sleep, here is a whole new fertile globe, a lush planet of warm pastures, sparkling streams and waterfalls, a world bountiful with creatures, darting through alien green felicity. Our travellers walk entranced, stupefied, unable to believe their unaccustomed senses or their luck.

As I said, the story asks for too much luck; it would never happen. And yet, isn't that what *has* happened to each one of us? We *have* woken after hundreds of millions of years asleep, defying astronomical odds. Admittedly we didn't arrive by spaceship, we arrived by being born, and we didn't burst conscious into the world but accumulated awareness gradually through babyhood. The fact that we slowly apprehend our world, rather than suddenly discover it, should not subtract from its wonder.

Of course I am playing tricks with the idea of luck, putting the cart before the horse. It is no accident that our kind of life finds itself on a planet whose temperature, rainfall and everything else are exactly right. If the planet were suitable for another kind of life, it is that other kind of life that would have evolved here. But we as individuals are still hugely blessed. Privileged, and not just privileged to enjoy our planet. More, we are granted the opportunity to understand why our eyes are open, and why they see what they do, in the short time before they close for ever. 10

Here, it seems to me, lies the best answer to those petty-minded scrooges who are always asking what is the *use* of science. In one of those mythic remarks of uncertain authorship, Michael Faraday is alleged to have been asked what was the use of science. 'Sir,' Faraday replied. 'Of what use is a new-born child?' The obvious thing for Faraday (or Benjamin Franklin, or whoever it was) to have meant was that a baby might be no use for anything at present, but it has great potential for the future. I now like to think that he meant something else, too: What is the use of bringing a baby into the world if the only thing it does with its life is just work to go on living? If everything is judged by how 'useful' it is—useful for staying alive, that is—we are left facing a futile circularity. There must be some added value. At least a part of life should be devoted to *living* that life, not just working to stop it ending. This is how we rightly justify spending taxpayers' money on the arts. It is one of the justifications properly offered for conserving rare species and beautiful buildings. It is how we answer those barbarians who think that wild elephants and historic houses should be preserved only if they 'pay their way'. And science is the same. Of course science pays its way; of course it is useful. But that is not *all* it is.

After sleeping through a hundred million centuries we have finally opened our eyes on a sumptuous planet, sparkling with colour, bountiful with life. Within decades we must close our eyes again. Isn't it a noble, an enlightened way of spending our brief time in the sun, to work at understanding the universe and how we have come to wake up in it? This is how I answer when I am asked—as I am surprisingly often—why I bother to get up in the mornings. To put it the other way round, isn't it sad to go to your grave without ever wondering why you were born? Who, with such a thought, would not spring from bed, eager to resume discovering the world and rejoicing to be a part of it?

The poet Kathleen Raine, who read Natural Sciences at Cambridge, specializing in Biology, found related solace as a young woman unhappy in love and desperate for relief from heartbreak:

> Then the sky spoke to me in language clear,
> familiar as the heart, than love more near.
> The sky said to my soul, 'You have what you desire!
>
> 'Know now that you are born along with these
> clouds, winds, and stars, and ever-moving seas
> and forest dwellers. This your nature is.
>
> 'Lift up your heart again without fear,
> sleep in the tomb, or breathe the living air,
> this world you with the flower and with the tiger share.'
>
> 'Passion' (1943)

There is an anaesthetic of familiarity, a sedative of ordinariness, which dulls the senses and hides the wonder of existence. For those of us not gifted in poetry, it is at least worth while from time to time making an effort to shake off the anaesthetic. What is the best way of countering the sluggish habituation brought about by our gradual crawl from babyhood? We can't actually fly to another planet. But we can recapture that sense of having just tumbled out to life on a new world by looking at our own world in unfamiliar ways. It's tempting to use an easy example like a rose or a butterfly, but let's go straight for the alien deep end. I remember attending a lecture, years ago, by a biologist working on octopuses, and their relatives the squids and cuttlefish. He began by explaining his fascination with these animals. 'You see,' he said, 'they are the Martians.' Have you ever watched a squid change colour?

Television images are sometimes displayed on giant LED (Light Emitting Diode) hoardings. Instead of a fluorescent screen with an electron beam scanning side to side over it, the LED screen is a large array of tiny glowing lights, independently controllable. The lights are individually brightened or dimmed so that, from a distance, the whole matrix shimmers with moving pictures. The skin of a squid behaves like an LED screen. Instead of lights, squid skin is packed with thousands of tiny bags filled with ink. Each of these ink bags has miniature private muscles to squeeze it. With a puppet string leading to each one of these separate muscles, the squid's nervous system can control the shape, and hence the visibility, of each ink sac.

In theory, if you wire-tapped the nerves leading to the separate ink pixels and stimulated them electrically via a computer, you could play out Charlie Chaplin movies on the squid's skin. The squid doesn't do that, but its brain does control the wires with precision and speed, and the skinflicks that it shows are spectacular. Waves of colour chase across the surface like clouds in a speeded-up film; ripples and eddies race over the living screen. The animal signals its changing emotions in quick time: dark brown one second, blanching ghostly white the next, rapidly modulating interwoven patterns of stipples and stripes. When it comes to changing colour, by comparison chameleons are amateurs at the game.

The American neurobiologist William Calvin is one of those thinking hard today about what thinking itself really is. He emphasizes, as others have done before, the idea that thoughts do not reside in particular places in the brain but are shifting patterns of activity over its surface, units which recruit neighbouring units into populations becoming the same thought, competing in Darwinian fashion with rival populations thinking alternative thoughts. We don't see these shifting patterns, but presumably we would if neurones lit up when active. The cortex of the brain, I realize, might then look like a squid's body surface. Does a squid think with its skin? When a squid suddenly changes its colour pattern, we suppose it to be a manifestation of mood change, for signalling to another squid. A shift in colour announces that the squid has switched from an aggressive mood, say, to a fearful one. It is natural to presume that the change in mood took place in the brain, and caused the change in colour as a visible manifestation of internal thoughts, rendered external for purposes of communication. The fancy I am adding is that the squid's thoughts themselves may reside nowhere but in the skin. If squids think with their skins they are even more 'Martian' than my colleague realized. Even if that is too far-fetched a speculation (it is), the spectacle of their rippling colour changes is quite alien enough to jolt us out of our anaesthetic of familiarity.

Squids are not the only 'Martians' on our own doorstep. Think of the grotesque faces of deep-sea fish, think of dust mites, even more fearsome were they not so tiny; think of basking sharks, just fearsome. Think, indeed, of chameleons with their catapult-launched tongues, swivelling eye turrets and cold, slow gait. Or we can capture that 'strange other world' feeling just as effectively by looking inside ourselves, at the cells that make up our own bodies.

A cell is not just a bag of juice. It is packed with solid structures, mazes of intricately folded membranes. There are about 100 million million cells in a human body, and the total area of membranous structure inside one of us works out at more than 200 acres. That's a respectable farm.

What are all these membranes doing? They seem to stuff the cell as wadding, but that isn't all they do. Much of the folded acreage is given over to chemical production lines, with moving conveyor belts, hundreds of stages in cascade, each leading to the next in precisely crafted sequences, the whole driven by fast-turning chemical cogwheels. The Krebs cycle, the 9-toothed cogwheel that is largely responsible for making energy available to us, turns over at up to 100 revolutions per second, duplicated thousands of times in every cell. Chemical cogwheels of this particular marque are housed inside mitochondria, tiny bodies that reproduce independently inside our cells like bacteria. As we shall see, it is now widely accepted that the mitochondria, along with other vitally necessary structures within cells, not only resemble bacteria but are directly descended from ancestral bacteria who, a billion years ago, gave up their freedom. Each one of us is a city of cells, and each cell a town of bacteria. You are a gigantic megalopolis of bacteria. Doesn't that lift the anaesthetic's pall?

As a microscope helps our minds to burrow through alien galleries of cell   20
membranes, and as a telescope lifts us to far galaxies, another way of coming out of the anaesthetic is to return, in our imaginations, through geological time. It is the inhuman age of fossils that knocks us back on our heels. We pick up a trilobite and the books tell us it is 500 million years old. But we fail to comprehend such an age, and there is a yearning pleasure in the attempt. Our brains have evolved to grasp the time-scales of our own lifetimes. Seconds, minutes, hours, days and years are easy for us. We can cope with centuries. When we come to millennia—thousands of years—our spines begin to tingle. Epic myths of Homer; deeds of the Greek gods Zeus, Apollo and Artemis; of the Jewish heroes Abraham, Moses and David, and their terrifying god Yahweh; of the ancient Egyptians and the Sun God Ra: these inspire poets and give us that *frisson* of immense age. We seem to be peering back through eerie mists into the echoing strangeness of antiquity. Yet, on the time-scale of our trilobite, those vaunted antiquities are scarcely yesterday.

Many dramatizations have been offered, and I shall essay another. Let us write the history of one year on a single sheet of paper. That doesn't leave much room for detail. It is roughly equivalent to the lightning 'Round-up of the Year' that newspapers trot out on 31 December. Each month gets a few sentences. Now on another sheet of paper write the history of the previous year. Carry on back through the years, sketching, at a rate of a year per sheet, the outline of what happened in each year. Bind the pages into a book and number them. Gibbon's *Decline and Fall of the Roman Empire* (1776–88) spans some 13 centuries in six volumes of about 500 pages each, so it is covering the ground at approximately the rate we are talking about.

'Another damned, thick square book. Always scribble,
scribble, scribble! Eh! Mr Gibbon?'

William Henry,
First Duke of Gloucester (1829)

That splendid volume *The Oxford Dictionary of Quotations* (1992), from which I
have just copied this remark, is itself a damned thick, square doorstop of a
book, and about the right size to take us back to the time of Queen Elizabeth I.
We have an approximate yardstick of time: 4 inches or 10 cm of book thickness
to record the history of one millennium. Having established our yardstick,
let's work back to the alien world of geological deep time. We place the book
of the most recent past flat on the ground, then stack books of earlier centuries
on top of it. We now stand beside the pile of books as a living yardstick. If we
want to read about Jesus, say, we must select a volume 20 cm from the ground
or just above the ankle.

A famous archaeologist dug up a bronze-age warrior with a beautifully
preserved face mask and exulted: 'I have gazed upon the face of Agamemnon.'
He was being poetically awed at his penetration of fabled antiquity. To find
Agamemnon in our pile of books, you'd have to stoop to a level about halfway
up your shins. Somewhere in the vicinity you'd find Petra ('A rose-red city,
half as old as time'), Ozymandias, king of kings ('Look on my works, ye
Mighty, and despair') and that enigmatic wonder of the ancient world the
Hanging Gardens of Babylon. Ur of the Chaldees, and Uruk the city of the legendary hero Gilgamesh had their day slightly earlier and you'd find tales of
their foundation a little higher up your legs. Around here is the oldest date of
all, according to the seventeenth-century archbishop James Ussher, who calculated 4004 BC as the date of the creation of Adam and Eve.

The taming of fire was climacteric in our history; from it stems most of
technology. How high in our stack of books is the page on which this epic discovery is recorded? The answer is quite a surprise when you recall that you
could comfortably sit down on the pile of books encompassing the whole of
recorded history. Archaeological traces suggest that fire was discovered by our
Homo erectus ancestors, though whether they made fire, or just carried it about
and used it we don't know. They had fire by half a million years ago, so to consult the volume in our analogy recording the discovery you'd have to climb up
to a level somewhat higher than the Statue of Liberty. A dizzy height, especially given that Prometheus, the legendary bringer of fire, gets his first mention a little below your knee in our pile of books. To read about Lucy and our
australopithecine ancestors in Africa, you'd need to climb higher than any
building in Chicago. The biography of the common ancestor we share with
chimpanzees would be a sentence in a book stacked twice as high again.

But we've only just begun our journey back to the trilobite. How high
would the stack of books have to be in order to accommodate the page where
the life and death of this trilobite, in its shallow Cambrian sea, is perfunctorily

celebrated? The answer is about 56 kilometres, or 35 miles. We aren't used to dealing with heights like this. The summit of Mount Everest is less than 9 km above sea level. We can get some idea of the age of the trilobite if we topple the stack through 90 degrees. Picture a bookshelf three times the length of Manhattan island, packed with volumes the size of Gibbon's *Decline and Fall*. To read your way back to the trilobite, with only one page allotted to each year, would be more laborious than spelling through all 14 million volumes in the Library of Congress. But even the trilobite is young compared with the age of life itself. The first living creatures, the shared ancestors of the trilobite, of bacteria and of ourselves, have their ancient chemical lives recorded in volume 1 of our saga. Volume 1 is at the far end of the marathon bookshelf. The entire shelf would stretch from London to the Scottish borders. Or right across Greece from the Adriatic to the Aegean.

Perhaps these distances are still unreal. The art in thinking of analogies for   25 large numbers is not to go off the scale of what people can comprehend. If we do that, we are no better off with an analogy than with the real thing. Reading your way through a work of history, whose shelved volumes stretch from Rome to Venice, is an incomprehensible task, just about as incomprehensible as the bald figure 4,000 million years.

Here is another analogy, one that has been used before. Fling your arms wide in an expansive gesture to span all of evolution from its origin at your left fingertip to today at your right fingertip. All the way across your midline to well past your right shoulder, life consists of nothing but bacteria. Many-celled, invertebrate life flowers somewhere around your right elbow. The dinosaurs originate in the middle of your right palm, and go extinct around your last finger joint. The whole story of *Homo sapiens* and our predecessor *Homo erectus* is contained in the thickness of one nail-clipping. As for recorded history; as for the Sumerians, the Babylonians, the Jewish patriarchs, the dynasties of Pharaohs, the legions of Rome, the Christian Fathers, the Laws of the Medes and Persians which never change; as for Troy and the Greeks, Helen and Achilles and Agamemnon dead; as for Napoleon and Hitler, the Beatles and Bill Clinton, they and everyone that knew them are blown away in the dust from one light stroke of a nail-file.

> The poor are fast forgotten,
> They outnumber the living, but where are all their bones?
> For every man alive there are a million dead,
> Has their dust gone into earth that it is never seen?
> There should be no air to breathe, with it so thick,
> No space for wind to blow, nor rain to fall;
> Earth should be a cloud of dust, a soil of bones,
> With no room even, for our skeletons.
>   Sacheverell Sitwell, 'Agamemnon's Tomb' (1933)

Not that it matters, Sitwell's third line is inaccurate. It has been estimated that the people alive today make up a substantial proportion of the humans that have ever lived. But this just reflects the power of exponential growth. If we count generations instead of bodies, and especially if we go back beyond humankind to life's beginning, Sacheverell Sitwell's sentiment has a new force. Let us suppose that each individual in our direct female ancestry, from the first flowering of many-celled life a little over half a billion years ago, lay down and died on the grave of her mother, eventually to be fossilized. As in the successive layers of the buried city of Troy, there would be much compression and shaking down, so let us assume that each fossil in the series was flattened to the thickness of a 1 cm pancake. What depth of rock should we need, if we are to accommodate our continuous fossil record? The answer is that the rock would have to be about 1,000 km or 600 miles thick. This is about ten times the thickness of the earth's crust.

The Grand Canyon, whose rocks, from deepest to shallowest, span most of the period we are now talking about, is only around one mile deep. If the strata of the Grand Canyon were stuffed with fossils and no intervening rock, there would be room within its depth to accommodate only about one 600th of the generations that have successively died. This calculation helps us to keep in proportion fundamentalist demands for a 'continuous' series of gradually changing fossils before they will accept the fact of evolution. The rocks of the earth simply don't have room for such a luxury—not by many orders of magnitude. Whichever way you look at it, only an extremely small proportion of creatures has the good fortune to be fossilized. As I have said before, I should consider it an honour.

> The number of the dead long exceedeth all that shall live. The night of time far surpasseth the day, and who knows when was the Aequinox? Every houre addes unto that current Arithmetique, which scarce stands one moment . . . Who knows whether the best of men be known, or whether there be not more remarkable persons forgot than any that stand remembred in the known account of time?
>
> Sir Thomas Browne, *Urne Buriall* (1658) ◢

Reflections and Inquiries

1. How convincingly does Dawkins support Mervyn Peake's claim that "to live at all is miracle enough"? How would Dawkins define the word *miracle* in this context? How do you?

2. What motivates Dawkins to get up in the morning? Is this your reason as well? Why or why not?

3. What causes the familiar to have an "anaesthetic" effect on people?

4. Why doesn't the fossil record reveal a more complete picture of the pageant of past life on earth, according to Dawkins?

Reading to Write

To what extent does Dawkins's thesis support or challenge the existence of a spiritual or divine aspect to life? Argue your premise in a short essay.

Science vs. Religion in Future Constitutional Conflicts | Delos B. McKown

To what extent has science displaced religion? In the following essay, Delos B. McKown, a professor of philosophy at Auburn University, argues that science has disproved religious claims and, as a result, has rendered religion obsolete. More fundamentally, religion—specifically Christianity—is unsupported by what McKown calls "the dominant mode of modern knowledge"—that is, by rigorous methods of objective reasoning and investigation known as the scientific method.

The Founding Fathers gave us an utterly secular Constitution, yet one that protects the free exercise of religion more surely than the free exercise of science. Thomas Jefferson and James Madison, though they were cool toward much in religion, were fervent on the behalf of freedom, including the freedom to be or not to be religious. Cognizant of past and present threats to religion from government, they were also aware of past and present threats to government from religion. The religion clauses of the First Amendment took shape accordingly.

Although Jefferson and Madison were aware of the sectarian strife that would simmer, if not boil over, in a free society, they were content that it would be so, hoping only that it would nullify itself politically. It never occurred to them that progress in "science and useful arts" (i.e., technology) would, one day, so provoke and dismay religion as to be endangered by it. As deists, they believed the study of nature to be the surest way to the creator's mind. Thus, the major premise of religion, God's existence, seemed inviolable by science. Moreover, perceiving no danger to science from religion, our forefathers took no preventive measures. The unforeseen result is that religion is constitutionally favored over science. . . .

Source: McKown, Delos B. "Science vs. Religion in Future Constitutional Conflicts." *Free Inquiry* (Summer 1984): 12–17. Rpt. in *Science & Religion: Opposing Viewpoints.* San Diego: Greenhaven, 1988. 66–71. Reprinted by permission of *Free Inquiry.*

Religion's Threat to Science

Even as our forefathers foresaw no threat of science versus religion worth precluding, so multitudes today perceive none either, believing that science and religion, properly understood, do not conflict. No less a scientist than Stephen Jay Gould has endorsed this mistake. Although he did not show how a true religion (presumably compatible with science) can be extracted from the swarming mass of false religions, one can guess what it would involve—namely, a creator who made the world as it is because of his purpose(s) for it. But, this is no more than deism.

Deism, however, is not a proper paradigm for most existing religions. It is too spare, ideal, and rarefied to resemble very much the garden varieties in which people actually believe. The price Gould pays in supplying a religion that does not conflict with science is the price of extreme attenuation, of draining religion of its blood and guts, as it were.

Viewed from a religion with guts, a religion whose blood is boiling at present, i.e., from the standpoint of American fundamentalism, there is no conflict between science and religion either. Of course the price science would have to pay in making good on this absurd claim is nothing less than its own dismemberment. An astronomer recently estimated that if creationist claims were true, about 50 percent of his introductory course in astronomy would have to be deleted, a disaster approximating that with which creationism threatens biology. Geology would also be gutted, and archaeology and anthropology would suffer substantially, as would much, if not most, of the study of prehistory. Any aspect of science relying on radiometric dating techniques would be emasculated, and not even linguistics would go unscathed.

Real Religion

People often have trouble comprehending that, for many believers, real religion, if not true religion (whatever that might be), involves some form or another of scriptural literalism. For multitudes of Christians, belief in the inerrancy of the Bible is, religiously, on a par with belief in the existence of God and the redemption of Christ. There are, of course, ways in which science and religion cannot conflict that involve unrelated functions. For example, science does not address itself to saving souls or to performing rites of passage, and religion does not attempt to elucidate electromagnetics or to release the atom's energy. But, given scriptures that make unsupported pronouncements on the nature of the universe, the earth, life, and humankind; given people whose religion includes, as a major doctrine, belief in scriptural inerrancy; and given constitutional guarantees for the free exercise of any real, heartfelt religion, conflict between science and religion is inevitable. Given its inevitability, one wonders how intense and extensive the conflict will become. It is important to notice that the conflict is already intense and extensive and that it will almost certainly get worse in the foreseeable future. . . .

Christianity is scientifically unsupported and probably unsupportable, philosophically suspect at best and disreputable at worst, and historically fraudulent.

To say that Christianity is scientifically unsupportable is not to say that scientists must be atheists or hostile to religion, nor that teleology is logically incompatible with every cosmology. What it says has been well put by Ralph A. Alpher: "Surely if a necessity for a god-concept in the universe ever turns up, that necessity will become evident to the scientist." Scientific investigation as such does not begin with this concept; it leads to no such concept and is not ever likely to do so.

Sheer indifference to theology, however, is not the only characteristic of modern science. At times it is hostile, as the Medawars have shown:

> [T]he physicists were in the main very well disposed towards God, the geneticists are not.
> It is upon the notion of *randomness* that geneticists have based their case against a benevolent or malevolent deity and against there being any overall purpose or design in nature.

Sensing the coming dark night for Western religion, Freud wrote:

> Humanity has in the course of time had to endure from the hands of science two great outrages upon its naive self-love. The first was when it realized that our earth was not the center of the universe. . . . The second was when biological research robbed man of his particular privilege of having been specially created, and relegated him to a descent from the animal world.

How long can it go unnoticed that Christianity is unsupported (and is   10
probably unsupportable) by the dominant mode of modern knowledge? At present the religious right does not see science as its true nemesis but rather as a tiny band of secular humanists, satanically inspired of course. Perhaps the scales will fall from their eyes one day and they will see perspicuously. Perhaps some, or even many, liberal Jews and Christians will join them in perspicuous viewing. What will happen to science and science education then?

No Support from Philosophy

When the empirical rug is pulled from under a person, the most likely landing is philosophy—for sophisticates at least. But, nowadays, philosophy is not a welcome place to land. No longer the handmaiden of theology, it probes theology's major premise with impunity. Put epigrammatically, the invisible and nonexistent look much alike, so much so that when intending to speak of the invisible, the theologian may be speaking of the nonexistent. How shall we know? What referent, if any, does "God" name univocally? Unless and until theologians show us that they are speaking of more than their own concepts, it is pointless to continue, even though they go on and on endlessly.

When one is denied logical proofs for the existence of God and thus forced to depend upon faith alone, the next lower landing is so-called religious experience. Since all the religions of the world are validated in at least part by the experiences of their devotees, what is the evidentiary nature of these experiences relative to the truth of a religion in general or to any of its separable doctrines? We in the West who have lately learned more of Islam can scarcely doubt that this great faith is often supported by vital, if not fanatic, feelings. Yet this faith denies the Trinity, the virgin birth, and the death of Jesus by crucifixion—doctrines that are powerfully validated by the religious experiences of Christians. Experiences that validate contradictory doctrines cannot but be suspect. Concerning theism in general and Christianity in particular, one must conclude that they are philosophically suspect at best, disreputable at worst.

A Historical Fraud

The last and perhaps most distressing part of the litany of modern knowledge is that Christianity is historically fraudulent. The fraud at issue, of course, is pious fraud nonetheless. Morton Smith observes tartly that, whenever "a theologian talks of a 'higher truth,' he is usually trying to conceal a lower falsehood." Three examples of pious fraud must suffice here.

First, it can no longer be maintained that the church is founded on the New Testament; rather the church compiled the New Testament, and out of intensely partisan documents written by churchmen with theological axes to grind. Moreover, orthodox Christianity preserved only those documents that furthered its theological and hierarchical ends, suppressing those it took to be inimical. No wonder we know so little of the historical Jesus! But, then, if we knew him better, we might admire him less.

Second, much in the Gospels concerning Jesus is suspect. Neither history nor biography, they were written that their recipients might believe in him (John 20:31). Intent on convincing Jews of Jesus' messiahship, the Gospel (and other New Testament) writers wrenched passages and prophecies out of the Jews' own scriptures and made them apply willy-nilly to Jesus. This massive misuse of the Old Testament amounts to outright fraud. Taking scriptural license into account plus fabricated birth stories, suspiciously different resurrection tales, and many inconsistencies, Albert Schweitzer concluded, "The Jesus of Nazareth who came forward publicly as the Messiah, preached the ethic of the Kingdom of God, who founded the Kingdom of Heaven on earth, and died to give his work its final consecration, never had any existence."

Third, the church has always represented Christianity as the religion of and from Jesus, but it is not the religion of Jesus. That religion was Judaism, the religion he shared with the original Jerusalem church (Acts 21:17–31). Nor is orthodox Christianity the religion from Jesus. It is the religion about Jesus emanating from St. Paul's paranormal experiences, unmitigated gall, and desire to dominate the movement (Gal. 1:11, 2:11–16; 2 Cor. 11–12). So different is the contrivance of Paul from Jesus' religion that we can say (paraphrasing

15

Jeremy Bentham) that, with respect to Jesus, Paul was at the beginning of his Christianity what Judah was at the end of his. One could go on and on, but enough is enough.

To get the point, simply let the litany ring out again: Christianity is scientifically unsupported and probably unsupportable, at best, disreputable at worst, and historically fraudulent. . . .

The schools cannot teach modern science without adopting the rational empiricism that underlies it, nor can they teach scientific method without aiding and abetting the secularism that follows in its wake. The contents and attitudes of public school curricula that so aggrieve religious rightists have not been caused by a handful of secular humanists but by the general secularism that has followed science as surely as have its technological applications. Religious rightists, incapable of recognizing this and casting about for something else to blame, have seized on what they like to call "the godless religion of secular humanism." . . . How absurd! Nevertheless, that is the dilemma in which the public schools are caught, particularly now, as new emphasis is being placed on improved science education. . . .

The impossible dream is that scientific inquiry and the acquisition and diffusion of knowledge in general, and in the public schools in particular, might have constitutional guarantees equivalent to those enjoyed by religion. It is very hard, however, to foresee an amendment that says Congress shall not subordinate scientific information to religious information or prohibit the free dissemination of the former, or one that says Congress must promote scientific knowledge even at the expense of religious sensibilities.

Better Science Education

Without waiting for such a guarantee, we should (1) work to improve and expand science education across the board in the public schools; (2) seek ways, including the possible use of professional sanctions, to help safeguard the integrity of science instruction in public schools and to shield science teachers against uninformed public opinion or other political pressures; (3) explore with various scientific organizations the possibility of the nonprofit production and publication of science textbooks for the public schools as an economic weapon against unprincipled commercial publishers; (4) attempt to involve scientists and their professional organizations, as never before, in curriculum development and improvement in the public schools; (5) attempt, formally and informally, through education, to increase Americans' appreciation of science and to heighten their awareness of its advantages to the nation and its citizens; (6) join or support organizations committed to the separation of church and state; and (7) work through education to help wean Americans from their traditional religion, especially in its fundamentalistic, literalistic, and authoritarian manifestations.

Weaning Americans from their traditional religion will, of course, be most difficult. A recent article in *U.S. News & World Report* began as follows: "Sensing a gnawing disillusionment with science and secularism as the driving forces in U.S. society, churches are growing more aggressive in proclaiming spirituality that is the root of their very existence," and went on to say that there "is a newfound determination by those of religious faith to 'search out the sacred' in a society that has increasingly moved away from its religious underpinnings." Thus, while some of us press ahead, welcoming more science and secularity, others work to reestablish the reign of religion.

A Total Break Is Needed

Jacques Monod deserves the final word for the compassionate acuteness of his diagnosis of current Western culture. He wrote:

> Modern societies accepted the treasures and the power that science laid in their laps. But they have not accepted—they have scarcely even heard— its profounder message: the defining of a new and unique source of truth, and the demand for a thorough revision of ethical premises, for a total break with the animist tradition, the definitive abandonment of the "old covenant," the necessity of forging a new one. Armed with all the powers, enjoying all the riches they owe to science, our societies are still trying to live by and to teach systems of values already blasted at the root by science itself.

> No society before ours was ever rent by contradictions so agonizing. ◪

Reflections and Inquiries

1. How valid, in your opinion, is McKown's evidence in support of his claim that conflict between science and religion is inevitable?

2. Do you agree or disagree with Ralph A. Alpher's assertion that if, in effect, God exists, that fact should be made evident through scientific investigation? What is the basis for your agreement or disagreement?

3. What evidence does McKown use to support his claim that Christianity is historically fraudulent? How valid or sufficient is this evidence, in your opinion? (You may wish to review the evaluation of evidence in Chapter 2, pages 33–34.)

4. Why, according to McKown, is Scripture historically unreliable?

5. What underlies the public's disillusionment with science? Do you share in this disillusionment? Why or why not?

Reading to Write

According to McKown, if science accepts the claim that there is no conflict between itself and religion, it would cause "its own dismemberment. How valid is McKown's assertion, based on the evidence he provides? Write a short essay outlining your position.

Unresolved Problems
of Evolution | Henry M. Morris

Henry M. Morris, a former chair of the Department of Civil Engineering at Virginia Polytechnic Institute, has also served as president of the Institute for Creation Research in San Diego. As a creationist, Morris attempts to show that while science in general does not contradict holy writ, evolution does. Worse, he argues, evolution is harmful to young people because it undermines Christian values. In the following selection from his book, *The Troubled Waters of Evolution,* Morris focuses on what he takes to be unresolved problems generated by an evolutionary view of life.

Modern creationists recognize and accept all the observed biological changes which evolutionists offer as proof of evolution. New varieties of plants and animals can be developed rather quickly by selection techniques, but creationists point out that no new basic *kind* has ever been developed by such processes. Mutations are fairly common, but not transmutations. A moth species may change from predominantly light-colored to predominantly dark-colored, as a result of natural selection operating on Mendelian variants in a changed environment, but the moth does not become a dragon-fly, or even a different species of moth! Fruit-flies may develop numerous new mutants as a result of irradiation, but after a thousand successive generations of such treatment, they are still fruit-flies!

Evolutionists, however, object to this argument, insisting that the few thousand years of recorded history are insufficient time to permit new kinds to evolve. For this, millions of years are required, and so we should not expect to *see* new kinds evolving.

Creationists in turn insist that this belief is not scientific evidence but only a statement of faith. The evolutionists seem to be saying: "Of course, we cannot really *prove* evolution, since this requires ages of time, and so, therefore, you should accept it as a proved fact of science!" Creationists regard this as an odd type of logic, which would be entirely unacceptable in any other field of science.

As a matter of fact, it is not true that time alone will produce evolution. The common opinion that anything can happen, no matter how improbable, if enough time is available, is obviously incorrect. For example, a pile of bricks and lumber would never "evolve" into a building by the random interplay of environmental forces acting upon it, no matter how many billions of years it might lie there on the construction site. On the contrary, it would beyond question "*de*-volve," and go back to dust.

Source: Morris, Henry M. "Unresolved Problems of Evolution." *The Troubled Waters of Evolution.* 2nd ed. San Diego, Ca.: Creation-Life Publishers, 1982. 16–22. Reprinted by permission of the author.

Here it is necessary to introduce the concept of entropy, which creationists   5
insist makes evolution on any significant scale quite impossible. Entropy
(from two Greek words meaning "turning inward") is a measure of disorder,
or randomness. The Law of Increasing Entropy, known also as the Second Law
of Thermodynamics, states that *every* system (physical, biological, or anything
else) tends toward a state of increasing entropy. This is why machines run
down, why houses and roads wear out, and why organisms get old and die.
As time goes on, disorder increases. The great British scientist, Sir Arthur Eddington, called this law Time's Arrow. That is, as time flows onward, the "arrow" of available energy for future processes always points downward. The
whole universe, in fact, is "running down," heading toward an eventual "heat
death," in which all forms of energy will have been degraded into uniform,
low-temperature heat dispersed through space, no longer capable of accomplishing the work of maintaining the innumerable processes of the cosmos.

Creationists point out that this Second Law, accepted by all scientists and
confirmed by thousands of experiments on all types and sizes of systems, is
exactly the converse of the principle of evolution, according to which everything is moving upward from primeval chaos to future perfection. Therefore,
they ask, how can evolution and entropy both be universal laws? But there is
no doubt that the Second Law has always been confirmed quantitatively,
wherever it can be tested.

It is true, of course, that there can be *apparent* exceptions to the Second
Law, in so-called "open systems." Thus, a seed may grow up into a tree or a
pile of bricks and lumber into a building. An outside source of energy is necessary for this to occur—sunlight in the case of the seed, construction machinery and workmen in the case of the building. But even then, this apparent
growth is only local and temporary, not universal and eternal. *Most* seeds die,
and even the few that become trees also *eventually* die. The building, too, will
eventually go back to the dust.

The evolutionist agrees, but he also says that, since the earth is an open
system, there is enough incoming solar energy to maintain the evolutionary
process over the "few" billion years of geologic time before the earth finally
dies. It may be, some also say, that even though all processes now tend toward
increasing entropy, perhaps in the past they were different.

But again, to the creationist, this is a strange type of reasoning for scientists. Science is supposed to proceed from confirmed facts of experimental observation. How can processes which now *always* involve *increasing* entropy
justify belief in past evolutionary processes of *decreasing* entropy?

Furthermore, even local and temporary increases in order require more   10
than merely an open system with energy available in the environment. *Always*,
in addition, there must be a program (or code, or pattern, or template) built
into the embryonic system to direct the conversion of the environmental
energy into meaningful growth of order in the system. In the case of the
seed, this requirement is met in part by the marvelous genetic code, the

intricately-ordered structure of the DNA molecules of the genes of the germ cell. This amazing biochemical system could never have created itself and yet it is absolutely necessary for the system to grow and it always directs the in-flowing energy into the production of a plant (or animal) of the same basic kind as the parents—even when mutational "mistakes" in the transmission of this information result in somewhat deformed or otherwise damaged offspring.

The question is: "What, or where, is the infinitely complex program which would be required to convert the primeval disorder into the infinitely-complex ordered structure of the universe and its living creatures?" The evolutionist at this point pleads ignorance, saying such questions are not proper questions for science to ask.

The creationist, of course, says the logical answer is an infinitely-capable Programmer! But if such an Infinite Intelligence exists, then He would be too intelligent to create man by such an infinitely cruel, wasteful, inefficient process as evolution!

In addition to a program, any system experiencing a growth of order must also involve an energy conversion of some kind for transforming the environmental energy into the growth phenomenon. For the seed, this is the amazingly-complex, little-understood process known as *photosynthesis*. This process could never create itself, or just randomly happen, but there it is! Order never spontaneously arises out of disorder.

It is not sufficient to say, as the evolutionist does, that the sun's energy is great enough to maintain the process of evolution. The essential, and unanswered, question is: "*How* does the sun's energy maintain the process of evolution? What is the specific mechanism of 'evolutionary photosynthesis' that converts solar energy into the transformation of particles into atoms, then into molecules and stars and galaxies, complex molecules into replicating molecules, simple cells into metazoan life, marine invertebrates into reptiles and birds and men, unthinking chemicals into conscious intelligence and abstract reasoning?" Again the creationist is convinced that special creation is a more scientific theory than evolution. He notes that the pile of bricks and lumber will never evolve by itself into a building, even though it also is an "open system" and the sun's energy bathing the construction site contains far more than enough energy to carry out the process of building the building. In fact, the building is far less complex than even the simplest form of living cell, not to mention the total organic world itself.

The evolutionist may somehow maintain his faith that the phenomena of   15
mutation (seemingly a disordering mechanism, in full accord with the Second Law) and natural selection (seemingly a conservational process which tends to weed out the misfits produced by mutation, thus maintaining the *status quo* in nature) supply the mechanism for evolving the whole world, but he ought to recognize that this is pure faith (or, better, wishful thinking), not science!

Gaps in the Fossils

But, at this point the evolutionist reminds the creationist of the fossil record and the long geological ages. The fossilized remains of plants and animals preserved in the sedimentary rocks of the earth's crust are cited to prove the historical *fact* of evolution, even though the precise mechanism may be obscure. Extinct trilobites and dinosaurs and cavemen presumably witness to the tortuous evolutionary struggle over hundreds of millions of years of geologic time. Furthermore, radioactive dating by uranium, potassium, and other minerals confirms the evolutionist's belief that the earth must be billions of years old.

But this evidence does not persuade the creationist either. He reminds the evolutionist that *extinction* does not prove *evolution!* The fossil record speaks eloquently of death, often catastrophic death. The fact that dinosaurs have become extinct tells us nothing about how they first came into existence.

Furthermore, essentially the same gaps that exist between basic kinds in the present world exist also in the fossil world (e.g., the gap between cats and dogs, pines and oaks, sharks and whales, etc.). Multitudes of fossils exist, representing the same kinds of animals as in the present world (as well as extinct kinds, such as dinosaurs and trilobites), but none has been found in between these basic kinds, or leading up to them! This strikes the creationist as a highly improbable circumstance if indeed all basic kinds have evolved by slow stages from a common ancestral form, as the evolutionist insists. There ought rather to be a continuous intergrading series, instead of discrete kinds, both in the present world and in the fossils, if evolution is really true.

Is the Earth Really That Old?

Neither is the modern scientific creationist much impressed by the supposed great age of the earth's geologic formations. He reminds us that the only real *history* that has been recorded from earlier times extends back just a few thousand years. Any events that took place before that must be deduced indirectly by extrapolating some present-day process (e.g., radioactive decay of uranium into lead, soil erosion, canyon-cutting, delta deposition, etc.) back into the distant past, to arrive at an approximate date when those events took place.

But to do this, several assumptions have to be made: (1) the condition of the components of the process when it first began to operate has to be known (but this is impossible, since no observers were present then); (2) the system must always have been a "closed system," so that no external events could affect the process (but this is impossible, since there is in nature no such thing as a truly closed system); (3) the assumption of *uniformitarianism* must be applied, by which the process is assumed always to operate at the same uniform rate, throughout all ages (but this is impossible, since all processes are statistical in nature, and their rates can and do vary and change whenever any of the many factors controlling them vary and change).

Furthermore, creationists object to the screening process by which evolutionists discard all natural processes which do *not* give great ages for the events of earth history. There are many such processes (e.g., influx of helium into the atmosphere, influx of uranium into the ocean, influx of meteoritic dust to the earth, and many others) which indicate the earth is quite young! Even many uranium and potassium ages turn out to be practically zero, but these are invariably discarded or explained away on the basis of supposed contamination or alteration.

Still further, the creationist suspects that the fossil record and the sedimentary rocks, instead of speaking of a long succession of geologic ages, may tell rather of just *one* former age, destroyed in a single great worldwide aqueous cataclysm. Several objective facts suggest this: (1) the fact that the geologic "ages," as identified primarily by their fossils, are found in quite an indiscriminate variety of arrangements at different localities around the world, with any succession possible—any "age" missing, or even laid on top of any supposedly more "recent" age; (2) the fact that rocks of any physical character—limestone, shale, sandstone, metamorphic, igneous, loose and unconsolidated, hard and indurated, etc.—may be found indiscriminately in any so-called "age"; (3) the fact that any given local formation seems almost always to indicate geologic processes (e.g., volcanism, glaciation, tectonism, sedimentation, etc.) operating at far higher, more catastrophic intensities than is the case in the modern world; (4) the fact that fossils are often, in all "ages," found buried together in great numbers, under conditions absolutely requiring cataclysmic extinction and rapid burial; (5) the fact that the traditions of all nations and tribes around the world describe just such a primeval watery cataclysm as the geologic formations seem to require.

The Faith of the Evolutionist

The evolutionist may finally admit that his theory does still have many serious unsolved problems. Nevertheless, he feels it is the only proper belief, since belief in special creation in effect gives up on the problems, relying on a force outside present scientific phenomena to explain the origin of these phenomena.

The creationist acknowledges this. He finally must accept creation and a Creator by faith, since the process of special creation is not accessible to scientific observation.

But neither is the historical process of evolution, he reminds the evolutionist. Evolution also must be accepted on faith, and that faith is more arbitrary than that of the creationist. Evolutionary faith must be maintained in spite of the Second Law of Thermodynamics, the clearcut distinction between kinds, the very limited nature of observed biological changes, the deteriorative nature of mutations, the many contradictions in the fossil record, the catastrophic appearance of most geologic formations, and many other problems. These phenomena are all perfectly consistent with creationism, of course.

In any case, creation at the very least has as much plausibility as a scientific model of origins as does evolution. Therefore, creationists are saying with

25

increasing clarity these days, creation should be taught in the public schools on at least an equal basis with evolution. ◪

Reflections and Inquiries

1. How do creationists and evolutionists differ in their views on the origins of species?

2. How do creationists and evolutionists differ in their respective assessments of the age of the earth? Why is age such an important factor for both groups?

3. Why do creationists turn to the Second Law of Thermodynamics as evidence against the theory of evolution? How might an evolutionist counterargue this charge?

4. Why is the fossil record unreliable to creationists?

Reading to Write

Morris argues that special creation is more scientifically sound than evolution. How well does he support this claim, in your opinion? Write a point-by-point defense or refutation of Morris's use of evidence to support his thesis.

Darwinism Defined: The Difference Between Fact and Theory | Stephen Jay Gould

A prolific author of more than fifteen books and hundreds of articles, Stephen Jay Gould is the Alexander Agassiz Professor of Zoology and a professor of geology at Harvard University where he is also Curator of Invertebrate Paleontology at the Museum of Comparative Zoology. His collection of essays, *The Panda's Thumb* (1980), won the 1981 American Book Award for Science. As one of the world's foremost spokespersons for evolutionary biology, Gould has made national headlines in his defense of teaching evolution in the public schools. In the following essay, he explains why evolution is a fundamental principle of biology.

Source: Gould, Stephen Jay. "Darwinism Defined: The Difference Between Fact and Theory." *Discover* Jan. 1987:161–67. Reprinted by permission of the author.

Charles Darwin, who was, perhaps, the most incisive thinker among the great minds of history, clearly divided his life's work into two claims of different character: establishing the fact of evolution, and proposing a theory (natural selection) for the mechanism of evolutionary change. He also expressed, and with equal clarity, his judgment about their different status: confidence in the facts of transmutation and genealogical connection among all organisms, and appropriate caution about his unproved theory of natural selection. He stated in the *Descent of Man:* "I had two distinct objects in view; firstly, to show that species had not been separately created, and secondly, that natural selection had been the chief agent of change . . . If I have erred in . . . having exaggerated its [natural selection's] power . . . I have at least, as I hope, done good service in aiding to overthrow the dogma of separate creations."

Fact and Theory

Darwin wrote those words more than a century ago. Evolutionary biologists have honored his fundamental distinction between fact and theory ever since. Facts are the world's data; theories are explanations proposed to interpret and coordinate facts. The fact of evolution is as well established as anything in science (as secure as the revolution of the earth about the sun), though absolute certainty has no place in our lexicon. Theories, or statements about the causes of documented evolutionary change, are now in a period of intense debate—a good mark of science in its healthiest state. Facts don't disappear while scientists debate theories. As I [have previously written] . . . , "Einstein's theory of gravitation replaced Newton's but apples did not suspend themselves in midair pending the outcome." . . .

In this period of vigorous pluralism and intense debate among evolutionary biologists, 'I am greatly saddened to note that some (distinguished commentators among non-scientists, in particular Irving Kristol in a *New York Times* Op Ed piece of Sept. 30, 1986 ("Room for Darwin and the Bible"), so egregiously misunderstand the character of our discipline and continue to confuse this central distinction between secure fact and healthy debate about theory. . . .

Direct Evidence of Evolutionary Change

Our confidence in the fact of evolution rests upon copious data that fall, roughly, into three great classes. First, we have the direct evidence of small-scale changes in controlled laboratory experiments of the past hundred years (on bacteria, on almost every measurable property of the fruit fly *Drosophila*), or observed in nature (color changes in moth wings, development of metal tolerance in plants growing near industrial waste heaps), or produced during a few thousand years of human breeding and agriculture. Creationists can scarcely ignore this evidence, so they respond by arguing that God permits limited modification within created types, but that you can never change a cat into a dog (who ever said that you could, or that nature did?).

The Fossil Record

Second, we have direct evidence for large-scale changes, based upon sequences in the fossil record. The nature of this evidence is often misunderstood by non-professionals who view evolution as a simple ladder of progress, and therefore expect a linear array of "missing links." But evolution is a copiously branching bush, not a ladder. Since our fossil record is so imperfect, we can't hope to find evidence for every tiny twiglet. (Sometimes, in rapidly evolving lineages of abundant organisms restricted to small areas and entombed in sediments with an excellent fossil record, we do discover an entire little bush—but such examples are as rare as they are precious.) In the usual case, we may recover the remains of side branch number 5 from the bush's early history, then bough number 40 a bit later, then the full series of branches 156–161 in a well preserved sequence of younger rocks, and finally surviving twigs 250 and 287.

In other words, we usually find sequences of structural intermediates, not linear arrays of ancestors and descendants. Such sequences provide superb examples of temporally ordered evolutionary trends. Consider the evidence for human evolution in Africa. What more could you ask from a record of rare creatures living in terrestrial environments that provide poor opportunity for fossilization? We have a temporal sequence displaying clear trends in a suite of features, including threefold increase of brain size and corresponding decrease of jaws and teeth. (We are missing direct evidence for an earlier transition to upright posture, but wide-ranging and unstudied sediments of the right age have been found in East Africa, and we have an excellent chance to fill in this part of our story.) What alternative can we suggest to evolution? Would God—for some inscrutable reason, or merely to test our faith create five species, one after the other (*Australopithecus afarensis, A. africanus, Homo habilis, H. erectus,* and *H. sapiens*), to mimic a continuous trend of evolutionary change?

Or, consider another example with evidence of structurally intermediate stages—the transition from reptiles to mammals. The lower jaw of mammals contains but a single bone, the dentary. Reptiles build their lower jaws of several bones. In perhaps the most fascinating of those quirky changes in function that make pathways of evolution, the two bones articulating the upper and lower jaws of reptiles migrate to the middle ear and become the malleus and incus (hammer and anvil) of mammals.

Creationists, ignorant of hard evidence in the fossil record, scoff at this tale. How could jaw bones become ear bones, they ask. What happened in between? An animal can't work with a jaw half disarticulated during the stressful time of transition.

The fossil record provides a direct answer. In an excellent series of temporally ordered structural intermediates, the reptilian dentary gets larger and larger, pushing back as the other bones of a reptile's lower jaw decrease in size. We've even found a transitional form with an elegant solution to the problem of remaking jaw bones into ear bones. This creature has a double articulation—one between the two bones that become the mammalian hammer and anvil (the old reptilian joint), and a second between the squamosal and dentary bones (the modern mammalian condition). With this built-in redundancy, the emerging mammals could abandon one connection by moving two bones into the ear, while retaining the second linkage, which becomes the sole articulation of modern mammals.

Pervasive Quirks

Third, and most persuasive in its ubiquity, we have the signs of history preserved within every organism, every ecosystem, and every pattern of biogeographic distribution, by those pervasive quirks, oddities, and imperfections that record pathways of historical descent. These evidences are indirect, since we are viewing modern results, not the processes that caused them, but what else can we make of the pervasive pattern? Why does our body, from the bones of our back to the musculature of our belly, display the vestiges of an arrangement better suited for quadrupedal life if we aren't the descendants of four-footed creatures? Why do the plants and animals of the Galapagos so closely resemble, but differ slightly from, the creatures of Ecuador, the nearest bit of land 600 miles to the east, especially when cool oceanic currents and volcanic substrate make the Galapagos such a different environment from Ecuador (thus removing the potential argument that God makes the best creatures for each place, and small differences only reflect a minimal disparity of environments)? The similarities can only mean that Ecuadorian creatures colonized the Galapagos and then diverged by a natural process of evolution.

10

This method of searching for oddities as vestiges of the past isn't peculiar to evolution, but a common procedure of all historical science. How, for example, do we know that words have histories, and haven't been decreed by some all-knowing committee in Mr. Orwell's bureau of Newspeak? Doesn't the bucolic etymology of so many words testify to a different life style among our ancestors? In this article, I try to "broadcast" some ideas (a mode of sowing seed) in order to counter the most "egregious" of creationist sophistries (the animal *ex grege*, or outside the flock), for which, given the *quid pro quo* of business, . . . [I am paid] an "emolument" (the fee that millers once received to grind corn).

I don't want to sound like a shrill dogmatist shouting "rally round the flag boys," but biologists have reached a consensus, based on these kinds of data, about the fact of evolution. When honest critics like Irving Kristol misinterpret this agreement, they're either confusing our fruitful consonance about the fact of evolution with our vibrant dissonance about mechanisms of change, or they've misinterpreted part of our admittedly arcane technical literature.

One such misinterpretation has gained sufficient notoriety that we crave resolution both for its own sake and as an illustration of the frustrating confusion that can arise when scientists aren't clear and when commentators, as a result of hidden agendas, don't listen. Tom Bethell argued in *Harper's* (February 1985) that a group of young taxonomists called pattern cladists have begun to doubt the existence of evolution itself.

This would be truly astounding news, since cladistics is a powerful method dedicated to reforming classification by using only the branching order of lineages on evolutionary trees ("propinquity of descent" in Darwin's lovely phrase), rather than vague notions of overall similarity in form or function. (For example, in the cladistic system, a lungfish is more closely related to a horse than to a salmon because the common ancestor of lungfish and horse is more recent in time than the link point of the lungfish-horse lineage with the branch leading to modern bony fishes, including salmon.)

Cladists use only the order of branching to construct their schemes of relationships; it bothers them not a whit that lungfish salmon look and work so much alike. Cladism, in other words, is the purest of all genealogical systems for classification, since it works only with closeness of common ancestry in time. How preciously ironic then, that this most rigidly evolutionary of all taxonomic systems should become the subject of such extraordinary misunderstanding—as devised by Bethell, and perpetuated by Kristol when he writes: ". . . many younger biologists (the so-called 'cladists') are persuaded that the differences among species—including those that seem to be closely related—are such as to make the very concept of evolution questionable."

Ill-Conceived Scientific Procedure

This error arose for the following reason. A small splinter group of cladists (not all of them, as Kristol claims)—"transformed" or "pattern" cladists by their own designation—have adopted what is to me an ill-conceived definition of scientific procedure. They've decided, by misreading Karl Popper's philosophy, that patterns of branching can be established unambiguously as a fact of nature, but that processes causing events of branching, since they can't be observed directly, can't be known with certainty. Therefore, they say, we must talk only of pattern and rigidly exclude all discussion of process (hence "pattern cladistics").

This is where Bethell got everything arse-backwards and began the whole confusion. A philosophical choice to abjure all talk about process isn't the same thing as declaring that no reason for patterns of branching exists. Pattern cladists don't doubt that evolution is the cause behind branching; rather, they've decided that our science shouldn't be discussing causes at all.

Now I happen to think that this philosophy is misguided; in unguarded moments I would even deem it absurd. Science, after all, is fundamentally about process; learning why and how things happen is the soul of our discipline. You can't abandon the search for cause in favor of a dry documentation of pattern. You must take risks of uncertainty in order to probe the deeper questions, rather than stopping with sterile security. You see, now I've blown our cover. We scientists do have our passionate debates—and I've just poured forth an example. But as I wrote earlier, this is a debate about the proper approach to causes, not an argument about whether causes exist, or even whether the cause of branching is evolution or something else. No cladist denies that branching patterns arise by evolution.

This incident also raises the troubling issue of how myths become beliefs through adulterated repetition without proper documentation. Bethell began by misunderstanding pattern cladistics, but at least he reports the movement as a small splinter, and tries to reproduce their arguments. Then Kristol picks up the ball and recasts it as a single sentence of supposed fact—and all cladists have now become doubters of evolution by proclamation. Thus a movement, by fiat, is turned into its opposite—as the purest of all methods for establishing genealogical connections becomes a weapon for denying the mechanism that all biologists accept as the cause of branching on life's tree: evolution itself. Our genealogy hasn't been threatened, but my geniality has almost succumbed. . . .

What challenge can the facts of nature pose to our own decisions about the moral value of our lives? We are what we are, but we interpret the meaning of our heritage as we choose. Science can no more answer the questions of how we ought to live than religion can decree the age of the earth. Honorable and discerning scientists (most of us, I trust) have always understood that the limits to what science can answer also describe the power of its methods in their proper domain. Darwin himself exclaimed that science couldn't touch the problem of evil and similar moral conundrums: "A dog might as well speculate on the mind of Newton. Let each man hope and believe what he can."   20

There is no warfare between science and religion, never was except as a historical vestige of shifting taxonomic boundaries among disciplines. Theologians haven't been troubled by the fact of evolution, unless they try to extend their own domain beyond its proper border (hubris and territorial expansionism aren't the sins of scientists alone.) . . .

Similarly, most scientists show no hostility to religion. Why should we, since our subject doesn't intersect the concerns of theology? I strongly dispute Kristol's claim that "the current teaching of evolution in our public schools does indeed have an ideological bias against religious belief." Unless at least half my colleagues are inconsistent dunces, there can be—on the most raw and direct empirical grounds—no conflict between science and religion. I know hundreds of scientists who share a conviction about the fact of evolution, and teach it in much the same way. Among these people I note an entire spectrum of religious attitudes—from devout daily prayer and worship to resolute atheism. Either there's no correlation between religious belief and confidence in evolution—or else half these people are fools.

A Shared Struggle for Wisdom

The common goal of science and religion is our shared struggle for wisdom in all its various guises. I know no better illustration of this great unity than a final story about Charles Darwin. This scourge of fundamentalism had a conventional church burial—in Westminster Abbey no less. J. Frederick Bridge, Abbey organist and Oxford don, composed a funeral anthem especially for the occasion. It may not rank high in the history of music, but it is, as my chorus director opined, a "sweet piece." (I've made what may be the only extant recording of this work, marred only by the voice of yours truly within the bass section.) Bridge selected for his text the finest biblical description of the common aim that will forever motivate both the directors of his building and the inhabitants of the temple of science—wisdom. "Her ways are ways of pleasantness and all her paths are peace" (Proverbs 3:17). ◪

Reflections and Inquiries

1. According to Gould, in what way is evolution a fact? In what way is it a theory?

2. Creationists have difficulty with the notion that one species can mutate into another. What does Gould point to in the fossil record that proves this indeed can occur?

3. Gould "confesses" that scientists debate theories all the time, but how does he distinguish this kind of debating from the creationists' kind?

4. What does Gould mean by "the common goal of science and religion is our shared struggle for wisdom in all its various guises"? What do you suppose Gould means by *wisdom* in this context?

Reading to Write

In a short paper, compare Gould's assessment of the fossil record as a source of evidence for evolution with Henry M. Morris's assessment in the preceding selection. In your conclusion, decide which assessment seems most convincing and explain why.

The Real Message of Creationism | Charles Krauthammer

According to creationists, the theory of evolution has no more solid grounding in undisputed fact than the Biblical story of creation, which at least is the word of God (and therefore beyond disputation). Thus, being on equal footing with evolution, creationism has a rightful place in the science classroom as an alternative theory of human origin. Biologists, however, argue that creationism cannot possibly be on equal footing with science because creationism accepts as a *precondition* of inquiry the fact that God created the earth and all life on it. There can be no preconditions in scientific inquiry, scientists argue. In the following essay, Charles Krauthammer, an eminent journalist and contributing writer for *Time,* argues for a middle ground: While creationism may not qualify as science, it still deserves inclusion in the schools.

Source: Krauthammer, Charles. "The Real Message of Creationism." *Time* 22 Nov. 1999: 120. © 1999 Time Inc. Reprinted by permission.

*At the 1925 Scopes Trial in Dayton, Tennessee, Clarence Darrow (left) defended John
Scopes, the teacher arrested for teaching theories of evolution in a public school. He is
seen here with William Jennings Bryan who represented the State of Tennessee in defense
of Biblical Creationism.*

When the Kansas Board of Education voted recently to eliminate evolution from the state science curriculum, the sophisticates had quite a yuk.
One editorial cartoon had an ape reclining in a tree telling his mate, "We are
descended from the Kansas School Board." The decision has been widely de-
rided as a sign of resurgent Middle American obscurantism, a throwback to
the Scopes "monkey trial."

Well, to begin with, the Scopes trial is not the great fable the rather fictional *Inherit the Wind* made it out to be. The instigators of the trial were not
bluenosed know-nothings wanting to persecute some poor teacher for teaching evolution. They were officials of the American Civil Liberties Union so eager for a test case to overturn a new Tennessee law prohibiting the teaching of
evolution that they promised to pay the expenses of the prosecution! The
A.C.L.U. advertised for a volunteer and found one John Scopes, football coach
and science teacher, willing to take the rap. He later said he was not sure
whether he'd ever even taught any evolution.

Son of Scopes is not quite what it seems either. The twist in the modern
saga is the injection of creationism as the scientific alternative to evolution. So,

let's be plain. Creationism, which presents *Genesis* as literally and historically true, is not science. It is faith crudely disguised as science.

It is not science because it violates the central scientific canon that a theory must, at least in principle, be disprovable. Creationism is not. Any evidence that might be brought—fossil, geological, astronomical—to contradict the idea that the universe is no more than 6,000 years old is simply explained away as false clues deliberately created by God at the very beginning.

Why? To test our faith? To make fools of modern science? This is hardly even good religion. God may be mysterious, but he is certainly not malicious. And who but a malicious deity would have peppered the universe with endless phony artifacts designed to confound human reason?

Creationism has no part in the serious curriculum of any serious country. Still, I see no reason why biblical creation could not be taught in the schools—not as science, of course, but for its mythic grandeur and moral dimensions. If we can assign the *Iliad* and the *Odyssey*, we certainly ought to be able to assign *Genesis*.

But can we? There's the rub. It is very risky to assign *Genesis* today. The A.C.L.U. might sue. Ever since the Supreme Court decision of 1963 barring prayer from the public schools, any attempt to import not just prayer but biblical studies, religious tenets and the like into the schools is liable to end up in court.

That is why the Kansas school board decision on evolution is so significant. Not because Kansas is the beginning of a creationist wave—as science, creationism is too fundamentally frivolous and evolution too intellectually powerful—but because the Kansas decision is an important cultural indicator.

It represents the reaction of people of faith to the fact that all legitimate expressions of that faith in their children's public schooling are blocked by the new secular ethos. In a society in which it is unconstitutional to post the Ten Commandments in school, creationism is a back door to religion, brought in under the guise—the absurd yet constitutionally permitted guise—of science.

This pedagogic sleight of hand, by the way, did not originate with religious folk. Secularists have for years been using biology instruction as a back door for inculcating their values. A sex-ed class on the proper placement of a condom is more than instruction in reproductive mechanics. It is a seminar—unacknowledged and tacit but nonetheless powerful—on permissible sexual mores.

Religion—invaluable in America's founding, forming and flowering—deserves a place in the schools. Indeed, it had that place for almost 200 years. A healthy country would teach its children evolution and the Ten Commandments. The reason that Kansas is going to have precisely the opposite—the worst of both worlds— is not because Kansans are primitives, but because a religious people has tried to bring the fruits of faith, the teachings and higher values of religion, into the schools and been stymied.

The result is a kind of perverse Law of Conservation of Faith. Block all teaching of religious ideas? O.K., we'll sneak them in through biology.

This is nutty. It has kids looking for God in all the wrong places. For the purposes of a pluralist society, the Bible is not about fact. It is about values. If we were a bit more tolerant about allowing the teaching of biblical values as ethics, we'd find far less pressure for the teaching of biblical fables as science. ◪

Reflections and Inquiries

1. What is Krauthammer's reason for saying that "creationism . . . is not science"? Do you agree or disagree? How might Henry M. Morris (see pages 498–503) respond?

2. What does it mean that a theory "must be disprovable" to qualify as science?

3. Krauthammer interprets the Kansas Board of Education's decision to eliminate evolution from the state's public school curriculum to be a public reaction against the "new secular ethos" that seems to be blocking expressions of faith in the schools. Do you agree that such secular resistance to faith exists? Explain.

4. Religion, asserts Krauthammer, "deserves . . . a place in the schools." Do you agree or disagree? If the former, how would you reconcile it with the separation of church and state?

Reading to Write

In a short essay, defend or challenge Krauthammer's claim that "the Bible is not about fact. It is about values." How convincingly does Krauthammer support this claim? How should *fact* and *values* be defined in this context?

Fecundity | Annie Dillard

In the following excerpt from her celebrated, Pulitzer Prize–winning book, *Pilgrim at Tinker Creek*, the nature writer, poet, literary critic, and novelist Annie Dillard captures the tension many of us feel between the biological inevitability and necessity of death and the emotional need to triumph over death. Death, one might say, is the arena in which intellect and spirit are engaged in continual combat. Does one win out over the other?

Source: Dillard, Annie. From Chapter 10, Section II, of *Pilgrim at Tinker Creek. Three by Annie Dillard.* New York: Harper Perennial, 1990. 170–74. Copyright © 1974 by Annie Dillard. Reprinted by permission of HarperCollins Publishers, Inc.

W. C. Fields called death "the Fellow in the Bright Nightgown." He shuffles around the house in all the corners I've forgotten, all the halls I dare not call to mind or visit for fear I'll glimpse the hem of his shabby, dazzling gown disappearing around a turn. This is the monster evolution loves. How could it be?

The faster death goes, the faster evolution goes. If an aphid lays a million eggs, several might survive. Now, my right hand, in all its human cunning, could not make one aphid in a thousand years. But these aphid eggs—which run less than a dime a dozen, which run absolutely free—can make aphids as effortlessly as the sea makes waves. Wonderful things, wasted. It's a wretched system. Arthur Stanley Eddington, the British physicist and astronomer who died in 1944, suggested that all of "Nature" could conceivably run on the same deranged scheme. "If indeed she has no greater aim than to provide a home for her greatest experiment, Man, it would be just like her methods to scatter a million stars whereof one might haply achieve her purpose." I doubt very much that this is the aim, but it seems clear on all fronts that this is the method.

Say you are the manager of the Southern Railroad. You figure that you need three engines for a stretch of track between Lynchburg and Danville. It's a mighty steep grade. So at fantastic effort and expense you have your shops make nine thousand engines. Each engine must be fashioned just so, every rivet and bolt secure, every wire twisted and wrapped, every needle on every indicator sensitive and accurate.

You send all nine thousand of them out on the runs. Although there are engineers at the throttles, no one is manning the switches. The engines crash, collide, derail, jump, jam, burn. At the end of the massacre you have three engines, which is what the run could support in the first place. There are few enough of them that they can stay out of each others' paths.

You go to your board of directors and show them what you've done. And what are they going to say? You know what they're going to say. They're going to say: it's a hell of a way to run a railroad. 5

Is it a better way to run a universe?

Evolution loves death more than it loves you or me. This is easy to write, easy to read, and hard to believe. The words are simple, the concepts clear— but you don't believe it, do you? Nor do I. How could I, when we're both so lovable? Are my values then so diametrically opposed to those that nature preserves? This is the key point.

Must I then part ways with the only world I know? I had thought to live by the side of the creek in order to shape my life to its free flow. But I seem to have reached a point where I must draw the line. It looks as though the creek is not buoying me up but dragging me down. Look: Cock Robin may die the most gruesome of slow deaths, and nature is no less pleased; the sun comes up, the creek rolls on, the survivors still sing. I cannot feel that way about your death, nor you about mine, or either of us about the robin's—or even the barnacles'. We value the individual completely, and nature values him not a whit. It looks for the moment as though I might have to reject this creek life unless I want to be utterly brutalized. Is human culture with its values my only real home after all? Can it possibly be that I should move my anchor-hold to the side of a library? This direction of thought brings me abruptly to a fork in the road where I stand paralyzed, unwilling to go on, for both ways lead to madness.

Either this world, my mother, is a monster, or I myself am a freak.

Consider the former: the world is a monster. Any three-year-old can see how unsatisfactory and clumsy is this whole business of reproducing and dying by the billions. We have not yet encountered any god who is as merciful as a man who flicks a beetle over on its feet. There is not a people in the world who behaves as badly as praying mantises. But wait, you say, there is no right and wrong in nature; right and wrong is a human concept. Precisely: we are moral creatures, then, in an amoral world. The universe that suckled us is a monster that does not care if we live or die—does not care if it itself grinds to a halt. It is fixed and blind, a robot programmed to kill. We are free and seeing; we can only try to outwit it at every turn to save our skins.

This view requires that a monstrous world running on chance and death, careening blindly from nowhere to nowhere, somehow produced wonderful us. I came from the world, I crawled out of a sea of amino acids, and now I must whirl around and shake my fist at that sea and cry Shame! If I value anything at all, then I must blindfold my eyes when I near the Swiss Alps. We must as a culture disassemble our telescopes and settle down to backslapping. We little blobs of soft tissue crawling around on this one planet's skin are right, and the whole universe is wrong.

Or consider the alternative.

Julian of Norwich, the great English anchorite and theologian, cited, in the manner of the prophets, these words from God: "See, I am God: see, I am in all things: see, I never lift my hands off my works, nor ever shall, without end. How should anything be amiss?" But now not even the simplest and best of us sees things the way Julian did. It seems to us that plenty is amiss. So much is amiss that I must consider the second fork in the road, that creation itself is blamelessly, benevolently askew by its very free nature, and that it is only human feeling that is freakishly amiss. The frog that the giant water bug sucked had, presumably, a rush of pure feeling for about a second, before its brain turned to broth. I, however, have been sapped by various strong feelings about the incident almost daily for several years.

Do the barnacle larvae care? Does the lacewing who eats her eggs care? If they do not care, then why am I making all this fuss? If I am a freak, then why don't I hush?

Our excessive emotions are so patently painful and harmful to us as a species that I can hardly believe that they evolved. Other creatures manage to have effective matings and even stable societies without great emotions, and they have a bonus in that they need not ever mourn. (But some higher animals have emotions that we think are similar to ours: dogs, elephants, otters, and

10

15

the sea mammals mourn their dead. Why do that to an otter? What creator could be so cruel, not to kill otters, but to let them care?) It would seem that emotions are the curse, not death—emotions that appear to have devolved upon a few freaks as a special curse from Malevolence.

All right then. It is our emotions that are amiss. We are freaks, the world is fine, and let us all go have lobotomies to restore us to a natural state. We can leave the library then, go back to the creek lobotomized, and live on its banks as untroubled as any muskrat or reed. You first. ◪

Reflections and Inquiries

1. State in your own words the essence of the dilemma that Dillard dramatizes in this piece. Do you agree that the dilemma is a valid one, or do you consider it to be, to use the term from logic (see Chapter 5), a false dichotomy? Why or why not?

2. What is the purpose of the Southern Railroad analogy? How well, in your opinion, does it capture evolutionary selection? What other analogy might Dillard have used?

3. Dillard refers to human emotions as "excessive," and as "painful and harmful to us as a species." Do you think she is being ironic? If so, what clues does she give you? If not, then why does she feel this way about emotions?

4. What point is Dillard making in her last paragraph?

Reading to Write

Annie Dillard is one of several authors who have attempted to reconcile "random" nature with "purposeful" humanity. Write a comparison between Annie Dillard's approach and those of one or more of the following authors:

- Ralph Waldo Emerson, *Nature*, Boston, 1836

- Henry David Thoreau, *Walden*, Boston, 1854

- Pierre Teilhard de Chardin, *Science and Christ*, 1965, trans. René Hague, New York: Harper, 1968

- Loren Eiseley, *The Unexpected Universe*, New York: Harcourt, 1969

- Chet Raymo, *Honey from Stone: A Naturalist's Search for God*, New York: Dodd, 1987

- Barbara Brown Taylor, *The Luminous Web: Essays on Science and Religion*, Boston: Cowley, 2000

Too Much Confrontation: Why Creationism Should Not Be Taught Alongside Evolution | Mark Rodriguez

Creationists argue that an evolutionary approach to the origins of life is as much a belief as supernatural creation because of the lack of sufficient evidence. Evolutionists counterargue that there is sufficient evidence, that evolution is not a belief because it makes no predetermined assumptions and is always subjecting hypotheses to rigorous testing. Are these two views so contradictory that they cannot be taught together? Would doing so violate the separation of church and state, thereby violating the civil rights of students? Mark Rodriguez, a student at Santa Clara University, argues this premise in the following essay.

There are two opposing views of how life arose on this planet, evolutionist and creationist. The evolutionist view believes that the universe came into being merely by chance over a succession of millions of years. The creationist side believes that the world was created supernaturally. Patrick Marks explains the evolutionist view that life began purely by chance:

Completely random, accidental chemical reactions in the oceans produced self-replicating molecular machines—single-celled life forms. Over many millions of years accidental mutations gradually produced more and more complex life forms until the earth was teeming with unique and varied creatures of every description, including bipedal primates, called human beings, which possessed self-awareness.

Duane Gish explains the creationist view:

All living things were brought into being by the acts of a Creator. Sharp boundaries separate major taxonomic groups. Variation exists only within established groups. No transitional forms exist between groups in higher categories. (135)

Both groups have been in constant, heated debate as to which record of creation should be taught in public schools. As it stands, only evolution is being taught. Creationists consider this unfair and are fighting for equal representation. Creationists feel that to teach one side without the other in our pluralistic democratic society is a violation of academic and religious freedom.

But if creationism was allowed to be taught in our public schools, that would be a direct violation of one's civil rights. According to the First Amendment, "There shall be a separation between church and state." Creationism, which regards the creation of life as a supernatural act of God, is a religious view and therefore should not be taught in public schools. Creationists argue that there are many violations of the First Amendment, such as the observance of an essentially religious holiday like Thanksgiving or Christmas, or putting the words "In God We Trust" on U.S. currency. This is not an example of possible indoctrination, but teaching creationism in a biology classroom could be.

Also, if creationism was allowed to be taught in public schools, there would be excessive, disruptive arguments over which creation story should be taught since every religion has its own story as to how life began on this world. As it stands, most advocates of creationism are Christians. With so many different religions such as Buddhism, Judiasm, and Hinduism, there is no way to choose just one story on which all religions could agree. And if it were left up to the state to choose a single creation story, then those not of that religion would feel that their own beliefs were either wrong or of little or no importance. That would violate their civil rights. A science class, on the other hand, deals with general truths that are obtained through the scientific method, and are not based on personal beliefs.

To keep from violating one's civil rights, creationism should be taught as an elective or special course. Students should have a right to choose whether they wish to learn about creationism in addition to evolution. These courses should also be taught no earlier than in senior year of high school, since these ideas are complex and hard to understand.

Works Cited

Gish, Duane "Creation, Evolution and the Historical Evidence." *American Biology Teacher* 35 (Mar. 1973): 135.

Marks, Patrick C. "Darwin and the Devil's Advocate." 2000. 5 Jan. 2001 <http://www.darwin-devils-advocate.com/toc.htm.>

Reflections and Inquiries

1. How well does Rodriguez defend his claim that teaching creationism alongside evolution violates students' civil rights? How might one counterargue Rodriguez's claim?

2. Do you agree or disagree with Rodriguez's recommendation that creationism should be offered only as an elective? Why?

3. Support or challenge Rodriguez's assertion that "a science course . . . deals with general truths that are obtained through the scientific method, and are not based on personal beliefs."

Reading to Write

After reading as much as you can about creationism and evolution, write a position paper in which you argue that creationism and evolution are or are not sufficiently compatible to be taught together in a biology class.

Connections Across the Clusters

To what extent is the creation–evolution debate a censorship issue? A privacy issue? (See Clusters 3 and 8, respectively.)

Writing Projects

1. Write a detailed examination of the "argument from design" debate, starting, perhaps, with its originator William Paley (see his *Natural Theology* [1802]). Give equal attention to both sides of the argument. In your conclusion, decide which side offers the most compelling argument and explain why.

2. Write an essay in which you describe your own efforts to reconcile scientific understanding with religious faith.

Suggestions for Further Reading

Davies, Paul. *God and the New Physics.* New York: Simon, 1983.

Gould, Stephen Jay. "Evolution as Fact and Theory." *Hen's Teeth and Horse's Toes.* New York: Norton, 1983. 253–62.

———. *Rocks of Ages: Science and Religion in the Fullness of Life.* New York: Ballantine, 1999.

Larson, Edward J. *Trial and Error: The American Controversy over Creation Evolution.* New York: Oxford UP, 1985.

Polkinghorne, John. *One World: The Interaction of Science and Theology.* Princeton: Princeton UP, 1988.

Raymo, Chet. *Skeptics and True Believers: The Exhilarating Connection Between Science and Religion.* New York: Walker & Co., 1998.

Ruse, Michael. "Answering the Creationists: Where They Go Wrong and What They're Afraid Of." *Free Inquiry* 18 (Spring 1998): 28–33.

Teilhard de Chardin, Pierre. *Science and Christ.* Trans. Rene Hague. New York: Harper, 1965.

6 | Is Multicultural Education Necessary?

Introduction

Ideas about education, like ideas about religion and politics, tend to be categorized as "conservative" or "liberal." Thus stereotyped, they tend to become oversimplified as well. While it is true that to be conservative generally means to find value in traditional practices and that to be liberal generally means to be willing to change existing practices in light of changing values and circumstances, it does not necessarily follow that one view must exclude the other.

Multiculturalism—the study of the way that different cultures and groups interact in a particular context (educational, economic, political)—has shed important light on the possibilities of human progress and cooperation. In education, it has called attention to possible correlations between cultural heritage, sexual orientation, socioeconomic background and learning; between proficiency in a primary or secondary language and learning; between culturally bound teaching methods and learning. The following selections present a range of critical stances on multicultural approaches to education and serve to guide readers toward making more informed judgments on these important issues.

Addressing Issues of Multiple Identities for Women of Color on College Campuses

Angela D. Ferguson and
Mary F. Howard-Hamilton

Diversity is often discussed in simplistic terms. The term is often used in generalized ways in reference to inclusion of African Americans, Latinos, and so on in white communities with little or no attention given to the complex diversity within such groups. One example is sexual identity—problematic itself in a campus community, but especially problematic within a recognized ethnic group, such as African American women. In the following study, Angela D. Ferguson and Mary F. Howard-Hamilton call attention to the multiple-identity situations these women face.

Campus organizations and student groups are frequently established based on a single identity without recognition or discussion of the multiple characteristics many students embrace. Oftentimes, students identify with others based on immutable or visible characteristics relative to gender and race. For example, it is not uncommon to have student groups on campuses that focus on women's issues, African American issues, Latino issues, or international students' concerns and issues. Although these groups serve the needs of many college students, they are generally based on the assumption that their members represent a homogeneous group and that all members share common concerns. Group members may indeed share common concerns; however, discussions of or attention to diversity issues within organizations and social groups may not occur.

Henry Louis Gates (1996) cogently stated that people "speak as if race is something blacks have, sexual orientation is something gays and lesbians have, gender is something women have, ethnicity is something so called 'ethnics' have" (p. 3). Thus, if persons do not fit "neatly" into the aforementioned categories, they are not acknowledged as sharing group membership in any particular group. Moreover, if they do not openly identify with the above categories, people assume they do not have any worries about the various identities. This conclusion is far from true because everyone in our society is part of the multicultural salad bowl (Pope, 1995). Gates (1996) argued for an inclusive definition of multiculturalism of which gay, lesbians, and bisexuals are a part because: (a) the identity stages that racial groups must attain are comparable for sexual minorities; (b) multicultural counseling skills are transferable;

Source: Ferguson, Angela D., and Mary F. Howard-Hamilton. "Addressing Issues of Multiple Identities for Women of Color on College Campuses." *Toward Acceptance: Sexual Orientation Issues on Campus.* Ed. Vernon A. Wall and Nancy J. Evans. Lanham: UP of America, 2000. 283–97. Reprinted by permission.

(c) there is a cultural environment among lesbians and gays; and (d) the impact of oppression on gays and lesbians as well as the majority culture affects their careers, psychosocial development, and overall life.

In this chapter we discuss the issues specifically related to African American lesbian and bisexual women and how the integration of race, gender, and sexual orientation forms a confluence of characteristics that should be addressed to enhance sensitivity among student affairs practitioners, faculty, and students. Multicultural theoretical perspectives are discussed to provide a base for examining these issues. Strategies for inclusion related to training and interventions are presented.

Multicultural Perspectives in Student Affairs

Multicultural theoretical perspectives have their "roots in the racial civil rights movement of the 1960's and early 1970's" (Helms & Richardson, 1997, p. 62). Along with providing credibility for African American rights (Hutnik, 1991), this movement helped increase awareness of other undervalued, hidden, multiply oppressed groups of people in American society. The growing presence of women, men and women of color, openly LGBT students, and non-traditional students on college campuses has helped to serve as a catalyst in challenging earlier theoretical concepts of student development and their application to human behavior and mental health (Chickering & Reisser, 1993).

Early multicultural theoretical and empirical literature began changing traditional frameworks of understanding individuals by including the exploration of racial identity development (Atkinson, Morten, & Sue, 1998; Cross, 1991; Helms, 1993). This literature helped mental health and student affairs professionals gain an understanding of important characteristics and psychological dynamics involved in developing a non-White racial identity. Racial identity models that have focused specifically on non-European American individuals have examined the sociopolitical dynamics of each group's race, how racial issues are perceived and dealt with (Carter, 1995), and how social consequences of oppression and prejudice impact self-esteem.

Gender identity development models have surfaced since the emergence of the feminist movement. Gender role identity varies within and among cultural groups, and many cultures, including European American, continue to value stereotypic gender expectations and ideologies (Fassinger & Richie, 1997), particularly when intense and pervasive patriarchal values are embraced (Greene, 1994). Many women of color perceive their family as the primary social unit and a source of emotional refuge from racism in the dominant culture (Greene, 1994). Consequently, many lesbians of color may choose not to jeopardize connection with family members and with the ethnic community system by identifying themselves as lesbian. Kanuha (1990) stated that due to racism and the need for people of color to form alliances against it, "lesbians of color are inextricably bound to their racial-ethnic communities and therefore to men of color" (p. 172).

Several sexual orientation models (Cass, 1979; Coleman, 1982; Troiden, 1989) have appeared in the psychological literature. They outline the developmental tasks by which the individual comes to accept her or his sexual orientation. These models have also been useful in understanding the complex and all too often misunderstood development of a nonheterosexual identity. However, these approaches have been criticized for their insensitivity to diverse groups in terms of race/ethnicity, age, gender, and those who exhibit a bisexual orientation (McCarn & Fassinger, 1996). Tremble, Schneider, and Appathurai (1989) noted that "the study of the gay and lesbian experience in North America has been most often the study of the White, middle-class experience. Until recently, the impact of ethnic and racial differences among gay males and lesbians has remained largely unexamined" (p. 253).

Issues Impacting Lesbian and Bisexual Women of Color

Many college students struggle to adapt to a very new environment, one that may appear indifferent to and rejecting of their individuality, race, and culture. Many are also in the process of learning about and understanding issues related to sexuality and intimacy (Evans & D'Augelli, 1996), and are generally unfamiliar with the issues related to sexual orientation (Eldridge & Barnett, 1991). Moreover, many cultures have religious and/or familial values and principles that are not similar to traditional American dating rituals thereby restricting the individual's awareness and expression of sexuality relative to the culturally dominant groups on campus.

Developing a lesbian, gay, or bisexual relationship may be "a more complex process than achieving an intimate heterosexual relationship because of the invisibility of lesbian and gay couples in our society" (Evans, Forney, & Guido-DiBrito, 1998, p. 97). Consequently, many gay men, lesbians, and bisexual students have not had the opportunity of dating or developing romantic relationships with same-sex partners. This developmental task of developing and forming intimate relationships may be more challenging for lesbian and bisexual women of color due to the complexity of race, gender, and cultural factors.

As a group, lesbian and bisexual women of color include ethnically   10
and culturally diverse individuals. African American, Black American of Caribbean descent, Latina, Asian American, Native American, Asian Indian, and Pacific Islander women comprise a few of the ethnic groups that may be considered "women of color." Cultural values and practices, belief systems, and gender values vary among the large group of women who consider themselves lesbian (Greene, 1994). Sexual orientation to date does not have a uniform definition and is not perceived similarly by the heterosexual community or the gay, lesbian, or bisexual communities (Ferguson, 1995). Definitions of sexual orientation may vary, in part, due to the fact that many cultures have a wide range of perceptions and attitudes about sexual behavior (Espin, 1984; Smith, 1997) depending on factors such as gender, religion, and social status. Moreover, Greene (1997) noted that sexuality is contextual and that ". . . what

it means to be a gay man or a lesbian will be related to the meaning assigned to sexuality in the culture" (p. 218). Gender roles and expectations are significantly impacted by cultural and religious values, customs, and beliefs.

Lesbian and bisexual women of color are often attempting to integrate at least three social identities that have historically been stigmatized and oppressed: race, gender, and sexual orientation. The effects of race, ethnicity, and gender may differentially affect lesbian and bisexual women of color's coming-out process. For some women who are in the process of developing racial, ethnic, and gender identities while at the same time coming out, the effects of racism, homophobia, and sexism may uniquely impact their cognitive, emotional, and behavioral transitions relative to developing any one of their identities (Ferguson, 1995). Additionally, Morales (1989) noted that throughout their lives, ethnic gay and lesbian individuals have to relate to three different reference groups: "the gay/lesbian community, the ethnic community, and the predominantly heterosexual White mainstream society" (p. 22). The lesbian and bisexual woman of color on college campuses is visible and invisible in multiple ways. Many of her peers are typically focused on one or perhaps two of her social identities: race/ethnicity and gender, with little attention to the possibility of her having a non-heterosexual identity. As a result, her race/ethnicity is often the primary visible identity to heterosexual White and racial/ethnic communities, as well as to White gay, lesbian, and bisexual communities. She is invisible in that her sexual orientation can be minimized or ignored by the same communities. This visibility/invisibility continuum presents lesbians of color with unique challenges on college campuses in terms of self-identity, group membership, group identification, and community inclusion/exclusion. Integrating themselves on a college campus is therefore more complex than simply experiencing "adjustment issues" to a new environment.

Issues Impacting Lesbian and Bisexual African American Women

The paramount issue facing bisexual and lesbian African American women is inclusion. Where do I belong and who will support me and my identity? Within certain lesbian movements, some African American lesbians and bisexuals have felt that the espoused belief in justice for all women was not inclusive of women of color (Louise, 1989). For African American lesbians in particular, it is often difficult to find acceptance among the African American population because lesbianism is largely incompatible with female role expectations based on traditional African American values (Loiacano, 1989). Moreover, many African American lesbians and bisexuals perceive the African American community as very homophobic and rejecting of them (Mays & Cochran, 1988). Yielding to social pressure, many lesbians and bisexual women of African descent attempt to follow social expectations by marrying. An early study found that 47% of African American lesbians and 13% of African American gay males have been married a least once (Bell & Weinberg,

1978). More recently, Ferguson (1995) surveyed 181 women of African descent who identified as lesbian and found that approximately 67% of the women had been in a committed relationship with a man at some time in their lives. Additionally, approximately 39% of the women reported that they have children. Greene (1994) summarized that African American lesbians may ". . . have continued contact with men and with heterosexual peers to a greater extent than their White counterparts" (p. 246). African American lesbians' adherence to gender roles (for instance, marriage, children, commitment to men) may allow them to perceive themselves as part of their cultural and ethnic community, rather than feeling separated and isolated because of their sexual orientation (Ferguson, 1995).

Sexual attraction to men and forming a family have been embedded in the heterosexual community to mean that a woman is "normal" (Greene, 1994). Developmentally, African American women are attempting to negotiate teenage and adult expectations, as well as the meaning of womanhood for themselves and with their peers. Feeling "abnormal" may significantly prevent women from developing confidence, leadership skills, and socially visible roles on campus. Consequently, the question of belonging to which group(s) often poses a salient dilemma for many African American women who embrace a "non-heterosexual" sexual orientation.

Garnets and Kimmel (1993) found several themes relevant for understanding cultural influence on the identity of lesbians and gays. These themes are:

1. **Religion**—The African American community rallies around the church, which brings about racial pride in identity and solidarity among its members. However, the religious community often ostracizes African American gays and lesbians.

2. **Gender roles**—It is difficult for women to carry out androgynous or nontraditional roles.

3. **Family structure**—Coming out to family may mean the loss of a major support system. Many individuals therefore remain closeted.

4. **Identity formation**—Integration of multiple identities (race, gender, and sexual orientation) may engender a conflicting value system not only about themselves but what they may teach to others.

5. **Integration into the majority culture**—This may mean "an ongoing management of conflicting allegiances between those groups that represent the expression of intimacy and those that provide ethnic foundation" (Garnets & Kimmel, 1993, p. 334).

Strategies for Inclusion

Where does the woman of color who embraces a lesbian or bisexual identity go for support on campus? Student affairs faculty and practitioners are in a

15

position to help create and implement curricular changes, programs, and services to be more inclusive of this population.

The authors of the *NASPA Perspective on Student Affairs* (1987) presented several assumptions and beliefs that shape the student affairs profession. In the belief that "each student has worth and dignity" (p. 10) administrators were reminded that:

> It is imperative that students learn to recognize, understand, and celebrate human differences. Colleges can, and indeed must help their students become open to the differences that surround them: race, religion, age, gender, culture, physical ability, language, nationality, sexual preference [sic], and lifestyle. These matters are learned best in collegiate settings that are rich with diversity and they must be learned if the ideals of human worth and dignity are to be advanced. (p. 10)

Addressing Multicultural Issues in Student Affairs Preparation

Based upon this philosophy, student affairs graduate preparation programs should be helping students understand and embrace the dramatic changes in the demographic complexion of the student population on college campuses (Talbot, 1996). Talbot examined current graduate training programs and found that many of the students define and view diversity narrowly. Populations that they included in their definitions were "women, African Americans, and adult learners" (p. 174). The students rarely mentioned other racial/ethnic groups or lesbians, bisexuals, or gay men. Additionally, Talbot stated that "several students indicated that gay, lesbian, and bisexual issues were almost 'taboo'; bringing up the topic usually caused tension" (p. 174). Many instructors assert that they lack the knowledge, interest, or time to prepare appropriate literature and information that is inclusive of diversity (Vazquez, 1997). The students interviewed in Talbot's (1996) study stated that in-class discussions about multiculturalism were promoted by the students rather than being faculty generated. These findings are alarming because the faculty who teach in graduate preparation programs are not preparing new practitioners with effective communication and intervention strategies for the diverse student body on today's college campuses. This lack of diversity training is antithetical to the guiding philosophy statements put forth by the field which state that student affairs practitioners should do no harm to the students they serve (ACPA, 1993). When personal identity is ignored by using only the traditional theories and attempting to apply them to all cultural groups, educators are doing harm to the students with whom they work by not acknowledging or embracing their unique characteristics.

Once a multicultural training model has been developed, programs must also consider the various topical areas to be included in not only a multicultural course, but in all areas of student affairs preparation. Some programs may be presenting culture-specific information in a manner that prohibits inclusion of people with multiple identities. Consequently, "students may learn to stereotype clients if only normative information is presented without adequate consideration of within-group differences" (Ridley, Espelage, & Rubinstein, 1997, p. 136). Addressing issues of identity development, for example, would require student affairs administrators and faculty to acknowledge the fact that racial identity may differ due to the individual's gender and sexual orientation; gender identity may differ due to race/ethnicity and sexual orientation; and sexual orientation identity may differ due to gender and race/ethnicity. Training programs must emphasize the importance of examining identity theories concurrently and acknowledge the complexity of integrating multiple social identities and multiple forms of oppression. As students gain an understanding of this complex process, they may begin to move beyond "knowledge and sensitivity"; they can begin to learn practical applications of multicultural approaches and move toward developing multicultural skills (Ridley et al., 1997, p. 136).

Lesbian and bisexual women of color need to find allies and supportive networks to insure their success on campus. This goal can be accomplished if training programs prepare practitioners to become sensitive to racial/gendered individuals as well as to understand diversity issues and factors both between and within racial, gender, and sexual orientation group members.

Many student affairs practitioners know it is important to "walk the walk and talk the talk," but do they really know how to be assertive in uncomfortable situations? Increasing comfort in such situations is one reason why the infusion of a multicultural curriculum and specific course work is so important in our field. Curricula that incorporate a multicultural perspective in theory courses, research, consultation, career, supervision, and counseling courses would assist graduate students in their preparation to work with issues of diversity. Assisting students to recognize and understand oppression based on "isms," their biases and misperceptions about their own and others' culture, and the relevance of sociopolitical and sociocultural contexts would provide them with an awareness that "all people have been shaped by membership in one or more cultures and that these cultural roots or origins influence people's values, behavior, and perception of events" (Pope, Reynolds, & Cheatham, 1997, p. 62). Courses that emphasize the idea of diversity as including multiple identities would help to sensitize students to becoming aware that people do not exist under one identity, but may also be attempting to integrate identities that may be mutually stigmatizing.

Curricula that utilize an integrative approach in which training involves a didactic component (cognitive) and an experiential (affective) component would assist students in recognizing the ways in which their own cultural realities and internalizations interact and affect their work with others (Brown, 1993; Comas-Diaz, 1994). This approach would assist students in becoming more flexible and pluralistic in their teaching and research practices, and pro-

20

gram development. Moreover, it would allow student affairs practitioners to gain an understanding of their own cultural development.

McEwen and Roper (1994) suggested that "incorporating multicultural-ism into preparation programs should heighten multicultural awareness and knowledge of graduate students and faculty; embracing multiculturalism represents honest scholarship, rather than scholarship void of consideration of multicultural issues" (p. 49). In addition to coursework and personal exploration, student affairs practitioners should become familiar with the lesbian and bisexual community around them. Talbot (1996) stressed that students in graduate preparation programs should have direct contact and exposure to diverse students, faculty, and staff. For example, personal interaction and participation in dialogues to find out what issues and concerns plague African American lesbian and bisexual women will increase cohesion among these students and administrators. In addition, becoming familiar with community groups off campus can help student affairs administrators and practitioners guide students to referral sources if needed.

Building Bridges of Support Through Student Affairs Practice

Based upon the reviewed literature, several suggestions for providing a supportive environment for comfort and inclusion among African American lesbians are offered. Administrators can make a strong supportive pronouncement for lesbian, bisexual, and gay rights by supporting the inclusion of a sexual orientation statement in the university nondiscrimination policy. Faculty can assist in this process by becoming members of committees that are developed to address the issue of homophobia and heterosexism on campus. Additionally, strategies to address sensitivity to heterosexism in the classroom, similar to the sexual harassment policies already developed, should be designed by faculty and administrators in a collaborative effort. Demonstrating faculty and administrative support shows students that there is solidarity and advocacy towards this issue.

A support group for lesbian and bisexual women of color should be accessible to students in addition to larger organizations that are inclusive of LGBT students regardless of race or gender. This is one way that lesbians and bisexuals have gained integration of their multiple identities (Garnets & Kimmel, 1993). Garnets and Kimmel stated that such a network provides a sense of community by: (a) creating new extended families that are more sensitive to their needs (p. 336); (b) increasing visibility by acknowledging their presence among the larger racial/ethnic and gay and lesbian populations; and (c) helping them to consolidate efforts toward ameliorating oppression in the respective communities they interact with on a continual basis. It is imperative that some type of network for women of color be established due, in part, to the fact that this cohort is less likely to seek assistance from counselors, thus intensifying their isolation, tension, and loneliness on campus (Greene, 1994).

Inclusion of bisexual women of color should be a focal point for the group [25] because "the gay and especially the lesbian community is embracing bisexuality as never before" (Nichols, 1994, p. 157). If necessary, a group for bisexual women should be established for psychological, social, and emotional support. The bisexual orientation paradigm is relatively new to researchers, practitioners, and counselors. Very little has been written regarding the needs of this population. However, individuals embracing a bisexual identification have unique needs that are separate from those of lesbians and this "paradigm recognizes that sexual orientation is multidimensional; this conception not only includes attraction, behavior, and identity, but also allows for fluid identity over the life cycle" (Nichols, 1994, p. 167).

Establishing "safe places" in classrooms, residential housing, workshops, and student organizations for students to discuss a variety of issues and concerns can help support individuals with multiple identities. Continuing the trend of limiting discussions to "Black" issues, "women's" issues, or "gay, lesbian, bisexual" issues without regard to integrating these issues perpetuates the monolithic, unidimensional paradigm that currently exists. Becoming aware that "Black" issues also include women's and gay, lesbian, and bisexual concerns is an important step in raising the conscience of the campus community.

Conclusion

Traditional student affairs and psychological research historically has excluded or minimized the importance of the individual's social identities (i.e., ethnicity, gender, sexual orientation) and their relationship within individuals' psychological, interpersonal, leadership, and social development. The effects of racism, sexism, and homophobia may differentially affect lesbian and bisexual women of color, and oftentimes in erratic and contradictory ways. As they seek to develop friendships and social activities, the existing separate campus organizations and activities (for example, Black organizations, women's organizations, Greek organizations) may prevent lesbian and bisexual women of color from experiencing themselves as "whole" persons.

Racism, sexism, and heterosexism are forms of oppression perpetrated by respective majority/dominant groups. Moreover, sexism and heterosexism are also forms of oppression in both the communities of color and in the gay/lesbian communities, respectively. Lesbian and bisexual women of color are often in the position of juggling multiple identities and multiple oppressions (Ferguson, 1995). Each social identity carries its own type of oppression, which may be conflicting with another social identity. Being a member of one oppressed group may evoke feelings of fear, denial, or anger that may cause the individual to disavow any membership in another oppressed group (Tajfel, 1981). These factors play a part in how the individual may perceive the salience and importance of a particular social identity relative to the stressors, environment, and people in her life (Ferguson, 1995), and may inhibit her academic and personal/interpersonal growth.

The gay, bisexual, and lesbian population has many within-group differences that should be recognized and addressed in all aspects of student development and student activities on campus. Just as many racial/ethnic groups are lumped into one monolithic categorization of behaviors or beliefs, so are lesbians, gays, and bisexuals. Continued research and further data are imperative to provide information on the supportive services needed for lesbians and bisexuals of color on college campuses in order to expand our understanding of ways to enrich, transform, and develop multicultural efforts in the field.

References

American College Personnel Association (1993). American College Personnel Association: Statement of ethical principles and standards. *Journal of College Student Development, 34,* 89–92.

Atkinson, D. R., Morten, G., & Sue, D. W. (Eds.). (1998). *Counseling American minorities: A cross-cultural perspective* (5th ed.). Boston: McGraw Hill.

Bell, A., & Weinberg, M. (1978). *Homosexuality: A study of diversity among men and women.* New York: Simon & Schuster.

Brown, L. S. (1993). Anti-domination training as a central component of diversity in clinical psychology education. *Clinical Psychologist, 46,* 83–87.

Carter, R. T. (1995). *The influence of race and racial identity in psychotherapy.* New York: Wiley.

Cass, V. C. (1979). Homosexual identity formation: A theoretical model. *Journal of Homosexuality, 15,* 13–23.

Chickering, A. W., & Reisser, L. (1993). *Education and identity* (2nd ed.). San Francisco: Jossey-Bass.

Coleman, E. (1982). Developmental stages of the coming out process. In J. Gonsiorek (Ed.), *Homosexuality and psychotherapy: A practitioner's handbook of affirmative models* (pp. 31–44). New York: Haworth.

Comas-Diaz, L. (1994). An integrative approach. In L. Comas-Diaz & B. Greene (Eds.), *Women of color: Integrating ethnic and gender identities in psychotherapy* (pp. 287–318). New York: Guilford Press.

Cross, W. E., Jr. (1991). *Shades of Black: Diversity in African-American identity.* Philadelphia, PA: Temple University Press.

Eldridge, N. S., & Barnett, D. C. (1991). Counseling gay and lesbian students. In N. J. Evans & V. A. Wall (Eds.), *Beyond tolerance: Gays, lesbians and bisexuals on campus* (pp. 147–178). Alexandria, VA: American College Personnel Association.

Espin, O. M. (1984). Cultural and historical influences on sexuality in Hispanic/Latina women: Implications for psychotherapy. In C. Vance (Ed.), *Pleasure and danger: Exploring female sexuality* (pp. 149–163). London: Routledge & Kegan Paul.

Evans, N. J., & D'Augelli, A. R. (1996). Lesbians, gay men, and bisexual people in college. In R. C. Savin-Williams & K. M. Cohen (Eds.). *The lives of lesbians, gays, and bisexuals: Children to adults* (pp. 201–226). Fort Worth, TX: Harcourt Brace.

Evans, N. J., Forney, D. S., & Guido-DiBrito, F. (1998). *Student development in college: Theory, research, and practice.* San Francisco: Jossey-Bass.

Fassinger, R. E., & Richie, B. S. (1997). Sex matters: Gender and sexual orientation in training for multicultural counseling competency. In D. B. Pope-Davis & H. L. K. Coleman (Eds.), *Multicultural counseling competencies* (pp. 83–110). Thousand Oaks, CA: Sage.

Ferguson, A. D. (1995). *The relationship between African American lesbians' race, gender, and sexual orientation and self-esteem.* Unpublished doctoral dissertation, University of Maryland, College Park.

Gates, H. L. (1996). The ethics of identity. *Pathways, 20* (3), 3–4.

Garnets, L., & Kimmel, D. (Eds.). (1993). *Psychological perspectives on lesbian and gay male experiences.* New York: Columbia University Press.

Greene, B. (1994). Lesbian women of color: Triple jeopardy. In L. Comas-Diaz & B. Greene (Eds.), *Women of color: Integrating ethnic and gender identities in psychotherapy* (pp. 389–427). New York: Guilford.

Greene, B. (Ed.). (1997). *Psychological perspectives on lesbian and gay issues: Vol. 3. Ethnic and cultural diversity among lesbians and gay men* (pp. 297–300). Thousand Oaks, CA: Sage.

Helms, J. E. (1993). *Black and White racial identity: Theory, research, and practice.* Westport, CT: Praeger.

Helms, J. E., & Richardson, T. Q. (1997). How "multiculturalism" obscures race and culture as differential aspects of counseling competency. In D. B. Pope-Davis & H. L. K. Coleman (Eds.), *Multicultural counseling competencies* (pp. 60–82). Thousand Oaks, CA: Sage.

Hutnik, N. (1991). *Ethnic minority identity.* New York: Oxford University Press.

Kanuha, V. (1990). Compounding the triple jeopardy: Battering in lesbian of color relationships. *Women and Therapy, 9,* 169–183.

Loiacano, D. K. (1989). Gay identity issues among Black Americans: Racism, homophobia, and the need for validation. *Journal of Counseling and Development, 68,* 21–25.

Louise, V. (1989). Coming out. In J. Penelope & S. Wolfe (Eds.), *The original coming out stories.* Freedom, CA: The Crossing Press.

Mays, V., & Cochran, S. (1988). The Black woman's relationship project: A national survey of Black lesbians. In M. Shernoff & W. Scott (Eds.), *The sourcebook on lesbian/gay health care* (2nd ed., pp. 54–62). Washington, DC: National Lesbian and Gay Health Foundation.

McCarn, S. R., & Fassinger, R. E. (1996). Revisioning sexual minority identity development formation: A new model of lesbian identity and its implications for counseling and research. *The Counseling Psychologist, 24,* 508–534.

McEwen, M. L., & Roper, L. D. (1994). Incorporating multiculturalism into student affairs preparation programs: Suggestions from the literature. *Journal of College Student Development, 35,* 46–53.

Morales, E. S. (1989). Ethnic minority families and minority gays and lesbians. *Journal of Homosexuality, 17,* 217–239.

National Association of Student Personnel Administrators (1987). *A perspective on student affairs.* Washington, DC: Author.

Nichols, M. (1994). Therapy with bisexual women: Working on the edge of emerging cultural and personal identities. In M. P. Mirkin (Ed.), *Women in context: Toward a feminist reconstruction of psychotherapy* (pp. 149–169). New York: Guilford.

Pope, M. (1995). The "salad bowl" is big enough for us all: An argument for the inclusion of lesbians and gay men in any definition of multiculturalism. *Journal of Counseling and Development, 73,* 301–304.

Pope, R. L., Reynolds, A. L., & Cheatham, H. E. (1997). American College Personnel Association strategic initiative on multiculturalism: A report and proposal. *Journal of College Student Development, 38,* 62–66.

Ridley, C. R., Espelage, D. L., & Rubinstein, K. J. (1997). Course development in multicultural counseling. In D. B. Pope-Davis & H. L. K. Coleman (Eds.), *Multicultural counseling competencies* (pp. 131–158). Thousand Oaks, CA: Sage.

Smith, A. (1997). Cultural diversity and the coming-out process. In B. Greene (Ed.), *Psychological perspectives on lesbian and gay issues: Vol. 3. Ethnic and cultural diversity among lesbians and gay men* (pp. 297–300). Thousand Oaks, CA: Sage.

Talbot, D. M. (1996). Master's student's perspective on their graduate education regarding issues of diversity. *NASPA Journal, 33,* 163–178.

Tajfel, H. (1981). *Human groups and social categories: Studies in social psychology.* Cambridge: Cambridge University Press.

Tremble, B., Schneider, M., & Appathurai, C. (1989). Growing up gay or lesbian in a multicultural context. *Gay and Lesbian Youth, 17,* 253–267.

Troiden, R. R. (1989). The formation of homosexual identities. *Journal of Homosexuality, 17,* 43–73.

Vazquez, L. A. (1997). A systemic multicultural curriculum model: The pedagogical process. In D. B. Pope-Davis & H. L. K. Coleman (Eds.), *Multicultural counseling competencies* (pp. 159–183). Thousand Oaks, CA: Sage. ◪

Reflections and Inquiries

1. What tends to be oversimplified in traditional ethnic-group designations, according to Ferguson and Howard-Hamilton?

2. What problems of sexual identity might some African American women face?

3. Why is it so difficult for African American lesbians to find acceptance within traditional African American communities?

4. How can college communities help women with their sexual identities?

5. Reflect on the importance of identity within a specific ethnic group—your own, perhaps. Why is it necessary—or unnecessary—to identify and describe them?

6. What do you consider to be the most influential elements in identity formation? Which of them are in greatest need of cultivation in college communities? Why?

Reading to Write

Write a critical evaluation of Ferguson's and Howard-Hamilton's recommendations for how campus organizations can help gay, lesbian, and bisexual students fit in.

Two Languages Are Better Than One

Wayne P. Thomas
and Virginia P. Collier

Some educators argue that bilingual education fails because teachers cannot properly teach students to be experts in the language of instruction while simultaneously learning the subject of instruction. But Wayne P. Thomas and Virginia P. Collier set out to prove that thesis wrong. According to these educators, students serve as peer tutors for each other and are able to stimulate natural language acquisition because they keep the level of interaction intellectually stimulating. Thomas is Professor of Research and Evaluation Methods at George Mason University. Collier is Professor of Bilingual, Multicultural, and ESL Education at George Mason University. Both authors are researchers with the U.S. Department of Education's Center for Research on Education, Diversity, and Excellence.

Among the underachieving youth in U.S. schools, students with no proficiency in English must overcome enormous equity gaps, school achievement tests in English show. Over the past three decades, schools have developed a wide range of programs to serve these English learners. After much experimentation, U.S. schools now have clear achievement data that point to the most powerful models of effective schooling for English learners. What is astounding is that these same programs are also dynamic models for school reform for all students.

Imagine how the 21st century will look. Our world will surely be in constant change, for we are facing this pattern now. The predictions of the near future also depict an interconnected world, with global travel and instant international communications. Right now, many U.S. businesses seek employees proficient in both English and another language. Students who graduate with monocultural perspectives will not be prepared to contribute to their societies, for cross-cultural contact is at an all-time high in human history as population mobility continues throughout the world (Cummins in Ovando and Collier 1998). Thus, majority and minority language students together must prepare for a constantly changing world.

Tapping the Power of Linguistic Diversity

For more than three decades, as we have struggled to develop effective models for schooling English learners, we have mostly considered the choices available to us from a deficit perspective. That is, we have often viewed English learners as a "problem" for our schools (oh, no—they don't know English), and so we "remediate" by sending them to a specialist to be "fixed." In the remedial program, English learners receive less access to the standard

Source: Thomas, Wayne P., and Virginia P. Collier. "Two Languages Are Better Than One." *Educational Leadership* 55 (Dec. 1997): 23–27. Reprinted with permission of the Association for Supervision and Curriculum Development. Copyright © 1985 by ASCD. All rights reserved.

grade-level curriculum. The achievement and equity gap increases as native English speakers forge ahead while English learners make less progress. Thus, underachieving groups continue to underachieve in the next generation. Unfortunately, the two most common types of U.S. school services provided for English learners—English as a Second Language (ESL) pullout and transitional bilingual education—are remedial in nature. Participating students and teachers suffer often from the social consequences of this perception.

But when the focus of any special school program is on academic enrichment for all students, the school community perceives that program positively, and students become academically successful and deeply engaged in the learning process. Thus, enrichment programs for English learners are extremely effective when they are intellectually challenging and use students' linguistic and cultural experiences as a resource for interdisciplinary, discovery learning (Chiang 1994, Ovando and Collier 1998, Thomas and Collier 1997). Further, educators who use the enrichment models that were initially developed for English learners are beginning to see the power of these models for *all* students.

A History of Bilingual Enrichment

These innovative enrichment models are called by varying names—*dual language, bilingual immersion, two-way bilingual,* and *developmental bilingual education.* We recommend these models as forms of mainstream education through two languages that will benefit all students. Let's examine the history of their development and some basic characteristics of these models.

Initially, the first two 20th-century experiments with bilingual education in the United States and Canada in the early 1960s came about as a result of parental pressure. Both of these experiments were enrichment models. In Canada, English-speaking parents who wanted their children to develop in both French and English initiated what became known as immersion education. Immersion is a commitment to bilingual schooling throughout grades K–12 in which students are instructed 90 percent of the school day during kindergarten and grade 1 in the *minority* language chosen for the program, and 10 percent of the day in the majority language (English). The hands-on nature of academic work in the early grades is a natural vehicle for proficiency development of the minority language.

Immersion programs emphasize the less dominant language more than English in the first years, because the minority language is less supported by the broader society, and academic uses of the language are less easily acquired outside school. Gradually, with each subsequent grade, the program provides more instruction in the majority language until children learn the curriculum equally through both languages by grade 4 or 5. By grade 6, students have generally developed deep academic proficiency in both languages, and they can work on math, science, social studies, and language arts at or above grade level in *either* language. From the 1960s to the 1990s, immersion bilingual schooling has grown immensely popular in Canada and has achieved high rates of success with majority and minority students, students of middle- and low-income families, as well as students with learning disabilities (Cummins and Swain 1986, Genesee 1987).

About the same time that the first immersion program started in Canada, Cubans arriving in Miami, Florida, initiated the first U.S. experiment with two-way bilingual education in 1963. The term *two-way* refers to two language groups acquiring the curriculum through each other's languages; *one-way* bilingual education refers to one language group receiving schooling through two languages (Stern 1963). Intent on overthrowing Fidel Castro and returning to their country, the Cuban arrivals established private bilingual schools to develop their children's English and maintain their Spanish. The public schools, losing significant enrollment, chose to develop bilingual classes to attract students back. As English-speaking parents enrolled their children in the classes, two-way, integrated bilingual schooling emerged as a new program model in the United States. These classes provided a half day of the grade-level curriculum in Spanish and a half day in English, now known as the 50–50 model of two-way.

Over time, these two experiments have expanded to many states in the United States as school communities recognize the benefits for all students. The immersion model, originally developed in Canada for majority language speakers, has become known as the *90–10* two-way model in the United States because during the first two years both language groups receive 90 percent of the instruction through the *minority* language.

Students as Peer Language Models

Key to the success of all two-way programs is the fact that both language groups stay together throughout the school day, serving as peer tutors for each other. Peer models stimulate natural language acquisition for both groups because they keep the level of interaction cognitively complex (Panfil 1995). Research has consistently demonstrated that academic achievement is very high for all groups of participants compared to control groups who receive schooling only through English. This holds true for students of low socioeconomic status, as well as African-American students and language-minority students, with those in the 90–10 model achieving even higher than those in the 50–50 model (Lindholm 1990, Lindholm and Aclan 1991, Thomas and Collier 1997).

The Role of Careful Planning

What are other essential characteristics of this school reform? An important principle is clear curricular separation of the two languages of instruction. To maintain a continuous cognitive challenge, teachers do not repeat or translate lessons in the second language, but reinforce concepts taught in one language across the two languages in a spiraling curriculum. Teachers alternate the language of instruction by theme or subject area, by time of day, by day of the week, or by the week. If two teachers are teaming, each teacher represents one

10

language. When two teachers share and exchange two classes, this is a cost-effective, mainstream model that adds no additional teachers to a school system's budget. In contrast, ESL pullout is the most costly of all program models for English learners because extra ESL resource teachers must be added to the mainstream staff (Crawford 1997).

Successful two-way bilingual education includes

- a minimum of six years of bilingual instruction;
- focus on the core academic curriculum rather than on a watered-down version;
- quality language arts instruction in both languages;
- separation of the two languages for instruction;
- use of the non-English language for at least 50 percent of the instructional time and as much as 90 percent in the early grades;
- an additive bilingual environment that has full support of school administrators;
- a balanced ratio of students who speak each language (for example, 50–50 or 60–40, preferably not to go below 70–30;
- promotion of positive interdependence among peers and between teachers and students;
- high-quality instructional personnel; and
- active parent-school partnerships (Lindholm 1990).

Demographics influence the feasibility of two-way programs, because the students in each language group serve as peer teachers for each other. A natural choice for many U.S. schools is a Spanish-English two-way program, because Spanish speakers are most often the largest language group. In the 204 two-way bilingual schools identified in the United States in a 1997 survey, other languages of instruction in addition to Spanish include, in order of frequency, Korean, French, Cantonese, Navajo, Japanese, Arabic, Portuguese, Russian, and Mandarin Chinese (Montone et al. 1997).

Closing the Equity Gap Through Bilingual Enrichment

What makes these programs work? To answer this question, let's look at the students who are initially the lowest achievers on tests in English. Most school policymakers commonly assume that students need only a couple of years to learn a second language. But while these students make dramatic progress in English development in the first two years, English language learners are competing with a moving target, the native English speaker, when tested in English.

The average native English speaker typically gains 10 months of academic growth in one 10-month school year in English development because first

15

language acquisition is a natural work in progress throughout the school years, not completed until young adulthood. Although some score higher and some lower, on average they also make a year's progress in a year's time in mathematics, science, and social studies. Thus students not yet proficient in English initially score three or more years below grade level on the tests in English because they cannot yet demonstrate in their second language all that they actually know. These students must outgain the native speaker by making one and one-half years progress on the academic tests in their second language for each of six successive school years (a total of nine years progress in six years) to reach the typical performance level of the constantly advancing native English speaker.

When students do academic work in their primary language for more than two to three years (the typical support time in a transitional bilingual program), they are able to demonstrate with each succeeding year that they are making more gains than the native English speaker—and closing the gap in achievement as measured by tests in English across the curriculum. After five to six years of enrichment bilingual schooling, former English learners (now proficient in English) are able to demonstrate their deep knowledge on the academic tests in English across the curriculum, as well as in their native language, achieving on or above grade level (Thomas and Collier 1997).

Bridging the Gap to a Better Tomorrow

Why is such progress for English learners important for our schools? Language-minority students are predicted to account for about 40 percent of the school-age population by the 2030s (Berliner and Biddle 1995). It is in our pragmatic self-interest to ensure their success as young adults, for they will be key to a robust economy to pay retirement and medical benefits for today's working adults. We must close the equity gap by providing enrichment schooling for all. For native English speakers as well as language-minority students, the enrichment bilingual classes appear to provide a constant stimulus and intellectual challenge similar to that of a gifted and talented class. The research evidence is overwhelmingly clear that *proficient* bilinguals outperform monolinguals on school tests (Collier 1995). Crossing cultural, social class, and language boundaries, students in a bilingual class develop multiple ways of solving human problems and approach ecological and social science issues from a cross-national perspective. These learners acquire deep academic proficiency in two languages, which becomes a valuable resource in adult professional life. And they learn to value each other's knowledge and life experiences—leading to meaningful respect and collaboration that lasts a lifetime.

References

Berliner, D. C., and B. J. Biddle. (1995). *The Manufactured Crisis: Myths, Fraud, and the Attack on America's Public Schools.* Reading, Mass.: Addison Wesley.

Chiang, R. A. (1994). "Recognizing Strengths and Needs of All Bilingual Learners: A Bilingual/Multicultural Perspective." *NABE News 17,* 4: 11, 22–23.

Collier, V. P. (1995). *Promoting Academic Success for ESL Students: Understanding Second Language Acquisition for School*. Elizabeth: New Jersey Teachers of English to Speakers of Other Languages-Bilingual Educators.

Crawford, J. (1997). *Best Evidence: Research Foundations of the Bilingual Education Act*. Washington, D.C.: National Clearinghouse for Bilingual Education.

Cummins, J., and M. Swain. (1986). *Bilingualism in Education*. New York: Longman.

Genesee, F. (1987). *Learning Through Two Languages: Studies of Immersion and Bilingual Education*. Cambridge, Mass: Newbury House.

Lindholm, K. J. (1990). "Bilingual Immersion Education: Criteria for Program Development." In *Bilingual Education: Issues and Strategies*, edited by A. M. Padilla, H. H. Fairchild, and C. M. Valadez. Newbury Park, Calif.: Sage.

Lindholm, K. J., and Z. Aclan. (1991). "Bilingual Proficiency as a Bridge to Academic Achievement: Results from Bilingual/Immersion Programs." *Journal of Education* 173: 99–113.

Montrone, C., D. Christian, and A. Whitcher. (1997). *Directory of Two-Way Bilingual Programs in the United States*. Rev. ed. Washington, D.C.: Center for Applied Linguistics.

Ovando, C. J., and V. P. Collier. (1998). *Bilingual and ESL Classrooms: Teaching in Multicultural Contexts*. 2nd ed. New York: McGraw-Hill.

Panfil, K. (1995). "Learning from One Another: A Collaborative Study of a Two-Way Bilingual Program by Insiders with Multiple Perspectives." *Dissertation Abstracts International* 56-10A. 3859 (University Microfilms No. AA196-06004).

Stern, H. H., ed. (1963). *Foreign Languages in Primary Education: The Teaching of Foreign or Second Languages to Younger Children*. Hamburg, Germany: International Studies in Education, UNESCO Institute for Education.

Thomas, W. P., and V. P. Collier. (1997). *School Effectiveness for Language Minority Students*. Washington, D.C.: National Clearinghouse for Bilingual Education. ◾

Reflections and Inquiries

1. What "enormous equity gaps" must students with no English proficiency overcome? What would be the best way to overcome such equity gaps, according to Thomas and Collier?

2. The authors assert that program enrichment rather than the students' learning problems should be the focus of a bilingual education classroom. What is the point of changing emphasis in this manner? How valid is such a change in emphasis, in your opinion?

3. Why do the authors advocate peer-learner models? How do they work best?

4. What does it mean when the level of peer-student interaction is kept "cognitively complex"? Why is this important?

Reading to Write

Review Thomas's and Collier's criteria for "quality instruction" in a successful bilingual education program. Then discuss in a short essay which two or three of these criteria are most important and why.

Language and Literature from a Pueblo Indian Perspective | Leslie Marmon Silko

Leslie Marmon Silko is a Native American novelist and essayist whose first novel, *Ceremony* (1977), the story of a half-breed and veteran of World War II who tries to restore his war-damaged psyche by turning to ancient rituals, has been called one of the greatest twentieth-century novels about modern Indian life. Silko, of Laguna Pueblo, Mexican, and white ancestry, attended reservation schools as a child and graduated from the University of New Mexico in 1969. In the following essay, she discusses the fundamental differences between Anglo and Native American experience with language and stresses the need for Anglo educators responsible for teaching Native American youth to recognize these differences.

Where I come from, the words that are most highly valued are those which are spoken from the heart, unpremeditated and unrehearsed. Among the Pueblo people, a written speech or statement is highly suspect because the true feelings of the speaker remain hidden as he reads words that are detached from the occasion and the audience. I have intentionally not written a formal paper to read to this session because of this and because I want you to hear and to experience English in a nontraditional structure, a structure that follows patterns from the oral tradition. For those of you accustomed to a structure that moves from point A to point B to point C, this presentation may be somewhat difficult to follow because the structure of Pueblo expression resembles something like a spider's web—with many little threads radiating from a center, crisscrossing each other. As with the web, the structure will emerge as it is made and you must simply listen and trust, as the Pueblo people do, that meaning will be made.

I suppose the task that I have today is a formidable one because basically I come here to ask you, at least for a while, to set aside a number of basic approaches that you have been using and probably will continue to use in approaching the study of English or the study of language; first of all, I come to ask you to see language from the Pueblo perspective, which is a perspective that is very much concerned with including the whole of creation and the whole of history and time. And so we very seldom talk about breaking language down into words. As I will continue to relate to you, even the use of a specific language is less important than the one thing—which is the "telling," or the storytelling. And so, as Simon Ortiz has written, if you approach a Pueblo person and want to talk words or, worse than that, to break down an individual word into its components, ofttimes you will just get a blank stare, because we don't think of words as being isolated from the speaker, which, of course, is one element of the oral tradition. Moreover, we don't think of words as being alone: Words are always with other words, and the other words are almost always in a story of some sort.

Today I have brought a number of examples of stories in English because I would like to get around to the question that has been raised, or the topic that has come along here, which is what changes we Pueblo writers might make with English as a language for literature. But at the same time I would like to explain the importance of storytelling and how it relates to a Pueblo theory of language.

So first I would like to go back to the Pueblo Creation story. The reason I go back to that story is because it is an all-inclusive story of creation and how life began. Tséitsínako, Thought Woman, by thinking of her sisters, and together with her sisters, thought of everything which is, and this world was created. And the belief was that everything in this world was a part of the original creation, and that the people at home realized that far away there were others—other human beings. There is even a section of the story which is a prophesy—which describes the origin of the European race, the African, and also remembers the Asian origins.

Starting out with this story, with this attitude which includes all things, I would like to point out that the reason the people are more concerned with story and communication and less with a particular language is in part an outgrowth of the area [pointing to a map] where we find ourselves. Among the twenty Pueblos there are at least six distinct languages, and possibly seven. Some of the linguists argue—and I don't set myself up to be a linguist at all—about the number of distinct languages. But certainly Zuni is all alone, and Hopi is all alone, and from mesa to mesa there are subtle differences in language—very great differences. I think that this might be the reason that what particular language was being used wasn't as important as what a speaker was trying to say. And this, I think, is reflected and stems or grows out of a particular view of the story—that is, that language *is* story. At Laguna many words have stories which make them. So when one is telling a story, and one is using words to tell the story, each word that one is speaking has a story of its own too. Often the speakers or tellers go into the stories of the words they are using to tell one story so that you get stories within stories, so to speak. This structure becomes very apparent in the storytelling, and what I would like to show you later on by reading some pieces that I brought is that this structure also informs the writing and the stories which are currently coming from Pueblo people. I think what is essential is this sense of story, and story within story, and the idea that one story is only the beginning of many stories, and the sense that stories never truly end. I would like to propose that these views of structure and the dynamics of storytelling are some of the contributions which Native American cultures bring to the English language or at least to literature in the English language.

First of all, a lot of people think of storytelling as something that is done at bedtime—that it is something that is done for small children. When I use the

5

term "storytelling," I include a far wider range of telling activity. I also do not limit storytelling to simply old stories, but to again go back to the original view of creation, which sees that it is all part of a whole; we do not differentiate or fragment stories and experiences. In the beginning, Tséitsínako, Thought Woman, thought of all these things, and all of these things are held together as one holds many things together in a single thought.

So in the telling (and today you will hear a few of the dimensions of this telling) first of all, as was pointed out earlier, the storytelling always includes the audience and the listeners, and, in fact, a great deal of the story is believed to be inside the listener, and the storyteller's role is to draw the story out of the listeners. This kind of shared experience grows out of a strong community base. The storytelling goes on and continues from generation to generation.

The Origin story functions basically as a maker of our identity—with the story we know who we are. We are the Lagunas. This is where we came from. We came this way. We came by this place. And so from the time you are very young, you hear these stories, so that when you go out into the wider world, when one asks who you are, or where are you from, you immediately know: We are the people who came down from the north. We are the people of these stories. It continues down into clans so that you are not just talking about Laguna Pueblo people, you are talking about your own clan. Within the clans there are stories which identify the clan.

In the Creation story, Antelope says that he will help knock a hole in the earth so that the people can come up, out into the next world. Antelope tries and tries, and he uses his hooves and is unable to break through; and it is then that Badger says, "Let me help you." And Badger very patiently uses his claws and digs a way through, bringing the people into the world. When the Badger clan people think of themselves, or when the Antelope people think of themselves, it is as people who are of *this* story, and this is *our* place, and we fit into the very beginning when the people first came, before we began our journey south.

So you can move, then, from the idea of one's identity as a tribal person into clan identity. Then we begin to get to the extended family, and this is where we begin to get a kind of story coming into play which some people might see as a different kind of story, though Pueblo people do not. Anthropologists and ethnologists have, for a long time, differentiated the types of oral language they find in the Pueblos. They tended to rule out all but the old and sacred and traditional stories and were not interested in family stories and the family's account of itself. But these family stories are just as important as the other stories—the older stories. These family stories are given equal recognition. There is no definite, pre-set pattern for the way one will hear the stories of one's own family, but it is a very critical part of one's childhood, and it continues on throughout one's life. You will hear stories of importance to the family—sometimes wonderful stories—stories about the time a maternal uncle got the biggest deer that was ever seen and brought back from the mountains. And so one's sense of who the family is, and who you are, will then extend from that—"I am from the family of my uncle who brought in this wonderful

10

deer, and it was a wonderful hunt"—so you have this sort of building or sense of identity.

There are also other stories, stories about the time when another uncle, perhaps, did something that wasn't really acceptable. In other words, this process of keeping track, of telling, is an all-inclusive process which begins to create a total picture. So it is very important that you know all of the stories—both positive and not so positive—about one's own family. The reason that it is very important to keep track of all the stories in one's own family is because you are liable to hear a story from somebody else who is perhaps an enemy of the family, and you are liable to hear a version which has been changed, a version which makes your family sound disreputable—something that will taint the honor of the family. But if you have already heard the story, you know your family's version of what *really* happened that night, so when somebody else is mentioning it, you will have a version of the story to counterbalance it. Even when there is no way around it—old Uncle Pete did a terrible thing—by knowing the stories that come out of other families, by keeping very close watch, listening constantly to learn the stories about other families, one is in a sense able to deal with terrible sorts of things that might happen within one's own family. When a member of one's own family does something that cannot be excused, one always knows stories about similar things which happened in other families. And it is not done maliciously. I think it is very important to realize this. Keeping track of all the stories within the community gives a certain distance, a useful perspective which brings incidents down to a level we can deal with. If others have done it before, it cannot be so terrible. If others have endured, so can we.

The stories are always bringing us together, keeping this whole together, keeping this family together, keeping this clan together. "Don't go away, don't isolate yourself, but come here, because we have all had these kinds of experiences"—this is what the people are saying to you when they tell you these other stories. And so there is this constant pulling together to resist what seems to me to be a basic part of human nature: When some violent emotional experience takes place, people get the urge to run off and hide or separate themselves from others. And of course, if we do that, we are not only talking about endangering the group, we are also talking about the individual or the individual family never being able to recover or to survive. Inherent in this belief is the feeling that one does not recover or get well by one's self, but it is together that we look after each other and take care of each other.

In the storytelling, then, we see this process of bringing people together, and it works not only on the family level, but also on the level of the individual. Of course, the whole Pueblo concept of the individual is a little bit different from the usual Western concept of the individual. But one of the beauties of the storytelling is that when something happens to an individual, many people will come to you and take you aside, or maybe a couple of people will come and talk to you. These are occasions of storytelling. These occasions of storytelling are continuous; they are a way of life.

Storytelling lies at the heart of the Pueblo people, and so when someone comes in and says, "When did they tell the stories, or what time of day does the storytelling take place?" that is a ridiculous question. The storytelling goes on constantly—as some old grandmother puts on the shoes of a little child and tells the child the story of a little girl who didn't wear her shoes. At the same time somebody comes into the house for coffee to talk with an adolescent boy who has just been into a lot of trouble, to reassure him that *he* got into that kind of trouble, or somebody else's son got into that kind of trouble too. You have this constant ongoing process, working on many different levels.

One of the stories I like to bring up about helping the individual in crisis is a recent story, and I want to remind you that we make no distinctions between the stories—whether they are history, whether they are fact, whether they are gossip—these distinctions are not useful when we are talking about this particular experience with language. Anyway, there was a young man who, when he came back from the war in Vietnam, had saved up his Army pay and bought a beautiful red Volkswagen Beetle. He was very proud of it, and one night drove up to a place right across the reservation line. It is a very notorious place for many reasons, but one of the more notorious things about the place is a deep arroyo behind the place. This is the King's Bar. So he ran in to pick up a cold six-pack to take home, but he didn't put on his emergency brake. And his little red Volkswagen rolled back into the arroyo and was all smashed up. He felt very bad about it, but within a few days everybody had come to him and told him stories about other people who had lost cars to that arroyo. And probably the story that made him feel the best was about the time that George Day's station wagon, with his mother-in-law and kids in the back, rolled into that arroyo. So everybody was saying, "Well, at least your mother-in-law and kids weren't in the car when it rolled in," and you can't argue with that kind of story. He felt better then because he wasn't alone anymore. He and his smashed-up Volkswagen were now joined with all the other stories of cars that fell into that arroyo.

There are a great many parallels between Pueblo experiences and the remarks that have been made about South Africa and the Caribbean countries—similarities in experiences so far as language is concerned. More specifically, with the experience of English being imposed upon the people. The Pueblo people, of course, have seen intruders come and intruders go. The first they watched come were the Spaniards; while the Spaniards were there, things had to be conducted in Spanish. But as the old stories say, if you wait long enough, they'll go. And sure enough, they went. Then another bunch came in. And old stories say, well, if you wait around long enough, not so much that they'll go, but at least their ways will go. One wonders now, when you see what's happening to technocratic-industrial culture, now that we've used up most of the sources of energy, you think perhaps the old people are right.

But anyhow, our experience with English has been different because the Bureau of Indian Affairs schools were so terrible that we never heard of Shake-

15

speare. There was Dick and Jane, and I can remember reading that the robins were heading south for winter, but I knew that all winter the robins were around Laguna. It took me a long time to figure out what was going on. I worried for quite a while about the robins because they didn't leave in the winter, not realizing that the textbooks were written in Boston. The big textbook companies are up here in Boston and *their* robins do go south in the winter. But this freed us and encouraged us to stay with our narratives. Whatever literature we received at school (which was damn little), at home the storytelling, the special regard for telling and bringing together through the telling, was going on constantly. It has continued, and so we have a great body of classical oral literature, both in the narratives and in the chants and songs.

As the old people say, "If you can remember the stories, you will be all right. Just remember the stories." And, of course, usually when they say that to you, when you are young, you wonder what in the world they mean. But when I returned—I had been away from Laguna Pueblo for a couple of years, well more than a couple of years after college and so forth—I returned to Laguna and I went to Laguna-Acoma high school to visit an English class, and I was wondering how the telling was continuing, because Laguna Pueblo, as the anthropologists have said, is one of the more acculturated pueblos. So I walked into this high school English class and there they were sitting, these very beautiful Laguna and Acoma kids. But I knew that out in their lockers they had cassette tape recorders, and I knew that at home they had stereos, and they were listening to Kiss and Led Zeppelin and all those other things. I was almost afraid, but I had to ask—I had with me a book of short fiction (it's called *The Man to Send Rain Clouds* [New York: Viking Press, 1974]), and among the stories of other Native American writers, it has stories that I have written and Simon Ortiz has written. And there is one particular story in the book about the killing of a state policeman in New Mexico by three Acoma Pueblo men. It was an act that was committed in the early fifties. I was afraid to ask, but I had to. I looked at the class and I said, "How many of you heard this story before you read it in the book?" And I was prepared to hear this crushing truth that indeed the anthropologists were right about the old traditions dying out. But it was amazing, you know, almost all but one or two students raised their hands. They had heard that story, just as Simon and I had heard it, when we were young. That was my first indication that storytelling continues on. About half of them had heard it in English, about half of them had heard it in Laguna. I think again, getting back to one of the original statements, that if you begin to look at the core of the importance of the language and how it fits in with the culture, it is the *story* and the feeling of the story which matters more than what language it's told in. ◪

Reflections and Inquiries

1. Silko compares the structure of Pueblo discourse to a spider web. Does the comparison work, in your opinion? Explain how it does or does not.

2. Storytelling, according to Silko, lies at the root of Pueblo expression. Why is storytelling so important?

3. In Pueblo culture, what is the relationship of the speaker to the story being told? What is significant, in terms of communication goals, about this relationship?

4. How, according to Pueblo belief, can the story "be inside the listener"? What are the implications of such an assertion?

Reading to Write

Write an essay in which you speculate on ways the Pueblo and Anglo approaches to language might work together to help underprepared students.

Speaking a Public Language | Richard Rodriguez

The son of Mexican immigrant workers, Richard Rodriguez in 1981 published his autobiography, *Hunger of Memory,* which has stirred considerable controversy for its antibilingual education stance. In his book, Rodriguez describes his move from a socially disadvantaged and alienated Spanish-speaking child thrust into English-only classrooms in Sacramento to a professor of English literature and writer twenty years later. In the following excerpt from the book, Rodriguez presents his reasons for upholding English-only instruction in American schools.

Supporters of bilingual education today imply that students like me miss a great deal by not being taught in their family's language. What they seem not to recognize is that, as a socially disadvantaged child, I considered Spanish to be a private language. What I needed to learn in school was that I had the right—and the obligation—to speak the public language of *los gringos.* The odd truth is that my first-grade classmates could have become bilingual, in the conventional sense of that word, more easily than I. Had they been taught (as upper-middle-class children are often taught early) a second language like Spanish or French, they could have regarded it simply as that: another public language. In my case such bilingualism could not have been so quickly achieved. What I did not believe was that I could speak a single public language.

Without question, it would have pleased me to hear my teachers address me in Spanish when I entered the classroom. I would have felt much less afraid. I would have trusted them and responded with ease. But I would have

---

delayed—for how long postponed?—having to learn the language of public society. I would have evaded—and for how long could I have afforded to delay?—learning the great lesson of school, that I had a public identity.

Fortunately, my teachers were unsentimental about their responsibility. What they understood was that I needed to speak a public language. So their voices would search me out, asking me questions. Each time I'd hear them, I'd look up in surprise to see a nun's face frowning at me. I'd mumble, not really meaning to answer. The nun would persist, 'Richard, stand up. Don't look at the floor. Speak up. Speak to the entire class, not just to me!' But I couldn't believe that the English language was mine to use. (In part, I did not want to believe it.) I continued to mumble. I resisted the teacher's demands. (Did I somehow suspect that once I learned public language my pleasing family life would be changed?) Silent, waiting for the bell to sound, I remained dazed, diffident, afraid.

Because I wrongly imagined that English was intrinsically a public language and Spanish an intrinsically private one, I easily noted the difference between classroom language and the language of home. At school, words were directed to a general audience of listeners. ('Boys and girls.') Words were meaningfully ordered. And the point was not self-expression alone but to make oneself understood by many others. The teacher quizzed: 'Boys and girls, why do we use that word in this sentence? Could we think of a better word to use there? Would the sentence change its meaning if the words were differently arranged? And wasn't there a better way of saying much the same thing?' (I couldn't say. I wouldn't try to say.)

Three months. Five. Half a year passed. Unsmiling, ever watchful, my teachers noted my silence. They began to connect my behavior with the difficult progress my older sister and brother were making. Until one Saturday morning three nuns arrived at the house to talk to our parents. Stiffly, they sat on the blue living room sofa. From the doorway of another room, spying the visitors, I noted the incongruity—the clash of two worlds, the faces and voices of school intruding upon the familiar setting of home. I overheard one voice gently wondering, 'Do your children speak only Spanish at home, Mrs. Rodriguez?' While another voice added, 'That Richard especially seems so timid and shy.'

That Rich-heard!

With great tact the visitors continued, 'Is it possible for you and your husband to encourage your children to practice their English when they are home?' Of course, my parents complied. What would they not do for their children's well-being? And how could they have questioned the Church's authority which those women represented? In an instant, they agreed to give up the language (the sounds) that had revealed and accentuated our family's closeness. The moment after the visitors left, the change was observed. '*Ahora*, speak to us *en inglés*,' my father and mother united to tell us.

At first, it seemed a kind of game. After dinner each night, the family gathered to practice 'our' English. (It was still then *inglés*, a language foreign

5

to us, so we felt drawn as strangers to it.) Laughing, we would try to define words we could not pronounce. We played with strange English sounds, often overanglicizing our pronunciations. And we filled the smiling gaps of our sentences with familiar Spanish sounds. But that was cheating, somebody shouted. Everyone laughed. In school, meanwhile, like my brother and sister, I was required to attend a daily tutoring session. I needed a full year of special attention. I also needed my teachers to keep my attention from straying in class by calling out, *Rich-heard*—their English voices slowly prying loose my ties to my other name, its three notes, *Ri-car-do*. Most of all I needed to hear my mother and father speak to me in a moment of seriousness in broken—suddenly heartbreaking—English. The scene was inevitable: One Saturday morning I entered the kitchen where my parents were talking in Spanish. I did not realize that they were talking in Spanish however until, at the moment they saw me, I heard their voices change to speak English. Those *gringo* sounds they uttered startled me. Pushed me away. In that moment of trivial misunderstanding and profound insight, I felt my throat twisted by unsounded grief. I turned quickly and left the room. But I had no place to escape to with Spanish. (The spell was broken.) My brother and sisters were speaking English in another part of the house.

Again and again in the days following, increasingly angry, I was obliged to hear my mother and father: 'Speak to us *en inglés*.' (*Speak.*) Only then did I determine to learn classroom English. Weeks after, it happened: One day in school I raised my hand to volunteer an answer. I spoke out in a loud voice. And I did not think it remarkable when the entire class understood. That day, I moved very far from the disadvantaged child I had been only days earlier. The belief, the calming assurance that I belonged in public, had at last taken hold.

Shortly after, I stopped hearing the high and loud sounds of *los gringos*. A more and more confident speaker of English, I didn't trouble to listen to *how* strangers sounded, speaking to me. And there simply were too many English-speaking people in my day for me to hear American accents anymore. Conversations quickened. Listening to persons who sounded eccentrically pitched voices, I usually noted their sounds for an initial few seconds before I concentrated on *what* they were saying. Conversations became content-full. Transparent. Hearing someone's *tone* of voice—angry or questioning or sarcastic or happy or sad—I didn't distinguish it from the words it expressed. Sound and word were thus tightly wedded. At the end of a day, I was often bemused, always relieved, to realize how 'silent,' though crowded with words, my day in public had been. (This public silence measured and quickened the change in my life.)

At last, seven years old, I came to believe what had been technically true   10 since my birth: I was an American citizen.

But the special feeling of closeness at home was diminished by then. Gone was the desperate, urgent, intense feeling of being at home; rare was the experience of feeling myself individualized by family intimates. We remained a loving family, but one greatly changed. No longer so close; no longer bound tight by the pleasing and troubling knowledge of our public separateness. Neither my older brother nor sister rushed home after school anymore. Nor did I. When I arrived home there would often be neighborhood kids in the house. Or the house would be empty of sounds.

Following the dramatic Americanization of their children, even my parents grew more publicly confident. Especially my mother. She learned the names of all the people on our block. And she decided we needed to have a telephone installed in the house. My father continued to use the word *gringo.* But it was no longer charged with the old bitterness or distrust. (Stripped of any emotional content, the word simply became a name for those Americans not of Hispanic descent.) Hearing him, sometimes, I wasn't sure if he was pronouncing the Spanish word *gringo* or saying gringo in English.

Matching the silence I started hearing in public was a new quiet at home. The family's quiet was partly due to the fact that, as we children learned more and more English, we shared fewer and fewer words with our parents. Sentences needed to be spoken slowly when a child addressed his mother or father. (Often the parent wouldn't understand.) The child would need to repeat himself. (Still the parent misunderstood.) The young voice, frustrated, would end up saying, 'Never mind'—the subject was closed. Dinners would be noisy with the clinking of knives and forks against dishes. My mother would smile softly between her remarks; my father at the other end of the table would chew and chew at his food, while he stared over the heads of his children.

My *mother!* My *father!* After English became my primary language, I no longer knew what words to use in addressing my parents. The old Spanish words (those tender accents of sound) I had used earlier—*mamá* and *papá*—I couldn't use anymore. They would have been too painful reminders of how much had changed in my life. On the other hand, the words I heard neighborhood kids call *their* parents seemed equally unsatisfactory. *Mother* and *Father; Ma, Papa, Pa, Dad, Pop* (how I hated the all-American sound of that last word especially)—all these terms I felt were unsuitable, not really terms of address for *my* parents. As a result, I never used them at home. Whenever I'd speak to my parents, I would try to get their attention with eye contact alone. In public conversations, I'd refer to 'my parents' or 'my mother and father.'

My mother and father, for their part, responded differently, as their children spoke to them less. She grew restless, seemed troubled and anxious at the scarcity of words exchanged in the house. It was she who would question me about my day when I came home from school. She smiled at small talk. She pried at the edges of my sentences to get me to say something more. (What?) She'd join conversations she overheard, but her intrusions often stopped her children's talking. By contrast, my father seemed reconciled to the new quiet. Though his English improved somewhat, he retired into silence. At dinner he spoke very little. One night his children and even his wife helplessly giggled at his garbled English pronunciation of the Catholic Grace before Meals.

15

Thereafter he made his wife recite the prayer at the start of each meal, even on formal occasions, when there were guests in the house. Hers became the public voice of the family. On official business, it was she, not my father, one would usually hear on the phone or in stores, talking to strangers. His children grew so accustomed to his silence that, years later, they would speak routinely of his shyness. (My mother would often try to explain: Both his parents died when he was eight. He was raised by an uncle who treated him like little more than a menial servant. He was never encouraged to speak. He grew up alone. A man of few words.) But my father was not shy, I realized, when I'd watch him speaking Spanish with relatives. Using Spanish, he was quickly effusive. Especially when talking with other men, his voice would spark, flicker, alive with sounds. In Spanish, he expressed ideas and feelings he rarely revealed in English. With firm Spanish sounds, he conveyed confidence and authority English would never allow him.

The silence at home, however, was finally more than a literal silence. Fewer words passed between parent and child, but more profound was the silence that resulted from my inattention to sounds. At about the time I no longer bothered to listen with care to the sounds of English in public, I grew careless about listening to the sounds family members made when they spoke. Most of the time I heard someone speaking at home and didn't distinguish his sounds from the words people uttered in public. I didn't even pay much attention to my parents' accented and ungrammatical speech. At least not at home. Only when I was with them in public would I grow alert to their accents. Though, even then, their sounds caused me less and less concern. For I was increasingly confident of my own public identity.

I would have been happier about my public success had I not sometimes recalled what it had been like earlier, when my family had conveyed its intimacy through a set of conveniently private sounds. Sometimes in public, hearing a stranger, I'd hark back to my past. A Mexican farmworker approached me downtown to ask directions to somewhere. '¿Hijito . . . ?' he said. And his voice summoned deep longing. Another time, standing beside my mother in the visiting room of a Carmelite convent, before the dense screen which rendered the nuns shadowy figures, I heard several Spanish-speaking nuns—their busy, singsong overlapping voices—assure us that yes, yes, we were remembered, all our family was remembered in their prayers. (Their voices echoed faraway family sounds.) Another day, a dark-faced old woman—her hand light on my shoulder—steadied herself against me as she boarded a bus. She murmured something I couldn't quite comprehend. Her Spanish voice came near, like the face of a never-before-seen relative in the instant before I was kissed. Her voice, like so many of the Spanish voices I'd hear in public, recalled the golden age of my youth. Hearing Spanish then, I continued to be a careful, if sad, listener to sounds. Hearing a Spanish-speaking family walking behind me, I turned to look. I smiled for an instant, before my glance found the Hispanic-looking faces of strangers in the crowd going by.

Today I hear bilingual educators say that children lose a degree of 'individuality' by becoming assimilated into public society. (Bilingual schooling was popularized in the seventies, that decade when middle-class ethnics began to resist the process of assimilation—the American melting pot.) But the bilingualists simplistically scorn the value and necessity of assimilation. They do not seem to realize that there are *two* ways a person is individualized. So they do not realize that while one suffers a diminished sense of *private* individuality by becoming assimilated into public society, such assimilation makes possible the achievement of *public* individuality.

The bilingualists insist that a student should be reminded of his difference from others in mass society, his heritage. But they equate mere separateness with individuality. The fact is that only in private—with intimates—is separateness from the crowd a prerequisite for individuality. (An intimate draws me apart, tells me that I am unique, unlike all others.) In public, by contrast, full individuality is achieved, paradoxically, by those who are able to consider themselves members of the crowd. Thus it happened for me: Only when I was able to think of myself as an American, no longer an alien in *gringo* society, could I seek the rights and opportunities necessary for full public individuality. The social and political advantages I enjoy as a man result from the day that I came to believe that my name, indeed, is *Rich-heard Road-ree-guess.* It is true that my public society today is often impersonal. (My public society is usually mass society.) Yet despite the anonymity of the crowd and despite the fact that the individuality I achieve in public is often tenuous—because it depends on my being one in a crowd—I celebrate the day I acquired my new name. Those middle-class ethnics who scorn assimilation seem to me filled with decadent self-pity, obsessed by the burden of public life. Dangerously, they romanticize public separateness and they trivialize the dilemma of the socially disadvantaged.

My awkward childhood does not prove the necessity of bilingual education. My story discloses instead an essential myth of childhood—inevitable pain. If I rehearse here the changes in my private life after my Americanization, it is finally to emphasize the public gain. The loss implies the gain: The house I returned to each afternoon was quiet. Intimate sounds no longer rushed to the door to greet me. There were other noises inside. The telephone rang. Neighborhood kids ran past the door of the bedroom where I was reading my schoolbooks—covered with shopping-bag paper. Once I learned public language, it would never again be easy for me to hear intimate family voices. More and more of my day was spent hearing words. But that may only be a way of saying that the day I raised my hand in class and spoke loudly to an entire roomful of faces, my childhood started to end.

20

Reflections and Inquiries

1. How does Rodriguez distinguish between "public" and "private" language? Do you agree with this distinction? Why or why not?

2. Describe Rodriguez's reaction to his parents' decision to stop speaking Spanish. Is it consistent or inconsistent with his views about bilingual education? Explain.

3. What exactly is Rodriguez referring to when he mentions "the new quiet" he experienced from his family following the nuns' visit?

4. What had to happen before Rodriguez could experience "full public individuality"? Are any factors besides language-based ones relevant to this change, in your opinion?

Reading to Write

Are the losses Rodriguez describes worth the gains? In a short essay, defend or argue against this manner of language acquisition. How might Rodriguez's experience have been different and less distressing?

The Politics of Remediation | Mike Rose

The teaching of writing and reading has been a major problem in American schools. Students who come from underprivileged backgrounds or for whom English is their second language have often been held back or, worse, considered "backward" for their inability to keep up with privileged or native speakers. Mike Rose, who directs the Writing Center at the University of California, Los Angeles, has worked intensively with such students, discovering that many are bright and possess great potential to succeed in school if teachers take the time to understand their needs. In the following selection, Rose describes his experience working with students in ways that pay more attention to them as individuals from different (often disadvantaged) backgrounds rather than in ways directed toward inadequacies in their verbal skills.

... My students knew they were considered poor readers. We were approaching the last session I would have with them, and I wanted to leave them with something snappy that would allow them, if just for an hour, to gain entry to the sophisticated vocabulary that would probably serve to intimidate them for some time to come. Here's the lesson I came up with, pretty con-

---

Source: From Rose, Mike. "Literate Stirrings." *Lives on the Boundary.* New York: Free, 1989. 105–11. Reprinted with the permission of The Free Press, a Division of Simon & Schuster, Inc. Copyright © 1989 by Mike Rose.

trived, I admit, but it was fun to play out. I printed on strips of art paper words that had unusual spellings or that would sound funny if exaggerated slightly:

Macabre

Eulogy

Misanthrope

Lampoon

Paranoid

And so on. I also clipped out pictures that could accompany each word: For example, for *eulogy* I used a picture of a priest reading from a Bible at a funeral. I spread out the words on the table—saving the pictures for later—and told the children these were big, important, snazzy words, and they were to pick one that looked weird or was spelled funny or that hit them in any way. They then had to explain why they chose their words. Finally, I gave the meanings of the words and spread out the pictures before them, asking them to find a picture they thought went with their words. After all this rigmarole, they were to write a story to fit the words and pictures they had chosen.

Rodrigo picked out a picture of a man, eyes wide, with his hand over his mouth. Rodrigo's word was *macabre:*

> This man used to like girls very much. One night he was driving a truck when he saw a girl and stopped. He went over to see the girl. When he saw her face, it looked like a horse! He ran as fast as he could! He jumped into the truck really scared, and he never liked girls again.

We labeled this "Rodrigo's Macabre Story," and it, like all the essays before, went up on the cafeteria wall. Danny wrote the word *misanthrope* over the two pictures he chose: one of a boxer posed for a punch and another of a TV private eye elbowing a man across the face.

> These dudes think that they are smart, but they aren't. These dudes hate everybody! They look mean. They kill. And most of all, they are dumb.

And Delores chose *lampoon.* Delores was tall and overweight and wore glasses that were a little too large for her face. In a moment of sweet revenge, she turned her own catalog of insult toward the boy who sat next to her in her regular class, displaying one of the motives that has perennially impelled writers to write:

> Hi everybody. Guess what I am writing about? I am writing a lampoon of Tommy! He looks so funny. Let me tell you how he looks, O.K.? He has four eyes, and long hair, and is so fat that he has to wear a size 60! In town he can't even fit through the door. They have to push him out! And you should see his hands. They are so big that they could cover your

face. And he is only nine years old! And boy, I tell you, he is so big that we hate him. You know what we call him? Fat-head Fatty!

That afternoon Casey came running up to me in the schoolyard: "Hey, I wrote something for you all on my own!" and held out a piece of paper, folded in four. Casey was one of my favorites. He was an affable boy with sandy hair, a perennially scraped elbow, and an awful home. His father was long gone, and his mother cocktailed and sometimes didn't come home for two- and three-day stretches. Casey was rambunctious and was always getting in trouble—not serious, nasty trouble, but fooling around, talking-in-class trouble, little bruises on the shins of Conduct. I would look at him during our class and think of Dave Snyder, the guy I tip-tapped through biology at Mercy High. I listened to the defensive wit he had developed about his mother and simultaneously wanted to laugh with him and hold him close to me: "Last year, my mother gave us turkey dinners," he told Ben and me just before Thanksgiving holiday. "*TV* turkey dinners! But she gave us two apiece." Here he paused for a beat, "After all, it *was* Thanksgiving."

So here was Casey with a story for his teacher. "I'll be damned," I thought, "I've flicked the switch." I unfolded the note as Casey looked on:

> Mike
> How are you. Do you want to tripout today. I have a lid of wead. I will meet you in the park. You are a kool guy. I am going to take a crap.
>
> > so long
> > your buddy
> > Casey

Jesus! What in the hell—what am I gonna say? Was he really carrying marijuana? Worry flipped quickly to anger. Casey was pushing—pushing. . . . And as I stood there, I saw . . . as though rising out of confusion, I saw that Casey was doing what so many of my high school friends loved to do: freak the teacher. And he'd succeeded. I pretended to read the note a moment longer, giving myself a chance to come up with something. I pointed to the end of the last sentence and looked solemnly down at him: "You know, Casey, you spelled 'crap' perfectly. Congratulations." "Awwww," he said, "you're no fun," and started laughing. I tapped my fingers on his head and grunted, and then he and I walked out onto the wide, grassy field to talk, man to man, about the risky methods people devise to show their need and their affection.

☑   ☑   ☑

I used versions of this curriculum again with other groups of students, tinkering with it, being more cautious with the "Everyday People" slide show, streamlining the exercise with the big words. Still, whatever adjustments I made, there were lots of ways, I can see now, that the curriculum fell short, even considering the general limitations of time. While there was some continuity between the exercises, each didn't build carefully on the ones preceding

5

it, didn't take full advantage of what was developing in prior lessons. The "Rocky Raccoon" exercise, for example, tapped knowledge of plot line and story structure, and there were some students who should have had a further chance to use what they knew.

Another problem was that the curriculum was somewhat self-enclosed. While it did not prohibit children from drawing on their interests and the events in their own lives, it failed to elicit creatively the tales and folklore and genres that were part of their various families and cultures. Finally, I could have done much more than I did to get the children to reflect on this mutual venture into literacy. How would they explain the work they were now doing? What did it mean to create stories? Were they noticing any changes in the way they wrote? Could I get them to reconsider the attitudes they must have developed about themselves as readers and writers?

But for all the limitations of my fledgling curriculum—its short-sightedness, its fragmentation—something unusual was going on. The essays many of the children were producing, flawed as they were, were not jibing with the various assessments of their ability that I had heard and read. A series of achievement tests and the grades and comments of assorted teachers had designated these students as having significant problems with written language. By the fourth or fifth grade, they had been pretty thoroughly defined as limited. The question, then, was what was the nature of the curriculum and the assessments that provided the base for this definition?

The English curricula that I saw, and the English textbooks particularly, were almost entirely oriented toward grammatical analysis. Subskills. Every year the children faced about two hundred pages that required them to circle or underline subjects or verbs or pronouns; that directed them to fill in the correct noun or pronoun or verb form; that asked them to read lists of sentences and indicate if they were simple or compound or if their purpose was to tell, raise a question, or exclaim; that told them to indicate whether a noun was singular or plural, simple or compound, common or proper; that told them to indicate the tense of verbs, to label action verbs and linking verbs, and to decline irregular verbs. And the tests they took measured how well they had learned to do these tasks.

There ended up being little room in such a curriculum—unless the inventive teacher created it—to explore the real stuff of literacy: conveying something meaningful, communicating information, creating narratives, shaping what we see and feel and believe into written language, listening to and reading stories, playing with the sounds of words. Writing and reading are such private acts that we forget how fundamentally social they are: We hear stories read by others and we like to tell others about the stories we read; we learn to write from others and we write for others to read us. The curriculum I saw drained the life out of all this, reduced literacy to the dry dismembering of language—not alive, not communicative at all. The children's textbooks were colorful, and little boys and girls and dogs and cats cavorted around the exercises, but the exercises themselves were not all that distant from the ancient descriptive grammar books I had learned about in graduate school—grammars that analyzed language down to its smallest parts and invented a meticulous, even finicky, classification system to contain them. This was a science of language that was "not . . . intended to help with teaching," as the historian H. I. Marrou once observed. It was an exercise that was "all analysis and no synthesis," pursued for its own pedantic ends.

It seemed to me that such a curriculum was especially troublesome for children like the ones in my class: children who had not been prepped in their homes to look at language in this dissected, unnatural way; children for whom English was a foreign language; children of particularly mobile families who fell out of the curricular lockstep demanded by this approach to language; children who might have some problems with their vision or with the way they process written language; children who, like me long ago, just didn't see the sense in such analysis, and, before long, were missing it, not getting it and falling behind. And so these children would fail at the kind of literacy activities the school system had woven throughout its curriculum and turn off to writing and reading in general. But that did not mean that they were illiterate.   10

Given that cognitive growth does not proceed in miraculous leaps, my curriculum was clearly not kicking these children's development into fast-forward. It had to be eliciting and shaping something that was already there. Hank could write his sequel to "Rocky Raccoon" because he knew something about Westerns. Mark deployed his vivid imagination in a wild-child narrative to create a boy who hunts deer, bears, and birds. Danny relied on a dopey and familiar joke to produce a comic dialogue about deflating muscles. And Delores—Delores rambled, but she wrote the most elaborate essay her teacher had yet seen her produce. She appropriated slapstick and hyperbole to the delicious purpose of lampooning the fathead who made her life miserable. There were times, then, when emotions and desires and all sorts of child knowledge about movies and sitcoms and slapstick and family stories blended in complex ways to yield a piece of writing that belied the schools' assessments of these students' literacy. ▨

Reflections and Inquiries

1. What do you think was Rose's purpose for assigning his "fancy words" lesson to his students?

2. Much of Rose's teaching seems to extend beyond the classroom. Give an example of this and evaluate its usefulness.

3. What does Rose identify as a major problem with English textbooks? Why is it a problem for him? Do you agree or disagree with his position?

4. Identify and discuss what Rose refers to as "the real stuff" of literacy.

5. How does Rose capitalize on his students' own experiences as a way of improving their literacy skills? How effective a teaching technique is this, in your opinion?

Reading to Write

Write an analysis of Rose's teaching methods. What specifically does Rose do or say that helps marginalized or underprepared learners improve their writing? You will want to read other sections of *Lives on the Boundary* to gain a comprehensive view of Rose's insights and classroom or tutorial strategies.

Equality and the Classics | Dinesh D'Souza

In the following excerpt from his controversial critique of multicultural educational practices in U.S. universities, Dinesh D'Souza argues against the displacement of Western classics by non-Western ones. This premise feeds into his larger view, developed in his book *Illiberal Education,* that multiculturalism is merely a façade for a new kind of racist policy in academe—racist in that it mandates multicultural study and manipulates admissions policies based on race, ethnicity, and gender. D'Souza, a native of India, studied at Dartmouth and Princeton Universities, where he edited conservative newspapers. He was a domestic policy analyst under President Reagan and a research fellow at the American Enterprise Institute.

. . . Universities can address their curricular problems by devising a required course or sequence for entering freshmen which exposes them to the basic issues of equality and human difference, through a carefully chosen set of classic texts that deal powerfully with those issues. Needless to say, non-Western classics belong in this list when they address questions relevant to the subject matter. Such a solution would retain what Matthew Arnold termed "the best that has been thought and said," but at the same time engage the contemporary questions of ethnocentrism and prejudice in bold and provocative fashion.

It seems that currently both the teaching of Western classics as well as the desire to study other cultures have encountered serious difficulties in the curriculum. As the case of Stanford illustrates, an uncritical examination of non-Western cultures, in order to favorably contrast them with the West, ends up as a new form of cultural imperialism, in which Western intellectuals project their own domestic prejudices into faraway countries, distorting them beyond

---

Source: From D'Souza, Dinesh. "Equality and the Classics." *Illiberal Education: The Politics of Race and Sex on Campus.* New York: Free, 1991. 254–57. Reprinted with permission of The Free Press, a Division of Simon & Schuster, Inc. Copyright © 1991 by Dinesh D'Souza.

recognition to serve political ends. Even where universities make a serious effort to avoid this trap, it remains questionable whether they have the academic expertise in the general undergraduate program to teach students about the history, religion, and literature of Asia, Africa, and the Arab world.

The study of other cultures can never compensate for a lack of thorough familiarity with the founding principles of one's own culture. Just as it would be embarrassing to encounter an educated Chinese who had never heard of Confucius, however well versed he may be in Jefferson, so also it would be a failure of liberal education to teach Americans about the Far East without immersing them in their own philosophical and literary tradition "from Homer to the present." Universal in scope, these works prepare Westerners to experience both their own, as well as other, ideas and civilizations.

The problem is that many of the younger generation of faculty in the universities express lack of interest, if not contempt, for the Western classics. Either they regard the books as flawed for their failure to endorse the full emancipation of approved minorities, or they reject their metaphysical questions as outdated and irrelevant. Naturally, young people will not investigate these texts, which are often complex and sometimes written in archaic language, if they do not believe their efforts will be repaid. Unfortunately, many undergraduates today seem disinclined to read the classics, but not because they oppose or detest them. Their alienation is more radical: they are indifferent to them. For them the classics have retreated into what Lovejoy called "the pathos of time."

Yet a survey of these books immediately suggests that many of them are fully aware of, and treat with great subtlety, the problems of prejudice, ethnocentrism, and human difference. Long before Willie Horton raised, in American minds, the specter of a dark-skinned man sexually assaulting a white woman, Iago raised this possibility with Brabantio. Will he allow his "fair daughter" to fall into "the gross clasps of a lascivious Moor"? If he does not intervene, Iago warned, "You'll have your daughter covered with a Barbary horse." *Othello* and the *Merchant of Venice,* Shakespeare's Venetian plays, are both subtle examinations of nativism and ethnocentrism. Both engage issues of ethnic and sexual difference. They reflect a cosmopolitan society's struggle to accommodate the alien, while maintaining its cultural identity. Othello is the tragedy of a foreign warrior who depended on Desdemona's love to legitimate his full citizenship in his new country—when Iago casts that love into doubt, not just his marriage but his identity was fundamentally threatened. By contrast with Othello, Shylock is the outsider who refused to integrate, and pressed his principles into uncompromising conflict with those of Christian civilization. These timeless examples of the tension between community and difference are precisely what young people today should confront, and respond to in terms of their own experience.

The relevance of the classical tradition to questions of beauty and equality and freedom has not gone unrecognized by perceptive black thinkers and writers. Traveling in Vienna, W. E. B. Du Bois wrote, "Here Marcus Aurelius,

5

the Roman Caesar died; here Charlemagne placed the bounds of his empire that ruled the world five centuries. . . . Around Vienna the intrigues and victories of Napoleon centered. . . . And here, after the downfall of the great Tyrant, sat the famous congress which parcelled out the world and declared the African slave a stench in the nostrils of humanity." Du Bois saw the grandeur and degradation in a single unifying thought—slavery was the West's tragic flaw; yet it was tragic precisely because of the greatness of the civilization that encompassed it.

Paul Robeson recalled that his father took him "page by page through Virgil and Homer and other classics." As a result, Robeson says, "a love of learning, a ceaseless quest for truth in all its fulness—this my father taught." Robeson believed that the Latin and Greek classics were just as much the treasure of the American black as of the American white. When Robeson played Othello on Broadway, he created a national sensation. Audiences found *Othello*, in Robeson's words, "painfully immediate in its unfolding of evil, innocence, passion, dignity and nobility, and contemporary in its overtones of a clash of cultures, and of the partial acceptance and consequent effect upon one of a minority group." Othello's jealousy thus "becomes more credible, the blow to his pride more understandable, the final collapse of his individual world more inevitable." In 1943–44 Robeson's *Othello* set a record for a Shakespearean play on Broadway, running for almost three hundred consecutive performances.

◪   ◪   ◪

For a variety of reasons, university presidents and deans will not implement even the most obvious and sensible reform proposals. First, being for the most part bureaucrats rather than intellectual leaders, they lack the vision and imagination to devise new and innovative policies, preferring to continue familiar programs and echo their accompanying bromides. Second, university officials feel physically and morally intimidated by minority activists; as a result, the activists set the agenda and timorous administrators usually go along. Third, and perhaps most serious, many no longer believe in the emancipation brought about by liberal education, and are quite willing to sacrifice liberal principles to achieve expedient ends.

The liberal university is a distinctive and fragile institution. It is not an all-purpose instrument for social change. Its function is indeed to serve the larger society which supports and sustains it, yet it does not best do this when it makes itself indistinguishable from the helter-skelter of pressure politics, what Professor Susan Shell of Boston College terms "the academic equivalent of Tammany Hall." Nothing in this book should be taken to deny the legitimate claim of minorities who have suffered unfairly, nor should reasonable aid and sympathy be withheld from them. But the current revolution of minority victims threatens to destroy the highest ideals of liberal education, and with them that enlightenment and understanding which hold out the only prospects for racial harmony, social justice, and minority advancement. . . . ◪

Reflections and Inquiries

1. Why does D'Souza think that Western intellectuals' efforts to include an examination of non-Western cultures in the curriculum constitutes "a new form of cultural imperialism"? Do you agree or disagree with this charge, and why?

2. According to D'Souza, young faculty members lack interest in, or even show contempt for, traditional Western classics. Why? Have you found this to be the case in your experience?

3. Compare D'Souza's use of evidence to support his views with Lawrence W. Levine's in the selection that follows. Which of the two authors provides the most convincing support for his thesis? What errors in reasoning, if any, do you detect in one or both of these authors?

4. D'Souza places much of the blame for curriculum design problems on university presidents and deans. Is this a valid charge? Bring up the matter with the dean or president at your school and weigh his or her responses against those of D'Souza's.

Reading to Write

What grounding in Western classics (for example, Homer's *Iliad* or *Odyssey*, Dante's *Divine Comedy*, any of Shakespeare's plays) have you had? Do you agree with D'Souza that they can offer as much insight into multicultural issues as non-Western classics? Write an essay agreeing or disagreeing with D'Souza's premise.

A Historian in Wonderland: Through the Looking Glass | Lawrence W. Levine

In diametric opposition to Dinesh D'Souza, who argues that the inclusion of non-Western works into the Western school curriculum is unnecessary because the Western classics are universal in theme and scope, Lawrence W. Levine argues that the shift to multicultural books and ideas reflects the changing values of U.S. culture. Once suspected as irrelevant, so-called non-Western works are much more reflective of contemporary U.S. society and hence just as essential as the traditional classics. Levine is the Margaret Byrne Professor of History, emeritus, at the University of California, Berkeley, a recipient of the MacArthur Prize Fellowship, and a member of the American Academy of Arts and Letters.

Source: From Levine, Lawrence W. "Through the Looking Glass." *The Opening American Mind: Canons, Culture, and History.* Boston: Beacon, 1996. 20–33. © 1996 by Lawrence W. Levine. Reprinted by permission of Beacon Press, Boston.

The "traditional" curriculum that prevailed so widely in the decades be-tween the World Wars, and whose decline is lamented with such fervor by the conservative critics, ignored most of the groups that compose the American population whether they were from Africa, Europe, Asia, Central and South America, or from indigenous North American peoples. The primary and often exclusive focus was upon a narrow stratum of those who came from a few Northern and Western European countries whose cultures and mores suppos-edly became the archetype for those of all Americans in spite of the fact that in reality American culture was forged out of a much larger and more diverse complex of peoples and societies. In addition, this curriculum did not merely teach Western ideas and culture, it taught the *superiority* of Western ideas and culture; it equated Western ways and thought with "Civilization" itself. This tendency is still being championed by contemporary critics of the university. "Is it Eurocentric to believe the life of liberty is superior to the life of the bee-hive?" Charles Krauthammer inquired in his justification of the European con-quest of the Americas. Without pretending to have studied the cultures of Asia or Africa in any depth, Secretary of Education William Bennett did not hesitate to inform the faculty and students of Stanford University that "the West is a source of *incomparable* intellectual complexity and diversity and depth."

To say that a curriculum that questions these parochial assumptions is somehow anti-Western or anti-intellectual is to misunderstand the aims of ed-ucation. If in fact the traditions of Western science and humanities mean what they say, modern universities are performing precisely the functions institu-tions of higher learning should perform: to stretch the boundaries of our un-derstanding; to teach the young to value our intellectual heritage not by rote but through comprehension and examination; to continually and perpetually subject the "wisdom" of our society to thorough and thoughtful scrutiny while making the "wisdom" of other societies and other cultures accessible and subject to comparable scrutiny; to refuse to simplify our culture beyond recognition by limiting our focus to only one segment of American society and instead to open up the *entire* society to thoughtful examination.

To require more careful study and more convincing documentation for the charges against the university is not to be pedantic or picayune; it is to hold the critics of the university to the same scholarly standards and the same hu-manistic values they claim the university itself has abandoned. The irony is that the critics of the contemporary university too often have become parodies of the very thing they're criticizing: ideologues whose research is shallow and whose findings are widely and deeply flawed by exaggerated claims, vituper-ative attacks, defective evidence, and inadequate knowledge of the history of the university in the United States and of the process by which canons and curricula have been formed and reformed since the beginning of American higher education.

While performing the high task of protecting knowledge and scholarly standards against "barbarians," it is obviously not always possible to observe the purest scholarly standards oneself. Dinesh D'Souza's "research" technique, for example, is summed up by the following incident. While visiting the Berkeley campus of the University of California, he wanted to speak with "Asian American students" as part of his investigation. Students of Asian ancestry then constituted roughly one-third of the undergraduates at Berkeley, but D'Souza had trouble locating interviewees: "It is not easy to find an Asian student willing to talk at Berkeley. I passed up two or three who would talk only on condition of anonymity. I approached one student waiting for the library to open, but he was too eager not to miss a minute of reading time. Eventually I found Thuy Nguyen, a cheerful woman who turned out to be a student at UC-Davis. She knew all about Berkeley, though; she was visiting her friend Cynthia Dong, an undergraduate there." Thus his *entire* direct testimony from "Berkeley" students of Asian descent—a designation covering a wide variety of peoples and cultures—comes from a student enrolled not at Berkeley but at the University of California at Davis, a campus sixty miles away. Ironically, D'Souza's approach is all too typical of those whose concern about the declining standards and ideals of the academic world has led them to level blistering attacks against it.

After a tour of universities Charles Sykes reported back that "tens of thousands of books and hundreds of thousands of journal articles . . . bloat libraries with masses of unread, unreadable, and worthless pablum." Alas, we never learn whether Mr. Sykes knows this because he himself has performed the heroic task of carefully examining the tens of thousands of books and hundreds of thousands of articles, or if he is synthesizing the Herculean labors of other investigators who remain anonymous, or if he is merely *assuming* that so many books and articles that sit so inertly on library shelves simply *must* be "worthless pablum." Robert Hughes too can't resist the trap of pretending to be able to sum up the scholarly world without having done more than dip the edge of a toenail into it. "With certain outstanding exceptions like Edward Said, Simon Schama or Robert Darnton," he declared, "relatively few of the people who are actually writing first-rate history, biography or cultural criticism in America have professorial tenure." Since in his entire volume Hughes cites only six works of history directly in his notes, it is impossible to discern how he arrived at this ludicrous judgment of the discipline of history which is in one of its most exciting and original periods and has in the past several decades produced large numbers of significant works that have advanced our thinking about the past considerably.

Without taking the trouble to conduct an actual investigation, Martin Anderson, a Fellow at the Hoover Institution, decided: "The work of scholars that is relevant to the critical issues facing Americans is almost nonexistent." This self-generated observation led him to the conclusion that "taken as a whole, academic research and writing is the greatest intellectual fraud of the twentieth century." Based upon precisely the same sort of self-referential "analysis," the historian Page Smith concluded that "the vast majority of the so-called re-

5

search turned out in the modern university is essentially worthless," though obviously he could have had no actual familiarity with "the vast majority" of university research, most of which is in fields he knew nothing about. Similarly, Allan Bloom presented no evidence whatever to document his assertions that students today appreciate classical music less than they did thirty years ago, or that sexual liberation has robbed them of their ability to relate to the novels of the past, or that students no longer think about or want to visit the countries of western Europe. Bloom's "research," apart from his own limited personal experience, was primarily internal, conducted largely in the archives of his own mind and the precincts of the sensibilities of the ancient writers as he envisioned them.

In his influential polemic *Tenured Radicals*, Roger Kimball spoke about the "decanonization" of dead, White, European men in recent years but presented no evidence that writers like Shakespeare are actually studied less now than they were before the 1960s. In fact, the most exhaustive surveys of college and university literature courses conducted in 1984–85 and again in 1990 provide no documentation for this accusation made so frequently by conservative critics. The earlier survey concluded that "courses are added to expand the curriculum, not to replace traditional offerings, which remain in place as core requirements for the English major." Of the courses that 80 percent of the English departments insisted their majors take, the three most frequently required were survey courses in British literature, American literature, and Shakespearian drama. The 1990 survey of over nine hundred English teachers indicated that courses in nineteenth-century American literature featured such authors as Nathaniel Hawthorne, Henry David Thoreau, Herman Melville, and Ralph Waldo Emerson, while previously neglected writers like Frederick Douglass and Harriet Beecher Stowe made their way into the curriculum very gradually. "The major works and authors remain preeminent in the courses surveyed," the report concluded. The ways in which curricular change and tradition can and do coexist and constitute the substance of the contemporary university are simply ignored in the impassioned culture of hyperbole which pictures Alice Walker and Toni Morrison displacing Shakespeare.

Like Allan Bloom, Kimball and many of his fellow critics jump from rhetoric to assumption, from assumption to assertion, from assertion to fact. Author after author, critic after critic have recited the catechism concerning how the New Left has captured the academic world. One searches in vain for evidence, for citations, for documentation. Some truths, it seems, are too obvious to require the needless paraphernalia of scholarship. But not too obvious to need constant reiteration so that once again the unproven assertion becomes "documented" through the sheer force of repetition. In 1992, the historian John Diggins asserted that "in the field of American history . . . a liberal Ph.D. who subscribed to consensus instead of class conflict, or a white male conservative who admired Madison more than Marx, had about as much chance of getting hired on some faculty as Woody Allen of starting as point guard for the

Knicks." Though Diggins's claim was unaccompanied by any evidence whatever, Lynn Cheney in her 1992 report as chairman of the National Endowment for the Humanities cited it as a "fact" to document her own allegation that a political agenda now often dominated universities and their faculties. Similarly, Professor Jerry Z. Muller has written that political correctness "is a consequence of the institutionalization within the academy of a cohort of New Leftists who came of age politically in the 1960s, who lecture on egalitarianism while practicing elitism, and who exert disproportionate influence through their organizational zeal and commitment to academic politics," and cited Diggins's own totally unsupported assertion that the New Left dominates as his sole "proof." This kind of uninformed and under-researched generalizing is done ostensibly *in defense* of the university by those who seem to understand, or at least to care, little about its purposes, standards, and approaches.

Charges of political advocacy against the university are made also through the process of transforming norms into extremes. Hostility to the writings of "Dead White European Males" is attributed to any scholar who would supplement the canon with the work of those who have been traditionally excluded from it. Afrocentrism and multiculturalism are made synonymous by simply ignoring the large and sophisticated body of recent scholarship on ethnicity which has nothing to do with Afrocentrism *or* Eurocentrism. Practices and processes that have long exemplified the academe are made to appear to be the contemporary fruits of advocacy. Thus vigorously debating the orthodoxies of prior days, or supplementing and replacing canonical texts and subjects, or altering and experimenting with curricula, or using abstruse theories and complex language, or constructing courses to accommodate the changing nature of the student body, or responding to the major social, cultural, and political forces of the day are treated as evidence of the university's current degradation when in fact they have been endemic in the American academic world. Peter Shaw has complained of "resistance to authority of all kinds" in the modern university: "Literary critics rejected traditional interpretations, scholars found the formal limitations of their disciplines stifling, and humanists objected to the established canon of great works." This condition, of course, is hardly peculiar to our own time but has been an evolving characteristic of American universities throughout the nineteenth and twentieth centuries. Universities are about teaching the methods and dispositions necessary to criticize, question, and test authority.

Similarly, when Gertrude Himmelfarb criticizes many of her fellow historians for daring to "impose upon the past their own determinacy," for acting as if "the past has to be deconstructed and constructed anew," she is, in fact, describing the well-established process of historiography. Historians have always reconstructed the past on the basis of new information, new research, new theories, new approaches, new understandings; on the basis of what the historian Jack Hexter once called the "tracking devices" of their own time. The current emphasis on social and cultural history which so troubles contemporary critics

10

is no more permanent than were past emphases on political, intellectual, economic, or diplomatic history. Neither is it any more—or less—politically motivated. It reflects, as earlier historiographies have reflected, the questions, problems, issues that touch our time and help us make sense of the world. It also reflects the fact that history today is written, as it has always been written, by human beings who are part of their own societies and cultures.

Perhaps the most common of the charges that the contemporary university is guilty of behavior that differentiates it qualitatively from its predecessors and makes it an exception in the history of American higher education are those revolving around what has been called "political correctness" (PC) which has allegedly cast a pall on freedom of expression and action on the American campus. Lynn Cheney has argued that today's students "can disagree with professors. But to do so is to take a risk." In fact, when was it *not* risky for a socialist student to confront her economics professor who was teaching about the wonders of the free market, for an atheist student to confront his professor of religion who was teaching about the wonders of monotheism, or for African American students to confront their professor of history who was teaching about the wonders of the Founding Fathers, many of whom were slaveholders? This has always been the case in the university. Those professors who would welcome vigorous debate and disagreement on fundamentals often fail to get it either because students don't think this is their place, or because of those of their colleagues who don't welcome it and have taught students to repress their dissident urges. Students have always had to learn to accommodate to the whims and prejudices of professors, to the attitudes and sensitivities of fellow students, and to the values and beliefs of the larger society; to, that is, the complex of considerations that today is referred to much too simply as "political correctness."

The trouble with critics like Cheney is that they have made this long-standing condition in the academe a partisan one (unique to the Left) and an exceptional one (unique to our time). From reading Cheney and most of her fellow critics, you would never dream that there existed a conservative Republican professor or a centrist Democratic professor who stifled freedom of thought and inquiry in the classroom, who intimidated students into silence, who felt it was a student's function to listen and a professor's to dominate the discourse, who was confident of having the True Word to impart to a captive student audience. The problem Cheney is describing—of students fearing to risk debate—is neither new nor confined to one part of the political spectrum, nor is it unique to our time, nor is it particularly virulent in our time, nor does it really characterize the contemporary university which is a more varied, more open, more dynamic place to be in and near than ever before. This problem is inherent in the university which is a dual institution: on the one hand a center of free inquiry and discourse, on the other hand a center of intellectual authority—two characteristics that don't mesh easily and often lead to contradictory or inconsistent behavior. Ironically, it is most often Cheney's fellow conservative critics who have invoked authority in their vision of the class-room. Thus Gertrude Himmelfarb has argued that "it is reasonable and proper to ask students, even scholars, . . . to accept, at least provisionally, until dis-proved by powerful evidence, the judgment of posterity about great writers and great books. This calls for an initial suspension of private judgment in fa-vor of authoritative opinion, the collective opinion of generations."

It surely was much simpler when the university community was a homo-geneous one, not because there was more freedom but because homogeneity ensured that there was more unanimity about what constituted acceptable ideas and behavior; because, that is, there was *more,* not less, of what today is called political correctness. When Allan Bloom blamed the radical students of the 1960s for opening the university to the "vulgarities present in society at large," he conveniently ignored the truth that long before the student move-ments universities had hardly transcended the larger society's "vulgarities" but had in fact mirrored its often prejudiced, repressive, and "politically cor-rect" attitudes toward gender, race, and ethnicity in their admissions policies, their hiring practices, and their curricula.

But the American university no longer is and never again will be homoge-neous, and much of what we have seen recently in terms of speech codes and the like are a stumbling attempt to adapt to this new heterogeneity. The major consequence of the new heterogeneity on campuses, however, has not been re-pression but the very opposite—a flowering of ideas and scholarly innovation unmatched in our history. Charles Sykes quotes the educator Robert Maynard Hutchins's dictum that the liberal arts should free the student "from the prison-house of his class, race, time, place, background, family, and even his nation," and goes on to argue that universities today have reversed Hutchins's definition by focusing on race, class, gender, and sexual orientation. On the contrary, today's universities with their diverse student bodies, faculties, and curricula have done more to free us from the confines of self-absorption than Hutchins could have imagined. The problem with Hutchins's vision is that like Bloom's, it was coupled to a homogeneous university community of fac-ulty and students largely from the same class and background who were al-lowed to assume that *they* were the model and everyone else the deviants, that *they* possessed culture which everyone else lacked. What so troubles many conservatives is the modern university's presumption in believing that it can actually educate a wide array of people and help free them from the prison house of stereotypes and assumptions—those they hold of others and those others hold of them.

The British historian Sir Lewis Namier observed that "the crowning at-tainment of historical study is a historical sense—an intuitive understanding of how things do not happen." It is exactly this understanding of how things do *not* happen that the leading critics of the contemporary university lack. Thus they freely spin their facile theories of how the survivors of the New Left lost the political wars but won their ultimate triumph by capturing the uni-versity and transforming it from an institution of culture and learning to a

15

high-handed and inflexible purveyor of Political Correctness. The problem with such notions—aside from the fact that they are promulgated, to borrow Carl Becker's memorable phrase, without fear and without research—is that they are telling examples of how things do not happen. Universities in the United States are not transformed by small cabals of political and social radicals who somehow (the process is never revealed) capture venerable private and public institutions of higher learning, convert them to their own agendas, overwhelm and silence the vast majority of their colleagues while boards of regents and trustees benignly look on, and mislead generations of gullible and passive college youth who are robbed of their true heritage and thus compelled to stumble forth into the larger world as undereducated and uncultured dupes mouthing the platitudes taught them by the band of radical mesmerists posing as college professors. "I have never fully understood the notion that faculty could brainwash me into believing whatever they wanted me to," a Stanford undergraduate testified. "Reading Hitler did not make me a fascist; reading Sartre did not make me an existentialist. Both simply enabled me to think about those philosophies in ways I hadn't previously." It should not take a great deal of reflection to realize that neither college students nor college faculties nor college administrations operate in the manner posited by the apocalyptic and conspiratorial views of the contemporary university. This is not how things happen in the American university and to comprehend why some people are convinced that they do we might ponder Richard Hofstadter's notions of the "paranoid style" in American politics.

In no sense did Hofstadter equate what he called the paranoid style with psychological pathology. He argued that while clinical paranoia describes an individual who is convinced of the existence of a hostile and conspiratorial world "directed specifically *against him*," the paranoid style involves belief in a conspiracy "directed against a nation, a culture, a way of life." Hofstadter found this style recurring throughout American history in the anti-Masonic and anti-Catholic crusades, and in such manifestations of anti-Communism as McCarthyism and the John Birch Society. But there is nothing particularly retrograde about the style; one can find it in aspects of abolitionism, of Populism, and of antiwar movements as well. It is less tied to particular political goals than to a way of seeing the world, a way of understanding how things work by invoking the process of conspiracy. "The paranoid spokesman," according to Hofstadter, "sees the fate of this conspiracy in apocalyptic terms. . . . He is always manning the barricades of civilization. He constantly lives at a turning point: it is now or never in organizing resistance to conspiracy. Time is forever just running out. . . . The apocalypticism of the paranoid style runs dangerously near to hopeless pessimism, but usually stops just short of it."

I would argue that this manner of envisioning reality has frequently characterized those who resisted the changes taking place in American higher education, and never more so than during the past several decades. Perhaps the most unfortunate aspect of this mode of analysis is not merely that it's incorrect but that it's so simple and pat and that we learn little, if anything, from it.

"We are all sufferers from history," Hofstadter concluded, "but the paranoid is a double sufferer, since he is afflicted not only by the real world, with the rest of us, but by his fantasies as well."

What is wrong with the dominant critiques is not that they are mistaken in every instance, nor that there aren't things to criticize in contemporary universities. Of course there are. We need to integrate learning more fully and to have more sequential courses that build on one another. We need to minimize the use of inaccessible jargon wherever possible, particularly in those fields where jargon has become a way of life. We need to make a greater effort to communicate with colleagues in other disciplines, with students, and with the general public. We need to ensure that teaching ability is considered seriously in all faculty personnel decisions. We need to learn how to respond to the considerable challenge of teaching the most wide-ranging and heterogeneous body of students in the history of American higher education. The problem is that the charges against the university are so hyperbolic, so angry, so conspiracy-minded, and so one-sided they can find almost nothing positive to say. They see little if any good coming out of the new research and teaching on race and gender, the multifaceted study of American culture, the attempts to more completely understand the world and its peoples and cultures, the exciting development of a student body and faculty that are increasingly becoming more representative of the nation's population.

There *is* fragmentation in the United States; there *is* distrust; there *is* deep anger—and much of this is reflected in and acted out in universities, but none of it is *caused* by universities or by professors or by young people. Nevertheless, all three are easy scapegoats for the problems of the larger society. The many changes taking place in the nation's universities have created awkward moments pregnant with the possibilities of progress but also containing an abundance of room for egregious mistakes, and universities have had their share of both. But to collect dozens of anecdotes illustrating the stumbling of many universities in the face of new pressures and challenges—while ignoring all of their many successful adjustments and innovations—and to parade these stories forth as indicative of the great problem we face is mistaken. Those who do so disregard the fact that the real fragmentation confronting this society has nothing to do with the university, which is one of the more successfully integrated and heterogeneous institutions in the United States, and everything to do with the reality that forms of fragmentation—social, ethnic, racial, religious, regional, economic—have been endemic in the United States from the outset. In our own time this historic fragmentation has been exacerbated because a significant part of our population has been removed from the economy and turned into a permanent underclass with no ladders leading out of its predicament and consequently little hope.

Americans' complicated and ambivalent attitudes toward the university   20
have created the myth that universities are not part of the "real" world, and many professors, pleased at the notion that they were apart from and therefore

more "objective" about the surrounding society, have been willing to go along with this illusion and to varying extents have even come to believe it. In truth, as this study will illustrate again and again, universities are never far removed from the larger society. To have a literature of crisis built upon the university and the young as *the* enemy, as *the* creators of fragmentation, discontent, and social turmoil, is so bizarre as to almost, but not quite, defy understanding. Rather than face the complex of reasons for our present state of unease, it is easier and certainly much more comforting to locate the source of our dilemma in an institution—the university—that has always been deeply suspect in the United States, in a group—professors—who have always been something of an anomaly in a theoretically egalitarian land, and in a generation—college youth—who have always made us nervous because they never *seem* to be our exact replicas.

The trouble with the widespread apocalyptic view of the sudden takeover of the university by forces essentially alien to its basic spirit is that this vision removes the American university from the context of its own extended history and transforms long-term processes of change and development into short-term accidents. When the Mock Turtle asked Alice to explain where she came from, the Gryphon exclaimed impatiently, "No, no! The adventures first, explanations take such a dreadful time." Contemporary critics of the university have shown a similar impatience. Explanations *do* take time, but they remain essential. To understand where the university is we have to understand where it has been and how its present state was constructed. There is no quicker or easier way to proceed; to fathom today requires some awareness of yesterday. In the process we will learn not only about higher education, we will discover truths about our culture and, hopefully, about ourselves as well. ◢

Reflections and Inquiries

1. What problems does Levine see with the research methods of certain conservative defenders of the Western curriculum, such as Dinesh D'Souza, Charles Sykes, and Roger Kimball? How convincingly does Levine support his claim that these research methods are defective?

2. According to Levine, "Students have always had to learn to accommodate to the whims and prejudices of professors." Drawing from your own experience, do you agree or disagree that it is more difficult to accommodate to the whims of "politically correct" professors?

3. Why does Levine invoke Richard Hofstadter's notion of "the paranoid style" of politics in describing the attitudes of the critics of multicultural education?

4. What does Levine advocate in the way of better dialogue between the critics and the defenders of multicultural education?

Reading to Write

What long-standing myths about the university help prevent deeper understanding of the relationship between higher education and society, according to Levine? In a short essay, suggest what can be done to dispel these myths.

STUDENT ESSAY

The Importance of Multicultural Education in Global Society | Chris Garber

In a multicultural society, educators have come to realize, one's social identity cannot be ignored. One's race, cultural heritage, gender, and socioeconomic milieu are fundamental ingredients in acquiring a sense of self. Without finding ways of connecting this sense of self to what one is being taught in the classroom, learning may be impeded. In the following essay, Chris Garber, a first-year business major at Santa Clara University, critiques the arguments against multicultural education and calls attention to its benefits.

> People speak as if race is something blacks have, sexual orientation is something gays and lesbians have, gender is something women have, ethnicity is something so called "ethnics" have . . . Thus, if persons do not fit "neatly" into the aforementioned categories, they are not acknowledged as sharing group membership in any particular group. Moreover, if they do not openly identify with the above categories, people assume that they do not have any worries about the various identities.
>
> —Henry Louis Gates (Ferguson and Howard-Hamilton 284)

By 2030, educators estimate language-minority students will make up 40 percent of children in school (Thomas and Collier 26). This statistic represents not only the increasing diversity of the population in the United States, but also a pressing need within the educational community to reevaluate its focus. Currently, an entire portion of the school age population does not benefit from the system of education in our country. Since this group grows larger every year, curriculum needs to be adapted to meet the needs of a more diverse group of students.

Although a concrete, universal definition remains elusive, most educators understand that multicultural education is a method of teaching that exposes students to a wide variety of cultures, traditions, and social groups in an attempt to help them better understand how they fit into society. This also includes bilingual education, which seeks to increase students' proficiency in English while at the same time maintaining their connection with their first language. Multicultural education has grown in popularity throughout the past 15 years as student populations have grown increasingly diverse. The need stems from the fact that "traditional student affairs and psychological research historically has excluded or minimized the importance of the individual's social identities (i.e., ethnicity, gender, sexual orientation) and their relationship within individuals' psychological, interpersonal, leadership, and social development" (Ferguson and Howard-Hamilton 293). It is detrimental to assume that a child who does not know English would benefit from the same type of education as a student who has been speaking English his or her entire life. Multicultural education seeks to allow all students to benefit equally from education.

The debate on this issue remains complex, and as a result it is easier to avoid rather than discuss or address. Activists bring up the fearful image of the "melting pot" in argument against multicultural education. In this social model, programs use education to mold the various cultures of America into one homogeneous group deemed socially acceptable by dominant society. This results in the loss of the history and traditions of the many ethnic groups who inhabit our nation. Supporters believe in order to "make it" in society, minority students are forced to abandon their heritage, thus giving up their personal and cultural identities (Nieto 10). They fear that multicultural education will serve only to destroy the cultural differences making each of us unique. Another accusation against multicultural education is it completely undermines the integrity of the history of Western thought and achievement. Critics shrug off multiculturalism as an identity crisis of the minority population which threatens to destroy Western culture (Giroux 505).

In his book, *The Disuniting of America*, Arthur M. Schlessinger states a contrasting argument as he explores the effects of multiculturalization on society. He comes to the conclusion that while cultural diversity promotes human interaction, the overemphasis of these differences leads to conflict. First, it creates a group Schlessinger refers to as the "militants of ethnicity"—people caught up in upholding cultural differences who become alienated from society and instill social unrest. Second, cultural separation results in "balkinization": a disuniting of society that eventually leads to social breakdown on the premise that no one will be able to relate to any cultural group but their own. Schlessinger argues that the only way to achieve social diversity without the fragmentation of society is to create an education system that lifts up cultural differences and teaches tolerance and understanding. Only through a system of multicultural education can people gain the cross-cultural experience necessary to interact in today's international world.

Multicultural education benefits and improves our society. In "Two Languages Are Better than One," Wayne P. Thomas and Virginia P. Collier argue for multicultural education because, "in the remedial program, English learners receive less access to the standard grade-level curriculum. The achievement

5

and equity gap increases as native English speakers forge ahead while English learners make less progress" (23). The current system of education proves culturally inadequate since it widens the gap in student achievement rather than closes it. Our current programs for bilingual education involve either separating English learners from the school population or minimizing their exposure to core material. Both options alienate them from their peers and deny them the education they need and deserve.

In his book, *Hunger of Memory,* Richard Rodriguez writes about the changes in his life as a result of bilingual education. He explains that the biggest barrier in the English learner's quest for acceptance in society remains the sense of separation between his or her culture and the American life he or she is pursuing. Rodriguez insists, "full individuality is achieved, paradoxically, by those who are able to consider themselves members of the crowd. Thus it happened for me: Only when I was able to think of myself as an American, no longer an alien in *gringo* society, could I seek the rights and opportunities necessary for full public individuality" (27). An educational program making all members feel like they belong builds a stronger and less fragmented community. Once a sense of public identity is achieved, the individual understands his or her societal role and can better interact with other people. In this way, education represents the pathway to becoming a member of society.

The argument against multicultural education has taken a number of different forms. Henry A. Giroux's essay, "Democracy and the Discourse of Cultural Difference: Towards a Politics of Border Pedagogy," emphasizes one of the more powerful movements by conservative intellectuals who claim multiculturalism works against the entire institution of Western thought. They argue multicultural proponents hold distorted attitudes that emphasize bigotry and prejudice in Western culture rather than its great achievements. Furthermore, they label multiculturalism as a crisis within the value system of American culture that destroys the "common culture" that has resulted from hundreds of years of shared international discovery. Giroux quotes Roger Kimball, who states:

> Implicit in the politicizing mandate of multiculturalism is an attack on the idea of common culture, the idea that, despite our many differences, we hold in common an intellectual, artistic, and moral legacy, descending largely from the Greeks and the Bible, supplemented and modified over centuries by innumerable contributions from diverse lands and peoples. It is this legacy that has given us our science, our political institutions, and the monuments of artistic and cultural achievement that define us as a civilization. Indeed, it is this legacy, insofar as we live up to it, that preserves us from chaos and barbarism. And it is precisely this legacy that the multiculturalist wishes to dispense with. (519)

Kimball points out that discoveries of people from all nations founded the modern world. Thus, he explains, modern civilization is by definition diverse and emphasizing these differences is unnecessary. Kimball sees multiculturalism replacing the shared identity developed through humankind's achievements. Furthermore, he concludes, the emphasis of cultural differences does not provide common ground, and therefore it dismantles the foundation of modern civilization.

Gloria Anzaldúa, in her book *Borderlands/La Frontera: The New Mestiza,* argues a different point with ramifications similar to Kimball's. She explains that American education forces other cultures to give up their identities for the sake of fitting into popular society. While her ideas place importance on customs and heritage, she does not support multicultural education. She sees it as a method of assimilation diluting the full importance of cultural independence. She explains, "Chicanos and other people of color suffer economically for not acculturating. This voluntary (yet forced) alienation makes for psychological conflict, a kind of dual identity—we don't identify with the Anglo-American cultural values and we don't totally identify with the Mexican cultural values" (43). Anzaldúa claims that forcing outside rules on minority cultures does not draw them in as expected, but rather pushes them away through the destruction of their social identity. As a result, they cannot relate to other social groups and move to the fringes of society. In addition, by losing their cultural identity, they have difficulty if they want to go back to their original beliefs.

Both Anzaldúa's and Kimball's ideas assume multicultural education cannot provide the benefits found in either the institution of Western thought or the cultural history of minority populations. Kimball's statement ignores the argument that accepted Western thought ignores the ideas of minorities while claiming to represent the entire population. The argument is not what would happen if multicultural education is widely implemented, but rather what will happen if it is not. Giroux states, "what is at stake is not the defense or repudiation of a common culture, but the creation of a democratic society in which differences are affirmed and interrogated rather than dismissed as essentialist or disruptive" (509). Without a broader education base, our society will not gain the cultural acceptance necessary for the coming age of diversity, and Schlessinger's fear of "balkanization" could become a reality.

Anzaldúa's pessimistic view of multicultural education can be counterargued by Rodriguez, who wrote, "Those middle-class ethnics who scorn assimilation seem to me filled with decadent self-pity, obsessed by the burden of public life. Dangerously, they romanticize public separateness and they trivialize the dilemma of the socially disadvantaged" (27). He explains separatists have become convinced that minorities cannot emerge as members of mainstream society. By citing personal examples, his story argues that one gains personal identity through cultural acceptance and understanding. Further, he states while his family life at home changed as a result of his learning English, "there are *two* ways a person is individualized" (26). While an individual's private sense and his or her dependence on cultural heritage diminishes with multicultural education, this loss makes the gain of a greater understanding of the self in relation to the rest of the world possible. In the end, the gain results in the

10

forming of a public identity—a sense of belonging within mass society, which Rodriguez claims is essential to being an active member of a community.

For students in the multicultural age of America, English cannot be a second language. It needs to be a tool that, when combined with a student's first language, not only makes the student a part of American society but allows him or her to achieve at a higher level than possible without it. In light of this, there are a number of ways multicultural education could be implemented to best improve each student's experience.

For example, in "Strength Through Cultural Diversity," multicultural expert Ronald Takaki proposes that courses encouraging diversity should be offered at universities to fulfill social science or humanities requirements as core classes. In this way, students would receive diversity education without having to take extra classes or commit more time to study (Heuberger, Gerber, and Anderson 109). Angela D. Ferguson and Mary F. Howard-Hamilton call for a similar solution in their discussion of college diversity but assert that faculty need to reaffirm their commitment to supporting a diverse student population. They also seek the implementation of courses and programs that not only support diversity but also "emphasize the idea of diversity as including multiple identities [and] sensitize students to becoming aware that people do not exist under one identity" (291). This argument seeks not only a broader curriculum base but also seeks programs supporting ethnic students as well as those of different sexual orientations. It reminds us that a classroom experience can cover only so much information and that the variables included in a person's identity are infinite, necessitating personalized support and interaction. Furthermore, Leslie Marmon Silko writes from a Pueblo Indian perspective, a culture based in storytelling. She states, "if you begin to look at the core of the importance of the language and how it fits in with the culture, it is the *story* and the feeling of the story which matters more than what language it's told in" (58). Multicultural education should not emphasize the evident differences in language and customs but rather accentuate the common themes that can be better explored by bringing in diverse works. Commenting on a broad scale, Thomas and Collier see that bilingual education would be beneficial to the entire school age population, not just communities including English learners. "The research evidence is overwhelmingly clear that *proficient bilinguals outperform monolinguals on school tests*" (26). With this in mind, multicultural education represents an improvement on the modern education system not only for minority students but for all. A wide-scale implementation of multicultural and bilingual programs can serve only to enhance the experience of English-speaking students while at the same time rectifying the crime being committed by a system serving only the majority.

It is essential that the American education system keep up with the changing needs of our students. As globalization spreads throughout the modern world, contact and interaction with other cultures will become part of daily life. Students need to be given the tools to allow intercultural relations to take place. This can be accomplished by changing curriculum and implementing programs that broaden the scope of topics covered, as well as enacting bilingual programs to make education more effective for the entire school age population. The result is a student who is not only better educated but ready to critically assess, with an open mind and an open heart, situations involving people from all walks of life.

Works Cited

Anzaldúa, Gloria. "How to Tame a Wild Tongue." *Ways of Reading: An Anthology for Writers*. Eds. David Bartholomae and Anthony Petrosky. 5th ed. Boston: Bedford, 1999. 36–45.

Ferguson, Angela D., and Mary F. Howard-Hamilton. "Addressing Issues of Multiple Identities for Women of Color on College Campuses." *Toward Acceptance: Sexual Orientation Issues on Campus*. Ed. Vernon A. Wall and Nancy J. Evans. Lanham: UP of America, 2000. 283–97.

Giroux, Henry A. "Democracy and the Discourse of Cultural Difference: Towards a Politics of Border Pedagogy." *British Journal of Sociology of Education* 12 (1991): 501–20.

Heuberger, Barbara, Diane Gerber, and Reed Anderson. "Strength Through Cultural Diversity." *College Teaching* 47 (1999): 107–14.

Nieto, Sonia. "Affirming Diversity." *National Education Association Today* 18 (2000): 10.

Rodriguez, Richard. *Hunger of Memory*. Boston: Godine, 1982.

Schlesinger, Arthur M. *The Disuniting of America: Reflection on a Multicultural Society*. New York: W. W. Norton, 1991.

Silko, Leslie Marmon. "Language and Literature from a Pueblo Indian Perspective." *English Literature: Opening Up the Canon*. Ed. Leslie A. Fiedler and Houston A. Baker, Jr. Baltimore: Johns Hopkins UP, 1981. 52–58.

Thomas, Wayne P., and Virginia P. Collier. "Two Languages Are Better than One." *Educational Leadership* 55 (Dec. 1997–Jan. 1998): 23–26. ◼

Reflections and Inquiries

1. What are Garber's principal arguments against multicultural education? How convincingly does he refute them?

2. Garber argues that English cannot be a second language for students in America. Why not? Do you agree or disagree?

3. According to Garber, "A wide-scale implementation of multicultural and bilingual programs can serve only to enhance the experience of English-speaking students." Why? Do you agree or disagree?

Reading to Write

After reading about multicultural education programs, curricular and extracurricular, investigate your school's programs. Examine any brochures and catalogs associated with these programs. What do you see as their strengths and shortcomings? Write an essay evaluating one or more of these programs, suggesting improvements if you feel they are warranted.

Connections Across the Clusters

1. Make a case for the advancement of multicultural education through distance learning via the Internet. (See Cluster 1.)

2. How might multicultural education influence the teaching and practice of science, specifically space science? (See Cluster 4.) The making of connections between science and religion? (See Cluster 5.)

Writing Projects

1. Visit your campus's multicultural center or a minority-student organization and obtain information about its most pressing problems. Then write an essay in which you examine these problems, their effect on student learning and student life, the efforts to solve the problems, and what work remains to be done.

2. Examine the course offerings in your major from the perspective of multicultural learning. Write an essay in which you propose changes, such as adding new courses that focus on minorities and their works or revising existing courses so they embrace multicultural matters.

Suggestions for Further Reading

Bloom, Allan David. *The Closing of the American Mind: How Higher Education Has Failed Democracy and Impoverished the Souls of Today's Students*. New York: Simon, 1987.

Giroux, Henry A. *Schooling and the Struggle for Public Life: Critical Pedagogy in the Modern Age*. Minneapolis: University of Minnesota Press, 1988.

Harper's Symposium. "Who Needs the Great Works?" *Harper's* Sept. 1989: 43–52.

Hofstadter, Richard. *The Paranoid Style in American Politics and Other Essays*. New York: Knopf, 1965.

Kates, Gary. "The Classics of Western Civilization Do Not Belong to Conservatives Alone." *Chronicle of Higher Education* 5 July 1989: A46.

Kimball, Roger. *Tenured Radicals: How Politics Has Corrupted Our Higher Education*. New York: Harper, 1990.

Krauthammer, Charles. "Hale Columbus, Dead White Male." *Time* 27 May 1991: 74.

Sykes, Charles J. *The Hollow Men: Politics and Corruption in Higher Education*. Washington, DC: Regnery, 1990.

Introduction

Like book censorship, media censorship of any kind has the potential of violating freedom-of-speech rights. But unlike books, visual media—television, movies, CD-ROMs and video games—have a much greater impact on children and young adolescents. Every hour a child devotes to reading books is offset by as many as ten hours devoted to some visual medium, most often television.

Educators and psychologists are concerned that detrimental behavior may be caused in part by such excessive exposure to countless situations involving acts of violence. Even when such acts are punished, they nonetheless may affect a child's ability to develop compassion, to solve problems civilly and cooperatively, or to appreciate the complexity of human nature, which tends to be grossly oversimplified to fit the format of sixty-minute TV dramas full of cliffhangers (which occur, naturally, just before commercial breaks!).

The following articles examine the issue of media violence from several different perspectives. By open-mindedly taking each perspective seriously, you may arrive at a sensible way of dealing with this controversial social issue.

New Insights into Media Violence | Rose A. Dyson

Canada, like the United States, is involved in an effort to control media violence—and like the United States that effort is met with much opposition from private enterprise, especially from the media industries.

In the following excerpt from her study of media violence undertaken as a doctoral student at the University of Toronto's Institute for Studies in Education, Rose A. Dyson examines the efforts being made to control violent content programming—in the context of civil liberty—in both United States and Canada, and concludes with an assessment of the progress being made.

Source: From Dyson, Rose A. "New Insights into Media Violence." *Mind Abuse: Media Violence in an Information Age.* Montreal: Black Rose, 2000. 168–92. Rrprinted with the kind permission of Black Rose Books, Montreal, www.web.net/blackrosebooks.

The obvious question is why, with so many warnings for several decades now about where communications technology without responsible regulation is leading us, has there been so little progress on the problem of violent content? The fact that self-serving responses from industry have consistently clouded consensus on the research demonstrating harmful effects is one reason. But many men and women, health professionals, educators and otherwise, in a number of countries, have agreed upon excesses involving media violence causing social harm and have tried to do something about it.

Nevertheless, confusion over what constitutes harm and how it should be addressed is still predominant. What these trends do, is illuminate the need to reexamine our civil liberties, redefine what we mean by censorship, accelerate the Cultural Environmental Movement (CEM) and implement the kind of proposals which would take us in a new direction advocated by the CEM and other similar organizations.

What Have We Learned?

In her book, *Boys Will Be Boys: Breaking the Links Between Masculinity and Violence,* published in 1992, Miriam Miedzian considered the pattern of dedication and commitment to change exhibited by a number of groups acting in the public interest in the United States over a period of 20 years. These groups included Action for Children's Television (ACT), the National Coalition on Television Violence (NCTV), the American Medical Association (AMA), the National Parent-Teacher Association (NPTA) and the National Council of the Churches of Christ (NCCC), all of whom have declared themselves over the years as being opposed to censorship. This, in her view, was the key reason for their lack of progress. Despite their activism, these groups have not, adequately clarified what they mean by the word censorship or stressed the point that they are *for* responsible regulation. They have used too strict an interpretation of the First Amendment. As a result, tireless efforts to influence the Federal Communications Commission (FCC) to use its rule-making and licensing power to decrease television violence his had little effect.

In Canada, patterns of protest and subsequent diffusion of them by vested interests have been similar. When the LaMarsh Commission conducted its hearings in 1977, it was reported that over 8,000 people attended. More than 800 participants made either oral or written presentations or both. Over half of these came from community groups and individuals not affiliated with specific institutions in education, research, religious organizations, industry or government. Although since then, there has been some ongoing public activity in attempts to address the problem of media violence in Canada, for the most part, the momentum of public concern built up by the LaMarsh inquiry has not been sustained. This has occurred largely for two reasons. First, the work of the Commission was immediately discredited by the news media, and second, the initial leadership of the LaMarsh Center established at York University in Toronto ignored the central purpose for which it was intended and developed its own agenda for research on the subject of violence.

Canadians Concerned About Violence In Entertainment (C-CAVE) itself was formed in 1983, five years after the Commission's Report was released, largely as an outgrowth of encouragement and support from its American counterpart, NCTV, founded by Illinois based, child psychiatrist, Thomas Radecki. The organization has always been linked with other Canadian organizations attempting to improve the quality of popular culture and reduce levels of violence in society, particularly for women and children. It has never, however, enjoyed the same kind of support and generous funding as other organizations, such as the Alliance for Children and Television (ACT) and the Association for Media Literacy (AML), focused exclusively on alternative television programming for children or values-free analysis of the media.[1] As a result, its mandate to provide public education on what the research shows on media violence, based on overwhelming evidence pointing toward harmful effects, and solutions that include strategies to address systemic violence as well as alternative programming and individual responsibility, has been marginalized.

In 1990, when the issue of media violence began, once again, to receive attention on a widespread basis in Canada, dozens of additional community-based groups sprung up, and while they lasted helped to amplify calls for change that went beyond the parent, the teacher, and alternative programming. Unfortunately, there has not been much lasting impact. Similarly, although the number of individual researchers and journalists with an appreciation of how mass media work in contemporary society has grown, this has been offset by increasing evidence of desensitization, particularly among young journalists, such as those reviewing video games. For many this entertainment has been normalized through diets of media, heavily laced with "action" from a very early age, and is having an impact on their social orientation, in spite of the fact that, as a generation, they are better educated and much less inclined to accept conventional notions of "censorship" than their predecessors were two decades ago. Also, although more women are now employed within the media industries and have brought new feminist perspectives to issues, framing them in different ways, some, like their young male counterparts, argue in defense of violent content.

In 1998, in *The New York Times*, American journalist Lawrie Mifflin discussed evidence of unprecedented levels of excesses in television programming while public outcry appeared to be diminishing.[2] At the same time, similar observations were made in Canada's national newspaper, *The Globe and Mail* by journalist Sandra Martin. She wrote of trends in popular culture involving unprecedented excesses in the use of sexual themes. Nevertheless, analysis in both cases was still carefully framed to conclude with emphasis on "opposition to censorship."[3] This pattern tends to repeat itself over and over again in ways that seem designed more to placate editors than because they offer sound conclusions to the overall analysis. As long as this unvaried approach is adhered to, eloquent hand-wringing, whether it is practiced by mainstream journalists or community activists will only continue to serve the hegemonic purposes of dominant interests.

In the United States, the Littleton, Colorado, massacre, reminiscent of the Montreal Polytechnical Institute shootings in Canada, in 1989, helped to galvanize all sectors of American society into responses to the mushrooming problems of violence in society. While American print coverage focused on the re-introduction of gun control legislation, another round of Senate hearings on media violence, passage of a juvenile justice bill designed to prevent and punish youth crime at the state and federal levels, voluntary removal of violent video games by arcade owners, and negligence lawsuits, in Canada, it was predominantly on successful "containment" of subsequent eruptions of school violence by police and school officials.[4] While in Manitoba a $100,000 awareness campaign was launched to "help" the industry based Entertainment Software Rating Board, formed in 1994, keep violent and sexually explicit video games out of the hands of children, in Ontario, with an election underway, Minister of Consumer and Commercial Relations for the Harris Government, David Tsubouchi, concluded that the subject was a non issue.[5]

In Canada, evidence of Federal Government interest in issues involving media violence is, now, virtually non-existent. The Canadian Radio-television and Telecommunications Commission (CRTC), in its report on the Internet, concluded that there were already adequate Criminal Code provisions and self-regulation to handle on-line crimes such as the production of hate literature and child pornography. Besides, said Ms. Bertrand, Chair of the federal regulator, regulation would "cripple" Canada's vibrant, competitive and productive Internet industries.[6] In Ottawa, federal officials reached a "compromise" with Americans over the issue of Canadian advertising allowances in their split-run magazines with Heritage Minister, Sheila Copps, promising tax breaks for everyone regardless of content.[7] The Toronto Police morality squad declined an opportunity to lay obscenity charges against the sexually violent book *American Psycho*, in this case citing the Butler decision as their *reason* while the entire matter was ignored by the media despite a news release from C-CAVE.[8]

Meanwhile, media scholars, community activists and concerned journalists with a more critical perspective continue to exchange views and calls for decisive action to stem the flow of profit driven cultural commodities with lifestyles and conflict resolution strategies which are plunging us into world wide chaos, whether it is in Kosovo, Colorado, or Taber, Alberta. Clearly the Internet is offering new channels for quick and widespread information exchange that is unfiltered by the agendas of dominant corporate interests and this unprecedented window of opportunity must be utilized and extended as effectively and quickly as possible.

Responsible Re-Regulation

Promises of industry self-regulation, alone, without government intervention have never worked well. In the United States, in October, 1990, the 20,000 members of ACT had convinced Congress to pass the Children's Television Act. The law, which came into effect a year later, stipulated that broadcasters had to serve the educational and informational needs of children or face the risk of losing their broadcast licenses. However in December, 1992, *Maclean's* reported that by August of that year, a review by consumer groups of 58 stations revealed that no broadcasters had produced new programming to comply with the law. "Instead, they had simply re-labeled existing programs, in many cases cartoons, as educational."[9]

In 1996, in the middle of the presidential campaign, a similar pledge was extracted by Clinton from the American broadcasters to commit to a minimum of three hours of "quality" children's programming each week, but again, with no clear assurance that progress on implementation of this new policy would be closely monitored. In June, 1999, based on findings released by The Annenberg Public Policy Center of the University of Pennsylvania, which has tracked the quality of children's television programming on U.S. TV networks since 1996, it was found that one in five television shows aimed at young people has little or no educational value at all.[10] Minor signs of improvement were, however, noted. In 1998, 26 percent of the shows were deemed to be of low quality compared with 36 percent in 1997.

These same patterns of extremely marginal change for the better have been evident in Canada as well. Objections to the violence in the television program for children, *Teenage Mutant Ninja Turtles,* were diffused by replacing it with the *Mighty Morphin Power Rangers,* which is similar in content. For Global Television, accommodating the CBSC ruling on the program being too violent for Canadian television meant minor modifications to, basically, the same thematic material with even the title itself retained, until some months later it was discontinued entirely, ostensibly due to costs involved in making the modifications. Until stringent guidelines and enforcement are provided by government acting in the public interest this kind of insignificant modification in programming content will continue to flourish.

Community Dialogue with Industry:
How Meaningful Is It?

In the 1970s a major setback experienced by community activists on the subject of media violence, both Canadian and American, resulted from the wave of deregulation that characterized the "Reagan years." Deregulation of children's television programming led to a scenario where many half-hour programs became 30 minute commercials, filled with violence, most of them infiltrating Canadian airwaves. In the process, some of the avenues for dialogue that were established in that decade in Hollywood were dismantled simply because they were no longer required. Campaigns to reduce sex and violence, though highly publicized, enjoyed only brief success because the trend toward deregulation was accompanied by the justification that the public interest would be better served if marketplace forces were allowed to operate freely. By the late 1980s, as Kathryn Montgomery has explained, "skillfully fashioned industry strategies had transformed advocacy groups from a disruptive force into what network executives referred to as a 'feedback system.'"[11]

In Canada, C-CAVE first established communication with the CAB in the early 1980s and provided input for the new code of violence which was approved by the CRTC in 1994. In the end, however, the code fell short of expectations by a considerable margin. At that time, through their societal issues chairman, Peter O'Neill, the industry based association sought assistance in "coordinating a list of concerns" and those of other groups with whom C-CAVE worked. These were then discussed in a closed circuit TV dialogue among broadcasters in 1994, with a videotaped copy of the conference later given to the author. Essentially the dialogue involved an exchange of recycled information among industry spokesmen on various initiatives being undertaken to address the issue of media violence in response to pressure from community organizations.

In compiling the list of "suggestions and concerns"—among them the reminder of findings demonstrating that adults as well as children are affected by violence—Joan DeNew, founder of C-CAVE, informed O'Neill that several activists had flatly refused to "dialogue" with the CAB at all because they considered it a waste of time. In terms of serious policy implementations for self-regulation through widespread adherence to its conduct code approved in 1994, nothing has yet occurred to change their minds. Although C-CAVE sustained a series of meetings with industry spokesmen until Peter O'Neill was downsized as a result of an industry merger in 1997, which were attended by representatives from other community based organizations as well, in the end, nothing was accomplished. O'Neill's identified replacement, CTV Vice President, Bev Oda, has not demonstrated any interest at all in sustaining this dialogue. An invitation to Ms. Oda to participate in a panel coordinated by the author for the 1998 Canadian Communications Conference at the University of Ottawa on "Regulation of the Media for the Good of the Public" was accepted but subsequent follow-up phone calls were ignored.

These experiences resonate with Montgomery's warning that even when members of the industry are willing to "dialogue" with advocacy groups, as part of their continuing strategy for deflecting pressure, without effective political leverage, these groups are unlikely to have their demands and concerns taken seriously.[12] Along with many others, she has stressed that the economic marketplace is not synonymous with a marketplace of ideas and that present trends are paving the way for the marginalization of more and more groups of citizens. The challenge now, in all countries, particularly as film, television and video production converges and locations for this economic activity mushroom around the world, is to reinvent and extend these channels for communication and to avoid previous pitfalls. This needs to happen between all sectors of society, including industry, with firmly established links and networks between community activists on a local, national and international basis under the auspices of international umbrella organizations such as those first initiated by the International Coalition Against Violent Entertainment (I-CAVE) and currently being built upon within the Cultural Environment Movement (CEM).

In Canada, such an opportunity was nominally provided by Bill Graham, chairman of the House of Commons Standing Committee on Foreign Affairs and International Trade. In the early months of 1999, he conducted a series of cross-country consultations on international trade priorities and concerns in preparation for major World Trade Organization (WTO) ministerial conferences planned for later in the year, but there is no evidence that Graham, himself, understands the impact of globalization on cultural issues. At an International Forum on *The Challenges of Globalization* held at Bishop's University in Lennoxville, Quebec, in conjunction with the Congress for the Social Sciences and Humanities in June, 1999, when he spoke at a luncheon, he was flippant and dismissive of any links between harmful cultural products and more liberalized trading patterns, despite receipt of numerous submissions on the subject from the author in the past, which included the aforementioned consultations.

In the Report itself, entitled *Canada and the Future of the World Trade Organization,* the only reference made to C-CAVE at all in the chapter on cultural issues, is within the context of an old issue concerning control of content, such as violence portrayed in audiovisual media, manifesting itself in a new way because of technological change. Said the authors, "It has a trade dimension because of the ease with which digital signals can cross borders."[13] This was hardly a new, ground breaking observation on the problem. What is now urgently needed is some representation on the cultural industries Sectoral Advisory Group on International Trade (SAGIT), lauded in the Report as a key component in preparations for the future from the non-profit sector of the cultural community, so that appropriate regulations for the protection of cultural sovereignty *and* the cultural environment can be introduced into trade talks on a global basis.

From the standpoint of public education, broad, transparent public consultations are needed in order for the crucial choices and decisions that are now facing all countries and international bodies engaged in increasingly complex, multilateral and regional trade liberalization processes to be better understood. But they are essential to serious collaboration between representatives in all sectors of society committed to meeting the challenges of the new information age and the impact of violent content upon it.

Minor steps taken so far for North American co-operation on strategies such as blocking devices for parents must be reinforced. Despite widespread concerns that the telecommunications bill approved by the U.S. Congress in 1996 paves the way for media conglomerates to seize greater control of the emerging information superhighway and sets a precedent for similar bills in other jurisdictions, the bill endorses emerging V-chip technology, This is an important gain if only because it is an acknowledgment from industry that media violence is, indeed, harmful. It signals a slight departure from previous assertions that research findings are inconclusive or that the problem is a moral issue only and should be dealt with entirely by parents. In other words, however minuscule, it is an indication of some movement toward consensus from government and industry as well as parents and educators that we, in fact, have a serious and growing health and social problem.

Unfortunately, the section within this U.S. telecommunications bill, which would have made it a crime for people to knowingly send "indecent" material to minors over the Internet through the Communications Decency Act (CDA), was struck down almost immediately.[14] However, when the successful court challenge was reported on in the September, 1996, issue of *Internet World*, there was also reference to ways in which the problem, once acknowledged only in the home and school was growing within the work place as well, as Internet "addiction" siphoned time and energy away from job related activity. This was a clear indication that the problem is growing and not about to go away on its own.

When the U.S. Supreme Court ruled the CDA unconstitutional in 1997, Congress responded in 1998 by passing the Child Online Protection Act, which would criminalize the posting of any material deemed "harmful to minors" on a commercial Internet website. Critics of the Act continue to claim its effect on speech would not be much different from that of the CDA, an assertion the lower courts have basically agreed with, and the new legislation is now pending a hearing in the Third Circuit Court of Appeals.[15]

Bills have also been introduced requiring any library or school receiving federal funds to install filtering software on any computer terminal accessible to the general public. Again, in 1998, a federal district court ruled that a library in Virginia had violated the guarantee of free speech when it decided to install the Internet filter X-Stop on all of its computer terminals and called for such devices only on computers designated for use by children. In spite of this fierce opposition, American legislators continue to cast about for solutions in the post-Littleton mood and are, so far, undeterred by arguments that the only answer to bad speech is more speech.[16]

Advertiser Boycotts

While speech alone is not and cannot be the whole answer, the potential for useful information exchange on issues of mutual concern on an international basis is growing. In 1994, exchanges between the Norwegian YMCA and Canadian community organizations on CAB codes of conduct helped to in-

25

form the campaign launched in Canada, in October, 1996, urging advertisers to boycott two new violent series in the TV season that fall. Letters were mailed to seventy of Canada's largest advertisers, in which the Coalition for Responsible Television (CRTV) urged companies to boycott the ultra violent series "Poltergeist: The Legacy," purchased by CTV, and "Millennium," purchased by Global TV.

The CRTV pointed out that working with the CRTC and broadcasters had not proven to be even remotely productive and that a new direction was needed. Simultaneously, the public was urged to "point the finger of blame for harmful programming at the corporations who underwrite violent shows with their advertising dollars" and to demand greater responsibility and accountability from them for what goes on the air. "Without advertising," said co-president, Jacques Brodeur, "programming cannot exist." One year later "Poltergeist" was taken off the air due to "poor ratings" according to CAB spokesman, Peter ONeill, and "Millennium" was moved from a 9 o'clock to a 10 o'clock time slot. In May, 1997, a CRTV news bulletin announced the results of its campaign encouraging the boycott. Out of 25 sponsors of the television program, *Millennium*, 13 agreed to pull their ads.[17] Meanwhile, in the business section of *The Globe and Mail* it was reported that Peter Swain, President of Media Buying Services Ltd. in Toronto, had issued the following warning:

> Advertisers are becoming more sensitive to the negative implications of being associated with violent programming . . . in most corporate board rooms it's not worth the price of admission to be seen as exploiting violence. It's too dangerous . . . It doesn't take much to create a bandwagon effect and go after an advertiser.[18]

Similar attempts on the part of C-CAVE, working in cooperation with both the CRTV and the CEM, to remove the Howard Stern show from the air on Q107-FM in Toronto and CHOM-FM in Montreal by encouraging advertiser boycotts, have also been somewhat successful. The Stern Show was taken off the air in Montreal, prevented from proliferating throughout the country, canceled for late night television in Toronto by CHUM Ltd., and although he remains on the air in Toronto, an extra producer has been hired to screen out what the CBSC deems to be unacceptable on the basis of Canadian codes of conduct.

In this case, partial success was due to some assistance and cooperation from competing radio station owners as well. Ironically, the success from these advertiser boycotts has come under criticism within the Cultural Environment Movement itself. At the second International Convention, held at Ohio University in March, 1999, these Canadian initiatives were criticized by American media scholars concerned that industry sources of funding for research projects might be threatened by advertiser boycotts.

Re-examining Our Civil Liberties

As early as 1969, in the United States Lange and his colleagues made the point that the policies of the First Amendment can no longer be secured simply by keeping the government out. They also argued that analysis is not values-free in research any more than reporting is in journalism. This is an observation that is repeated more and more often in recent literature on a whole host of social and environmental issues. Warnings are also being made that freedom of expression is, paradoxically, in grave danger *because* there is a lack of serious response to the problem of media violence. One of these surfaced in Comstock's 1991 analysis of research on knowledge, beliefs and perceptions resulting from greater exposure to violent media. He and his colleagues concluded that it is associated with an ideology favorable to the use of force and indifference to civil liberties.

Many scholars have argued that traditional media give us our perceptions of the world around us and have challenged the enduring myth that media provide "a free marketplace" in which everyone's ideas and opinions can be aired. In democracies, developed on the basis of classic liberalism, the media are expected to take an active role in the process of governance through criticism and vigilant observance. These functions have traditionally been encouraged by giving the press and other media of expression the same freedom of speech that we enjoy as individuals. Yet, today more than ever there is evidence that this is no longer tenable as more and more ownership of the media is concentrated into fewer and fewer hands. Certainly there are some mitigating influences from alternative and independent media, made possible by the wider availability of new communications technology, but for the most part, the mainstream media are controlled by dominant corporate interests unresponsive to social concerns.

The prevailing mood of the general populace tends to be one of confusion   30
and resignation on the basis of beliefs that effective regulation is not possible either because of the nature of new technology or because of the potential threat of "censorship." Others, including Canadian financial journalist, Linda McQuaig, argue that new communications technology, such as the Internet, offer greater potential than ever before for regulation in the interest of people rather than corporations and financial institutions.[19] Simplistic definitions merely add to the problem of public confusion and mitigate progress toward effective, long-term solutions that address issues of content as well as issues of ownership, copyright and privacy.

In fact, there is increasing evidence that censorship works best when it is least recognized. The cornerstone of a successful democracy is that its members learn to obey the rules that they collectively give themselves. Also, they must learn to *recognize* the rules that they have collectively given themselves, and distinguish them from rules that are being imposed upon them by dominant corporate interests under the guise of collective freedom and choice for everyone. One of the most important jobs facing adult educators today in the provision of public education is facilitating a better understanding of this crucial distinction. The main emphasis must include challenging the notion that corporations or enterprises are "persons" and therefore entitled to liberties guaranteed to persons. Anatol Rapoport, founder of a four-year peace and conflict studies program at the University of Toronto, and author of *The Origins of Violence* has spelled out some of the fundamental differences involved. There are stringent laws against killing persons.

> Corporations are routinely killed by other corporations (as in "hostile take-overs"), and there are no legal defenses against such "murders." Corporations can change heads. They do not have a natural life span. Unlike persons corporations don't have children, at any rate, are not responsible for lives of entities that might be regarded as their children. Therefore arguments invoking "freedom of expression," which must be taken seriously when applied to human individuals, should have no force with regard to corporations.[20]

Legal scholar, Stephen Sedley, has argued that there is little to be learned about either the philosophy or the policy of civil liberties from the general run of mass media and that there is a danger in letting political commentators and leading writers dictate or even shape our views on the subject. Most of the principles now accepted and supported by the media were, in fact, fought for and won by predecessors with a much broader concept of freedom of speech. Press freedom, for example, is seldom echoed by much press stridency in defense of the freedom of others to voice their views in a similar manner. Every day, newspaper editors decide which news items will be included and which ones will be rejected. Are they not practicing a form of censorship? Basic civil liberties have always had to be fought for in society on a more popular, widespread basis.

In his analysis of the political economy of the mass media, Noam Chomsky does not blame the press for limited discourse in Western society and explains that it has happened in every society since biblical times. Anyone who refuses to be subordinated to power will be marginalized and, while there are huge differences between the mechanisms and severity of social control in different societies, what is striking, he explained to *Peace Magazine* editor Metta Spencer in an interview, in 1995, in Toronto, is that the results are much the same in both free and totalitarian societies.

Certainly *principle* in defining civil liberties is fundamental, but it is not a unitary body of timeless criteria. It is a complex and shifting concept. The way in which anti-racism has become a principle because consensus has made it one is an example. Slavery is no longer perceived as a "right," as it still was by white European males who drafted the First Amendment in the United States. The genesis, consensus, and rationale of principles and rights are a complicated web of divergent ideas and movements over a period of decades that change as time passes. We have experienced modifications in our collective perceptions involving rights and freedoms in relation to cigarette smoking.

There are countless examples of how language, defined as "sexist" is being tolerated less than it once was.

At the same time, ecotheologians such as Thomas Berry in the U.S. are calling into question the concept of democracy itself and recommending that it be replaced with the concept of "biocracy." In such a framework our entire legal system, which now fosters a sense of human beings having rights on a level that ignores the rights of other species in the natural world and the rights of future generations of humans, would need to be reexamined According to Berry, "all our professions and institutions must be judged primarily by the extent to which they foster a mutually enhancing human-earth relationship."[21]

As a society, we have become more critical of what we perceive to be infringements on our basic freedoms and less cognizant of our duties, responsibilities, and obligations as citizens. In 1993, on behalf of the Government of Ontario, police superintendent Kenneth Turriff reported on his review of public perceptions of duties, responsibilities and obligations for Canadian citizenship. He argued that democracy, as we now know it, was in danger because of both the growing public demand for more privileges from "the system" and the Government's attempt to satisfy these demands.

From his computer search, Turriff discovered that the majority of treatises on freedom that included reference to either duties, responsibilities, or obligations, were written in the 1940s and that these gradually faded in number as the search moved into the area of publications of the 1970s, 1980s and 1990s. He also noted that "following the proclamation of the Charter of Rights and Freedoms in 1982, the primary focus of the literature pertaining to citizenship is on rights and freedoms." What Turriff's observations underscore is an increasingly simplified perception of what it means to live in a democratic society.

The diminishing appreciation for the cost of freedom, its importance in our lives and the ease with which it may be lost, needs to be reversed. More vigilant protection of our basic civil liberties becomes especially urgent upon close examination of the current information-based economy, not only because of the extra-ordinarily powerful influence the new communications technologies exert, but because of the growing complexity which surrounds their converging erosion of our democratic way of life. More questions need to be asked as to whether or not it is possible to pursue democracy and social justice at all when corporations are allowed to control so much wealth and power.

Following initiatives for a "Democracy Teach-In" at university campuses throughout the United States in October, 1996, Vigdor Schreibman reported on the CEM listserv that the breakdown of American democracy was visible everywhere. At the same time, he said, it was being pervasively denied because of its complexity and because of the "calamitous implications for the American myth."[22] In a survey done one month earlier it was discovered that very few faculty members appeared to be willing to speak out either in public or on their own campuses. This, in turn, was leading to a lack of student interest and activities in anything other than sports. The ideals of young Americans didn't even seem to include democratic politics anymore. Instead, they were adopting the attitude that there is no rational purpose for them to participate in a rigged and lopsided political system. Said Schreibman, "The bottom line is clear: when the next American generation becomes this nation's leaders, in the absence of fundamental reform, there will remain not even the ancient dream of democracy."

In this context the legal challenge launched against the Canadian Government by British Columbia lawyer, Connie Fogal, and the Defense of Canadian Liberty Committee in April, 1998, over negotiations of the Multilateral Agreement on Investment (MAI) then at the Paris based OECD, and now back at the WTO, offers an important opportunity for clarification of civil liberties, rights, and protection. In this case both the content of the Agreement and the process engaged in by the Canadian Government are being challenged. It is being argued that the MAI is a mechanism and structure that restricts—possibly even eliminates—the capacity of the Government to make and continue domestic law in the interest of citizens and the public good; that it paves the way for the spending of public monies without parliamentary approval; and that it is a vehicle which would eliminate adherence to the Constitutional framework and imperatives of Canada. Essentially, it would give:

> [S]overeign rights, without responsibilities, to international corporations and financial institutions, and it impedes, if not eradicates, mechanisms to maintain control over local, provincial property and civil rights, and renders impotent our judiciary with respect to these matters. . . . It will have the effect of granting corporations, non-natural persons as well as the minority of natural persons, rights over Canadians, their governments, and their courts, when those same corporations may be foreign owned and controlled by foreign "parent" affiliates.[23]

The kind of concerns, which the MAI has sparked globally, are precipitating a re-examination of democratic principles which may ultimately help to save them.

Progress Toward Harm Based Definitions

Many Americans have pointed out, that in helping to frame the First Amendment, Thomas Jefferson emphasized that their legal system must be responsive to changing historical conditions.[24] In 1986, in his book, *Amusing Ourselves to Death*, Neil Postman called for a ban on political commercials along with cigarette and liquor commercials. For those objecting on the basis that such a ban would violate the First Amendment he suggested a compromise not unlike the one proposed by Joyce Nelson for the CRTC two years later: "Require all political commercials to be preceded by a short statement to the effect that common sense has determined that watching political commercials is hazardous to the intellectual health of the community."[25] Throughout the world the rights of tobacco companies to advertise their products under the guise of freedom of expression are being challenged and these trends need to he broadened to encompass other toxic cultural messages as well.

In Canada, despite progress on harm based legislation for the protection of women and children, the debate over freedom of expression surrounding issues of pornography and the harmful impact of advertising on children is far from over. Although the courts are beginning to acknowledge that collective freedom from fear and abuse must take precedence over someone's right to amuse himself in any way he chooses, or sell anything for profit, regardless of the consequences, as ruled in the Butler and Irwin Toy cases, there is still very little evidence of real change in business and social practices. In 1999, the Butler decision was actually used as an excuse by the Toronto Police Force to ignore distribution and sales of the ultra violent novel *American Psycho*.

In her analysis of the debate over censorship as it applies to pornography, American legal scholar, Catherine Mackinnon, has discussed "the sexual politics of the First Amendment." She argues that, "Written by white men who owned slaves and regarded women as chattels it was drafted to guarantee *their* freedom to keep something they felt at risk of losing."[26] In actual fact it is harm-based rather than content-based and society at large is still fraught with disagreement as to whether women are or should be subordinated to men, especially in a sexual context. "The struggle against pornography," says Mackinnon, "is an abolitionist struggle to establish that just as buying and selling human beings never was anyone's property right, buying and selling women and children is no one's civil liberty."[27] Mackinnon has led the debate within the legal community, joining the themes of harm and equality in an effort to remove female pornography from the realm of First Amendment protection. Her assessment of the ongoing struggle against pornography, within the context of entrenched perceptions of civil liberties skewed in favor of dominant male interests, applies equally in the ongoing struggle against violence in the media. Just as pornography eroticizes hierarchy, media violence glamorizes it. In both cases the central dynamic is inequality on the basis of dominant-submissive relations.

In fact, the problem is reaching unprecedented proportions. When she testified on behalf of the Mahaffy and French families during their application hearing to have a section of the Criminal Code that allows the public access to evidence altered, Mackinnon said the tapes of the sexual assaults and murders of their daughters were no different from the ones on video store shelves only in this case we all knew how they had been made. As with other forms of pornography where bondage is often used to heighten the male's aggression and sexual arousal, it is extremely damaging to society.[28] There is no difference if the victimization involves real people as opposed to staged performers.

Despite warnings over the past decade from researchers, such as Miedzian, O'Connor, Dyer and Grossman on how civilian youth is socialized to be warlike and violent, the profit-driven appeal of violence as an industrial ingredient on a global basis continues to serve a patriarchal, male-dominated model for social and political organization. As many scholars including Berry have observed, the term "patriarchy" is now useful "to designate the deepest and most destructive level of determination in the Western perception of reality and value."[29] Subsequent criticism of these manifestations are now widely identified with the rising consciousness of women which, in turn, has given rise to popular post-secondary studies in "ecofeminism." Scilla Elworthy, founder of the Oxford Research Group in England, offers an insightful analysis of these connections in her book, published in 1996, about women entitled *Power & Sex.*

Freedom of Expression Not Corporate Freedom of Enterprise

The premise that better distinctions have to be made between individual freedom of expression and corporate freedom of enterprise is rapidly becoming a cruel understatement. Confusion between the two which allows for the blatant exploitation of children's value-systems, as in the case of "O.J. Halloween" costume items marketed for children in the fall of 1994 during the height of publicity surrounding the trial of O.J. Simpson in the State of California, along with distortions of civil liberties in mockeries made of fair-trial rights, as occurred in the Bernardo, Homolka and Simpson trials, must be better addressed by adult educators.[30]

There are other dimensions to media excesses which must also be addressed. It was not only the legal principle involving the "presumption of innocence" which was eroded by media opportunism when American Olympian athlete, Tonya Harding, was charged as an accomplice in the attack on rival skater Nancy Kerrigan as they both competed for prominence in the 1994 Winter Games. In that case, systemic violence which has infused professional sports was also a factor as it was when Canadian competitive athlete Ben Johnson was charged in 1988 with the illegal use of steroids, The pressure to win, fueled by the glamour of media attention, exacerbates and promotes these kind of deviancies.[31]

A more recent example emerged with the accidental death of World Wrestling Federation (WWF) performer, Owen Hart of Calgary, Alberta, in May, 1999, when a cable wire snapped while he was being lowered into the ring for a match in Kansas City, Missouri. It drew attention to the extra ordinary lengths to which Federation promoters will go in order to create a spectacle and draw audiences—all under the guise of "spectator sport."[32]

These examples illustrate how the ethical underpinnings to some of our basic institutions are in need of critical reexamination if we are serious about reclaiming our democratic freedoms in the current cultural environment. At the very least, it must be acknowledged, that while our news gathering media preoccupy themselves with sensationalism and trivial details, we are being unfairly distracted from more urgent matters such as the growing threats to our long term survival as a species from other forms of environmental degradation. But until we address the issue of cultural degradation it is unlikely that we will make much progress in other areas. Furthermore, as American

45

Technical Consultant Jeff Robbins argued at the *New World Order Conference* in Toronto, in June, 1999:

> Television, arguably the hands-down most successful and powerful panderer to the principle of least effort ever invented, is also the number one engine driving consumption around the globe . . . advancing technology is rendering people and human social structures increasingly addicted to consumption. It is this exponentially mounting dependency that will render futile any and all proposals for a sustainable future unless recognized and dealt with very soon.[33]

As Berry has pointed out, the creation of a new cultural coding in an ecological context is the current challenge in our collective human experience.

Notes

1. Haslett Cuff, 1998, May 2, *The Globe and Mail,* p. C6.
2. 1998, April 6.
3. 1998, May 4, p. D1.
4. Chan, 1999; Mitchell, 1999; Obmascik, 1999.
5. Howell, 1999; Kuxhaus, 1999; C-CAVE, 1999.
6. Tuck, 1999, May 18, *The Globe and Mail,* p. A1.
7. Scoffield, 1999, May 2, *The National Post,* p. A3.
8. C-CAVE, May 26, 1999.
9. Jenish, 1992, Dec. 7, *Maclean's Magazine,* p. 44.
10. Children's TV . . . , 1999, June 29, *The Globe and Mail,* p. C2.
11. Montgomery, 1989, p. 216.
12. Montgomery, 1989, p. 222.
13. Canada, June, 1999.
14. U.S. bill rips, 1996, Feb. 2, *The Globe and Mail,* p. A11.
15. Brown, 1999.
16. Brown, 1999.
17. Canadian Teachers Federation/CRTV, 1996.
18. "TV violence," 1997.
19. McQuaig, L. 1998. *The Cult of Impotence,* Toronto, London. NY: Viking.
20. Personal communication, December 7, 1995.
21. Berry, 1988, p. 212.
22. Schreibman, V. 1996. Oct. 21, personal communication.
23. Fogal. C., 1998, April 26, cfogal@netcom.ca; dweston@island.net
24. Miedzian, 1991; Postman, 1986; Schiller, 1989; Tofflet, 1980.
25. Postman, 1985, p. 159.
26. Mackinnon, 1987, p. 206.
27. Mackinnon, 1997, p. 213.
28. Rankin, 1996, p. A8.
29. Berry, 1988, p. 141.
30. "Sister-in-law," 1994, Oct. 18, *The Toronto Star,* p. A20.
31. Rasminsky, 1994, Feb. 10, *The Globe and Mail,* p. A25.
32. Mitchell, 1999, May 25, *The Globe and Mail,* p. A1.
33. Robbins, 1999, June 5. ◢

Reflections and Inquiries

1. Why didn't the 1989 Montreal Polytechnical Institute shootings have the same galvanizing effect on Canadians as the 1998 Littleton, Colorado massacre had on Americans?

2. What loophole did the media industry use to avoid strictures passed by the Children's Television Act of 1990?

3. Why, according to Dyson, is it a myth to consider broadcasting as a "free marketplace"?

4. Why is "corporate freedom of enterprise" not a part of "freedom of expression," according to Dyson? Why is it necessary to make a distinction?

Reading to Write

1. Dyson quotes media expert Kathryn Montgomery as saying that "the economic marketplace is not synonymous with a marketplace of ideas." In a short paper, defend or challenge this assertion in the context of the media violence issue, using Dyson's findings and your own outside reading.

2. Write an essay in which you attempt to define "harmful programming." Refer to Dyson's study and one or two others. Also allude to actual TV programs, past and present, for examples.

Statement Linking Media Violence to Violence in Kids Draws Criticism | Cheryl Arvidson

In 2000, four major health organizations, including the American Medical Association and the American Academy of Child & Adolescent Psychiatry, issued a statement attesting to overwhelming evidence of a connection between media violence and violent behavior in children. But a number of experts, including one psychiatrist, are not convinced that a significant connection exists. Journalist Cheryl Arvidson summarizes both sides of the issue in the following report.

Source: Arvidson, Cheryl. "Statement Linking Media Violence to Violence in Kids Draws Criticism." *The Freedom Forum Online.* 31 July 2000. Reprinted with permission of The Freedom Forum.

The decision by four major health organizations to issue a statement linking violent television shows, movies, music lyrics and video games to violence in children was a political one, not one based on conclusive scientific evidence, according to censorship foes and academics who have studied the existing research on violence and the media.

It's absolutely predictable in the current political climate," said Henry Jenkins, a professor of comparative media studies at the Massachusetts Institute of Technology, about the statement released last week in Washington at a Capitol Hill news conference convened by Sen. Sam Brownback, R-Kan.

"The mixture of the post-Columbine moral climate coupled with an election year is designed to feed the 'culture war' rhetoric," Jenkins said, referring to last year's massacre of 12 students and a teacher by two teen gunmen in a Denver suburb. "It feeds into the hands of various political groups that would like to set themselves up against popular culture for political gain."

"The question I have is, Where's the news here?" said Robert Corn-Revere, a First Amendment specialist with the Washington law firm of Hogan & Hartson. "This isn't based on some new research or new finding. It's not a medical or scientific statement. It's a political statement."

The four organizations issuing the statement—the American Medical Association, the American Academy of Pediatrics, the American Psychological Association, and the American Academy of Child & Adolescent Psychiatry said that more than 1,000 studies "point overwhelmingly to a causal connection between media violence and aggressive behavior in some children." 5

"The conclusion of the public health community, based on over 30 years of research, is that viewing entertainment violence can lead to increases in aggressive attitudes, values and behavior, particularly in children," the statement said.

"I know the research is not as definitive as people suggest it is and claim it is," said Joan Bertin, executive director of the National Coalition Against Censorship. "Why there is this movement in the medical community I don't know . . . but obviously, somebody has been doing some organizing."

Dr. Edward J. Hill, a spokesman for the American Medical Association, flatly disputed suggestions that the health groups were making a political statement. But he did acknowledge that the statement was issued at the behest of Brownback and some of his congressional colleagues who "wanted to raise the level of public awareness of the epidemic of violence and the youth of America."

"What's the political advantage of the American Medical Association to go out and talk about a link between media violence and violence?" Hill asked. "I don't see any political advantage to that. I think we have a professional and moral responsibility to point out that there is that link, and parents have to be extremely aware of this link. I think that is extremely responsible."

But Jonathan Freedman, a professor in the University of Toronto Department of Psychology who has studied the research on media violence and vio- 10 lent behavior, said he found the statement of the AMA and other health groups to be "irresponsible."

"It's incredible," he said. "The scientific evidence does not support what they are saying. In fact they claim that it does, and that is simply incorrect in my opinion."

Freedman said that although some studies suggest a causal link between entertainment violence and violent acts in children, "the majority of them do not. Normally, in science, you expect to get consistent results. It's irresponsible for any scientist to say that given the distribution of (these) results, this is proven."

Freedman, a psychologist, said he wouldn't be so upset if the medical groups had issued a statement saying they believed there was a link "based on our intuitions and experience. But putting it in terms of what scientific evidence shows is irresponsible and absolutely wrong. I would challenge the AMA to bring forth any member of their board who has read it (the research).

"First, you have to be trained to read it," he continued. "I imagine the doctors would have a great deal of difficulty reading this kind of research. Even if they were trained to do it, they would have to take the time to do it. It would take a year to read the research carefully. I don't blame them for not reading it; I just blame them for making a statement that suggests they have read it."

Hill, the AMA spokesman, conceded that neither he nor anyone on the   15
board had read the research, "but we have a science department that gives us the information that we utilize. We have to depend upon that science department. I suspect that our science department has thoroughly read that material."

Hill said suggestions that the scientific evidence is not definitive reminded him of the earlier debate over evidence linking tobacco to cancer.

"Forty years ago they said exactly the same thing about tobacco," he said. "Obviously, it has been quite proven that we were not irresponsible. This is another example of that type of rhetoric. They're condemning the quality of science behind this link that we think is a causal link between media violence and real violence in some people."

But Freedman said it was "really insulting" to compare the studies on television, movie, music or video game violence to the smoking and cancer studies. "There the evidence is extremely powerful and consistent and convincing. That is not the case with this kind of (violence) research," he said.

Bertin said that for several years, social scientists have sought to cast the media violence/youth violence debate as the same type of discussion identified cigarettes and guns as public health threats.

"The cause and effect between cigarettes and health and guns and health   20
are clear," she said. "But here, the link between viewing violence in some entertainment format and engaging in a criminal act is not at all clear."

Jenkins, who said he approached the question from the viewpoint of a "humanist" who studies issues of culture, said he was troubled when lawmakers trumpet "fairly simple-minded political solutions to complex problems."

"We're not dealing with this (youth violence) as a complex, cultural concern that requires multiple types of research to be brought together," he said. "That is not to say the media has no effect, it's just that it is much more complicated than the causal claim" cited by the health organizations.

Both Jenkins and Bertin said that when a group as prestigious as the AMA flatly endorses a link between media violence and violence in children, it raises the stakes in the debate and makes it more difficult to get to the heart of the problem.

"It's very, very hard to argue against the AMA because of the aura of authority that we ascribe to medicine and science in our current culture, which means to me the AMA should be more careful" in the positions it takes, Jenkins said. "I'm simply skeptical that my doctor has more to say than I do about the cultural causes of these problems. It's making judgments about things [the doctor] isn't qualified to evaluate."

Although most people "know instinctively that this (media violence) is   25
not what causes people to become violent and it's much more complicated than that . . . it is going to concern people," Berlin said. "It must be countered. I think to the casual observer, it certainly is going to have an influence."

"I wish these organizations had exerted better judgment than to start releasing statements about causal effects," agreed Corn-Revere, the First Amendment lawyer. "With some very limited exceptions, not even the social scientists who conduct the studies make such claims."

Bertin said one way to counter the argument of the health groups is to "go at it the other way and get the people who actually engage in crime and try to work backwards to determine what are the causative actions that actually precipitated this crime. They hardly ever talk about the media. That might be one way to bring a little more clarity to the discussion.

"I don't want to be an apologist for crummy television and movies," she continued. "That's not the point. The point is these claims of causation are not well founded, and they terribly . . . oversimplify a very complex problem."

Bertin said she was not suggesting that "there isn't an occasional person for whom this stimulus is important, but most people think . . . that the person for whom that kind of stimulus is the operative event is like an accident waiting to happen. If it weren't the TV show, it could be a comic book. That person is looking for an excuse, and finds it in the media he chooses to view."

Jenkins said the problem with current research on media violence and be-   30
havior is that cultural studies cannot be conducted in a sterile laboratory environment in the same way other medical research is done. For example, he said, "very few of us consume violent media in a sterile laboratory" and cultural factors have a major impact on how an individual reacts. Also, he said, just studying a "neurological response" does not factor in "how people interpret, translate, make sense of the type of violence they are consuming."

The studies also fail to make distinctions between the impact of different types of media violence on different age groups, he said, adding that the studies also measure only the immediate response to violence, but the effect may be quite different after some time has passed.

"There is no direct process we can follow between consuming media violence and committing violent crime," he said. "I think the really good work . . . is very cautious and very qualified." ◪

Reflections and Inquiries

1. On what grounds does Arvidson assert that the health organizations' statement linking media violence to violence in children is a political one? How did the health experts making the statement counterargue? Whose views seem most convincing, and why?

2. One health expert, psychology professor Jonathan Freedman, finds the statement to be irresponsible. On what grounds does he make this assertion?

3. What is problematic about "claims of causation," according to some critics of the statement?

4. What makes research into the media violence effects on children so difficult, according to media expert Henry Jenkins?

Reading to Write

Given the complexity of establishing a causal link between media violence and violence in children, write a paper in which you argue for the best way to proceed. Should we do nothing to curb the kinds or frequency of violence in video games, TV shows, or movies? Why? Or should we take the opposite track and censor excessively violent shows (assuming we can reach consensus on what "excessively violent" means)? Should we design new kinds of experiments? What kinds?

Major Studios Used Children to Test-Market Violent Films | Doreen Carvajal

When nine motion picture studies submitted confidential documents to a government commission assigned to investigate ways in which entertainment with violent content was marketed, it was learned that children were being used to test-market movies and other media products they would not be allowed to purchase on their own. Efforts to control this abuse of the system may prove difficult because the motion picture and video game industries, not a federal agency, determine industry standards, reflected in the G/PG-13/R/ rating system. In the following investigative report, *New York Times* journalist Doreen Carvajal discloses some surprising facts about the appeal of media violence to children and teenagers.

Before the Hollywood Pictures unit of Disney released the R-rated Sylvester Stallone movie *Judge Dredd*, about urban anarchy and street war, the studio tested the film before a focus group that included more than 100 youths ages 13 to 16.

MGM/United Artists tested commercials for *Disturbing Behavior*, an R-rated horror thriller about troublemaking teenagers transformed into upstanding citizens, before more than 400 12- to 20-year-olds. A survey reported that they felt the "stand-out scene" was one of a blonde bashing her head into a mirror.

Columbia Tristar's researchers interviewed 50 children ages 9 to 11 to evaluate concepts for the sequel to *I Know What You Did Last Summer*, a tale of a serial slasher equipped with an outsized ice hook.

"There is evidence to indicate that attendance in the original movie dipped down to the age of 10," explained a memorandum from the National Research Group, the dominant market research organization for major studios. "Therefore, it seems to make sense to interview 10- to 11-year-olds."

These incidents and others are recorded in confidential marketing documents submitted by nine movie studios to the government commission that investigated the marketing of violent entertainment to children and teenagers, who are frequent moviegoers. Those documents show that some of the biggest companies in Hollywood routinely recruited scores of teenagers and children as young as 9 to evaluate story concepts, commercials, theatrical trailers and rough cuts for R-rated movies.

Yesterday [September 26, 2000], the movie industry's trade association, the Motion Picture Association of America, announced steps to restrict its marketing of R-rated films to under-age children. Among them is a pledge not to use children under 17 in test screenings unless they are accompanied by an adult. An R-rated movie requires that anyone under 17 be accompanied by an adult because of explicit violent or sexual content. The rating, like all movie ratings, is the industry's own standard, subject only to its own policing.

Jack Valenti, the trade association's chairman, said a report by the Federal Trade Commission has prompted studios to take "a fresh new look at the way we market films."

The industry's program is the latest reaction to the commission's sharply critical report of marketing practices in the movie, music, and video-game industries. Citing regulations prohibiting it from releasing trade secrets, the report did not reveal the names of the entertainment companies involved or the details of the marketing campaigns. Those are contained in the supporting documents, which were obtained by *The New York Times.*

Eight movie studio executives are scheduled to testify today [September 27, 2000] before the Senate Commerce Committee about their policies. At the first committee hearing, two weeks [earlier], Mr. Valenti conceded that perhaps marketing people "stepped over the line" but argued that the location of that line was "ill lit, hazily observed." . . .

In their own marketing plans submitted to the trade commission, the major movie studios offered a window into practices that can begin almost as soon as a movie is conceived. Preliminary test screenings are conducted months before films appear in theaters.

Recruiters hunt for moviegoers in movie lines or malls offering free tickets to people who match the age and ethnic profile set by the studios. And the results ultimately can shape promotions, advertising, and decisions for a movie sequel. . . .

. . . Toy tie-ins to PG-13 movies, which caution that violent material may be "inappropriate" for children under 13, broaden the promotion of those films to children as young as 4. . . .

In the case of *Judge Dredd,* Hollywood Pictures tested the film with a broad group that included a subset of 13- to 16-year-olds. The participants were asked to rate everything from the movie's music and action to its ending and its hero, played by Mr. Stallone. Participants also rated every movie scene, including a robot ripping off a man's arms and a plane crashing into a prison.

Later, the company's researchers tested the movie's five commercials before 1,800 people, who included participants as young as 12. And those surveys, along with the earlier movie ratings, detected a clear pattern of enthusiasm among one age group: young teenagers, particularly males. . . .

The goal, as outlined in a memorandum from National Research Group, was plain: "to determine who are the most intense fans of the movie by age, gender, ethnicity, et cetera, and what drives their zeal. The results will help define the primary and secondary targets and what about the movie most appeals to them. It will also provide information on the key aspects of the original movie most liked and guidance for direction of the second movie."

Columbia was even more aggressive about focusing on a younger audience for the futuristic science-fiction thriller *The Fifth Element*, a PG-13 film that starred Bruce Willis as a 23rd century ex-soldier and cabdriver turned galactic hero.

The studio sought to advertise the movie on the children's network Nickelodeon. MTV Networks, which oversees Nickelodeon, refused to allow an advertisement because it considered the movie inappropriate for its viewers, who are mostly under 12.

"There are several gun battles, a couple of fight sequences and some devastating bomb blasts," an MTV executive wrote to representatives of Columbia. "Finally the sexual situations are well removed from Nickelodeon's sphere—the talk show host performing cunnilingus on a female singer."

The studio unsuccessfully appealed the ban, arguing in part that the science-fiction genre required a suspension of belief and that the violence would be suspect to "the children of today who are more sophisticated." In addition, it noted in a memorandum, "This film needs the audience that Nickelodeon provides to be successful."

The quest for the under-17 market reflects certain realities of moviegoing   20
habits. Studies from the Motion Picture Association of America indicate, for example, that the group ages 12 to 17 accounts for 17 percent of movie audiences, a figure disproportionate to their actual share of the population, which is 10 percent.

When MGM/United Artists was preparing to release its R-rated film *Disturbing Behavior*, researchers started tracking the interest and awareness among a sampling of 331 10- to 20-year-olds and a broader group of 400 12- to 59-year-olds.

Later, the studio screened two 30-second commercials among 438 moviegoers 12 to 20. In a scene-by-scene rating of the commercials, viewers evaluated such fleeting moments as a "needle toward clamped eye" and a girl bashing her head into a mirror.

"The stand-out scenes continue to be the blonde hitting her head in the mirror," the researchers reported. . . .

Perhaps the most blunt and candid appraisal of the youthful audience for violent entertainment comes in two marketing memorandums for restricted video games called Turok and Duke Nukem Zero Hour, which features a foul-mouthed alien-annihilator who, according to promotional material, is notable for "spitting more one-liners than Rodney Dangerfield while building the body count." Both carry an M rating, which bars their sale to children under 17. Like movie ratings, video ratings are the industry's own, not regulated by law. . . .

In another marketing plan, Acclaim Entertainment, the makers of the   25
M-rated Turok series, explains why the primary audience for the video remains males 12 to 17, even through these consumers cannot buy the material by themselves. The Turok series has sold more than 3 million units on the strength of weapons features like the "all-powerful Chest-Burster."

"Turok has an M rating, which may discourage parents from buying the game and hinder clearance of a commercial airing in shows primarily for children under 12," observed the marketing report. "However, the younger the audience, the more likely they are to be influenced by TV advertising. Adults are more likely to evaluate software purchases based on more extensive research." ◾

Reflections and Inquiries

1. What rationale do motion picture executives give for testing R-rated films on children much younger than seventeen?

2. Even though the head of the Motion Picture Association of America, Jack Valenti, admits that marketing researchers "stepped over the line" by testing R-rated movies on underage children, he also adds that it was difficult to locate that line. Discuss the logic or illogic of this response.

3. What sorts of reactions do children and teenagers have on the films tested on them?

4. What realities of moviegoing habits are reflected by the effort to test R-rated films on an under-seventeen population?

Reading to Write

Drawing from information provided by Carvajal's report, write an essay supporting or criticizing the motion picture industry's marketing research practices.

TV Isn't Violent Enough | Mike Oppenheim

Perhaps experiencing violence vicariously through books, movies, and games is good for us. Aristotle used the word *catharsis* to describe the purging effect that witnessing something horrific (such as Oedipus's blinding himself after realizing his tragic misdeeds) has on our emotions. Such emotional release might *prevent* us from being violent ourselves. Freelance writer and physician Mike Oppenheim works with this idea in the following essay. Could it be true that if the media depicted violence more accurately and graphically—as in real life—we would find it completely unappealing?

Source: Oppenheim, Mike. "TV Isn't Violent Enough." *TV Guide* 11 Feb. 1984: 20–21. Reprinted with permission from TV Guide Magazine Group, Inc., © 1984 TV Guide Magazine Group, Inc., February 1984. TV GUIDE is a registered trademark of TV Guide Magazine Group, Inc.

Caught in an ambush, there's no way our hero (Matt Dillon, Eliot Ness, Kojak, Hoss Cartwright . . .) can survive. Yet, visibly weakening, he blazes away, and we suspect he'll pull through. Sure enough, he's around for the final clinch wearing the traditional badge of the honorable but harmless wound: a sling.

As a teenager with a budding interest in medicine, I knew this was nonsense and loved to annoy my friends with the facts.

"Aw, the poor guy! He's crippled for life!"

"What do you mean? He's just shot in the shoulder."

"That's the worst place! Vital structures everywhere. There's the blood   5 supply for the arm: axillary artery and vein. One nick and you can bleed to death on the spot."

"So he was lucky."

"OK. If it missed the vessels it hit the brachial plexus: the nerve supply. Paralyzes his arm for life. He's gotta turn in his badge and apply for disability."

"So he's *really* lucky."

"OK. Missed the artery. Missed the vein. Missed the nerves. Just went through the shoulder joint. But joint cartilage doesn't heal so well. A little crease in the bone leaves him with traumatic arthritis. He's in pain the rest of his life—stuffing himself with codeine, spending his money on acupuncture and chiropractors, losing all his friends because he complains all the time. . . . Don't ever get shot in the shoulder. It's the end. . . ."

Today, as a physician, I still sneer at TV violence, though not because of any moral objection. I enjoy a well-done scene of gore and slaughter as well as   10 the next viewer, but "well-done" is something I rarely see on a typical evening in spite of the plethora of shootings, stabbings, muggings, and brawls. Who can believe the stuff they show? Anyone who remembers high-school biology knows the human body can't possibly respond to violent trauma as it's usually portrayed.

☒   ☒   ☒

On a recent episode, Matt Houston is at a fancy resort, on the trail of a vicious killer who specializes in knifing beautiful women in their hotel rooms in broad daylight. The only actual murder sequence was in the best of taste: all the action off screen, the flash of a knife, moans on the sound track.

In two scenes, Matt arrives only minutes too late. The hotel is alerted, but the killer's identity remains a mystery, Absurd! It's impossible to kill someone instantly with a knife thrust—or even render him unconscious. Several minutes of strenuous work are required to cut enough blood vessels so the victim bleeds to death. Tony Perkins in *Psycho* gave an accurate, though abbreviated, demonstration. Furthermore, anyone who has watched an inexperienced farmhand slaughter a pig knows that the resulting mess must be seen to be believed.

If consulted by Matt Houston, I'd have suggested a clue: "Keep your eyes peeled for someone panting with exhaustion and covered with blood. That might be your man."

Many Americans were puzzled at the films of the assassination attempt on President Reagan. Shot in the chest, he did not behave as TV had taught us to expect ("clutch chest, stagger backward, collapse"). Only after he complained of a vague chest pain and was taken to the hospital did he discover his wound. Many viewers assumed Mr. Reagan is some sort of superman. In fact, there was nothing extraordinary about his behavior. A pistol is certainly a deadly weapon, but not predictably so. Unlike a knife wound, one bullet can kill instantly—provided it strikes a small area at the base of the brain. Otherwise, it's no different: a matter of ripping and tearing enough tissue to cause death by bleeding. Professional gangland killers understand the problem. They prefer a shotgun at close range.

☑   ☑   ☑

The trail of quiet corpses left by TV's good guys, bad guys, and assorted ill-tempered gun owners is ridiculously unreal. Firearms reliably produce pain, bleeding, and permanent, crippling injury (witness Mr. Reagan's press secretary, James Brady: shot directly in the brain but very much alive). For a quick, clean death, they are no match for Luke Skywalker's light saber.   15

No less unreal is what happens when T. J. Hooker, Magnum, or a Simon brother meets a bad guy in manly combat. Pow! Our hero's fist crashes into the villain's head. Villain reels backward, tipping over chairs and lamps, finally falling to the floor, unconscious. Handshakes all around. . . . Sheer fantasy! After hitting the villain, our hero would shake no one's hand. He'd be too busy waving his own about wildly, screaming with the pain of a shattered fifth metacarpal (the bone behind the fifth knuckle), an injury so predictable it's called the "boxer's fracture." The human fist is far more delicate than the human skull. In any contest between the two, the fist will lose.

The human skull is tougher than TV writers give it credit. Clunked with a blunt object, such as the traditional pistol butt, most victims would not fall conveniently unconscious for a few minutes. More likely, they'd suffer a nasty scalp laceration, be stunned for a second or two, then be extremely upset. I've sewn up many. A real-life, no-nonsense criminal with a blackjack (a piece of iron weighing several pounds) has a much better success rate. The result is a large number of deaths and permanent damage from brain hemorrhage.

☑   ☑   ☑

Critics of TV violence claim it teaches children sadism and cruelty. I honestly don't know whether or not TV violence is harmful, but if so the critics have it backward. Children can't learn to enjoy cruelty from the neat, sanitized mayhem on the average series. There isn't any! What they learn is far more malignant: that guns or fists are clean, efficient, exciting ways to deal with a difficult situation. Bang!—you're dead! Bop!—you're unconscious (temporarily)!

"Truth-in-advertising" laws eliminated many absurd commercial claims. I often daydream about what would happen if we had "truth in violence"—if every show had to pass scrutiny by a board of doctors who had no power to censor but could insist that any action scene have at least a vague resemblance to medical reality ("Stop the projector! . . . You have your hero waylaid by three Mafia thugs who beat him brutally before he struggles free. The next day he shows up with this cute little Band-aid over his eyebrow. We can't pass that. You'll have to add one eye swollen shut, three missing front teeth, at least twenty stitches over the lips and eyes, and a wired jaw. Got that? Roll 'em . . .").

Seriously, real-life violence is dirty, painful, bloody, disgusting. It causes   20
mutilation and misery, and it doesn't solve problems. It makes them worse. If we're genuinely interested in protecting our children, we should stop campaigning to "clean up" TV violence. It's already too antiseptic. Ironically, the problem with TV violence is: It's not violent enough. ◪

Reflections and Inquiries

1. Oppenheim published his essay in 1984 and is alluding to TV shows of that time. Does his premise still hold true with regard to current TV shows? Give examples one way or another.

2. Why are depictions of gun murders on TV often "ridiculously unreal"?

3. What specifically makes the typically unrealistic depictions of TV murders much more dangerous than realistic ones?

4. Is Oppenheim being entirely serious when he says that TV isn't violent enough? Why or why not?

Reading to Write

How convincing is Oppenheim's support of his thesis? Write an essay in which you defend or challenge his views, referring to his reasons as well as those from one or two other sources.

Violent Content on Television | W. James Potter

In the following study, W. James Potter, a professor of communication at Florida State University and author of Media Literacy, identifies twenty-four facets of television violence, which he divides into four categories: (1) presence of violence on TV, (2) the characters perpetrating the violent acts, (3) the contexts in which the violence occurs, and (4) patterns of TV violence in other countries.

Social scientists have published more than 60 separate analyses of violent content on television around the world (see Tables 4.1 and 4.2). These content analyses began almost as early as television broadcasting itself, and they continue today. They have been especially numerous since 1980. Although most of these studies have been conducted by independent scholars—usually university professors—some have been conducted by citizen action groups (Center for Media and Public Affairs, 1994; Lichter & Lichter, 1983; "NCTV Says," 1983); some have been funded by industry groups (Cole, 1995, 1996; *National Television Violence Study*, 1997, 1998) or private foundations (Kunkel et al., 1988); and some have been conducted by the television industry itself (Columbia Broadcasting System, 1980).

Within this activity, three content analysis projects stand out as major because of their groundbreaking nature, their size, and their influence. First is the series of content analyses of physical violence by George Gerbner and his colleagues at the University of Pennsylvania. This study is noteworthy because the same methods were used each year for 22 years beginning in 1967. Second, Bradley Greenberg and his colleagues conducted a 3-year analysis of television programming in the mid-1970s. This study is important, because it broadened the examination of physical violence to include verbal aggression and other forms of antisocial activity. Third is the *National Television Violence Study* (NTVS), which was funded for 3 years by the National Cable Television Association. Although it narrowed the focus again to physical violence, it analyzed narratives at three levels: macro level (the entire program), midlevel (the scene), and micro level (the violent act). It also had the best sample of any content analysis of television. Its composite week of more than 3,000 hours of programming for each of 3 years is a representative sample of all television programming across 23 channels in all parts of the day.

The content analysis literature on media violence has focused almost exclusively on the medium of television. One exception is the work of Clark and Blankenburg (1972), who compared violence across several mass media: movies, television, novels, popular magazine fiction, comic books, and newspapers.

TABLE 4.1	**Content Analyses of Television Violence in the United States**	
Year	*Author(s)*	*Source*
1954	Head, S. W.	*Quarterly of Film, Radio, and Television* 9, 175–194
1954	Smythe, D. W.	*Public Opinion Quarterly* 18, 143–156
1961	Schramm, Lyle, & Parker	*Television in the lives of our children*
1963	Lyle & Wilcox	*Journal of Broadcasting*, 7, 157–166
1972	Clark & Blankenburg	*Television and social behavior*, vol. 1, 188–243
1972	Gerbner, G.	*Television and social behavior*, vol. 1, 28–187
1973	Dominick, J.	*Public Opinion Quarterly* 37, 241–250
1976	Gerbner & Gross	*Journal of Communication* 26(2), 172–199
1976	Poulos, Harvey, & Liebert	*Psychological Reports* 39, 1047–1057
1976	Slaby, Quarfoth, & McConnachie	*Journal of Communication* 26(1), 88–96
1977	CBS, Office of Social Research	(nothing cited in book's original references)
1977	Franzblau, Sprafkin, & Rubinstein	*Journal of Communication* 27(2), 164–170
1977	Gerbner, Gross, Eleey, Jackson-Beck, Jeffries-Fox, & Signorielli	*Journal of Communication* 27(2), 171–180
1978	Gerbner, Gross, Jackson-Beck, Jeffries-Fox, & Signorielli	*Journal of Communication* 28(3), 176–207
1979	Harvey, Sprafkin, & Rubinstein	*Journal of Broadcasting* 23, 179–189
1980	Columbia Broadcasting System	*Network prime time violence tabulation for 1978–79 season*
1980	Gerbner, Gross, Morgan, & Signorielli	*Journal of Communication* 30(3), 10–29
1980	Gerbner, Gross, Signorielli, & Morgan	*Journal of Communication* 30(1), 37–47
1980	Greenberg, Edison, Korzenny, Fernandez-Collado, & Atkin	*Life on television*, 99–128
1982	Gerbner, Gross, Morgan, & Signorielli	*Journal of Communication*, 32(2), 100–127
1982	Kaplan, S. J. & Baxter, L. A.	*Journalism Quarterly* 59, 478–482
1983	Estep & Macdonald	*Journalism Quarterly* 60, 293–300
1983	Lichter, L. S. & Lichter, S. R.	*Prime time crime*
1983	"NCTV Says"	*Broadcasting Magazine*, March 22, p. 63

(continued)

TABLE 4.1	*(continued)*	
Year	*Author(s)*	*Source*
1985	Baxter, Riemer, Landini,	*Journal of Broadcasting & Electronic Media*
	Leslie, & Singletary	*29*, 333–340
1986	Brown & Campbell	*Journal of Communication 36(1)*, 94–106
1986	Gerbner, Gross, Morgan, & Signorielli	*Perspectives in media effects*, 17–40
1986	Sherman & Dominick	*Journal of Communication 36(1)*, 79–93
1987	Potter, W. J. & Ware, W.	*Communication Research 14*, 664–686
1992	Lichter, S. R. & Amundson, D.	*A day of television violence*
1993	Sommers-Flanagan, Sommers-Flanagan, & Davis	*Sex Roles 28*, 745–753
1994	Center for Media and Public Affairs	*Violence in prime time television*
1994	Oliver, M. B.	*Journal of Broadcasting & Electronic Media 38*, 175–192
1995	Cole, J.	*The UCLA television violence monitoring report*
1995	Potter, Vaughan, Warren, Howley, Land, & Hagemeyer	*Journal of Broadcasting & Electronic Media 39*, 496–516
1996	Cole, J.	*The UCLA television violence monitoring report*
1997	*National Television Violence Study*	Vol. 1
1997	Potter, Warren, Vaughan, Howley, Land, & Hagemeyer	*Communication Research Reports 14*, 116–124
1998	Cole, J.	*The UCLA television violence monitoring report*
1998	Kunkel, Farinola, Cope, Donnerstein, Biely, & Zwarun	*Rating the TV ratings*
1998	*National Television Violence Study*	Vol. 2
1999	*National Television Violence Study*	Vol. 3

TABLE 4.2   **Summary of Content Findings**

The Presence of Violence in the Television World

1. Prevalence of violence is widespread.
2. Prevalence of violence varies across types of programs.
3. Rates of violence are high.
4. Rates of violence fluctuate across different types of programs.
5. Rates are higher for verbal violence than for physical violence.
6. As for duration, violence appears in only a small percentage of time in television programming.
7. Rates are shifting from major to minor types of violence.
8. Violent crime is much more frequent on TV than in real life.

Profiles of Characters Involved with Violence

9. Most perpetrators are males.
10. Most perpetrators are white.
11. Most perpetrators are middle-aged.
12. Victims and perpetrators are similar demographically.
13. A high proportion of the violence is committed by "good" characters.

The Context of Violent Portrayals

14. Most of the violence is intentional, and usually the motives are not prosocial.
15. Consequences for the victims are rarely shown.
16. The perpetrators often are not punished.
17. Much of the violence is justified.
18. Weapons are often found in violent acts.
19. The presentation style is rarely graphic and explicit.
20. Much of the violence is portrayed in a humorous context.
21. Violence is often shown in a fantasy context or in an unrealistic pattern.

Patterns in Countries Other Than the United States

22. The United States leads the world in the prevalence of violence on television.
23. Character portrayals generally conform to U.S. patterns.
24. Context generally conforms to U.S. patterns.

But despite this narrow focus on one medium, the literature still exhibits a wide diversity of methodological features. This variety is one of the most positive characteristics of the content analysis literature. When we see some findings emerge consistently across many different studies, we can be confident that those findings are fairly robust.

The following sections list 24 findings in four categories: (a) the presence of violence in the television world, (b) profiles of characters involved with violence, (c) the context of violent portrayals, and (d) patterns in countries other than the United States.

The Presence of Violence in the Television World

1. *Prevalence of violence is widespread.* Regardless of the definition, the units of analysis, the sample, or the types of coders, content analyses consistently find that violence is prevalent across the entire television landscape. Such has been found to be the case across a wide range of studies by academics (e.g., see Gerbner, Gross, Morgan, & Signorielli, 1980; Greenberg, Edison, Korzenny, Fernandez-Collado, & Atkin, 1980; *National Television Violence Study*, 1997, 1998; Potter et al., 1995; Potter & Ware, 1987; Schramm, Lyle, & Parker, 1961; Smythe, 1954; Williams, Zabrack, & Joy, 1982), citizen activists (Lichter & Lichter, 1983; "NCTV Says," 1983), and members of the television industry itself (Columbia Broadcasting System, 1980).

For example, Gerbner and Signorielli (1990), looking back over the 22 years of their content analyses, reported that 80% of all analyzed shows (three networks during prime time and Saturday morning) contained violence. The NTVS found violence in 60% of the 9,000 programs it analyzed across 23 channels and 3 years (Smith et al., 1999). The Center for Media and Public Affairs (1994) found that 68% of all series contained at least one violent scene.

2. *Prevalence of violence varies across types of programs.* Although violence is found across the entire television landscape, certain types or shows exhibit a higher prevalence than others (Smith et al., 1999; Wilson et al., 1997, 1998). The NTVS found that premium cable channels show the highest prevalence of violence, with 85% of its programs containing some physical violence, followed by basic cable channels (59%), independent channels (55%), commercial broadcast networks (44%), and public broadcast stations (18%). As for genres, 90% of all movies contained some violence, followed by drama series (72%), children's series (66%), music videos (31%), reality-based programs (30%), and comedy series (27%).

- *Nonfiction.* Lyle and Wilcox (1963) analyzed Los Angeles television and found that 17.5% of the items were stories about crime, major news accidents, and disasters. This figure compared to only 13.2% of stories devoted to these categories in four local newspapers. Several years later, Clark and Blankenburg (1972) found the same results in an analysis of national television news and four large newspapers, with 44.6% of the stories on television displaying violence, whereas only 25.0% of the stories in newspapers dealt with violence. More recently, the NTVS found that 38% of its 384 ana-lyzed nonfiction programs contained visual violence, and another 18% con-tained talk about violence (Whitney et al., 1997).

- *Music Videos.* There is also a high prevalence of violence in music videos. For example, Baxter, Riemer, Landini, Leslie, and Singletary (1985) analyzed 62 MTV videos and found that 53% contained violence. Sherman and Dominick (1986) analyzed 166 concept (nonperformance) videos and found that more than 56% of all videos contained some violence. Brown and Campbell (1986) analyze 112 videos on MTV and Black Entertainment Tele-vision and found that half of all characters engaged in some form of antiso-cial behavior. Sommers-Flanagan, Sommers-Flanagan, and Davis (1993) broke their 40 MTV videos down into 313 segments and found that only 6% of all segments showed explicit aggression, but another 25% of segments contained implicit aggression.

- *Children's Programming.* Schramm et al. (1961) found that more than half of the programs children were most likely to watch displayed violence that played an important part in the narratives. Gerbner says that children's Sat-urday morning programs are by far the most violent genre (Gerbner & Si-gnorielli, 1990). From 1967 to 1985, 94% of all children's (weekend daytime) programming contained violence. In addition, 81.7% of all leading charac-ters were involved in violence (Signorielli, 1990).

3. *Rates of violence are high.* The number of violent acts per hour remains high across the television landscape in general, although the rate fluctuates from study to study and from year to year. Reported rates of physical aggres-sion range from a low of 5 acts per hour (Center for Media and Public Affairs, 1994) upward to 8.1 (Potter & Ware, 1987), 8.7 (Potter et al., 1995), 9.0 (Williams et al., 1982), 10.0 (Lichter & Amundson, 1992), and 14.6 (Greenberg et al., 1980). Some of this variation is due to differences in methods across studies.

When the definitions of violence, sampling, and units of analysis are re-peated each year, there are still fluctuations, as demonstrated by Gerbner and Signorielli (1990), who reported regular cycles of rates from 6.7 to 9.5 acts per hour over the 22 years of their analyses.

4. *Rates of violence fluctuate across different types of programs.* Such fluctua-tion is especially apparent when verbal violence is also documented. For ex-ample, Potter and Ware (1987) report higher rates of aggression (physical and verbal) in some program types, such as action adventure programs (44.3 acts per hour), compared with situation comedies (25.0), episodic series (15.9), and continuing series (14.8).

- *Nonfiction.* Rates of violence are high in nonfiction programming (Oliver, 1994; Potter et al., 1997), but usually not as high as in fictional programming (Lichter & Amundson, 1992; Potter et al., 1995; Smith et al., 1999; Wilson et al., 1997, 1998). For example, Potter et al. (1997) found the rate of antisocial activity on reality-based programs to be 32.5 acts per hour, and within the set of reality-based programming, national news shows had the highest rate, 44.5 acts per hour. Using the same definition, Potter et al. (1995) found the rate to be 38.2 for fictional programming.

- *Music Videos.* Sherman and Dominick (1986) analyzed 166 concept (nonperformance) videos and found an average of 2.9 acts per violent video.

- *Children's Programming.* Studies that compare violence across genres have consistently found Saturday morning cartoons to be the highest on physical violence. From the earliest days of television, the programming designated for children has exhibited very high rates of physical violence (Gerbner & Signorielli, 1990; Greenberg et al., 1980; Poulos, Harvey, & Liebert, 1976; Schramm et al., 1961; Smythe, 1954). Smythe found that children's drama had more than three times the rate of violence than general-audience drama (22.4 vs. 6.0 acts per hour), but that the highest rate (36.6) was in children's comedy drama. Gerbner and Signorielli said that children's Saturday morning programs are by far the most violent genre. From 1967 to 1985, children's programming exhibited a rate of 20.1 violent acts per hour, which is three times the average found on prime-time television (Gerbner & Signorielli, 1990). Greenberg et al. found that the rate of physical violence on Saturday morning cartoons (25.9 acts per hour) was 40% higher than for the next genre—action-adventure programs (18.3 acts per hour).

- *Situation Comedies.* Although situation comedies have low rates of physical violence, they consistently have the highest rates of verbal violence (Greenberg et al., 1980; Potter et al., 1997; Williams et al., 1982). For example, Greenberg found a rate of 33.2 acts of verbal violence per hour in the mid-1970s, and the same rate was found 20 years later (Potter & Vaughan, 1997).

5. *Rates are higher for verbal violence than for physical violence.* Studies that look at both physical and verbal forms of violence have consistently found verbal forms to occur more frequently. Williams et al. (1982) found a ratio of 1.1 acts of verbal aggression to every act of physical aggression in their analysis of American and Canadian prime-time television in 1980. Potter and Ware (1987) reported a ratio of 1.4:1 in prime-time television in 1985. Greenberg et al. (1980) reported a ratio of about 1.8:1. Potter and Vaughan (1997) found a ratio of 2.4:1. Of course, definitions and samples differ across these studies, but even so, the findings are so robust that they continue to emerge: Verbal aggression is at least as prevalent as physical aggression on television.

6. *As for duration, violence appears in only a small percentage of time in television programming.* Less than 5% of programming time is violent. For example, Gerbner. Gross, Signorielli, Morgan, and Jackson-Beeck (1979b) examined 10 years of data and found a range of 2.2 to 3.7 min/hr (an average of 2.4). Thus, only 4% of the time was there violence on the screen in the United States. The NTVS found a difference in duration depending on the type of program. With reality-based shows (public affairs, talk, documentaries, but not breaking news), 3.3%

of program time contained visual violence, and another 2.4% exhibited talk about violence (Whitney et al., 1997). In fictional programs, the duration was much higher (12.9%), largely because the coding of fictional violence included the time for threats that built up to the violent act (Wilson et al., 1997).

7. *Rates are shifting from major to minor types of violence.* To see this trend, we need to consider both physical and verbal forms of violence. For example, Potter and Vaughan (1997) replicated the study of Greenberg et al. (1980) to see if rates of different types of violence changed from the mid-1970s to the mid-1990s. They found that overall rates of physical violence stayed the same (12.7 vs. 12.3 acts per hour), but rates of verbal violence had climbed (from 22.8 to 27.0). This change is even more clear with two genres in particular. With situation comedies, the rate of physical violence stayed the same (7.2 acts per hour), but the rate of verbal violence went up from 33.5 to 41.9 acts per hour. With action-adventure programs, physical violence stayed about the same (18.2 vs. 21.5), but verbal violence went up (from 22.0 to 28.6).

8. *Violent crime is much more frequent on TV than in real life.* In his analysis of prime-time drama and comedy, Dominick (1973) reported that 60% of all programs portrayed at least one crime, with murder and assault ranked as the two most frequent crimes. In real life, burglary and larceny are the two most prevalent crimes.

Oliver (1994) reported that in reality-based police shows, 87% of criminal suspects were associated with violent crimes, but only 13% of all crimes in the real world are violent; therefore these TV shows greatly overrepresent violent crime. On television, 49.7% of all crimes were murders, compared to less than 0.2% in the United States. The TV world also displays inflated percentages of robbery (19.5% on TV vs. 5.0% in real life) and aggravated assault (14.8% vs. 7.0%).

Profiles of Characters Involved with Violence

9. *Most perpetrators are males.* It is much more rare to see a female committing an act of violence compared to a male (Dominick, 1973; Gerbner, Gross, Morgan, & Signorielli, 1980; Greenberg et al., 1980; National Television Violence Study, 1997, 1998; Potter et al., 1995; Potter & Ware, 1987; Poulos et al., 1976; Williams et al., 1982). The percentage of perpetrators who are males ranges from about 71% to 85%. For example, Poulos et al. analyzed the content of children's Saturday morning television programs and found that 71% of all characters (376 human and 142 animal characters) were male. They said, "Inasmuch as males tended to be portrayed as more aggressive but less sympathetic or understanding than females, the image of males as both more potent and more callous than females is being perpetuated" (p. 1055).

10. *Most perpetrators are white.* It is much more rare to see an ethnic minority committing an act of violence compared to a white character (Dominick, 1973; Gerbner, Gross, Signorielli, & Morgan, 1980; Greenberg et al., 1980; *National Television Violence Study*, 1997, 1998; Potter et al., 1995; Potter & Ware, 1987; Poulos et al., 1976; Sherman & Dominick, 1986; Williams et al., 1982). The proportion of aggressors who are white is typically about 75% to 90%.

11. *Most perpetrators are middle-aged.* In most content analysis studies, middle-aged characters, defined as between the ages of 20 and 50, commit about 75% to 95% of all violent acts (Dominick, 1973; Gerbner, Gross, Signorielli, & Morgan, 1980; Greenberg et al., 1980; *National Television Violence Study,* 1997, 1998; Potter et al., 1995; Potter & Ware, 1987; Sherman & Dominick, 1986; Williams et al., 1992).

12. *Victims and perpetrators are similar demographically.* Victims are likely to be white, middle-aged males (Greenberg et al., 1980; *National Television Violence Study,* 1997, 1998; Potter et al., 1995; Potter & Ware, 1987; Sherman & Dominick, 1986; Williams et al., 1982). However, the analyses of Gerbner, Gross, Signorielli, and Morgan (1980) show that women are more likely to be victims than perpetrators (Signorielli, 1990).

13. *A high proportion of the violence is committed by "good" characters.* The Center for Media and Public Affairs (1994) reports that "violence on television is typically not a tool of evil . . . most violence in network shows is committed by positive characters" (p. 12). This conclusion is based on the center's finding that much of the violence (42%) is committed primarily by "positive" characters, whereas negative or criminal characters account for 20% of the violence and neutral characters for 17%. "Good" characters are sometimes operationalized as heroes, and when they are, heroes are found to commit as many antisocial acts as villains do (Potter & Ware, 1987).

In the realm of crime, Dominick (1973) found that almost one third of all law enforcers committed violence on entertainment television. On reality-based crime shows, such as *Cops* and *America's Most Wanted,* Oliver (1994) reported that although 51% of police officers used aggressive behaviors, only 19% of criminal suspects did.

However, this pattern was not found in the NTVS project (Wilson et al., 1997, 1998). In those analyses, 45% of perpetrators were bad characters and 24% were good characters. Why the discrepancy? Two explanations are possible. First, perhaps the difference can be traced to the type of violence. For example, Potter and Ware (1987) reported that in general, 26% of antisocial acts are committed by heroes, 28% by villains, and 46% by secondary characters. But when we look at only serious violence, the pattern changes: Negative characters commit 37%, positive characters 25%. Another explanation is that the NTVS greatly expanded the number of channels examined beyond the major broadcast networks. Perhaps the good characters are the largest proportion of perpetrators on the major networks, and the bad characters take over on the other channels.

The Context of Violent Portrayals

14. *Most of the violence is intentional, and usually the motives are not prosocial.* Rarely is violence portrayed as an accident (Dominick, 1973; Larsen, Gray, & Fortis, 1968; *National Television Violence Study,* 1997, 1998; Potter et al., 1995, 1997; Smith et al., 1999; Williams et al., 1982; Wilson et al., 1997, 1998).

As for motives in fictional shows, Williams et al. (1982) reported that in

97% of violent acts on television, the perpetrators intended harm. Potter et al. (1995) found that 58% of the acts were malicious and 33% were inconsiderate. In addition, in half the acts, the motive was to hurt the victim either physically or emotionally. Dominick (1973) reported that the most popular motives for crime are greed (32%) and avoidance of detection (31%). The *National Television Violence Study* (1997, 1998) found that most of the violent interactions were intentionally motivated, by personal gain (30%), protection of life (26%), or anger (24%) (Smith et al., 1999; Wilson et al., 1997, 1998). In nonfiction, Potter et al. (1997) found that 60% of motives for violence consisted of maliciousness.

Another way to examine motives is to make a distinction between motives 25
that are internal (desires of characters) and those that are external (forced by one's role or by others). Estep and Macdonald (1983) reported that 24% of motives for antisocial acts on the top-rated television shows were internal. Using a broader sample of all prime-time programming several years later, Potter and Ware (1987) found that 39% were internally motivated; that is, violent acts were not forced by external conditions such as threats, poverty, and so on.

15. *Consequences for the victims are rarely shown.* In most portrayals of violence, the victim is not shown in pain or suffering (Center for Media and Public Affairs, 1994; Dominick, 1973; *National Television Violence Study,* 1997, 1998; Potter et al., 1995; Sherman & Dominick, 1986; Williams et al., 1982). In fictional programming, Williams et al. (1982) reported that more than 81% of violent acts depicted no impairment to the victims. In 76% of violent scenes, no physical outcome of the violence was shown, and 90% of the scenes showed no emotional impact on characters (Center for Media and Public Affairs, 1994). The *National Television Violence Study* reported that in 47% of all violent interactions absolutely no harm was shown, and in 58% of violent scenes, the target showed no pain. In addition, in only 16% of all programs with violence was there a portrayal of long-term negative consequences such as psychological, financial, or emotional harm (Smith et al., 1999; Wilson et al., 1997, 1998). The same pattern was found in music videos. Sherman and Dominick (1986) reported that in almost 80% of all violence in performance music videos, no outcome of the violence was shown.

In nonfictional programming, Potter et al. (1997) found that 53.4% of the violent acts had no consequences for the victim, and 17.2% had only minor consequences. News programs were more likely to show major harmful consequences than were other types of nonfictional programming. The *National Television Violence Study* reported that 87% of acts of visual violence in reality-based programs showed no long-term negative consequences (Whitney et al., 1997).

16. *The perpetrators often are not punished.* Rarely are negative consequences to the perpetrators shown (Dominick, 1973; Potter et al., 1995, 1997; Potter & Ware, 1987; Smith et al., 1999; Wilson et al., 1997, 1998). For example, Potter and Ware found that only 12% of violent acts were portrayed as being punished. The *National Television Violence Study* reported that 19% of violent interactions in fictional programming were shown as punished, and another

8% were shown with both reward and punishment immediately after the action. When looking at the entire show, the rates of punishment were higher, because another 40% of perpetrators were punished at the end of the show (Smith et al., 1999; Wilson et al., 1997, 1998). Still, about 37% of the perpetrators remain unpunished anywhere in the program for committing a violent act.

As for nonfiction, Potter et al. (1997) reported that 77.4% of the violent acts are not punished in any way. Dominick (1973) found that although most criminals are usually tracked down and caught, only 5% are shown during a trial or even have their trial mentioned during the drama. Furthermore, almost one third of all law enforcers commit violence on entertainment television, and they are never punished. In reality-based programming, 67% of acts show no punishment (Wartella, Whitney, et al., 1998; Whitney et al., 1997).

Much of the violence on television is portrayed as successful, except for violence perpetrated by criminals (Estep & Macdonald, 1983; Oliver, 1994; Williams et al., 1982). For example, Williams et al. found that the most common reaction to aggression by victims was to allow the violence to occur without striking back (29.1%) or to withdraw from the encounter (15.8%). 30

"There is a definite tendency for television programs to project content in which socially approved goals are most frequently achieved by methods that are not socially approved," observed Larsen et al. (1968, p. 100). The exception to this pattern of the successful use of violence is with criminals. In reality-based crime shows, violent crime is usually portrayed as unsuccessful. For example, Oliver (1994) reported that about 78% of crimes on these shows are cleared (perpetrators are arrested), and in the remaining 22% the suspect eludes arrest. This pattern of frequently arresting perpetrators is not matched by real-world statistics, which show that only 18% of crimes are cleared by an arrest, The same unrealistic pattern is found in fictional crime drama. Estep and Macdonald (1983) analyzed crime dramas in the 1980–1981 season and found that 72% of the murder suspects and 60% of the robbery suspects were portrayed as arrested, and a large percentage of crimes were resolved with the criminal suspect's death (14% of murder suspects, 19% of robbery suspects). These findings are consistent with those of Dominick (1973), who reported that 88% of crimes in prime-time fiction were portrayed as solved.

This high level of success and low level of punishment tells viewers that violence is not bad. Larsen et al. (1968) concluded that "a state of anomie is consistently being portrayed on television dramatic programming" (p. 111).

17. *Much of the violence is justified.* The amount of justification changes depending on the perspective from which it is judged. Potter and Ware (1987) found that 93% of violent instances were justified from the perspective of the perpetrator—not by society. That is, if the perpetrator was portrayed as regarding the violent act as warranted, the coder recorded it as justified. But if the perpetrator displayed a negative feeling, such as remorse, the act was coded as unjustified from the character's point of view.

The results would be different if the judgment of justification were made from the point of view of society. The NTVS defined justification primarily in terms of motives: Violence used to protect oneself or one's family or to retaliate against an attack was regarded as justified. With this perspective on justification, the NTVS found that 32% of all violent interactions were judged to be justified by the coders (Wilson et al., 1998).

18. *Weapons are often found in violent acts.* The NTVS said that in fictional   35
programming, guns are used in one fourth of all violent interactions, and that other kinds of weapons are used in another one third of all violent interactions. The most prevalent form of violence, however, was natural means—the use of nothing more than the perpetrator's body (Smith et al., 1999; Wilson et al., 1997, 1998).

In reality-based programming, guns were used in 44% of visually depicted violent interactions (Wartella, Whitney, et al., 1998; Whitney et al., 1997). In music videos, 35% of the violent acts were committed with a weapon (Sherman & Dominick, 1986).

19. *The presentation style is rarely graphic and explicit.* The NTVS (Wilson et al., 1997, 1998) found that within fictional programming, rarely (10% of the time) is violence shown graphically—that is, shown closer than in a distant shot. Less than 3% of all violent scenes feature a close-up of the violence. In addition, only 15% of violent scenes showed any blood or gore.

In reality-based programming, violence is graphic in only 7% of acts, and intense in only 10% of acts (Wilson et al., 1997, 1998). In contrast, in 38% of instances in which people talked about violence, the descriptions were graphic (Wartella, Whitney, et al., 1998; Whitney et al., 1997).

20. *Much of the violence is portrayed in a humorous context.* Humor is a common context for violence (*National Television Violence Study*, 1997, 1998; Potter et al., 1995; Signorielli, 1990; Smythe, 1954; Williams et al., 1982). For example, Smythe found that about one fourth of all acts and threats of violence were committed in a humorous context, and that the humorous context was more common in programs for children than in those for a general audience. In Gerbner's analyses from 1967 to 1985, children's (weekend daytime) programming was found to have the highest rates of violence, but 73% of that programming presented violence in at least a partly comic context, compared to only 20% of prime-time programming using a comic context to present violence (Signorielli, 1990). More recently, the NTVS found that 39% of violent interactions occur in a humorous context in fictional programming, but only 3% of acts in reality-based programs are coupled with humor (Wartella, Whitney, et al., 1998; Whitney et al., 1997). Potter and Warren (1998) found that when presented in a humorous context, the violence also appeared with other contextual factors that tended to trivialize it.

21. *Violence is often shown in a fantasy context or in an unrealistic pattern.* The   40
National Television Violence Study reported that about half of the violent acts were shown in a fantasy context, such as with anthropomorphized animals and puppets (Smith et al., 1999; Wilson et al., 1997, 1998). But the concept of realism is more complex than simply determining whether or not there are puppets.

Potter et al. (1995) explored this issue by examining violent content from the perspectives of replicated and contextual reality. As for replicated reality, they found that most of the aggression was at the less serious end of the spectrum, with serious assaults and deaths relatively rare compared to less serious assaults and verbal violence. As for the serious violence of a criminal nature, males are represented as perpetrators more than females, which is realistic. But African Americans are underrepresented, as are younger perpetrators. As for contextual reality, there were some differences between true fantasy shows (cartoons, science fiction, etc.) and shows with realistic settings. Fantasy violence is more likely to be humorous, less likely to be punished, and more likely to have a perpetrator with a malicious intent.

Rates of violent crime are much higher than rates of nonviolent crime, a pattern that is opposite to that of crime in the real world (Dominick, 1973; Oliver, 1994). In addition, Oliver found that on reality-based police shows, demographics deviate from the real world significantly. Among television police officers, only 9% are African American, but in the real world 17% of all police officers are African American. Among criminal suspects, the demographics are very similar to real-world criminal suspects. In addition, white characters were more likely to be portrayed as police officers than as criminal suspects, whereas African American and Latino characters were more likely to be portrayed as criminal suspects than as police officers.

Contextual reality was assessed in terms of how closely television portrayals follow the pattern of how violence unfolds in real life. Potter et al. (1995) point out a substantial difference in the patterns in the area of consequences of violence. In real life, violence carries serious physical, emotional, and psychological consequences. But in the television world, the portrayal of violence largely neglects the harmful consequences for the victims (Center for Media and Public Affairs, 1994; Dominick, 1973; *National Television Violence Study*, 1997, 1998; Potter et al., 1995; Sherman & Dominick, 1986; Williams et al., 1982). Television presents to viewers a very unrealistic picture of the nature of violence.

Patterns in Countries Other Than the United States

22. *The United States leads the world in the prevalence of violence on television.* Violence is less prevalent on TV in countries other than the United States (Cumberbatch, Lee, Hardy, & Jones, 1987; Gunter, 1987; Iwao, de Sola Pool, & Hagiwara, 1981a; Kapoor, Kang, Kim, & Kim, 1994; Mustonen & Pulkkinen, 1993). In Great Britain, for example, Cumberbatch et al. used Gerbner's definition of violence and found that only about 30% of all programs contained any violence and that the overall rate was 1.7 acts per hour. The Broadcasting Standards Council (1993) reported higher figures, saying that 52% of programs contained violence, with an average of 4.0 scenes per hour. The highest rate was found on national news (7.5 scenes per hour); the rate for children's programming was 2.6.

In Korea, only one third of prime-time programs were found to contain vi-   45
olence. In addition, less than 8% of all leading characters were involved in violence (Kapoor et al., 1994).

In Finland, Mustonen and Pulkkinen (1993) examined a complete week of
broadcasting, including news and sports and found that there were 3.5 aggressive acts per hour across all programs, 5.6 in fictional programming. The
physical forms of violence made up the majority, 2.7 acts per hour. Mustonen
and Pulkkinen found cartoons to have the highest hourly rate, as well as the
highest ratings of brutality across all genres. They attributed much of the aggression to importation from other countries. Among programs produced in
Finland, the rate of violence was 1.5 acts per hour, whereas imported programs had a much higher rate: 5.6 acts per hour for programs imported from
Europe, 12.1 for programs imported from North America.

An eight-country comparison in Asia with Western television found that
Asian television in general contains fewer incidents of violence but that suffering is glorified and blood is frequently shown (Goonasekera & Lock, 1990;
Hagiwara, 1990). However, the two cultures were the same in the pattern of
heroes and villains being equally likely to commit violence. Heroes, however,
are shown suffering much more in Asian television.

Duration appears to be shorter in other countries. For example, in Finland,
Mustonen and Pulkkinen (1993) found that about 2.4% of overall programming (3.9% of fictional programming) was violent. In Japan, Iwao et al. (1981a)
found that on average 2.3 min/hr of programming time, or about 4% of all
programming time, was violent.

☑   ☑   ☑

Exceptions. There are several exceptions to the overall finding that violence is
lower on television in countries other than the United States. In Australia, for
example, McCann and Sheehan (1985) found patterns similar to those in the
United States. Using Gerbner's definition of violence, they analyzed the content of 59 hours (80 programs) and found that 79% of cartoons, 73% of all fictional programming, and only 4% of nonfiction programming contained
violence. On average there were 5.4 violent episodes per hour; the rate for cartoons was 10.2 (the highest rate), for fiction 7.2, and for nonfiction 0.4.

Williams et al. (1982) found 18.5 acts of aggression per hour in North   50
American television. Much of their sample came from U.S. programming, and
this programming was higher in conflict and aggression than Canadian programming. Furthermore, the duration of the aggressive scenes from U.S. television was substantially greater.

In Japan, Iwao et al. (1981a) used Gerbner's definition and found the pres-
ence of violence to be about the same in Japan as in the United States. They
found violence in 81% of programs, compared to Gerbner's 80% in the United
States; in Japan, 2.3 min/hr were violent, compared with 2.4 in the United
States; and the proportion of characters committing violence was 46.3% in
Japan, compared with 46.0% in the United States. Cartoons were found to

have the highest rate of violent scenes per hour (14.3)—even higher than samurai dramas (8.7). Iwao et al. also found that highly violent shows were generally less popular among viewers, so over time the rate of violence dropped (Iwao, de Sola Pool, & Hagiwara, 1981b).

Studies that have looked at both fictional and nonfictional programming in countries other than the United States find much more violence in fictional programming (Broadcasting Standards Council, 1995; Mustonen & Pulkkinen, 1993). These findings match the findings from the United States (Lichter & Amundson, 1992; Potter et al., 1995, 1997).

23. *Character portrayals generally conform to U.S. patterns.* As with U.S. television, a very high percentage of aggressors in foreign-television violence are males (70% to 95%), and seldom are they younger than 20 or older than 50 (Cumberbatch et al., 1987; Kapoor et al., 1994; Mustonen & Pulkkinen, 1993; Williams et al., 1982).

In Finland, "aggressors were two times more likely to be 'baddies' than 'goodies'" (Mustonen & Pulkkinen, 1993, p. 181). The same is true in Japan (Iwao, et al., 1981a) and Korea (Kapoor et al., 1994). But in Australia, the pattern of good characters as aggressors is more prevalent; McCann and Sheehan (1985) found that heroes were the aggressors in 42% of episodes, and villains were the aggressors in 54%. In addition, heroes were the victims in 66% of acts, and villains were the victims in 29%.

In Israel, most of the characters involved in violence were male and middle-aged (20–39 years old). In addition, whereas perpetrators were much more likely to be bad characters, victims were equally likely to be bad or good (Shinar, Parnes, & Caspi, 1972).

24. *Context generally conforms to U.S. patterns.* As for motives, Mustonen and Pulkkinen (1993) found that spontaneous acts of aggression were much more frequent (57%) than planned aggression (27%) and that the percentage of first-strike acts (76%) was much higher than that of retaliatory acts (12%). They said that "TV narration emphasized the act of aggression much more than its consequences. Aggressive acts were used as a climax point of a story. They were usually stressed with detailed visual cues, ravishing music, or other sound effects, while a noticeable proportion (36%) of the consequences were presented only as hints or not shown at all" (p. 181).

In Great Britain, the Broadcasting Standards Council (1993) reported that 17% of violent scenes were comic, 59% showed harmful consequences within the scene, and 40% showed some form of weapon being used to inflict harm.

In Japan, violence was shown with a high use of guns, unrealism, and justification (Forum for Children's Television, 1988). In addition, the rate of verbal violence was higher than that of physical violence (Forum for Children's Television, 1982). But on Japanese television, victims are usually shown suffering. "The protracted agony that characters suffer shocks U.S. viewers of Japanese TV and leaves them convinced that Japanese TV is much more violent than their own" (Iwao et al., 1981b, p. 31).

In Israel, the weapon was usually natural means, and harmful consequences for the victims are seldom portrayed (Shinar et al., 1972).

Conclusion

The examination of violence on television has been an active area of research,   60
generating more than 60 published content analyses, most of which have been
conducted in the past 20 years. The findings indicate that television shown in
all parts of the world contains a great deal of violence and that this violence
usually is portrayed in an antisocial manner; that is, the portrayals contain
many elements that would lead viewers to experience negative effects. ■

Reflections and Inquiries

1. Of the twenty-four facets of TV violence Potter identifies, which are the
   most relevant for determining how influential TV violence is on young
   people? Why?

2. What do you find is the most startling fact about violence in children's television programming? Why?

3. Potter discusses the frequency of "verbal violence" in comedy shows. Is this
   a valid category of media violence? Explain.

4. Why is the question of justification of TV violence problematic?

Reading to Write

Potter's analysis clarifies what constitutes violence. Does it also give you
insight into why such violent content is harmful to young people? Write an
essay in which you try to resolve this latter issue.

Toxic Lessons | Jean Tepperman

The following piece outlines key concerns that educators and parents have
about the influence that violent TV programming has on children. It poses
four questions: (1) Does media violence encourage violent behavior? (2) How
does TV violence mislead? (3) Who, among children, are most influenced by
media violence? (4) How do children typically react to media violence?

Does Media Violence Promote Violent Behavior?

"Since 1955, about 1,000 studies, reports, and commentaries concerning the
impact of television violence have been published. The accumulated research

Source: Tepperman, Jean. "Toxic Lessons: What Do Children Learn from Media
Violence?" *Children's Advocate,* Jan–Feb, 1997. Published in the January–February 1997
edition of *The Children's Advocate Newspaper,* produced by Action Alliance for Children.
Reprinted by permission.

clearly demonstrates a correlation between viewing violence and aggressive behavior."

That statement, made by the American Psychological Association in 1992, summarized its comprehensive review of research on the effects of media violence. Other organizations including the American Medical Association, National Institutes of Mental Health, and the U.S. Centers for Disease Control came to similar conclusions.

One key study that showed the connection between media violence and real violence was the one by Dr. Leonard D. Eron. He followed a group of young people for 22 years and found that those who watched more television at age eight were more likely, at age 30, to have committed more serious crimes, to be more aggressive when drinking, and to punish their children more harshly than others. Others have repeated Eron's study and found similar results throughout the United States and other countries as well.

Another researcher, University of Washington epidemiologist Brandon Centerwall, surveyed young male felons imprisoned for committing violent crimes. Between one-quarter and one-third reported having consciously imitated crime techniques they saw on television.

"Laboratory" studies, says Ronald Slaby, media-violence expert at the Education Development Center, also show that media violence has an "aggressor effect." Children who watch a violent TV show, for example, act more aggressive immediately after the show.

How Does TV Violence Mislead Young People?

Children and youth are affected by the sheer quantity of violence on TV and in the movies. But perhaps more damaging are the false messages that media violence sends.

- *Violence is often rewarded and seldom has negative consequences.* According to the 1992 National Television Violence Study by Mediascope, perpetrators go unpunished in 73 percent of all violent scenes on television.

- *Violence is everywhere.* Slaby tells the story of a preschooler who was informed of the death of her friend's father. "Who killed him?" she asked. Her question reflected the assumption, drawn from television, that violence was the normal cause of death.

- *Violence is justified.* Much of the violence on television is committed by the "hero" of the show. The National Television Violence Study found that aggression by "good guys" is rarely punished; even "bad guys" are punished only 62 percent of the time. *Power Rangers,* like countless war movies, teaches that violence by "good guys" is not only justified but heroic.

- *Violence is funny.* Laugh tracks in shows like *The Three Stooges* often follow actions like whacking someone over the head. Children's cartoons are especially likely to present violence as funny.

- *Violence is pleasurable.* Clint Eastwood, in *Dirty Harry,* finds violence so enjoyable that he encourages people to provoke him— a violent act would "make my day."

Which Young People Are Most Susceptible to Influence by Media Violence?

Three factors are strong predictors, according to Slaby:

1. *Identifying with one of the characters.* The response, therefore, depends on which character the viewer identifies with. Since aggressors in the media are usually male and females are usually victims, for example, boys are more likely to respond with aggression and girls with fear.

2. *Interpreting what they see as realistic and relevant to their own lives.* Media violence is more likely to have a strong effect, therefore, on children who see violence in their lives. It also has a stronger effect on young children, who lack the real-life experience to judge whether something they see is realistic.

3. *Personal fantasizing about the characters on a violent show.* Daydream "reruns" increase the influence of scenes a child has watched.

In addition, says Slaby, the context in which violence is presented is crucial. In Shakespeare's tragedies and in TV shows like the popular Civil War series, violence is shown realistically, with its suffering and tragic aftermath. But such realistic, "prosocial" portrayals of violence account for only about 4 percent of TV programming.

How Do Most Children and Young People React to Media Violence?

Most people, of course, don't become violent when they watch TV or movie violence. But they may be affected in other ways. Slaby lists four effects of media violence:

- an *aggressor* effect—encouraging violent behavior

- a *victim* effect—increasing fearfulness

- a *bystander* effect—leading to callousness, accepting violence as normal

- an *appetite* effect—building a desire to watch more violence.

These effects combine, says media expert George Gerbner of the Annenberg Center for Public Policy, University of Pennsylvania, to create a "mean world syndrome," a perception that the community and society in which we live are frightening and crime-ridden.

On a personal level, according to Gerbner, these fears lead to alienation and isolation. On a policy level, they fuel support for "repressive policies and increased incarceration." Violence-prevention expert Deborah Prothrow-Stith of the Harvard School of Public Health, says media violence both reflects and contributes to a growing "culture of meanness," a fertile ground for real-life violence. ☑

Reflections and Inquiries

1. Given the summative nature of this article, how convincing is the evidence Tepperman provides to support the link between violent programming and violent behavior in children?

2. Which fact in each of the four categories is most significant to you? Least significant? Why?

3. In what ways are Tepperman's findings corroborated or contradicted by findings reported by some of the other writers you have read in this cluster?

Reading to Write

After viewing several TV shows, compare your findings with regard to the violence depicted with Tepperman's findings. Write an essay in which you supplement or contrast Tepperman's findings with your own.

Murder, Mayhem, Politics and Commerce
The Influence of the Media in the United States | Gay Hollis

In the following essay, Gay Hollis argues that evidence for excessive media influence clearly exists and that the danger lies in its potential to manipulate us in ways that rob us of our individuality. Hollis is a teacher and debate coach at Taylor High School in Katy, Texas.

He bragged to all his friends that his kill ratio would break every previous record. Nothing was going to stop him this time. Though he was only fourteen years old, the steely glint of determination in his eyes told them that he really meant what he said.

John Mohavic carefully prepared himself for his murderous mission. He stockpiled ammunition, selecting and arranging his weapons. He checked his sights, his navigational gear, and his bulletproof armor plat-

---

Source: Hollis, Gay. "Murder, Mayhem, Politics: The Influence of the Media in the United States, 1999." Reprinted by permission of the author.

ing. Satisfied with the state of his arsenal, he set out from the old warehouse into a dark, cluttered alley.

He rounded the corner and came out into the street. Snow began to fall. The moist flakes twinkling past New York's neoned hustle and bustle cast a spell of transfixing beauty over the entire cityscape. But he had no eyes for beauty. The dispossessed seldom do.

Around the next corner, the first sight that greeted him was a street fight. A small crowd had gathered to watch two emaciated black youths lunge and slash at each other with cheap gravity-blade knives.

But John moved on barely glancing at the violent scene before him. 5
He had a job to do, and nothing was going to deter him from that task.

He made his way around toward Times Square, then Broadway. It was almost midnight now, and the streets seemed to come alive. A garish kaleidoscope of flashing lights mixed with the wheedling jive of hawkers and the choked cacophony of the dense traffic.

Finally, he arrived at the Port Authority terminal and began to wait for the airport transit bus. Before the bus arrived, however, two security guards, suspicious of the bulk beneath his trench coat, walked toward John. He didn't hesitate. Raising his automatic weapon, he mowed them down with a series of short, sharp blasts

Pandemonium broke out in the crowded station. Bystanders ran for cover, screaming as the blood pooled beneath the two officers. A boom box was dropped in the center of the waiting area, still blasting raucous rap music.

Almost immediately, several more security guards came running down the long corridor off to John's right. He opened fire again. This time, several spectators were shot along with the officers. A mother traveling with three children was caught in the crossfire. She was killed instantly when her temple was struck by a hollow-point round—her brains splattering across the Formica counter behind her.

Quickly reloading, John turned to escape. But now officers charged 10
him from all directions. A fierce fight broke out. There was nowhere to run.

Inevitably, John was hit. Again and again bullets tore through his flesh. Yet he continued to fire his weapon madly until the very end. Finally an armored patrol car swung into position directly in from of him, and he was done for.

Game over. Insert two quarters to play again. (Huckabee, 1998)

She appears to be the all-American girl. She is a bubbly, vivacious blonde high school senior whose clothing seems to set the fashion trend. During the day she is a mild-mannered student with a smile that could melt even the coldest heart, but by night she becomes something entirely different: she is the Slayer, the "chosen one" whose duty is to protect the world from the demons who try to enter the world through the hell-mouth (located in lovely Sunnydale, California). Cashing in on the popularity of Gothic themes among the nation's teenagers, the WB series *Buffy the Vampire Slayer* features a character who makes nightly patrols of the local cemeteries to stake the night's newly created vampires. Buffy counts among her closest friends a werewolf, a witch/computer geek, and a vampire boyfriend. With their help, and with the help of sleek karate moves and combat training, Buffy shreds hordes of demons each week through hand-to-hand combat as teenagers cheer while she assaults them both verbally and physically. However, this graphically violent television series, clearly designed for a teenage audience, is only a watered-down version of the violence children are inundated with daily through the media.

Americans, far more than any other group of people in the world today, are faced with the pervasiveness of the media. Nielson Media Research estimates that TV receivers are found in 99 percent of all households in the United States and that the average television set is on more than 7 hours a day (Albarran and Chan-Olmstead, 1988). This apparent overwhelming fascination Americans have with the media has created concern in two basic areas. First, as movies, television programming, and even children's video games have become increasingly focused on graphic violence, there is growing concern about the effects of prolonged exposure to these violent scenes on our country's children. Second, as mergers and acquisitions have reduced ownership of media resources including television broadcasting, newspapers, and movies to only a handful of corporations, there is also concern over the control and manipulation of information available to the American public.

Media Violence

Perhaps no singular event has done more to focus attention on the prevalence of violence in the media than the tragic deaths of students and faculty at Columbine High School in Littleton, Colorado, early this year. While there is no definitive answer that would explain why Dylan Klebold and Eric Harris spent nearly a year planning and then executing a massacre of their classmates—certainly many cultural and societal issues were involved as well as other teenage angst issues—it is clear that these two young men as well as other teens like Michael Carneal, the shooter in the Paducah, Kentucky, school killings, were clearly influenced by images in the entertainment industry.

Television Violence

The American Medical Association long ago acknowledged the relationship between prolonged exposure to what it calls "virtual violence" (violence that appears in various forms of media entertainment such as television, music, film, video, computer, and cyberspace) and violence in society. In a statement prepared for the 1995 U.S. Senate Committee on Commerce, Science, and Transportation, the AMA explained:

15

It is a shocking fact that by the time children leave elementary school, they have seen 8,000 killings and 100,000 other violent acts portrayed on television, according to the Center for Media and Public Affairs. The same source reports that by the age of 18, the typical American child will have witnessed 40,000 killings and 200,000 acts of violence on television. It is a well accepted principle that children learn behavior by example. The pairing of learning by example with the decreased physiologic response is what makes this exposure of such great concern. (AMA, 1995)

Other studies have supported the same conclusions. Psychologist Leonard Eron noted similar effects in his statement before the U.S. Senate.

Over 35 years of laboratory and real-life studies provide evidence that televised violence is a cause of aggression among children, both contemporaneously, and over time. Television violence affects youngsters of all ages, both genders, at all socio-economic levels, and all levels of intelligence. The effect is not limited to children who are already disposed to being aggressive, and it is not restricted to the United States. The fact that the same finding of a relation between television violence and aggression in children has been found in study after study, in one country after another, cannot be ignored. (Eron, 1995)

Moreover, American children are exposed to violence from every medium. In addition to the death and mayhem they witness on television, they listen to music that advocates drug use and violence against police and authority in general. Much of today's popular music also portrays women as objects of sex and violence, often at the same time.

Movies

Movies have also become increasingly violent, frequently spawning copycats who reenact the scenes from these movies in real-life incidents. There was a great deal of talk about banning the movie *Natural Born Killers* after a series of robbery and murders appeared across the country similar to those glorified in the movie. In addition, many observers have been struck by the similarities displayed in the recent rash of school shootings with events in movies that have enjoyed popular teen followings. Images of a trench coat-clad Leonardo DiCaprio pulling out a shotgun and blowing away his classmates in a dream sequence of *The Basketball Diaries* and of an ultra-suave Keanu Reeves carefully selecting and lining his black trench coat with a variety of high-powered guns in *The Matrix* eerily parallel the events of both Paducah, Kentucky, and Littleton, Colorado.

Video Games

Adding to the controversy in these and other cases involving teen violence   20
is the specter of graphic video games. Journalist John Leo explains this phenomenon:

The conventional argument is that this is a harmless activity among children who know the difference between fantasy and reality. But the games are often played by unstable youngsters unsure about the difference. Many of these have been maltreated or rejected and left alone most of the time (a precondition for playing the games obsessively). Adolescent feelings of resentment, powerlessness, and revenge pour into the killing games. In these children, the games can become a dress rehearsal for the real thing. (Leo, 1999)

Moreover, psychologist and retired Army officer David Grossman sees much more dire effects of these games. He thinks "point and shoot" video games are similar to strategies used in the military to break down a soldier's aversion to killing. According to Leo, evidence suggests that these games played an important role in the recent school shootings.

Video games are much more powerful versions of the military's primitive discovery about overcoming the reluctance to shoot. Grossman says Michael Carneal, the schoolboy shooter in Paducah, Kentucky, showed the effects of video-game lessons in killing. Carneal coolly shot nine times, hitting eight people, five of them in the head or neck. Head shots pay a bonus in many video games. Now the Marine Corps is adapting a version of Doom, the hyperviolent game played by one of the Littleton killers, for its own purposes.

Leo goes on to add:

More realistic touches in video games help blur the boundary between fantasy and reality—guns carefully modeled on real ones, accurate-looking wounds, screams, and other sound effects, even the recoil of a heavy rifle. Some newer games seem intent on erasing children's empathy and concern for others. Once the intended victims of video slaughter were mostly gangsters or aliens. Now some games invite players to blow away ordinary people who have done nothing wrong—pedestrians, marching bands, an elderly woman with a walker. In these games, the shooter is not a hero, just a violent sociopath. One ad for a Sony game says: "Get in touch with your gun-toting, testosterone-pumping, cold-blooded murdering side." (Leo, 1999)

Grossman sums up this issue. "We have to start worrying about what we are putting into the minds of our young. Pilots train on flight simulators, drivers on driving simulators, and now we have our children on murder simulators" (qtd. in Leo, 1999).

Merging Media

In addition to the violence in our society, which many experts believe is related to the influence of the media, many others are concerned about the ramifications of the trend in recent years toward massive consolidation within the communications industries. SMU Professor Alan B. Albarran attributes the growth of media conglomerates to the 1996 Telecommunications Act. "The growing merger activity is a direct result of the 1996 Telecommunications Act, which eliminated a number of regulatory barriers in terms ownership limits, especially in the cable and telecommunications industries. Over time, these actions will further consolidate many market segments (Albarran, 1998)."

This type of consolidation is illustrated by media critic Ben H. Bagdikian, who explains:

> Predictions of massive consolidation are based on extraordinary changes in recent years. At the end of World War II, for example, 80 percent of the daily newspapers in the United States were independently owned, but by 1989 the proportion was reversed, with 80 percent owned by corporate chains. In 1981 twenty corporations controlled most of the business of the country's 11,000 magazines, but only seven years later that number had shrunk to three corporations. Today, despite more than 25,000 outlets in the United States, twenty-three corporations control most of the business in daily newspapers, magazines, television, books, and motion pictures. The same dominant corporations in these major fields appear in other, often newer, media. It is the open strategy of major media owners to own as many different kinds of media as possible—newspapers, magazines, broadcasting, books, movies, cable, recordings, video cassettes, movie houses, and copyright control of the archival libraries of past work in all these fields. (Bagdikian, 1993)

For example, Time Warner Inc.'s $7.6 billion purchase of Turner Broadcasting Systems, Inc. in 1996 created the largest media firm in the world with strong cable distribution, programming, and print divisions. Walt Disney Company's $19 billion acquisition of Capital Cities/ABC Inc. in 1995 created the second largest media conglomerate, with extraordinary strengths in programming, broadcasting, and cablecasting. Viacom Inc.'s $8.4 billion purchase of Paramount Pictures in 1994 brought together a major cable and video firm with a premier television and film producer, and its $8.4 billion acquisition of Blockbuster that year brought in video and audio retail outlets and additional film library resources (Picard). 25

Control of Information

But why should the public be concerned about this trend? As Bagdikian explains it:

> An alarming pattern emerges. On one side is information limited by each individual's own experience and effort; on the other, the unseen affairs of the community, the nation, and the world, information needed by the individual to prevent political powerlessness. What connects the two are the mass media, and that system is being reduced to a small number of

closed circuits in which the owners of the conduits—newspapers, magazines, broadcast stations, and all the other mass media—prefer to use
material they own or that tends to serve their own economic purposes.
(Bagdikian, 1997)

Furthermore, as news becomes the business of corporate America, greater
emphasis is being placed on the bottom line. Economic efficiency has led what
has been deemed a "homogenization" of the news. Since many of these corporations own multiple information outlets, it is cheaper and easier to use the
same sources for all of the outlets. Picard explains this process.

In terms of news, dominant ideologies governing the definition of news
and how it should be covered create the opportunities for the creation of
economies of scale in the collection and distribution of news. As a result,
commercial firms designed to collect news and information and then sell
it to media have developed, providing services to any media that will
buy. These news and feature syndicates now provide the bulk of materials of newspapers and magazines, although many readers presume that
their favorite publications produce their own materials.

(He adds:)

These types of interactions between media firms have an unfortunate result: a large proportion of news and information comes from the same
sources. It is merely packaged and reused by various media, creating a
homogenization of material. Even when major commercialized media
create their own material, they do so with the same ideologies of news
and information. Thus, the perspectives and breadth of coverage are limited. (Picard, 1998)

Another problem related to the control of information is associated with
how the media deals with specific issues. Too often, in today's concentrated
media environment, the public is most likely to read or hear about what events
provide the most economic benefit to the corporation. This has the effect of
rendering the public susceptible to manipulation both for political and commercial reasons.

Political reality for citizens is created by mediated communications, and
most of what is communicated through media are "fantasies" contrived
by politicians and interest groups that wish to manipulate opinion. Media convey these fantasies in ways designed to make a profit. For these
reasons, webs of media influence are created that produce a distorted
picture of politics, a picture intended to entertain, reassure, and manipulate by providing more style than substance. This problem is compounded by highly market-driven approaches to television and print
news. Information is selected that entertains and diverts rather than an-

alyzes significant issues and problems in society. News that "sells" becomes an overriding concern, and extensive efforts are made to find and convey news in ways that support financial goals of companies. (Picard, 1998)

Cross-Promotion

The concentrated corporate control of the media raises an additional issue. As these corporations place their fingers in many pies, they put themselves in a position to cross-promote their goods and services. This is done in a variety of ways. The most obvious way this is achieved is through unified promotional campaigns.

> Today, most of the leading movie studios are also owners in other media, and, thanks to the free-market amnesia about anti-trust law, have once again started buying up movie houses to guarantee audiences for their own films and keep out competitors' pictures. In 1948 the United States Supreme Court found ownership of movie theaters by the major movie studios a violation of antitrust law. The U.S. Department of Justice in recent years has ignored that finding and by 1988 a few major studios had bought control of more than a third of all the movie screens in the country. (Bagdikian, 1997)

Another important area of cross-promotion has to do with media regulation itself. Since the media control the public's access to information, it has been quite successful in subtly manipulating the public into supporting the interests of the corporation. As Picard explains this process:

> As government has spent a great deal of effort wrestling with regulations regarding media in recent years, associations and coalitions funded by media companies have lobbied feverishly to promote the interests of the private commercial firms. Media associations—especially the National Cable Television Association and the National Association of Broadcasters—have produced campaigns and even advertisements supporting their policy interests. These have been distributed nationwide for their members to broadcast and cablecast on their stations and systems. The ads urge support for the associations' positions and ask viewers to contact Congress and the FTC with that support. (Picard, 1998)

Additionally, these corporations can use their newscasts (the service) to subtly promote the products produced by other sectors of the company. For example, the widely publicized Barbara Walters interview of Michael Jackson, which drew one of the largest audiences in television history, was timed to coincide with the release of Jackson's new album whose label was also owned by the same corporation. The program also carried three advertisements for the record (Jamieson, 1997).

Conclusion

Clearly, the evidence exists that the media conglomerates exert far too much influence on American society today. Recent changes in legislation, promoted by the communications industry itself, have only opened the door to increased influence and manipulation of the public and of the political process.

Buffy, the vampire slayer, is the nightmare of Sunnydale's various demons. Unless the power of the media is curtailed, American citizens may soon wake up to find these corporate conglomerates driving our nightmares of an Orwellian society where Big Brother watches us and tells us what to think under the guise of the news.

Works Cited

Albarran, Alan B., and Sylvia M. Chan-Olmstead. "The United States and the Global Marketplace." *Global Media Economics.* Ed. Alan B. Albarran and Sylvia M. Chan-Olmstead. Ames: Iowa State UP, 1998.

American Medical Association. Statement in *Television Violence:* Hearings before the U.S. Senate Committee on Commerce, Science, and Transportation, July 12, 1995.

Bagdikian, Ben H. *The Media Monopoly.* Beacon: Boston, 1997.

Eron, Leonard. *Violence on Television:* Hearings before the U.S. Senate Committee on Commerce, Science, and Transportation. 1995.

Huckabee, Mike *Kids Who Kill.* Nashville: Broadman, 1998.

Jamieson, Kathleen and Karlyn Campbell. *The Interplay of Influence.* Belmont: Wadsworth, 1997.

Leo, John. "When Life Imitates Video." *U.S. News & World Report* 3 May 1999.

Picard, Robert G. "Media Concentration, Economics, and Regulation." *The Politics of News /The News of Politics.* Ed. Denis McQuail and Pippa Norris. Washington: CQ, 1998.

Zillman, Dolf. "The Psychology of the Appeal of Portrayals of Violence." *Why We Watch.* Jeffrey H. Goldstein, editor. Oxford University Press: New York. 1998. ◢

Reflections and Inquiries

1. What purpose is served by Hollis's quotation from Mike Huckabee's *Kids Who Kill?* How well does it prepare the reader for what follows?

2. Hollis divides her argument into subheadings. How effectively do they organize her arguments?

3. What are "merging media," and why are they of concern?

4. According to Hollis, "as news becomes the business of corporate America, greater emphasis is being placed on the bottom line." What does she mean by this statement? Why does Hollis consider it a serious issue?

Reading to Write

Write a detailed critique of Hollis's use of evidence to defend her thesis. Is it sufficient? Appropriate? Timely (in relation to the year in which it was written, 1999)? You may wish to search for additional sources Hollis might have found useful.

Connections Across the Clusters

1. Are media violence issues at all relevant to distance learning? (See Cluster 1.) To multicultural education issues? (See Cluster 6). To privacy issues? (See Cluster 8.) How?

2. To what extent is the effort to control violent content in movies, video games, and TV shows an act of justifiable censorship? Of unjustifiable censorship? (See Cluster 3.)

Writing Projects

1. Write an analysis of violence in one kind of TV programming, such as cartoons or police dramas. Is all the TV violence you see depicted harmful, or do you wish to make such distinctions as, say, "benign," "questionable," and "dangerously influential" violence? Justify your claims by referring to relevant statistics and expert testimony.

2. Write a position paper in which you defend or refute the following claim: "Violence depicted in comedy routines or cartoons is harmless to children." Support your assertions with specific examples and testimony from appropriate experts.

Suggestions for Further Reading

Buckingham, David. "Electronic Child Abuse? Rethinking the Media's Effects on Children." *Ill Effects: The Media/Violence Debate.* Ed. Martin Barker and Julian Petley. London: Routledge, 1997. 32–47.

Murdock, Graham. "The Television and Delinquency Debate." *Screen Education* 30 (Spring 1979): 51–67.

———. "Visualizing Violence: Television and the Discourse of Disorder." *Rethinking Communication.* Vol. 2. London: Sage, 1989. 226–49.

Rosengren, Karl E., and Swen Windahl. *Media Matter: TV Use in Childhood Adolescence.* Norwood: Ablex, 1989.

Rowland, Willard D., Jr. *The Politics of TV Violence: Policy Uses of Communication Research.* Beverly Hills: Sage, 1983.

Siano, Brian. "Frankenstein Must Be Destroyed: Chasing the Monster of TV Violence." *The Humanist* 54 (Jan.–Feb. 1994): 20–25.

8 | Can We Preserve Our Privacy in the Internet Age?

Introduction

Turn on your computer and you automatically leave an electronic trail of your most private activities. Employers may monitor the e-mail their employees dispatch from the workplace. Private businesses easily trace Web site hits to their points of origin. Every one of the seventy million Internet users has his or her activities monitored by scrupulous as well as unscrupulous individuals and groups, and no one is under any obligation to inform them of it. Most searchers are scrupulous. The FBI, for example, although it has a means of searching everyone's e-mail at any time, does not bring in law enforcement officials unless it spots something truly criminal. Even so, the fact that a government agency can pry into our private business is unsettling to many. Welcome to the age of surveillance!

Is it possible, or even worthwhile, to find ways of preserving our privacy in this age? Should we put a stop to employers' random drug testing or psychological testing? The following articles examine these thorny privacy issues from several different perspectives.

The Searchable Soul | *Harper's Magazine* Forum:
Mark Costello, Michael Moynihan,
Ron Sege, Alan Westin, and Colin Harrison

In the following discussion forum, four professionals from law, government, and academe staged a formal discussion with moderator and *Harper's* deputy editor Colin Harrison. The participants raise privacy issues all of us worry about—for example, what, if anything, is the government doing about electronic invasion of individual privacy, such as the placing of "cookies"—

Source: Costello, Mark, Michael Moynihan, Ron Sege, Alan Westin, and Colin Harrison. "The Searchable Soul: Privacy in the Age of Information Technology." Forum. *Harper's* Jan. 2000: 57–68. Copyright © 1999 by *Harper's Magazine.* All rights reserved. Reproduced from the January 2000 issue by special permission.

encoded files—on the computers of Internet users to keep track of sites visited, frequency of visits, and users' personal information disclosed at those
sites? Forum participant Mark Costello has served as a prosecutor in the Manhattan District Attorney's Office. Michael Moynihan, who served in the U.S.
Treasury and Commerce Departments from 1995–1999, helped design President Clinton's Internet regulation policy. Ron Sege is executive vice president
of Lycos, an Internet portal company. Alan Westin, professor emeritus of Public Law and Government at Columbia University, helped pass the Federal
Privacy Act of 1974.

As the new century begins, at least 70 million Americans are using the Internet, each of them producing data as rapidly as he or she consumes it,
each tracked by technologies ever more able to collate the smallest preference
or the greatest desire. Hope, fear, curiosity, joy—in some form, all our emotions and impulses have become digitized, retrievable, and displayed for sale.

Our essential records (age, address, credit rating, marital status, etc.) also
are increasingly captured in electronic form, and are thus more vulnerable to
the efficiencies of scale and the uses of commerce. One Web site, for example,
promises, for the meager sum of seven dollars, to scan "over two billion
records to create a single comprehensive report on an individual."

Worried that capitalism and technology will continue to seize what remains of our policy, *Harper's Magazine* invited four experts to discuss what we
might expect.

The following discussion was held over lunch at the Savoy restaurant in
Manhattan.

> Mark Costello is a former prosecutor in the Manhattan District Attor-
> ney's Office and the U.S. Department of Justice, and is the author, writing
> under the pseudonym John Flood, of *Bag Men*, a novel.

> Michael Moynihan served in the U.S. Treasury and Commerce depart-
> ments from 1995 to 1999 and was one of the principal architects of the
> Clinton Administration's Internet regulation policy. He is now a senior
> fellow at the Center for Strategic and International Studies.

> Ron Sege is the executive vice president of Lycos, the Internet portal
> company, and is responsible for the Web sites in the Lycos Network.

> Alan Westin is professor emeritus of public law and government at Co-
> lumbia University and the author of *Privacy and Freedom* (1967). He was
> instrumental in the passage of the Federal Privacy Act of 1974, which
> regulates government use of personal data held in government records.

> Colin Harrison is deputy editor of *Harper's Magazine*. He served as
> moderator.

Cookies, Magic, and the Golden Egg

Colin Harrison: Suddenly, I'm worried. Like so many other Americans, I'm   5
using the Internet a lot now and am enjoying its complexity and enormity—even its chaos. But I'm aware that with every click I'm being watched, perhaps as I've never been watched before. When I consider my cyber future, how should I conceptualize my privacy?

Alan Westin: Let's put the question in historical context. If you start with the Greek city-state and run through the Middle Ages into early parliamentary institutions and then to the American Republic, privacy remained largely unchanged by technology. When the Framers wrote the Bill of Rights, they had notions about physical search and seizure and limits on the records that could be collected and used. Our laws contain the first modern code balancing privacy against other interests such as disclosure and protective surveillance. But in the 1960s we reached a watershed. That was the moment computer systems began to arrive with large-scale databases and remote terminals. Now we're in the second modern revolution in privacy. The Internet is transforming the way people reveal themselves.

Michael Moynihan: On the one hand, technology has miniaturized what's needed to store immense amounts of information, and, on the other, it linked up those repositories of information all around the world. Now information can be pulled together from diverse sources very rapidly. Today, for example, the tax returns of the entire country could be placed on several CD-ROMs. Soon almost everything about anyone—home movies, old snapshots, college test scores—will be storable in a small amount of space. The Internet itself I compare to a gigantic tape recorder that runs twenty-four hours a day, but the fact that people are able to log on and chat using anonymous names or quasi-anonymous screen names means that they have a tendency to talk about themselves without realizing that everything they're saying is being recorded. The same thing is true in the workplace, where e-mail and, in some cases, voice mail can be archived. Because of the transactional capability of the Internet, people willingly provide information about themselves, for which companies reward them. We are moving into a period when your personal information is something that has value, and if you withhold it you are denying yourself opportunity. Merchants can almost always sell something for less if they're willing to take your personal information and sell it as a commodity. These forces are immense, and still only in their infancy.

Harrison: Why isn't my government protecting me?

Moynihan: Well, the government *is* taking action but, in typical fashion, is moving slowly and without consistency. In the United States, we have a tradition of distributed government, and so a comprehensive privacy protection policy is unlikely to ever occur here. For example, your video-tape rental records are, like your library books, generally protected by law, but your health records are generally not. There's no reason to expect that there will be any simple fix to the privacy issue. In Europe they are looking at severely limiting the distribution of personal data by private companies, but, oddly enough, they have paid no attention to what the government does with your data—which underscores the fact that people's concern about privacy ultimately has to do with whom they fear. In the United States we have a long tradition of healthy wariness about the government getting our data. In Europe people are comfortable with the government knowing everything about them but are concerned about catalogue companies getting their data. And although most Americans may feel they get too many catalogues, ultimately they like catalogues and other shopping options, and don't mind sharing their data with merchants. The federal government is likely to take some steps but nothing comprehensive.

Harrison: I, for one, very much mind the companies mining my life for   10
data. I fear them much more than I fear the government, which is a huge, ponderous, conflicted organism that has to get a court order to find out anything interesting about me, whereas Ron and his industry can find out a lot about me without any legal mechanism.

Moynihan: The government can use the power of law to extract information from you. You may supply information to private industry, but much of what enters databases throughout the world comes involuntarily when you get your driver's license or fill out a government form, because you're required to provide your social security number, which has become an effective key to your personal information—your height, weight, address, and eye color. About half the states sell that information to database companies. The Senate has passed legislation that would restrict this, but it has many exceptions.

Westin: One of the questions we ask in survey research is this: When you think about threats to your privacy, which are you most concerned about—government or business? We found that 55 percent cite government, 43 percent cite business, and a few people say both or neither. That tells you the government still is perceived as the greater potential threat, though that 43 percent is a very solid minority.

Ron Sege: Forgive me, but there's a paradox in this discussion. My company serves about half of the country's Internet users on a monthly basis—some 32 million users out of a total of 70 million. Like any good business, we survey our users to try to understand the aspects of our service they like the most and would like to see us improve. Far and away the leading features our users are interested in are related to personalization. The very power of the Internet is its ability to get you what you want and what you need. For me to give you MyLycos, you have to tell me something about yourself. Our users understand

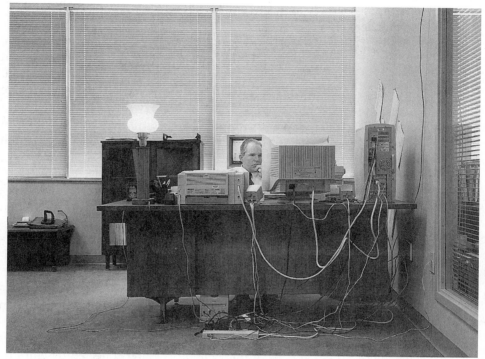

According to some experts, privacy is no longer possible in the age of computers and the Internet.

that. We have a strict opt-in policy for all of the individual data that we collect about our users. You volunteer to tell us everything. Yes, we cookie you, but we cookie you strictly for the purpose of gathering broad, statistically significant information. We don't target individual users based on information that we collect about them without their knowledge.

Westin: Are you reassured by this?

Sege: The power of the Internet is based on the fact that the vast majority of our users choose to provide us with information. We've got to be careful not to kill the goose that laid the golden egg. Nothing is more individual than a pair of Levi's that have been sewn especially for me based on my exact measurements taken with some laser measurement system in my local store. Right? All that's possible as a consequence of technology, but the only way I get that pair of Levi's is if I provide some very personal information to the manufacturer. So we just have to make sure that we don't take this notion of protecting privacy too far and hit it with a meat cleaver so that it keeps guys like me from innovating and providing users with technology they can benefit from.

Moynihan: But doesn't the real magic come when you can take information that people supply and combine it with what you find out about them somewhere else?

Sege: Right. That collaborative filtering technology *is* available if you want it. Now, it's true that the ultimate power of the Web potentially lies in my ability to store and reduce your query strings—what you type into my search box—and then give you information based on what I've learned about your behavior. That's very, very powerful. And what I can learn from these query strings will yield unprecedented amounts of information on behavior in America. But I won't use that information for any purpose other than what you've been told about and have agreed to.

Moynihan: If you're able to harness that power and come up with tantalizing commercial offers, that would not bother me. I'd have great concern, however, if, having assembled that data, you provided it to others who might be judging me on one basis or another—for example, to a bank evaluating a credit application or to an insurance company deciding what rates to charge me.

Westin: What you're doing, Michael, is distinguishing between risk assessment and marketing. Risk assessment in a rationalistic, egalitarian society has to be based on objective information about people's creditworthiness, their insurability, and their employability. What worries the average person is what information is being collected by employers, insurance companies, and banks in order to make those judgments. Passing around your personal information affects your rights and benefits and opportunities. Marketing, on the other hand, is a different domain. People differ in the degree to which they're comfortable opening themselves up to personalization. But many are, in fact, willing to give up personal information.

Sege: I don't know that the Internet has changed the nature of the problem   20 fundamentally. From the dawn of the credit-card database, companies have had tremendous insight into your behavior. Certainly the Internet allows us to collect more nuances—in fact, I can understand your preferences based on how you search my database—but the principles are the same.

The King's Men and the Mice

Harrison: Mark, as a federal prosecutor, wouldn't you want the information Ron is gathering?

Mark Costello: I'd want it. Should I have it? No. Remember, when the government gets information, only a tiny percentage of it is used in criminal prosecutions. The government conducts about 60 million background checks a year. So the government is out there making judgments about people in all kinds of contexts, and the more information the better. Of course this information is valuable. That's the danger.

Harrison: If your job is to catch criminals and put them in prison, why shouldn't you have it?

Costello: Because I might have to investigate a thousand people, of which ten might be indictable bad guys. What about the other 990? A lot of people are suspect but innocent. The other injury is that technology has made surveillance invisible. This is the technological difference Alan mentioned. For hundreds of years in England and the United States, you couldn't be searched without knowing you were being searched. If the king's men kicked down my door, well, I knew it. With wiretapping in the 1920s, it first became possible to be unsurveillably surveilled.

Westin: Actually, with the telegraph-tapping in the 1850s you had the beginning of the surreptitious tap. But you're quite right, the telephone made it ubiquitous.

Costello: And in cyberspace that is true power. Now why is unsurveilled surveillance more corrosive than the old notion of the king's men knocking down my door? The reason is because you never know when or if it's happening to you. I've seen studies showing that something like 20 or 30 million Americans think they've been wiretapped in a given year.

Moynihan: When in fact the actual number is about 2,000.

Westin: That's the actual number of warrants issued under federal and state court orders. It would not be true to say that that's the number of wiretaps. There are a lot of illegal ones by private detectives, for business espionage, etc.

Costello: The point is that there's a perception of surveillance that far outstrips the reality of surveillance, and this is because surveillance is now invisible.

Moynihan: Indeed, in a totalitarian state that technique is able to exert an effect on people's consciousness. It was not possible for the countries in Eastern Europe to monitor everyone, but the perception of being monitored effectively kept people in line.

Westin: Despite all the technology of the Fifties and Sixties and Seventies, most of the studies of totalitarian regimes—from the Soviet Union to Cuba—pointed out that what really mattered was neighborhood surveillance, the fact that every building and every office had an informer. It was the organization of ratting on your neighbor that really made people worry the most. George Orwell noted that it was the informer *plus* the telescreen that made the Big Brother society.

Harrison: Now people crave the telescreen, in effect inducing their own surveillance.

Sege: Let me just make sure people understand the state of the art on the Internet as it relates to this topic. First, I cannot trace your individual activities without your identifying yourself to me. All I can do is trace the activities of your computer. This is an important distinction, particularly as it relates to law enforcement. Having identified you, I could then look at your cookies on the hard drive and see which other Web sites you'd visited. There isn't a one-to-one correspondence between the computer and the individual in the vast majority of cases. Households often have one computer, but three people use it.

Westin: All that will change. In a few years we will have biometric identifiers when people sign on to their computers. *That* world will be the new world.

Sege: I think it's farther out than a few years, but my point is that today I can identify the computer and I cannot identify the user. The second point is, whereas it's true that I have enough computer power to store, reduce, and analyze all of the static demographic data I get from my users, there still is not enough computer power on earth for me to store, reduce, analyze, and use the search query string data. So Lycos throws off about one terabyte of information a week of search-related data, but there's no way we can process and store all that information and focus in on one individual user.

Moynhihan: Over time, the computer capacities will grow exponentially. Today's terabyte is tomorrow's megabyte.

Westin: Let's come back to law. The idea that the Internet will remain law-proof is one of the sillier notions, given that we have one million lawyers who will help make sure that doesn't happen. One thing that is dramatically different is that the consumer traditionally had very little power over the collection of his or her information and its use by business. The law said that this information is protected by the First Amendment: customer lists belong to the business that collects them, and the individual has no property rights to the consumer information that's collected. This is all changing. That information is so valuable now that a whole new industry of infomediaries and others are appearing, saying: We are going to represent you, be your agent. You give us your information, and we will parcel it out at fees that we will then share with you. So if you travel to France and August is the month you travel, that's so valuable to travel companies and others that we'll sell that for X dollars, and you'll get two thirds of it and we'll get one third of it. The era in which your personal information was a free good in the old economic sense, like free air and free water once were, is no longer here. One more point. We have to be careful not to talk about all people and how they feel about this. In fact, we find a solid division of the American public into three groups on this issue. You have privacy fundamentalists, about 25 percent, who are very worried about privacy, don't want to give out their consumer information, and would reject discounts. At the opposite end you have about 20 percent whom we call the privacy unconcerned. Couldn't care less. Give them five cents off, they'll give you their complete genealogical history—no problem. In

35

between you've got the 55 percent we call the privacy pragmatists. And the questions that concern them are: What benefit are you giving me, the consumer? What's the risk I run that you're going to misuse my information? What safeguards do you promise? If they trust you, they'll give you the information; if they don't trust you but want the benefit, then they'll bring law and the government into it and say, I want the benefit, but the risk is too great for me to trust you, so I want a statute to protect me.

Moyniahan: My sense is that the cat is out of the bag.

Sege: Why do you say that?

Moynihan: Because to function in the information economy these days, you're compelled to provide your personal information. I'll give you an example. At first I did not want to join the local affinity card program at my local supermarket, thinking, Why do I want to tell Safeway how much yogurt I'm buying? But I soon recognized that if I had the affinity card, I would get a 50 percent discount on a lot of items. It didn't take long for me to sign up.

Westin: All you're saying is that you put an economic value on your privacy and that it mattered to you when you weighed getting the benefit. I don't agree that everybody is going to fall into line for the discount or the opportunity.

Moynihan: The right to withhold your personal information is an important one that we should protect, but over time the underlying technological trends are such that we will end up divulging a great deal of information simply to participate in the economy.

Sege: Go back to your example of the corner grocery store and carry it over to the Internet. The Internet is actually very liberating, because unlike the corner grocery store, which you have to go to, the Internet allows you to steer clear of those merchants who don't have a privacy policy that you support.

Moynihan: You're suggesting that consumers will shop for a privacy policy. That presupposes they will put privacy ahead of price or selection and will expect companies to honor their policies.

Harrison: Is there any kind of privacy protection that you could not overcome, Mark, working for the Justice Department?

Costello: There's virtually none—with a court order. I think, broadly, that Alan would agree that, in the context of wiretapping, the legal framework created in 1969 has worked. You see very few rogue wiretaps by government agents, and the number of legal wiretaps dramatically dropped, partially because of the law, partially because J. Edgar Hoover finally died. There are different measures of injury, however, and this is where I part company with Alan and Michael. First there is a perception by people, perhaps not well-founded, that they are being watched. As we said, there are 2,000 wiretaps a year in this country,

give or take, by the government. There are 30 million people who believe that they've been wiretapped. We all agree that it is deeply corrosive for a society to feel as if it's being watched. And so even if the
people at this table and elsewhere can put together a framework that is
reasonable for controlling this great gathering of information, the perception of surveillance will be there. When it's invisible surveillance,
when you can't see when you're being seen, the corrosive effect is
greatly multiplied. The other problem is that the body of Internet law
will be made by the United States, yet the Internet is an international
phenomenon. Although ultimately phone-based, it is fundamentally
unlike old Ma Bell. You can move an Internet service provider to the
Caribbean or the Far East, and suddenly the United States Department
of Justice or Department of the Treasury is irrelevant.

Moynihan: But as a practical matter, the ISPs are not relocating their servers
to the Caribbean, because it's much simpler for AOL to keep them in
Virginia. Once a business reaches a certain size, it's not practical to
move servers.

Westin: Professor Peter Swire, now Clinton's counselor for privacy, says
that on the Internet, organizations with Web sites can be elephants or
mice. Mice are very small, scurry fast, are hard to get hold of. Elephants, on the other hand, can be seen, they're slow, and you can grab
them. Let's regulate the elephants, he suggests, the AOLs, the Mi-
crosofts, the Lycoses—the big boys. If we spend all our attention on the
mice in the Caribbean and the Far East, we're never going to make any
progress. So if you want to set norms and standards, pay attention
to the companies that have 18 million people on their server, not to
one guy in his garage who offers what seems to be a tremendous
anonymizer.

Harrison: One nasty mouse can cause a lot of trouble. We've got people
spreading viruses, professional rumor-mongers, for-hire spooks—lots
of mice out there.

Data, Predestination, and a Man with a Certain Chin

Moynihan: Alan, I think you're very optimistic about the ability of govern-   50
ment to solve this problem. Even if legislation is passed to deal with the
most problematic areas—health records, for example—the underlying
trend is for information to become more and more accessible. Government won't deal with that. We have to ask ourselves what this means
for our society, because America was founded on the notion that you
could start anew. If you didn't like Europe or the East Coast, you could
move west. You could leave behind old preconceptions or truths—that
you were a disbeliever or in debt—and try again. That was the allure of
the frontier.

Harrison: Where there was no information about you.

Moynihan: Exactly. The actual frontier is long gone, of course. Frederick Jackson Turner's famous 1893 speech to the American Historical Association told us that. But as Turner expected, the idea of the frontier endured. Jack Kerouac found it years later in the freedom of the American road, and, ironically, many West Coasters and other pioneers believed they had found it in cyberspace. Except it turns out that cyberspace lives in computers, which also are good at searching and remembering.

Westin: It's more complicated. With the frontier, you left the community that knew you, but the minute you got to the new community, you were known. There was a second historical trend, the anonymization of urban life. In many ways it's a more powerful tradition. As the famous German expression put it, "City air makes you free."

Moynihan: That's true. People historically left the small community to find freedom in cities, but as we've moved into a global village (as opposed to a city), where information is known about you, I think we are fundamentally leaving behind that era when you could reinvent yourself by moving, when in effect, you could vote with your feet.

Costello: Part of what's frightening is that we have information-gathering and -storage ability that is international in scope and therefore beyond laws, either good or bad, and follows you wherever you go. You'll have a paradoxical and perhaps unprecedented situation, unlike any other community or the frontier, in which a lot will be known about you by people who don't know you at all.   55

Moynihan: The risk is that we could become a society in which your future is predestined at birth. When if you come, informationally, from a certain neighborhood, that information becomes a self-fulfilling prophecy, defining the sort of offers that you receive, your credit opportunities, your school choices, even the banner ads you see when you get to a certain Web site. When the scope of your future is limited by information in your profile at each step of your life.

Harrison: Data predestination.

Sege: Again, we're stating the situation in the worst possible light. Go back to the results of our user surveys. People see the Internet more than anything as an opportunity to receive more relevant information and more targeted goods and services. Their quality of life is higher. Our unprecedented prosperity for the last ten-odd years has been because we've driven so much inefficiency out of our society. A lot of that has resulted from personalization.

Harrison: Ron, is there any information about people you *won't* take, even when it's offered voluntarily?

Sege: We only take information that we ask for, so by definition we don't take information that we don't ask for. For example, we have a site called Lycos Zone, which is designed for children under the age of twelve. We don't collect any information on kids in Lycos Zone.   60

Harrison: I'm just trying to find blocks of information that are sacred.

Sege: First of all, passing anonymous information content through is differ- ent from passing personalized information. We don't distribute any personalized information about anybody without that person's con- sent. Now, for aggregated blocks of anonymous data, we routinely dis- close the results of a month of search query strings—what the most popular search terms were in the last month, that kind of thing. So that's all anonymous, and I don't think it's relevant to the discussion. But one problem we have is trying to figure out how the First Amend- ment applies to all of this.

Moynihan: I expect that ultimately some genetic information will be pro- tected. That issue is going to be incredibly important in the twenty- first century.

Westin: We should recognize, though, that there's no information, no mat- ter how personal or how sensitive, that some individuals will not dis- close in what they think is the proper protective context. For example, in disease chat rooms people share cancer experiences with people they trust, because they, too, had the disease. There's no such thing as infor- mation per se that individuals will not disclose. It depends to whom they are disclosing it.

Moynihan: But they would probably be very concerned about sharing the same information with employers or life insurers.   65

Westin: Of course.

Moynihan: The question is, How do you begin to draw those distinctions? For example, if someone is doing a search on a disease, presumably he or she is interested in that disease. How do you protect that information from being handed over to a company that would be making judg- ments based on it?

Harrison: Suppose I run an insurance company and I come to you, Ron, and say, I will pay you top dollar to mine the search strings to find the 4 mil- lion people interested in lupus.

Moynihan: You can buy the search word.

Harrison: Okay, I'll buy the search word for lupus, and I will pay you to   70 provide me with all the people on your network who are interested in lupus. Of course, I am going to take that data and correlate it with other data to determine whom I'm going to sell insurance to.

Westin: Remember a couple of things: one, you're not going to know the name of the person, you're only going to know his or her e-mail ad- dress or screen name or—

Sege: For a search engine you only will know the computer the person uses.

Moynihan: Ron, if an individual logs in at Lycos to use some of your per- sonalized services, then you could know the person right down to his or her middle initial.

Sege: You could.

Harrison: I grant you that the information is not going to be perfect, but I,   75
the insurance company, have other ways of filtering it.

Westin: Under state law you have to have personalized information to make an underwriting decision. If my cousin has lupus or my wife has lupus and I go to a lupus Web site, you'd violate the law if you made any judgment about me, Alan Westin, on your life insurance policy, based on assumptions from which Web sites I visit.

Harrison: Suppose I have a way of filtering out the information to make it accurate?

Sege: I wouldn't provide it.

Harrison: Why?

Sege: As a matter of policy.   80

Harrison: Your privacy policy?

Sege: Our Lycos privacy policy, which is available on our Web site. We do not sell that information or provide it to third parties without your consent or without following what's specified in our privacy policy.

Moynihan: But Ron, to what extent will your principles hold up in the commercial marketplace? One can envision a situation a couple of years from now in which a search engine is acquired by a large conglomerate that happens to own financial services, as well as insurance operations, to whom that data might be extremely valuable. How do we protect against that?

Westin: By the perception of the marketplace and because of the privacy advocates' vigilance. When a conglomerate like Citigroup was formed, they issued a privacy promise, which they registered with the federal regulators as well as posted on their Web site, that said: We will never use health information from our Travelers subsidiary for any decision that has to do with banking or financing. Now, why did they do that? They did it as self-denial, because they would have *loved* to put that information together. They did it because of the perception that they would not have happy customers if they used people's health information that way.

Moynihan: There's a tendency to gloss over what really goes on, because   85
underwriting does involve information from the medical information bureau, which may not be an Internet-driven thing but is a similarly large database.

Westin: Not about individuals.

Moynihan: It is precisely about individuals.

Westin: You're talking about the MIB database, which contains the results of your applications to a life insurance company and whether they have turned you down. So if they declined you because you had cancer, there's a code in there that's evident when you apply to another life insurance company.

Costello: The bottom line is that if this information can be gathered and has a dollar value, it will eventually be sold.

Westin: Unless forbidden by the marketplace or law.   90

Costello: But the laws of the United States, in which you have such faith, are just not as relevant as they were five or ten years ago. Because if I can sell this information for $100 million I will go to the Bahamas. That is called capitalism.

Sege: Then why do I have the privacy policy I have? Because I believe it will maximize the value of the firm over the long term. And if I start selling this information, then customers are going to go someplace else.

Costello: And then you get to the next sort of specter, which is an argument for being skeptical about the comfort of the law, even wise law made by wise people. The next specter is government. Your company policies mean nothing if I've got a court order, Ron. You give me the information or you go to jail, period. And I'm not aware of any piece of information that I can't gather by subpoena, court order, search warrant, whatever. With some of this information, I don't even need a court order, I don't even need to go to a judge, I can just get a subpoena. When I was a prosecutor I had a stack of them sitting in my desk.

Moynihan: There's also informal cooperation between law enforcement and business.

Costello: Absolutely. When you talk about DNA, there's obviously going to   95
be a tremendous change. A story appeared today in the *New York Times* about a rapist. They have his semen specimen; they don't know who he is but they know what he's like. Imagine the implications of that. In fact, the NYPD would like to collect DNA on every one of the 400,000 arrests they make every year. Eventually they would build up an enormous profile of arrested persons.

Westin: I'm not so sure that I would start with the premise that crime scene DNA is a piece of private information. I would say that such information is public. Somebody has committed a crime and has left the equivalent of a fingerprint.

Moynihan: But it's an opening to a potentially invasive search to find the matching strand.

Costello: Let's say that the DNA shows that the man has poor eyesight and a certain type of chin. You'll now have people who wear glasses and have a certain type of chin being forced to provide alibis.

Westin: Yes, the same way a witness who saw the crime would say, I think the person wore glasses and had a cleft chin. It's not any different from the fact that law enforcement pursues any clue. But the problem is the data bank. Will we allow government to create stored DNA databases on many, many people?

Moynihan: Once the government has captured data, as it does when it   100
processes W-2 statements, that data is available for other purposes. Currently the W-2 statements have people's incomes and addresses, and recently that data has been opened up for the enforcement of particular legal actions that society has deemed important—for example,

tracking down deadbeat dads. There will always be reasons to open up that data. The question is, Where do you draw the line? I think that we can't expect that the line will always be in the same place. It's going to fluctuate, and the trend is for it to recede.

Costello: It will reflect the prejudices of who's looking at it. The people who are using this information will be flawed. One concrete example is in the case of the law-enforcement response to the Internet. In the last three years most Internet prosecutions have involved child pornography. The vast majority of people who have been prosecuted or arrested or purged have been gay males. Is this because gay males like pornography more than other people? No, it's because this is who law enforcement has gone after. We could talk about a good legal framework and a bad one, but ultimately these efforts are going to be washed away by the bigger trends of profit, geography, the global nature of the Internet, and the fact that information flows.

Moynihan: I would overlay on this discussion the point that we are currently at peace in the United States, and we do not have any of the pressures toward relinquishing data that would come into play were we engaged in a war. I think the historical evidence is pretty strong that when you have a major war going on, there is a general transfer of rights from the individual to the government, which is charged with fighting and winning war. We are fortunate now that we don't have the problem, and there does seem to have been a distribution of computing power to individuals so that they now can run software to protect their privacy, and so forth. But we have to keep in mind that if you move into an environment in which the government is threatened externally, some of that freedom could be retracted.

Westin: If terrorism in the United States were to get really serious, the FBI director could say: You know, we're going to need the encryption keys, and we'll set up a public key system. We'll give it to courts, and we'll give it to the Department of Commerce. He'd argue that the ability of Americans to walk down the street in peace will depend on it. That would be a very powerful argument. Wait until the first subway attack with gas.

Moynihan: It would totally turn the debate upside down. Scruples would vanish. We need to remember that we are living in an environment that is the most conducive to privacy in decades, yet privacy is decreasing.

Costello: The basic technological rule of thumb is that law enforcement and government are generally five years behind the times—actually more like ten—but it's remarkable how a lot of the tools that Ron doesn't think about for a second are going to find their way into government use. Things like packet sniffing, which by their nature involve looking at everything flowing down the Internet. A lot of these tools, including the DNA stuff that we've talked about, are going to find their way into the hands of law enforcement. It's not clear to me that people are ready

105

for that. And then if there's a terrorist incident, a hacker plague, or a China paranoia, that's only going to make the government more aggressive.

Unknown at Last?

Harrison: Given these pressures on our privacy, what will some of the responses of civilization be? Will we all use encryptors? What will we be doing?

Westin: We will have very powerful tools with which individuals assert their privacy. We now have anonymizers and encryption techniques, and we will have organizations that will exist to be your interface with the world. They will give you a coded identity, get the information or goods you want, and pass it on to you, without the information or goods supplier ever knowing you. Privacy management is going to be one of the great growth industries of the next decade.

Moynihan: Privacy will be available for a price, but only a few will pay to protect it. In the future the truly elite will use old-fashioned rotary telephones, stay out of reach of cell phones, and never get paid. It's the rest of us that are tied in to this information economy. One tool that doesn't alter the underlying trend but will help protect our freedom—and here the Internet is a fantastically positive force—is transparency. The essence of cronyism or totalitarianism is information asymmetry, when an elite knows everything about you but you know nothing about it. That leads to injustice and, often, incompetence by an unaccountable elite. So one thing we need to do is to subject elites to the same scrutiny they subject us to. The other thing is to build into computers qualities that overcome the uncertainty of all knowledge—the forbearance, understanding, and leaps of faith that let us forgive enemies, erase debt, and, from time to time, throw away what the data is telling us.

Westin: The people who have always been the most attractive for surveillance and penetration of privacy have been the elites. In the days of Rome and Greece and Elizabethan England, it was the rich and powerful who were the targets of both gossip and surveillance. Ironically, it's the well-to-do who have the resources to go into the country to get away or to have the gated community and have surveillance protection, but they're also the ones who are the targets of the media and law-enforcement investigation. And that will always continue, because people want to know what Madonna has shopped for or who the ruler is sleeping with.

Harrison: So one lesson is, if you want to be unknown, don't make any money. Work outside the economy.   110

Westin: You raise another issue when you say "outside the economy." It's long been known that people pay cash if they don't want to have transactions recorded. Ten years from now, many people will use digital cash. Their transactions will be absolutely anonymous.

Moynihan: Alan, there's no true anonymity when it comes to money. For technical reasons, money always has a trail of crumbs behind it. I don't think anyone should count on anonymous digital cash proliferating.

Costello: You can't have completely anonymous cash, because it has to be linked to you to prove you own it. If there is a record of it somewhere, it will never be beyond the reach of the government. Also, because we've recognized that using cash is a way to conceal your activities from the government, using cash has now become something that causes the government to look at you. If an untraceable form of e-cash is ever invented, the first thing government would do is get a list of all the people who use it.

Harrison: Ron, what information do you protect about yourself?

Westin: That's an intrusive question.   115

Harrison: I know it's an intrusive question.

Sege: It's a violation of my privacy.

Harrison: Are you willing to tell us?

Sege: What type of information do I protect? Actually, I'd like to state both sides of the equation. I tend to provide preference information about myself: where I like to travel, what I like to eat, what form of transportation I like. I protect and feel most zealous about medical information.

Costello: I think my biggest concern is that—wait, you're not recording this   120
are you? I wouldn't want any of this to get out.

Westin: With or without a court order.

Costello: I don't find I'm terribly concerned about so-called preference information.

Sege: You don't mind making it available?

Costello: I just don't care whether you know that I do or don't like Levi's. I find that some of the strangest sorts of personal information come out in the old-fashioned way—you know, living among neighbors, the fact that people I don't know living on my street know my children very well, and so forth. But I've been through so many background checks in my life, so I guess I've been—

Harrison: Violated already.   125

Costello: Yeah, I'm already a husk.

Westin: There's no information about me that I'll not willingly reveal to the right person. I'll tell my medical practitioner anything about me if it will help my care. I'll tell my insurance company what I think is a fair trade-off in order for them to know how to make a judgment about my insurability. So it all depends to whom the information is going to be revealed. Our surveys show that people are most sensitive about financial and medical information, and financial usually beats out medical by a couple of points.

Harrison: Do you go to any particular steps to protect your information vulnerability?

Westin: I always look to see who's asking me for the information, and if I think that they're not entitled to it, I don't give it to them. I will not patronize an establishment that asks me for information I'm not prepared to give. For example, it annoys the hell out of me that an insurance carrier will want to see my medical history to decide whether I'm entitled to get some treatment and some third party is going to be looking at my medical history. But I understand that's the world of health care today, and I can't opt out of that system.

Harrison: How about you, Michael?   130

Moynihan: In order to get me to answer that question you should give me a discount on something. But seriously, perhaps from having worked in the government in Washington, I've become aware that there is no privacy. As Mark said, almost anything, if it's not available, can be readily obtained. So although I might like to protect certain information, I've gone ahead and gotten a Safeway card.

Harrison: You're trying to hide in plain sight?

Moynihan: So to speak. Which I think may be what most people will end up having to do.

Internet Glossary

anonymizer *n:*   an Internet service that strips all identifying information from a user's Internet transactions, allowing anonymous e-mailing, Web browsing, and newsgroup posting.

biometric identifiers *n:*   a class of digital identification technologies that includes voice printing, retinal scanning, and fingerprint imaging; because *biometric identifiers* are digital, they can be indexed and searched.

collaborative filtering *n:*   an automated process of recommending data to a user based on the recommendations of other users who have demonstrated similar preferences, judgments, etc.; *collaborative filtering systems* have been used to provide communities of users with recommendations for books, music, movies, Web pages, newsgroup postings, and other Internet content.

cookie *n:*   an encoded file placed by a Web server on an Internet user's computer; the *cookie* may contain visitation statistics (number of visits, time, and date), personal information supplied by the user (name, address, password, credit card number, preferences), or other information; *vt:*   to place a cookie on a user's computer; to covertly track someone using a digital signifier.

encryption *n:*   the process of converting data into unreadable code; *encrypted data* requires a cipher key to be retranslated back to a readable format; *unencrypted data* is called plain or clear text.

Sources for internet glossary: WorldWide Language Institute <www.wwli.com>; Webopedia Online Computer Dictionary <www.pcwebopedia.com>; Stephen Jenkins <homepages.enterprise.net/ jenko/Glossary/G.htm>; U.S. Patent Office.

packet *n:*   a unit of data sent over a digital computer network; a sequence of *packets* can contain user names, passwords, e-mails, addresses, data-base records, and entire files.

packet-sniffing *n:*   the process of monitoring data traveling over a network; *packet-sniffers* are especially effective on smaller local networks (such as business and university Ethernets), where all network transmission data passes continuously through every computer on the network.

query string *n:*   a line of encoded text, concatenated to the end of a Web address, that delivers a specialized command to the Web server; a *query string* can also provide the server with information the user has inputted into Web page forms as well as information about previous Web pages and sites the user has visited.

search engine *n:*   an online database of records containing Web page addresses, titles, and content summaries: information in a *search engine* is either submitted by Web page authors or gathered directly from the Web using automated search programs.

terabyte *n:*   a unit of measurement for data storage (1 terabyte = 1,024 gigabytes = 1,048,576 megabytes) roughly equivalent to 38 miles of file cabinets full of information. ◪

Reflections and Inquiries

1. Why is individual privacy virtually impossible to maintain if one uses the Internet?

2. How do most people perceive "surveillance"? How, according to Costello, does the reality of surveillance differ from the way it is perceived?

3. Some of the discussants allude to George Orwell and Big Brother. To what extent, if at all, has our culture come to resemble that of the totalitarian state depicted in Orwell's novel *1984?*

4. According to Moynihan, "to function in the information economy . . . you're compelled to provide your personal information." What does he mean by this? Do you agree or disagree? Why?

5. Why is it difficult, if not impossible, to create a national privacy policy for the Internet?

Reading to Write

1. Write a brief summary of each Forum participant's contribution to the discussion of privacy.

2. In a short essay, attempt to resolve the paradox between ensuring customer privacy and ensuring customer satisfaction via disclosure of personal information.

Privacy in the Workplace | Rodger Doyle

> Because employers have a legal right to monitor their employees, workplace privacy is a complicated issue. The following news article reports on efforts by individual states to increase privacy protection for workers. Rodger Doyle is a frequent contributor to *Scientific American* and is the author of the *Atlas of Contemporary America* (Facts on File, 1994).

The U.S. Constitution gives substantial protection to privacy in the home but not where Americans make a living. A 1998 survey of 1,085 corporations conducted by the American Management Association shows that more than 40 percent engaged in some kind of intrusive employee monitoring. Such monitoring includes checking of e-mail, voice mail and telephone conversations; recording of computer keystrokes; and video recording of job performance. Random drug testing is done by 61 percent of those surveyed. Psychological testing, which often attempts to probe intimate thoughts and attitudes, is done by 15 percent of corporations. Genetic testing, which creates the potential for discrimination on a vast scale, is practiced by only 1 percent but, in the absence of a federal law preventing the practice, could become far more widespread if the cost continues to decline.

According to a 1996 survey by David F. Linowes and Ray C. Spencer of the University of Illinois, a quarter of 84 Fortune 500 companies surveyed released confidential employee information to government agencies without a subpoena, and 70 percent gave out the information to credit grantors. Paradoxically, about three fourths of companies barred employees from seeing supervisors' evaluations of their performance, and one fourth forbade them from seeing their own medical records.

Employers are understandably concerned with raising worker productivity, preventing theft, avoiding legal liability for the actions of employees and preventing corporate espionage. These concerns have largely been given far more weight by the courts than the privacy rights of workers, reflecting the reality that federal laws generally do not give strong protection to workers. One of the few exceptions is the Employee Polygraph Protection Act of 1988, which bars polygraph testing except in certain narrow circumstances. Many scientists consider polygraph testing to be unreliable, yet it has been used as the basis for firing employees.

To make up for federal inadequacy, some states have enacted their own statutes. Federal law takes precedence, but where state laws provide greater protection, employers are usually subject to both. The map shows states that ban various activities, including paper-and-pencil honesty tests, which have

Source: Doyle, Rodger. "By the Numbers: Privacy in the Workplace." *Scientific American* Jan. 1999. © 1999 Rodger Doyle. Reprinted with permission.

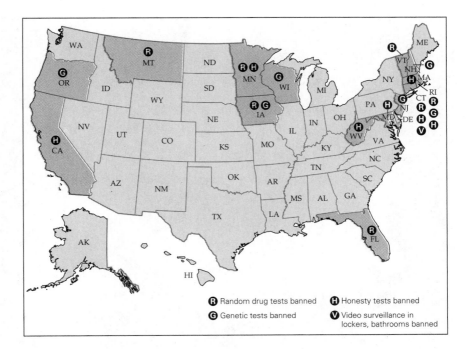

R Random drug tests banned   H Honesty tests banned
G Genetic tests banned   V Video surveillance in
                                                        lockers, bathrooms banned

not been scientifically validated. No state gives strong privacy protection to workers using e-mail, voice mail or the telephone, nor does any state prohibit intrusive psychological testing. The map illustrates that state laws provide only spotty overall support for worker privacy. Surprisingly, it also shows that worker protection from state laws is weak in the seven states stretching from New York to Missouri, where unions are strongest.

Can the legitimate concerns of employers be reconciled with the privacy concerns of workers? In the early 1990s Senator Paul Simon of Illinois and Representative Pat Williams of Montana attempted to do just that with the Privacy for Consumers and Workers Act. Key provisions require that employers clearly define their privacy policies, refrain from monitoring personal communication, refrain from video monitoring in locker rooms or bathrooms, and notify workers when telephone monitoring is in progress (except for quality control). The act, which represented a compromise by unions, employees and civil-rights organizations, was shelved after the Republicans took over Congress in 1994.

A leading privacy activist, Robert Ellis Smith, publisher of *Privacy Journal*, believes the bill is still worthy of passage but would add more provisions, such as stipulating that employers would have to spell out in advance the reasons for monitoring, discontinue it when the reasons no longer apply and destroy tapes of any innocent employee who was monitored. Linowes and Spencer suggest that any new law regulating data privacy be backed up with the threat of punitive damage awards. Lewis Maltby of the American Civil

5

An employee's movements are monitored by a surveillance camera.

Liberties Union suggests that unless or until a national workplace privacy law can be passed, corporations try to be less intrusive. For example, they could discontinue video surveillance in locker rooms and bathrooms and end secret monitoring of employees unless there is suspicion of severe misconduct. ◢

Reflections and Inquiries

1. To what extent does the U.S. Constitution ensure individual privacy?

2. Why do you suppose the Employee Polygraph Protection Act was successfully passed by Congress in 1988?

3. What specific kinds of workplace privacy protection do Senator Paul Simon and Representative Pat Williams seek with their Privacy for Consumers and Workers Act?

4. What kinds of abusive invasions of privacy might occur if workers' privacy is not protected?

Reading to Write

Write a defense or refutation of the need for privacy in the workplace, using the information provided by this article and by the most current information you can locate.

Shahar v. Bowers | Ellen Alderman and
Lifestyle Monitoring | Caroline Kennedy

> Privacy issues can sometimes take an ironic twist, as in the case of a lesbian who was fired from a job before she started it when the employer got word that the woman was planning to marry another woman. As the following narrative of the case discloses, the woman's attorney realized that attempting to sue on the basis of violation of privacy was not the way to proceed. Ellen Alderman and Caroline Kennedy are practicing attorneys from Main and New York respectively. They are the authors of *In Our Defense: The Bill of Rights in Action*. Both are graduates of the Columbia University School of Law.

After graduating magna cum laude from Tufts University in Boston in 1986, Robin Brown wanted to live in a city with warmer weather and good jobs for women. She chose Atlanta, Georgia. Robin was hired to be the program director for the B'nai B'rith Youth Organization, and later took a job as a paralegal, but her long-range goal was to work in the public sector.

In December 1986, Robin attended a winter solstice party, which is, as she puts it, "the politically correct version of a Christmas party." There, she was introduced to Francine Greenfield, known as Fran, who had moved to Atlanta from New York to get her Ph.D. in clinical psychology. Robin and Fran fell in love. As their relationship developed, they bought a house together, got a couple of dogs, and settled down to pursue their respective careers.

Robin considered applying to a graduate school in social work, but in September 1988 wound up instead at Emory Law School as the winner of a Woodruff Fellowship, a prestigious full academic scholarship. Robin did well at Emory. She made the dean's list every semester, received two American Jurisprudence Awards (given to the student in each course who received the highest grade), and was selected as an editor of the *Law Review*. Robin also passed the Georgia Bar Exam while she was still in her third year of law school, and graduated sixth in her class of over two hundred students.

While in law school, Robin decided she would like to do criminal work after graduation. She was also concerned about having a secure, steady job and earning enough money to help support Fran while she completed graduate

---

Source: Alderman, Ellen, and Caroline Kennedy. "*Shahar v. Bowers*: Lifestyle Monitoring." *The Right to Privacy.* New York: Knopf, 1995. 294–302. © 1995 by Ellen Alderman and Caroline Kennedy. Used by permission of Alfred A. Knopf, a division of Random House, Inc.

school. During her second year at Emory, Robin applied and was accepted for a summer job in the office of the attorney general for the state of Georgia, Michael Bowers.

Robin enjoyed the work that summer, especially the criminal appeals and death penalty cases. Deciding how to integrate her personal life with Fran into everyday office socializing, however, required thought and a plan of action. It was a process Robin says many gay people in the workforce must go through.

For her part, she did not want to avoid talk of her personal life alto-gether—that seemed unnatural. She could, as some people she knew did, dis-cuss her private life but constantly edit her descriptions. For example, she could refer to Fran as a "friend" or the two of them as "we" and avoid references to "she" or "her." But that, too, seemed unnatural, not to mention exhausting.

Robin decided that for her, the best approach was to steer a middle course. "Wherever I would work, I would want to be honest about who I am. But that doesn't mean I want to come in the first day and put a big sign on my door," she says. "So what I usually do is try to get to know people—sort of get a feel-ing for when they're liking me and thinking okay things about me. Then, once I've got that established, if I come out to them, hopefully they won't rule me out as a person."

Robin eventually came out to her fellow summer law clerks and three or four permanent employees in the office, including her supervisor. As far as Robin could tell, her sexual orientation did not cause much of a stir among those who knew. And by the end of the summer, Robin had received an offer from the attorney general to become a full-time prosecutor in his office. She happily accepted.

Nineteen ninety-one was to be a big year for Robin for another reason as well. For some time, Robin and Fran had been meeting with a rabbi to discuss sanctifying their relationship through a religious marriage ceremony. They fi-nally chose a date—July 28—after Robin's graduation but before the start of her job. The weekend celebration was to take place on a campground at Table Rock State Park in the South Carolina mountains. Robin and Fran had made all the arrangements. They expected about a hundred people, including their parents, grandparents, and friends. Fran had invited the entire psychology de-partment from the federal penitentiary where she was working, and Robin had invited a couple of people from the attorney general's office.

As part of the ceremony, Robin and Fran had also decided to change their names. "We weren't satisfied with any of the combinations of Brown and Green we came up with, so we decided to take a name that had a different kind of meaning for us than variations of our fathers' names would have," says Fran. They chose Shahar, which in biblical Hebrew means "an act of seek-ing God" and in modern Hebrew translates as "dawn."

In mid-June 1991, Robin called Bob Coleman, the deputy attorney general in charge of administration, to confirm her starting date (September 23) and her division assignment (division 3, criminal appeals and death penalty work) and to inform him of her upcoming name change. "I had this big thing about changing my name," says Robin. "I thought I just couldn't go in and have a new name. I decided to say, 'I'm getting married and I'm changing my name.' Just like that. I didn't know him well enough to get into it with him, and I assumed he would say, 'Congratulations. Okay, what's your new name going to be?' And he would change my paperwork and that would be the end of it."

"But," she says, "what happened was, he got very excited when I told him I was getting married. Then I found out through the grapevine a few weeks later that he had been running around the office telling everyone that I was getting married. The assumption behind it was that I was marrying a man. Certainly, when I said to him, 'I'm getting married and I'm changing my name,' I didn't think he would think I was marrying a woman. But it was very difficult because I didn't know him well enough to say, 'Bob, I'm having a ceremony with my female partner.' I didn't feel comfortable telling him that."

"I was horrified because it meant that when I got to the job, they would all be saying, 'Oh, I heard you got married,' and I would be in this awkward position over and over again—'Do I tell them that I married a woman, or do I let it go?' If he had just said 'Congratulations,' then I would have come to work and I would have been able to come out at my own pace. . . . I just didn't really think it through."

But as it turned out, she didn't have to. A couple of weeks later, on July 9, Bob Coleman's secretary called to ask Robin to come down to the office for a brief meeting. When Robin got to Coleman's office the next day, he was there with Stephanie Manis, another deputy attorney general. Coleman handed Robin an envelope and said her job offer was being withdrawn. Robin asked if she could speak with Michael Bowers personally and was told his schedule was full. That was it. She was fired before she had started work.

"I really think I was in a state of shock," says Robin, haltingly. "I mean, I just remember feeling so hot, and my body just kind of shaking—it's sort of mind-blowing. I had done very well in law school. I could have had a lot of choices of where to work. I *wanted* to work for them. And my work was good. There was never any question of [whether] I did a good job for them. It was like a bomb going off in my face.

"I left. I opened the letter. I saw what it said," Robin continues. The letter read:

> I regret to inform you that I must withdraw the State Law Department's offer of employment. . . . This action has become necessary in light of information which has only recently come to my attention relating to a purported marriage between you and another woman. As the chief legal officer of this state, inaction on my part would constitute tacit approval of this purported marriage and jeopardize the proper functioning of this office.

"I went to a pay phone and called Fran. Then I called my parents. I called the director of career services at Emory. I went to an appointment which I cut short. Then I came home and Fran had left work and come home."

Fran says she, too, was shocked. "Just absolutely shocked. The timing made it worse, coming about two weeks before the ceremony. We were already in a state of total confusion. Unlike traditional families, we were doing it ourselves, all of it. So there was a lot of stress. Plus, Robin's job was our income. We had these tickets to go to Greece for a month, and I know what I earn working part-time just doesn't cut it. We were spending all our money on this wedding. The idea was that Robin was going to have a decent-paying job. And then it was, no job."

In deciding how to respond to Michael Bowers, Robin faced a dilemma. On the one hand, she says, "I felt like he was baiting me, like, 'Come on, sue me. I'm putting it in writing for you.'" but she was aware of the personal difficulties she would face as an open lesbian bringing a lawsuit against a popular politician in a conservative community. Robin says she was concerned she would be used as a "pawn to advance his political career." On the other hand, she felt that if she did not take official action, she would always "be left with this feeling of being a victim."

The heart of the case lay in Shahar's claim that her sexual orientation bore   20
no relationship to the quality of her work, and that her job offer could not be withdrawn solely because of activities conducted outside the office. At first, it seemed to be a quintessential privacy claim. Her private life had nothing to do with her job. Instead, Robin's case became a prime example of the *limitations* of the right to privacy. And in what some would call a twist of fate, and others a setup, Michael Bowers was the reason why.

Michael Bowers is a somewhat infamous figure in the struggle for gay rights. His rise to prominence began in 1982, when Georgia police entered the home of a man named Michael Hardwick and found Hardwick in bed with another man. Hardwick was arrested and charged with violating the state's sodomy law. At that time, Georgia's sodomy law, like those of many states, defined sodomy as "any sexual act involving the sex organs of one person and the mouth or anus of another." It applied to heterosexuals as well as homosexuals and carried a prison sentence of up to twenty years. Hardwick challenged the law as unconstitutional. He argued that private sexual behavior between consenting adults was within the zone of privacy that the Supreme Court had created in other decisions involving contraception and abortion. Michael Bowers, as Georgia's attorney general, fought to keep the sodomy law on the books. Bowers argued that homosexual sodomy was not within the zone of privacy that protected heterosexual reproductive decisions.

The Supreme Court agreed with Bowers. In a 5-to-4 decision, the Court refused to recognize a "fundamental right to engage in homosexual sodomy." The dissenters, led by justice Harry Blackmun, rejected that characterization of the case. Blackmun wrote: "What the Court really has refused to recognize is the fundamental interest all individuals have in controlling the nature of their intimate associations with others. . . . [This] poses a far greater threat to the values most deeply rooted in our Nation's history than tolerance of nonconformity could ever do."

After their defeat in *Hardwick,* gay rights advocates retreated from the right to privacy as the legal rationale for their cause. For example, current battles over gays in the military are usually litigated under the Equal Protection Clause as cases of discrimination, not as violations of the right to privacy. Paradoxically, too, the loss in the courts reflected the growing strength of the gay rights movement and a new social reality. Maybe as a practical as well as a legal matter, "privacy" was not the answer. In the 1990s, according to Ruth Harlow, Shahar's lawyer and the associate director of the ACLU's Lesbian and Gay Rights Project, "Privacy is not really what we are looking for."

Instead, Harlow describes the central issue in Shahar's case as "allowing us to live in the public realm, just like everyone else does, and not having to keep private decisions about who we have relationships with, or what we do in the context of our religion." In other words, Robin should be able to steer a middle course and talk freely with people at work once she gets to know them, rather than constantly having to hide her personal life.

Harlow says, "Robin Shahar was doing the same thing that heterosexual people do all the time. She had mentioned entering into a relationship with her partner, and that they were going to take a trip together. These are the kinds of things that people talk about every day, but if it happens to be in the context of a lesbian or gay relationship, it becomes a different issue. . . . So the right to privacy just [doesn't] mesh with our whole theory of what the case is about."

Instead, Robin claimed that the withdrawal of her job offer violated her freedom of religion and association (under the First Amendment) and unlawfully discriminated against her on the basis of her sexual orientation. First, Shahar argued that the ceremony was purely religious n nature; it was performed by a rabbi; it was private; it was conducted far from the office in a remote location; and it was not a legally recognized marriage, only a religious ceremony. Secondly, Robin argued that her relationship with Fran and their private gathering were both protected by the constitutional right of intimate association. The right has been developed in a number of court cases involving the traditional family unit, but Robin broke new legal ground by arguing that her relationship with Fran should also be protected. Finally, she argued that she had a straightforward case of discrimination: Michael Bowers withdrew the job offer simply because she was a lesbian. The case became a rallying point not only for gay rights advocates but also for workplace privacy advocates concerned about employers' control over the off-duty behavior of their employees, whether it be sexual practices, religious affiliations, or recreational activities.

For his part, Bowers rejected Shahar's claims of freedom of religion and association. He argued that it was the homosexual nature of the marriage, not Robin's religious beliefs or practices, that had led to the withdrawal of her job

25

offer. He pointed out that he had not prevented the ceremony, and that Robin remained free to associate with Fran or whomever she wished. Finally, he said that withdrawing Shahar's job offer was not an act of discrimination but, under the circumstances, the only reasonable response from the state's chief legal officer. Bowers pointed out that he had broad discretion over the hiring, firing, and administration of the Law Department. The attorneys who work for him are the legal counselors for the state. They must defend and enforce the laws of Georgia, including the sodomy law.

Bowers relied heavily on his role in the *Hardwick* decision and his visibility as a defender of public morality. He claimed that if the department had to prosecute a sodomy case in the future, or litigate a civil case involving benefits for homosexual partners, Robin's presence in the department would undermine public confidence in the department's ability to enforce the laws in general, because presumably she herself would be in violation of a law. He stated in his deposition: "The natural consequence of a marriage is some sort of sexual conduct. I would think, to most people, and if it's homosexual, it would have to be sodomy."

Bowers contended that Robin's ceremony was a public political statement of the type prohibited by departmental regulations, not a private religious ceremony. As Dorothy Kirkley, the lawyer representing Michael Bowers, put it, "In every job there are some constraints on what you do given the legal responsibility of the office, its duties, the fishbowl nature, the culture, the work ethic, whatever. Your conduct has to be calibrated to be appropriate to the office where you work . . . particularly in a place like the attorney general's office, which is very public, very visible in the state of Georgia."

Bowers had been forced, he claimed, to choose between compromising his position by approving Shahar's public conduct, or withdrawing her job offer. In fact, some people in the Law Department saw Robin as a political activist who had applied to work for Bowers precisely because of his visibility—in other words, she had set him up.   30

Not surprisingly, Shahar objected to Bowers' interpretation of the facts. She portrays herself not as a crusader, but as naïve. Her primary objection, however, was to the assumption that she was a lawbreaker simply because she was a lesbian. She pointed out that she had not been accused of sodomy, and there was no evidence that she had engaged in such behavior. She claimed it was discriminatory to assume that she, as a lesbian, had engaged in sodomy, while not assuming the same of heterosexual attorneys.

Furthermore, argued Robin, whether or not she was a homosexual had no bearing on whether she could perform the job of staff attorney, even in a case involving sodomy. "I can think of very few lawyers who would have the luxury of being in a job where they would believe in every case they were handling, where they would always think that they were on the right side of a case," she says. "Part of what I have to deal with as a lawyer is that I'm going to get certain cases that I'm just not going to agree with. But nonetheless, I have to advocate on behalf of my client to the best of my ability. And it's offensive to think that, because I'm a lesbian, I'm not going to be able to put my personal beliefs aside to advocate on behalf of my client."

One of the most hotly debated issues in the case was which legal standard should be used to measure Michael Bowers' action. Shahar argued that because her fundamental rights (freedom of religion and freedom of association) had been infringed, the most demanding standard should be applied. In order to justify his withdrawal of her job offer, Shahar argued, the state had to show that it had a *compelling* interest in refusing to employ her, and that Bowers had taken the most limited step necessary to achieve that goal.

Bowers contended that a different analysis should be applied. When government is acting as an employer (as opposed to when it is acting on behalf of all citizens), its actions should be measured by balancing the employee's interest—here, Robin's interest in her same-sex marriage—against the government's interest in the efficient delivery of public services.

On October 7, 1993, the federal district court in Atlanta issued its opinion. 35° In potentially significant language, it found that Robin and Fran's relationship is protected by the Constitution's right of intimate association. The court also agreed with Shahar that she had "pursued her desired association only at the price of her employment."

The question then boiled down to whether Bowers justifiably imposed that price. On this issue, the court agreed with Bowers and applied the balancing test. The court found that the ceremony was public, not private, and that continued employment of Shahar could undermine "the efficient and credible operation of the Department which requires attorneys to refrain from any conduct which appears improper or inconsistent with Department efforts in enforcing Georgia law."

The court concluded that "the unique circumstances of this case show that [Bowers'] interest in the efficient operation of the Department outweigh [Shahar's] interest in her intimate association with her female partner." Robin was out of a job.

Robin Shahar went to work for the city of Atlanta's Law Department and is appealing her case. ◪

Reflections and Inquiries

1. Why do you suppose Bowers explicitly stated his reasons, in writing, to Robin Brown-Shahar for firing her?

2. What was the rationale behind the Georgia Supreme Court's decision to reject Shahar's claim that her sexual orientation bore no relationship to the quality of her work?

3. What rights other than privacy did Ruth Harlow (Shahar's attorney) see Bowers as having violated? How did Bowers counterrespond? Which claim seems most relevant, in your opinion?

4. What was the rationale behind the federal district court's final ruling?

Reading to Write

Given the information presented in the *Shahar v. Bowers* case, defend or challenge the assumption that government employees must abide by laws regulating their sexual preferences or practices.

Privacy and Intimate Information | Ferdinand Schoeman

Privacy is often assumed to be a value, but how? What are its social implications? Is it better to disclose ourselves to others or to keep secrets? Is it possible for privacy and the need for public disclosure to coexist harmoniously? Is it even possible to generalize about these matters, or are they strictly dependent on particular circumstances? Questions such as these arise when we consider privacy from a philosophical perspective. In the following essay, Ferdinand Schoeman, an expert in the philosophy of law, examines these questions in the context of intimate information about individuals.

I knew the mass of men conceal'd
Their thought, for fear that if reveal'd
They would by other men be met
With blank indifference, or with blame reproved;
    from Matthew Arnold's "The Buried Life"

Privacy itself is suspect as a value. It makes deception possible and provides the context for concealing things about which we may feel ashamed or guilty. Embarrassed by this feature, defenders of privacy often argue that privacy is a necessary response to a social and political world that is insufficiently understanding, benevolent, respecting, trustworthy, or caring. I shall call this rationale for privacy "reactive." This response assumes that we would no longer care who knows the most intimate facts about ourselves were the world morally improved. Some have even suggested that, divorced from its prudential motivation, a proclivity for privacy should be seen as an attitude that impedes the realization of a sense of community and at the same time makes the individual more vulnerable to selective disclosures on the part of others. [If everything about a person is already known by others, that person need not fear revelations. If he (or she) discovers that others are more like him than he first suspected, he is less subject to the intimidations engendered by a sense of comparative inferiority.]

Source: Schoeman, Ferdinand David. "Privacy and Intimate Information." *Philosophical Dimensions of Privacy: An Anthology.* Ed. Ferdinand David Schoeman. New York: Cambridge UP, 1984. 403–418. Copyright © 1984 by Cambridge University Press. Reprinted with the permission of Cambridge University Press.

Philosophers and legal theorists have discussed privacy as valuable independent of its effectiveness in protecting persons from a morally harsh world. Charles Fried,[1] Robert Gerstein, [2] James Rachels,[3] and Richard Wasserstrom,[4] have elaborated the ways in which the intimate qualities of some interpersonal relationships would not be possible outside the context of privacy. Ruth Gavison,[5] Jeffrey Reiman,[6] Richard Wasserstrom,[7] Robert Gerstein,[8] and Stanley Benn[9] have pointed out how certain intimate dimensions of the self (having to do with the creation or discovery of moral character) would be truncated or debased without respect accorded to the individual's claim to control personal information. In the vein of these theorists, I would like to add to the discussion of the place of privacy as a value independent of its feature of protecting people from an imperfect social world. In this chapter I will elaborate themes others have introduced as well as suggest some new ones. Essentially I hope to show that on balance, outside of special contexts, revelation of self is not to be thought of as desirable in itself and may be detrimental. I hope to persuade readers that respect for privacy marks out something morally significant about what it is to be a person and about what it is to have a close relationship with another. Put abstractly, I shall argue that respect for privacy reflects a realization that not all dimensions of self and relationships gain their moral worth through their promotion of independently worthy ends.

I

I shall begin by discussing the question of whether revelation of self is good, except in those special contexts when it enables others to injure one's interests. Let me begin with the presumption that, prudent mistrust aside, more knowledge about a person is better. One implication of this view, a view entertained by Richard Wasserstrom[10] and endorsed by Richard Posner,[11] is that it is a better state of the world, other things being equal, if when I go to the dry cleaners to pick up my pants the attendant and I also share our innermost feelings and attitudes, despite the fact that we have no close relationship. The claim is that even outside the context of an especially close relationship, it is somewhat better for people to know more about one another than it is for them to know less. This attitude strikes me as most implausible but enlightening. It can be used to illustrate how much of what is good about people sharing and knowing one another intimately is contextually dependent.

As things now stand, people generally reveal intimate parts of their lives only to persons in contexts in which some special involvement is anticipated. It is, accordingly, very awkward to be going about one's business and be confronted with a plea or expectation for personal involvement which, by hypothesis, is unoccasioned by the relationship. Although sometimes welcome, generally such pleas are disturbing for they seem to give us less control over where we will expend our emotional resources. The reason for being reserved in these situations is not fear of being harmed by the content of one's revelations, but rather a realization that such situations call for something personally important to be given without first assuring that it is given freely. It does not seem plausible to suggest that it would be better if people generally revealed intimacies without really caring about the emotional attachments normally associated with such revelations; the very intimacies such revelations characteristically promote would have a harder time surfacing if they were deprived of their social and personal significance.

Three exceptions to this position should be noted and explained. First, there are times when a person so desperately needs the concern of others that something like an insistence on intimacy is legitimized. (Crisis may occasion temporary intimacy.) This concession in no way goes to showing that in normal situations such revelations are appropriate. Second, the publication of personal diaries, autobiographies, poems, confessions, and the like, though revealing of personal intimacies, hardly seems to warrant moral disapproval, as the position here advocated about reserve would seem to suggest. In response, we can observe that unlike personal disclosure, the publication of personal information leaves others completely free emotionally to take whatever attitude they want toward the writer. Even though the point of the writing may be to affect others in a personal way, there is still the distance that publication imposes that differentiates this communication from person-to-person revelations. Third, it may be pointed out that we often talk to complete strangers about intimate matters and that the frequency with which this occurs suggests that something important is being missed in the analysis presented. In considering this argument, it is important to notice that a stranger is someone uninvolved in the web of one's ordinary social relationships and someone one expects to stay uninvolved. Thus to a certain extent, revelations to a complete stranger are largely equivalent to publication because the expectation of involvement is so remote. The stranger provides an objective perspective—a perspective people admittedly find very useful to confront. The fact that one is in a position to tell a stranger things of an intimate nature does not suggest that it would be good to tell the same things to someone with whom one has an ongoing relationship. Our relationship with these people would become very different if intimate sharing were made a part of it. (Below I take up the question of the desirability of redefining relationships so as to include such intimacy.)

The emphasis in discussion of these exceptions has been on the demands revelations place upon the listener. Now, I shall discuss in detail difficulties for the person who is doing the revealing. Essentially, I shall argue that what is revealed in abstract contexts may not be at all what the revealer intends to convey.

What makes information private or intimate for a person is not just a function of the content of the information; it is also a function of the role the information plays for the person. One facet of this role is that the information is to be regarded as special and thus only revealed in certain contexts—contexts in which the very giving of the information is valued as a special act, and where the information so given will be received sympathetically. We tend to think of private information as pertaining to primarily embarrassing or wrongful conduct or thoughts. I think that what makes things private is in large part their importance to our conceptions of ourselves and to our relationships with others. To entrust another with intimate information is not primarily to provide the other with an arsenal that could prove detrimental to ourselves if revealed to the world. Perhaps the most significant aspect of what the revealer of intimate information has to convey is that *the information matters deeply to himself.* Typically, this involves a trust that the other will not regard the revelation as inconsequential, as it would be to the world at large. What is conveyed to someone uninvolved is different in an essential way from what is intimately conveyed. Selective self-disclosure provides the means through which people envalue personal experiences which are intrinsically or objectively valueless.

Perhaps the closest analogy to what I am trying to express about intimate information is our attitude toward a holy object—something that is appropriately revealed only in special circumstances. To use such an object, even though it is a humble object when seen out of context, without the idea of its character in mind is to deprive the object of its sacredness, its specialness. Such an abuse is regarded as an affront, often requiring ritual procedures to restore the object's sacred character. (Note that there are certain uses which are permitted even though not devotional in nature: use for educational purposes, for example.)

Supportive of this analogy between the private and the sacred are some literary treatments of privacy invasions. Incursions into one's privacy, one finds, are described as *pollutions* or *defilements*. In Henry James's novel *The Reverberator* we find Gaston Probert trying to explain to his finacée, Francie Dosson, just what her revelations of family matters to, and the subsequent publication in, a society newspaper has meant to his family. Gaston puts it this way: "They were the last, the last people in France, to do it to. The sense of excruciation—or pollution."[12] We also find the theme of privacy invasion as defilement explored in Athol Fugard's play, *A Lesson from Aloes*. The South African secret police have ransacked Piet and Gladys Bezuidenhout's house. They discover Gladys's diary and read it, despite the fact that there is nothing significant in it to anybody but Gladys. Gladys, trying to explain to her husband just how defiling the experience was, speaks as follows:[13]

> There, I've cancelled those years, I'm going to forget I ever lived them. They weren't just laundry lists, you know. There were very intimate and personal things in those diaries, things a woman only talks about to herself. Even then it took me a lot of trust and courage to do that. I know I never had much either, but I was learning. *(Her hysteria begins to surface again)* You were such a persuasive teacher, Peter! "Trust, Gladys. Trust yourself. Trust Life." There's nothing left of that. *(She brandishes her diary)* Must I tell you what I've been trying to do with this all day? Hide it. It's been behind the dressing table . . . under the mattress.
>
> Can you think of somewhere really safe? Where nobody would find it, including yourself? There isn't is there? Do you know what I would really like to do with this? Make you eat it and turn it into shit . . . then

maybe everybody would leave it alone. Yes, you heard me correctly. Shit! I've learned how to use my dirty words. And just as well, because there's no other adequate vocabulary for this country. Maybe I should do that in case they come again. A page full of filthy language. Because that is what they were really hoping for when they sat down with my diaries. Filth! . . .

If you were to tell me once more that they won't come again . . . ! To start with, I don't believe you, but even if I did, that once was enough. You seem to have a lot of difficulty understanding that, Peter. It only needs to happen to a woman once, for her to lose all trust she ever had in anything or anybody. They violated me, Peter. I might just as well have stayed in that bed, lifted up my nightdress and given them each a turn. I've shocked you. Good! Then maybe now you understand.

Not only is it a violation of an individual if intimate information is forced or tricked out of the person, or if a confidence is betrayed, as the literary examples here illustrate, but even the person himself who feels something special about this information may be insufficiently sensitive to the role of this information in his own mind. (Perhaps we should say that a person can violate his own privacy.) Probably every person has had the experience of telling another something very important, something that is unappreciated as special by the listener. This information, we learn, is really only meant for those who will treat it as something that matters *because it matters to the speaker.* Otherwise the most we have is a good or interesting story; often not even that. By being shared with others who cannot really appreciate the personal significance of certain information, such information loses some of its special character for the revealers. The kind of connectedness that is a prerequisite for intimate sharing must be present for this kind of appreciation to emerge. Otherwise the effort at communicating will misfire.

I have been arguing that the revelation of intimate information should be regarded as appropriate only in certain contexts, and that indeed, in a sense this kind of revelation *cannot* take place outside such a context. When it does take place outside the proper setting, a sense of violation is occasioned, whether the revelation was voluntary or not. Let me now address the question: Would the world be a better place if everyone shared the kind of relationship in which it was appropriate to make private disclosures? In response, let me begin by noting that different kinds of relationships require different qualities of persons. For instance, qualities which make persons good friends may make them unsuitable for a supervisor–supervisee relationship. There need not be any defect in the persons either as friends or as workers; qualities required in each relationship may be mutually exclusive. For a host of reasons, personal characteristics may determine that a person feels more comfortable in, and gains more out of, certain personal settings than others. Such concerns cannot be irrelevant to the capacity and desirability for intimacy. It is worth noting that in many of our important relationships emotional distance between the parties is crucial. For instance in a lawyer–client relationship, a psychotherapist–patient relationship, or even a student–teacher relationship it is not ideal that there be unbounded emotional involvement between the parties. These relationships require an objectivity of judgment that would be counterproductive to eliminate. Conversely, such professional detachment would be inappropriate in relationships in which identification with the other is a central feature of the relationships, as in parent–child relationships, friendships, and marriages.

People have, and it is important that they maintain, different relationships with different people. Information appropriate in the context of one relationship may not be appropriate in another. Such observations have been captured by sociological notions such as "audience segregation," "role," and "role credibility."[14] Such notions have been introduced to help describe or explain how the effectiveness of our relationships to various people in diverse contexts depends on limited access to persons or, more precisely, on access to limited dimensions of persons. Though some of our important relationships and aspirations involve intimacy with others, some are focused on really quite limited and objective interactions. As Ruth Gavison has argued,[15] part of our capacity to work with others in professional contexts may depend on remaining uninvolved in personal, political, moral, and religious aspects of the other. Accordingly, if a person finds the discussion of his own or anyone else's intimate life inappropriate in many contexts, it is not necessarily because he has anything to be ashamed about or anything for which he should feel guilty. It is that there are various dimensions of a person which it is important to develop, only some of which may involve intimate sharing. The integrity of different spheres of a person, and the ultimate integrity of the person, depends on that person's capacity to focus on one dimension at a time. This defense of privacy has nothing to do with lack of trust or good will generally, or with any fact about the moral imperfections of the world.

Some writers have equated nondisclosure of self to others as tantamount to fraud, hypocrisy, deceit.[16] Keeping people ignorant about what one is like in spheres they are not part of, or have no reasonable claim to knowledge about, is in no way morally tainted behavior. Generally, so long as a person does not misrepresent himself to those who, within the relevant domain, reasonably rely on his projected image, that person is not acting deceptively.

Related to the concern that role segregation is deceptive or hypocritical is the claim that it would be better if people exhibited coherence across the different roles they maintain. For instance, what one is like as a professional would in relevant ways be indicative of what one is like as a family member, as a citizen, as a friend, as an athlete, and so on. Though what I shall have to say here is admittedly sketchy and speculative, there does seem to be evidence of a psychological nature that relates to this issue. Different conceptions of what it is to be a person do bear on the issue of an individual's personality coherence and the role of privacy. According to the commonsense view, there is a core personality that is integrated but puts on various guises (for various purposes) in particular contexts. The picture is of a character standing behind various masks, none of which is really the actor, with the ability of discarding all the personae and revealing the true core. From this view, we can distinguish authentic responses of an individual from those that are role-governed, context-dependent, and inauthentic. On this account, privacy serves to protect a person's intimate self through concealment. Privacy permits pretense.

There is another view according to which there may be no unified core   15
personality that exhibits authentic or inauthentic responses to circumstances. Instead there are diverse facets of personality that are brought into play in various contexts. These facets of self are not personae that some central self dons in its inauthentic mode. Rather these selves actually constitute the person. A person is something like a corporation of context-dependent characters. Any coherence between dimensions is something achieved and not something naturally implicit in the person.

On this second view it is still possible for people to be deceptive or inauthentic. The reference self is simply not the central core; it is the particular dimension of self that is specific to the prevailing context. Roles are not the masks of personality but the very medium within which personality is attributable to people. Privacy from this perspective supplies the condition for the expression and fulfillment of different dimensions of self, all of which may be equally real. It is important to emphasize that the attribution of dimensionality to individuals does not mean that people are multiple personalities in a clinical sense. Rather this view states that one may operate with different values and sensitivities in these different modes without being either schizophrenic or deceptive.

Psychologists who have advanced this second view of the self have done so on the basis of clinical and experimental findings.[17] Their most dramatic evidence is that certain consequences that would be anticipated on the basis of the commonsense view of self are frequently not what is found. On the commonsense view an individual's behavior in one setting should be quite predictable on the basis of his behavior in other settings. This is not the case. What is found is that knowledge about a person in one context is of little predictive value when anticipating behavior in dissimilar contexts. Instead, what proves to be a better predictor of behavior is knowledge of how others, however varied in personality, have behaved in the particular context at issue. Knowing the context of behavior and knowing how others have responded to this context prove to be more reliable indicators of behavior than does knowing how an individual has behaved in other contexts. There is more uniformity in behavior among different individuals in the same context than there is in the same person over a range of different contexts.

This evidence may suggest that there is no core self; one of the key functions that the core self is supposed to serve is to account for the consistency of behavior through diverse contexts and times. If the effect is not present, there is less reason to posit the cause. The results of the experiments cited above suggest there is some basis for thinking that privacy may play a central role in personality development. Privacy may provide the contexts in which various facets of personality can develop.

There are situations which require unusually high coherence between roles or even require that there be only one role in the agent's life. Someone who joins a monastic order has apparently committed himself to leading only a monastic life, or at least to doing only things consistent with that life. People who present themselves in such roles indicate to others that all their dimensions can be expected to conform to the ideals of their self-proclaimed ideal self. Such roles may preclude much of what would normally count as private domains. Although there are obviously things to admire about such choices, it is also apparent that there are costs in terms of aspects of the self that must be foregone.

II

Are there domains of life which are inherently private? Several positions have been developed in the literature in answer to this question. According to some, what it is that is regarded as private is culturally determined and respect for a person's privacy is primarily symbolic in significance.[18] According to a related position, what is private is determined by each particular relationship.[19] Relationships define which parts of another's life one can legitimately inquire into and which are beyond one's legitimate ken. According to still others, what is private is determined by what area of one's life does not, or tends not to, affect the significant interests of others.[20]

The last criterion is subject to the following difficulty. Whatever one might claim as private can cease being such if others manage to generate a stake in that state of affairs. With such a criterion one no longer maintains control over what would otherwise seem a private part of one's life. For instance, so long as one is in a position to make a large bet on any matter relating to another's life, that matter ceases to be private because of the interest one acquires in uncovering this facet of another's life. Additionally, if we think of the large investments certain institutions have in tracking down intimate details of various people's lives, we should have to concede that these details are not really private after all. While we may want to be somewhat utilitarian in considering how much weight to give to individual privacy claims, I think that there is little persuasive about the position that the "self-regarding" aspects of life are at the same time the private aspects.

A related criterion of the private, it could be suggested, is that it be the domain of a person's life which the individual is generally in the best position to manage well. Assigning rights over this area to anyone else, the suggestion continues, would result in lower overall benefits. One may concede the point that individuals should control those parts of their lives which they can best manage without thinking that this constitutes a criterion of the private. Although a physician might be in the best position to regulate how we should care for our bodies, this remains a private matter.

Although there are many things that we regard as private, some of these things seem essentially private because they are central to us—because they define what we are emotionally, physically, cognitively, and relationally. We might say about these categories that we consider information relating to them presumptively private. Other values may offset our interest in protecting an individual's privacy in any particular context, nonetheless, roughly speaking, one's private sphere in some sense can be equated with those areas of a person's life which are considered intimate or innermost. Though categories like parent, poet, and patriot have the meaning they do in a social context, it is their centrality to identity which makes these roles part of a person's private dimension.

This view is my basis for rejecting the second criterion of the private mentioned above: the view that each relationship defines what is private to it. It may be true that depending on our relationship we will regard some pieces of information appropriate for some to inquire into and others not. This fact does not settle what it is that is private. Even if we think that it is appropriate for a psychiatrist or a spouse to ask us about various things, this does not mean that such topics are not private matters. It is just that the norms permit some people access to our private domains.

The position advocated here might be challenged by observing that qualities such as age, race, family status, profession, and general appearance are central to us even though we do not generally regard these as private. And other characteristics are taken as private even though they do not have much to do with what is central to our lives or with the integrity of our intimate selves, for example, annual income. The qualities that I mention as central but which are not regarded generally as private are those that would be either very difficult to conceal if one were to have any social existence at all, or else central to one's public role and thus counterproductive to keep private for that reason. With respect to those things that are not central to people but about which people feel a sense of privacy, these might generally be regarded as sensitive topics because of the reactive concerns we all share or because of socially conditioned norms. In any event, in saying that the realm of the intimate is essentially private or marks off what is the private realm, I am not saying that there are not other bases for people feeling private about certain matters. Everyone would concede that much of what people regard as private is a culturally conditioned sensitivity. The issue is whether culturally distinctive norms determine all of what is regarded as private, and I am arguing that the answer to this is no.

Numerous lawyers and philosophers have accused those who introduce privacy terminology when discussing state regulation of birth control and abortion as confused.[21] Still, if one thinks that whether a married couple uses birth control is a *private matter* and for that reason not within the proper domain of state regulation, the sense of privacy I am advocating is vindicated. Even if some pressing need legitimized state involvement with such decisions, they would remain private decisions in the sense that they related to intimate elements of life. (They would cease to be private in the sense of answering

25

who had final legal authority to make decisions here.)[22] The centrality of decisions concerning birth control and abortion to intimate relationships and intimate aspects of oneself *makes* such issues privacy issues.

One might ask how am I differentiating the notion of the private from the notion of the intimate. Although I have regraded the intimate as a criterion of the private, labeling something as part of one's private realm indicates that there are norms of nonintrusion which apply to that area of a person's life. Labeling an area one of intimacy does not carry the same normative associations. The relationship between the two is, however, internal.

III

I have argued that respect for privacy enriches social and personal interaction by providing contexts for the development of varied kinds of relationships and multiple dimensions of personality. I have also suggested that while one can usually share informational aspects of oneself without apparent limit, sharing what is significant to one about this information is effectively limited to special kinds of relationships, and that we have independent reasons for not taking as an ideal the generalization of such special relationships to encompass all our interactions with others. Let me now move on.

The general point I wish to advance in this section is that respect for privacy signifies our recognition that not all dimensions of persons or relationships need to serve some independently validated social purpose. A private sphere of valuation must be morally recognized. My position involves two arguments. First, part of what is meant by respecting persons as persons is the acknowledgment that what has meaning for one individual thereby gains presumptive moral value independent of its promotion of socially valuable ends. Second, the personal basis of value is best kept located in the private realm generally; otherwise it will atrophy and be subsumed by public standards of value.

I start with the thesis that the individual is a source of value. A number of considerations are important to keep in mind. First, if the only morally recognizable point of a person's activities were to consist in the degree to which his activities assisted other people's projects, we would have a self-defeating and groundless situation. Some things must be good for persons, independent of their effects on others, or else there would be no point to helping others in the first place. Second, what is important to a person about pursuing goals is not only the objective relevance of the goals themselves but also their personal relevance—the fact that they are his goals.[23] It would be wrong to say of a person that his attachment to his objective should not count in assessing whether it is worth his while to pursue that end. And it would be wrong to say that his attachment should have no independent bearing on others' evaluations and pursuits. Without an individual's capacity to create value in something by valuing it, what we are left with is respect for values but no respect for persons as such. The respect for persons would be derivative only to the extent to which persons happened to value what was really and independently valuable. On such a view persons would have only instrumental or incidental value insofar as they promoted the right objectives. This is not to say that the fact that a person forms an objective is to be taken by others as a decisive reason for valuing and facilitating that objective. It is only to say that this valuation by the individual must be accorded moral weight independent, to a certain degree, of its overall consequences for society.

One could object to this position on the ground that what is valuable in an individual's idiosyncratic objectives is not the object of his or her loyalties as such, which may be neutral or detestable, but rather the *process through which the individual exercises autonomy.* Focusing on the desirability of autonomous choice provides sufficient basis for respect for individuals without having to further suppose that individuals add value to the objectives themselves by valuing them.[24] In response, one can observe that the values or loyalties one adheres to may not reflect autonomous choice in a direct sense and insofar as the agent sees it. For instance, a person may think that it is only through subjection to something over which he has no legitimate choice that he satisfies important objectives, for example, subjection to moral principles and rules or to divine commands. (One could then respond that even such first-order subjection reflects autonomy but at a higher level; the problem can be reiterated at each level.) Why should we judge that it is because a value reflects autonomous choice, and not inner meaning, that a person's objectives gain presumptive value? It seems much more plausible to suggest that whatever value autonomy has derives from its provision of prospects for meaningful existence than to say that the value of inner meaning derives from its reflection of autonomy.

It is no accident that some of our institutions that protect people's loyalties to ends which are potentially antagonistic to social well-being (such as testimonial privileges generally and the protection against self-incrimination specifically) generally were secured in a context of freedom of conscience,[25] which is an aspect of protection of intimacy. The essence of such struggles is the argument that there is within each individual some part that is not to be exploited even for socially or politically worthy ends. The medieval notion of *subsidiarity* can be usefully applied here. Subsidiarity involves regarding the political state as limited in its scope to certain domains of a person's life. This view specifically regards the state as not being competent to involve itself with determinations in matters of conscience or inner meanings generally. This position need not imply that the state does not have the ability or capacity to be effective in such areas. More pertinent to our concern is the theory's insistence that whatever the state's ability or capacity to mold consciences, it is violative of a person to do so.

Privacy, I wish to suggest, insulates individual objectives from social scrutiny. Social scrutiny can generally be expected to move individuals in the direction of the socially useful. Privacy insulates people from this kind of accountability and thereby protects the realm of the personal. When in conflict with social aims, private objectives tend to be devalued. For example, discussing parent–child relationships, nearly all the vast literature cites the best interest of the child as the sole basis for legitimizing parental control over the child. These discussions leave out entirely the interest parents and children alike have in maintaining intimate involvement (except as it promotes the child's well-being). This interest in intimacy must be taken into account when characterizing the moral basis for family autonomy. It is in such contexts that important aspects of personality develop. Something important is obscured when the family is seen as having primarily social, rather than personal, objectives.[26]

I believe it is important in a society for there to be institutions in which people can experience some of what they are without excessive scrutiny. Privacy is such an institution. Privacy involves norms that allow the pursuit and development of aims and relationships that count simply because the people involved find meaning in them. Privacy, I want to argue, provides the context for personal objectives being respected. I have suggested there is nothing wrong with people pursuing personally validated objectives, even though these do not serve the interest of everyone or enhance the autonomous status of others.

I have argued . . . that from a number of perspectives privacy is important   35 independent of its *reactive* function of protecting people from the morally unscrupulous, or merely suboptimal, qualities of others. Privacy is important with respect to the multidimensionality of persons and with respect for the personal or inner lives of people Dimensionality and inner meaning together provide the primary bases for defending the nonreactive importance of privacy.

Notes

For helpful comments and discussions I am indebted to Herbert Fingarette, Kent Greenawalt, Teri Bell, Michael Gardner, Sara Schechter-Schoeman, Evelyn B. Pluhar, and Linda Weingarten.

1. Charles Fried, "Privacy," 77 *Yale Law Journal* (1968) 475–93.
2. Robert Gerstein, "Intimacy and privacy," 89 *Ethics* (1978) 76–81.
3. James Rachels, "Why privacy is important," 4 *Philosophy and Public Affairs* (1975) 323–33.
4. Richard Wasserstrom, "Privacy: some arguments and assumptions," in Richard Bronaugh, ed., *Philosophical Law,* Westport, Conn.: Greenwood Press, 1978.
5. Ruth Gavison, "Privacy and the limits of law," 89 *Yale Law Journal* (1980) 421–71.
6. Jeffrey Reiman, "Privacy, intimacy, and personhood," 6 *Philosophy and Public Affairs* (1976) 26–44.
7. Richard Wasserstrom, "Privacy: some arguments and assumptions," in Richard Bronaugh, ed., *Philosophical Law,* Westport, Conn.: Greenwood Press, 1978.
8. Robert Gerstein, "Privacy and self-incrimination," 80 *Ethics* (1970) 87–101.
9. Stanley Benn, "Privacy, freedom and respect for persons," in J. R. Pennock and W. Chapman, eds., *Nomos XIII: Privacy,* New York, Atherton Press, 1971.
10. Richard Wasserstrom, "Privacy: some arguments and assumptions," in Richard Bronaugh, ed., *Philosophical Law,* Westport, Conn.: Greenwood Press, 1978.

11. Richard Posner, "The right to privacy," 12 *Georgia Law Review* (1978) 393–422.
12. Henry James, *The Reverberator,* New York: Grove Press, 1979, p. 190. See also Helen Lynd, *On Shame and the Search for Identity.* New York: Harcourt, Brace & Co., 1958.
13. Athol Fugard, *A Lesson from Aloes,* New York: Random House, 1981, pp. 27–28.
14. Erving Goffman, *The Presentation of Self in Everyday Life,* Garden City: Doubleday, 1959.
15. Ruth Gavison, "Privacy and the limits of law," 89 *Yale Law Journal* (1980) 87–101.
16. See the works of Posner, Wasserstrom, and Goffman already cited for expressions to this effect.
17. Walter Mischel, *Personality and Assessment,* New York: John Wiley, 1968, chapter 5.
18. Charles Fried, "Privacy," 77 *Yale Law Journal* (1968) 475–93.
19. James Rachels, "Why privacy is important," 4 *Philosophy and Public Affairs* (1975) 323–33.
20. H. J. McCloskey, "The political ideal of privacy," 21 *Philosophical Quarterly* (1971) 303–14, and "Privacy and the right to privacy," 55 *Philosophy* (1980) 17–38.
21. Louis Henkin, "Privacy and autonomy," 74 *Columbia Law Review* (1974) 1410–33; Ruth Gavison, "Privacy and the limits of law" 89 *Yale Law Journal* (1980) 421–71, esp. 438ff; Hyman Gross, "Privacy and autonomy," in J. R. Pennock and J. W. Chapman, eds., *Nomos XIII: Privacy,* New York: Atherton Press, 1971; and Human Gross, "The concept of privacy," 42 *New York University Law Review* (1967) 35–54.
22. Stanley I. Benn and Gerald Gaus, "The Public and the private: concepts and action," in Stanley I. Benn and Gerald Gaus, eds., *The Public and the Private in Social Policy,* London: Croon Helm and St. Martin's Press, 1983, pp. 3–27.
23. See Thomas Nagel, "The Limits of Objectivity," in Sterling McMurren, ed., *The Tanner Lectures on Human Values,* Salt Lake City: University of Utah Press, 1980, 75–140; Bernard Williams, "Persons, character and morality," in Amelie Rorty, ed., *Identity of Persons,* Berkeley: University of California Press, 1976, 197–216; and Samuel Scheffler, *The Rejection of Consequentialism,* Oxford: Oxford University Press, 1982, especially chapter 2.
24. Evelyn Pluhar suggested this problem in her "Commentary on 'privacy and intimate information,'" presented at the 1983 American Philosophical Association, Western Division, meetings.
25. See Leonard Levy, *Origins of the Fifth Amendment,* Oxford: Oxford University Press, 1968. Interestingly, even Jeremy Bentham, who was hostile to testimonial privileges generally, acknowledged the priest-penitent privilege since it recognized a Catholic's institutionally defined duty to confess transgressions, and thus was a requirement of religious freedom.
26. For an extensive defense of this claim see two works by Ferdinand Schoeman: "Rights of children, rights of parents, and the moral basis of the family," 91 *Ethics* (1980) 6–19, and "Childhood competence and autonomy," 12 *The Journal of Legal Studies* (1983) 267–87. ◪

Reflections and Inquiries

1. What is the basis for Schoeman's association of the private with the sacred?

2. In what contexts might social interaction be improved if individuals do not disclose intimate information?

3. Schoeman suggests that there is "no core self." What does he mean by this? How does it relate to the issue of privacy?

4. How does Schoeman distinguish the *private* from the *intimate?* What is significant about this distinction?

Reading to Write

1. Critique Schoeman's argument that the individual is a source of value.

2. Reflect on the relationship between privacy and disclosure as social values. Are they of equal or unequal importance? If the former, how should they be reconciled? If the latter, which value is most important, and why? Refer specifically to Schoeman's assertions.

The Globalization of Privacy Solutions

The Movement Towards Obligatory Standards for Fair Information Practices | Joel R. Reidenberg

Privacy policy is of international concern, and efforts are being made to establish global standards for fair use of private information. In the following article, Joel R. Reidenberg, an expert on international privacy practices and the technology of privacy, examines the problems in establishing such standards.

Varying jurisdictional approaches as well as different standards for the treatment of personal information will pose conflicts for the interrelated and international data processing arrangements of the twenty-first century. The European Union's directive on data protection (the "EU directive")[1] coupled with the Global Information Infrastructure (GII) raise the stakes for global solutions to the universally recognized need to maintain fair information practices in an information society. Yet, at the same time, the nature of twenty-first century information-processing arrangements will be complex and ill-suited for a single type of solution. This essay argues that data protection norms in Europe will promote obligatory standards for fair information practices in the United States as a consequence of the provisions found in European law and in the EU directive.

Source: Reidenberg, Joel R. "The Globalization of Privacy Solutions: The Movement towards Obligatory Standards for Fair Information Practices." *Visions of Privacy: Policy Choices for the Digital Age.* Eds. Colin J. Bennett and Rebecca Grant, Toronto: U. of Toronto, 1999. 217–28. Copyright © 1999 by Joel Reidenberg. Reprinted with permission of the publisher.

The European Pressure

The EU directive establishes a comprehensive legal foundation throughout Europe for the fair treatment of personal information and subjects international data flows from Europe to restrictions if the destination does not assure an 'adequate' level of protection.[2] It therefore exerts significant pressure on information rights, practices, and policies in North America.

Over the past twenty years, U.S. law has provided sporadic legal rights and remedies for information privacy.[3] Most regulatory efforts have constrained the government, while existing private sector standards derive largely from company-specific practices.[4] In essence the U.S. approach means that the existence and non-existence of meaningful data protection will be specific to particular circumstances.[5] The EU directive and the GII, thus, present critical challenges for U.S. policies and practices. Against the divergent structural background, the imposition by the EU directive both of harmonized European legal requirements for the fair treatment of personal information and of limitations on transborder data flows outside of Europe forces the U.S. government to recognize that American standards will be examined in Europe and forces U.S. companies to recognize that they will have to respect European legal mandates. Although there is uncertainty regarding the long-term application of the EU directive to particular contexts, multinational companies and the U.S. government will by necessity follow closely the implementation of the EU directive.

Although the EU directive provides an impetus for introspection by the United States as well as other countries outside Europe, the GII is also forcing American scrutiny of the treatment of personal information. Public opinion polls show that Americans care about privacy and are concerned about the treatment of personal information. This concern is noted particularly with respect to the development of online services. Similarly, companies are increasingly fearful of becoming the subject of the next data scandal and are beginning to see pro-active data protection policies as a commercial strategy. Businesses also express a critical need for confidence and security in the treatment of network information.

Nevertheless, the United States is not likely to adopt a comprehensive data protection law similar in content to the EU directive at the beginning of the new millennium. The ad hoc, reactive legal approach in the United States combined with an ingrained distrust of government are both unlikely to change without a major shift in political culture. For the foreseeable future, such a shift appears highly improbable. Instead, a proliferation of legal and extra-legal mechanisms are beginning to converge in a way that will proliferate the rules for the treatment of personal information within the United States. The nascent response, thus, to the twin pressures of the EU directive and the GII is a movement towards obligatory standards of fair information practice within the United States and a globalization of respect for mandatory principles of fair information practice.

5

Scrutiny and 'Adequacy'

The initial source for the extension within the United States of respect for mandatory principles of fair information practice will be the required European scrutiny of U.S. data protection. Because the EU directive is now law, comparisons between European data protection principles and U.S. standards of fair information practice must be made.[6] The EU directive requires that American standards of fair information practice be 'adequate' in order to permit transfers of personal information to the United States.[7] In the absence of directly comparable, comprehensive data protection legislation in the United States and the lack of explicit criteria for the determination of 'adequacy,' the assessment of the data flows to the United States is by necessity complex. Any general comparison would not be meaningful, as the context of information processing must be considered. More recently, the working party, created under the directive to advise the European Commission and composed of representatives from the European data protection agencies,[8] prepared a preliminary guidance note on the interpretation of 'adequacy' that similarly took a contextual view for future assessments.[9] A study of U.S. data protection conducted for the European Commission argued that the comparison should be made on the basis of 'functionally similar' treatment.[10] This approach matches an aggregation of targeted legal privacy rights, non-specific legal rights that have an impact on the treatment of personal information as well as the actual practices of data collectors in the United States against a core set of European standards. The result offers important points of convergence as well as divergence.[11]

In the context of the GII, data protection authorities will have significant difficulty applying European standards to trans-Atlantic data flows. As a practical matter, the diversity of activities, participants, and information-processing arrangements obscure clear analysis. The GII crosses sectoral and national regulatory boundaries, and crucial aspects of the treatment of personal information depend on esoteric technical characteristics. Even if a data protection authority wanted to investigate all contexts in each sector, the specialized expertise and the necessary resources are unlikely to be available.

Unless the European Union seeks to withdraw from international information flows, data protection authorities will face unexpected legal obstacles to export prohibitions. The relatively new world trade agreements embodied in the Final Act of the Uruguay Round, also known as the GATT 1994, include a sectoral accord on services, the General Agreement on Trade in Services (GATS). Because transnational information processing qualifies as a 'service,' the GATT 1994 provisions are likely to be a restraining force on European data export prohibitions. Restrictions on data flows applied against an entire country or against a specific sector within a country may violate these accords. Consistent with international trade agreements, GATS requires 'most-favoured nation treatment' that obligates signatory members to accord other signatories 'treatment no less favourable than it accords to like services and service suppliers of any other country.[12] Article 14 of the GATS expressly allows signatories to adopt measures for the protection of the privacy of individuals and the protection of confidentiality.[13] However, any such measures are still subject to the most-favoured nation clause. Similarly, the GATS Annex on Telecommunications allows signatories to take measures necessary to ensure 'security and confidentiality of messages' provided that such measures are not discriminatory.[14]

Any European restrictions on the flow of personal information must, thus, satisfy the tests of non-discrimination among third countries. For member states in the European Union to block information flows to one country with 'inadequate' privacy protection and not violate the principles of 'most-favoured nation' and non-discrimination, the member states must, at the same time, block information flows to all countries with similarly lacking privacy protection. In other words, to single out the information flows to a particular country without taking comparable action against other countries with similar privacy deficiencies is likely to constitute an impermissible discrimination.

By contrast, a focus on particular contexts, such as the treatment of caller identification information or the processing of particular information by a specific corporation, would be less likely to violate the non-discrimination obligation. The contextual analysis significantly diminishes any claim to discriminatory action on transborder data flows or to violations of 'most-favoured nation' status because the narrower the examination, the less likely it will be to find a comparable case treated in a more favourable way. Politically, the least problematic restrictions will thus come from case-by-case analysis and assessment.

Regardless of pressure from the EU directive, fair information practices in the United States face increasing public examination. Data protection scandals continue to attract attention. For example, within the past few years, NYNEX, one of the major American telephone companies, was publicly exposed for failing to implement customer subscriptions for number blocking on its caller identification service. The direct marketing industry has been criticized in the press for surreptitious data gathering activities on the Internet and for designing web sites to collect personal information from children. And Netscape was revealed to contain features that allow Internet web sites to read browsing patterns from the user's own hard drive.

At the same time, businesses are also concerned with privacy issues. Industry wants certainty of standards for the fair treatment of information. And, business needs confidence in the integrity of information.[15] Data protection around the world will be an essential element of 'good business practice' because the treatment of personal information is now an issue of business competitiveness. Already in Belgium, financial institutions have fought each other over the use of bank payment records to cross-sell products of affiliated companies.[16]

Companies based in the United States have also begun to recognize this key aspect of data protection. For example, Citibank has developed a data protection arrangement among affiliates for worldwide information processing that establishes a high competitive standard. Citibank implemented among its affiliates a series of contractual standards in the United States for the processing of railway card data originating in Germany.[17] Internet software providers are, likewise, seeking to incorporate privacy preferences in products. Microsoft, for example, has implemented filtering software for web sites in the Explorer 3.0 browser software. In essence, the sufficiency of standards of fair information practice within the United States is now on the political and business agenda.

The Confusing Governmental Response
in the United States

The U.S. governmental reaction, however, to the twin pressures from the EU directive and the GII is confusing. Despite the EU directive and the GII, the American regulatory philosophy remains wedded to targeted sectoral rules adopted in reaction to particular issues. The prospects for a comprehensive data protection law in the United States remain low. The U.S. government, particularly the federal government, has tried to give fresh thought to fair information practice issues, but the messages from policy decisions are neither coherent nor consistent.

In 1993, while the EU directive was still in draft form, Vice President Gore and the Clinton Administration launched the National Information Infrastructure initiative and created the Information Infrastructure Task Force (IITF). As part of the initiative, the IITF attempted an ambitious effort to define American standards of fair treatment of personal information for the information infrastructure. Because of the likelihood of increased foreign scrutiny of transborder data flows, the IITF examined the standards from the Council of Europe convention, the OECD guidelines, and the drafts of the EU directive with the intent to develop an American position consistent with global norms. By the end of 1995 the IITF issued a series of reports, non-binding policy statements, and guidelines that appear to compete with one another and result in the preservation of the federal regulatory status quo.[18] In 1996 and 1997 the Federal Trade Commission even took a brief foray into privacy policy and held widely publicized hearings that resulted in another government rehash of the debate over the effectiveness of self-regulation. Then, in fear of waning influence, the NTIA issued yet another explanation of self-regulation.[19]

More recently, individual states have begun to grapple with information infrastructure issues, and there is a growing movement to increase legal standards of fair information practice, particularly with respect to marketing uses of personal information. Interestingly, the EU directive is having an influence on the direction and drafting of proposals at the state level, as legislative staff consult the EU directive to find ideas and to strengthen support among representatives. In this election year, however, privacy issues are not likely to be a high priority.

Another more concrete response to the EU directive and the GII may be a

15

centralization of privacy policy within the federal government. The IITF presented a white paper in 1997 to address the issue of a data protection board.[20] The white paper presents a set of options for the institutional structure of privacy policy making, including the centralization of decision making. Because of the scrutiny of U.S. treatment of personal information, industry has a new incentive to seek international assistance from the U.S. government. If European regulators take the transborder data flow provisions seriously, the dispersion in the United States of jurisdiction for privacy issues coupled with inter-agency rivalries will ultimately encourage businesses to push for the creation of an executive branch data protection office. Otherwise, foreign data protection authorities will continue to have no appropriate U.S. counterpart with which to engage in problem solving and constructive dialogue. However, between budget pressures and ideological beliefs, a new independent agency with full regulatory powers has little chance of adoption. Instead, a consolidation of the dispersed functions in a single executive branch office is more likely to occur, and any powers for the private sector are likely to be limited to an ombudsman role.

In the likely event that European data protection authorities begin to block flows of personal information to the United States, a more specific American response can be expected. The U.S. government and industry groups will certainly raise initial objections to the principle of actual data transfer prohibitions. Some will strongly disagree with any foreign judgments of U.S. law and practice. Yet the American public reaction, and consequently the political pressure, will be much harder to anticipate. A data transfer prohibition that discloses a lack of fair treatment of personal information within the United States could greatly assist privacy advocates seeking additional U.S. protections. In addition, such decisions may split industry cohesion, as those companies with strong global data protection will have a commercial incentive to see businesses with poor practices thwarted in their international activities. Alternatively, the restraints may not be perceived within the United States as an appropriate level of response by European regulators to any identified problem with American data protection, and U.S business positions against regulatory protections for privacy may be strengthened politically.

For the long run, bilateral negotiations between the United States and the European Commission may assist the development of consistent U.S. government policies. Although the U.S. government has little to offer initially, given that domestic politics keep comprehensive data protection legislation off the negotiating table, the discussions themselves force the U.S. government and industry to confront the need to satisfy international privacy standards.

Globalizing Fair Treatment in Transborder Data Flows

The ambiguous state of fair information practice policy in the United States and the impending evaluation of U.S. processing activities, as required by the EU directive, together force data protection regulators, global companies, and their respective constituencies to achieve a workable consensus on satisfying fair information practice obligations for international data flows. In the global environment, the legal requirements of the EU directive will set the agenda; the treatment of personal information in Europe must conform to its mandates, and the personal information is not geographically constrained. As a result, two strategies may be offered to minimize conflicts over transborder data flows: (1) a new contractual model based on the liability of data exporters,[21] and (2) a technological approach based on the development and deployment of privacy conscious technical standards.

The contractual strategy offers a way to sustain European standards on the GII without the complexities of intensive regulatory intervention in a world of globally distributed information processing. Under the EU directive, an exporter of personal information could be held to violate the requirement of 'fair and lawful' processing if the exporter fails to assure that adequate information practices follow the data.[22] This means, for example, that a French data exporter would be liable in France under the standards imposed by French law for the treatment of the exported personal information regardless of where the data are processed. Under this interpretation, if an exporter cannot show that European standards are applied to the foreign processing, the exporter does not comply with the 'fair and lawful' processing requirements. contractual arrangements, then, become the key for data exporters to minimize the risk of European liability; data exporters will need to develop contracts that assure protection by data recipients.[23] This contractual strategy avoids the problems associated with enforcement and intercorporate agreements by individuals because it shifts the focus of contracts from protection of the individual to protection of the corporation itself.[24] At the same time, the liability approach maintains corporate responsibility and preserves local recourse for individuals against data exporters, rather than attempting to create rights against remote processors that will be hard to enforce.

This type of contractual strategy forces companies to assure fair treatment of personal information without the need for data protection regulators to make direct complex evaluations of foreign law. In the absence of contractual arrangements, data exporters will be unable to show 'fair and lawful' processing. To meet the burden of liability, companies will impose data protection obligations privately on data recipients. In practice, the legal strategy will require a serious commitment to supervision of foreign processing activities by data exporters. Without supervision, the data exporter remains widely exposed to liability at the place of export. This suggests an important role for codes of conduct both as a device to define contractually imposed standards for specific contexts and as a benchmark to measure compliance.[25] With this strategy 'information audits' become a critical self-preservation device for companies, while simultaneously avoiding the difficulties of extraterritorial inspection by data protection authorities and costly duplication of supervision by multiple data protection agencies. European data protection authorities may, for example, decide that an information audit certified by a trusted third party is the only way for a company to demonstrate 'fair and lawful' processing when personal data are exported. In any case, with this contractual strategy, European data protection authorities might accomplish the goal of assuring adequate treatment of personal information without many of the difficulties inherent to the assessment of foreign law.

The second strategy, a technological approach based on the development and deployment of privacy conscious technical standards, also offers an opportunity to embed fair information practices in the GII.[26] Technological choices establish default rules. For example, Netscape browser software allows Internet web sites to log visits on the user's computer hard drive and access that traffic information for profile purposes.[27] The feature is not publicized by Netscape, though technically savvy users can disable the logging capability without impeding their use of the Netscape browser.

The use of 'technologies of privacy' is essentially a business-driven solution that can be used to promote data protection goals and implement European obligations. Standards and architecture planning may in effect create binding privacy rules. For example, Internet web pages may adopt a common opt-out protocol, such as a small green box that can be clicked to erase a visitor's traffic data and thus preclude its use for secondary purposes. Similarly, protocols may be developed that anonymize personal information whenever possible.

The significance of technical protocols cannot be underestimated as a policy tool to develop binding standards of fair information practice. Two particularly noteworthy endeavours reflect complementary technical approaches. The Canadian Standards Association has elaborated a standard for fair information practice. The CSA model code integrates privacy as a technical quality standard. This standard emphasizes business policy and becomes a robust instrument as pressure mounts on the private sector to use the standard as a reference point in contracts. The CSA has sought to expand this approach by proposing a privacy quality standard at the International Organization for Standards (ISO). From Europe, data protection officials have endorsed the contribution to privacy that this standards initiative can offer.[28]

In the United States, however, the private sector has been more ambivalent; any such standard would require enforcement mechanisms against companies, mechanisms that do not presently exist within the U.S. framework. American industry has, instead, invested heavily in the promotion of architectural standards that would seek to incorporate privacy policies within Internet transmission protocols. Labelling and filtering technologies along with standard formats for data profiles present possibilities for the assurance of fair information practices. If implemented, the choices and structure of such architectural mechanisms will offer binding rules for participants. The proper design and implementation, thus, raise critical issues for data protection.[29] Nevertheless, as in the case of the CSA model code, European data protection authorities do see possibilities for the labelling and filtering approach.[30] The recognition and implementation of new technical strategies can reduce the potential regulatory conflicts for international information flows.

Conclusions

As information becomes the key asset of the twenty-first century, the treatment of personal information and the verification of compliance with fair standards become critical for public confidence in network activities.[31] In spite of the confusing U.S. government response to the GII and the EU directive, the possible solutions for international information flows exert a tremendous pressure towards obligatory standards. Liability coupled with contractual arrangements and network architecture impose significant rules on information processing. Narrow developments in U.S. government policy, greater corporate attention to fair information practices, new contractual arrangements, and network system default rules will collectively decrease the divergent characteristics of fair information practice standards in the United States from those of the EU directive. Yet the more seriously European data protection authorities take international data flows and the more extensively the public debates the GII, the greater the pressure will be towards these obligatory standards in the United States.

Notes

1. European Union, *Directive 95/46/EC of the European Parliament and of the Council on the Protection of Individuals with Regard to the Processing of Personal Data and on the Free Movement of Such Data* (Brussels: Official Journal L281, 24 Oct. 1995).
2. Ibid., Article 25–6.
3. See Paul Schwartz and Joel R. Reidenberg, *Data Privacy Law: A Study of U.S. Data Protection* (Charlottesville: Michie, 1996).
4. Ibid.
5. Ibid.
6. European Union, *Directive 95/46/EC,* Article 25.
7. Ibid.
8. See European Union *Directive 95/46/EC,* Article 29.
9. Working Party on the Protection of Individuals with Regard to the Processing of Personal Data, *Discussion Document: First Orientations on Transfers of Personal Data to Third Countries—Possible Ways Forward in Assessing Adequacy* (26 January 1997).
10. See Schwartz and Reidenberg, *Data Privacy Law.*
11. Ibid.
12. See *General Agreement on Tariffs and Trade,* Annex 1B: General Agreement on Trade in Services (GATS) (MTN/FA II-A1B), Article 2.
13. Ibid., Article 14 (c)(ii).
14. Ibid., Annex on Telecommunications, Article 5.4
15. Encryption controversies reflect this critical aspect of standards for fair information practices. In Congress recent proposals seek to confront the encryption issues.
16. See *Aff.* OCCH c. Générale de Banque, Trib. de comm. de Bruxelles, Chbre. des actions en cass, slle des référés, 15 sept. 1994 (Belgium) reprinted in *Droit de l'informatique et des télécoms* (1994–4), 46–50; Aff. Feprabel at Fédération des courtiers en Assurance c.

Kredietbank NV, Trib. de comm. d'Anvers, 7 juillet 1994 (Belgium), reprinted in *Droit de l'informatique et des télécoms* (1994–4), 51–5. Significantly, individuals did not bring these cases. Instead, the bank competitors successfully sued, based in part on the data protection prescriptions against secondary use of personal information.

17. See Alexander Dix, *The German Railway Card: A Model Contractual Solution of the 'Adequate level of Protection' Issue,* Proceedings of the 18th International Conference of Data Protection Commissioners, Ottawa, 1996.

18. See, e.g., U.S. Department of Commerce, NTIA, *Privacy and the NII: Safeguarding Telecommunications-Related Personal Information* (Washington, DC: Department of Commerce, Oct. 1995); IITF, *Report of the Privacy Working Group, Privacy and the NII: Principles for Providing and Using Personal Information* (Oct. 1995); U.S. Advisory Council, *First Report: Common Ground* (1995) (containing section on 'Privacy and Security').

19. See U.S. Department of Commerce, *Privacy and Self-Regulation in the Information Age* (Washington, DC: U.S. Department of Commerce, NTIA, 1997) (available at: http://www.ntia.doc.gov/reports/privacy/privacy_rpt.htm).

20. U.S. National Information Infrastructure Task Force, *Options for Promoting Privacy on the National Information Infrastructure* (April 1997) (available at: http://www.iitf.nist.gov/ipc/privacy.htm).

21. For an extended discussion, see Schwartz and Reidenberg, *Data Privacy Law;* see also Joel R. Reidenberg, 'Setting Standards for Fair Information Practice in the U.S. Private Sector,' *Iowa Law Review* 80: (1996), 497, 545–50.

22. See Schwartz and Reidenberg, *Data Privacy Law.*

23. Ibid.

24. Ibid.

25. For a discussion of the usefulness of codes of conduct and standards, see Colin Bennett, *Implementing Privacy Codes of Practice: A Report to the Canadian Standards Association* (Rexdale, ON: Canadian Standards Association, 1995).

26. See Joel R. Reidenberg, *Governing Networks and Rule-Making in Cyberspace, Emory Law Journal* 45 (1996), 911, 927–8.

27. Usually the data are stored in the Netscape directory in a file <cookies.txt.>.

28. See Working Party on the Protection of Individuals with Regard to the Processing of Personal Data, *Opinion 1/97 on Canadian Initiatives Relating to Standardization in the Field of Protection of Privacy Set Up by Directive 95/46/EC of the European Parliament and the Council of 24 October 1995,* (29 May 1997), stating that the Canadian and ISO initiatives 'significantly contribute to the protection of fundamental rights and privacy on a world-wide basis.'

29. See Joel R. Reidenberg, 'The Use of Technology to Assure Internet Privacy: Adapting Labels and Filters for Data Protection,' *Lex Electronica* 1:1, available at: http://www.lex-electronica.org/reidenb.html.

30. In both the April and September 1997 meetings the International Working Group on Data Protection in Telecommunications examined the Platform for Internet Content Selection and the Platform for Privacy Preferences technologies being developed by the World Wide Web consortium.

31. See Joel R. Reidenberg and François Gamet-Pol, *The Fundamental Role of Privacy and Confidence in the Network, Wake Forest Law Review* 30 (1995), 105. ▉

Reflections and Inquiries

1. How do the EU directive and GII technology conflict with existing U.S. privacy policy?

2. What recent privacy-related incidents may generate enough public pressure for the United States to adopt international policy guidelines?

3. Why is the United States resistant to influence from the EU directive and GII?

4. How might technologies of privacy be implemented successfully?

Reading to Write

1. How convincingly does Reidenberg present the rationale for the United States to abide by EU/GII standards? Write a detailed critique of his argument.

2. Write an essay on the value of the EU directive and the GII, using the information Reidenberg provides, plus information from other sources.

STUDENT ESSAY

Privacy? What Privacy? | Tina Lennox

Internet privacy has begun to sound like an oxymoron. Thanks to sophisticated hackers and high-tech devices for monitoring Web site accessing, individual privacy may seem like a hopeless ideal. But as Tina Lennox, a first-year business student at Santa Clara University, argues in the following paper, there may be ways even in today's high-tech age to prevent invasion of privacy.

Many would agree that privacy is important in corporate life. According to Ferdinand Schoeman, "Privacy is important . . . for the personal or inner lives of people" (416). Schoeman believes that respecting people's privacy shows moral strength. Unfortunately, the modern world greedily seeks information about people—the more the better, and there is usually no problem getting it. Privacy no longer exists, not even in a theoretical state. From the workplace to the Internet, the invasion of personal information is at an all-time high. "A 1998 survey of 1,085 corporations conducted by the American Management Association shows that more than 40 percent engaged in some kind of intrusive employee monitoring" (Doyle). Employers monitor actions through the "checking of e-mail, voice mail and telephone conversations; recording of computer keystrokes; and video recording of job performance" (4). The intrusion does not stop here as random drug testing, psychological testing, and genetic testing are practiced.

Even more pervasive and disturbing, "advances in database technology, marketing technology, and the sudden growth and capabilities of digital networks are creating new opportunities for direct marketers and raising new privacy issues" (Kirsh). The Internet is a powerful tool. Its large-scale influence has made it both a threat and a benefit. As a threat, the Internet demonstrates that privacy cannot be preserved in a high-tech age.

Simple tasks such as "surfing the net" and sending e-mails can broadcast personalized information about the sender to nosy viewers. These viewers fall into one of three categories according to Jim Aspinwall in his article, "The Complete Guide to Internet Privacy." The first is composed of "thrill-seeking kids" who merely wish "to annoy users and overwhelm networks." The second is known as the "system-crackers" or "script-kiddies." These hackers keep pushing their luck until they get caught. They find unsecured servers and take advantage of their weaknesses. Passwords are stolen, protection is disabled, systems are crashed, and network files are viewed and copied. The last group is the serious, sophisticated cyber-criminals. This group searches for vital corporate or government information. All three groups contribute to the ever-growing insecurity of Internet users.

The main targets of hackers are commercial sites. Through these sites, detailed information on an individual's credit, health, financial status, purchasing patterns, and personal preferences are made available on centralized computer databases. There are also cases of stolen identities where social security numbers and credit card numbers are used to buy goods, receive government benefits, and commit crimes. Aspinwall cites the case of BackOrifice, in which a sophisticated hacker silently records all activity on a personal computer and eventually takes over the entire system. Often, a site uses "cookies" to retain information on individual consumers. Cookies are small text files with plain and/or coded information on sites previously visited. They may either stay on the local hard drive for years or only be stored as temporary bits of information that disappear when the browser is closed (Aspinwall). As Steve Gibson of Gibson Research states, "when you are connected to the Internet, the Internet is also connected to you" (Aspinwall).

Through the Internet, merchants can reuse and sell personal information. Advertising companies such as DoubleClick, Inc., receive this data and use it to specialize their online billboards. DoubleClick dominates the online ad market with rapidly growing global online advertisement, spending currently up to $7.7 billion (Weston). Other companies sell customer prescription information to drug companies. HMO's, banks, and security firms have access to insurance records and, ultimately, medical records. Thought to be highly personal and confidential, medical records are one of the least protected records in America, according to Brendon Weston.

Although consumers complain about the lack of privacy on the Internet, they continue to utilize its resources day in and day out. A 1994 survey states that 82 percent of people polled were concerned about threats to personal privacy (Kirsh). While 51 percent were concerned about the creation of subscriber profiles on viewing and purchasing patterns online, 52 percent were interested in receiving information and advertising tailored to their particular interests (Kirsh). These two statistics contradict each other. By completing financial statements and forms through the Internet, these hypocritical consumers are dangling themselves over the open fire. Understandably, modern communities have become very dependent on the Internet for commerce and entertainment desires alike. It's fast, easy, efficient, and loaded with information. The only solution now is to use the Internet intelligently and carefully.

Federal laws now protect the rights of online users. The Electronic Privacy Commission Act (EPCA) protects consumers against the unauthorized surveillance of privileged electronic messages and the release to third parties of message content. It restricts government access to customer records on interactive service providers as well. During the Clinton presidency, the national Plan for Information Systems Protection was developed. It addresses the vulnerability of systems to cyber-terrorism and makes recommendations for security measures. On January 20, 2001, H.R. 237 was unveiled. Established by the House of Representatives members Chris Cannon and Anna Eshoo, the Internet Privacy Enhancement Act requires commercial sites and e-businesses to disclose how they use and secure information collected. Sites must also provide ways to safeguard against inappropriate and illegal use of the information by marketers or others. The inclusion of a disclosure statement that tells customers where the information goes and gives them the right to prevent their information from going to marketing is another policy of the act. "Consumers shouldn't have to reveal their life story every time they surf the web. This legislation will help to assure the security that Americans expect when it comes to privacy. . . . The bill doesn't regulate the Internet; it empowers the consumer" (Eshoo). The Federal Trade Commission has increased its penalty authority in online violations with civil penalties ranging from $22,000 to $500,000 (Eshoo). Promising future bills cover more restrictive privacy requirements, increased penalties, and greater burden on businesses through frequent reports and limits on activities.

While the government is taking small steps toward resolving consumer privacy issues, a great deal of responsibility lies on the individual, who can take steps to safeguard information from hackers and third-party onlookers. First, there are a number of Internet connection methods to choose from. With a standard modem, one anonymous dial-up customer out of millions is chosen and a random Internet protocol (IP) address is assigned to fit the computer's hardware. When logged off, the customer and address are gone completely. This type of modem is safer than a Digital Subscribe Line (DSL) or cable connection that is literally always on. DSL and cable connections use one to two permanent IP addresses and host names that work in conjunction with their specific computer. A hacker looking in on these lines of communication would find it easy to track down a user and user profile.

Second, precautionary measures can be taken by installing security patches. Practicing safe habits on computers will help guard information.

With a DSL or cable connection, the modem should be disconnected from the computer when not in use. This way the hacker can get absolutely no information from the dead modem line. Programs such as Zone-Alarm post warnings when an application tries to make a connection or external sites are trying to connect to the computer through the Internet. Virus protection programs similar to McAfee Virus Scan and Norton AntiVirus should be run weekly. Since many Internet e-mail servers are not secure, the Pretty Good Privacy Firewall Program (PGP) can be used to create a private encryption key for oneself and a public key to share with others so that they can decode the mail on the other end. Clients should be wary of the file attachments sent by unknown users. Even mail from family and friends may contain viruses that a quick scan would exterminate.

The capabilities for computers and Internet servers have far surpassed   10
consumer and producer expectations. Legislation has been passed, but to trifling ends. Ellen Alderman and Caroline Kennedy, authors of *The Right to Privacy*, make this observation:

> Perhaps the biggest problem with the statutory scheme is that there is no overall privacy policy behind it. As even a partial list of privacy laws indicates, they address a hodgepodge of individual concerns. The federal statutory scheme most resembles a jigsaw puzzle in which the pieces do not fit. That is because the scheme was put together backwards. Rather than coming up with an overall picture and then breaking it up into smaller pieces that mesh together, Congress has been sporadically creating individual pieces of legislation that not only do not mesh neatly but also leave gaping holes. (qtd. in Kirsh)

While privacy can never again be fully preserved, one cannot give in to the pressures of the high-tech age. It is a struggle between humans and machines. While machines have become increasingly powerful and capable, they can never compete with the abilities of the human mind. It is difficult to protect personal information in this high-tech age, but one cannot give up. It is cowardly just to lie down and let hackers and prying companies walk all over an individual's rights. The people need to continue passing legislation regarding Internet privacy issues and taking steps to safeguard themselves and their personal information. There need to be regularly scheduled, independent review groups to promote online privacy practices, the coalition of existing industry organizations, and privacy advocacy groups as well as individuals with support from government agencies, and consumer understanding and involvement with online privacy issues. Online improvements must be demanded and new standards strictly upheld for anything to change. Although Big Brother may be watching, individual responsibility and action must still continue.

Works Cited

Aspinwall, Jim. "The Complete Guide to Internet Privacy." *Mother Earth News* Nov. 2000: 1.

Doyle, Rodger. "Privacy in the Workplace." Jan. 2001. March 2001. <http://www.sciam.com/1999/01999issue/01999numbers.html>.

Eshoo, Anna G. "Reps. Eshoo and Cannon Unveil Internet Privacy Legislation." *FDCH Press Releases* Jan. 2001.

Kirsh, Ellen. "Recommendations for the Evolution of Netland: Protecting Privacy in a Digital Age." *JCMC Abstracts* 2 (Sept. 1996).

Schoeman, Ferdinand David. "Privacy and Intimate Information." *Philsophical Dimensions of Privacy: An Anthology.* Ed. Ferdinand David Schoeman. Cambridge, Eng.: Cambridge UP, 1984. 402–16.

Weston, Brendan. "Cookie Recipes." *Canadian Business* Dec. 2000. ◪

Reflections and Inquiries

1. According to Lennox, "privacy no longer exists." Do you agree or disagree? Why?

2. Why do hackers mainly target commercial Internet sites?

3. Why does Lennox call Internet users who value privacy "hypocritical"? Is this a fair criticism? Why or why not?

4. What can be done, according to Lennox, to help restore individual privacy?

Reading to Write

Read articles that discuss the concerns about Internet or workplace privacy shared by young adults. Next, conduct a campus survey to determine the range and seriousness of privacy concerns among your fellow students. Write a paper in which you compare the students' chief concerns with those of the published findings. What differences, if any, do you detect? What may account for these differences or lack of them?

Connections Across the Clusters

1. What kinds of privacy protection might be needed for students involved in distance learning? (See Cluster 1.)

2. How might minority students be protected by privacy laws? (See Cluster 6.)

Writing Projects

1. Write an essay in which you discuss the need for individual privacy in the workplace or on campus. What can employers or academic administrators do to ensure such privacy protection?

2. Examine the concept of privacy in terms of the different kinds of privacy that exist. Do some kinds deserve more protection than others? Why?

3. Examine privacy protection from the standpoint of gender, ethnicity, sexual preference, or religious convictions. What special protection measures need to be taken in these contexts?

Suggestions for Further Reading

Bok, Sissela. *Secrets: On the Ethics of Concealment and Revelation.* New York: Pantheon, 1982.

Branscomb, Anne Wells. *Who Owns Information?* New York: Basic, 1994.

Elder, David A. *The Law of Privacy.* New York: Clark Boardman, 1991.

Garrow, David J. *Liberty and Sexuality.* New York: Macmillan, 1994.

Gavison, Ruth. "Privacy and the Limits of Law." *Yale Law Journal* 89 (1980): 421–71.

Hixson, Richard F. *Privacy in a Public Society.* New York: Oxford UP, 1987.

Rachels, James. "Why Privacy Is Important." *Philosophy and Public Affairs* 4 (1975): 323–33.

Rothfeder, Jeffrey. *Privacy for Sale.* New York: Simon, 1992.

Seipp, David J. *The Right to Privacy in American History.* Cambridge: Harvard UP, 1987.

Introduction

Many of the greatest works ever written or spoken are arguments. Whether philosophical (Plato's "Allegory of the Cave"), spiritual (Edwards's "Sinners in the Hands of an Angry God"), sociopolitical (Douglass's "I Hear the Mournful Wail of Millions"), legal (the *Roe* v. *Wade* case on abortion), or scientific (Carson's *Silent Spring*), insight into physical and divine nature has been most effectively propagated through effective argument. Clarity of thesis, definition, and explanation; thoroughness and accuracy of evidence; eloquence; and lucidity of the manner of delivery or style—these are the rhetorical techniques that transform ideas into understanding.

As you study the following masterpieces of argument, ask yourself three questions:

1. What do you find most effective or distinctive about the author's approach to the subject matter?

2. How has he or she combined objective, factual information with subjective persuasive power?

3. Why do these arguments still make for valuable reading even though some of them are centuries old?

Allegory of the Cave | Plato

In his masterful dialogue, *The Republic*, Plato (428–347 B.C.E.) attempts to show that a rational relationship exists among the cosmos, the human soul, and the state. Qualities such as justice, good, and beautiful must coexist harmoniously in life. Politics, law, education, art, and literature are the means by which we come to perfect these qualities of the good life. In Book Seven of the dialogue,

Source: Plato. "Allegory of the Cave." *The Republic*. Trans. Benjamin Javett and Lewis Campbell. Oxford: Clarendon, 1894. 293–99. VII. 514–518.

Socrates argues his case for the potential of educators to lead humanity out of the darkness of deceptions and superficial appearances into the light of higher truth. This "Allegory of the Cave," as it has come to be known, is one of the most powerful meditations on the relationship between appearance and reality and of the importance of education in society.

SOCRATES, GLAUCON.
The den, the prisoners: the light at a distance;

And now, I said, let me show in a figure how far our nature is enlightened or unenlightened:—Behold! human beings living in an underground den, which has a mouth open towards the light and reaching all along the den; here they have been from their childhood, and have their legs and necks chained so that they cannot move, and can only see before them, being prevented by the chains from turning round their heads. Above and behind them a fire is blazing at a distance, and between the fire and the prisoners there is a raised way; and you will see, if you look, a low wall built along the way, like the screen which marionette players have in front of them, over which they show the puppets.

I see.

the low wall, and the moving figures of which the shadows are seen on the opposite wall of the den.

And do you see, I said, men passing along the wall carrying all sorts of vessels, and statues and figures of animals made of wood and stone and various materials, which appear over the wall? Some of them are talking, others silent.

You have shown me a strange image, and they are strange prisoners.

Like ourselves, I replied; and they see only their own shadows, or the shadows of one another, which the fire throws on the opposite wall of the cave?   5

True, he said; how could they see anything but the shadows if they were never allowed to move their heads?

And of the objects which are being carried in like manner they would only see the shadows?

Yes, he said.

And if they were able to converse with one another, would they not suppose that they were naming what was actually before them?

Very true.   10

The prisoners would mistake the shadows for realities.

And suppose further that the prison had an echo which came from the other side, would they not be sure to fancy when one of the passers-by spoke that the voice which they heard came from the passing shadow?

No question, he replied.

To them, I said, the truth would be literally nothing but the shadows of the images.

That is certain.

And now look again, and see what will naturally follow   15
if the prisoners are released and disabused of their error. At
first, when any of them is liberated and compelled suddenly
to stand up and turn his neck round and walk and look
towards the light, he will suffer sharp pains; the glare will
distress him, and he will be unable to see the realities of
which in his former state he had seen the shadows; and then
conceive some one saying to him, that what he saw before
was an illusion, but that now, when he is approaching nearer
to being and his eye is turned towards more real existence,
he has a clearer vision—what will be his reply? And you
may further imagine that his instructor is pointing to the objects as they pass and requiring him to name them,—will he

*And when released,
they would still per-
sist in maintaining the
superior truth of the
shadows.*

not be perplexed? Will he not fancy that the shadows which
he formerly saw are truer than the objects which are now
shown to him?

Far truer.

And if he is compelled to look straight at the light, will he
not have a pain in his eyes which will make him turn away
to take refuge in the objects of vision which he can see, and
which he will conceive to be in reality clearer than the things
which are now being shown to him?

True, he said.

*When dragged up-
wards, they would be
dazzled by excess of
light.*

And suppose once more, that he is reluctantly dragged
on a steep and rugged ascent, and held fast until he is forced
into the presence of the sun himself, is he not likely to be
pained and irritated? When he approaches the light his eyes
will be dazzled, and he will not be able to see anything at all
of what are now called realities.

Not all in a moment, he said.   20

He will require to grow accustomed to the sight of the
upper world. And first he will see the shadows best, next the
reflections of men and other objects in the water, and then
the objects themselves; then he will gaze upon the light of
the moon and the stars and the spangled heaven; and he will
see the sky and the stars by night better than the sun or the
light of the sun by day?

Certainly.

*At length they will see
the sun and under-
stand his nature.*

Last of all he will be able to see the sun, and not mere reflections of him in the water, but he will see him in his own
proper place, and not in another; and he will contemplate
him as he is.

Certainly.

He will then proceed to argue that this is he who gives   25 the season and the years, and is the guardian of all that is in the visible world, and in a certain way the cause of all things which he and his fellows have been accustomed to behold?

Clearly, he said, he would first see the sun and then reason about him.

They would then pity their old companions of the den

And when he remembered his old habitation, and the wisdom of the den and his fellow prisoners, do you not suppose that he would felicitate himself on the change, and pity them?

Certainly, he would.

And if they were in the habit of conferring honors among themselves on those who were quickest to observe the passing shadows and to remark which of them went before, and which followed after, and which were together; and who were therefore best able to draw conclusions as to the future, do you think that he would care for such honors and glories, or envy the possessors of them? Would he not say with Homer,

Better to be the poor servant of a poor master.
and to endure anything, rather than think as they do and live after their manner?

Yes, he said, I think that he would rather suffer anything   30
than entertain these false notions and live in this miserable manner.

Imagine once more, I said, such an one coming suddenly out of the sun to be replaced in his old situation; would he not be certain to have his eyes full of darkness?

To be sure, he said.

But when they returned to the den they would see much worse than those who had never left it.

And if there were a contest, and he had to compete in measuring the shadows with the prisoners who had never moved out of the den, while his sight was still weak, and before his eyes had become steady (and the time which would be needed to acquire this new habit of sight might be very considerable), would he not be ridiculous? Men would say of him that up he went and down he came without his eyes; and that it was better not even to think of ascending; and if any one tried to loose another and lead him up to the light, let them only catch the offender, and they would put him to death.

No question, he said.

The prison is the world of sight, the light of the fire is the sun.

This entire allegory, I said, you may now append, dear   35
Glaucon, to the previous argument; the prison house is the world of sight, the light of the fire is the sun, and you will not misapprehend me if you interpret the journey upwards to be the ascent of the soul into the intellectual world ac-

cording to my poor belief, which, at your desire, I have expressed—whether rightly or wrongly God knows. But, whether true or false, my opinion is that in the world of knowledge the idea of good appears last of all, and is seen only with an effort; and, when seen, is also inferred to be the universal author of all things beautiful and right, parent of light and of the lord of light in this visible world, and the immediate source of reason and truth in the intellectual; and that this is the power upon which he who would act rationally either in public or private life must have his eye fixed.

I agree, he said, as far as I am able to understand you.

Moreover, I said, you must not wonder that those who attain to this beatific vision are unwilling to descend to human affairs; for their souls are ever hastening into the upper world where they desire to dwell; which desire of theirs is very natural, if our allegory may be trusted.

Yes, very natural.

And is there anything surprising in one who passes from divine contemplations to the evil state of man, misbehaving himself in a ridiculous manner; if, while his eyes are blinking and before he has become accustomed to the surrounding darkness, he is compelled to fight in courts of law, or in other places, about the images or the shadows of images of justice, and is endeavoring to meet the conceptions of those who have never yet seen absolute justice?

Anything but surprising, he replied.

Anyone who has common sense will remember that the bewilderments of the eyes are of two kinds, and arise from two causes, either from coming out of the light or from going into the light, which is true of the mind's eye, quite as much as of the bodily eye; and he who remembers this when he sees anyone whose vision is perplexed and weak, will not be too ready to laugh; he will first ask whether that soul of man has come out of the brighter life, and is unable to see because unaccustomed to the dark, or having turned from darkness to the day is dazzled by excess of light. And he will count the one happy in his condition and state of being, and he will pity the other; or, if he have a mind to laugh at the soul which comes from below into the light, there will be more reason in this than in the laugh which greets him who returns from above out of the light into the den.

That, he said, is a very just distinction.

But then, if I am right, certain professors of education must be wrong when they say that they can put a knowledge into the soul which was not there before, like sight into blind eyes.

Marginal notes:

Nothing extraordinary in the philosopher being unable to see in the dark.

The eyes may be blinded in two ways, by excess or by defect of light.

The conversion of the soul is the turning round the eye from darkness to light.

40

They undoubtedly say this, he replied.   45

Whereas, our argument shows that the power and capacity of learning exists in the soul already; and that just as
the eye was unable to turn from darkness to light without
the whole body, so too the instrument of knowledge can
only by the movement of the whole soul be turned from the
world of becoming into that of being, and learn by degrees
to endure the sight of being, and of the brightest and best of
being, or in other words, of the good.

Very true.

And must there not be some art which will effect conversion in the easiest and quickest manner; not implanting the
faculty of sight, for that exists already, but has been turned
in the wrong direction, and is looking away from the truth?

Yes, he said, such an art may be presumed.

The virtue of wisdom has a divine power which may be turned either towards good or towards evil.

And whereas the other so-called virtues of the soul seem
to be akin to bodily qualities, for even when they are not
originally innate they can be implanted later by habit and
exercise, the virtue of wisdom more than anything else contains a divine element which always remains, and by this
conversion is rendered useful and profitable; or, on the other
hand, hurtful and useless. Did you never observe the narrow intelligence flashing from the keen eye of a clever
rogue—how eager he is, how clearly his paltry soul sees the
way to his end; he is the reverse of blind, but his keen eyesight is forced into the service of evil, and he is mischievous
in proportion to his cleverness?

Very true, he said.   50

But what if there had been a circumcision of such natures
in the days of their youth; and they had been severed from
those sensual pleasures, such as eating and drinking, which,
like leaden weights, were attached to them at their birth, and
which drag them down and turn the vision of their souls
upon the things that are below—if, I say, they had been released from these impediments and turned in the opposite
direction, the very same faculty in them would have seen the
truth as keenly as they see what their eyes are turned to now.

Very likely.

Neither the unedu-cated nor the overedu-cated will be good servants of the State.

Yes, I said; and there is another thing which is likely, or
rather a necessary inference from what has preceded, that
neither the uneducated and uninformed of the truth, nor yet
those who never make an end of their education, will be able
ministers of State; not the former, because they have no single aim of duty which is the rule of all their actions, private
as well as public; nor the latter, because they will not act at

all except upon compulsion, fancying that they are already dwelling apart in the islands of the blessed.

Very true, he replied.

Then, I said, the business of us who are the founders of the State will be to compel the best minds to attain that knowledge which we have already shown to be the greatest of all—they must continue to ascend until they arrive at the good; but when they have ascended and seen enough we must not allow them to do as they do now.

What do you mean?

Men should ascend to the upper world, but they should also return to the lower.

I mean that they remain in the upper world: but this must not be allowed; they must be made to descend again among the prisoners in the den, and partake of their labors and honors, whether they are worth having or not.

But is not this unjust? he said; ought we to give them a worse life, when they might have a better?

You have again forgotten, my friend, I said, the intention of the legislator, who did not aim at making any one class in the State happy above the rest; the happiness was to be in the whole State, and he held the citizens together by persuasion and necessity, making them benefactors of the State, and therefore benefactors of one another; to this end he created them, not to please themselves, but to be his instruments in binding up the State.

True, he said, I had forgotten.

The duties of philosophers.

Observe, Glaucon, that there will be no injustice in compelling our philosophers to have a care and providence of others; we shall explain to them that in other States, men of their class are not obliged to share in the toils of politics: and this is reasonable, for they grow up at their own sweet will, and the government would rather not have them. Being self-taught, they cannot be expected to show any gratitude for a culture which they have never received. But we have brought you into the world to be rulers of the hive, kings of yourselves and of the other citizens, and have educated you far better and more perfectly than they have been educated, and you are better able to share in the double duty. Where-

Their obligations to their country will induce them to take part in her government.

fore each of you, when his turn comes, must go down to the general underground abode, and get the habit of seeing in the dark. When you have acquired the habit, you will see ten thousand times better than the inhabitants of the den, and you will know what the several images are, and what they represent, because you have seen the beautiful and just and good in their truth. And thus our State, which is also yours, will be reality, and not a dream only, and will be administered in a spirit unlike that of other States, in which men fight with one another about shadows only and are distracted in the struggle for power, which in their eyes is a great good. Whereas the truth is that the State in which the rulers are most reluctant to govern is always the best and most quietly governed, and the State in which they are most eager, the worst.

Quite true, he replied.

And will our pupils, when they hear this, refuse to take their turn at the toils of State, when they are allowed to spend the greater part of their time with one another in the heavenly light?

They will be willing but not anxious to rule.

Impossible, he answered; for they are just men, and the commands which we impose upon them are just; there can be no doubt that every one of them will take office as a stern necessity, and not after the fashion of our present rulers of State.

The statesman must be provided with a better life than that of a ruler; and then he will not covet office.

Yes, my friend, I said; and there lies the point. You must contrive for your future rulers another and a better life than that of a ruler, and then you may have a well-ordered State; for only in the State which offers this, will they rule who are truly rich, not in silver and gold, but in virtue and wisdom, which are the true blessings of life. Whereas if they go to the administration of public affairs, poor and hungering after their own private advantage, thinking that hence they are to snatch the chief good, order there can never be; for they will be fighting about office, and the civil and domestic broils which thus arise will be the ruin of the rulers themselves and of the whole State.

65

Most true, he replied.

And the only life which looks down upon the life of political ambition is that of true philosophy. Do you know of any other?

Indeed, I do not, he said. ◼

Reflections and Inquiries

1. What is Plato's thesis in this allegory?

2. Why do you suppose Plato presents his argument as a dialogue? How does this approach contribute to the persuasive force of Plato's argument?

3. What physiological limitations of human vision does Plato use as an analogy to flawed understanding of reality? How accurate an analogy is it, in your opinion?

4. What criticism of education is Plato presenting to Glaucon?

5. How does Plato characterize the ideal legislator? How realistic a characterization is this, from your perspective?

Reading to Write

1. Reread the "Allegory of the Cave" and then present your own mini-dialogue between yourself (as a modern-day Plato) and a high school student. Topic: Why a liberal arts education is more valuable then mere training for a specific occupation.

2. Write an essay on Plato's conception of the soul, based on his discussion of it in this dialogue.

To His Coy Mistress | Andrew Marvell

Arguments can be presented poetically, as in the case of this famous late-seventeenth-century "carpe diem" poem, "To His Coy Mistress" ("mistress" meaning here "a woman of stature and authority"). Andrew Marvell (1621–1678) liked to debate difficult philosophical, political and—in the case of the following poem—moral issues poetically but without resolving them.

Had we but world enough, and time,
This coyness, lady, were no crime.
We would sit down, and think which way
To walk, and pass our long love's day.
Thou by the Indian Ganges' side   5
Should'st rubies find; I by the tide
Of Humber would complain*. I would
Love you ten years before the Flood,
And you should, if you please, refuse
Till the conversion of the Jews.   10
My vegetable* love should grow
Vaster than empires, and more slow;
An hundred years should go to praise
Thine eyes, and on thy forehead gaze;
Two hundred to adore each breast,   15
But thirty thousand to the rest;
An age at least to every part,
And the last age should show your heart.

*sing melancholy songs

*fertile, ample

Source: Marvell, Andrew. "To His Coy Mistress." *Andrew Marvell: The Complete English Poems.* New York: St. Martin's, 1974. 50–51.

For, lady, you deserve this state,
Nor would I love at lower rate.   20
    But at my back I always hear
Time's winged chariot hurrying near;
And yonder all before us lie
Deserts of vast eternity.
Thy beauty shall no more be found,   25
Nor, in thy marble vault, shall sound
My echoing song, then worms shall try
That long preserved virginity:
And your quaint honor turn to dust,
And into ashes all my lust.   30
The grave's fine and private place,
But none, I think, do there embrace.
    Now therefore, while the youthful hue
glow, luminescence Sits on thy skin like morning glew
And while thy willing soul transpires   35
At every pore with instant fires,
Now let us sport us while we may,
And now, like amorous birds of prey,
Rather at once our time devour,
Than languish in his slow-chapped power.   40
Let us roll all our strength and all
Our sweetness up into one ball,
And tear our pleasures with rough strife,
Through the iron gates of life.
Thus, though we cannot make our sun   45
Stand still, yet we will make him run. ◪

Reflections and Inquiries

1. Summarize the speaker's argument. How valid is it? How would you refute it?

2. Many consider this poem to be a satire. If so, what is it satirizing?

3. The poem uses a literary device called hyperbole (exaggeration). Where do you see examples of it? Why does the speaker use it?

4. Why does Marvell present his argument as a poem? Why not a prose manifesto instead?

5. The poem presents only one side of the argument. Why doesn't Marvell include the woman's counterresponse?

Reading to Write

1. Analyze the speaker's argument in terms of introduction, body of evidence, and conclusion.

2. Write a point-by-point counterargument (in verse or prose) from the woman's point of view.

A Modest Proposal | Jonathan Swift

> Originally published as a pamphlet in 1729 with the title "A Modest Proposal for Preventing the Children of Poor People in Ireland from Being a Burden to Their Parents or Country, and for Making Them Beneficial to the Public," this bitterly ironic proposal for alleviating the famine in Ireland was sparked by Jonathan Swift's intolerance of the hypocrisy of his native Ireland that preached the joys of parenthood and the sacredness of life while at the same time permitting economic corruption and famine. Swift (1667–1745), a political journalist and the author of *Gulliver's Travels* (1726), was also an ordained priest and Dean of St. Patrick's Cathedral, Dublin.

It is a melancholy object to those who walk through this great town or travel in the country, when they see the streets, the roads, and cabin doors, crowded with beggars of the female sex, followed by three, four, or six children, all in rags and importuning every passenger for an alms. These mothers, instead of being able to work for their honest livelihood, are forced to employ all their time in strolling to beg sustenance for their helpless infants, who, as they grow up, either turn thieves for want of work, or leave their dear native country to fight for the Pretender in Spain, or sell themselves to the Barbadoes.

I think it is agreed by all parties that this prodigious number of children in the arms, or on the backs, or at the heels of their mothers and frequently of their fathers, is in the present deplorable state of the kingdom a very great additional grievance; and therefore whoever could find out a fair, cheap, and easy method of making these children sound useful members of the commonwealth would deserve so well of the public as to have his statue set up for a preserver of the nation.

But my intention is very far from being confined to provide only for the children of professed beggars; it is of a much greater extent, and shall take in the whole number of infants at a certain age who are born of parents in effect as little able to support them as those who demand our charity in the streets.

Source: Swift, Jonathan. "A Modest Proposal." *Gulliver's Travels and Other Writings.* Ed. Lois A. Landa. Boston: Houghton Mifflin/Riverside Editions, 1960. 429–36.

As to my own part, having turned my thoughts for many years upon this important subject, and maturely weighed the several schemes of other projectors, I have always found them grossly mistaken in their computation. It is true, a child just dropped from its dam may be supported by her milk for a solar year, with little other nourishment; at most not above the value of two shillings, which the mother may certainly get, or the value in scraps, by her lawful occupation of begging; and it is exactly at one year old that I propose to provide for them in such a manner as instead of being a charge upon their parents or the parish, or wanting food and raiment for the rest of their lives, they shall on the contrary contribute to the feeding, and partly to the clothing, of many thousands.

There is likewise another great advantage in my scheme, that it will prevent those voluntary abortions, and that horrid practice of women murdering their bastard children, alas, too frequent among us, sacrificing the poor innocent babes, I doubt, more to avoid the expense than the shame, which would move tears and pity in the most savage and inhuman breast.

The number of souls in this kingdom being usually reckoned one million and a half, of these I calculate there may be about two hundred thousand couples whose wives are breeders, from which number I subtract thirty thousand couples who are able to maintain their own children, although I apprehend there cannot be so many under the present distress of the kingdom; but this being granted, there will remain an hundred and seventy thousand breeders. I again subtract fifty thousand for those women who miscarry, or whose children die by accident or disease within the year. There only remain an hundred and twenty thousand children of poor parents actually born. The question therefore is, how this number shall be reared and provided for, which, as I have already said, under the present situation of affairs, is utterly impossible by all the methods hitherto proposed. For we can neither employ them in handicraft or agriculture; we neither build houses (I mean in the country) nor cultivate land. They can very seldom pick up a livelihood by stealing till they arrive at six years old, except where they are of towardly parts; although I confess they learn the rudiments much earlier, during which time they can however be looked upon only as probationers, as I have been informed by a principal gentleman in the country of Cavan, who protested to me that he never knew above one or two instances under the age of six, even in a part of the kingdom so renowned for the quickest proficiency in that art.

I am assured by our merchants that a boy or a girl before twelve years old is no salable commodity, and even when they come to this age they will not yield above three pounds, or three pounds and half a crown at most on the Exchange; which cannot turn to account either to the parents or the kingdom, the charge of nutriment and rags having been at least four times that value.

I shall now therefore humbly propose my own thoughts, which I hope will not be liable to the least objection.

I have been assured by a very knowing American of my acquaintance in London, that a young healthy child well nursed is at a year old a most delicious, nourishing, and wholesome food, whether stewed, roasted, baked, or boiled, and I make no doubt that it will equally serve in a fricassee or a ragout.

I do therefore humbly offer it to public consideration that of the hundred and twenty thousand children, already computed, twenty thousand may be reserved for breed, whereof only one fourth part to be males, which is more than we allow to sheep, black cattle, or swine; and my reason is that these chil-   10
dren are seldom the fruits of marriage, a circumstance not much regarded by our savages, therefore one male will be sufficient to serve four females. That the remaining hundred thousand may at a year old be offered in sale to the persons of quality and fortune through the kingdom, always advising the mother to let them suck plentifully in the last month, so as to render them plump and fat for a good table. A child will make two dishes at an entertainment for friends; and when the family dines alone, the fore or hind quarter will make a reasonable dish, and seasoned with a little pepper or salt will be very good boiled on the fourth day, especially in the winter.

I have reckoned upon a medium that a child just born will weigh twelve pounds, and in a solar year if tolerably nursed increaseth to twenty-eight pounds.

I grant this food will be somewhat dear, and therefore very proper for landlords, who, as they have already devoured most of the parents, seem to have the best title to the children.

Infant's flesh will be in season throughout the year, but more plentiful in March, and a little before and after. For we are told by a grave author, an eminent French physician, that fish being a prolific diet, there are more children born in Roman Catholic countries about nine months after Lent than at any other season, therefore, reckoning a year after Lent, the markets will be more glutted than usual, because the number of popish infants is at least three to one in this kingdom; and therefore it will have one other collateral advantage, by lessening the number of Papists among us.

I have already computed the charge of nursing a beggar's child (in which list I reckon all cottagers, laborers, and four fifths of the farmers) to be about two shillings per annum, rags included; and I believe no gentleman would repine to give ten shillings for the carcass of a good fat child, which, as I have said, will make four dishes of excellent nutritive meat, when he hath only some particular friend or his own family to dine with him. Thus the squire will learn to be a good landlord, and grow popular among the tenants; the mother will have eight shillings net profit, and be fit for work till she produces another child.

Those who are more thrifty (as I must confess the times require) may flay   15
the carcass; the skin of which artificially dressed will make admirable gloves for ladies, and summer boots for fine gentlemen.

As to our city of Dublin, shambles may be appointed for this purpose in the most convenient parts of it, and butchers we may be assured will not be wanting; although I rather recommend buying the children alive, and dressing them hot from the knife as we do roasting pigs.

A very worthy person, a true lover of his country, and whose virtues I highly esteem, was lately pleased in discoursing on this matter to offer a refinement upon my scheme. He said that many gentlemen of his kingdom, having of late destroyed their deer, he conceived that the want of venison might be well supplied by the bodies of young lads and maidens, not exceeding fourteen years of age nor under twelve, so great a number of both sexes in every county being now ready to starve for want of work and service; and these to be disposed of by their parents, if alive, or otherwise by their nearest relations. But with due deference to so excellent a friend and so deserving a patriot, I cannot be altogether in his sentiments; for as to the males, my American acquaintance assured me from frequent experience that their flesh was generally tough and lean, like that of our schoolboys, by continual exercise, and their taste disagreeable; and to fatten them would not answer the charge. Then as to the females, it would, I think with humble submission, be a loss to the public, because they soon would become breeders themselves: and besides, it is not improbable that some scrupulous people might be apt to censure such a practice (although indeed very unjustly) as a little bordering upon cruelty; which, I confess, hath always been with me the strongest objection against any project, how well soever intended.

But in order to justify my friend, he confessed that this expedient was put into his head by the famous Psalmanazar, a native of the island Formosa, who came from thence to London about twenty years ago, and in conversation told my friend that in his country when any young person happened to be put to death, the executioner sold the carcass to persons of quality as a prime dainty; and that in his time the body of a plump girl of fifteen, who was crucified for an attempt to poison the emperor, was sold to his Imperial Majesty's prime minister of state, and other great mandarins of the court, in joints from the gibbet, at four hundred crowns. Neither indeed can I deny that if the same use were made of several plump young girls in this town, who without one single groat to their fortunes cannot stir abroad without a chair, and appear at the playhouse and assemblies in foreign fineries which they never will pay for, the kingdom would not be the worse.

Some persons of a desponding spirit are in great concern about that vast number of poor people who are aged, diseased, or maimed, and I have been desired to employ my thoughts what course may be taken to ease the nation of so grievous an encumbrance. But I am not in the least pain upon that matter, because it is very well known that they are every day dying and rotting by cold and famine, and filth and vermin, as fast as can be reasonably expected. And as to the younger laborers, they are now in almost as hopeful a condition. They cannot get work, and consequently pine away for want of nourishment to a degree that if at any time they are accidentally hired to common labor, they have not strength to perform it; and thus the country and themselves are happily delivered from the evils to come.

I have too long digressed, and therefore shall return to my subject. I think   20 the advantages by the proposal which I have made are obvious and many, as well as of the highest importance.

For first, as I have already observed, it would greatly lessen the number of Papists, with whom we are yearly overrun, being the principal breeders of the nation as well as our most dangerous enemies; and who stay at home on purpose to deliver the kingdom to the Pretender, hoping to take their advantage by the absence of so many good Protestants, who have chosen rather to leave their country than to stay at home and pay tithes against their conscience to an Episcopal curate.

Secondly, the poorer tenants will have something valuable of their own, which by law may be made liable to distress, and help to pay their landlord's rent, their corn and cattle being already seized and money a thing unknown.

Thirdly, whereas the maintenance of a hundred thousand children, from two years old and upwards, cannot be computed at less than ten shillings a piece per annum, the nation's stock will be thereby increased fifty thousand pounds per annum, besides the profit of a new dish introduced to the tables of all gentlemen of fortune in the kingdom who have any refinement in taste. And the money will circulate among ourselves, the goods being entirely of our own growth and manufacture.

Fourthly, the constant breeders, besides the gain of eight shillings sterling per annum by the sale of their children, will be rid of the charge of maintaining them after the first year.

Fifthly, this food would likewise bring great custom to taverns, where the vintners will certainly be so prudent as to procure the best receipts for dressing it to perfection, and consequently have their houses frequented by all the fine gentlemen, who justly value themselves upon their knowledge in good eating; and a skillful cook, who understands how to oblige his guests, will contrive to make it as expensive as they please.

Sixthly, this would be a great inducement to marriage, which all wise nations have either encouraged by rewards or enforced by laws and penalties. It would increase the care and tenderness of mothers toward their children, when they were sure of a settlement for life to the poor babes, provided in some sort by the public, to their annual profit instead of expense. We should see an honest emulation among the married women, which of them could bring the fattest child to the market. Men would become as fond of their wives during the time of their pregnancy as they are now of their mares in foal, their cows in calf, or sows when they are ready to farrow; nor offer to beat or kick them (as is too frequent a practice) for fear of a miscarriage.

Many other advantages might be enumerated. For instance, the addition of some thousand carcasses in our exportation of barreled beef, the propagation of swine's flesh, and improvements in the art of making good bacon, so much wanted among us by the great destruction of pigs, too frequent at our tables, which are no way comparable in taste or magnificence to a well-grown, fat, yearling child, which roasted whole will make a considerable figure at a lord mayor's feast or any other public entertainment. But this and many others I omit, being studious of brevity.

Supposing that one thousand families in this city would be constant customers for infants' flesh, besides others who might have it at merry meetings, particularly weddings and christenings, I compute that Dublin would take off annually about twenty thousand carcasses, and the rest of the kingdom (where probably they will be sold somewhat cheaper) the remaining eighty thousand.

I can think of no one objection that will possibly be raised against this proposal, unless it should be urged that the number of people will be thereby much lessened in the kingdom. This I freely own, and it was indeed one principal design in offering it to the world. I desire the reader will observe, that I calculate my remedy for this one individual kingdom of Ireland and for no other that ever was, is, or I think ever can be upon earth. Therefore let no man talk to me of other expedients: of taxing our absentees at five shillings a pound: of using neither clothes nor household furniture except what is of our own growth and manufacture; of utterly rejecting the materials and instruments that promote foreign luxury: of curing the expensiveness of pride, vanity, idleness, and gaming in our women: of introducing a vein of parsimony, prudence, and temperance: of learning to love our country, in the want of which we differ even from Laplanders and the inhabitants of Topinamboo: of quitting our animosities and factions, nor acting any longer like the Jews, who were murdering one anther at the very moment their city was taken: of being a little cautious not to sell our country and conscience for nothing: of teaching landlords to have at least one degree of mercy toward their tenants: lastly, of putting a spirit of honesty, industry, and skill into our shopkeepers; who, if a resolution could now be taken to buy only our native goods, would immediately unite to cheat and exact upon us in the price, the measure, and the goodness, nor could ever yet be brought to make one fair proposal of just dealing, though often and earnestly invited to it.

Therefore, I repeat, let no man talk to me of these and the like expedients,   30
till he hath at least some glimpse of hope that there will ever be some hearty and sincere attempt to put them in practice.

But as to myself, having been wearied out for many years with offering vain, idle, visionary thoughts, and at length utterly despairing of success, I fortunately fell upon this proposal, which, as it is wholly new, so it hath something solid and real, of no expense and little trouble, full in our own power, and whereby we can incur no danger in disobliging England. For this kind of commodity will not bear exportation, the flesh being of too tender a consistence to admit a long continuance in salt, although perhaps I could name a country which would be glad to eat up our whole nation without it.

After all, I am not so violently bent upon my own opinions as to reject any offer proposed by wise men, which shall be found equally innocent, cheap, easy, and effectual. But before something of that kind shall be advanced in contradiction to my scheme, and offering a better, I desire the author or authors will be pleased maturely to consider two points. First, as things now stand, how they will be able to find food and raiment for an hundred thousand useless mouths and backs. And secondly, there being a round million of creatures in human figure throughout this kingdom, whose sole subsistence put into a common stock would leave them in debt two millions of pounds sterling, adding those who are beggars by profession to the bulk of farmers, cottagers, and laborers, with their wives and children who are beggars in effect; I desire those politicians who dislike my overture, and may perhaps be so bold to attempt an answer, that they will first ask the parents of these mortals whether they would not at this day think it a great happiness to have been sold for food at a year old in this manner I prescribe, and thereby have avoided such a perpetual scene of misfortunes as they have since gone through by the oppression of landlords, the impossibility of paying rent without money or trade, the want of common sustenance, with neither house nor clothes to cover them from the inclemencies of the weather, and the most inevitable prospect of entailing the like or greater miseries upon their breed forever.

I profess, in the sincerity of my heart, that I have not the least personal interest in endeavoring to promote this necessary work, having no other motive than the public good of my country, by advancing our trade, providing for infants, relieving the poor, and giving some pleasure to the rich. I have no children by which I can propose to get a single penny; the youngest being nine years old, and my wife past childbearing. ◪

Reflections and Inquiries

1. Why do you suppose Swift chooses to express his views ironically? What advantage does irony have over a straightforward approach to the problem?

2. What social ills does Swift call attention to in his proposal?

3. Why does Swift refer to childbearing women as *breeders*?

4. How does Swift attempt to speak to the moral consciousness of his largely Catholic readership? What exactly is he saying to them via his proposal?

Reading to Write

Write an analysis of Swift's use of irony in this proposal. How, exactly, does it come across so powerfully?

Sinners in the Hands of an Angry God | Jonathan Edwards

One of the greatest of American theologians, Jonathan Edwards (1703–1758) is associated with a major religious revival in New England known as the Great Awakening. Edwards wished to propagate his idea of freedom of the will, based not only on Calvinist theology but also on his profound understanding of human psychology, largely influenced by the philosopher John Locke. In the following sermon, preached in Connecticut on Sunday, July 8, 1741, to an enthralled congregation, Edwards deploys his extraordinary literary and rhetorical skills to dramatize how utterly slender is the thread that holds us back from damnation.

Their foot shall slide in due time.

In this verse is threatened the vengeance of God on the wicked unbelieving Israelites, who were God's visible people, and who lived under the means of grace; but who, notwithstanding all God's wonderful works towards them, remained (as ver. 28.) void of counsel, having no understanding in them. Under all the cultivations of heaven, they brought forth bitter and poisonous fruit; as in the two verses next preceding the text.—The expression I have chosen for my text, *Their foot shall slide in due time,* seems to imply the following things, relating to the punishment and destruction to which these wicked Israelites were exposed.

1. That they were always exposed to *destruction;* as one that stands or walks in slippery places is always exposed to fall. This is implied in the manner of their destruction coming upon them, being represented by their foot sliding. The same is expressed, Psalm lxxiii. 18. "Surely thou didst set them in slippery places; thou castedst them down into destruction."

2. It implies, that they were always exposed to sudden unexpected destruction. As he that walks in slippery places is every moment liable to fall, he cannot foresee one moment whether he shall stand or fall the next; and when he does fall, he falls at once without warning: Which is also expressed in Psalm lxxiii. 18, 19. "Surely thou didst set them in slippery places; thou castedst them down into destruction: How are they brought into desolation as in a moment!"

3. Another thing implied is, that they are liable to fall *of themselves,* without being thrown down by the hand of another; as he that stands or walks on slippery ground needs nothing but his own weight to throw him down.

4. That the reason why they are not fallen already, and do not fall now, is   5

Source: Edwards, Jonathan. "Sinners in the Hands of an Angry God." *Jonathan Edwards: Representative Selections,* revised ed. Ed. with Introduction, Bibliography, and Notes by Clarence H. Faust and Thomas H. Johnson. New York: Hill and Wang, 1935; 1962. 155–72.

only that God's appointed time is not come. For it is said, that when that due time, or appointed time comes, *their foot shall slide.* Then they shall be left to fall, as they are inclined by their own weight. God will not hold them up in these slippery places any longer, but will let them go; and then, at that very instant, they shall fall into destruction; as he that stands on such slippery declining ground, on the edge of a pit, he cannot stand alone, when he is let go he immediately falls and is lost.

The observation from the words that I would now insist upon is this.—"There is nothing that keeps wicked men at any one moment out of hell, but the mere pleasure of God"—By the *mere* pleasure of God, I mean his *sovereign* pleasure, his arbitrary will, restrained by no obligation, hindered by no manner of difficulty, any more than if nothing else but God's mere will had in the least degree, or in any respect whatsoever, any hand in the preservation of wicked men one moment.—The truth of this observation may appear by the following considerations.

1. There is no want of *power* in God to cast wicked men into hell at any moment. Men's hands cannot be strong when God rises up. The strongest have no power to resist him, nor can any deliver out of his hands.—He is not only able to cast wicked men into hell, but he can most easily do it. Sometimes an earthly prince meets with a great deal of difficulty to subdue a rebel, who has found means to fortify himself, and has made himself strong by the numbers of his followers. But it is not so with God. There is no fortress that is any defence from the power of God. Though hand join in hand, and vast multitudes of God's enemies combine and associate themselves, they are easily broken in pieces. They are as great heaps of light chaff before the whirlwind; or large quantities of dry stubble before devouring flames. We find it easy to tread on and crush a worm that we see crawling on the earth; so it is easy for us to cut or singe a slender thread that any thing hangs by: thus easy is it for God, when he pleases, to cast his enemies down to hell. What are we, that we should think to stand before him, at whose rebuke the earth trembles, and before whom the rocks are thrown down?

2. They *deserve* to be cast into hell; so that divine justice never stands in the way, it makes no objection against God's using his power at any moment to destroy them. Yea, on the contrary, justice calls aloud for an infinite punishment of their sins. Divine justice says of the tree that brings forth such grapes of Sodom, "Cut it down, why cumbereth it the ground?" Luke xiii. 7. The sword of divine justice is every moment brandished over their heads, and it is nothing but the hand of arbitrary mercy, and God's mere will, that holds it back.

3. They are already under a sentence of *condemnation* to hell. They do not only justly deserve to be cast down thither, but the sentence of the law of God, that eternal and immutable rule of righteousness that God has fixed between him and mankind, is gone out against them, and stands against them; so that they are bound over already to hell. John iii. 18. "He that believeth not is condemned already." So that every uncoverted man properly belongs to hell; that

is his place; from thence he is, John viii. 23. "Ye are from beneath:" And thither he is bound; it is the place that justice, and God's word, and the sentence of his unchangeable law assign to him.

4. They are now the objects of that very same *anger* and wrath of God, that   10 is expressed in the torments of hell. And the reason why they do not go down to hell at each moment, is not because God, in whose power they are, is not then very angry with them; as he is with many miserable creatures now tormented in hell, who there feel and bear the fierceness of his wrath. Yea, God is a great deal more angry with great numbers that are now on earth: yea, doubtless, with many that are now in this congregation, who it may be are at ease, than he is with many of those who are now in the flames of hell.

So that it is not because God is unmindful of their wickedness, and does not resent it, that he does not let loose his hand and cut them off. God is not altogether such an one as themselves, though they may imagine him to be so. The wrath of God burns against them, their damnation does not slumber; the pit is prepared, the fire is made ready, the furnace is now hot, ready to receive them; the flames do now rage and glow. The glittering sword is whet, and held over them, and the pit hath opened its mouth under them.

5. The *devil* stands ready to fall upon them, and seize them as his own, at what moment God shall permit him. They belong to him; he has their souls in his possession, and under his dominion. The scripture represents them as his goods, Luke xi. 12. The devils watch them; they are ever by them at their right hand; they stand waiting for them, like greedy hungry lions that see their prey, and expect to have it, but are for the present kept back. If God should withdraw his hand, by which they are restrained, they would in one moment fly upon their poor souls. The old serpent is gaping for them; hell opens its mouth wide to receive them; and if God should permit it, they would be hastily swallowed up and lost.

6. There are in the souls of wicked men those hellish *principles* reigning, that would presently kindle and flame out into hell fire, if it were not for God's restraints. There is laid in the very nature of carnal men, a foundation for the torments of hell. There are those corrupt principles, in reigning power in them, and in full possession of them, that are seeds of hell fire. These principles are active and powerful, exceeding violent in their nature, and if it were not for the restraining hand of God upon them, they would soon break out, they would flame out after the same manner as the same corruptions, the same enmity does in the hearts of damned souls, and would beget the same torments as they do in them. The souls of the wicked are in scripture compared to the troubled sea, Isa. lvii. 20. For the present, God restrains their wickedness by his mighty power, as he does the raging waves of the troubled sea, saying, "Hitherto shalt thou come, but no further;" but if God should withdraw that restraining power, it would soon carry all before it. Sin is the ruin and misery of the soul; it is destructive in its nature; and if God should leave it without restraint, there would need nothing else to make the soul perfectly miserable.

The corruption of the heart of man is immoderate and boundless in its fury; and while wicked men live here, it is like fire pent up by God's restraints, whereas if it were let loose, it would set on fire the course of nature; and as the heart is now a sink of sin, so if sin was not restrained, it would immediately turn the soul into a fiery oven, or a furnace of fire and brimstone.

7. It is no security to wicked men for one moment, that there are no visible means of death at hand. It is no security to a natural man, that he is now in health, and that he does not see which way he should now immediately go out of the world by any accident, and that there is no visible danger in any respect in his circumstances. The manifold and continual experience of the world in all ages, shows this is no evidence, that a man is not on the very brink of eternity, and that the next step will not be into another world. The unseen, unthought-of ways and means of persons going suddenly out of the world are innumerable and inconceivable. Unconverted men walk over the pit of hell on a rotten covering, and there are innumerable places in this covering so weak that they will not bear their weight, and these places are not seen. The arrows of death fly unseen at noon-day; the sharpest sight cannot discern them. God has so many different unsearchable ways of taking wicked men out of the world and sending them to hell, that there is nothing to make it appear, that God had need to be at the expence of a miracle, or go out of the ordinary course of his providence, to destroy any wicked man, at any moment. All the means that there are of sinners going out of the world, are so in God's hands, and so universally and absolutely subject to his power and determination, that it does not depend at all the less on the mere will of God, whether sinners shall at any moment go to hell, than if means were never made use of, or at all concerned in the case.

8. Natural men's prudence and care to preserve their own lives, or the care of others to preserve them, do not secure them a moment. To this, divine providence and universal experience do also bear testimony. There is this clear evidence that men's own wisdom is no security to them from death; that if it were otherwise we should see some difference between the wise and politic men of the world, and others, with regard to their liableness to early and unexpected death: but how is it in fact? Eccles. ii. 16. "How dieth the wise man? even as the fool." 15

9. All wicked men's pains and *contrivance* which they use to escape hell, while they continue to reject Christ, and so remain wicked men, do not secure them from hell one moment. Almost every natural man that hears of hell, flatters himself that he shall escape it; he depends upon himself for his own security; he flatters himself in what he has done, in what he is now doing, or what he intends to do. Every one lays out matters in his own mind how he shall avoid damnation, and flatters himself that he contrives well for himself, and that his schemes will not fail. They hear indeed that there are but few saved, and that the greater part of men that have died heretofore are gone to hell; but each one imagines that he lays out matters better for his own escape than

others have done. He does not intend to come to that place of torment; he says within himself, that he intends to take effectual care, and to order matters so for himself as not to fail.

But the foolish children of men miserably delude themselves in their own schemes, and in confidence in their own strength and wisdom; they trust to nothing but a shadow. The greater part of those who heretofore have lived under the same means of grace, and are now dead, are undoubtedly gone to hell; and it was not because they were not as wise as those who are now alive: it was not because they did not lay out matters as well for themselves to secure their own escape. If we could speak with them, and inquire of them, one by one, whether they expected, when alive, and when they used to hear about hell, ever to be the subjects of that misery: we doubtless, should hear one and another reply, "No, I never intended to come here: I had laid out matters otherwise in my mind; I thought I should contrive well for myself: I thought my scheme good. I intended to take effectual care; but it came upon me unexpected; I did not look for it at that time, and in that manner; it came as a thief: Death outwitted me: God's wrath was too quick for me. Oh, my cursed foolishness! I was flattering myself, and pleasing myself with vain dreams of what I would do hereafter; and when I was saying, Peace and safety, then suddenly destruction came upon me."

10. God has laid himself under *no obligation*, by any promise to keep any natural man out of hell one moment. God certainly has made no promises either of eternal life, or of any deliverance or preservation from eternal death, but what are contained in the covenant of grace, the promises that are given in Christ, in whom all the promises are yea and amen. But surely they have no interest in the promises of the covenant of grace who are not the children of the covenant, who do not believe in any of the promises, and have no interest in the Mediator of the covenant.

So that, whatever some have imagined and pretended about promises made to natural men's earnest seeking and knocking, it is plain and manifest, that whatever pains a natural man takes in religion, whatever prayers he makes, till he believes in Christ, God is under no manner of obligation to keep him a moment from eternal destruction.

So that, thus it is that natural men are held in the hand of God, over the pit of hell; they have deserved the fiery pit, and are already sentenced to it; and God is dreadfully provoked, his anger is as great towards them as to those that are actually suffering the executions of the fierceness of his wrath in hell, and they have done nothing in the least to appease or abate that anger, neither is God in the least bound by any promise to hold them up one moment; the devil is waiting for them, hell is gaping for them, the flames gather and flash about them, and would fain lay hold on them, and swallow them up; the fire pent up in their own hearts is struggling to break out: and they have no interest in any Mediator, there are no means within reach that can be any security to them. In short, they have no refuge, nothing to take hold of; all that preserves them

20

every moment is the mere arbitrary will, and uncovenanted, unobliged forbearance of an incensed God.

Application
The use of this awful subject may be for awakening unconverted persons in this congregation. This that you have heard is the case of every one of you that are out of Christ.—That world of misery, that lake of burning brimstone, is extended abroad under you. There is the dreadful pit of the glowing flames of the wrath of God; there is hell's wide gaping mouth open; and you have nothing to stand upon, nor any thing to take hold of; there is nothing between you and hell but the air; it is only the power and mere pleasure of God that holds you up.

You probably are not sensible of this; you find you are kept out of hell, but do not see the hand of God in it; but look at other things, as the good state of your bodily constitution, your care of your own life, and the means you use for your own preservation. But indeed these things are nothing; if God should withdraw his hand, they would avail no more to keep you from falling, than the thin air to hold up a person that is suspended in it.

Your wickedness makes you as it were heavy as lead, and to tend downwards with great weight and pressure towards hell; and if God should let you go, you would immediately sink and swiftly descend and plunge into the bottomless gulf, and your healthy constitution, and your own care and prudence, and best contrivance, and all your righteousness, would have no more influence to uphold you and keep you out of hell, than a spider's web would have to stop a fallen rock. Were it not for the sovereign pleasure of God, the earth would not bear you one moment; for you are a burden to it; the creation groans with you; the creature is made subject to the bondage of your corruption, not willingly; the sun does not willingly shine upon you to give you light to serve sin and Satan; the earth does not willingly yield her increase to satisfy your lusts; nor is it willingly a stage for your wickedness to be acted upon; the air does not willingly serve you for breath to maintain the flame of life in your vitals, while you spend your life in the service of God's enemies. God's creatures are good, and were made for men to serve God with, and do not willingly subserve to any other purpose, and groan when they are abused to purposes so directly contrary to their nature and end. And the world would spew you out, were it not for the sovereign hand of him who hath subjected it in hope. There are black clouds of God's wrath now hanging directly over your heads, full of the dreadful storm, and big with thunder; and were it not for the restraining hand of God, it would immediately burst forth upon you. The sovereign pleasure of God, for the present, stays his rough wind; otherwise it would come with fury, and your destruction would come like a whirlwind, and you would be like the chaff of the summer threshing floor.

The wrath of God is like great waters that are dammed for the present; they increase more and more, and rise higher and higher, till an outlet is given;

and the longer the stream is stopped, the more rapid and mighty is its course, when once it is let loose. It is true, that judgment against your evil works has not been executed hitherto; the floods of God's vengeance have been withheld; but your guilt in the mean time is constantly increasing, and you are every day treasuring up more wrath; the waters are constantly rising, and waxing more and more mighty; and there is nothing but the mere pleasure of God, that holds the waters back, that are unwilling to be stopped, and press hard to go forward. If God should only withdraw his hand from the floodgate, it would immediately fly open, and the fiery floods of the fierceness and wrath of God, would rush forth with inconceivable fury, and would come upon you with omnipotent power; and if your strength were ten thousand times greater than it is, yea, ten thousand times greater than the strength of the stoutest, sturdiest devil in hell, it would be nothing to withstand or endure it.

The bow of God's wrath is bent, and the arrow made ready on the string,   25
and justice bends the arrow at your heart, and strains the bow, and it is nothing but the mere pleasure of God, and that of an angry God, without any promise or obligation at all, that keeps the arrow one moment from being made drunk with your blood. Thus all you that never passed under a great change of heart, by the mighty power of the Spirit of God upon your souls; all you that were never born again, and made new creatures, and raised from being dead in sin, to a state of new, and before altogether unexperienced light and life, are in the hands of an angry God. However you may have reformed your life in many things, and may have had religious affections, and may keep up a form of religion in your families and closets, and in the house of God, it is nothing but his mere pleasure that keeps you from being this moment swallowed up in everlasting destruction. However unconvinced you may now be of the truth of what you hear, by and by you will be fully convinced of it. Those that are gone from being in the like circumstances with you, see that it was so with them; for destruction came suddenly upon most of them; when they expected nothing of it, and while they were saying, Peace and safety: now they see, that those things on which they depended for peace and safety, were nothing but thin air and empty shadows.

The God that holds you over the pit of hell, much as one holds a spider, or some loathsome insect over the fire, abhors you, and is dreadfully provoked: his wrath towards you burns like fire; he looks upon you as worthy of nothing else, but to be cast into the fire; he is of purer eyes than to bear to have you in his sight; you are ten thousand times more abominable in his eyes, than the most hateful venomous serpent is in ours. You have offended him infinitely more than ever a stubborn rebel did his prince; and yet it is nothing but his hand that holds you from falling into the fire every moment. It is to be ascribed to nothing else, that you did not go to hell the last night; that you was suffered to awake again in this world, after you closed your eyes to sleep. And there is no other reason to be given, why you have not dropped into hell since you arose in the morning, but that God's hand has held you up. There is no other reason to be given why you have not gone to hell, since you have sat here in the house of God, provoking his pure eyes by your sinful wicked manner of attending his solemn worship. Yea, there is nothing else that is to be given as a reason why you do not this very moment drop down into hell.

O sinner! Consider the fearful danger you are in: it is a great furnace of wrath, a wide and bottomless pit, full of the fire of wrath, that you are held over in the hand of that God, whose wrath is provoked and incensed as much against you, as against many of the damned in hell. You hang by a slender thread, with the flames of divine wrath flashing about it, and ready every moment to singe it, and burn it asunder; and you have no interest in any Mediator, and nothing to lay hold of to save yourself, nothing to keep off the flames of wrath, nothing of your own, nothing that you ever have done, nothing that you can do, to induce God to spare you one moment.—And consider here more particularly,

1. *Whose* wrath it is: it is the wrath of the infinite God. If it were only the wrath of man, though it were of the most potent prince, it would be comparatively little to be regarded. The wrath of kings is very much dreaded, especially of absolute monarchs, who have the possessions and lives of their subjects wholly in their power, to be disposed of at their mere will. Prov. xx. 2. "The fear of a king is as the roaring of a lion: Whoso provoketh him to anger, sinneth against his own soul." The subject that very much enrages an arbitrary prince, is liable to suffer the most extreme torments that human art can invent, or human power can inflict. But the greatest earthly potentates in their greatest majesty and strength, and when clothed in their greatest terrors, are but feeble, despicable worms of the dust, in comparison of the great and almighty Creator and King of heaven and earth. It is but little that they can do, when most enraged, and when they have exerted the utmost of their fury. All the kings of the earth, before God, are as grasshoppers; they are nothing, and less than nothing: both their love and their hatred is to be despised. The wrath of the great King of kings, is as much more terrible than theirs, as his majesty is greater. Luke xii. 4, 5. "And I say unto you, my friends, Be not afraid of them that kill the body, and after that, have no more that they can do. But I will forewarn you whom you shall fear: fear him, which after he hath killed, hath power to cast into hell: yea, I say unto you, Fear him."

2. It is the *fierceness* of his wrath that you are exposed to. We often read of the fury of God; as in Isaiah lix. 18. "According to their deeds, accordingly he will repay fury to his adversaries." So Isaiah lxvi. 15. "For behold, the Lord will come with fire, and with his chariots like a whirlwind, to render his anger with fury, and his rebuke with flames of fire." And in many other places. So, Rev. xix. 15. we read of "the wine press of the fierceness and wrath of Almighty God." The words are exceeding terrible. If it had only been said, "the wrath of God," the words would have implied that which is infinitely dreadful: but it is "the fierceness and wrath of God." The fury of God! the fierceness of Jehovah! Oh, how dreadful must that be! Who can utter or conceive what such

expressions carry in them! But it is also "the fierceness and wrath of *Almighty* God." As though there would be a very great manifestation of his almighty power in what the fierceness of his wrath should inflict, as though omnipotence should be as it were enraged, and exerted, as men are wont to exert their strength in the fierceness of their wrath. Oh! then, what will be the consequence! What will become of the poor worms that shall suffer it! Whose hands can be strong? And whose heart can endure? To what a dreadful, inexpressible, inconceivable depth of misery must the poor creature be sunk who shall be the subject of this!

Consider this, you that are here present, that yet remain in an unregenerate state. That God will execute the fierceness of his anger, implies, that he will inflict wrath without any pity. When God beholds the ineffable extremity of your case, and sees your torment to be so vastly disproportioned to your strength, and sees how your poor soul is crushed, and sinks down, as it were, into an infinite gloom; he will have no compassion upon you, he will not forbear the executions of his wrath, or in the least lighten his hand; there shall be no moderation or mercy, nor will God then at all stay his rough wind; he will have no regard to your welfare, nor be at all careful lest you should suffer too much in any other sense, than only that you shall *not suffer beyond what strict justice requires.* Nothing shall be withheld, because it is so hard for you to bear. Ezek. viii. 18. "Therefore will I also deal in fury: mine eye shall not spare, neither will I have pity; and though they cry in mine ears with a loud voice, yet I will not hear them." Now God stands ready to pity you; this is a day of mercy; you may cry now with some encouragement of obtaining mercy. But when once the day of mercy is past, your most lamentable and dolorous cries and shrieks will be in vain; you will be wholly lost and thrown away of God, as to any regard to your welfare. God will have no other use to put you to, but to suffer misery; you shall be continued in being to no other end; for you will be a vessel of wrath fitted to destruction; and there will be no other use of this vessel, but to be filled full of wrath. God will be so far from pitying you when you cry to him, that it is said he will only "laugh and mock," Prov. i. 25, 26, &c.

How awful are those words, Isa. lxiii. 3, which are the words of the great God. "I will tread them in mine anger, and will trample them in my fury, and their blood shall be sprinkled upon my garments, and I will stain all my raiment." It is perhaps impossible to conceive of words that carry in them greater manifestations of these three things, *viz.* contempt, and hatred, and fierceness of indignation. If you cry to God to pity you, he will be so far from pitying you in your doleful case, or showing you the least regard or favour, that instead of that, he will only tread you under foot. And though he will know that you cannot bear the weight of omnipotence treading upon you, yet he will not regard that, but he will crush you under his feet without mercy; he will crush out your blood, and make it fly, and it shall be sprinkled on his garments, so as to stain all his raiment. He will not only hate you, but he will have you, in the utmost contempt: no place shall be thought fit for you, but under his feet to be trodden down as the mire of the streets.

30

3. The *misery* you are exposed to is that which God will inflict to that end, that he might show what that wrath of Jehovah is. God hath had it on his heart to show to angels and men, both how excellent his love is, and also how terrible his wrath is. Sometimes earthly kings have a mind to show how terrible their wrath is, by the extreme punishments they would execute on those that would provoke them. Nebuchadnezzar, that mighty and haughty monarch of the Chaldean empire, was willing to show his wrath when enraged with Shadrach, Meshech, and Abednego; and accordingly gave orders that the burning fiery furnace should be heated seven times hotter than it was before; doubtless, it was raised to the utmost degree of fierceness that human art could raise it. But the great God is also willing to show his wrath, and magnify his awful majesty and mighty power in the extreme sufferings of his enemies. Rom. ix. 22. "What if God, willing to show his wrath, and to make his power known, endure with much long-suffering the vessels of wrath fitted to destruction?" And seeing this is his design, and what he has determined, even to show how terrible the unrestrained wrath, the fury and fierceness of Jehovah is, he will do it to effect. There will be something accomplished and brought to pass that will be dreadful with a witness. When the great and angry God hath risen up and executed his awful vengeance on the poor sinner, and the wretch is actually suffering the infinite weight and power of his indignation, then will God call upon the whole universe to behold that awful majesty and mighty power that is to be seen in it. Isa. xxxiii. 12–14. "And the people shall be as the burnings of lime, as thorns cut up shall they be burnt in the fire. Hear ye that are far off, what I have done; and ye that are near, acknowledge my might. The sinners in Zion are afraid; fearfulness hath surprised the hypocrites," &c.

Thus it will be with you that are in an unconverted state, if you continue in it; the infinite might, and majesty, and terribleness of the omnipotent God shall be magnified upon you, in the ineffable strength of your torments. You shall be tormented in the presence of the holy angels, and in the presence of the Lamb; and when you shall be in this state of suffering, the glorious inhabitants of heaven shall go forth and look on the awful spectacle, that they may see what the wrath and fierceness of the Almighty is; and when they have seen it, they will fall down and adore that great power and majesty. Isa. lxvi. 23, 24. "And it shall come to pass, that from one new moon to anther, and from one sabbath to another, shall all flesh come to worship before me, saith the Lord. And they shall go forth and look upon the carcasses of the men that have transgressed against me; for their worm shall not die, neither shall their fire be quenched, and they shall be an abhorring unto all flesh."

4. It is *everlasting* wrath. It would be dreadful to suffer this fierceness and wrath of Almighty God one moment; but you must suffer it to all eternity. There will be no end to this exquisite horrible misery. When you look forward, you shall see a long for ever, a boundless duration before you, which will swallow up your thoughts and amaze your soul; and you will absolutely despair of ever having any deliverance, any end, any mitigation, any rest at all. You will know certainly that you must wear out long ages, millions of millions

of ages, in wrestling, and conflicting with this almighty merciless vengeance; and then when you have so done, when so many ages have actually been spent by you in this manner, you will know that all is but a point to what remains. So that your punishment will indeed be infinite. Oh, who can express what the state of a soul in such circumstances is! All that we can possibly say about it, gives but a very feeble, faint representation of it; it is inexpressible and inconceivable: For "who knows the power of God's anger?"

How dreadful is the state of those that are daily and hourly in the danger of this great wrath and infinite misery! But this is the dismal case of every soul in this congregation that has not been born again, however moral and strict, sober and religious, they may otherwise be. Oh that you would consider it, whether you be young or old! There is reason to think, that there are many in this congregation now hearing this discourse, that will actually be the subjects of this very misery to all eternity. We know not who they are, or in what seats they sit, or what thoughts they now have. It may be they are now at ease, and hear all these things without much disturbance, and are now flattering themselves that they are not the persons, promising themselves that they shall escape. If we knew that there as one person, and but one, in the whole congregation, that was to be the subject of this misery, what an awful thing would it be to think of! If we knew who it was, what an awful sight would it be to see such a person! How might all the rest of the congregation lift up a lamentable and bitter cry over him! But, alas! instead of one, how many is it likely will remember this discourse in hell? And it would be a wonder, if some that are now present should not be in hell in a very short time, even before this year is out. And it would be no wonder if some persons, that now sit here, in some seats of this meeting-house, in health, quiet and secure, should be there before to-morrow morning. Those of you that finally continue in a natural condition, that shall keep out of hell longest will be there in a little time! your damnation does not slumber; it will come swiftly, and, in all probability, very suddenly upon many of you. You have reason to wonder that you are not already in hell. It is doubtless the case of some whom you have seen and known, that never deserved hell more than you, and that heretofore appeared as likely to have been now alive as you. Their case is past all hope; they are crying in extreme misery and perfect despair; but here you are in the land of the living and in the house of God, and have an opportunity to obtain salvation. What would not those poor damned hopeless souls give for one day's opportunity such as you now enjoy!

And now you have an extraordinary opportunity, a day wherein Christ has thrown the door of mercy wide open, and stands in calling and crying with a loud voice to poor sinners; a day wherein many are flocking to him, and pressing into the kingdom of God. Many are daily coming from the east, west, north and south; many that were very lately in the same miserable condition that you are in, are now in a happy state, with their hearts filled with love to him who has loved them, and washed them from their sins in his own blood,

35

and rejoicing in hope of the glory of God. How awful is it to be left behind at such a day! To see so many others feasting, while you are pining and perishing! To see so many rejoicing and singing for joy of heart, while you have cause to mourn for sorrow of heart, and howl for vexation of spirit! How can you rest one moment in such a condition? Are not your souls as precious as the souls of the people at Suffield,* where they are flocking from day to day to Christ?

Are there not many here who have lived long in the world, and are not to this day born again? and so are aliens from the commonwealth of Israel, and have done nothing ever since they have lived, but treasure up wrath against the day of wrath? Oh, sirs, your case, in an especial manner, is extremely dangerous. Your guilt and hardness of heart is extremely great. Do you not see how generally persons of your years are passed over and left, in the present remarkable and wonderful dispensation of God's mercy? You had need to consider yourselves, and awake thoroughly out of sleep. You cannot bear the fierceness and wrath of the infinite God.—And you, young men, and young women, will you neglect this precious season which you now enjoy, when so many others of your age are renouncing all youthful vanities, and flocking to Christ? You especially have now an extraordinary opportunity; but if you neglect it, it will soon be with you as with those persons who spent all the precious days of youth in sin, and are now come to such a dreadful pass in blindness and hardness.—And you, children, who are unconverted, do not you know that you are going down to hell, to bear the dreadful wrath of that God, who is now angry with you every day and every night? Will you be content to be the children of the devil, when so many other children in the land are converted, and are become the holy and happy children of the King of kings?

And let every one that is yet of Christ, and hanging over the pit of hell, whether they be old men and women, or middle aged, or young people, or little children, now hearken to the loud calls of God's word and providence. This acceptable year of the Lord, a day of such great favours to some, will doubtless be a day of as remarkable vengeance to others. Men's hearts harden, and their guilt increases apace at such a day as this, if they neglect their souls; and never was there so great danger of such persons being given up to hardness of heart and blindness of mind. God seems now to be hastily gathering in his elect in all parts of the land; and probably the greater part of adult persons that ever shall be saved, will be brought in now in a little time, and that it will be as it was on the great out-pouring of the Spirit upon the Jews in the apostles' days; the election will obtain, and the rest will be blinded. If this should be the case with you, you will eternally curse this day, and will curse the day that ever you was born, to see such a season of the pouring out of God's Spirit, and will wish that you had died and gone to hell before you had seen it. Now undoubtedly it is, as it was in the days of John the Baptist, the axe is in an

---

*A town in the neighbourhood. [Edwards's note.]

extraordinary manner laid at the root of the trees, that every tree which brings not forth good fruit, may be hewn down and cast into the fire.

Therefore, let every one that is out of Christ, now awake and fly from the wrath to come. The wrath of Almighty God is now undoubtedly hanging over a great part of this congregation: Let every one fly out of Sodom: "Haste and escape for your lives, look not behind you, escape to the mountain, lest you be consumed." ☑

Reflections and Inquiries

1. What, according to Edwards, is keeping God from allowing sinners to descend into hell?

2. What recourse do sinners have to prevent their own eternal destruction?

3. Why does Edwards begin his sermon with a reference to Deuteronomy 32:35?

4. Why do you suppose Edwards gives such dramatic emphasis to God's anger?

Reading to Write

Do a stylistic analysis of this sermon. How does Edwards's use of certain kinds of sentence structure, metaphor, analogy, dramatization, word choice, repetition, and so on contribute to the emotional impact of his premise?

Keynote Address at the First Woman's Rights Convention   Elizabeth Cady Stanton

Barred from a world antislavery convention in London because they were women, Elizabeth Cady Stanton (1815–1902), an abolitionist and cofounder (with Susan B. Anthony) of the National Woman Suffrage Association (1869), teamed up with Lucretia Coffin Mott, founder of the Female Anti-Slavery Society in Philadelphia (1833), to organize the first Woman's Rights Convention in the United States in 1848. The following is an abridgment of Stanton's keynote address.

Source: From Stanton, Elizabeth Cady. "Keynote Address at the First Woman's Rights Convention, July 19, 1848." *A Treasury of the World's Greatest Speeches.* Ed. Houston Peterson. New York: Simon, 1965. 389–92.

Elizabeth Cady Stanton, left (1815– 1902), and Susan B. Anthony (1820– 1906) were two early champions of woman's rights.

"Man cannot fulfill his destiny alone, he cannot redeem his race unaided."

We have met here today to discuss our rights and wrongs, civil and political, and not, as some have supposed, to go into the detail of social life alone. We do not propose to petition the legislature to make our husbands just, generous, and courteous, to seat every man at the head of a cradle, and to clothe every woman in male attire. None of these points, however important they may be considered by leading men, will be touched in this convention. As to their costume, the gentlemen need feel no fear of our imitating that, for we think it in violation of every principle of taste, beauty, and dignity; notwithstanding all the contempt cast upon our loose, flowing garments, we still admire the graceful folds, and consider our costume far more artistic than theirs.

Many of the nobler sex seem to agree with us in this opinion, for the bishops, priests, judges, barristers, and lord mayors of the first nation on the globe, and the Pope of Rome, with his cardinals, too, all wear the loose flowing robes, thus tacitly acknowledging that the male attire is neither dignified nor imposing. No, we shall not molest you in your philosophical experiments with stocks, pants, high-heeled boots, and Russian belts. Yours be the glory to discover, by personal experience, how long the kneepan can resist the terrible strapping down which you impose, in how short time the well-developed muscles of the throat can be reduced to mere threads by the constant pressure of the stock, how high the heel of a boot must be to make a short man tall, and how tight the Russian belt may be drawn and yet have wind enough left to sustain life.

But we are assembled to protest against a form of government existing without the consent of the governed—to declare our right to be free as man is free, to be represented in the government which we are taxed to support, to have such disgraceful laws as give man the power to chastise and imprison his wife, to take the wages which she earns, the property which she inherits, and, in case of separation, the children of her love; laws which make her the mere dependent on his bounty. It is to protest against such unjust laws as these that we are assembled today, and to have them, if possible, forever erased from our statute books, deeming them a shame and a disgrace to a Christian republic in the nineteenth century. We have met

> To uplift woman's fallen divinity
> Upon an even pedestal with man's.

And, strange as it may seem to many, we now demand our right to vote according to the declaration of the government under which we live. This right no one pretends to deny. We need not prove ourselves equal to Daniel Webster to enjoy this privilege, for the ignorant Irishman in the ditch has all the civil rights he has. We need not prove our muscular power equal to this same Irishman to enjoy this privilege, for the most tiny, weak, ill-shaped stripling of twenty-one has all the civil rights of the Irishman. We have no objection to discuss the question of equality, for we feel that the weight of argument lies wholly with us, but we wish the question of equality kept distinct from the question of rights, for the proof of the one does not determine the truth of the other. All white men in this country have the same rights, however they may differ in mind, body, or estate.

The right is ours. The question now is: how shall we get possession of what rightfully belongs to us? We should not feel so sorely grieved if no man who had not attained the full stature of a Webster, Clay, Van Buren, or Gerrit Smith could claim the right of the elective franchise. But to have drunkards, idiots, horse-racing, rum-selling rowdies, ignorant foreigners, and silly boys fully recognized, while we ourselves are thrust out from all the rights that belong to citizens, it is too grossly insulting to the dignity of woman to be longer quietly submitted to. The right is ours. Have it, we must. Use it, we will. The pens, the tongues, the fortunes, the indomitable wills of many women are already pledged to secure this right. The great truth that no just government can be formed without the consent of the governed we shall echo and re-echo in the ears of the unjust judge, until by continual coming we shall weary him. . . .

There seems now to be a kind of moral stagnation in our midst. Philanthropists have done their utmost to rouse the nation to a sense of its sins. War, slavery, drunkenness, licentiousness, gluttony, have been dragged naked before the people, and all their abominations and deformities fully brought to light, yet with idiotic laugh we hug those monsters to our breasts and rush on to destruction. Our churches are multiplying on all sides, our missionary societies, Sunday schools, and prayer meetings and innumerable charitable and reform organizations are all in operation, but still the tide of vice is swelling, and threatens the destruction of everything, and the battlements of righteousness are weak against the raging elements of sin and death. Verily, the world waits the coming of some new element, some purifying power, some spirit of mercy and love. The voice of woman has been silenced in the state, the church, and the home, but man cannot fulfill his destiny alone, he cannot redeem his race unaided. There are deep and tender chords of sympathy and love in the hearts of the downfallen and oppressed that woman can touch more skillfully than man.

The world has never yet seen a truly great and virtuous nation, because in the degradation of woman the very fountains of life are poisoned at their source. It is vain to look for silver and gold from mines of copper and lead. It is the wise mother that has the wise son. So long as your women are slaves you may throw your colleges and churches to the winds. You can't have scholars and saints so long as your mothers are ground to powder between the upper and nether millstone of tyranny and lust. How seldom, now, is a father's pride gratified, his fond hopes realized, in the budding genius of his son! The wife is degraded, made the mere creature of caprice, and the foolish son is heaviness to his heart. Truly are the sins of the fathers visited upon the children to the third and fourth generation. God, in His wisdom, has so linked the whole human family together that any violence done at one end of the chain is felt throughout its length, and there, too, is the law of restoration, as in woman all have fallen, so in her elevation shall the race be recreated.

"Voices" were the visitors and advisers of Joan of Arc. Do not "voices" come to us daily from the haunts of poverty, sorrow, degradation, and despair, already too long unheeded. Now is the time for the women of this country, if they would save our free institutions, to defend the right, to buckle on the armor that can best resist the keenest weapons of the enemy—contempt and ridicule. The same religious enthusiasm that nerved Joan of Arc to her work nerves us to ours. In every generation God calls some men and women for the utterance of truth, a heroic action, and our work today is the fulfilling of what

5

has long since been foretold by the Prophet—Joel 2:28: "And it shall come to pass afterward, that I will pour out my spirit upon all flesh; and your sons and your daughters shall prophesy." We do not expect our path will be strewn with the flowers of popular applause, but over the thorns of bigotry and prejudice will be our way, and on our banners will beat the dark storm clouds of opposition from those who have entrenched themselves behind the stormy bulwarks of custom and authority, and who have fortified their position by every means, holy and unholy. But we will steadfastly abide the result. Unmoved we will bear it aloft. Undauntedly we will unfurl it to the gale, for we know that the storm cannot rend from it a shred, that the electric flash will but more clearly show to us the glorious words inscribed upon it, "Equality of Rights.". . . ◪

Reflections and Inquiries

1. Why does Stanton open with a reference to male and female modes of dress? What point does she make with her witty reference to the apparel of certain members of the clergy?

2. What laws does Stanton consider to be "a disgrace to a Christian republic"? Why?

3. What is the purpose of Stanton's allusion to Joan of Arc?

4. What consequences of female degradation does Stanton articulate?

Reading to Write

Examine Stanton's argument from an organizational perspective. Outline the sequence of points she makes, and then suggest a rationale for this sequence in relation to her thesis. How well does her opening prepare for what follows?

I Hear the Mournful Wail of Millions | Frederick Douglass

On July 4, 1852, Frederick Douglass (1817–1895), a former slave (he escaped to New England in his twenties) and member of the Massachusetts Antislavery Society who one day would discuss slavery with President Lincoln, was invited to commemorate Independence Day in Rochester, New York, with the following speech.

Source: Douglass, Frederick. "I Hear the Mournful Wail of Millions." *A Treasury of the World's Greatest Speeches.* Ed. Houston Peterson. New York: Simon, 1965. 478–82.

Fellow citizens, pardon me, allow me to ask, why am I called upon to speak here today? What have I, or those I represent, to do with your national independence? Are the great principles of political freedom and of natural justice, embodied in that Declaration of Independence, extended to us? and am I, therefore, called upon to bring our humble offering to the national altar, and to confess the benefits and express devout gratitude for the blessings resulting from your independence to us?

Would to God, both for your sakes and ours, that an affirmative answer could be truthfully returned to these questions! Then would my task be light, and my burden easy and delightful. For who is there so cold that a nation's sympathy could not warm him? Who so obdurate and dead to the claims of gratitude that would not thankfully acknowledge such priceless benefits? Who so stolid and selfish that would not give his voice to swell the hallelujahs of a nation's jubilee, when the chains of servitude had been torn from his limbs? I am not that man. In a case like that the dumb might eloquently speak and the "lame man leap as an hart."

But such is not the state of the case. I say it with a sad sense of the disparity between us. I am not included within the pale of this glorious anniversary! Your high independence only reveals the immeasurable distance between us. The blessings in which you, this day, rejoice are not enjoyed in common. The rich inheritance of justice, liberty, prosperity, and independence bequeathed by your fathers is shared by you, not by me. The sunlight that brought light and healing to you has brought stripes and death to me. This Fourth of July is yours, not mine. You may rejoice, I must mourn. To drag a man in fetters into the grand illuminated temple of liberty, and call upon him to join you in joyous anthems, were inhuman mockery and sacrilegious irony. Do you mean, citizens, to mock me by asking me to speak today? If so, there is a parallel to your conduct. And let me warn you that it is dangerous to copy the example of a nation whose crimes, towering up to heaven, were thrown down by the breath of the Almighty, burying that nation in irrevocable ruin! I can today take up the plaintive lament of a peeled and woe-smitten people!

"By the rivers of Babylon, there we sat down. Yea! we wept when we remembered Zion. We hanged our harps upon the willows in the midst thereof. For there, they that carried us away captive, required of us a song; and they who wasted us required of us mirth, saying, Sing us one of the songs of Zion. How can we sing the Lord's song in a strange land? If I forget thee, O Jerusalem, let my right hand forget her cunning. If I do not remember thee, let my tongue cleave to the roof of my mouth."

Fellow citizens, above your national, tumultuous joy, I hear the mournful wail of millions! whose chains, heavy and grievous yesterday, are, today, rendered more intolerable by the jubilee shouts that reach them. If I do forget, if I do not faithfully remember those bleeding children of sorrow this day, "may my right hand forget her cunning, and may my tongue cleave to the roof of my

5

mouth"! To forget them, to pass lightly over their wrongs, and to chime in with the popular theme would be treason most scandalous and shocking, and would make me a reproach before God and the world. My subject, then, fellow citizens, is *American slavery*. I shall see this day and its popular characteristics from the slave's point of view. Standing there identified with the American bondman, making his wrongs mine. I do not hesitate to declare with all my soul that the character and conduct of this nation never looked blacker to me than on this Fourth of July! Whether we turn to the declarations of the past or to the professions of the present, the conduct of the nation seems equally hideous and revolting. America is false to the past, false to the present, and solemnly binds herself to be false to the future. Standing with God and the crushed and bleeding slave on this occasion, I will, in the name of humanity which is outraged, in the name of liberty which is fettered, in the name of the Constitution and the Bible which are disregarded and trampled upon, dare to call in question and to denounce, with all the emphasis I can command, everything that serves to perpetuate slavery—the great sin and shame of America! "I will not equivocate; I will not excuse"; I will use the severest language I can command; and yet not one word shall escape me that any man, whose judgment is not blinded by prejudice, or who is not at heart a slaveholder, shall not confess to be right and just.

But I fancy I hear someone of my audience say, "It is just in this circumstance that you and your brother abolitionists fail to make a favorable impression on the public mind. Would you argue more and denounce less, would you persuade more and rebuke less, your cause would be much more likely to succeed." But, I submit, where all is plain, there is nothing to be argued. What point in the antislavery creed would you have me argue? On what branch of the subject do the people of this country need light? Must I undertake to prove that the slave is a man? That point is conceded already. Nobody doubts it. The slaveholders themselves acknowledge it in the enactment of laws for their government. They acknowledge it when they punish disobedience on the part of the slave. There are seventy-two crimes in the state of Virginia which, if committed by a black man (no matter how ignorant he be), subject him to the punishment of death; while only two of the same crimes will subject a white man to the like punishment. What is this but the acknowledgment that the slave is a moral, intellectual, and responsible being? The manhood of the slave is conceded. It is admitted in the fact that Southern statute books are covered with enactments forbidding, under severe fines and penalties, the teaching of the slave to read or to write. When you can point to any such laws in reference to the beasts of the field, then I may consent to argue the manhood of the slave. When the dogs in your streets, when the fowls of the air, when the cattle on your hills, when the fish of the sea and the reptiles that crawl shall be unable to distinguish the slave from the brute, then will I argue with you that the slave is a man!

For the present, it is enough to affirm the equal manhood of the Negro

Frederick Douglass (1817–1895) was a self-educated former slave who discussed the evils of slavery with Abraham Lincoln and served as a U.S. minister to Haiti.

race. Is it not astonishing that, while we are plowing, planting, and reaping, using all kinds of mechanical tools, erecting houses, constructing bridges, building ships, working in metals of brass, iron, copper, silver, and gold; that, while we are reading, writing, and ciphering, acting as clerks, merchants, and secretaries, having among us lawyers, doctors, ministers, poets, authors, editors, orators, and teachers; that, while we are engaged in all manner of enterprises common to other men, digging gold in California, capturing the whale in the Pacific, feeding sheep and cattle on the hillside, living, moving, acting, thinking, planning, living in families as husbands, wives, and children, and, above all, confessing and worshiping the Christian's God, and looking hopefully for life and immortality beyond the grave, we are called upon to prove that we are men!

Would you have me argue that man is entitled to liberty? that he is the rightful owner of his own body? You have already declared it. Must I argue the wrongfulness of slavery? Is that a question for republicans? Is it to be settled by the rules of logic and argumentation, as a matter beset with great difficulty, involving a doubtful application of the principle of justice, hard to be understood? How should I look today, in the presence of Americans, dividing and subdividing a discourse, to show that men have a natural right to freedom? speaking of it relatively and positively, negatively and affirmatively? To do so would be to make myself ridiculous and to offer an insult to your understanding. There is not a man beneath the canopy of heaven that does not know that slavery is wrong for him.

What, am I to argue that it is wrong to make men brutes, to rob them of their liberty, to work them without wages, to keep them ignorant of their relations to their fellow men, to beat them with sticks, to flay their flesh with the lash, to load their limbs with irons, to hunt them with dogs, to sell them at auction, to sunder their families, to knock out their teeth, to burn their flesh, to starve them into obedience and submission to their masters? Must I argue that a system thus marked with blood, and stained with pollution, is wrong? No! I will not. I have better employment for my time and strength than such arguments would imply.

What, then, remains to be argued? Is it that slavery is not divine; that God did not establish it; that our doctors of divinity are mistaken? There is blasphemy in the thought. That which is inhuman cannot be divine! Who can reason on such a proposition? They that can may; I cannot. The time for such argument is past.   10

At a time like this, scorching iron, not convincing argument, is needed. O! had I the ability, and could I reach the nation's ear, I would today pour out a fiery stream of biting ridicule, blasting reproach, withering sarcasm, and stern rebuke. For it is not light that is needed, but fire; it is not the gentle shower, but thunder. We need the storm, the whirlwind, and the earthquake. The feeling of the nation must be quickened; the conscience of the nation must be roused; the propriety of the nation must be startled; the hypocrisy of the nation must be exposed; and its crimes against God and man must be proclaimed and denounced.

What, to the American slave, is your Fourth of July? I answer: a day that reveals to him, more than all other days in the year, the gross injustice and cruelty to which he is the constant victim. To him, your celebration is a sham; your boasted liberty, an unholy license; your national greatness, swelling vanity; your sounds of rejoicing are empty and heartless; your denunciation of tyrants, brass-fronted impudence; your shouts of liberty and equality, hollow mockery; your prayers and hymns, your sermons and thanksgivings, with all your religious parade and solemnity, are, to Him, mere bombast, fraud, deception, impiety, and hypocrisy—a thin veil to cover up crimes which would disgrace a nation of savages. There is not a nation of savages. There is not a nation on the earth guilty of practices more shocking and bloody than are the people of the United States at this very hour.

Go where you may, search where you will, roam through all the monarchies and despotisms of the Old World, travel through South America, search out every abuse, and when you have found the last, lay your facts by the side of the everyday practices of this nation, and you will say with me that, for revolting barbarity and shameless hypocrisy, America reigns without a rival. ◪

Reflections and Inquiries

1. How does Douglass use the special occasion of Independence Day as a foundation for his address? How effectively does it come across?

2. What is significant about the first two words of his speech from an historical/political perspective? From a rhetorical one?

3. At one point, Douglass asserts, regarding the abolition of slavery, that "there is nothing to be argued." Why does he say this?

4. How does Douglass characterize the Fourth of July from the perspective of a slave?

Reading to Write

Write a comparative analysis of Douglass's speech with Martin Luther King's "Letter from Birmingham Jail," on pages 76–89. In what ways are they similar? Different? Include a discussion of their respective rhetorical strategies.

The Obligation to Endure | Rachel Carson

In 1962, marine biologist Rachel Carson (1907–1964), known for her beautifully written sea trilogy (*Under the Sea Wind,* 1941; *The Sea Around Us,* 1951; *The Edge of the Sea,* 1954), published her most famous work, *Silent Spring.* Her book almost single-handedly launched the modern environmental movement in the United States. It describes the devastating effects of pesticides on the environment. The title makes an ominous reference to the absence of birdsong as the result of massive bird deaths caused by DDT spraying. The book persuaded President John F. Kennedy to set up an office of environmental affairs, which eventually became the Environmental Protection Agency. In the following excerpt from *Silent Spring,* Carson introduces her case against the use of pesticides.

T he history of life on earth has been a history of interaction between living things and their surroundings. To a large extent, the physical form and the habits of the earth's vegetation and its animal life have been molded by the environment. Considering the whole span of earthly time, the opposite effect, in which life actually modifies its surroundings, has been relatively slight. Only within the moment of time represented by the present century has one species—man—acquired significant power to alter the nature of his world.

During the past quarter century this power has not only increased to one of disturbing magnitude but it has changed in character. The most alarming of all man's assaults upon the environment is the contamination of air, earth, rivers, and sea with dangerous and even lethal materials. This pollution is for the most part irrecoverable; the chain of evil it initiates not only in the world that must support life but in living tissues is for the most part irreversible. In this now universal contamination of the environment, chemicals are the sinister and little recognized partners of radiation in changing the very nature of the world—the very nature of this life. Strontium 90, released through nuclear explosions into the air, comes to earth in rain or drifts down as fallout, lodges in soil, enters into the grass or corn or wheat grown there, and in time takes up its abode in the bones of a human being, there to remain until his death. Similarly, chemicals sprayed on croplands or forests or gardens lie long in soil, entering into living organisms, passing from one to another in a chain of poisoning and death. Or they pass mysteriously by underground streams until they emerge and, through the alchemy of air and sunlight, combine into new forms that kill vegetation, sicken cattle, and work unknown harm on those who drink from once-pure wells. As Albert Schweitzer has said, "Man can hardly even recognize the devils of his own creation."

It took hundreds of millions of years to produce the life that now inhabits the earth—eons of time in which that developing and evolving the diversifying life reached a state of adjustment and balance with its surroundings. The environment, rigorously shaping and directing the life it supported, contained elements that were hostile as well as supporting. Certain rocks gave out dangerous radiation: even within the light of the sun, from which all life draws its energy, there were short-wave radiations with power to injure. Given time—time not in years but in millennia—life adjusts, and a balance has been reached. For time is the essential ingredient; but in the modern world there is no time.

The rapidity of change and the speed with which new situations are created follow the impetuous and heedless pace of man rather than the deliberate pace of nature. Radiation is no longer merely the background radiation of rocks, the bombardment of cosmic rays, the ultraviolet of the sun that have existed before there was any life on earth; radiation is now the unnatural creation of man's tampering with the atom. The chemicals to which life is asked to make its adjustment are no longer merely the calcium and silica and copper and all the rest of the minerals washed out of the rocks and carried in rivers to the sea; they are the synthetic creations of man's inventive mind, brewed in his laboratories, and having no counterparts in nature.

To adjust to these chemicals would require time on the scale that is nature's; it would require not merely the years of a man's life but the life of generations. And even this, were it by some miracle possible, would be futile, for

5

the new chemicals come from our laboratories in an endless stream; almost five hundred annually find their way into actual use in the United States alone. The figure is staggering and its implications are not easily grasped—500 new chemicals to which the bodies of men and animals are required somehow to adapt each year, chemicals totally outside the limits of biologic experience.

Among them are many that are used in man's war against nature. Since the mid-1940's over 200 basic chemicals have been created for use in killing insects, weeds, rodents, and other organisms described in the modern vernacular as "pests"; and they are sold under several thousand different brand names.

These sprays, dusts, and aerosols are now applied almost universally to farms, gardens, forests, and homes—nonselective chemicals that have the power to kill every insect, the "good" and the "bad," to still the song of birds and the leaping of fish in the streams, to coat the leaves with a deadly film, and to linger on in soil—all this though the intended target may be only a few weeds or insects. Can anyone believe it is possible to lay down such a barrage of poisons on the surface of the earth without making it unfit for all life? They should not be called "insecticides," but "biocides."

The whole process of spraying seems caught up in an endless spiral. Since DDT was released for civilian use, a process of escalation has been going on in which ever more toxic materials must be found. This has happened because insects, in a triumphant vindication of Darwin's principle of the survival of the fittest, have evolved super races immune to the particular insecticide used, hence a deadlier one has always to be developed—and then a deadlier one than that. It has happened also because, for reasons to be described later, destructive insects often undergo a "flareback," or resurgence, after spraying, in numbers greater than before. Thus the chemical war is never won, and all life is caught in its violent crossfire.

Along with the possibility of the extinction of mankind by nuclear war, the central problem of our age has therefore become the contamination of man's total environment with such substances of incredible potential for harm—substances that accumulate in the tissues of plants and animals and even penetrate the germ cells to shatter or alter the very material of heredity upon which the shape of the future depends.

Some would-be architects of our future look toward a time when it will be 10 possible to alter the human germ plasm by design. But we may easily be doing so now by inadvertence, for many chemicals, like radiation, bring about gene mutations. It is ironic to think that man might determine his own future by something so seemingly trivial as the choice of an insect spray.

All this has been risked—for what? Future historians may well be amazed by our distorted sense of proportion. How could intelligent beings seek to control a few unwanted species by a method that contaminated the entire environment and brought the threat of disease and death even to their own kind? Yet this is precisely what we have done. We have done it, moreover, for reasons that collapse the moment we examine them. We are told that the enormous and expanding use of pesticides is necessary to maintain farm production. Yet is our real problem not one of *overproduction?* Our farms, despite measures to remove acreages from production and to pay farmers *not* to produce, have yielded such a staggering excess of crops that the American taxpayer in 1962 is paying out more than one billion dollars a year as the total carrying cost of the surplus-food storage program. And is the situation helped when one branch of the Agriculture Department tries to reduce production while another states, as it did in 1958, "It is believed generally that reduction of crop acreages under provisions of the Soil Bank will stimulate interest in use of chemicals to obtain maximum production on the land retained in crops."

All this is not to say there is no insect problem and no need of control. I am saying, rather, that control must be geared to realities, not to mythical situations, and that the methods employed must be such that they do not destroy us along with the insects. ◪

Reflections and Inquiries

1. Why does Carson begin by emphasizing the interaction of living things on earth?

2. Why is much of the damage done to the environment by poisonous materials irreversible, according to Carson?

3. Despite massive use of deadly insecticides, harmful insects still prevail. Why?

4. Why is crop overproduction an environmental problem?

Reading to Write

Critique Carson's persuasive strategy. Does she make her case against the use of pesticides a convincing one, based on this excerpt? Why or why not? Read *Silent Spring* in its entirety to see if the additional information you were looking for is found there.

Roe v. Wade

*Original Transcript of the Argument
Before the United States
Supreme Court, 1972
410 U.S. 113 (1973)*

In 1970 a pregnant, unmarried woman living in Dallas, Texas, tried to obtain an abortion. Her request was denied under then existing Texas law. Adopting the pseudonym Jane Roe, she challenged that law on grounds that it violated her right to privacy. The case was successfully appealed before the U.S. Supreme Court in 1972–1973. As a result, the Supreme Court invalidated all state laws denying a woman the right to an abortion. However, this new ruling applied only to the first trimester of a woman's pregnancy. In the following excerpt from the latter half to the trial, Sarah Weddington (the attorney for Jane Roe), another couple, and a physician who had been under arrest for performing an abortion, argues with the Associate Justices whether a fetus is actually a person, whether abortion statutes are constitutional, and whether it is actually possible to determine with any degree of certainty where life actually begins.

Participants: Mrs. Sarah R. Weddington, Attorney for the Appellants [Jane Roe et al.]; Byron R. White, Associate Justice of the Supreme Court; Potter Stewart, Associate Justice of the Supreme Court; Harry A. Blackmun, Associate Justice of the Supreme Court.

Mrs. Sarah R. Weddington: Mr. Chief Justice [Warren Burger], and may it please the Court:

We are once again before this Court to ask relief against the continued enforcement of the Texas abortion statute. And I ask that you affirm the ruling of the three-judge [court] below which held our statute unconstitutional for two reasons: The first that it was vague, and the second that it interfered with the Ninth Amendment rights of a woman to determine whether or not she would continue to terminate a pregnancy. . . .

The first plaintiff was Jane Roe, an unmarried, pregnant girl, who had sought an abortion in the State of Texas and was denied it because of the Texas abortion statute, which provides an abortion is lawful only for the purpose of saving the life of the woman. . . .

In the original action she was joined by a married couple, John and Mary Doe. Mrs. Doe had a medical condition, her doctor had recommended, first, that she not get pregnant, and, second, that she not take the pill. . . .

5

Source: From *Roe* v. *Wade*. 410. U.S. 113. U.S. Sup.Ct. 1973 <http://members.aol.com/abtrbng2/oa/roeoa2.htm>.

As to the women, this is their only forum. They are in a very unique situation, for several reasons: First, because of the very nature of the interest involved. Their primary interest being the interest associated with the question of whether or not they will be forced by the State to continue an unwanted pregnancy. . . .

[T]here is a great body of cases decided in the past by this Court in the areas of marriage, sex, contraception, procreation, child-bearing, and education of children. Which says that there are certain things that are so much a part of the individual concern that they should be left to the determination of the individual. . . .

Again, this is a very special type case for the women, because of the very nature of the injury involved. It is an irreparable injury. Once pregnancy has started, certainly this is not the kind of injury that can be later adjudicated, it is not the kind of injury that can later be compensated by some sort of monetary reward.

These women who have now gone through pregnancy and the women who continue to be forced to go through pregnancy have certainly gone through something that is irreparable, that can never be changed for them. It is certainly great and it is certainly immediate.

Justice Byron R. White: Regardless of the purpose for which the [Texas]   10
statute [forbidding physicians from performing abortions] was originally enacted, or the purpose which keeps it on the books in Texas today, you would agree, I suppose, that one of the important factors that has to be considered in this case is what rights, if any, does the unborn fetus have?

Mrs. Weddington: That's correct. There have been two cases decided . . . that expressly hold that a fetus has no constitutional right. . . .

Mr. Justice White: Well, is it critical to your case that the fetus not be a person under the due process clause?

Mrs. Weddington: It seems to me that it is critical, first, that we prove this is a fundamental interest on behalf of the women, that it is a constitutional right. And, second—

Mr. Justice White: Well, yes, but about the fetus? . . . I'm just asking you, under the federal Constitution. Is the fetus a person, for the [purpose of the] protection of [the] due process [clause]?

Mrs. Weddington: All of the cases, the prior history of this statute, the com-   15
mon law history would indicate that it is not. The State has shown no—

Mr. Justice White: Well, what about—would you lose your case if the fetus was a person?

Mrs. Weddington: Then you would have a balancing of interest. . . . It seems to me that you do not balance constitutional rights of one person against mere statutory rights of another. . . . If the State could show that the fetus was a person under the Fourteenth Amendment, or under some other Amendment, or part of the Constitution, then you would have the situation of trying—you would have a State compelling interest which, in some cases, can outweigh a fundamental right. This is not the case in this particular situation. . . .

I think, had there been established that the fetus was a person under the Fourteenth Amendment or under constitutional protection, then there might be a differentiation. In this case there has never been established that the fetus is a person or that it's entitled to the Fourteenth Amendment rights of the protection of the Constitution. . . .

But here we have a person, the woman, entitled to fundamental constitutional rights as opposed to the fetus prior to birth, where there is no establishment of any kind of federal constitutional rights.

Mr. Justice Harry A. Blackmun: Well, do I get from this, then, that your case   20
depends primarily on the proposition that the fetus has no constitutional rights?

Mrs. Weddington: It depends on saying that the woman has a fundamental constitutional right and that the State has not proved any compelling interest for regulation in this area.

Even if the Court at some point determined the fetus to be entitled to constitutional protection, you would still get back into the weighing of one life against another.

Mr. Justice White: That's what's involved in this case? Weighing one life against another?

Mrs. Weddington: No, Your Honor. I say that would be what would be involved if the facts were different, and the State could prove that there was a person, for the constitutional right.

Mr. Justice Potter Stewart: Well, if—if—it were established that an unborn   25
fetus is a person, with the protection of the Fourteenth Amendment, you would have an almost impossible case here, would you not?

Mrs. Weddington: I would have a very difficult case. . . .

I think Mr. [Robert C.] Flowers [the attorney for the State of Texas, arguing that the statute barring doctors from performing abortions should be upheld] well made the point when he said that no one can say, Here is the dividing line; here is where life begins—life is here and life is not over here.

In a situation where no one can prove where life begins, where no one can show that the Constitution was adopted, that it was meant to protect fetal life, in those situations where it is shown that that kind of decision is so fundamentally a part of individual life of the family, of such fundamental impact on the person. . . .

Here a woman, because of her pregnancy, is often not a productive member of society. She cannot work, she cannot hold a job, she's not eligible for welfare, she cannot get unemployment compensation. And furthermore, in fact, the pregnancy may produce a child who will become a ward of the State. . . .

In this case, this Court is faced with a situation where there have   30
been fourteen three-judge courts that have ruled on the constitutionality of abortion statutes. Nine courts have favored the woman, five have
gone against her. Twenty-five judges have favored the woman, seventeen have gone against her. Nine circuit judges have favored the
woman, five have gone against her. Sixteen district court judges have
favored the woman, ten have gone against her.

No one is more keenly aware of the gravity of the issues or the
moral implications of this case, [but] it is a case that must be decided on
the Constitution. We do not disagree that there is a progression of fetal
development. It is the conclusion to be drawn from that upon which
we disagree.

We are not here to advocate abortion. We do not ask this Court to
rule that abortion is good or desirable in any particular situation.

We are here to advocate that the decision as to whether or not a particular woman will continue to carry or will terminate a pregnancy is a
decision that should be made by that individual, that in fact she has a
constitutional right to make that decision for herself, and that the State
has shown no interest in interfering with that decision. ◼

Reflections and Inquiries

1. How convincingly, in your opinion, does Weddington argue her view that it
   is not possible to determine where life begins?

2. Weddington argues that it is the woman's right, not the state's, to determine
   whether she should carry or terminate a pregnancy. On what grounds does
   Weddington build this claim?

3. Should an unborn fetus have constitutional rights? What are the difficulties
   behind an attempt to answer this question? Evaluate Weddington's manner
   of answering it.

Reading to Write

1. Write a defense of or counterargument to Weddington's concluding
   remarks.

2. Write a point-by-point evaluation of Weddington's assertions. Which points
   seem most or least convincing, and why?

The Character
of Hamlet's Mother | Carolyn G. Heilbrun

In the following gem of literary criticism, Carolyn G. Heilbrun cleverly demonstrates that Queen Gertrude, Hamlet's mother, is far from being the dim-witted, passive, weak, and sentimental woman that even the most distinguished (and male) Shakespearean scholars of the past have interpreted her as being—on the contrary, she is a shrewd and strong-willed (if lustful) woman. The essay is a fine example of the way a hitherto unacknowledged critical perspective (in this case a feminist one) can shed new light on even the most famous, most written-about play of all time. Heilbrun (b. 1926) is the Avalon Foundation Professor in the Humanities Emerita at Columbia University. She is the author of *Reinventing Womanhood* (1979), *Writing a Woman's Life* (1989), *The Education of a Woman: The Life of Gloria Steinem* (1995), and many other books, including the internationally known Kate Fansler mysteries (under her nom de plume, Amanda Cross).

If you have not read Shakespeare's *Hamlet* recently, it would be a good idea to do so first. Pay particular attention to the character of Gertrude and draw your own conclusions about her before evaluating the strengths or shortcomings of Heilbrun's argument.

The character of Hamlet's mother has not received the specific critical attention it deserves. Moreover, the traditional account of her personality as rendered by the critics will not stand up under close scrutiny of Shakespeare's play.

None of the critics of course has failed to see Gertrude as vital to the action of the play; not only is she the mother of the hero, the widow of the Ghost, and the wife of the current King of Denmark, but the fact of her hasty and, to the Elizabethans, incestuous marriage, the whole question of her "falling off," occupies a position of barely secondary importance in the mind of her son, and of the Ghost. Indeed, Freud and Jones see her, the object of Hamlet's Oedipus complex, as central to the motivation of the play.[1] But the critics, with no exception that I have been able to find, have accepted Hamlet's word "frailty" as applying to her whole personality, and have seen in her not one weakness, or passion in the Elizabethan sense, but a character of which weakness and lack of depth and vigorous intelligence are the entire explanation. Of her can it truly be said that carrying the "stamp of one defect," she did "in the general censure take corruption from that particular fault" (I.iv.35–36).

The critics are agreed that Gertrude was not a party to the late King's murder and indeed knew nothing of it, a point which, on the clear evidence of the play, is indisputable. They have also discussed whether or not Gertrude, guilty of more than an "o'er-hasty marriage," had committed adultery with Claudius before her husband's death. I will return to this point later on. Beyond discussing these two points, those critics who have dealt specifically with the Queen have traditionally seen her as well-meaning but shallow and feminine, in the pejorative sense of the word: incapable of any sustained rational process, superficial and flighty. It is this tradition which a closer reading of the play will show to be erroneous.

Professor Bradley describes the traditional Gertrude thus:

> The Queen was not a bad-hearted woman, not at all the woman to think little of murder. But she had a soft animal nature and was very dull and very shallow. She loved to be happy, like a sheep in the sun, and to do her justice, it pleased her to see others happy, like more sheep in the sun. . . . It was pleasant to sit upon her throne and see smiling faces around her, and foolish and unkind in Hamlet to persist in grieving for his father instead of marrying Ophelia and making everything comfortable. . . . The belief at the bottom of her heart was that the world is a place constructed simply that people may be happy in it in a good-humored sensual fashion.[2]

Later on, Bradley says of her that when affliction comes to her "the good in her nature struggles to the surface through the heavy mass of sloth."

Granville-Barker is not quite so extreme. Shakespeare, he says,

> gives us in Gertrude the woman who does not mature, who clings to her youth and all that belongs to it, whose charm will not change but at last fade and wither; a pretty creature, as we see her, desperately refusing to grow old. . . . She is drawn for us with unemphatic strokes, and she has but a passive part in the play's action. She moves throughout in Claudius' shadow; he holds her as he won her, by the witchcraft of his wit.[3]

Elsewhere Granville-Barker says, "Gertrude, who will certainly never see forty-five again, might better be 'old.' [That is, portrayed by an older, mature actress.] But that would make her relations with Claudius—and *their* likelihood is vital to the play—quite incredible" (p. 226). Granville-Barker is saying here that a woman about forty-five years of age cannot feel any sexual passion nor arouse it. This is one of the mistakes which lie at the heart of the misunderstanding about Gertrude.

Professor Dover Wilson sees Gertrude as more forceful than either of these two critics will admit, but even he finds the Ghost's unwillingness to shock her with knowledge of his murder to be one of the basic motivations of the play, and he says of her, "Gertrude is always hoping for the best."[4]

Now whether Claudius won Gertrude before or after her husband's death, it was certainly not, as Granville-Barker implies, with "the witchcraft of his wit" alone. Granville-Barker would have us believe that Claudius won her simply by the force of his persuasive tongue. "It is plain," he writes, that the Queen "does little except echo his [Claudius'] wishes; sometimes—as in the welcome to Rosencrantz and Guildenstern—she repeats his very words" (p. 227), though Wilson must admit later that Gertrude does not tell Claudius everything. Without dwelling here on the psychology of the Ghost, or the greater burden borne by the Elizabethan words "witchcraft" and "wit," we can plainly see, for the Ghost tells us, how Claudius won the Queen: the Ghost considers his brother to be garbage, and "lust," the Ghost says, "will sate itself in a celestial bed and prey on garbage" (I.v.54–55). "Lust"—in a woman of forty-five or more—is the key word here. Bradley, Granville-Barker, and to a lesser extent Professor Dover Wilson, misunderstand Gertrude largely because they are unable to see lust, the desire for sexual relations, as the passion, in the Elizabethan sense of the word, the flaw, the weakness which drives Gertrude to an incestuous marriage, appalls her son, and keeps him from the throne. Unable to explain her marriage to Claudius as the act of any but a weak-minded vacillating woman, they fail to see Gertrude for the strong-minded, intelligent, succinct, and, apart from this passion, sensible woman that she is.

To understand Gertrude properly, it is only necessary to examine the lines Shakespeare has chosen for her to say. She is, except for her description of Ophelia's death, concise and pithy in speech, with a talent for seeing the essence of every situation presented before her eyes. If she is not profound, she is certainly never silly. We first hear her asking Hamlet to stop wearing black, to stop walking about with his eyes downcast, and to realize that death is an inevitable part of life. She is, in short, asking him not to give way to the passion of grief, a passion of whose force and dangers the Elizabethans are aware, as Miss Campbell has shown.[5] Claudius echoes her with a well-reasoned argument against grief which was, in its philosophy if not in its language, a piece of commonplace Elizabethan lore. After Claudius' speech, Gertrude asks Hamlet to remain in Denmark, where he is rightly loved. Her speeches have been short, however warm and loving, and conciseness of statement is not the mark of a dull and shallow woman.

We next hear her, as Queen and gracious hostess, welcoming Rosencrantz and Guildenstern to the court, hoping, with the King, that they may cheer Hamlet and discover what is depressing him. Claudius then tells Gertrude, when they are alone, that Polonius believes he knows what is upsetting Hamlet. The Queen answers:

> I doubt it is no other than the main,
> His father's death and our o'er-hasty marriage. (II.ii.56–57)

This statement is concise, remarkably to the point, and not a little courageous. It is not the statement of a dull, slothful woman who can only echo her husband's words. Next, Polonius enters with his most unbrief apotheosis to brevity. The Queen interrupts him with five words: "More matter with less art" (II.ii.95). It would be difficult to find a phrase more applicable to Polonius. When this gentleman, in no way deterred from his loquacity, after purveying the startling news that he has a daughter, begins to read a letter, the Queen asks pointedly "Came this from Hamlet to her?" (II.ii.114).

We see Gertrude next in Act III, asking Rosencrantz and Guildenstern, with her usual directness, if Hamlet received them well, and if they were able to tempt him to any pastime. But before leaving the room, she stops for a word of kindness to Ophelia. It is a humane gesture, for she is unwilling to leave Ophelia, the unhappy tool of the King and Polonius, without some kindly and intelligent appreciation of her help:

> And for your part, Ophelia, I do wish
> That your good beauties be the happy cause
> Of Hamlet's wildness. So shall I hope your virtues
> Will bring him to his wonted way again,
> To both your honors. (III.i.38–42)

It is difficult to see in this speech, as Bradley apparently does, the gushing shallow wish of a sentimental woman that class distinctions shall not stand in the way of true love.

At the play, the Queen asks Hamlet to sit near her. She is clearly trying to make him feel he has a place in the court of Denmark. She does not speak again until Hamlet asks her how she likes the play. "The lady doth protest too much, methinks" (III.ii.240) is her immortal comment on the player queen. The scene gives her four more words: when Claudius leaps to his feet, she asks "How fares my Lord?" (III.ii.278).

I will for the moment pass over the scene in the Queen's closet, to follow her quickly through the remainder of the play. After the closet scene, the Queen comes to speak to Claudius. She tells him, as Hamlet has asked her to, that he, Hamlet, is mad, and has killed Polonius. She adds, however, that he now weeps for what he has done. She does not wish Claudius to know what she now knows, how wild and fearsome Hamlet has become. Later, she does not wish to see Ophelia, but hearing how distracted she is, consents. When Laertes bursts in ready to attack Claudius, she immediately steps between Claudius and Laertes to protect the King, and tells Laertes it is not Claudius who has killed his father. Laertes will of course soon learn this, but it is Gertrude who manages to tell him before he can do any meaningless damage. She leaves Laertes and the King together, and then returns to tell Laertes that his sister is drowned. She gives her news directly, realizing that suspense will increase the pain of it, but this is the one time in the play when her usual pointed conciseness would be the mark neither of intelligence nor kindness, and so, gently, and at some length, she tells Laertes of his sister's death, giving him time to recover from the shock of grief, and to absorb the meaning of her words. At Ophelia's funeral the Queen scatters flowers over the grave.

10

> Sweets to the sweet; farewell!
> I hop'd thou shouldst have been my Hamlet's wife.
> I thought thy bride-bed to have deck'd, sweet maid,
> And not t' have strew'd thy grave. (V.i.266–269)

She is the only one present decently mourning the death of someone young, and not heated in the fire of some personal passion.

At the match between Hamlet and Laertes, the Queen believes that Hamlet is out of training, but glad to see him at some sport, she gives him her handkerchief to wipe his brow, and drinks to his success. The drink is poisoned and she dies. But before she dies she does not waste time on vituperation; she warns Hamlet that the drink is poisoned to prevent his drinking it. They are her last words. Those critics who have thought her stupid admire her death; they call it uncharacteristic.

In Act III, when Hamlet goes to his mother in her closet his nerves are pitched at the very height of tension; he is on the edge of hysteria. The possibility of murdering his mother has in fact entered his mind, and he has just met and refused an opportunity to kill Claudius. His mother, meanwhile, waiting for him, has told Polonius not to fear for her, but she knows when she sees Hamlet that he may be violently mad. Hamlet quips with her, insults her, tells her he wishes she were not his mother, and when she, still retaining dignity, attempts to end the interview, Hamlet seizes her and she cries for help. The important thing to note is that the Queen's cry "Thou wilt not murder me" (III.iv.21) is not foolish. She has seen from Hamlet's demeanor that he is capable of murder, as indeed in the next instant he proves himself to be.

We next learn from the Queen's startled "As kill a king" (III.iv.30) that she has no knowledge of the murder, though of course there is only confirmation here of what we already know. Then the Queen asks Hamlet why he is so hysterical:

> What have I done, that thou dar'st wag thy tongue
> In noise so rude against me? (III.iv.39–40)

Hamlet tells her: it is her lust, the need of sexual passion, which has driven her from the arms and memory of her husband to the incomparably cruder charms of his brother. He cries out that she has not even the excuse of youth for her lust:

> O Shame! where is thy blush? Rebellious hell,
> If thou canst mutine in a matron's bones,
> To flaming youth let virtue be as wax
> And melt in her own fire. Proclaim no shame
> When the compulsive ardor gives the charge,
> Since frost itself as actively doth burn,
> And reason panders will. (III.iv.82–87)

This is not only a lust, but a lust which throws out of joint all the structure of human mortality and relationships. And the Queen admits it. If there is one quality that has characterized, and will characterize, every speech of Gertrude's in the play, it is the ability to see reality clearly, and to express it. This talent is not lost when turned upon herself:

> O Hamlet, speak no more!
> Thou turn'st mine eyes into my very soul,
> And there I see such black and grained spots
> As will not leave their tinct. (III.iv.88–91)

She knows that lust has driven her, that this is her sin, and she admits it. Not that she wishes to linger in the contemplation of her sin. No more, she cries, no more. And then the Ghost appears to Hamlet. The Queen thinks him mad again—as well she might—but she promises Hamlet that she will not betray him—and she does not.

Where, in all that we have seen of Gertrude, is there the picture of "a soft animal nature, very dull and very shallow"? She may indeed be "animal" in the sense of "lustful." But it does not follow that because she wishes to continue a life of sexual experience, her brain is soft or her wit unperceptive.

Some critics, having accepted Gertrude as a weak and vacillating woman, see no reason to suppose that she did not fall victim to Claudius' charms before the death of her husband and commit adultery with him. These critics, Professor Bradley among them (p. 166), claim that the elder Hamlet clearly tells his son that Gertrude has committed adultery with Claudius in the speech beginning "Ay that incestuous, that adulterate beast" (I.v.41ff). Professor Dover Wilson presents the argument:

> Is the Ghost speaking here of the o'er-hasty marriage of Claudius and Gertrude? Assuredly not. His "certain term" is drawing rapidly to an end, and he is already beginning to "scent the morning air." Hamlet knew of the marriage, and his whole soul was filled with nausea at the thought of the speedy hasting to "incestuous sheets." Why then should the Ghost waste precious moments in telling Hamlet what he was fully cognizant of before? . . . Moreover, though the word "incestuous" was applicable to the marriage, the rest of the passage is entirely inapplicable to it. Expressions like "witch-craft", "traitorous gifts", "seduce", "shameful lust", and "seeming virtuous" may be noted in passing. But the rest of the quotation leaves no doubt upon the matter. (p. 293)

Professor Dover Wilson and other critics have accepted the Ghost's word "adulterate" in its modern meaning. The Elizabethan word "adultery," however, was not restricted to its modern meaning, but was used to define any sexual relationship which could be called unchaste, including of course an incestuous one.[6] Certainly the elder Hamlet considered the marriage of Claudius and Gertrude to be unchaste and unseemly, and while his use of the word "adulterate" indicates his very strong feelings about the marriage, it would not to an Elizabethan audience necessarily mean that he believed Gertrude to have been false to him before his death. It is important to notice, too, that the Ghost does not apply the term "adulterate" to Gertrude, and he may well have considered the term a just description of Claudius' entire sexual life.

But even if the Ghost used the word "adulterate" in full awareness of its modern restricted meaning, it is not necessary to assume on the basis of this single speech (and it is the only shadow of evidence we have for such a conclusion) that Gertrude was unfaithful to him while he lived. It is quite probable that the elder Hamlet still considered himself married to Gertrude, and he is moreover revolted that her lust for him ("why she would hang on him as if increase of appetite had grown by what it fed on") should have so easily transferred itself to another. This is why he uses the expressions "seduce," "shameful lust," and others. Professor Dover Wilson has himself said "Hamlet knew of the marriage, and his whole soul was filled with nausea at the thought of the speedy hasting to incestuous sheets"; the soul of the elder Hamlet was undoubtedly filled with nausea too, and this could well explain his using such strong language, as well as his taking the time to mention the matter at all. It is not necessary to consider Gertrude an adulteress to account for the speech of the Ghost.

Gertrude's lust was, of course, more important to the plot than we may at first perceive. Charlton Lewis, among others, has shown how Shakespeare kept many of the facts of the plots from which he borrowed without maintaining the structures which explained them. In the original Belleforest story, Gertrude (substituting Shakespeare's more familiar names) was daughter of the king; to become king, it was necessary to marry her. The elder Hamlet, in marrying Gertrude, ousted Claudius from the throne.[7] Shakespeare retained the shell of this in his play. When she no longer has a husband, the form of election would be followed to declare the next king, in this case undoubtedly her son Hamlet. By marrying Gertrude, Claudius "popp'd in between th' election and my hopes" (V.ii.65), that is, kept young Hamlet from the throne. Gertrude's flaw of lust made Claudius' ambition possible, for without taking advantage of the Queen's desire still to be married, he could not have been king.

But Gertrude, if she is lustful, is also intelligent, penetrating, and gifted with a remarkable talent for concise and pithy speech. In all the play, the person whose language hers most closely resembles is Horatio. "Sweets to the sweet," she has said at Ophelia's grave. "Good night sweet prince," Horatio says at the end. They are neither of them dull, or shallow, or slothful, though one of them is passion's slave.

Endnotes

1. William Shakespeare, *Hamlet,* with a psychoanalytical study by Ernest Jones, M.D. (London: Vision Press, 1947), pp. 7–42.
2. A. C. Bradley, *Shakespearean Tragedy* (New York: Macmillan, 1949), p. 167.

3. Harley Granville-Barker, *Prefaces to Shakespeare* (Princeton: Princeton University Press, 1946), 1:227.

4. J. Dover Wilson, *What Happens in Hamlet* (Cambridge: Cambridge University Press, 1951), p. 125.

5. Lily B. Campbell, *Shakespeare's Tragic Heroes* (New York: Barnes & Noble, 1952), pp. 112–113.

6. See Bertram Joseph, *Conscience and the King* (London: Chatto & Windus, 1953), pp. 16–19.

7. Charlton M. Lewis, *The Genesis of Hamlet* (New York: Henry Holt, 1907), p. 36. ◾

Reflections and Inquiries

1. Heilbrun, unlike other Shakespearean critics before her, sees Gertrude as strong instead of frail. How convincingly does Heilbrun support this view? Why do you suppose the other critics—among the greatest in Shakespearean scholarship—would take the opposite view?

2. As part of her argumentative strategy, Heilbrun pays close attention to Elizabethan usage. Why is this important? What word in particular may have been misunderstood by earlier critics, and why?

3. What are, to you, the most compelling examples of Gertrude's independent mindedness, her ability to decide things on her own? Do you find yourself disagreeing with Heilbrun's characterization of Gertrude anywhere? Explain.

4. Heilbrun agrees that Gertrude is a slave to passion. Does this not contradict her claim that Gertrude is strong-willed? Why or why not?

Reading to Write

Read two or three additional contemporary critics' assessments of Gertrude. Look for commentary by both feminist and nonfeminist critics. Then write a comparative analysis of critical interpretations of Gertrude, concluding with the assessment you consider to be most insightful, and why.

Connections Across the Clusters

1. If Swift's "A Modest Proposal" were made into a TV drama, it is conceivable that many would try to ban it on the basis of excessive violence. Defend or challenge this view. (See Cluster 7.)

2. What does the *Roe* v. *Wade* case contribute to the privacy issue? (See Cluster 8.)

3. Discuss Frederick Douglass's and Elizabeth Cady Stanton's speeches in the context of multicultural learning. (See Cluster 6.)

4. How might Plato's "Allegory of the Cave" be used to resolve religious versus scientific ways of perceiving truth? (See Cluster 5.)

5. Assume that a school principal refuses to allow Andrew Marvell's "To His Coy Mistress" to be taught to sixth-grade students. Defend or challenge that principal's decision. (See Cluster 3.)

Writing Projects

1. Analyze the way Plato's allegory and Jonathan Edwards's sermon deal with spiritual truths. How would you describe their respective approaches to spirituality? What is most significant about each approach, in your opinion?

2. Write an essay that satirizes a social injustice. Use Swift's "A Modest Proposal" as a possible model.

3. Write a speech that calls attention to a current injustice in civil rights. Use Douglass's or Stanton's speech as a possible model.

Suggestions for Further Reading

Speeches and Sermons

Jesus. "The Sermon on the Mount," Matthew 5–7.

Ralph Waldo Emerson. "Divinity School Address" (1837) in *Selected Writings of Ralph Waldo Emerson*, ed. William H. Gilman. New American Library, 1965.

Abraham Lincoln. "The Gettysburg Address" (1863), in *A Treasury of the World's Great Speeches*, ed. Houston Peterson. New York: Grolier, 1964.

William Jennings Bryan. "Cross of Gold" (1896), in *A Treasury of the World's Great Speeches*, ed. Houston Peterson. New York: Grolier, 1964.

Eleanor Roosevelt. "Address to the Members of the American Civil Liberties Union" (1940). *Great American Speeches* [web site]. <http://www.pbs.org/greatspeeches/timeline/e_roosevelt_s.html>.

Elie Wiesel. "The Perils of Indifference" (1999). *Great American Speeches* [web site]. <http://www.pbs.org/greatspeeches/timeline/e_wiesel_s.html>

Trials

I.F. Stone. *The Trial of Socrates* (399 B.C.E.). New York: Little Brown, 1988.

W. P. Barrett. *The Trial of Jeanne d'Arc* (1431). Trans. Coley Taylor and Ruth H. Kerr. New York: Gotham, 1932.

A. Francis Steuart. *Trial of Mary Queen of Scots* (1586). London: William Hodge, 1923.

H. Montgomery Hyde. *The Trials of Oscar Wilde* (1895). London: William Hodge, 1948.

The World's Most Famous Court Trial: The Tennessee Evolution Case (Transcript of the Scopes Trial, 1925). Cincinnati: National, 1925.

Ann Tusa and John Tusa. *The Nuremberg Trial* (1946). New York: Atheneum, 1986.

Richard Rashke. *The Killing of Karen Silkwood: The Story Behind the Kerr-McGee Plutonium Case* (1979). Boston: Houghton, 1981.

Rodney A. Smolla. *Jerry Falwell v. Larry Flynt: The First Amendment on Trial* (1981). New York: St. Martin's, 1988.

Essays, Manifestoes, and Treatises

Niccolo Machiavelli. *The Prince* (1532). Trans. George Bull. New York: Penguin, 1961.

Henry David Thoreau. "Civil Disobedience" (1849). *The Portable Thoreau,* ed. Carl Bode. Penguin, 1977.

Charles Darwin. *On the Origin of Species* (1859). New York: Bantam, 1999.

Thorstein Veblen. *The Theory of the Leisure Class* (1899). Boston: Houghton, 1973.

Sigmund Freud. *Civilization and Its Discontents* (1930). Trans. James Strachey. New York: Norton, 1962.

George Orwell. "Politics and the English Language" (1946) *Selected Essays.* New York: Penguin, 1960.

Simone de Beauvoir. *The Second Sex.* Trans. H. M. Parshley. New York: Knopf, 1953.

C. P. Snow. *The Two Cultures & A Second Look.* Cambridge: Cambridge UP, 1959.

Margaret Mead and James Baldwin. *A Rap on Race.* New York: Lippincott, 1971.

Glossary of Rhetorical Terms

Ad hominem fallacy.   Literally, argument directed against the person. An error of reasoning in which the arguer attacks an individual's character or person as a way of attacking his or her ideas or performance.

Analogy.   Comparison made, for purpose of clarification, between two ideas sharing similar characteristics.

Analysis.   Breakdown of an idea into its constituent elements to facilitate comprehension.

Appeals.   The three means of persuasion described by Aristotle: *ethos* (referring to persuasion through character, ethics, values); *pathos* (referring to persuasion through emotions, feelings); and *logos* (referring to persuasion though logical reasoning). The three appeals often overlap in an argument.

Argument.   A discussion in which a claim is challenged or supported with evidence. *See also* Persuasion.

Bandwagon fallacy.   An error of reasoning that asserts that if an opinion is shared by a majority, the opinion must be correct.

Begging the question fallacy.   An error of reasoning that presents a disputable claim in a manner that suggests it is beyond dispute.

Brainstorming.   A form of prewriting in which one spontaneously records or utters ideas for a topic.

Categorization.   Arrangement or classification according to shared similarities.

Claim.   The idea or thesis that forms the basis of an argument.

Classical (or Aristotelian) argument.   A model of argument strategy that includes an introduction to the problem, a statement of the thesis or claim, a discussion of the evidence in support of the thesis, a refutation of opposing views, and a conclusion.

Clustering.   A form of prewriting in which one spontaneously writes down similar ideas and examples in circled groupings or *clusters,* or clumps and groups.

Composing process.   A reference to the multiple (but not necessarily sequential or otherwise orderly) activities of a writer in the act of completing a writing task. These activities typically involve such prewriting activities as brainstorming, freewriting, listing, and clustering; drafting activities such as preparing a first draft, revising, re-revising, and copyediting; and proofreading.

Data.   Another word for *evidence*. It can also refer to statistical evidence as opposed to expert testimonial, mathematical, or observational evidence.

Database.   An electronic list of references grouped by subject matter.

Deduction.   A mode of reasoning that begins with what is known to be true and seeks to determine the elements or premises that demonstrate the validity of that truth. *See also* Induction.

Definition.   In argumentative writing, definitions of technical terms are often necessary when the claim involves a specialized topic in law, the sciences, technology, business and industry. A definition often includes reference to a word or expression's origin (etymology), usage history, as well as standard lexical meaning.

Development.   Examining an idea in depth, using illustrations, cases in point, analysis, statistics, and other means of supporting assertions.

Discourse.   Sustained communication through oral or written language. There are three modes of discourse: (1) expository (or referential), which refers to explanation and analysis; (2) expressive, which refers to descriptive and dramatic writing; and (3) persuasive, which refers to the use of the Aristotelian appeals to change readers' minds about something. *See also* Appeals.

Either/Or fallacy.   An error of reasoning in which a many-sided argument is presented as having only two sides. Also known as the *false dichotomy.*

Enthymeme.   In deductive reasoning, a syllogism in which one of the premises goes unstated because it is assumed to be understood. In the enthymeme, "Socrates is mortal because he is a human being," the omitted-because-understood premise is "all human beings are mortal." *See also* Syllogism.

Ethos.   *See* Appeals.

Evidence.   Support for a claim. Evidence may be direct (data from surveys, experiments, research studies, and so on) or indirect (mathematical or logical reasoning). *See also* Proof.

Fallacy.   An error or flaw in logical reasoning.

False analogy or faulty analogy.   An error of reasoning that assumes the accuracy of an inaccurate (false) or inappropriate (faulty) comparison.

Fourth-term fallacy.   An error of reasoning in which one term is carelessly or deceptively substituted for another to force the assumption that both terms mean the same thing, thereby adding a "fourth term" to a syllogism, which can contain only three terms in their respective premises: major, middle, and minor. *See also* Syllogism.

Freewriting.   A form of prewriting in which one writes spontaneously and swiftly without regard to organization, development, usage, or mechanics.

Generalization.   A nonspecific, summative statement about an idea or situation. If a generalization does not account for some situations it is said to be *hasty* or *premature*. If a generalization is not accompanied by particular examples, it is said to be *unsupported*.

Glossing.   Making notes, such as comments or cross-references, in the margins of texts to enhance understanding as well as develop a critical stance on the ideas presented. Such notes are called *glosses*.

Hasty generalization.   *See* Generalization.

In-depth reading.   In critical reading, the stage of reading involving close attention to complexities of the topic, to subtle meanings, and to inferences; follows previewing. *See also* Previewing.

Induction.   Form of reasoning whereby one attempts a generalization or hypothesis after considering particular cases or samples, not before.

Linking.   In critical reading, the connecting of one part of a sentence with another to determine meaning and continuity of idea.

Listserv.   An online discussion group, acquired through subscription.

Mediation.   A form of argument that attempts to present fairly an objective discussion of opposing views before attempting to reach a conclusion.

Newsgroup.   An electronic bulletin board or forum. Also known as *usenet*.

Non sequitur.   Fallacy in which an assertion cannot logically be tied to the premise it attempts to demonstrate.

Paraphrase.   *See* Quotation.

Persuasion.   A form of argument that relies on using emotional appeals more than logical analysis to get readers or listeners to change their minds about something.

Plagiarism.   The use of others' ideas as if they were one's own. Plagiarism is a violation of international copyright law and therefore illegal.

Poisoning the well fallacy.   Attempting to corrupt an argument before the arguing begins.

Post hoc fallacy.   Shortened form of *post hoc ergo propter hoc* ("after the fact, therefore because of the fact"). An error of reasoning in which one attaches a causal relationship to a sequential one.

Premature generalization.   *See* Generalization.

Previewing.   The initial stage of critical reading consisting of prereading, skim-reading, and postreading. *See also* In-depth reading.

Proof.   A form of evidence involving mathematical deduction or the presentation of indisputable facts.

Proofreading.   Reading semifinal draft copy for errors in grammar, spelling, punctuation, capitalization, and the like.

Qualifier.   In Toulmin argument, a limitation imposed on a claim that makes it valid only under some or most circumstances, but not all. *See also* Toulmin argument.

Quotation.   The words of an authority used in argumentative writing to reinforce one's own views on a given topic. *Direct quotation* refers to verbatim citation of the author's words, which are placed in quotation marks. *Indirect quotation* or *paraphrase* refers to the author's idea without quoting verbatim. Both forms of quotation must be properly documented.

Red herring fallacy.   An error of reasoning in which one throws in an unrelated but similar seeming bit of information to throw readers or listeners off the track of the issue being argued.

Revising.   Substantive development or restructuring of a draft. Cf. "Proofreading"

Refutation.   The technique of representing fairly, and then demonstrating the shortcomings of, an assertion of variance with your own.

Research.   The process of searching, retrieving, and integrating information from outside sources to authenticate or reinforce one's argument.

Review.   A critical evaluation of an artistic work or exhibit, a new product, or a restaurant.

Rhetoric.   The art of or the techniques used in writing or speaking effectively. Aristotle defined rhetoric as the art of finding the best available means of persuasion in a given case.

Rhetorical rhombus.   A schematic for showing the elements involved in written or oral communication: Purpose, Audience, Writer, Subject.

Rogerian argument.   A mode of argument established by Carl Rogers in which arguers are urged to cooperate and to seek a common ground on which to negotiate their differences.

Serendipity.   In research, a fortunate coming together of ideas through unexpected discovery.

Slippery slope fallacy.   An error of reasoning in which one alludes to a sequence of highly unlikely consequences resulting from an observed or proposed situation.

Summary.   A highly condensed version of a work using or paraphrasing only the work's key points.

Syllogism.   A form of logical argument consisting of a major premise ("All stars are suns"), a minor premise ("Sirius is a star"), and a conclusion ("Therefore, Sirius is a sun").

Thesis.   The claim or main idea or premise of an argument.

Topic.   The specific subject of a paper.

Toulmin argument.   A strategy of argument developed by philosopher Stephen A. Toulmin in which it is understood that any claim is arguable because it is based on personal ethical values or warrants as well as an outside evidence or data.

Tracking.   In critical reading, shifting the perspective of meaning from sentence to word or from sentence to paragraph or from paragraph to whole essay.

Unsupported generalization.   *See* Generalization.

Warrant.   *See* Toulmin argument.

Index of Authors and Titles

Index of Terms